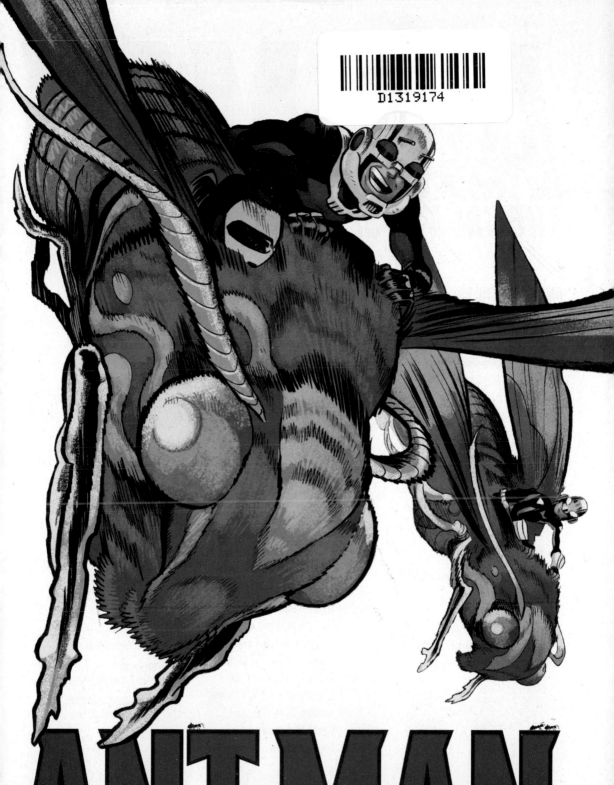

ANT-MAN

THE SAGA OF SCOTT LANG

ANT-MAN

THE SAGA OF SCOTT LANG

ANT-MAN & THE WASP: LIVING LEGENDS

WRITER: **Ralph Macchio**
ARTIST: **Andrea Di Vito**
COLOR ARTIST: **Laura Villari**
LETTERER: VC's **Travis Lanham**
COVER ART: **Andrea Di Vito** & **Laura Villari**

GUARDIANS TEAM-UP #7

WRITERS: **Nick Giovannetti** & **Paul Scheer**
ARTIST: **Shawn Crystal**
COLOR ARTIST: **Matthew Wilson**
LETTERER: VC's **Cory Petit**
COVER ART: **David Lopez**

ANT-MAN AND THE WASP #1-5

WRITER: **Mark Waid**
ARTIST: **Javier Garrón**
COLOR ARTIST: **Israel Silva**
LETTERER: VC's **Joe Caramagna**
COVER ART: **David Nakayama**

GIANT-MAN #1-3

WRITER: **Leah Williams**
ARTIST: **Marco Castiello**
COLOR ARTIST: **Rachelle Rosenberg**
LETTERER: VC's **Joe Sabino**
COVER ART: **Woo-Chul Lee**
Special Thanks to **Wil Moss**, **Sarah Brunstad**, **Raffaele Forte** & **Acunzo Vincenzo**

ANT-MAN #1-5

WRITER: **Zeb Wells**
ARTIST: **Dylan Burnett**
COLOR ARTIST: **Mike Spicer**
LETTERER: VC's **Cory Petit**
COVER ART: **Eduard Petrovich**

ASSISTANT EDITORS: **Xander Jarowey, Kathleen Wisneski** & **Lauren Amaro**
CONSULTING EDITOR: **Jordan D. White**
EDITORS: **Mark Basso, Katie Kubert, Nick Lowe, Jordan D. White, Chris Robinson** & **Darren Shan**

Ant-Man created by **Stan Lee, Larry Lieber** & **Jack Kirby**

COLLECTION EDITOR: **Jennifer Grünwald**

ASSISTANT EDITOR: **Daniel Kirchhoffer**

ASSISTANT MANAGING EDITOR: **Maia Loy**

ASSOCIATE MANAGER, TALENT RELATIONS: **Lisa Montalbano**

ASSOCIATE MANAGER, DIGITAL ASSETS: **Joe Hochstein**

VP PRODUCTION & SPECIAL PROJECTS: **Jeff Youngquist**

BOOK DESIGNER: **Adam Del Re**

SVP PRINT, SALES & MARKETING: **David Gabriel**

EDITOR IN CHIEF: **C.B. Cebulski**

ANT-MAN: THE SAGA OF SCOTT LANG. Contains material originally published in magazine form as ANT-MAN & THE WASP: LIVING LEGENDS (2018) #1, ANT-MAN AND THE WASP (2018) #1-5, GIANT-MAN (2019) #1-3, ANT-MAN (2020) #1-5 and GUARDIANS TEAM-UP (2015) #7. First printing 2022. ISBN 978-1-302-95065-1. Published by MARVEL WORLDWIDE, INC., a subsidiary of MARVEL ENTERTAINMENT, LLC. OFFICE OF PUBLICATION: 1290 Avenue of the Americas, New York, NY 10104. © 2022 MARVEL No similarity between any of the names, characters, persons, and/or institutions in this book with those of any living or dead person or institution is intended, and any such similarity which may exist is purely coincidental. **Printed in Canada.** KEVIN FEIGE, Chief Creative Officer; DAN BUCKLEY, President, Marvel Entertainment; DAVID BOGART, Associate Publisher & SVP of Talent Affairs; TOM BREVOORT, VP, Executive Editor; NICK LOWE, Executive Editor, VP of Content, Digital Publishing; DAVID GABRIEL, VP of Print & Digital Publishing; SVEN LARSEN, VP of Licensed Publishing; MARK ANNUNZIATO, VP of Planning & Forecasting; JEFF YOUNGQUIST, VP of Production & Special Projects; ALEX MORALES, Director of Publishing Operations; DAN EDINGTON, Director of Editorial Operations; RICKEY PURDIN, Director of Talent Relations; JENNIFER GRÜNWALD, Director of Production & Special Projects; SUSAN CRESPI, Production Manager; STAN LEE, Chairman Emeritus. For information regarding advertising in Marvel Comics or on Marvel.com, please contact Vit DeBellis, Custom Solutions & Integrated Advertising Manager, at vdebellis@marvel.com. For Marvel subscription inquiries, please call 888-511-5480. **Manufactured between 11/4/2022 and 12/6/2022 by SOLISCO PRINTERS, SCOTT, QC, CANADA.**

10 9 8 7 6 5 4 3 2 1

When the original Ant-Man, Hank Pym, retired from the job, electronics technician/burglar **SCOTT LANG** stole the costume to save his daughter. But when true villainy reared its head, Scott rose/shrunk to the occasion, proving himself worthy of the tech and the name. With his checkered past mostly behind him, Scott took on the size-changing, ant-communicating abilities of Ant-Man!

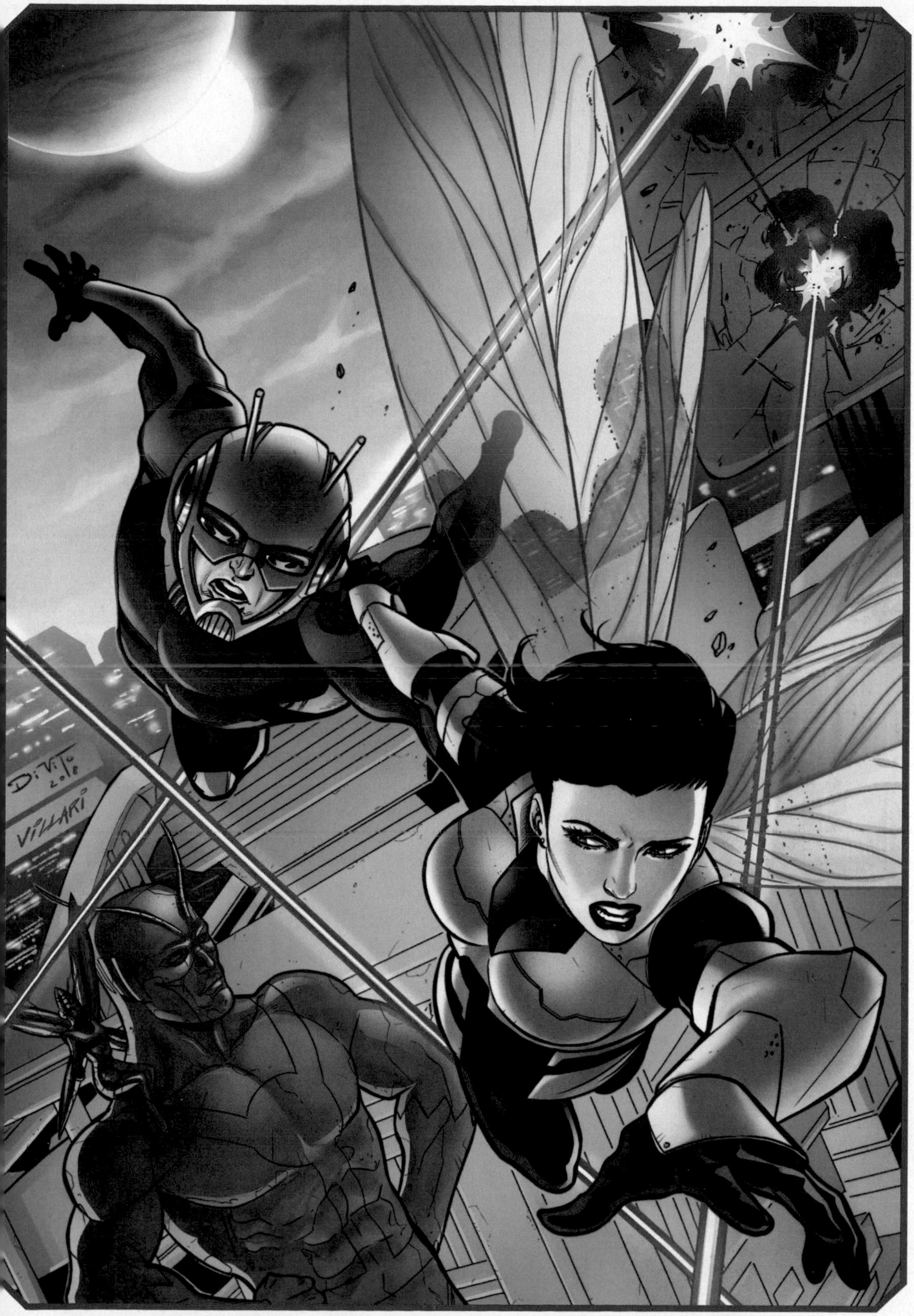

Di Vito 2018
Villari

ANT-MAN & THE WASP: LIVING LEGENDS

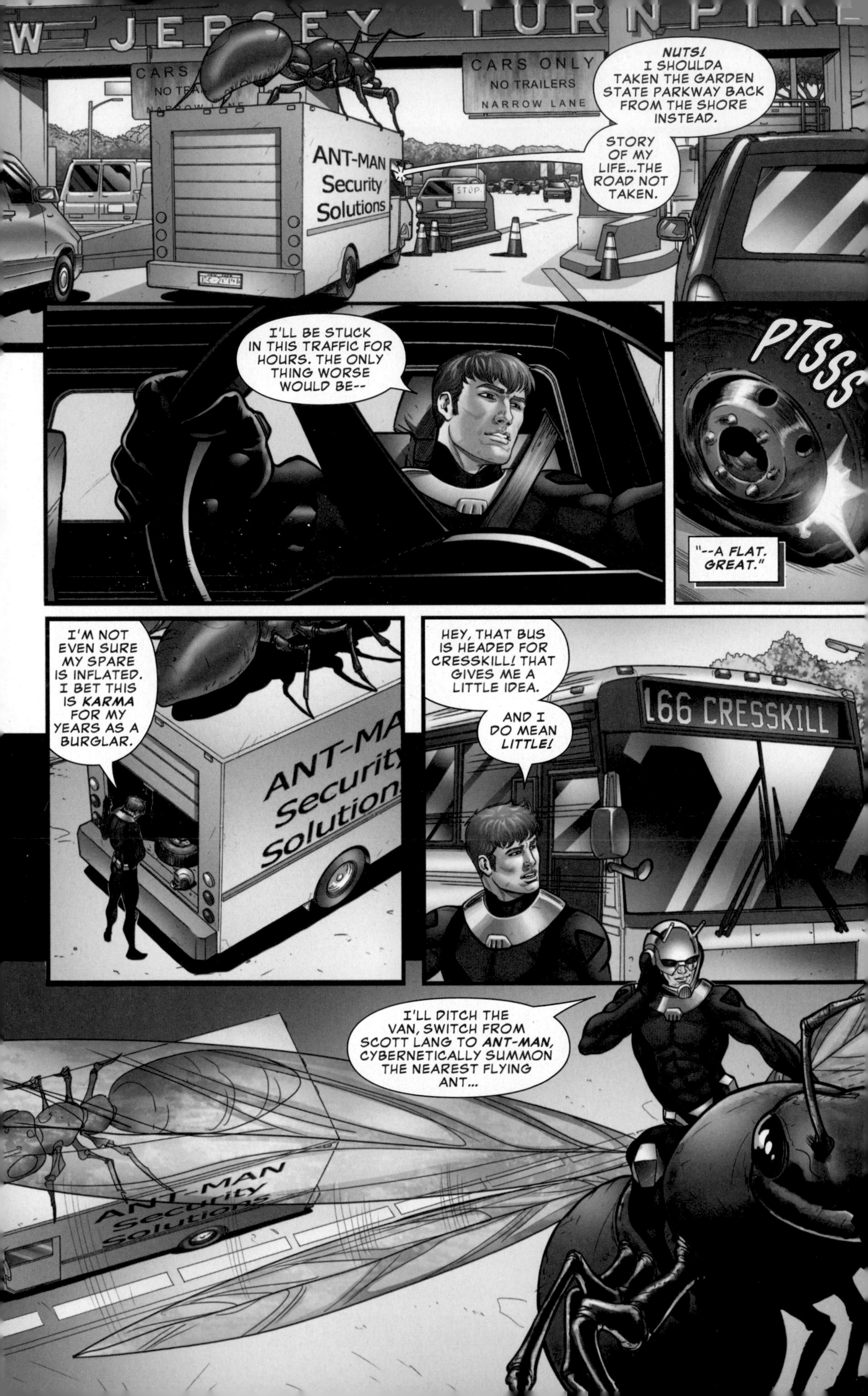

NEW JERSEY TURNPIKE
CARS ONLY NO TRAILERS NARROW LANE
ANT-MAN Security Solutions
STOP
NUTS! I SHOULDA TAKEN THE GARDEN STATE PARKWAY BACK FROM THE SHORE INSTEAD.
STORY OF MY LIFE...THE ROAD NOT TAKEN.
I'LL BE STUCK IN THIS TRAFFIC FOR HOURS. THE ONLY THING WORSE WOULD BE--
PTSSS
"--A FLAT. GREAT."
I'M NOT EVEN SURE MY SPARE IS INFLATED. I BET THIS IS KARMA FOR MY YEARS AS A BURGLAR.
HEY, THAT BUS IS HEADED FOR CRESSKILL! THAT GIVES ME A LITTLE IDEA.
AND I DO MEAN LITTLE!
166 CRESSKILL
I'LL DITCH THE VAN, SWITCH FROM SCOTT LANG TO ANT-MAN, CYBERNETICALLY SUMMON THE NEAREST FLYING ANT...

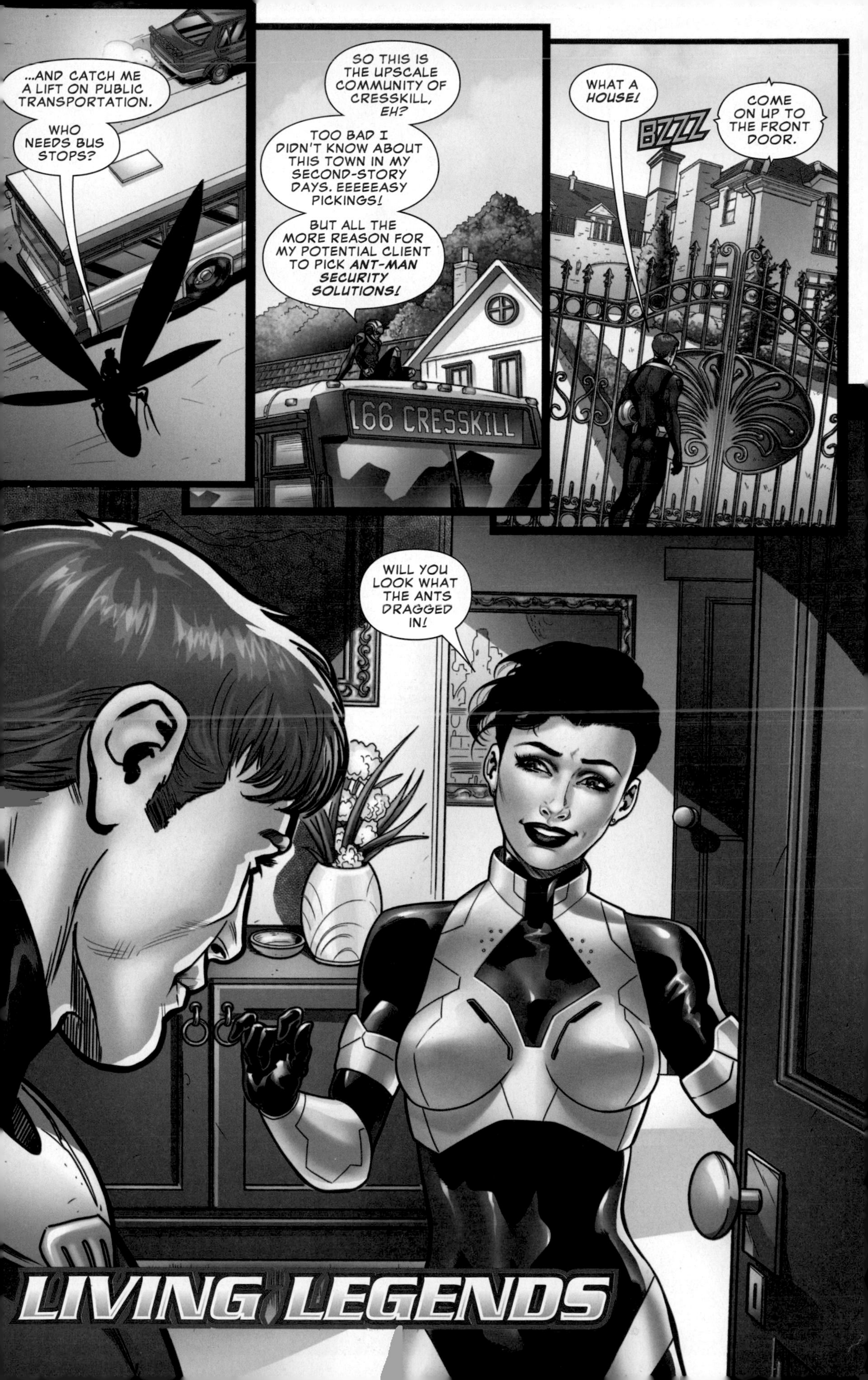
...AND CATCH ME A LIFT ON PUBLIC TRANSPORTATION.
WHO NEEDS BUS STOPS?
SO THIS IS THE UPSCALE COMMUNITY OF CRESSKILL, EH?
TOO BAD I DIDN'T KNOW ABOUT THIS TOWN IN MY SECOND-STORY DAYS. EEEEEASY PICKINGS!
BUT ALL THE MORE REASON FOR MY POTENTIAL CLIENT TO PICK ANT-MAN SECURITY SOLUTIONS!
166 CRESSKILL
WHAT A HOUSE!
BZZZ
COME ON UP TO THE FRONT DOOR.
WILL YOU LOOK WHAT THE ANTS DRAGGED IN!
LIVING LEGENDS

GIMME A HUG, HANDSOME! I *ALWAYS* SAID THAT HELMET HID YOUR *GOOD LOOKS!*

WHAT TOOK YOU SO LONG? AND I THOUGHT YOU TOLD ME TO GEAR UP FOR SOME "SECURITY TEST"?

YEAH, WELL, YOU SEE, JAN--

BWEEOOP BWEEEOOP

THAT'S NOT PART OF THE TEST.

ALWAYS SOME OLD PIECE OF HANK'S TECH GOING OFF AROUND THIS PLACE--

--BUT THIS ONE SEEMS TO BE COMING FROM THE COMMUNICATIONS ROOM.

MIND IF I TAG ALONG?

NO SECRETS HERE.

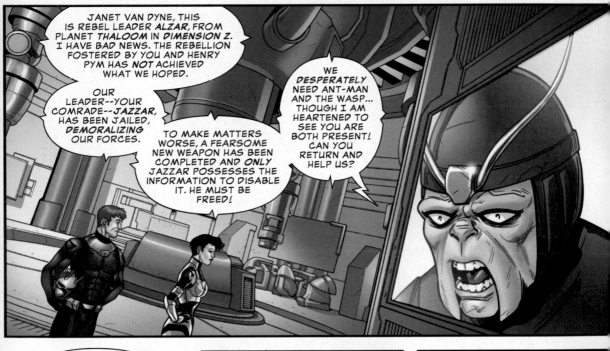

JANET VAN DYNE, THIS IS REBEL LEADER *ALZAR,* FROM PLANET *THALOOM* IN *DIMENSION Z.* I HAVE BAD NEWS. THE REBELLION FOSTERED BY YOU AND HENRY PYM HAS *NOT* ACHIEVED WHAT WE HOPED.

OUR LEADER--YOUR COMRADE--*JAZZAR,* HAS BEEN JAILED, *DEMORALIZING* OUR FORCES.

TO MAKE MATTERS WORSE, A *FEARSOME* NEW WEAPON HAS BEEN COMPLETED AND *ONLY* JAZZAR POSSESSES THE INFORMATION TO DISABLE IT. HE MUST BE *FREED!*

WE *DESPERATELY* NEED ANT-MAN AND THE WASP... THOUGH I AM HEARTENED TO SEE YOU ARE BOTH PRESENT! CAN YOU RETURN AND HELP US?

UMMM, WELL...I *AM* ANT-MAN. BUT--UH--I'M NOT *THAT* ANT-MAN. HANK PYM'S A BUDDY, Y'SEE, BUT I'M A DIFFERENT GUY ALTOGETHER.

ALZAR, HANK IS... *UNAVAILABLE.* BUT I UNDERSTAND THE *DIRE* NATURE OF YOUR PREDICAMENT.

I WON'T LET YOU DOWN. VAN DYNE OUT.

SOOOO...

HERE'S THE BRIEF VERSION. THIS DOOHICKEY IS AN INTER-DIMENSIONAL "ERASER" THAT TELEPORTS YOU BACK AND FORTH BETWEEN DIMENSIONS.

CUTZA, CALLED THE *LIVING ERASER,* USED IT TO HIJACK HANK AND ME TO DIMENSION Z.*

*WAY BACK IN *TALES TO ASTONISH* #49 --BACK-ISSUE BASSO

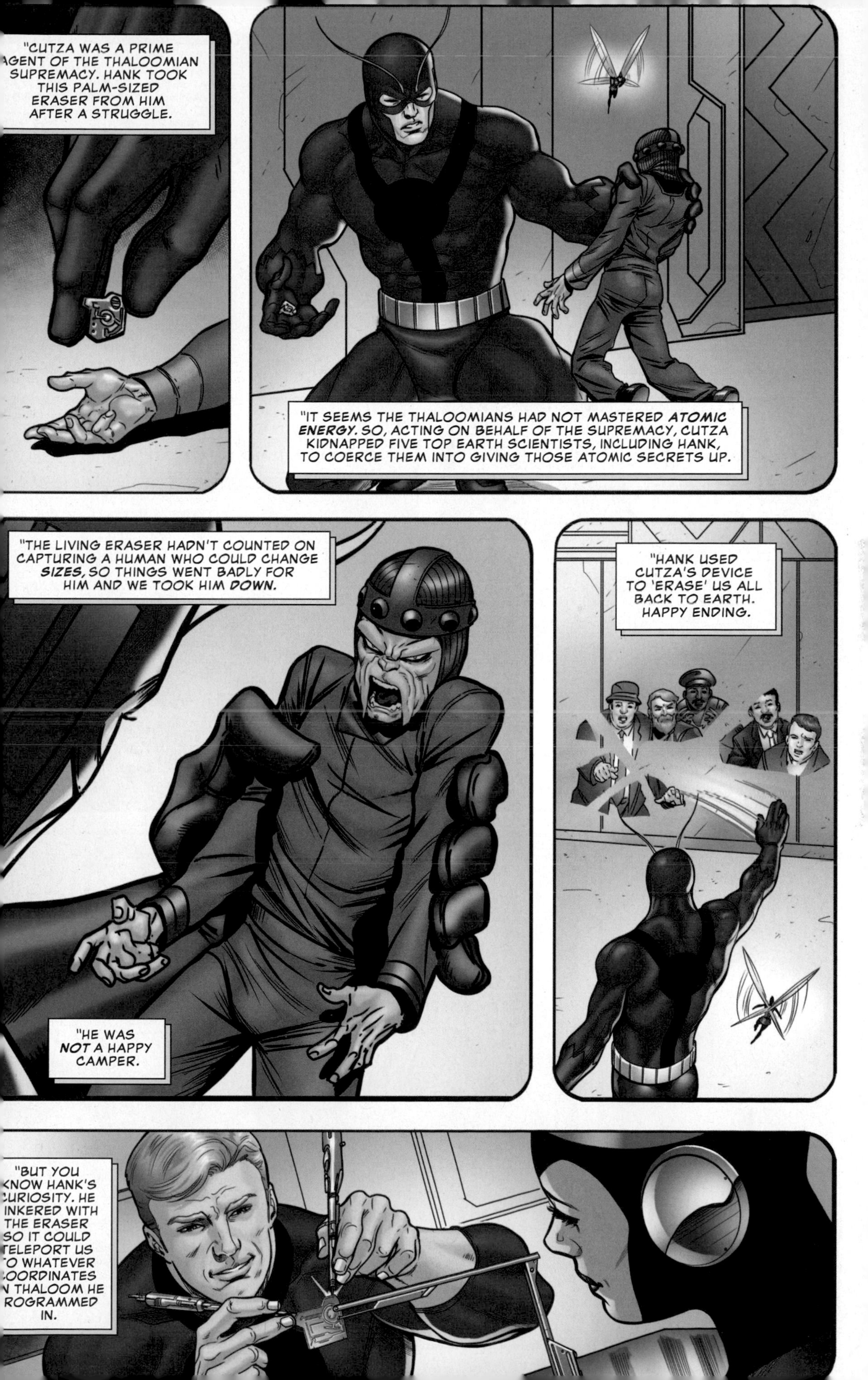
"CUTZA WAS A PRIME
AGENT OF THE THALOOMIAN SUPREMACY. HANK TOOK THIS PALM-SIZED ERASER FROM HIM AFTER A STRUGGLE.
"IT SEEMS THE THALOOMIANS HAD NOT MASTERED *ATOMIC ENERGY.* SO, ACTING ON BEHALF OF THE SUPREMACY, CUTZA KIDNAPPED FIVE TOP EARTH SCIENTISTS, INCLUDING HANK, TO COERCE THEM INTO GIVING THOSE ATOMIC SECRETS UP.
"THE LIVING ERASER HADN'T COUNTED ON CAPTURING A HUMAN WHO COULD CHANGE *SIZES,* SO THINGS WENT BADLY FOR HIM AND WE TOOK HIM *DOWN.*
"HE WAS *NOT* A HAPPY CAMPER.
"HANK USED CUTZA'S DEVICE TO 'ERASE' US ALL BACK TO EARTH. HAPPY ENDING.
"BUT YOU KNOW HANK'S CURIOSITY. HE TINKERED WITH THE ERASER SO IT COULD TELEPORT US TO WHATEVER COORDINATES IN THALOOM HE PROGRAMMED IN.

"SOON AFTER, WE ERASED OURSELVES INTO THE MIDST OF A HUGE *BATTLE* ON THALOOM.

"APPARENTLY, IN DEFEATING THE LIVING ERASER, WE'D *INSPIRED* A POWERFUL REBELLION AGAINST THE RULING DICTATORS.

"*JAZZAR* SAID THIS WAS A *CRUCIAL* BATTLE TO STOP THE COMPLETION OF A WEAPON FOR INVADING OTHER DIMENSIONS TO EXPAND THEIR EMPIRE... STARTING WITH OURS!

"THE ESSENTIAL COMPONENT WAS IN A WAREHOUSE, BUT IT *COULDN'T* BE TAKEN BECAUSE THE REBEL FORCES WERE PINNED DOWN.

"BUT A LITTLE LASER FIRE WASN'T GOING TO STOP ANT-MAN AND THE WASP.

"WE SLIPPED PAST THE SOLDIERS.

ZRPT

ZRPT

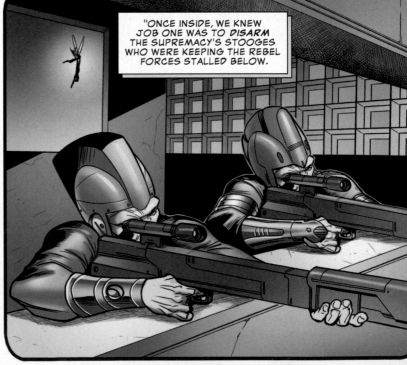

"ONCE INSIDE, WE KNEW JOB ONE WAS TO *DISARM* THE SUPREMACY'S STOOGES WHO WERE KEEPING THE REBEL FORCES STALLED BELOW.

"AND THAT'S JUST WHAT WE DID, IN RECORD TIME.

"THEY NEVER KNEW WHAT HIT THEM!

"THEN, ONLY ONE REMAINED-- A BRUTE ABOUT THE SIZE OF THE *HULK*.

"I GREW TO NORMAL HEIGHT TO KEEP HIM FOCUSED ON ME.

"THEN HANK SUDDENLY SHOT UP IN SIZE--AND THAT'S ALL SHE WROTE.

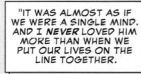

"IT WAS ALMOST AS IF WE WERE A SINGLE MIND. AND I *NEVER* LOVED HIM MORE THAN WHEN WE PUT OUR LIVES ON THE LINE TOGETHER.

"JAZZAR AND HIS REBELS CLAIMED WE SAVED BOTH EARTH *AND* THE THALOOMIAN REVOLUTION THAT DAY. WE WERE THEIR HEROES!"

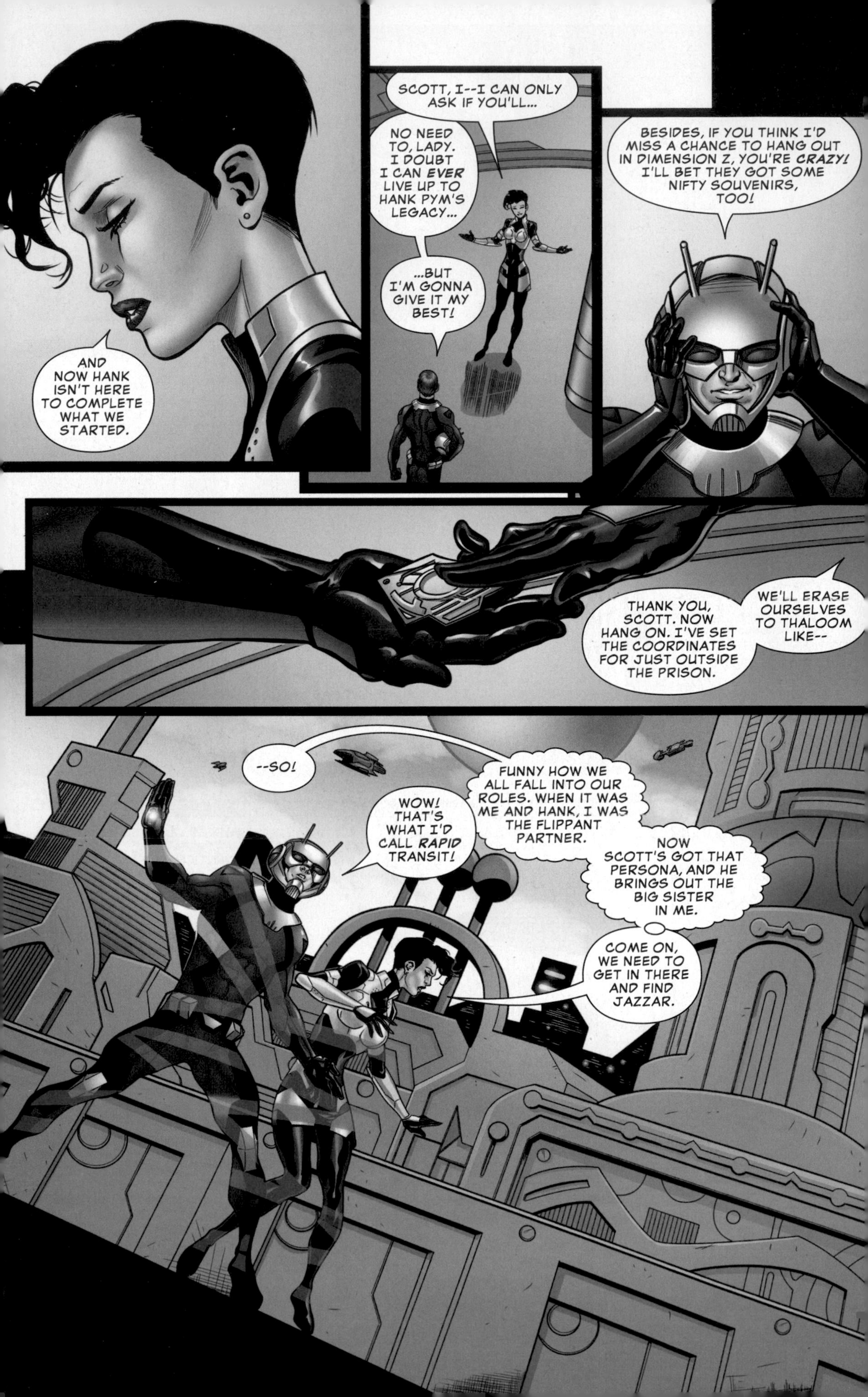
AND NOW HANK ISN'T HERE TO COMPLETE WHAT WE STARTED.
SCOTT, I--I CAN ONLY ASK IF YOU'LL...
NO NEED TO, LADY. I DOUBT I CAN EVER LIVE UP TO HANK PYM'S LEGACY...
...BUT I'M GONNA GIVE IT MY BEST!
BESIDES, IF YOU THINK I'D MISS A CHANCE TO HANG OUT IN DIMENSION Z, YOU'RE CRAZY! I'LL BET THEY GOT SOME NIFTY SOUVENIRS, TOO!
THANK YOU, SCOTT. NOW HANG ON. I'VE SET THE COORDINATES FOR JUST OUTSIDE THE PRISON.
WE'LL ERASE OURSELVES TO THALOOM LIKE--
--SO!
WOW! THAT'S WHAT I'D CALL RAPID TRANSIT!
FUNNY HOW WE ALL FALL INTO OUR ROLES. WHEN IT WAS ME AND HANK, I WAS THE FLIPPANT PARTNER.
NOW SCOTT'S GOT THAT PERSONA, AND HE BRINGS OUT THE BIG SISTER IN ME.
COME ON, WE NEED TO GET IN THERE AND FIND JAZZAR.

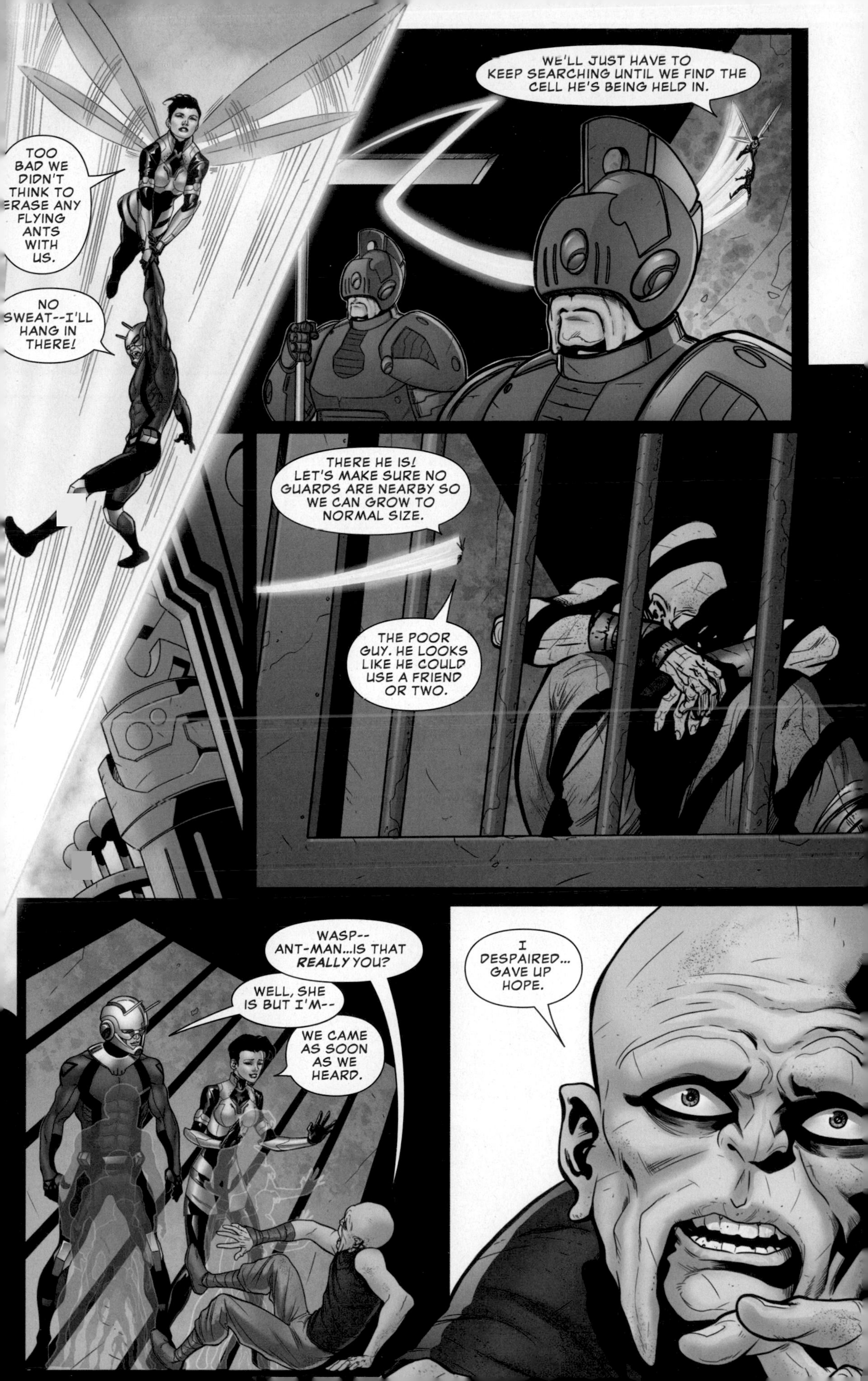

TOO BAD WE DIDN'T THINK TO ERASE ANY FLYING ANTS WITH US.
NO SWEAT--I'LL HANG IN THERE!
WE'LL JUST HAVE TO KEEP SEARCHING UNTIL WE FIND THE CELL HE'S BEING HELD IN.
THERE HE IS! LET'S MAKE SURE NO GUARDS ARE NEARBY SO WE CAN GROW TO NORMAL SIZE.
THE POOR GUY. HE LOOKS LIKE HE COULD USE A FRIEND OR TWO.
WASP-- ANT-MAN...IS THAT *REALLY* YOU?
WELL, SHE IS BUT I'M--
WE CAME AS SOON AS WE HEARD.
I DESPAIRED... GAVE UP HOPE.

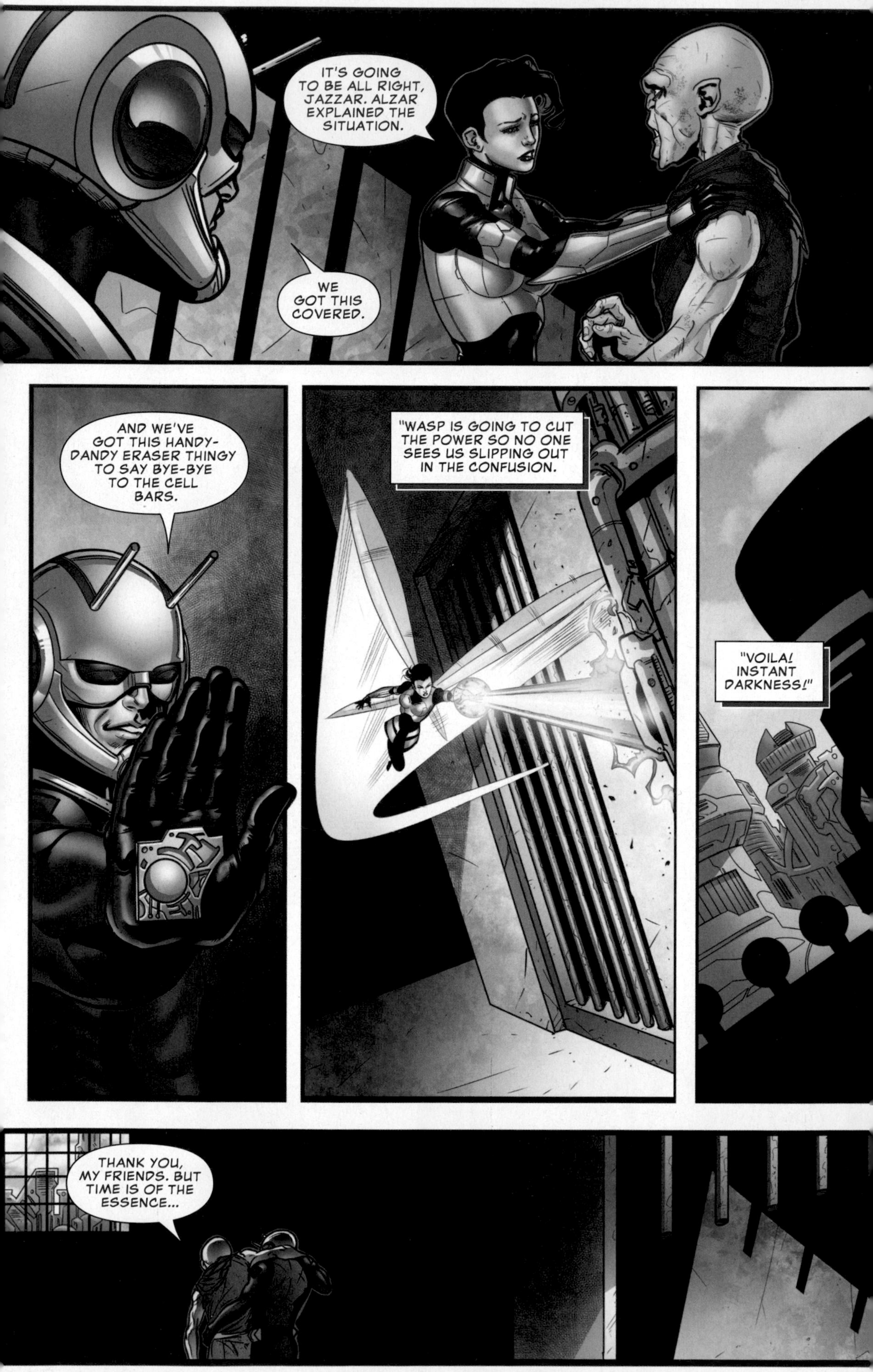
IT'S GOING TO BE ALL RIGHT, JAZZAR. ALZAR EXPLAINED THE SITUATION.
WE GOT THIS COVERED.
AND WE'VE GOT THIS HANDY-DANDY ERASER THINGY TO SAY BYE-BYE TO THE CELL BARS.
"WASP IS GOING TO CUT THE POWER SO NO ONE SEES US SLIPPING OUT IN THE CONFUSION.
"VOILA! INSTANT DARKNESS!"
THANK YOU, MY FRIENDS. BUT TIME IS OF THE ESSENCE...

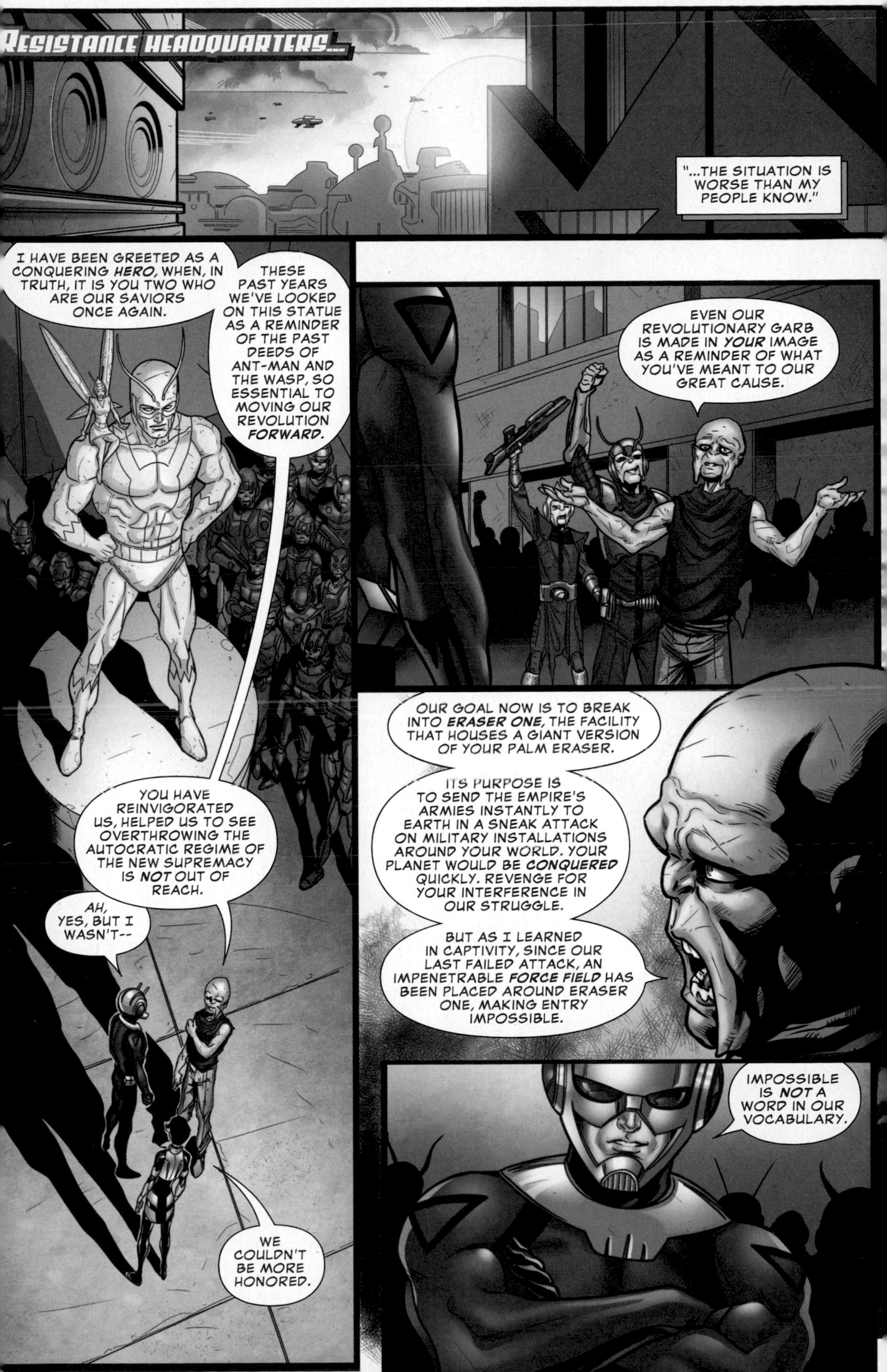
RESISTANCE HEADQUARTERS...
"...THE SITUATION IS WORSE THAN MY PEOPLE KNOW."
I HAVE BEEN GREETED AS A CONQUERING HERO, WHEN, IN TRUTH, IT IS YOU TWO WHO ARE OUR SAVIORS ONCE AGAIN.
THESE PAST YEARS WE'VE LOOKED ON THIS STATUE AS A REMINDER OF THE PAST DEEDS OF ANT-MAN AND THE WASP, SO ESSENTIAL TO MOVING OUR REVOLUTION FORWARD.
YOU HAVE REINVIGORATED US, HELPED US TO SEE OVERTHROWING THE AUTOCRATIC REGIME OF THE NEW SUPREMACY IS NOT OUT OF REACH.
AH, YES, BUT I WASN'T--
WE COULDN'T BE MORE HONORED.
EVEN OUR REVOLUTIONARY GARB IS MADE IN YOUR IMAGE AS A REMINDER OF WHAT YOU'VE MEANT TO OUR GREAT CAUSE.
OUR GOAL NOW IS TO BREAK INTO ERASER ONE, THE FACILITY THAT HOUSES A GIANT VERSION OF YOUR PALM ERASER.
ITS PURPOSE IS TO SEND THE EMPIRE'S ARMIES INSTANTLY TO EARTH IN A SNEAK ATTACK ON MILITARY INSTALLATIONS AROUND YOUR WORLD. YOUR PLANET WOULD BE CONQUERED QUICKLY. REVENGE FOR YOUR INTERFERENCE IN OUR STRUGGLE.
BUT AS I LEARNED IN CAPTIVITY, SINCE OUR LAST FAILED ATTACK, AN IMPENETRABLE FORCE FIELD HAS BEEN PLACED AROUND ERASER ONE, MAKING ENTRY IMPOSSIBLE.
IMPOSSIBLE IS NOT A WORD IN OUR VOCABULARY.

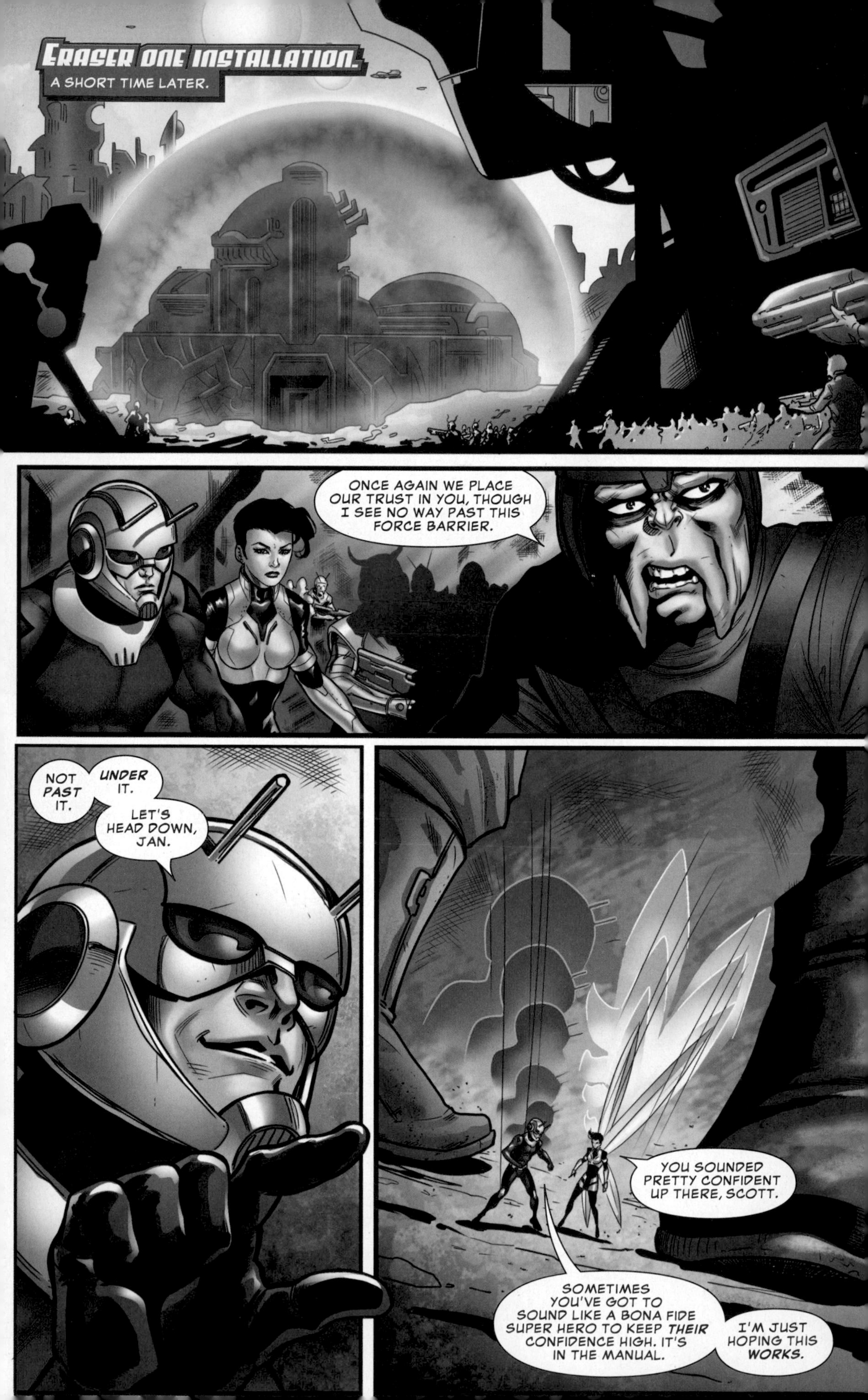
ERASER ONE INSTALLATION.
A SHORT TIME LATER.
ONCE AGAIN WE PLACE OUR TRUST IN YOU, THOUGH I SEE NO WAY PAST THIS FORCE BARRIER.
NOT PAST IT.
UNDER IT.
LET'S HEAD DOWN, JAN.
YOU SOUNDED PRETTY CONFIDENT UP THERE, SCOTT.
SOMETIMES YOU'VE GOT TO SOUND LIKE A BONA FIDE SUPER HERO TO KEEP THEIR CONFIDENCE HIGH. IT'S IN THE MANUAL.
I'M JUST HOPING THIS WORKS.

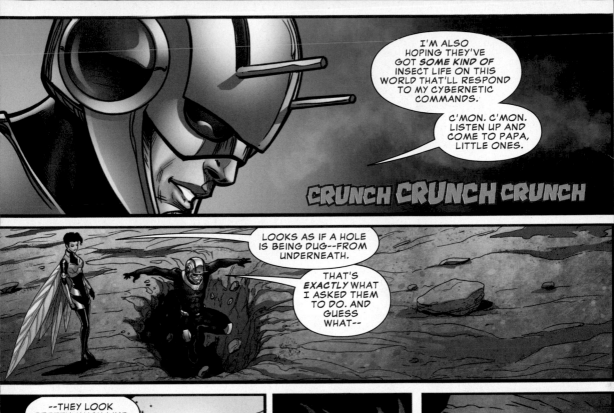

I'M ALSO HOPING THEY'VE GOT *SOME KIND OF* INSECT LIFE ON THIS WORLD THAT'LL RESPOND TO MY CYBERNETIC COMMANDS.

C'MON. C'MON. LISTEN UP AND COME TO PAPA, LITTLE ONES.

CRUNCH CRUNCH CRUNCH

LOOKS AS IF A HOLE IS BEING DUG--FROM UNDERNEATH.

THAT'S *EXACTLY* WHAT I ASKED THEM TO DO. AND GUESS WHAT--

--THEY LOOK PRETTY MUCH LIKE *OUR* ANTS.

NOW TO TUNNEL DOWN, DOWN, DOWN, UNTIL WE'RE UNDER THE LIMIT OF THE FORCE FIELD...

...AND UP THE OTHER SIDE!

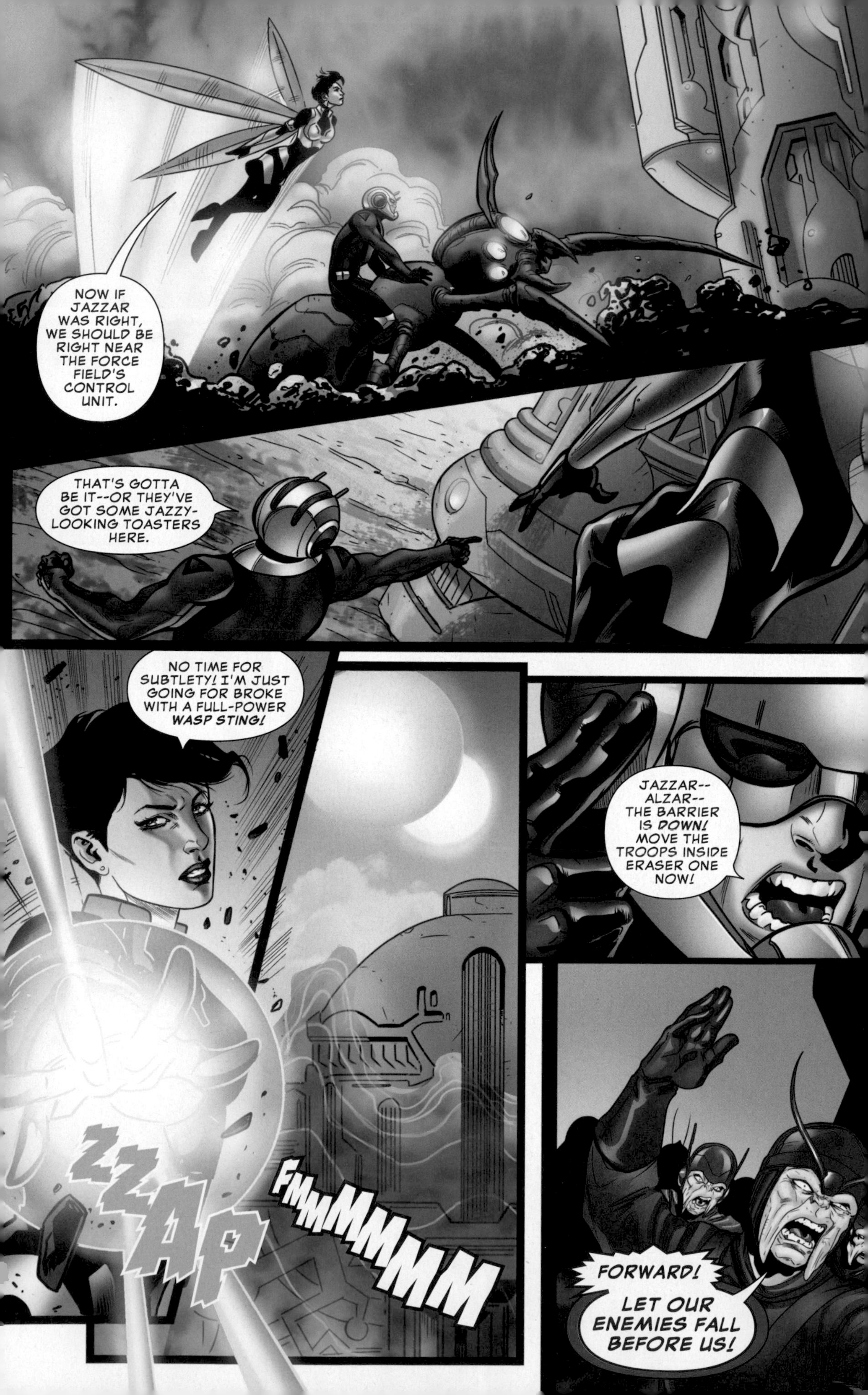
NOW IF JAZZAR WAS RIGHT, WE SHOULD BE RIGHT NEAR THE FORCE FIELD'S CONTROL UNIT.
THAT'S GOTTA BE IT--OR THEY'VE GOT SOME JAZZY-LOOKING TOASTERS HERE.
NO TIME FOR SUBTLETY! I'M JUST GOING FOR BROKE WITH A FULL-POWER WASP STING!
ZZZAP
FMMMMMMMM
JAZZAR-- ALZAR-- THE BARRIER IS DOWN! MOVE THE TROOPS INSIDE ERASER ONE NOW!
FORWARD!
LET OUR ENEMIES FALL BEFORE US!

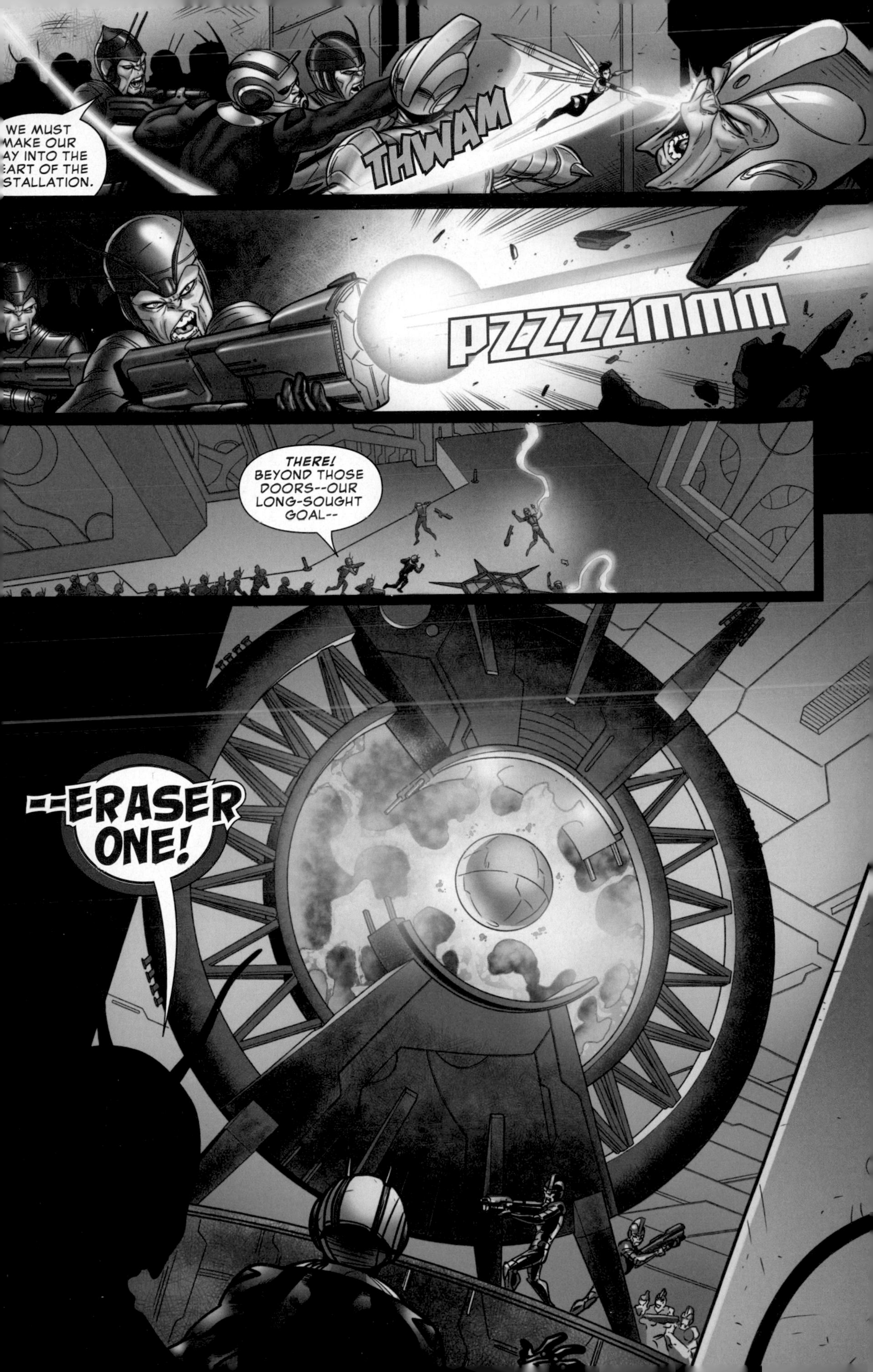

WE MUST
MAKE OUR
AY INTO THE
EART OF THE
STALLATION.
THWAM
PZZZZMMMM
THERE! BEYOND THOSE DOORS--OUR LONG-SOUGHT GOAL--
--ERASER ONE!

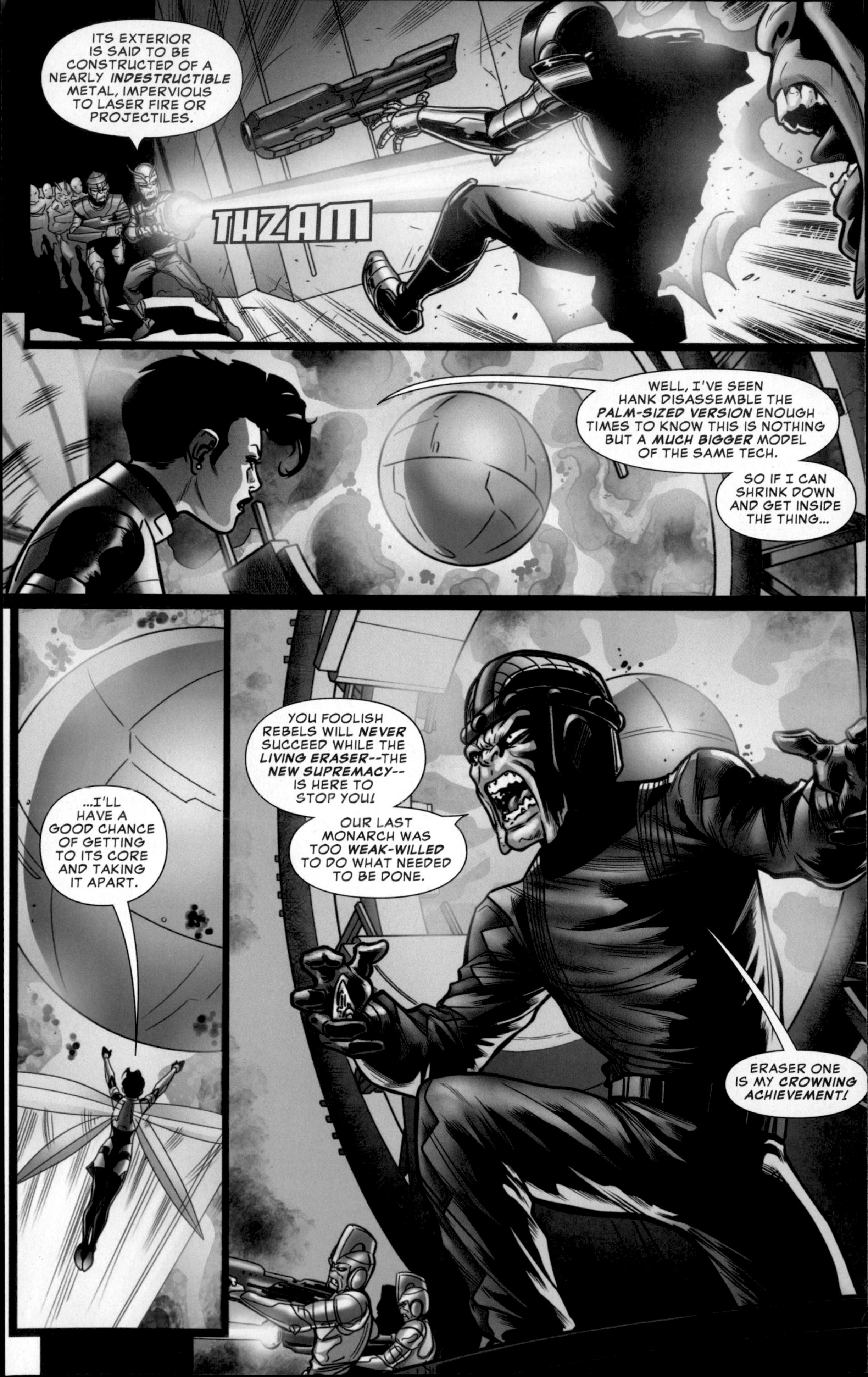
ITS EXTERIOR IS SAID TO BE CONSTRUCTED OF A NEARLY INDESTRUCTIBLE METAL, IMPERVIOUS TO LASER FIRE OR PROJECTILES.
THZAM
WELL, I'VE SEEN HANK DISASSEMBLE THE PALM-SIZED VERSION ENOUGH TIMES TO KNOW THIS IS NOTHING BUT A MUCH BIGGER MODEL OF THE SAME TECH.
SO IF I CAN SHRINK DOWN AND GET INSIDE THE THING...
...I'LL HAVE A GOOD CHANCE OF GETTING TO ITS CORE AND TAKING IT APART.
YOU FOOLISH REBELS WILL NEVER SUCCEED WHILE THE LIVING ERASER--THE NEW SUPREMACY--IS HERE TO STOP YOU!
OUR LAST MONARCH WAS TOO WEAK-WILLED TO DO WHAT NEEDED TO BE DONE.
ERASER ONE IS MY CROWNING ACHIEVEMENT!

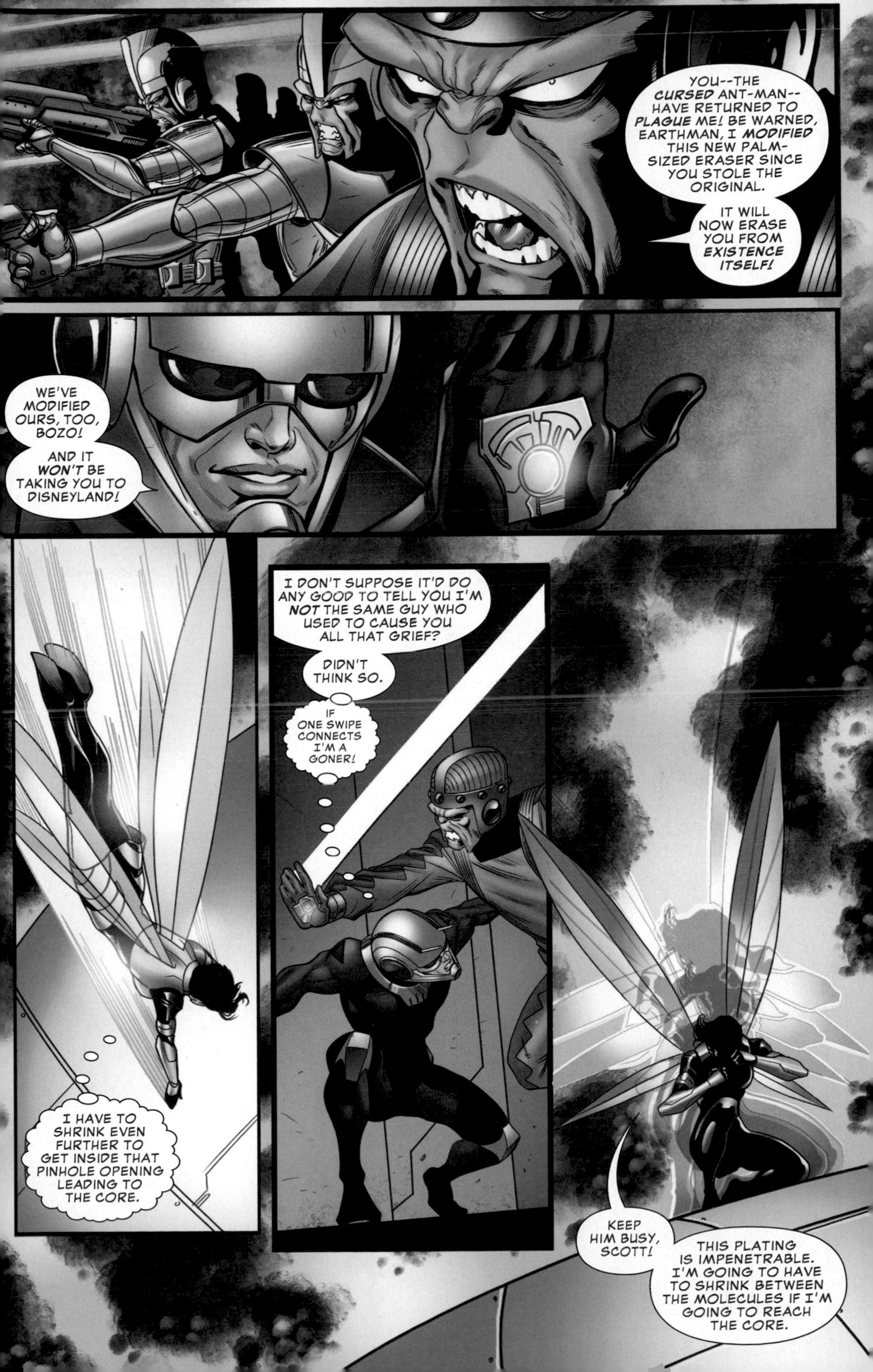
YOU--THE CURSED ANT-MAN--HAVE RETURNED TO PLAGUE ME! BE WARNED, EARTHMAN, I MODIFIED THIS NEW PALM-SIZED ERASER SINCE YOU STOLE THE ORIGINAL.
IT WILL NOW ERASE YOU FROM EXISTENCE ITSELF!
WE'VE MODIFIED OURS, TOO, BOZO!
AND IT WON'T BE TAKING YOU TO DISNEYLAND!
I HAVE TO SHRINK EVEN FURTHER TO GET INSIDE THAT PINHOLE OPENING LEADING TO THE CORE.
I DON'T SUPPOSE IT'D DO ANY GOOD TO TELL YOU I'M NOT THE SAME GUY WHO USED TO CAUSE YOU ALL THAT GRIEF?
DIDN'T THINK SO.
IF ONE SWIPE CONNECTS I'M A GONER!
KEEP HIM BUSY, SCOTT!
THIS PLATING IS IMPENETRABLE. I'M GOING TO HAVE TO SHRINK BETWEEN THE MOLECULES IF I'M GOING TO REACH THE CORE.

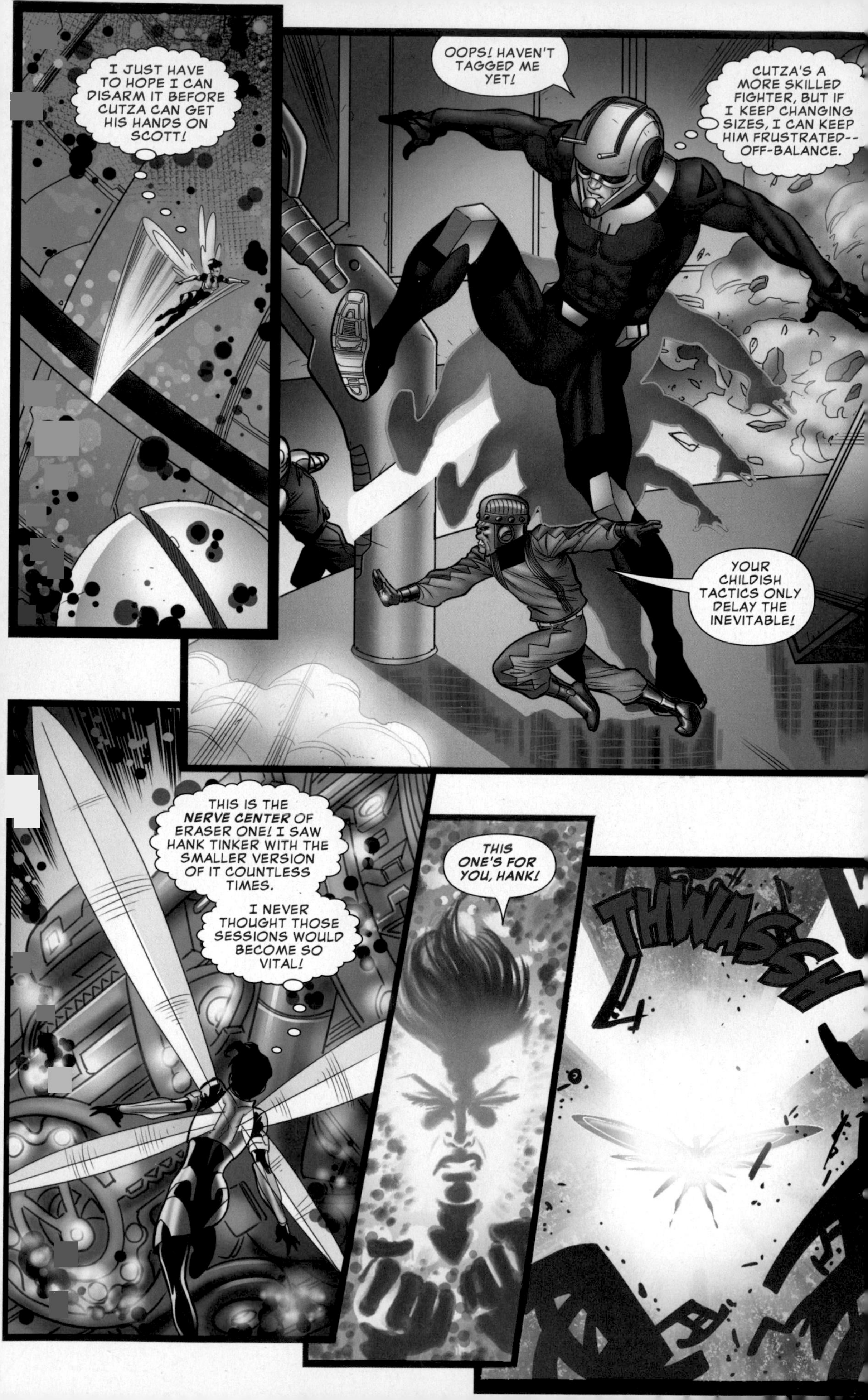

I JUST HAVE TO HOPE I CAN DISARM IT BEFORE CUTZA CAN GET HIS HANDS ON SCOTT!
OOPS! HAVEN'T TAGGED ME YET!
CUTZA'S A MORE SKILLED FIGHTER, BUT IF I KEEP CHANGING SIZES, I CAN KEEP HIM FRUSTRATED-- OFF-BALANCE.
YOUR CHILDISH TACTICS ONLY DELAY THE INEVITABLE!
THIS IS THE *NERVE CENTER* OF ERASER ONE! I SAW HANK TINKER WITH THE SMALLER VERSION OF IT COUNTLESS TIMES.
I NEVER THOUGHT THOSE SESSIONS WOULD BECOME SO VITAL!
THIS ONE'S FOR YOU, HANK!
THWASSH

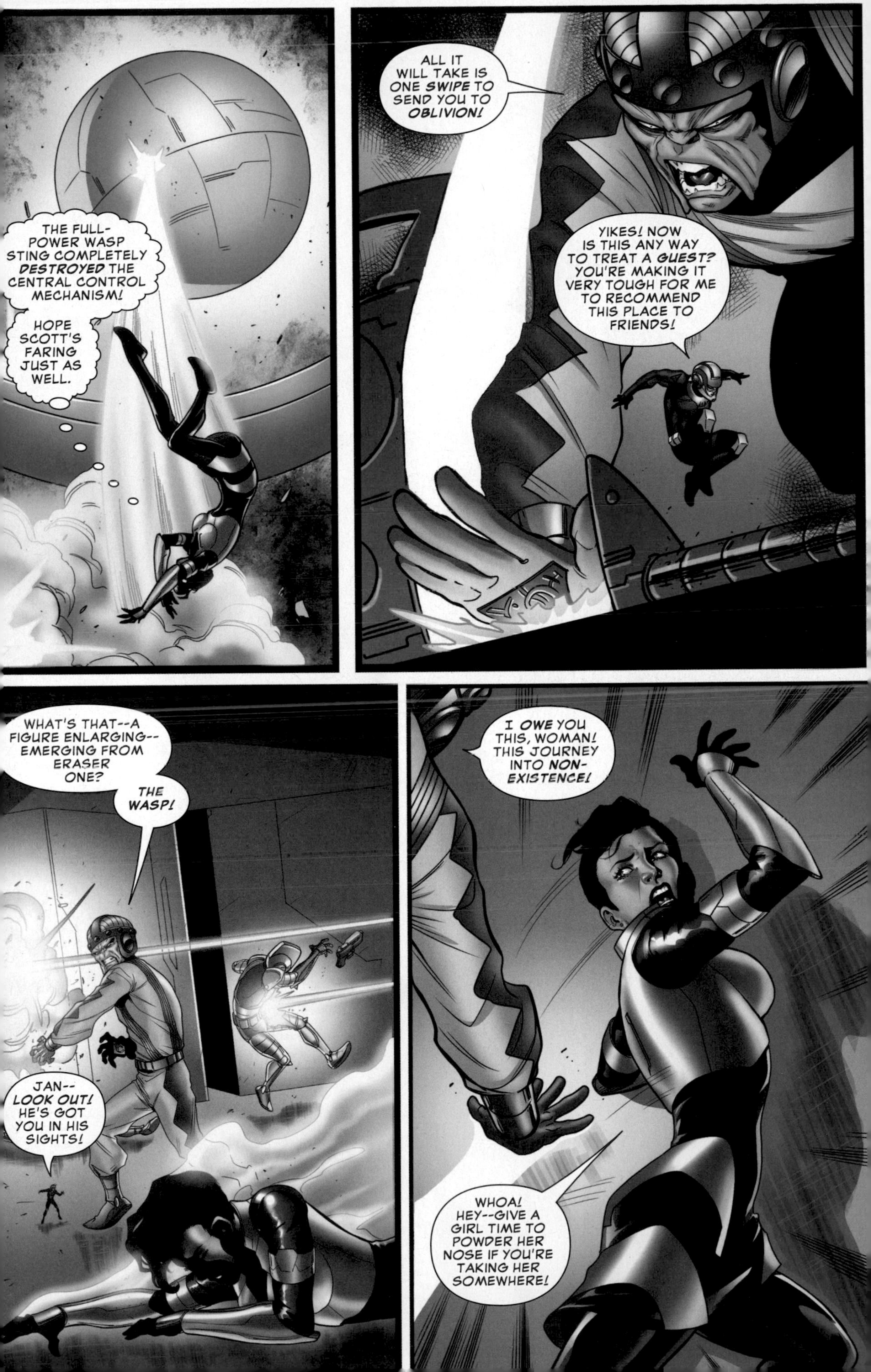
THE FULL-POWER WASP STING COMPLETELY DESTROYED THE CENTRAL CONTROL MECHANISM!
HOPE SCOTT'S FARING JUST AS WELL.
ALL IT WILL TAKE IS ONE SWIPE TO SEND YOU TO OBLIVION!
YIKES! NOW IS THIS ANY WAY TO TREAT A GUEST? YOU'RE MAKING IT VERY TOUGH FOR ME TO RECOMMEND THIS PLACE TO FRIENDS!
WHAT'S THAT--A FIGURE ENLARGING--EMERGING FROM ERASER ONE?
THE WASP!
JAN--LOOK OUT! HE'S GOT YOU IN HIS SIGHTS!
I OWE YOU THIS, WOMAN! THIS JOURNEY INTO NON-EXISTENCE!
WHOA! HEY--GIVE A GIRL TIME TO POWDER HER NOSE IF YOU'RE TAKING HER SOMEWHERE!

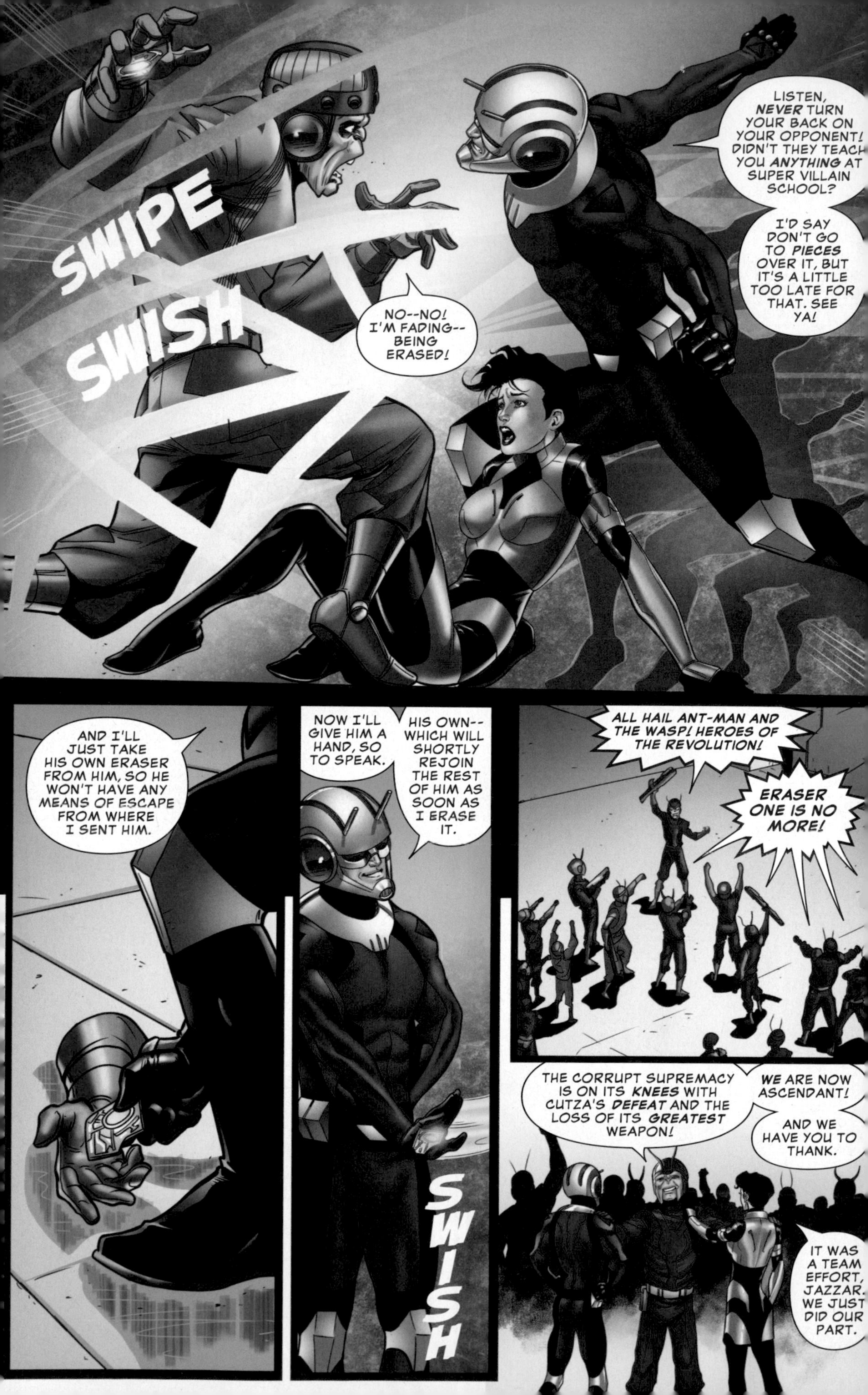
LISTEN, NEVER TURN YOUR BACK ON YOUR OPPONENT! DIDN'T THEY TEACH YOU ANYTHING AT SUPER VILLAIN SCHOOL?
I'D SAY DON'T GO TO PIECES OVER IT, BUT IT'S A LITTLE TOO LATE FOR THAT. SEE YA!
SWIPE
SWISH
NO--NO! I'M FADING--BEING ERASED!
AND I'LL JUST TAKE HIS OWN ERASER FROM HIM, SO HE WON'T HAVE ANY MEANS OF ESCAPE FROM WHERE I SENT HIM.
NOW I'LL GIVE HIM A HAND, SO TO SPEAK.
HIS OWN--WHICH WILL SHORTLY REJOIN THE REST OF HIM AS SOON AS I ERASE IT.
SWISH
ALL HAIL ANT-MAN AND THE WASP! HEROES OF THE REVOLUTION!
ERASER ONE IS NO MORE!
THE CORRUPT SUPREMACY IS ON ITS KNEES WITH CUTZA'S DEFEAT AND THE LOSS OF ITS GREATEST WEAPON!
WE ARE NOW ASCENDANT!
AND WE HAVE YOU TO THANK.
IT WAS A TEAM EFFORT, JAZZAR. WE JUST DID OUR PART.

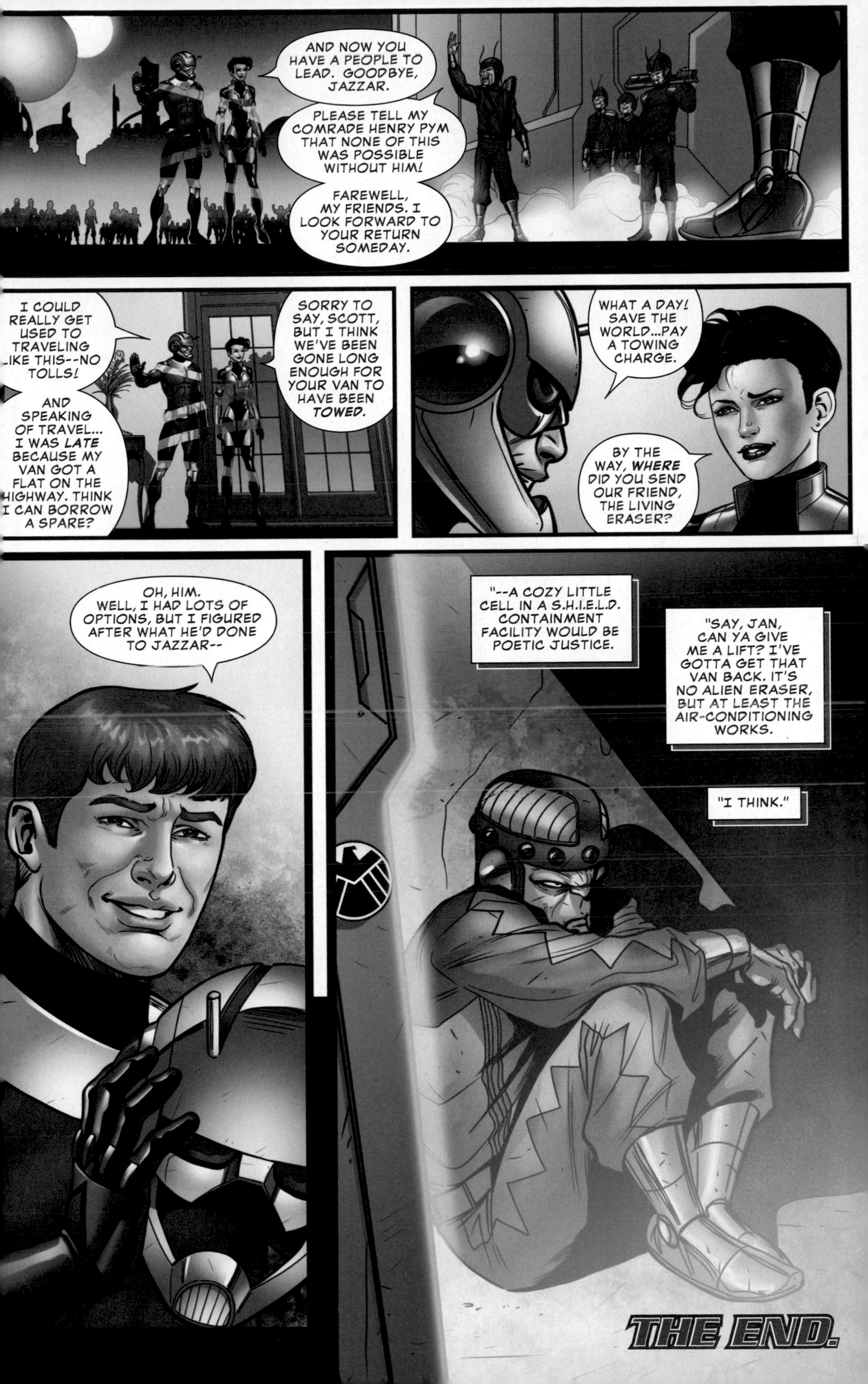
AND NOW YOU HAVE A PEOPLE TO LEAD. GOODBYE, JAZZAR.
PLEASE TELL MY COMRADE HENRY PYM THAT NONE OF THIS WAS POSSIBLE WITHOUT HIM!
FAREWELL, MY FRIENDS. I LOOK FORWARD TO YOUR RETURN SOMEDAY.
I COULD REALLY GET USED TO TRAVELING LIKE THIS--NO TOLLS!
AND SPEAKING OF TRAVEL... I WAS LATE BECAUSE MY VAN GOT A FLAT ON THE HIGHWAY. THINK I CAN BORROW A SPARE?
SORRY TO SAY, SCOTT, BUT I THINK WE'VE BEEN GONE LONG ENOUGH FOR YOUR VAN TO HAVE BEEN TOWED.
WHAT A DAY! SAVE THE WORLD...PAY A TOWING CHARGE.
BY THE WAY, WHERE DID YOU SEND OUR FRIEND, THE LIVING ERASER?
OH, HIM. WELL, I HAD LOTS OF OPTIONS, BUT I FIGURED AFTER WHAT HE'D DONE TO JAZZAR--
"--A COZY LITTLE CELL IN A S.H.I.E.L.D. CONTAINMENT FACILITY WOULD BE POETIC JUSTICE.
"SAY, JAN, CAN YA GIVE ME A LIFT? I'VE GOTTA GET THAT VAN BACK. IT'S NO ALIEN ERASER, BUT AT LEAST THE AIR-CONDITIONING WORKS.
"I THINK."
THE END.

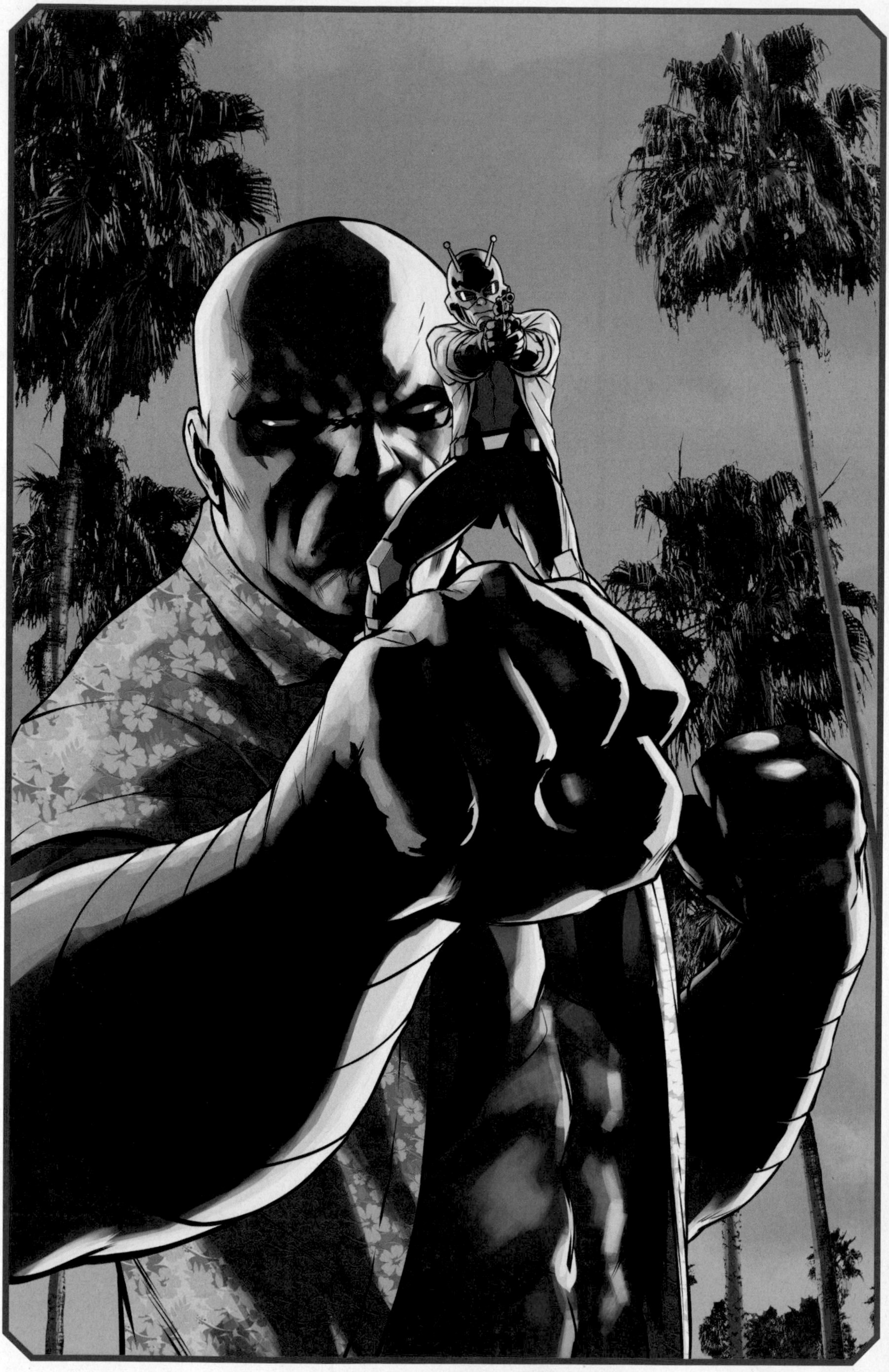

GUARDIANS TEAM-UP #7

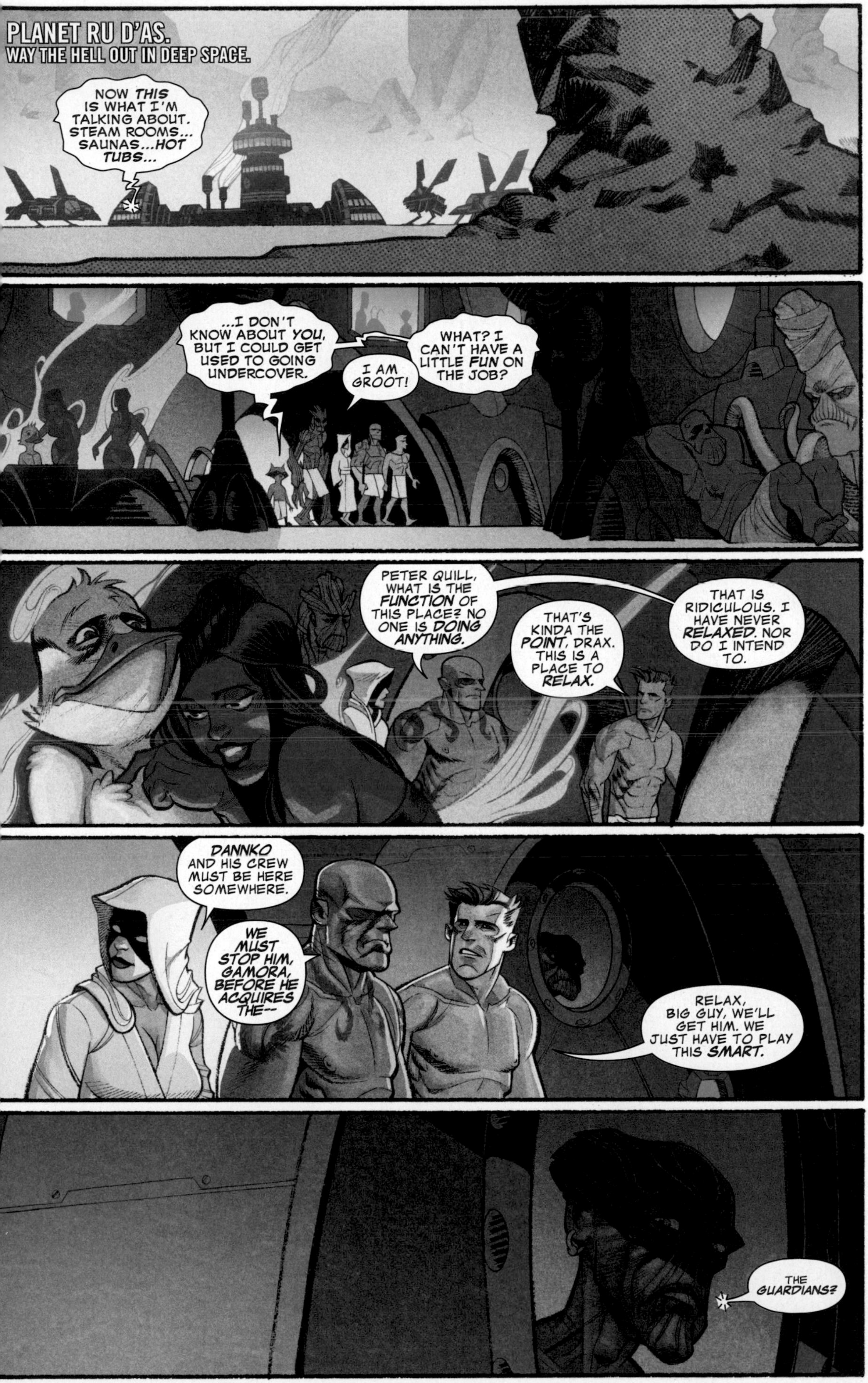
PLANET RU D'AS.
WAY THE HELL OUT IN DEEP SPACE.
NOW THIS IS WHAT I'M TALKING ABOUT. STEAM ROOMS... SAUNAS...HOT TUBS...
...I DON'T KNOW ABOUT YOU, BUT I COULD GET USED TO GOING UNDERCOVER.
WHAT? I CAN'T HAVE A LITTLE FUN ON THE JOB?
I AM GROOT!
PETER QUILL, WHAT IS THE FUNCTION OF THIS PLACE? NO ONE IS DOING ANYTHING.
THAT'S KINDA THE POINT, DRAX. THIS IS A PLACE TO RELAX.
THAT IS RIDICULOUS. I HAVE NEVER RELAXED. NOR DO I INTEND TO.
DANNKO AND HIS CREW MUST BE HERE SOMEWHERE.
WE MUST STOP HIM, GAMORA, BEFORE HE ACQUIRES THE--
RELAX, BIG GUY, WE'LL GET HIM. WE JUST HAVE TO PLAY THIS SMART.
THE GUARDIANS?

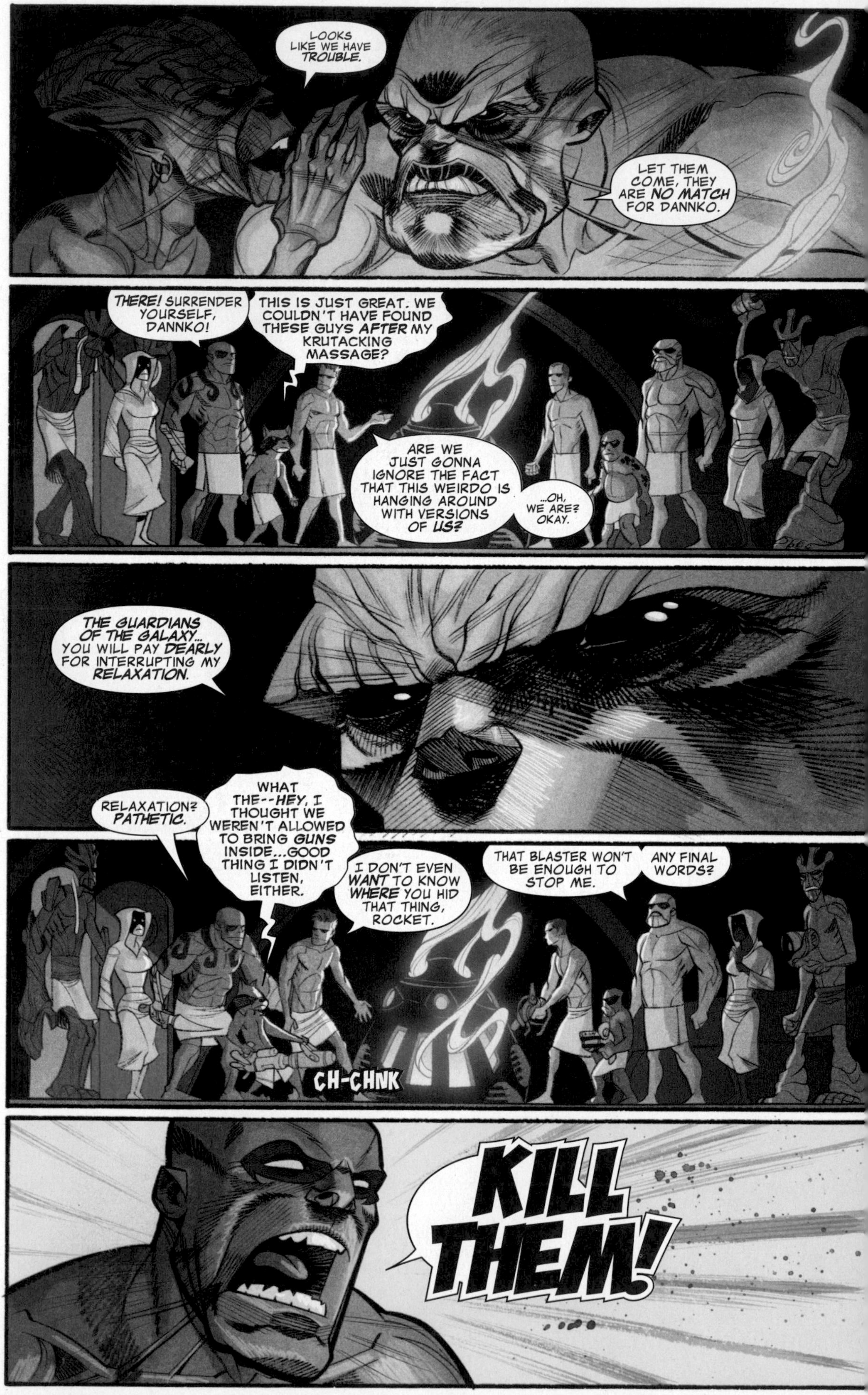
LOOKS LIKE WE HAVE TROUBLE.
LET THEM COME, THEY ARE NO MATCH FOR DANNKO.
THERE! SURRENDER YOURSELF, DANNKO!
THIS IS JUST GREAT. WE COULDN'T HAVE FOUND THESE GUYS AFTER MY KRUTACKING MASSAGE?
ARE WE JUST GONNA IGNORE THE FACT THAT THIS WEIRDO IS HANGING AROUND WITH VERSIONS OF US?
...OH, WE ARE? OKAY.
THE GUARDIANS OF THE GALAXY... YOU WILL PAY DEARLY FOR INTERRUPTING MY RELAXATION.
RELAXATION? PATHETIC.
WHAT THE--HEY, I THOUGHT WE WEREN'T ALLOWED TO BRING GUNS INSIDE...GOOD THING I DIDN'T LISTEN, EITHER.
I DON'T EVEN WANT TO KNOW WHERE YOU HID THAT THING, ROCKET.
THAT BLASTER WON'T BE ENOUGH TO STOP ME.
ANY FINAL WORDS?
CH-CHNK
KILL THEM!

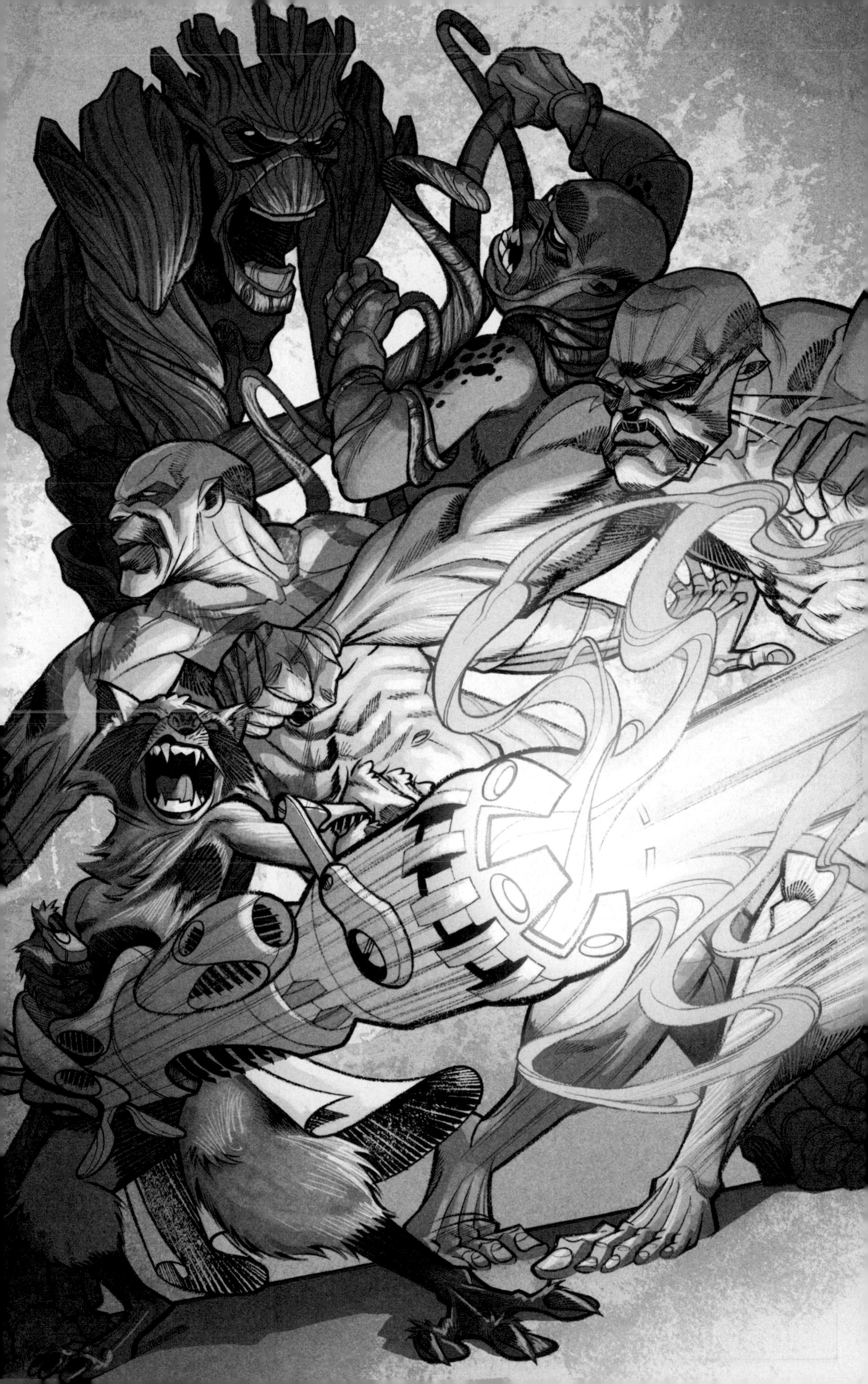

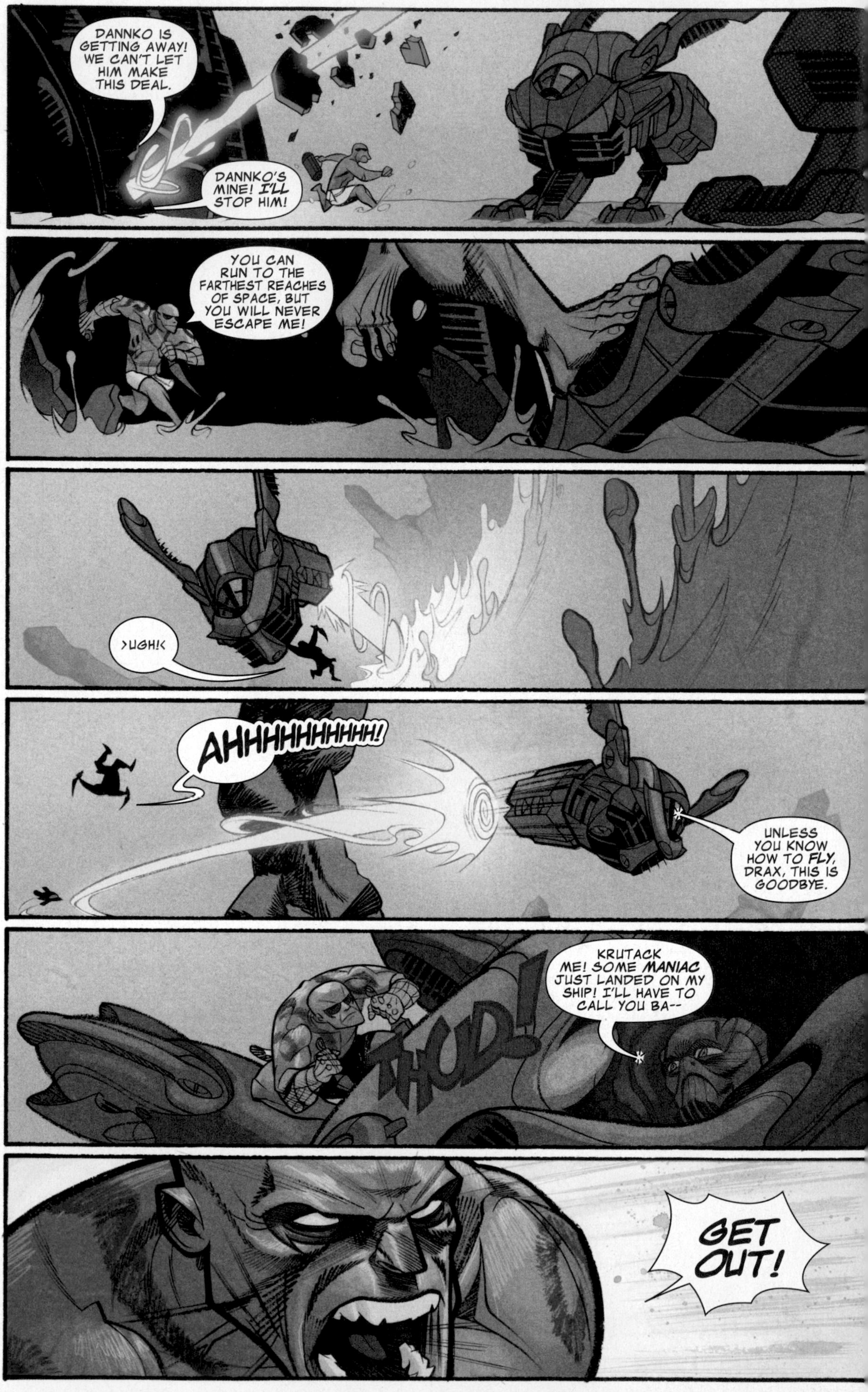
DANNKO IS GETTING AWAY! WE CAN'T LET HIM MAKE THIS DEAL.
DANNKO'S MINE! I'LL STOP HIM!
YOU CAN RUN TO THE FARTHEST REACHES OF SPACE, BUT YOU WILL NEVER ESCAPE ME!
>UGH!<
AHHHHHHHHHH!
UNLESS YOU KNOW HOW TO FLY, DRAX, THIS IS GOODBYE.
KRUTACK ME! SOME MANIAC JUST LANDED ON MY SHIP! I'LL HAVE TO CALL YOU BA--
THUD!
GET OUT!

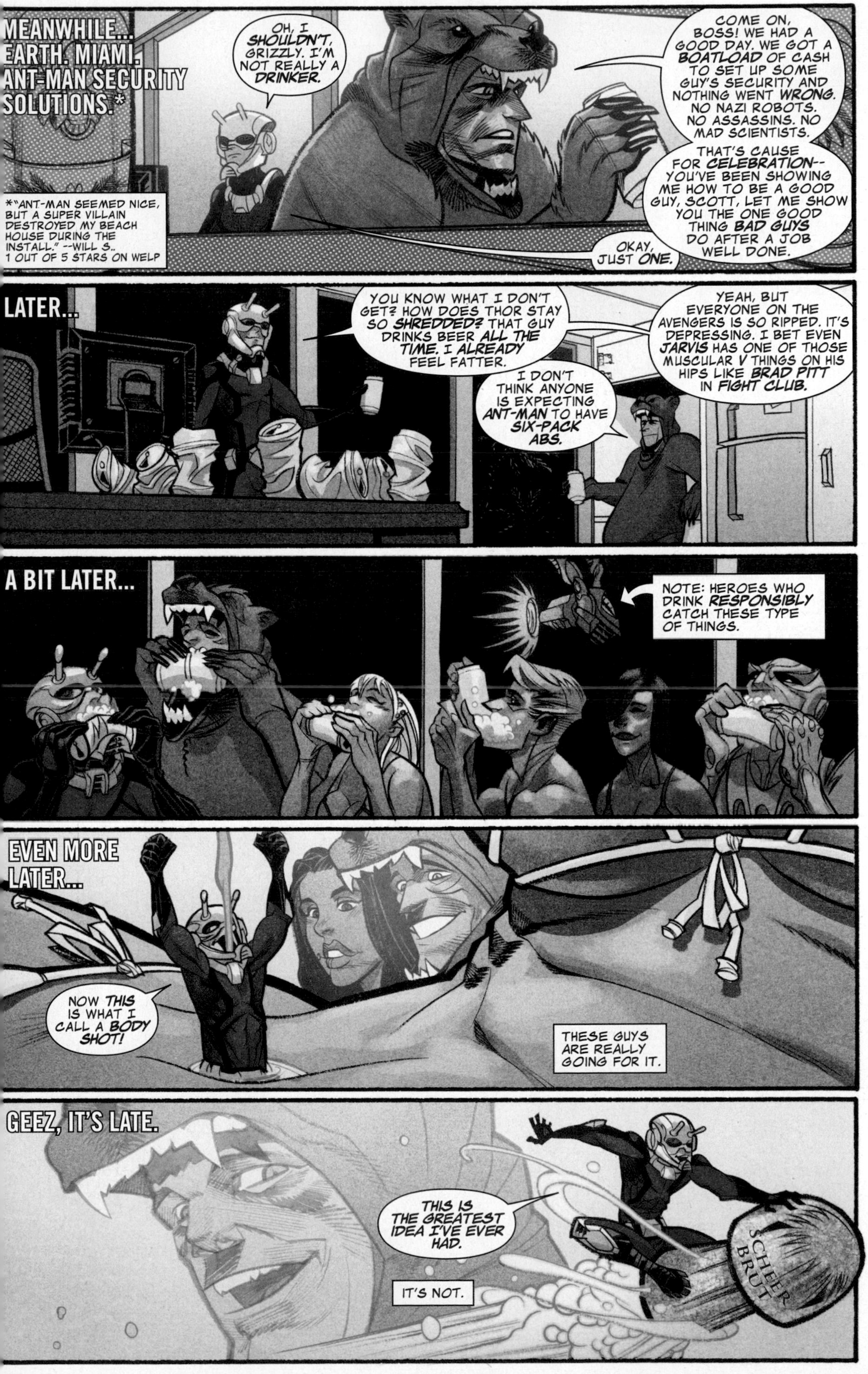
MEANWHILE... EARTH. MIAMI. ANT-MAN SECURITY SOLUTIONS.*
*"ANT-MAN SEEMED NICE, BUT A SUPER VILLAIN DESTROYED MY BEACH HOUSE DURING THE INSTALL." --WILL S.. 1 OUT OF 5 STARS ON WELP
OH, I SHOULDN'T, GRIZZLY. I'M NOT REALLY A DRINKER.
COME ON, BOSS! WE HAD A GOOD DAY. WE GOT A BOATLOAD OF CASH TO SET UP SOME GUY'S SECURITY AND NOTHING WENT WRONG. NO NAZI ROBOTS. NO ASSASSINS. NO MAD SCIENTISTS.
THAT'S CAUSE FOR CELEBRATION-- YOU'VE BEEN SHOWING ME HOW TO BE A GOOD GUY, SCOTT, LET ME SHOW YOU THE ONE GOOD THING BAD GUYS DO AFTER A JOB WELL DONE.
OKAY, JUST ONE.
LATER...
YOU KNOW WHAT I DON'T GET? HOW DOES THOR STAY SO SHREDDED? THAT GUY DRINKS BEER ALL THE TIME. I ALREADY FEEL FATTER.
I DON'T THINK ANYONE IS EXPECTING ANT-MAN TO HAVE SIX-PACK ABS.
YEAH, BUT EVERYONE ON THE AVENGERS IS SO RIPPED. IT'S DEPRESSING. I BET EVEN JARVIS HAS ONE OF THOSE MUSCULAR V THINGS ON HIS HIPS LIKE BRAD PITT IN FIGHT CLUB.
A BIT LATER...
NOTE: HEROES WHO DRINK RESPONSIBLY CATCH THESE TYPE OF THINGS.
EVEN MORE LATER...
NOW THIS IS WHAT I CALL A BODY SHOT!
THESE GUYS ARE REALLY GOING FOR IT.
GEEZ, IT'S LATE.
THIS IS THE GREATEST IDEA I'VE EVER HAD.
IT'S NOT.
SCHEER BRUT

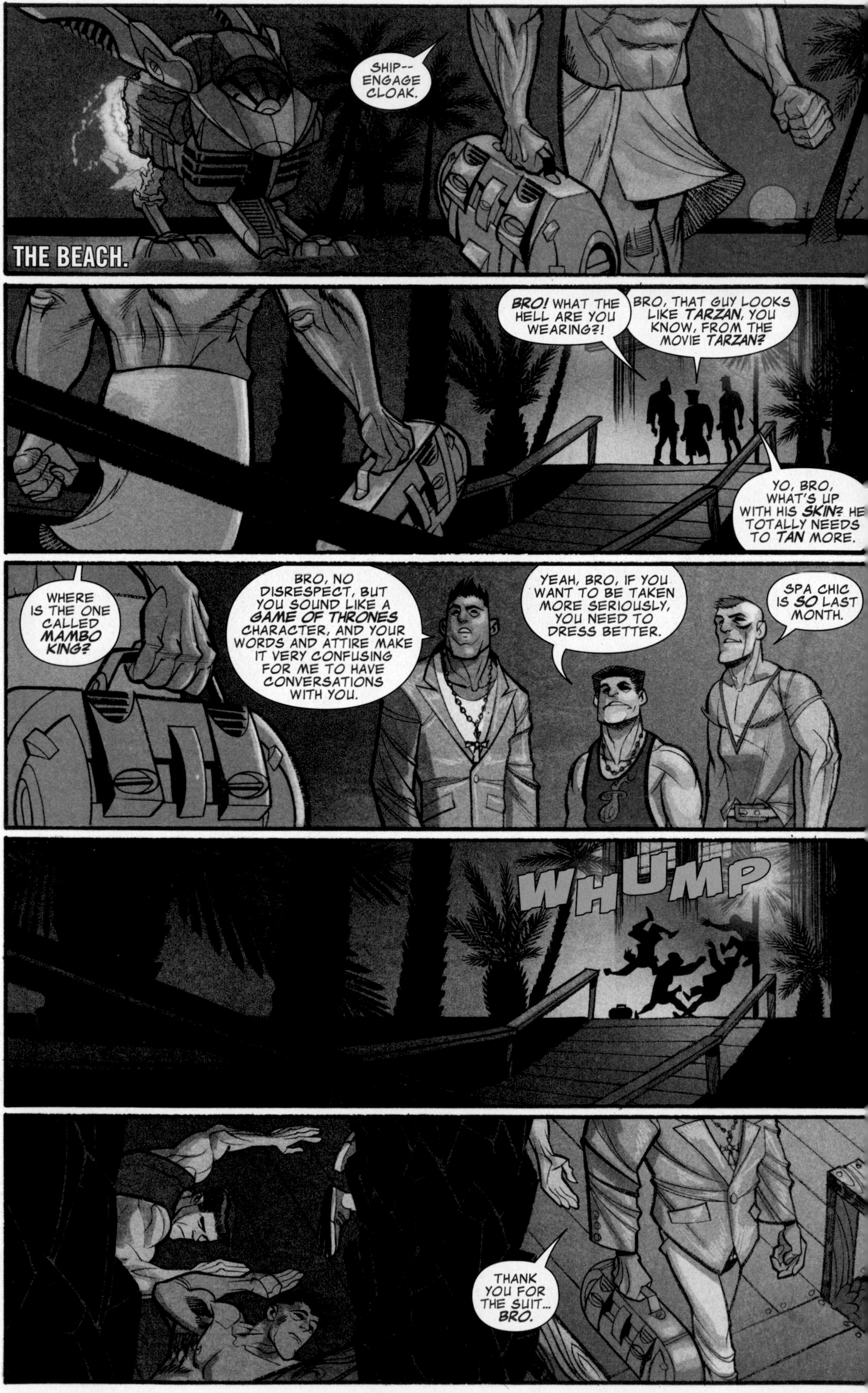
SHIP-- ENGAGE CLOAK.
THE BEACH.
BRO! WHAT THE HELL ARE YOU WEARING?!
BRO, THAT GUY LOOKS LIKE TARZAN, YOU KNOW, FROM THE MOVIE TARZAN?
YO, BRO, WHAT'S UP WITH HIS SKIN? HE TOTALLY NEEDS TO TAN MORE.
WHERE IS THE ONE CALLED MAMBO KING?
BRO, NO DISRESPECT, BUT YOU SOUND LIKE A GAME OF THRONES CHARACTER, AND YOUR WORDS AND ATTIRE MAKE IT VERY CONFUSING FOR ME TO HAVE CONVERSATIONS WITH YOU.
YEAH, BRO, IF YOU WANT TO BE TAKEN MORE SERIOUSLY, YOU NEED TO DRESS BETTER.
SPA CHIC IS SO LAST MONTH.
WHUMP
THANK YOU FOR THE SUIT... BRO.

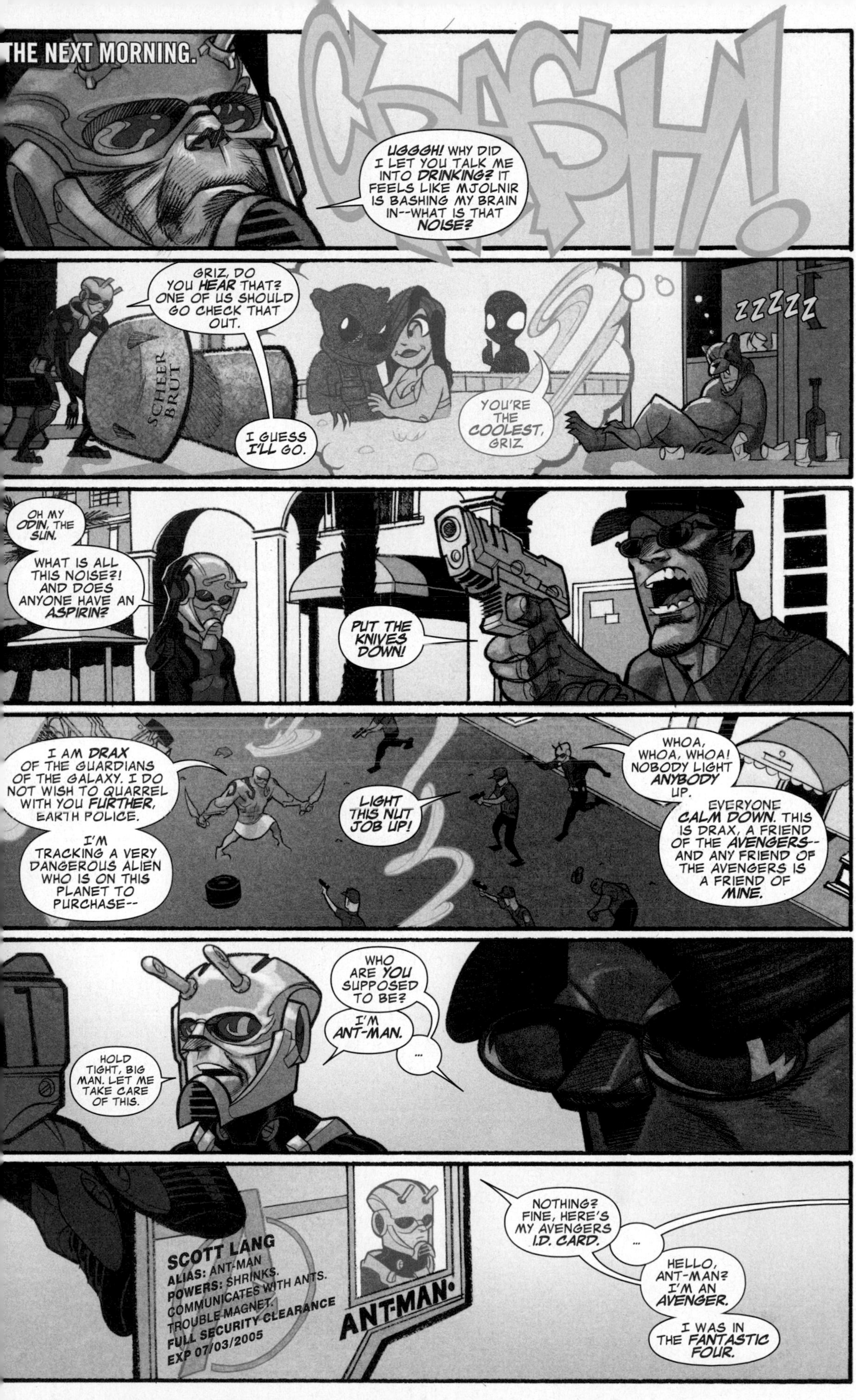
THE NEXT MORNING.
CRASH!
UGGGH! WHY DID I LET YOU TALK ME INTO DRINKING? IT FEELS LIKE MJOLNIR IS BASHING MY BRAIN IN--WHAT IS THAT NOISE?
GRIZ, DO YOU HEAR THAT? ONE OF US SHOULD GO CHECK THAT OUT.
SCHEER BRUT
I GUESS I'LL GO.
YOU'RE THE COOLEST, GRIZ.
ZZZZZ
OH MY ODIN, THE SUN.
WHAT IS ALL THIS NOISE?! AND DOES ANYONE HAVE AN ASPIRIN?
PUT THE KNIVES DOWN!
I AM DRAX OF THE GUARDIANS OF THE GALAXY. I DO NOT WISH TO QUARREL WITH YOU FURTHER, EARTH POLICE.
I'M TRACKING A VERY DANGEROUS ALIEN WHO IS ON THIS PLANET TO PURCHASE--
LIGHT THIS NUT JOB UP!
WHOA, WHOA, WHOA! NOBODY LIGHT ANYBODY UP.
EVERYONE CALM DOWN. THIS IS DRAX, A FRIEND OF THE AVENGERS--AND ANY FRIEND OF THE AVENGERS IS A FRIEND OF MINE.
HOLD TIGHT, BIG MAN. LET ME TAKE CARE OF THIS.
WHO ARE YOU SUPPOSED TO BE?
I'M ANT-MAN.
...
SCOTT LANG
ALIAS: ANT-MAN
POWERS: SHRINKS. COMMUNICATES WITH ANTS. TROUBLE MAGNET.
FULL SECURITY CLEARANCE
EXP 07/03/2005
ANT-MAN
NOTHING? FINE, HERE'S MY AVENGERS I.D. CARD.
...
HELLO, ANT-MAN? I'M AN AVENGER.
I WAS IN THE FANTASTIC FOUR.

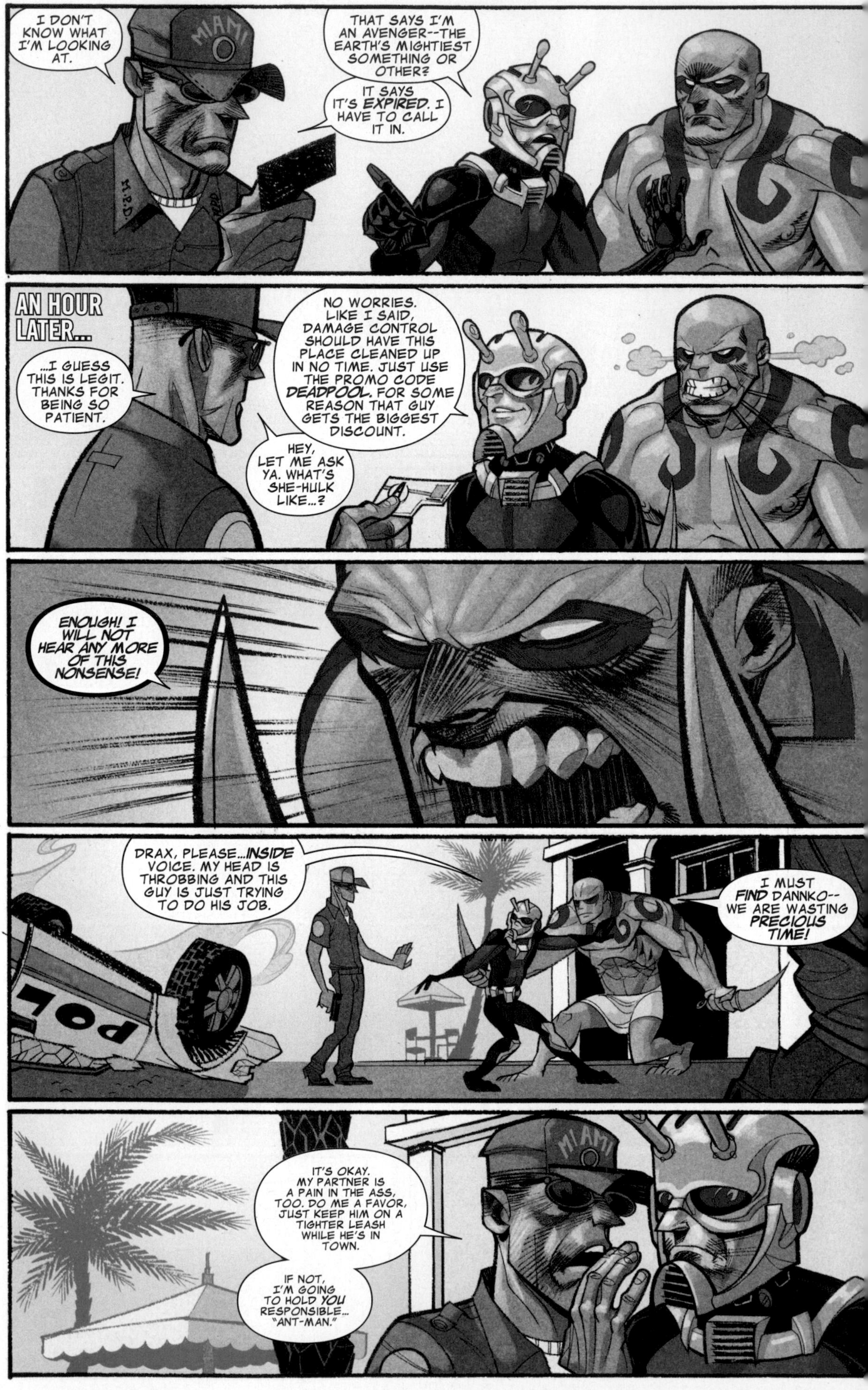
I DON'T KNOW WHAT I'M LOOKING AT.
THAT SAYS I'M AN AVENGER--THE EARTH'S MIGHTIEST SOMETHING OR OTHER?
IT SAYS IT'S EXPIRED. I HAVE TO CALL IT IN.
M.P.D.
AN HOUR LATER...
...I GUESS THIS IS LEGIT. THANKS FOR BEING SO PATIENT.
NO WORRIES. LIKE I SAID, DAMAGE CONTROL SHOULD HAVE THIS PLACE CLEANED UP IN NO TIME. JUST USE THE PROMO CODE DEADPOOL. FOR SOME REASON THAT GUY GETS THE BIGGEST DISCOUNT.
HEY, LET ME ASK YA. WHAT'S SHE-HULK LIKE...?
ENOUGH! I WILL NOT HEAR ANY MORE OF THIS NONSENSE!
DRAX, PLEASE...INSIDE VOICE. MY HEAD IS THROBBING AND THIS GUY IS JUST TRYING TO DO HIS JOB.
I MUST FIND DANNKO-- WE ARE WASTING PRECIOUS TIME!
POL
IT'S OKAY. MY PARTNER IS A PAIN IN THE ASS, TOO. DO ME A FAVOR, JUST KEEP HIM ON A TIGHTER LEASH WHILE HE'S IN TOWN.
IF NOT, I'M GOING TO HOLD YOU RESPONSIBLE... "ANT-MAN."

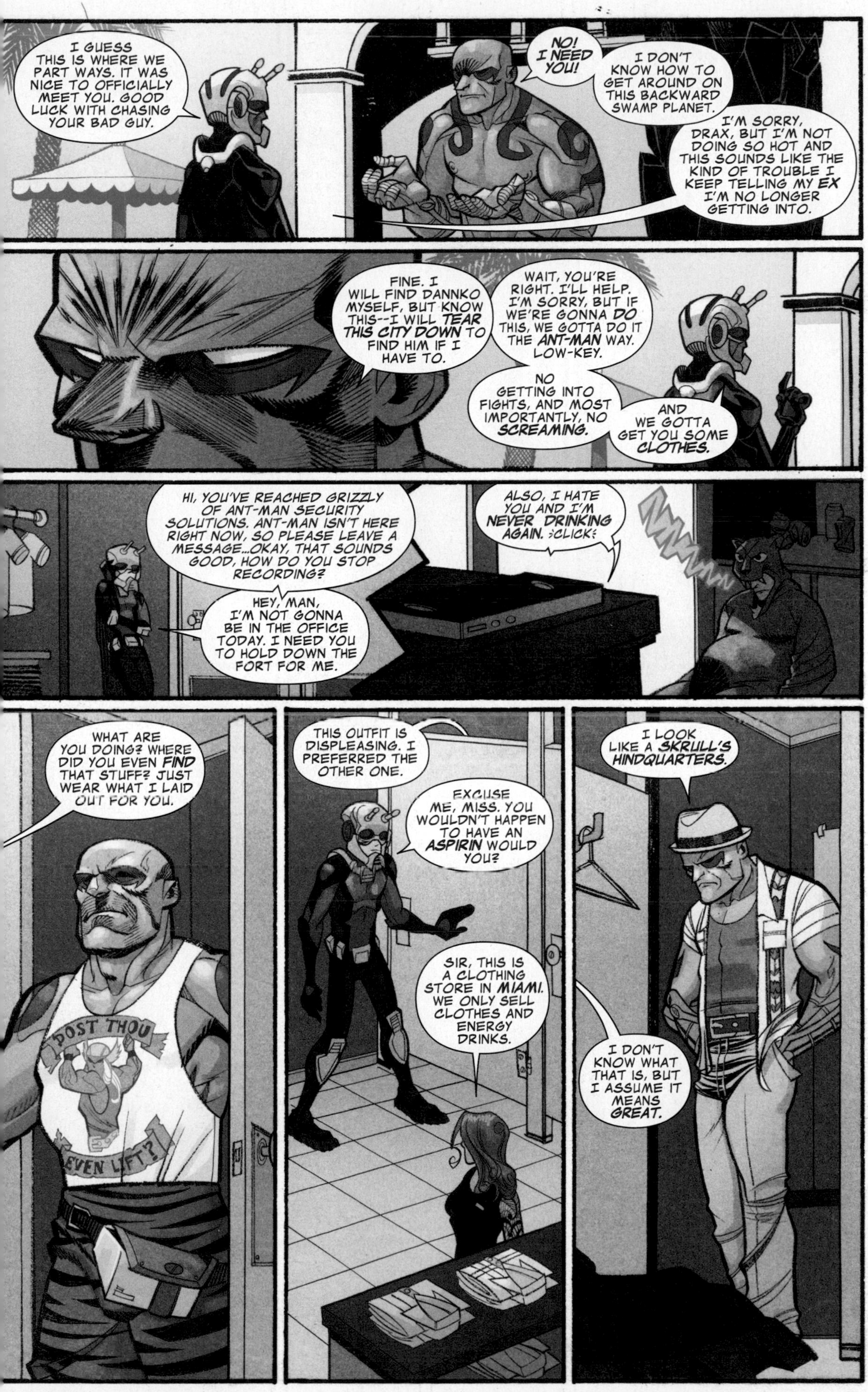
I GUESS THIS IS WHERE WE PART WAYS. IT WAS NICE TO OFFICIALLY MEET YOU. GOOD LUCK WITH CHASING YOUR BAD GUY.
NO! I NEED YOU!
I DON'T KNOW HOW TO GET AROUND ON THIS BACKWARD SWAMP PLANET.
I'M SORRY, DRAX, BUT I'M NOT DOING SO HOT AND THIS SOUNDS LIKE THE KIND OF TROUBLE I KEEP TELLING MY EX I'M NO LONGER GETTING INTO.
FINE. I WILL FIND DANNKO MYSELF, BUT KNOW THIS--I WILL TEAR THIS CITY DOWN TO FIND HIM IF I HAVE TO.
WAIT, YOU'RE RIGHT. I'LL HELP. I'M SORRY, BUT IF WE'RE GONNA DO THIS, WE GOTTA DO IT THE ANT-MAN WAY. LOW-KEY.
NO GETTING INTO FIGHTS, AND MOST IMPORTANTLY, NO SCREAMING.
AND WE GOTTA GET YOU SOME CLOTHES.
HI, YOU'VE REACHED GRIZZLY OF ANT-MAN SECURITY SOLUTIONS. ANT-MAN ISN'T HERE RIGHT NOW, SO PLEASE LEAVE A MESSAGE...OKAY, THAT SOUNDS GOOD, HOW DO YOU STOP RECORDING?
HEY, MAN, I'M NOT GONNA BE IN THE OFFICE TODAY. I NEED YOU TO HOLD DOWN THE FORT FOR ME.
ALSO, I HATE YOU AND I'M NEVER DRINKING AGAIN. *CLICK*
WHAT ARE YOU DOING? WHERE DID YOU EVEN FIND THAT STUFF? JUST WEAR WHAT I LAID OUT FOR YOU.
DOST THOU EVEN LIFT?
THIS OUTFIT IS DISPLEASING. I PREFERRED THE OTHER ONE.
EXCUSE ME, MISS. YOU WOULDN'T HAPPEN TO HAVE AN ASPIRIN WOULD YOU?
SIR, THIS IS A CLOTHING STORE IN MIAMI. WE ONLY SELL CLOTHES AND ENERGY DRINKS.
I LOOK LIKE A SKRULL'S HINDQUARTERS.
I DON'T KNOW WHAT THAT IS, BUT I ASSUME IT MEANS GREAT.

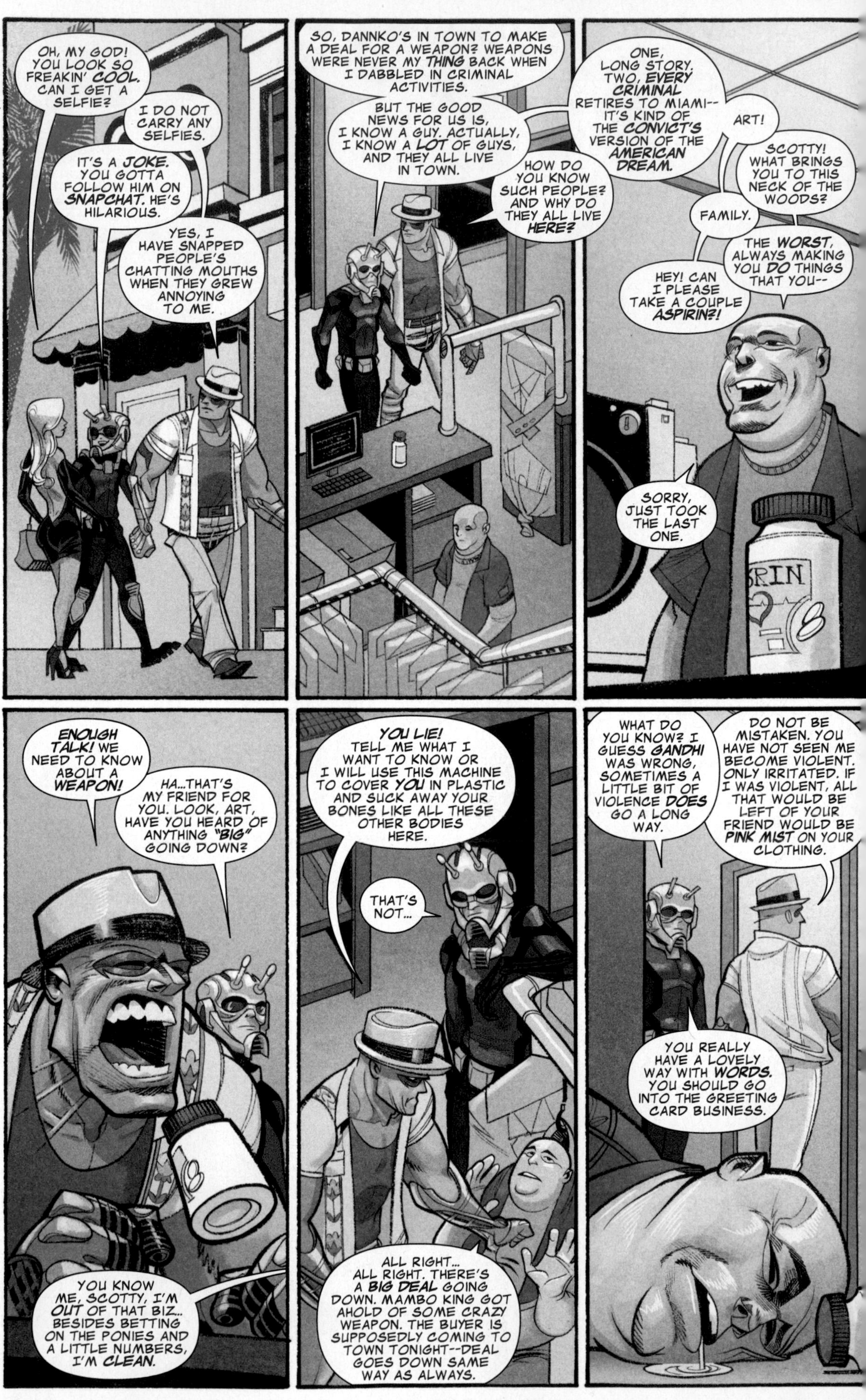
OH, MY GOD! YOU LOOK SO FREAKIN' COOL. CAN I GET A SELFIE?
I DO NOT CARRY ANY SELFIES.
IT'S A JOKE. YOU GOTTA FOLLOW HIM ON SNAPCHAT. HE'S HILARIOUS.
YES, I HAVE SNAPPED PEOPLE'S CHATTING MOUTHS WHEN THEY GREW ANNOYING TO ME.
SO, DANNKO'S IN TOWN TO MAKE A DEAL FOR A WEAPON? WEAPONS WERE NEVER MY THING BACK WHEN I DABBLED IN CRIMINAL ACTIVITIES.
BUT THE GOOD NEWS FOR US IS, I KNOW A GUY. ACTUALLY, I KNOW A LOT OF GUYS, AND THEY ALL LIVE IN TOWN.
HOW DO YOU KNOW SUCH PEOPLE? AND WHY DO THEY ALL LIVE HERE?
ONE, LONG STORY. TWO, EVERY CRIMINAL RETIRES TO MIAMI-- IT'S KIND OF THE CONVICT'S VERSION OF THE AMERICAN DREAM.
ART!
SCOTTY! WHAT BRINGS YOU TO THIS NECK OF THE WOODS?
FAMILY.
THE WORST, ALWAYS MAKING YOU DO THINGS THAT YOU--
HEY! CAN I PLEASE TAKE A COUPLE ASPIRIN?!
SORRY, JUST TOOK THE LAST ONE.
ENOUGH TALK! WE NEED TO KNOW ABOUT A WEAPON!
HA...THAT'S MY FRIEND FOR YOU. LOOK, ART, HAVE YOU HEARD OF ANYTHING "BIG" GOING DOWN?
YOU KNOW ME, SCOTTY, I'M OUT OF THAT BIZ... BESIDES BETTING ON THE PONIES AND A LITTLE NUMBERS, I'M CLEAN.
YOU LIE! TELL ME WHAT I WANT TO KNOW OR I WILL USE THIS MACHINE TO COVER YOU IN PLASTIC AND SUCK AWAY YOUR BONES LIKE ALL THESE OTHER BODIES HERE.
THAT'S NOT...
ALL RIGHT... ALL RIGHT. THERE'S A BIG DEAL GOING DOWN. MAMBO KING GOT AHOLD OF SOME CRAZY WEAPON. THE BUYER IS SUPPOSEDLY COMING TO TOWN TONIGHT--DEAL GOES DOWN SAME WAY AS ALWAYS.
WHAT DO YOU KNOW? I GUESS GANDHI WAS WRONG, SOMETIMES A LITTLE BIT OF VIOLENCE DOES GO A LONG WAY.
DO NOT BE MISTAKEN. YOU HAVE NOT SEEN ME BECOME VIOLENT. ONLY IRRITATED. IF I WAS VIOLENT, ALL THAT WOULD BE LEFT OF YOUR FRIEND WOULD BE PINK MIST ON YOUR CLOTHING.
YOU REALLY HAVE A LOVELY WAY WITH WORDS. YOU SHOULD GO INTO THE GREETING CARD BUSINESS.

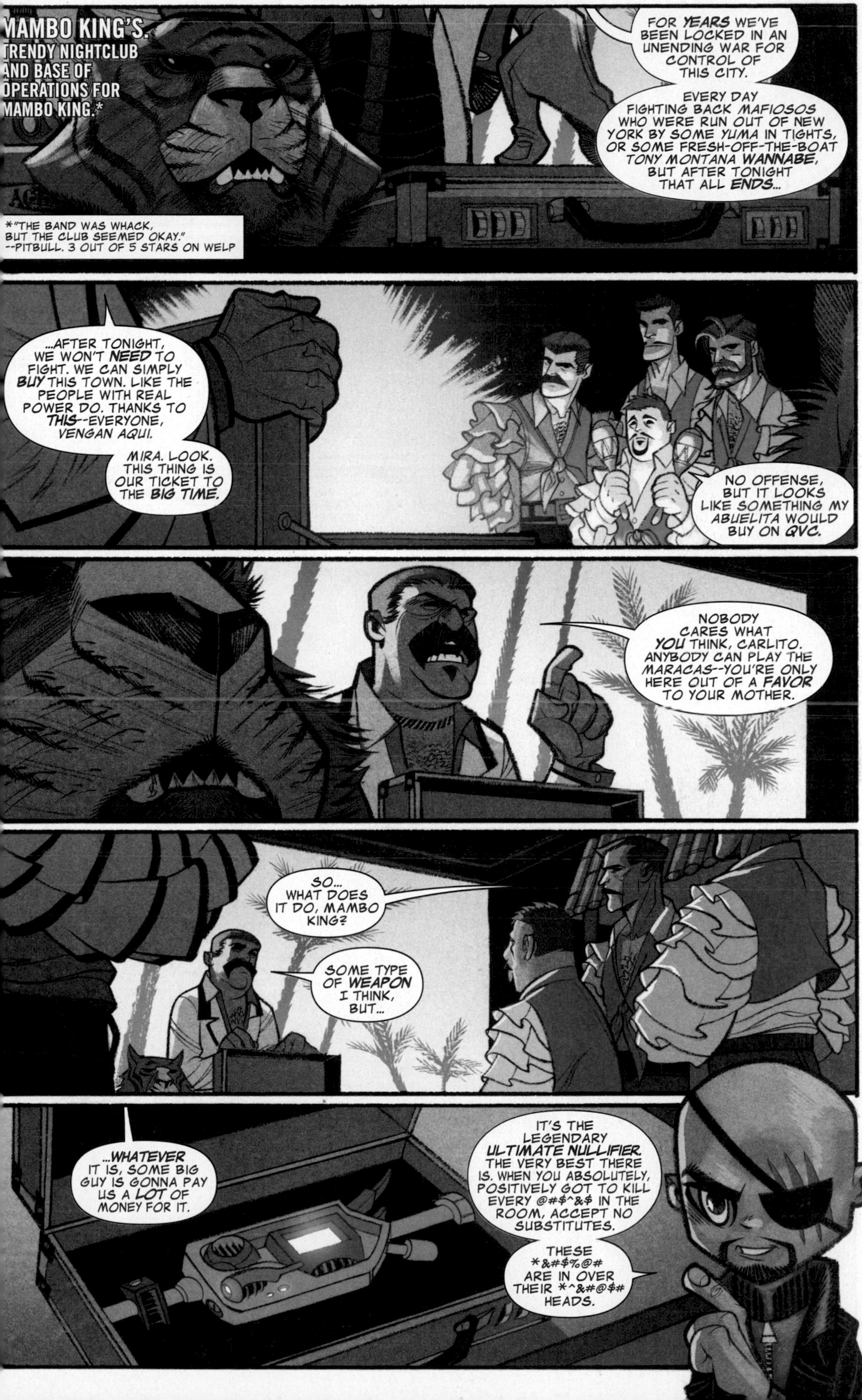
MAMBO KING'S. TRENDY NIGHTCLUB AND BASE OF OPERATIONS FOR MAMBO KING.*
*"THE BAND WAS WHACK, BUT THE CLUB SEEMED OKAY." --PITBULL. 3 OUT OF 5 STARS ON WELP
FOR YEARS WE'VE BEEN LOCKED IN AN UNENDING WAR FOR CONTROL OF THIS CITY.
EVERY DAY FIGHTING BACK MAFIOSOS WHO WERE RUN OUT OF NEW YORK BY SOME YUMA IN TIGHTS, OR SOME FRESH-OFF-THE-BOAT TONY MONTANA WANNABE, BUT AFTER TONIGHT THAT ALL ENDS...
...AFTER TONIGHT, WE WON'T NEED TO FIGHT. WE CAN SIMPLY BUY THIS TOWN. LIKE THE PEOPLE WITH REAL POWER DO. THANKS TO THIS--EVERYONE, VENGAN AQUI.
MIRA. LOOK. THIS THING IS OUR TICKET TO THE BIG TIME.
NO OFFENSE, BUT IT LOOKS LIKE SOMETHING MY ABUELITA WOULD BUY ON QVC.
NOBODY CARES WHAT YOU THINK, CARLITO. ANYBODY CAN PLAY THE MARACAS--YOU'RE ONLY HERE OUT OF A FAVOR TO YOUR MOTHER.
SO... WHAT DOES IT DO, MAMBO KING?
SOME TYPE OF WEAPON I THINK, BUT...
...WHATEVER IT IS, SOME BIG GUY IS GONNA PAY US A LOT OF MONEY FOR IT.
IT'S THE LEGENDARY ULTIMATE NULLIFIER. THE VERY BEST THERE IS. WHEN YOU ABSOLUTELY, POSITIVELY GOT TO KILL EVERY @#$^&$ IN THE ROOM, ACCEPT NO SUBSTITUTES.
THESE *&#$%@# ARE IN OVER THEIR *^&#@$# HEADS.

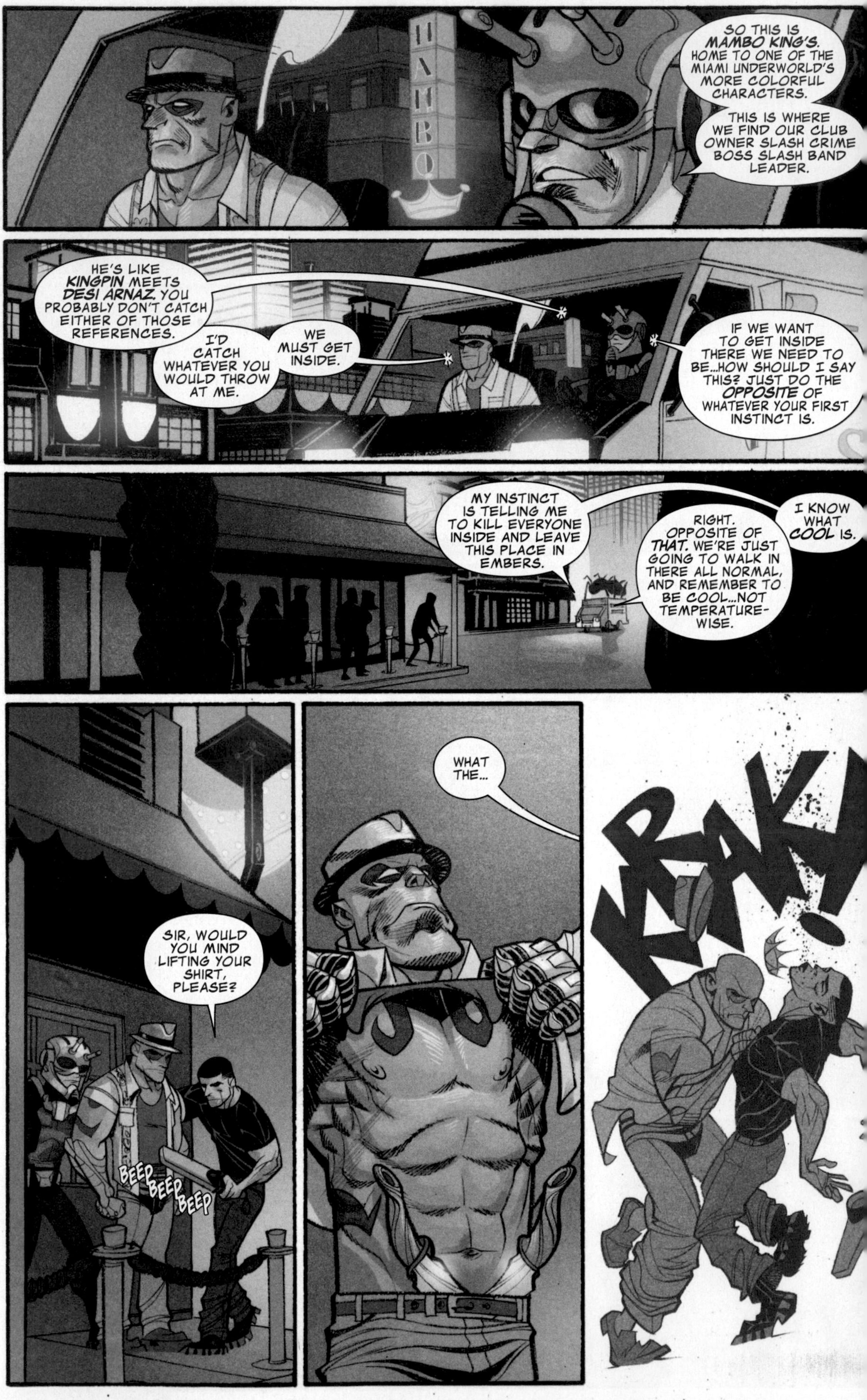
MAMBO
SO THIS IS MAMBO KING'S. HOME TO ONE OF THE MIAMI UNDERWORLD'S MORE COLORFUL CHARACTERS.
THIS IS WHERE WE FIND OUR CLUB OWNER SLASH CRIME BOSS SLASH BAND LEADER.
HE'S LIKE KINGPIN MEETS DESI ARNAZ. YOU PROBABLY DON'T CATCH EITHER OF THOSE REFERENCES.
I'D CATCH WHATEVER YOU WOULD THROW AT ME.
WE MUST GET INSIDE.
IF WE WANT TO GET INSIDE THERE WE NEED TO BE...HOW SHOULD I SAY THIS? JUST DO THE OPPOSITE OF WHATEVER YOUR FIRST INSTINCT IS.
MY INSTINCT IS TELLING ME TO KILL EVERYONE INSIDE AND LEAVE THIS PLACE IN EMBERS.
RIGHT. OPPOSITE OF THAT. WE'RE JUST GOING TO WALK IN THERE ALL NORMAL, AND REMEMBER TO BE COOL...NOT TEMPERATURE-WISE.
I KNOW WHAT COOL IS.
SIR, WOULD YOU MIND LIFTING YOUR SHIRT, PLEASE?
BEEP BEEP BEEP
WHAT THE...
KRAK!

I GUESS WE'RE NOT GOING IN THE FRONT DOOR...REMEMBER THAT TALK WE HAD ABOUT INSTINCTS?

YES, MY FIRST INSTINCT WAS TO MURDER HIM FOR WAVING THAT WAND IN MY FACE.

OH... OKAY. BABY STEPS. NOW WE WAIT.

LATER...

THAT'S HIM, THAT'S DANNKO!

WHOA! HE LOOKS LIKE A MEANER VERSION OF YOU WITH WAY BETTER FASHION SENSE.

WE NEED TO FIGURE OUT HOW TO GET IN THERE WITHOUT CAUSING A SCENE. IF WE SPOOK DANNKO OR THE MAMBO KING, WE RUN THE RISK OF THIS DEAL ACTUALLY GOING DOWN.

I HAVE AN IDEA.

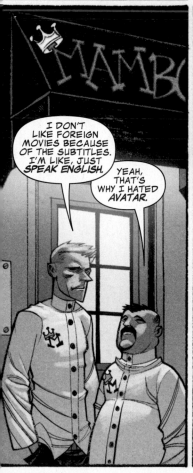

I DON'T LIKE FOREIGN MOVIES BECAUSE OF THE SUBTITLES. I'M LIKE, JUST SPEAK ENGLISH.

YEAH, THAT'S WHY I HATED AVATAR.

SORRY ABOUT THIS, GUYS!

IT'S FOR THE BEST!

SMAK

WHAP

WHAM

THAT LOOKED A LOT LIKE SOMETHING I WOULD DO.

THE DIFFERENCE IS, I USED VIOLENCE TO SAVE THE WORLD, YOU USE VIOLENCE TO ORDER A SANDWICH.

I NEVER ORDER ANYTHING. I TAKE.

EXACTLY.

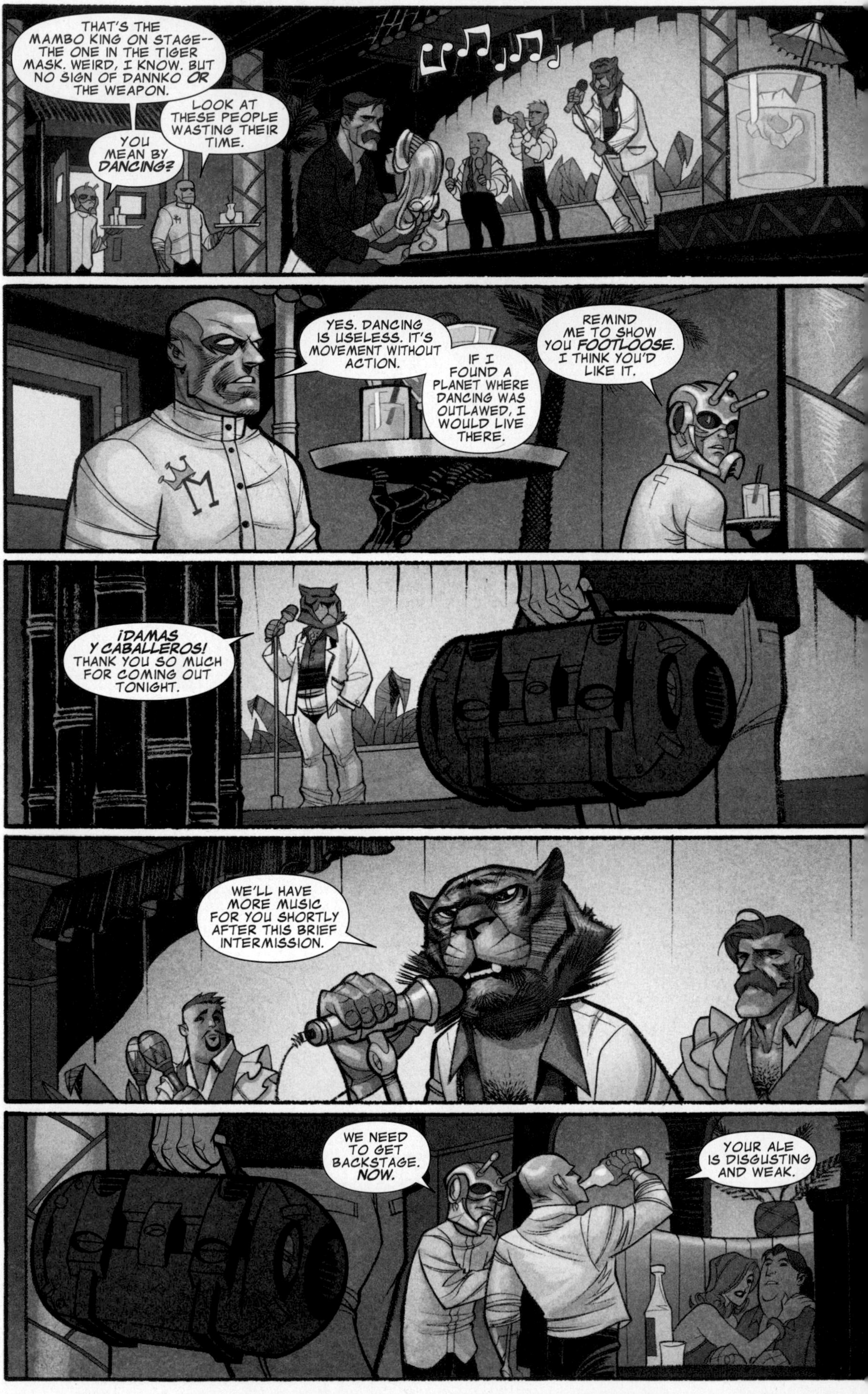
THAT'S THE MAMBO KING ON STAGE-- THE ONE IN THE TIGER MASK. WEIRD, I KNOW. BUT NO SIGN OF DANNKO OR THE WEAPON.
LOOK AT THESE PEOPLE WASTING THEIR TIME.
YOU MEAN BY DANCING?
YES. DANCING IS USELESS. IT'S MOVEMENT WITHOUT ACTION.
IF I FOUND A PLANET WHERE DANCING WAS OUTLAWED, I WOULD LIVE THERE.
REMIND ME TO SHOW YOU FOOTLOOSE. I THINK YOU'D LIKE IT.
¡DAMAS Y CABALLEROS! THANK YOU SO MUCH FOR COMING OUT TONIGHT.
WE'LL HAVE MORE MUSIC FOR YOU SHORTLY AFTER THIS BRIEF INTERMISSION.
WE NEED TO GET BACKSTAGE. NOW.
YOUR ALE IS DISGUSTING AND WEAK.

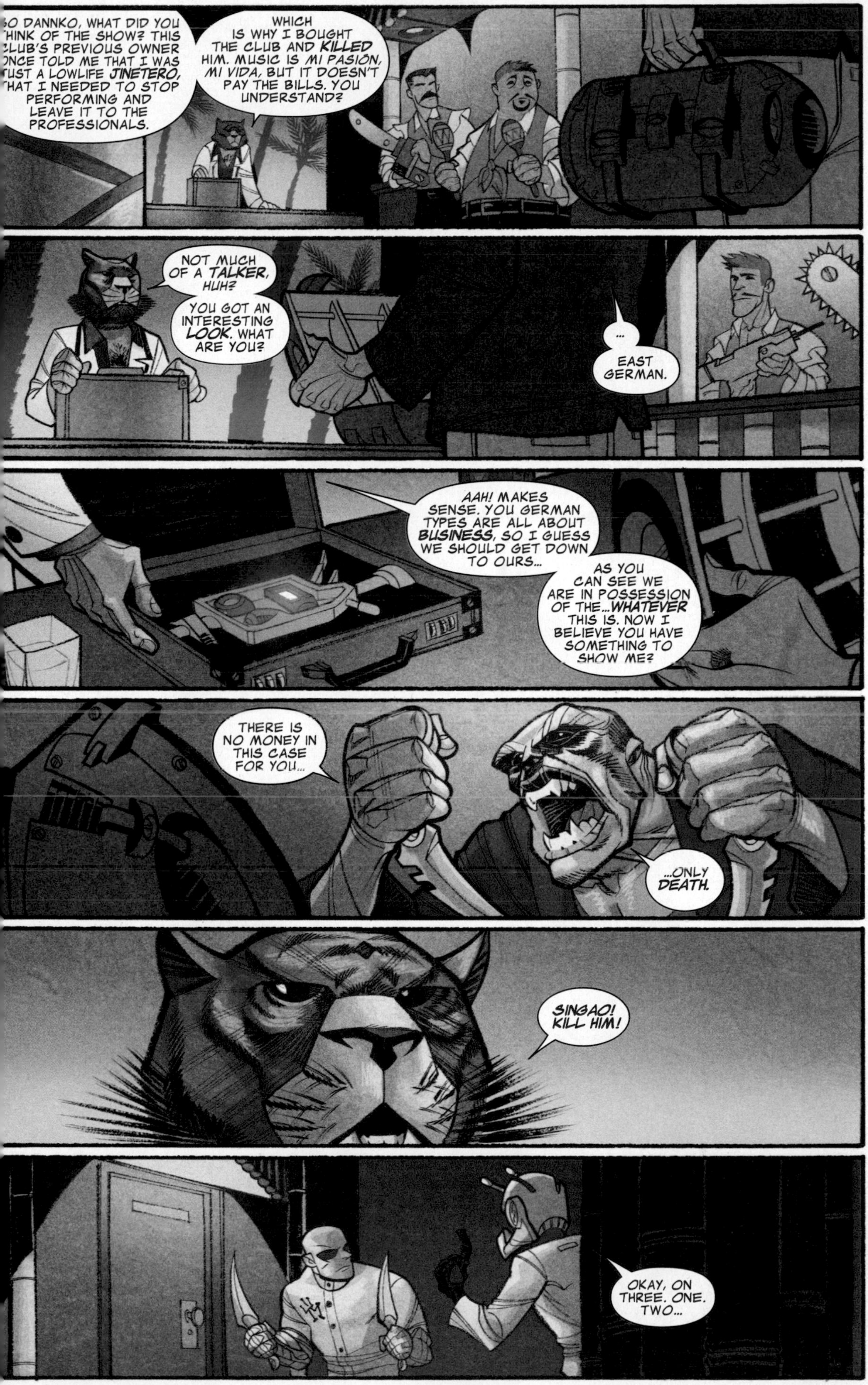
SO DANNKO, WHAT DID YOU THINK OF THE SHOW? THIS CLUB'S PREVIOUS OWNER ONCE TOLD ME THAT I WAS JUST A LOWLIFE JINETERO, THAT I NEEDED TO STOP PERFORMING AND LEAVE IT TO THE PROFESSIONALS.
WHICH IS WHY I BOUGHT THE CLUB AND KILLED HIM. MUSIC IS MI PASIÓN, MI VIDA, BUT IT DOESN'T PAY THE BILLS. YOU UNDERSTAND?
NOT MUCH OF A TALKER, HUH?
YOU GOT AN INTERESTING LOOK. WHAT ARE YOU?
...
EAST GERMAN.
AAH! MAKES SENSE. YOU GERMAN TYPES ARE ALL ABOUT BUSINESS, SO I GUESS WE SHOULD GET DOWN TO OURS...
AS YOU CAN SEE WE ARE IN POSSESSION OF THE...WHATEVER THIS IS. NOW I BELIEVE YOU HAVE SOMETHING TO SHOW ME?
THERE IS NO MONEY IN THIS CASE FOR YOU...
...ONLY DEATH.
SINGAO! KILL HIM!
OKAY, ON THREE. ONE. TWO...

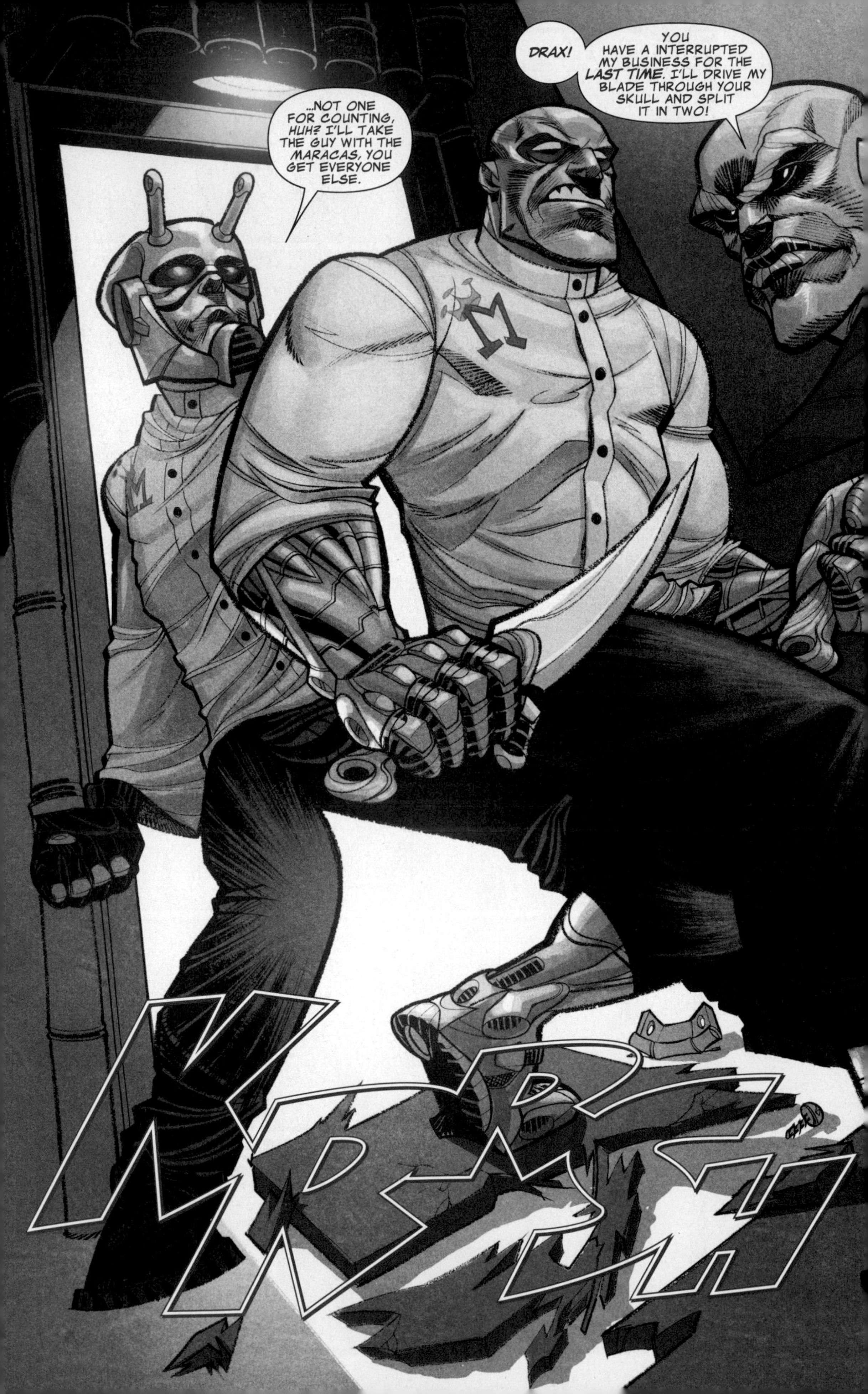
DRAX!
YOU HAVE A INTERRUPTED MY BUSINESS FOR THE LAST TIME. I'LL DRIVE MY BLADE THROUGH YOUR SKULL AND SPLIT IT IN TWO!
...NOT ONE FOR COUNTING, HUH? I'LL TAKE THE GUY WITH THE MARACAS, YOU GET EVERYONE ELSE.
KRRSH

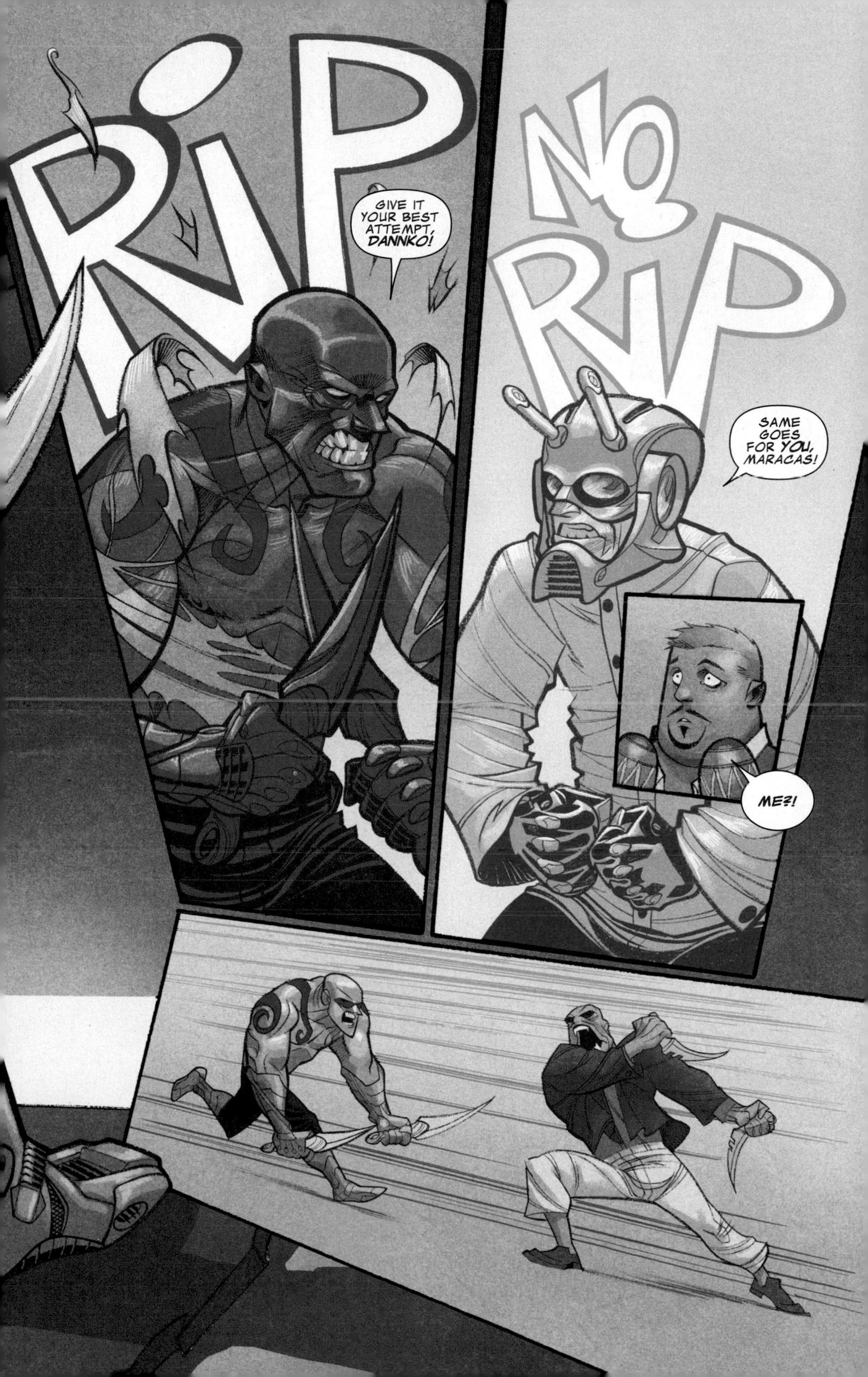
RIP
GIVE IT YOUR BEST ATTEMPT, DANNKO!
NO RIP
SAME GOES FOR YOU, MARACAS!
ME?!

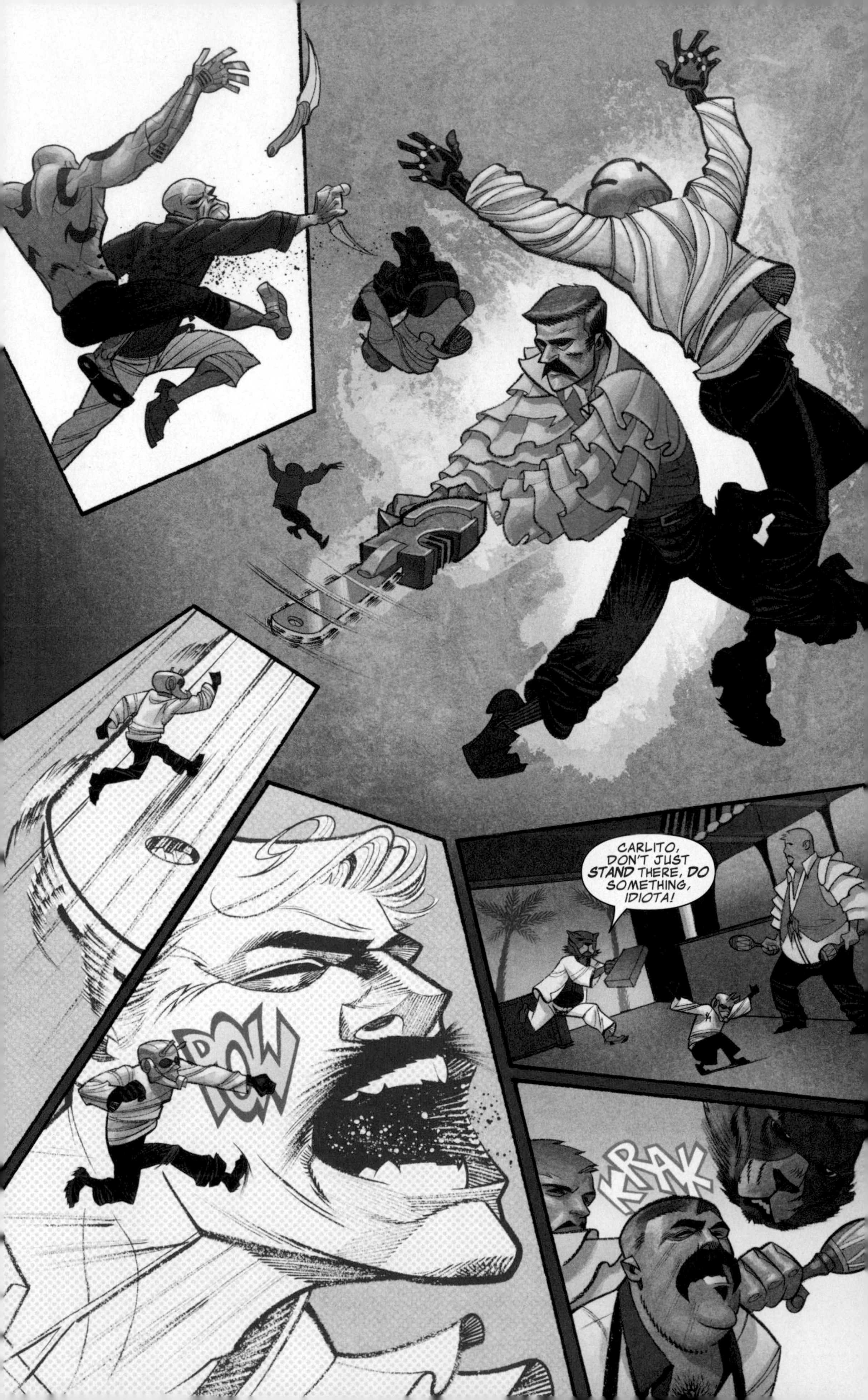
POW
CARLITO, DON'T JUST STAND THERE, DO SOMETHING, IDIOTA!
KRAK

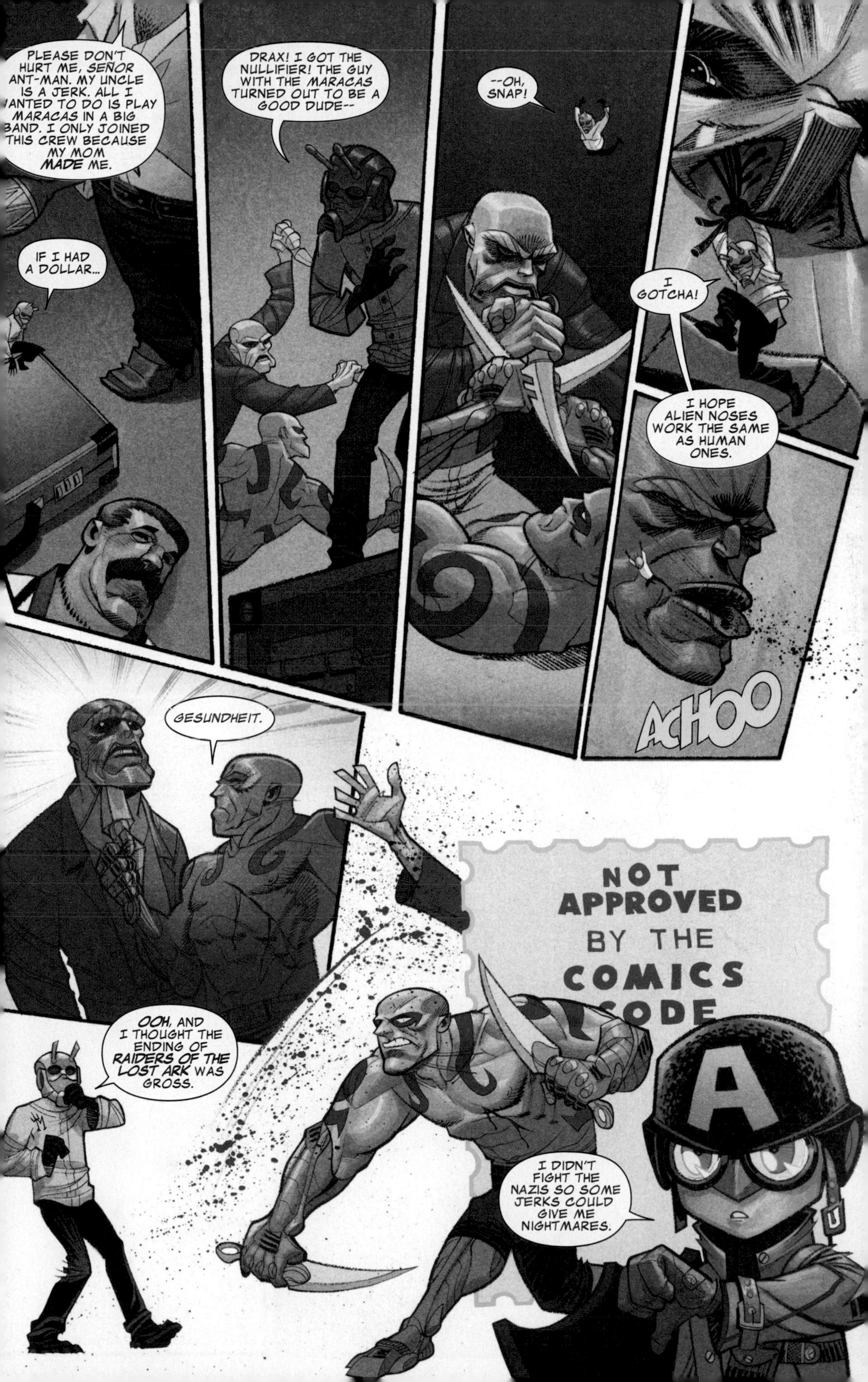
PLEASE DON'T HURT ME, SEÑOR ANT-MAN. MY UNCLE IS A JERK. ALL I WANTED TO DO IS PLAY MARACAS IN A BIG BAND. I ONLY JOINED THIS CREW BECAUSE MY MOM MADE ME.
IF I HAD A DOLLAR...
DRAX! I GOT THE NULLIFIER! THE GUY WITH THE MARACAS TURNED OUT TO BE A GOOD DUDE--
--OH, SNAP!
I GOTCHA!
I HOPE ALIEN NOSES WORK THE SAME AS HUMAN ONES.
ACHOO
GESUNDHEIT.
OOH, AND I THOUGHT THE ENDING OF RAIDERS OF THE LOST ARK WAS GROSS.
NOT APPROVED BY THE COMICS CODE
I DIDN'T FIGHT THE NAZIS SO SOME JERKS COULD GIVE ME NIGHTMARES.

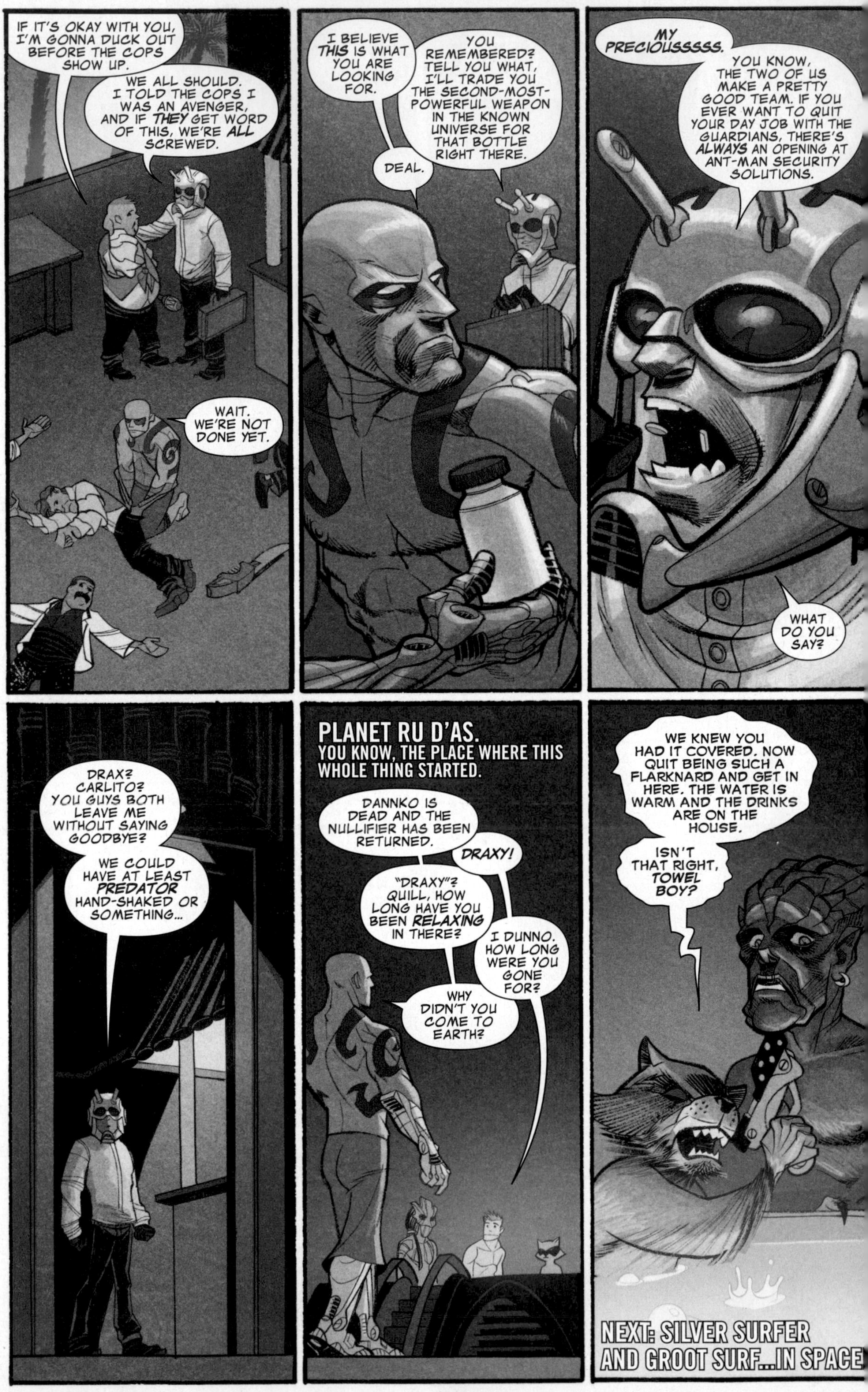
IF IT'S OKAY WITH YOU, I'M GONNA DUCK OUT BEFORE THE COPS SHOW UP.
WE ALL SHOULD. I TOLD THE COPS I WAS AN AVENGER, AND IF THEY GET WORD OF THIS, WE'RE ALL SCREWED.
WAIT. WE'RE NOT DONE YET.
I BELIEVE THIS IS WHAT YOU ARE LOOKING FOR.
YOU REMEMBERED? TELL YOU WHAT, I'LL TRADE YOU THE SECOND-MOST-POWERFUL WEAPON IN THE KNOWN UNIVERSE FOR THAT BOTTLE RIGHT THERE.
DEAL.
MY PRECIOUSSSSS.
YOU KNOW, THE TWO OF US MAKE A PRETTY GOOD TEAM. IF YOU EVER WANT TO QUIT YOUR DAY JOB WITH THE GUARDIANS, THERE'S ALWAYS AN OPENING AT ANT-MAN SECURITY SOLUTIONS.
WHAT DO YOU SAY?
DRAX? CARLITO? YOU GUYS BOTH LEAVE ME WITHOUT SAYING GOODBYE?
WE COULD HAVE AT LEAST PREDATOR HAND-SHAKED OR SOMETHING...
PLANET RU D'AS.
YOU KNOW, THE PLACE WHERE THIS WHOLE THING STARTED.
DANNKO IS DEAD AND THE NULLIFIER HAS BEEN RETURNED.
DRAXY!
"DRAXY"? QUILL, HOW LONG HAVE YOU BEEN RELAXING IN THERE?
I DUNNO. HOW LONG WERE YOU GONE FOR?
WHY DIDN'T YOU COME TO EARTH?
WE KNEW YOU HAD IT COVERED. NOW QUIT BEING SUCH A FLARKNARD AND GET IN HERE. THE WATER IS WARM AND THE DRINKS ARE ON THE HOUSE.
ISN'T THAT RIGHT, TOWEL BOY?
NEXT: SILVER SURFER AND GROOT SURF...IN SPACE

Teen science prodigy **NADIA** escaped the Russian assassin-training Red Room to search for her father, Hank Pym, in the United States. Pym's former wife, **JANET VAN DYNE**, became Nadia's stepmother and helped her claim her true inheritance: her father's shrinking technology and heroism. In Janet's honor, Nadia wears the mantle of the **WASP**!

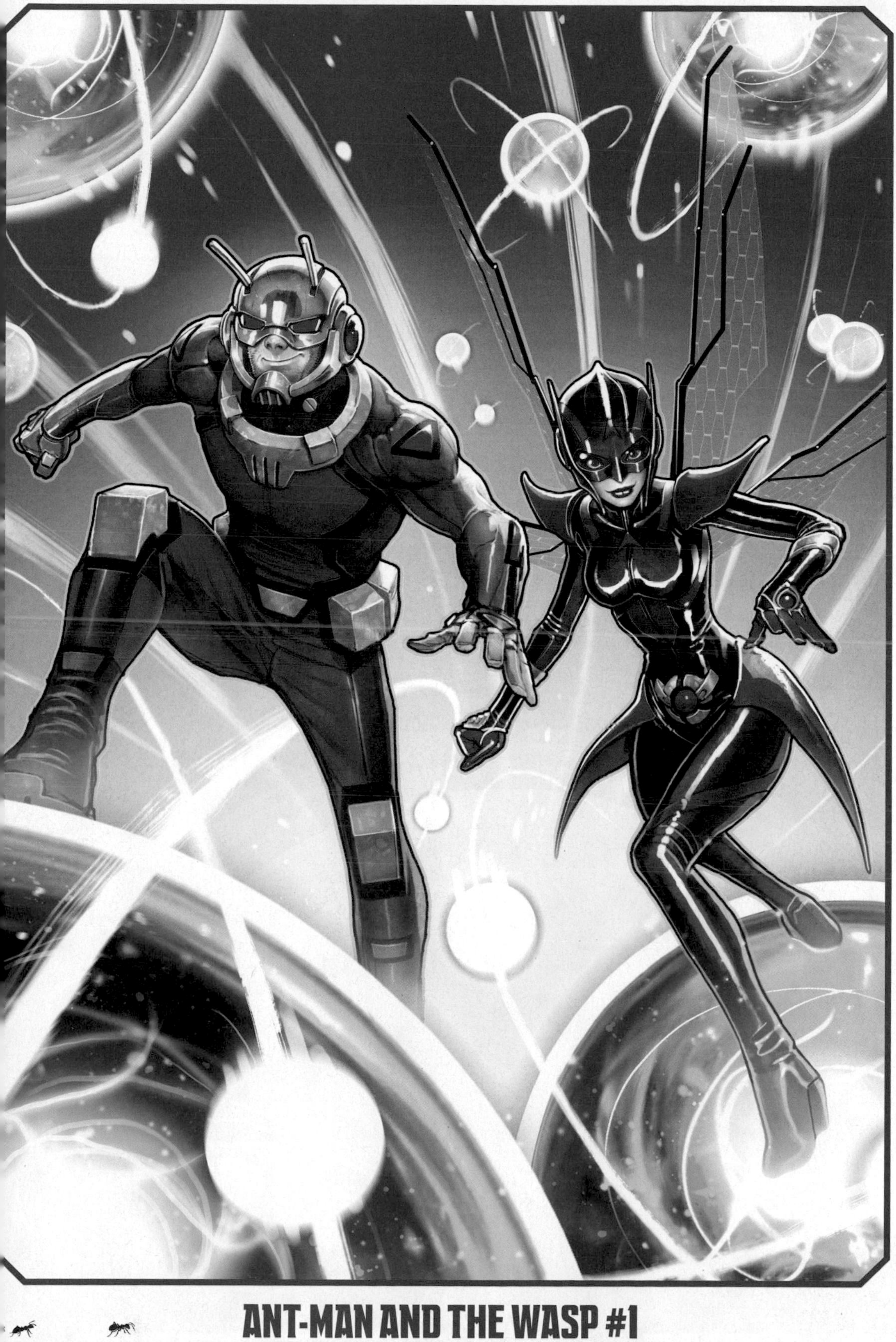

ANT-MAN AND THE WASP #1

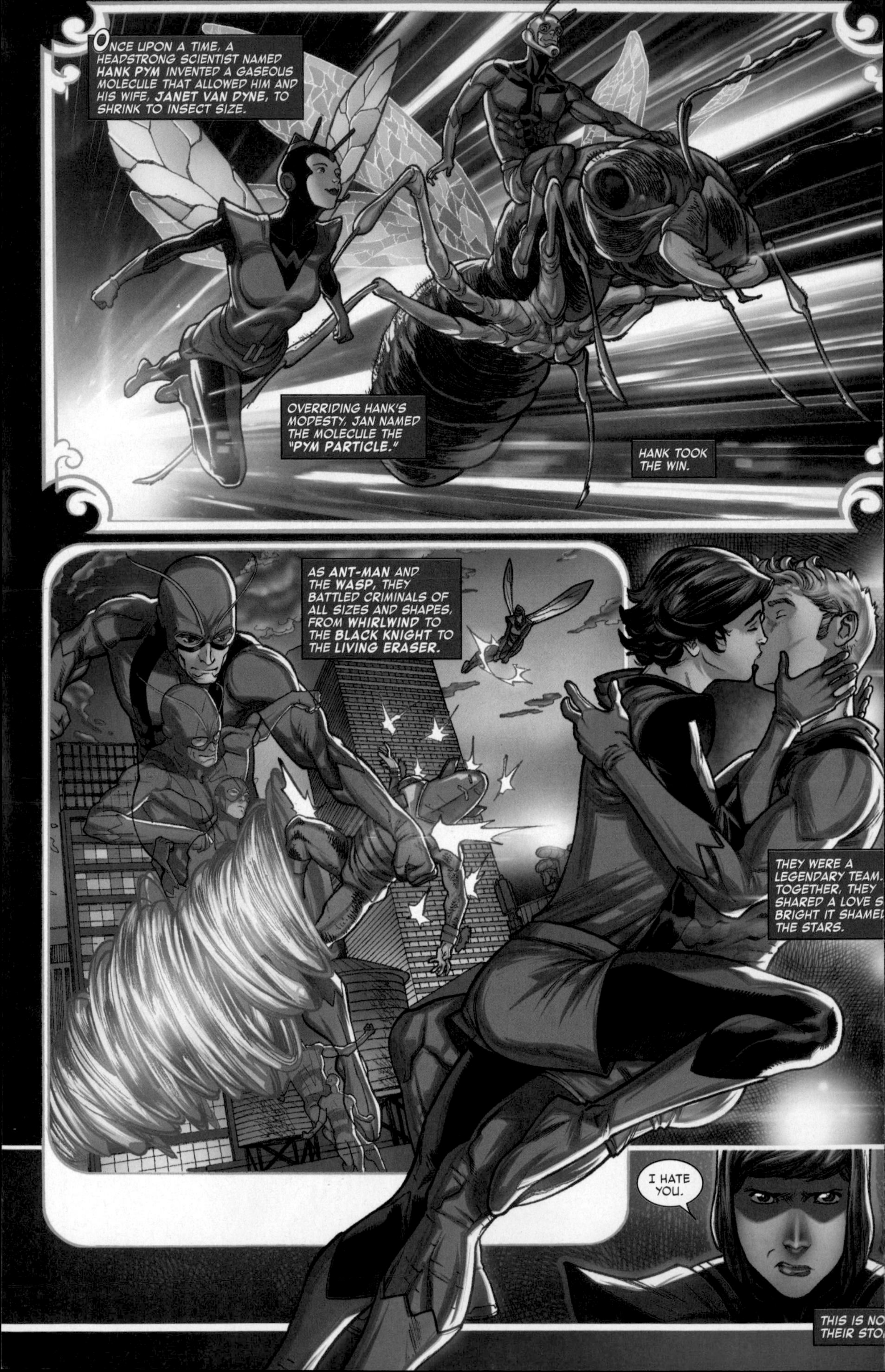
ONCE UPON A TIME, A HEADSTRONG SCIENTIST NAMED HANK PYM INVENTED A GASEOUS MOLECULE THAT ALLOWED HIM AND HIS WIFE, JANET VAN DYNE, TO SHRINK TO INSECT SIZE.
OVERRIDING HANK'S MODESTY, JAN NAMED THE MOLECULE THE "PYM PARTICLE."
HANK TOOK THE WIN.
AS ANT-MAN AND THE WASP, THEY BATTLED CRIMINALS OF ALL SIZES AND SHAPES, FROM WHIRLWIND TO THE BLACK KNIGHT TO THE LIVING ERASER.
THEY WERE A LEGENDARY TEAM. TOGETHER, THEY SHARED A LOVE S
I HATE YOU.

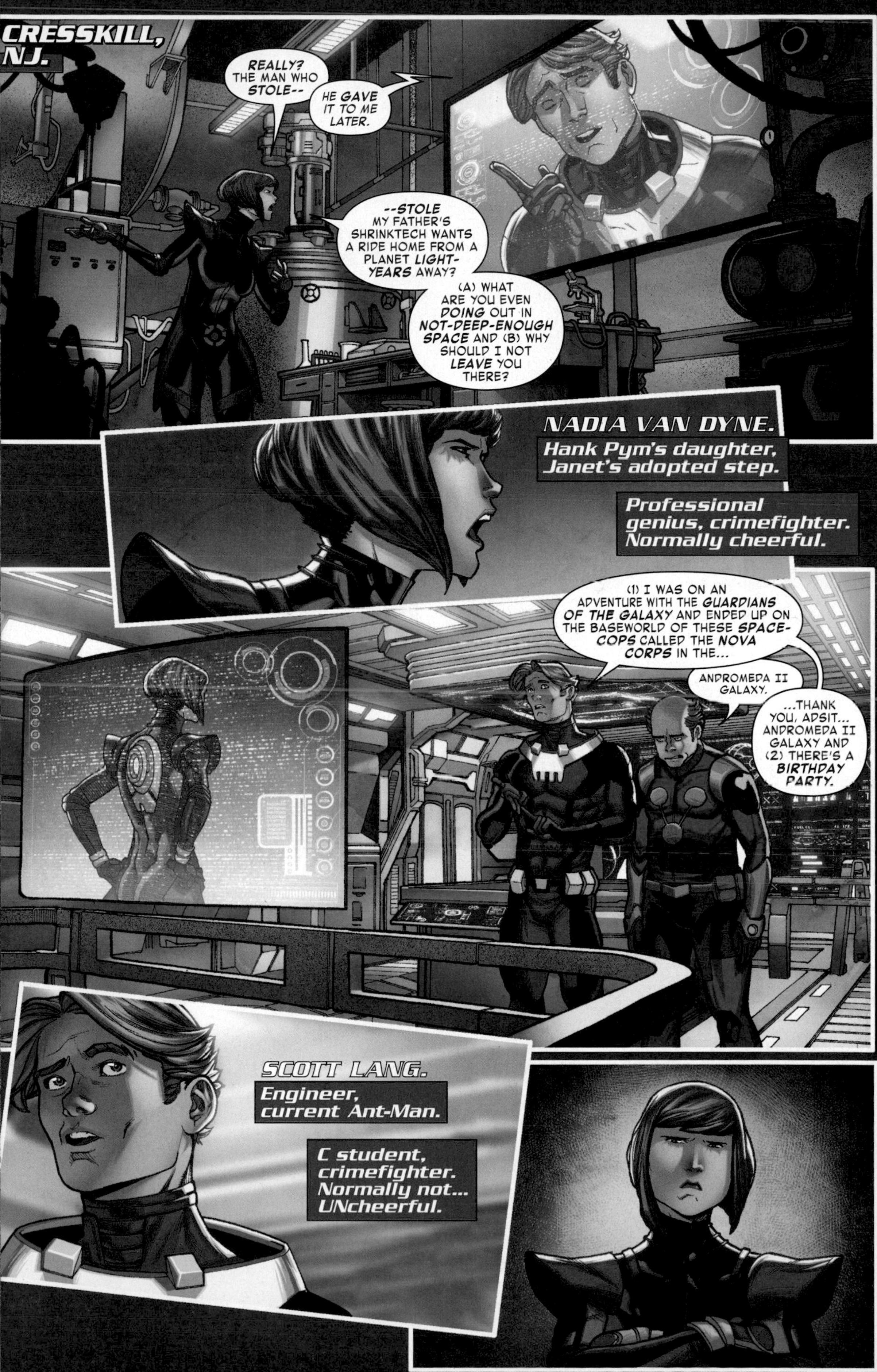
CRESSKILL, NJ.
REALLY? THE MAN WHO STOLE--
HE GAVE IT TO ME LATER.
--STOLE MY FATHER'S SHRINKTECH WANTS A RIDE HOME FROM A PLANET LIGHT-YEARS AWAY?
(A) WHAT ARE YOU EVEN DOING OUT IN NOT-DEEP-ENOUGH SPACE AND (B) WHY SHOULD I NOT LEAVE YOU THERE?
NADIA VAN DYNE.
Hank Pym's daughter, Janet's adopted step.
Professional genius, crimefighter. Normally cheerful.
(1) I WAS ON AN ADVENTURE WITH THE GUARDIANS OF THE GALAXY AND ENDED UP ON THE BASEWORLD OF THESE SPACE-COPS CALLED THE NOVA CORPS IN THE...
ANDROMEDA II GALAXY.
...THANK YOU, ADSIT... ANDROMEDA II GALAXY AND (2) THERE'S A BIRTHDAY PARTY.
SCOTT LANG.
Engineer, current Ant-Man.
C student, crimefighter. Normally not... UNcheerful.

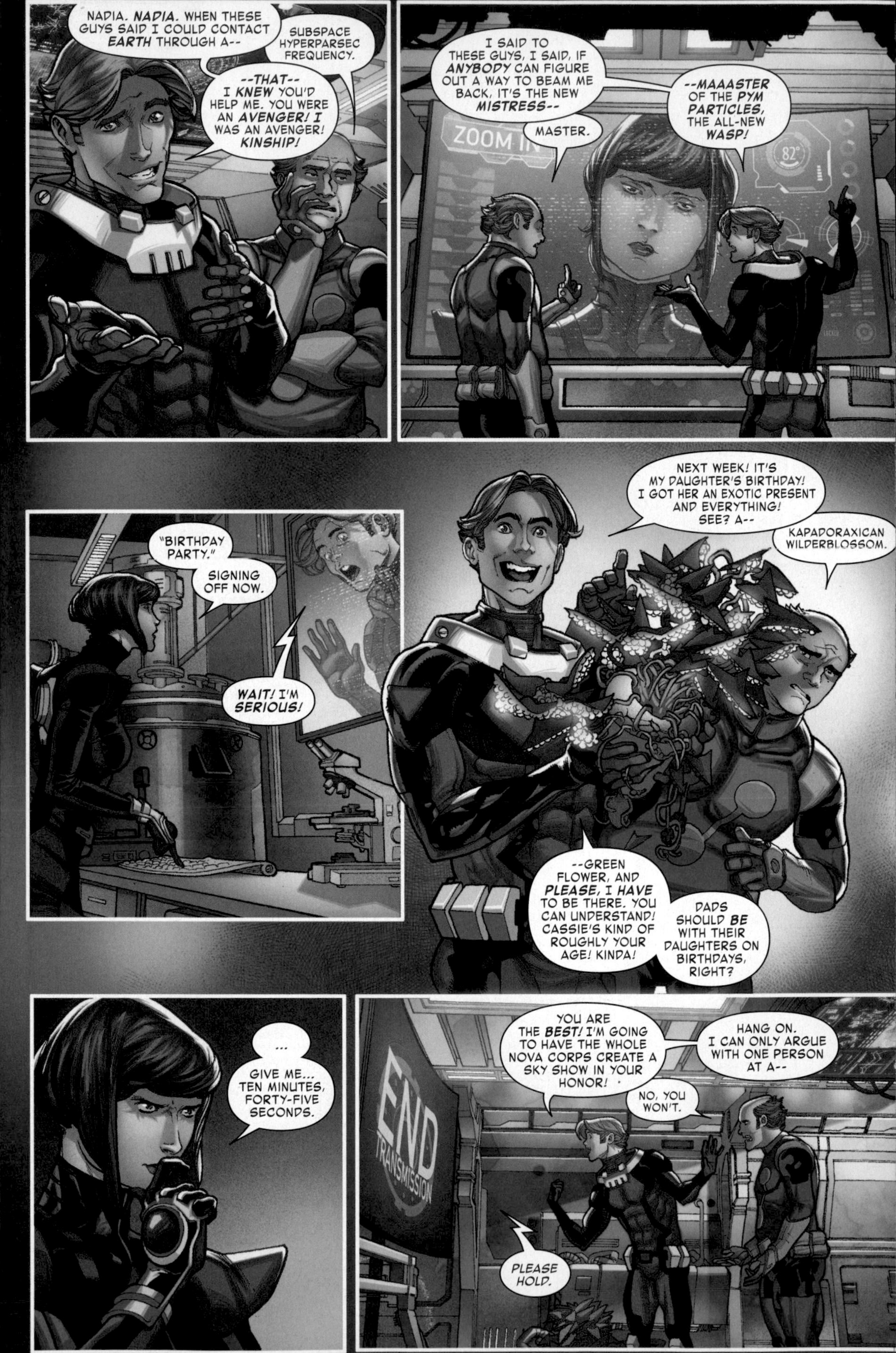
NADIA. NADIA. WHEN THESE GUYS SAID I COULD CONTACT EARTH THROUGH A--
SUBSPACE HYPERPARSEC FREQUENCY.
--THAT-- I KNEW YOU'D HELP ME. YOU WERE AN AVENGER! I WAS AN AVENGER! KINSHIP!
I SAID TO THESE GUYS, I SAID, IF ANYBODY CAN FIGURE OUT A WAY TO BEAM ME BACK, IT'S THE NEW MISTRESS--
MASTER.
--MAAASTER OF THE PYM PARTICLES, THE ALL-NEW WASP!
ZOOM IN
82°
NEXT WEEK! IT'S MY DAUGHTER'S BIRTHDAY! I GOT HER AN EXOTIC PRESENT AND EVERYTHING! SEE? A--
KAPADORAXICAN WILDERBLOSSOM.
"BIRTHDAY PARTY."
SIGNING OFF NOW.
WAIT! I'M SERIOUS!
--GREEN FLOWER, AND PLEASE, I HAVE TO BE THERE. YOU CAN UNDERSTAND! CASSIE'S KIND OF ROUGHLY YOUR AGE! KINDA!
DADS SHOULD BE WITH THEIR DAUGHTERS ON BIRTHDAYS, RIGHT?
...
GIVE ME... TEN MINUTES, FORTY-FIVE SECONDS.
END TRANSMISSION
YOU ARE THE BEST! I'M GOING TO HAVE THE WHOLE NOVA CORPS CREATE A SKY SHOW IN YOUR HONOR!
NO, YOU WON'T.
HANG ON. I CAN ONLY ARGUE WITH ONE PERSON AT A--
PLEASE HOLD.

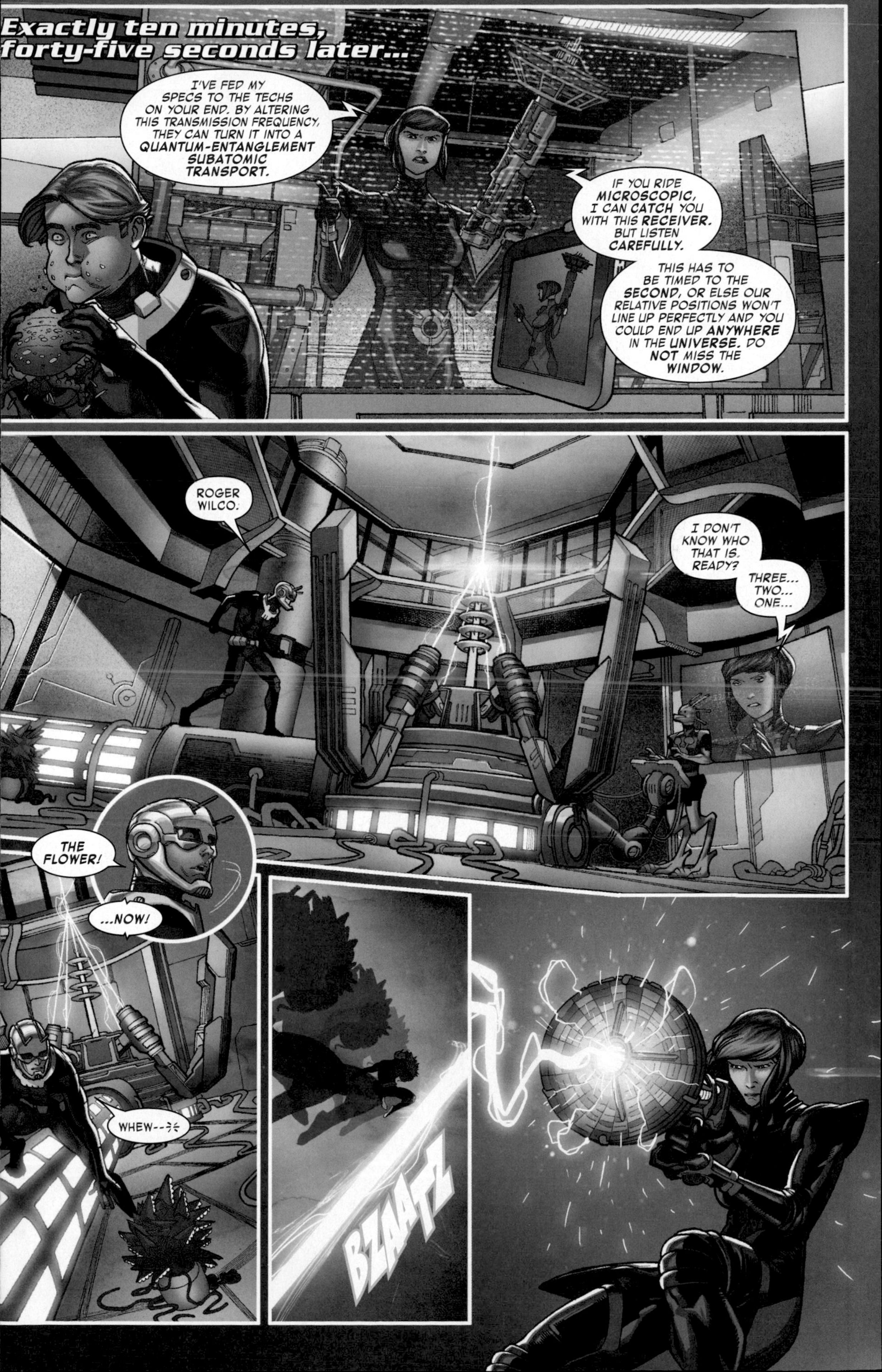
Exactly ten minutes, forty-five seconds later...
I'VE FED MY SPECS TO THE TECHS ON YOUR END. BY ALTERING THIS TRANSMISSION FREQUENCY, THEY CAN TURN IT INTO A QUANTUM-ENTANGLEMENT SUBATOMIC TRANSPORT.
IF YOU RIDE MICROSCOPIC, I CAN CATCH YOU WITH THIS RECEIVER. BUT LISTEN CAREFULLY.
THIS HAS TO BE TIMED TO THE SECOND, OR ELSE OUR RELATIVE POSITIONS WON'T LINE UP PERFECTLY AND YOU COULD END UP ANYWHERE IN THE UNIVERSE. DO NOT MISS THE WINDOW.
ROGER WILCO.
I DON'T KNOW WHO THAT IS. READY?
THREE... TWO... ONE...
THE FLOWER!
...NOW!
WHEW--
BZAATZ

HE MISSED THE WINDOW.

PANIC MODE DETECTED

HE MISSED THE WINDOW.

GREAT.

NOW I HAVE TO *FIND* HIM! HE CAN'T GET TO *ME*, BUT I CAN GET TO *HIM*--

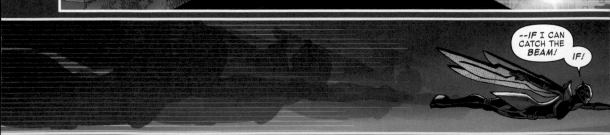

--IF I CAN CATCH THE BEAM! IF!

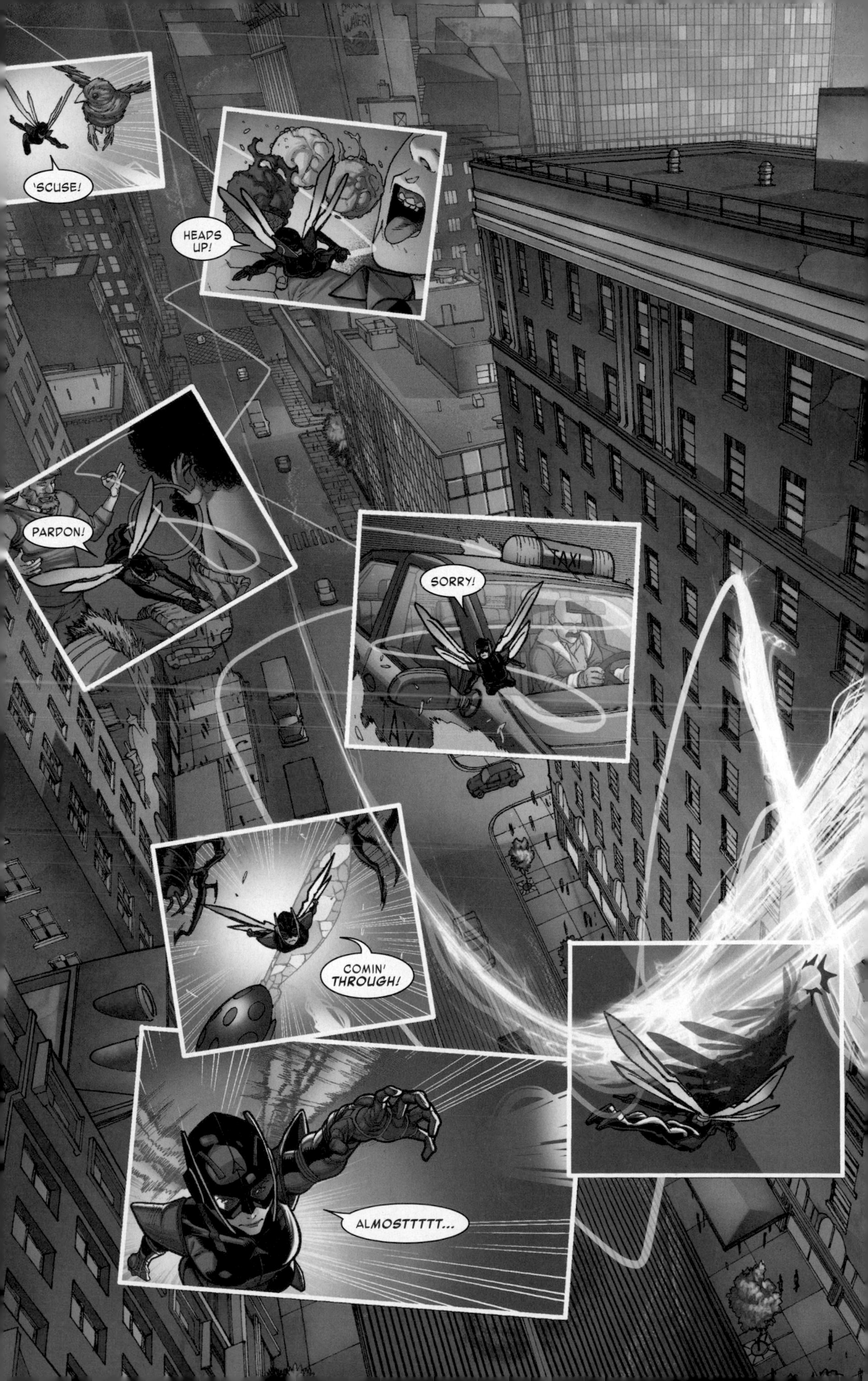
'SCUSE!
HEADS UP!
PARDON!
SORRY!
TAXI
COMIN' THROUGH!
ALMOSTTTTT...

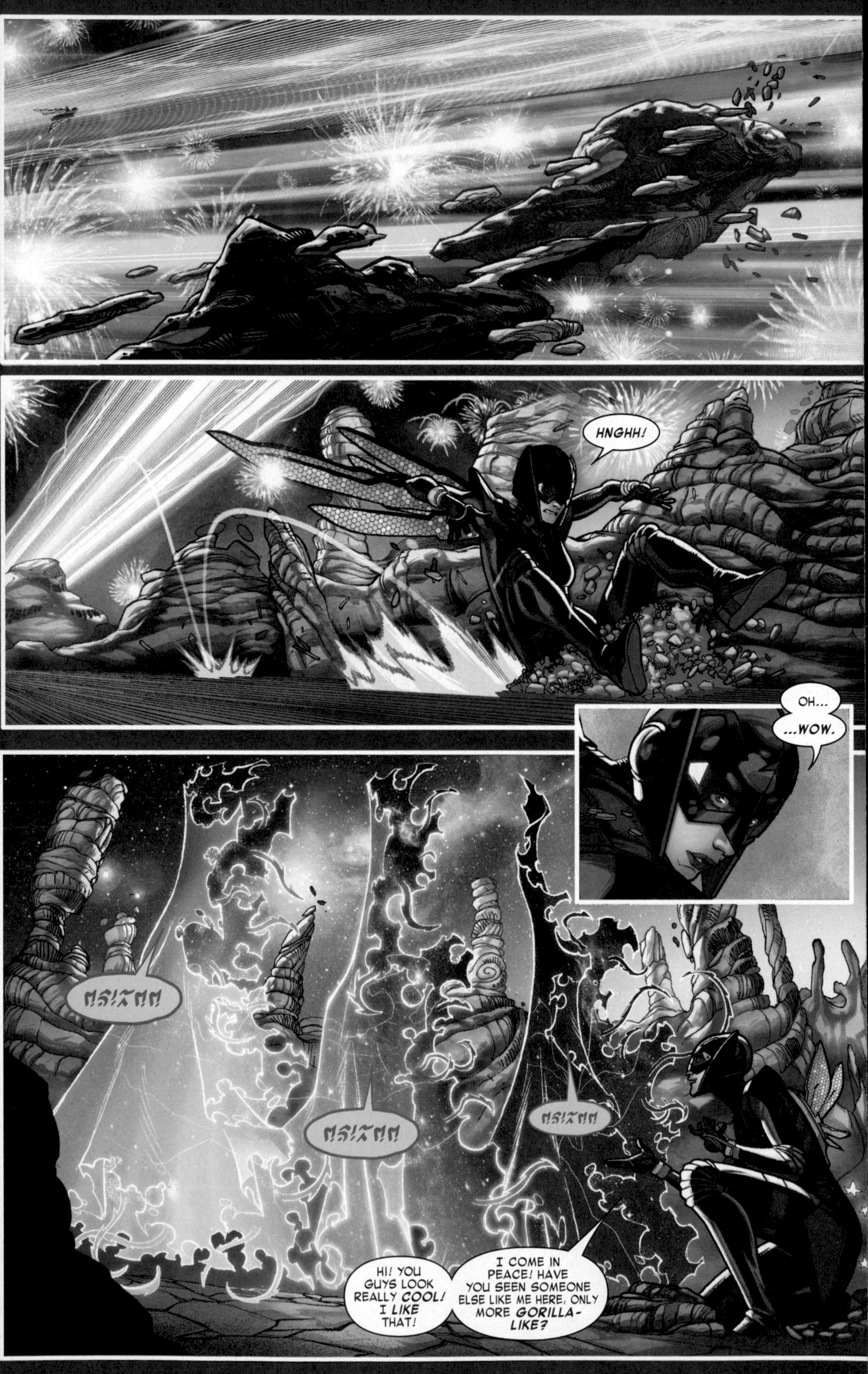
HNGHH!
OH...
...WOW.
HI! YOU GUYS LOOK REALLY COOL! I LIKE THAT!
I COME IN PEACE! HAVE YOU SEEN SOMEONE ELSE LIKE ME HERE, ONLY MORE GORILLA-LIKE?

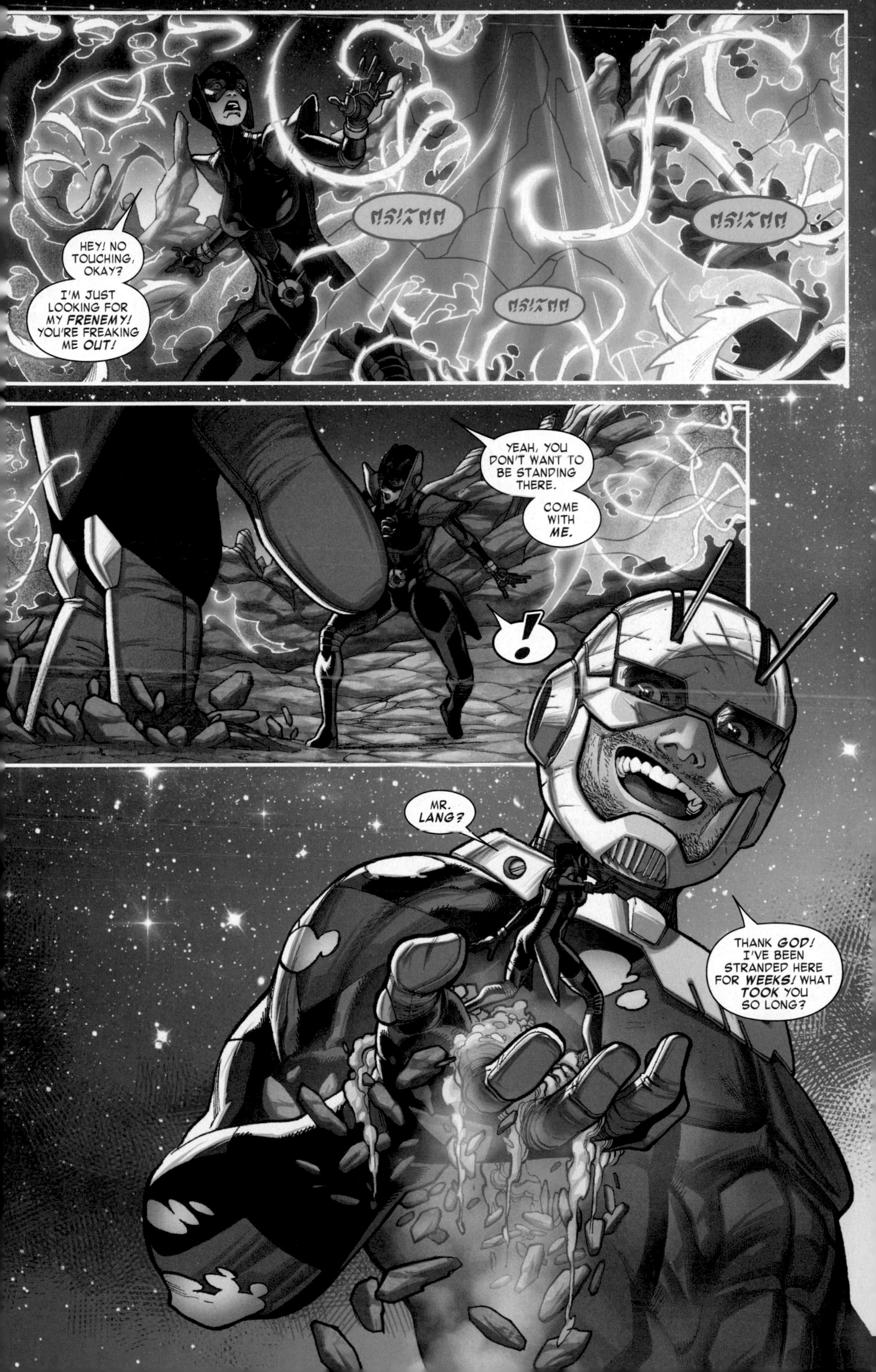

HEY! NO TOUCHING, OKAY?
I'M JUST LOOKING FOR MY *FRENEMY!* YOU'RE FREAKING ME *OUT!*
YEAH, YOU DON'T WANT TO BE STANDING THERE.
COME WITH *ME.*
!
MR. *LANG?*
THANK *GOD!* I'VE BEEN STRANDED HERE FOR *WEEKS!* WHAT *TOOK* YOU SO LONG?

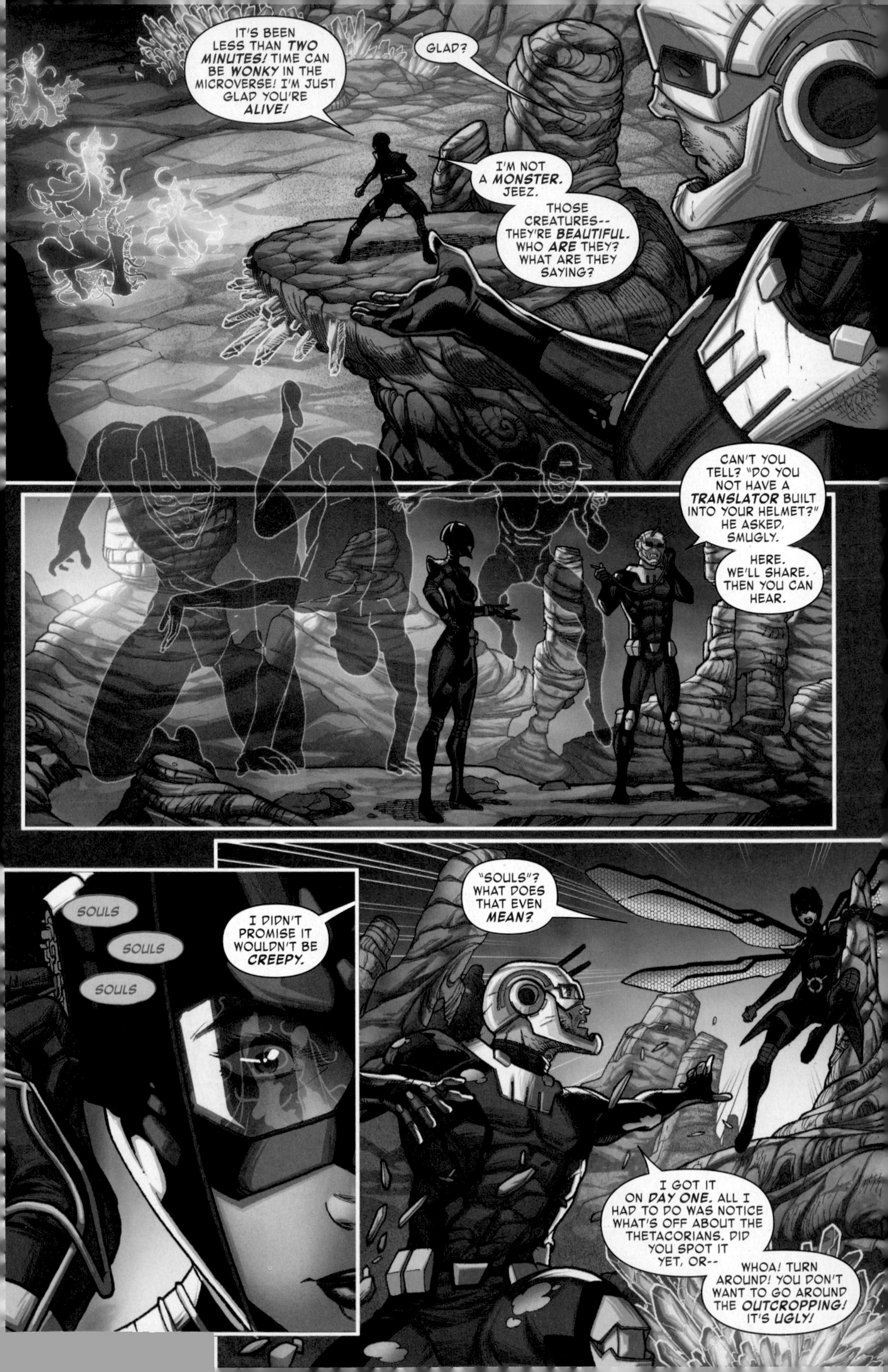
IT'S BEEN LESS THAN TWO MINUTES! TIME CAN BE WONKY IN THE MICROVERSE! I'M JUST GLAD YOU'RE ALIVE!
GLAD?
I'M NOT A MONSTER. JEEZ.
THOSE CREATURES-- THEY'RE BEAUTIFUL. WHO ARE THEY? WHAT ARE THEY SAYING?
CAN'T YOU TELL? "DO YOU NOT HAVE A TRANSLATOR BUILT INTO YOUR HELMET?" HE ASKED, SMUGLY.
HERE. WE'LL SHARE. THEN YOU CAN HEAR.
SOULS
SOULS
SOULS
I DIDN'T PROMISE IT WOULDN'T BE CREEPY.
"SOULS"? WHAT DOES THAT EVEN MEAN?
I GOT IT ON DAY ONE. ALL I HAD TO DO WAS NOTICE WHAT'S OFF ABOUT THE THETACORIANS. DID YOU SPOT IT YET, OR--
WHOA! TURN AROUND! YOU DON'T WANT TO GO AROUND THE OUTCROPPING! IT'S UGLY!

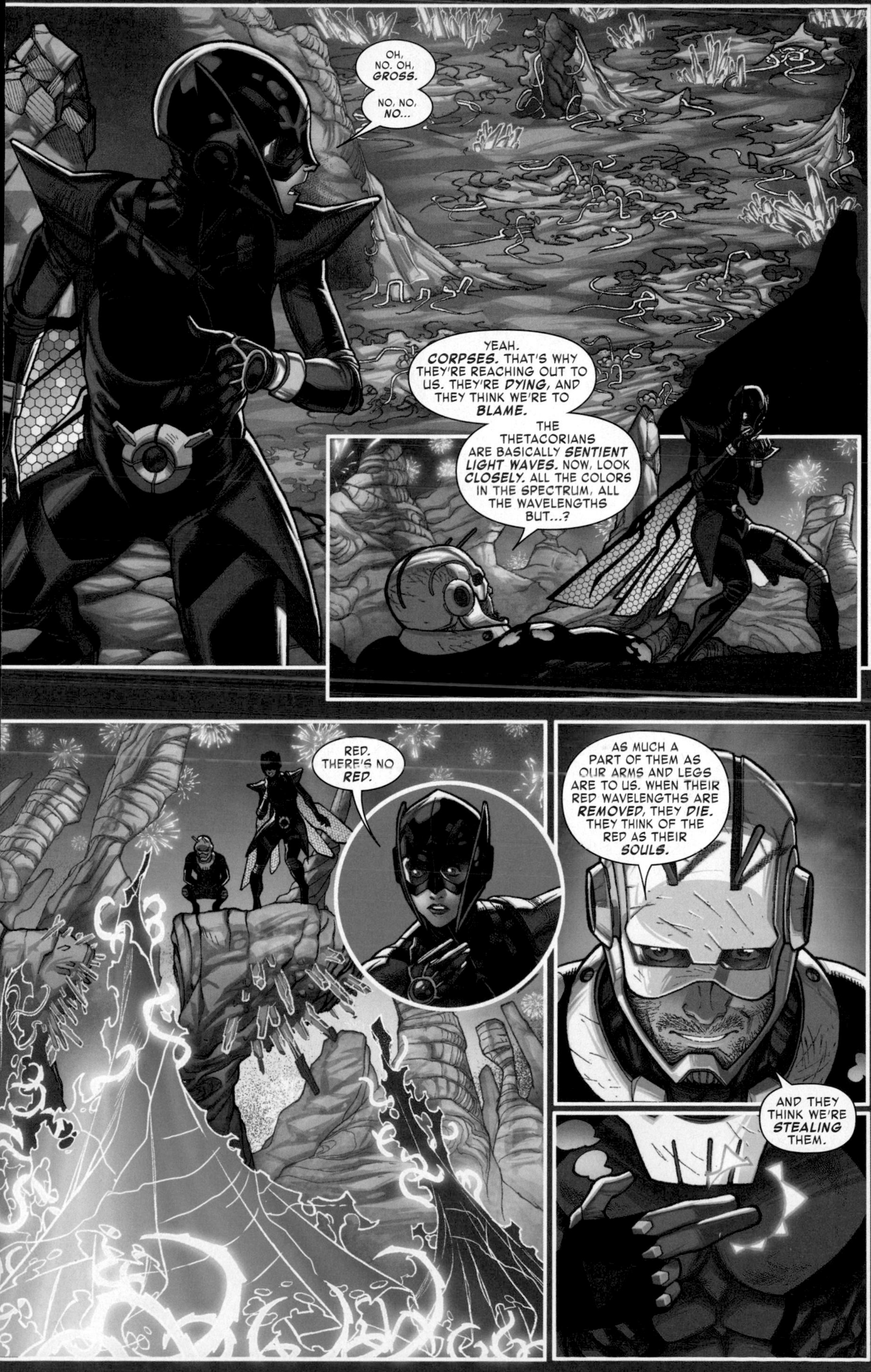

OH, NO. OH, GROSS.
NO, NO, NO...
YEAH. CORPSES. THAT'S WHY THEY'RE REACHING OUT TO US. THEY'RE DYING, AND THEY THINK WE'RE TO BLAME.
THE THETACORIANS ARE BASICALLY SENTIENT LIGHT WAVES. NOW, LOOK CLOSELY. ALL THE COLORS IN THE SPECTRUM, ALL THE WAVELENGTHS BUT...?
RED. THERE'S NO RED.
AS MUCH A PART OF THEM AS OUR ARMS AND LEGS ARE TO US. WHEN THEIR RED WAVELENGTHS ARE REMOVED, THEY DIE. THEY THINK OF THE RED AS THEIR SOULS.
AND THEY THINK WE'RE STEALING THEM.

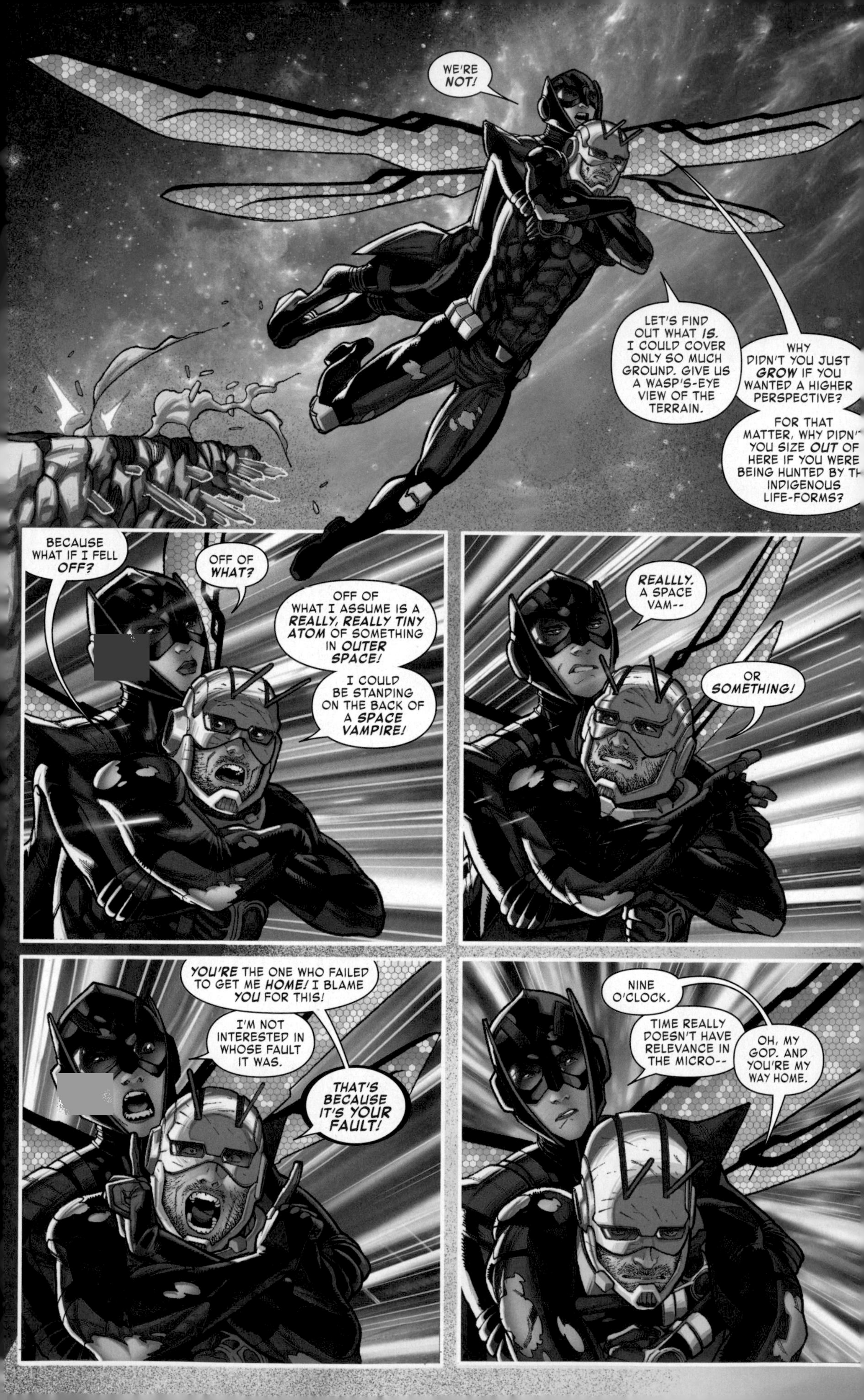
WE'RE NOT!
LET'S FIND OUT WHAT IS. I COULD COVER ONLY SO MUCH GROUND. GIVE US A WASP'S-EYE VIEW OF THE TERRAIN.
WHY DIDN'T YOU JUST GROW IF YOU WANTED A HIGHER PERSPECTIVE?
FOR THAT MATTER, WHY DIDN'T YOU SIZE OUT OF HERE IF YOU WERE BEING HUNTED BY THE INDIGENOUS LIFE-FORMS?
BECAUSE WHAT IF I FELL OFF?
OFF OF WHAT?
OFF OF WHAT I ASSUME IS A REALLY, REALLY TINY ATOM OF SOMETHING IN OUTER SPACE!
I COULD BE STANDING ON THE BACK OF A SPACE VAMPIRE!
REALLLY. A SPACE VAM--
OR SOMETHING!
YOU'RE THE ONE WHO FAILED TO GET ME HOME! I BLAME YOU FOR THIS!
I'M NOT INTERESTED IN WHOSE FAULT IT WAS.
THAT'S BECAUSE IT'S YOUR FAULT!
NINE O'CLOCK.
TIME REALLY DOESN'T HAVE RELEVANCE IN THE MICRO--
OH, MY GOD. AND YOU'RE MY WAY HOME.

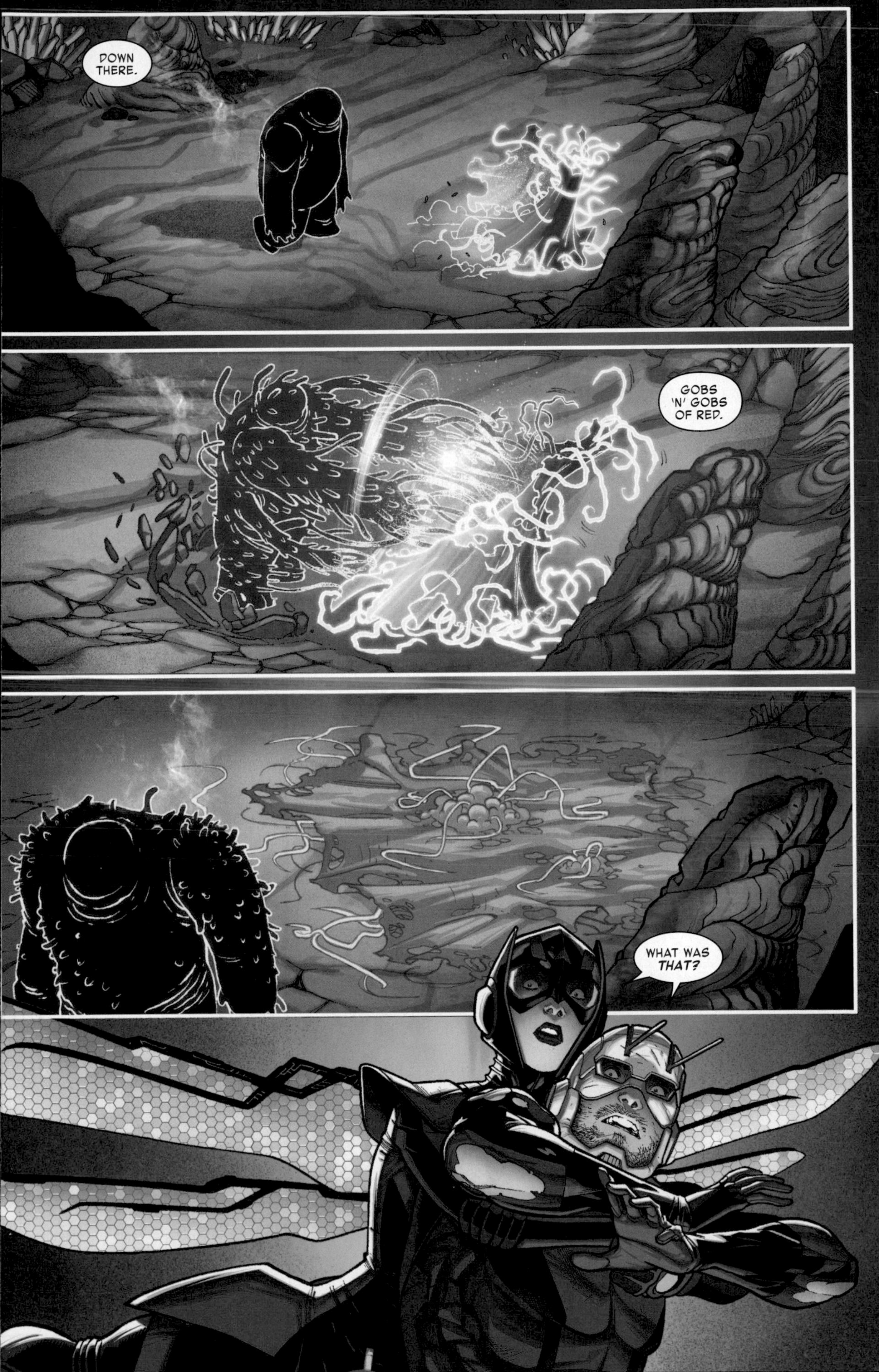
DOWN THERE.
GOBS 'N' GOBS OF RED.
WHAT WAS THAT?

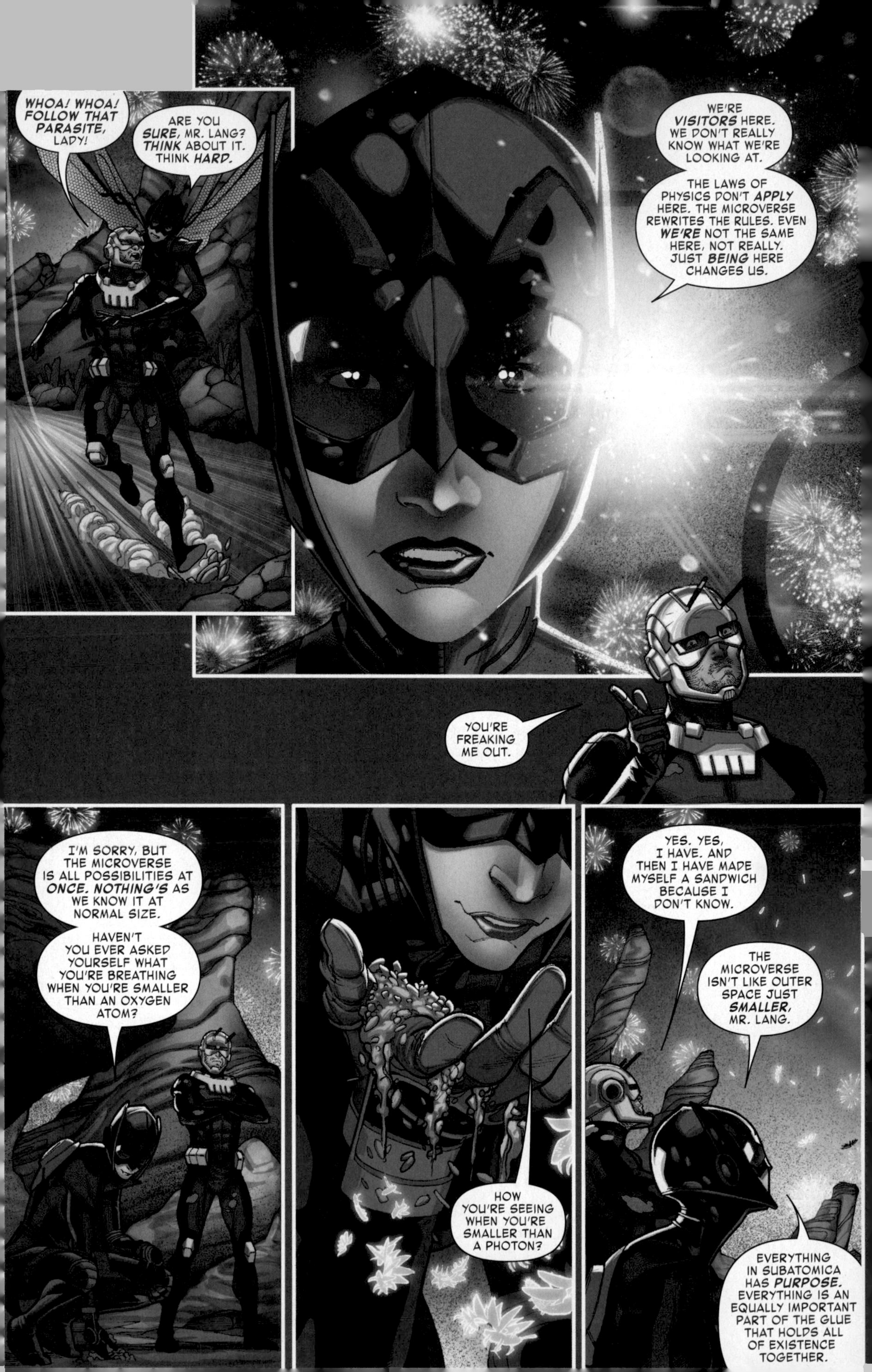
WHOA! WHOA! FOLLOW THAT PARASITE, LADY!
ARE YOU SURE, MR. LANG? THINK ABOUT IT. THINK HARD.
WE'RE VISITORS HERE. WE DON'T REALLY KNOW WHAT WE'RE LOOKING AT.
THE LAWS OF PHYSICS DON'T APPLY HERE. THE MICROVERSE REWRITES THE RULES. EVEN WE'RE NOT THE SAME HERE, NOT REALLY. JUST BEING HERE CHANGES US.
YOU'RE FREAKING ME OUT.
I'M SORRY, BUT THE MICROVERSE IS ALL POSSIBILITIES AT ONCE. NOTHING'S AS WE KNOW IT AT NORMAL SIZE.
HAVEN'T YOU EVER ASKED YOURSELF WHAT YOU'RE BREATHING WHEN YOU'RE SMALLER THAN AN OXYGEN ATOM?
HOW YOU'RE SEEING WHEN YOU'RE SMALLER THAN A PHOTON?
YES. YES, I HAVE. AND THEN I HAVE MADE MYSELF A SANDWICH BECAUSE I DON'T KNOW.
THE MICROVERSE ISN'T LIKE OUTER SPACE JUST SMALLER, MR. LANG.
EVERYTHING IN SUBATOMICA HAS PURPOSE. EVERYTHING IS AN EQUALLY IMPORTANT PART OF THE GLUE THAT HOLDS ALL OF EXISTENCE TOGETHER.

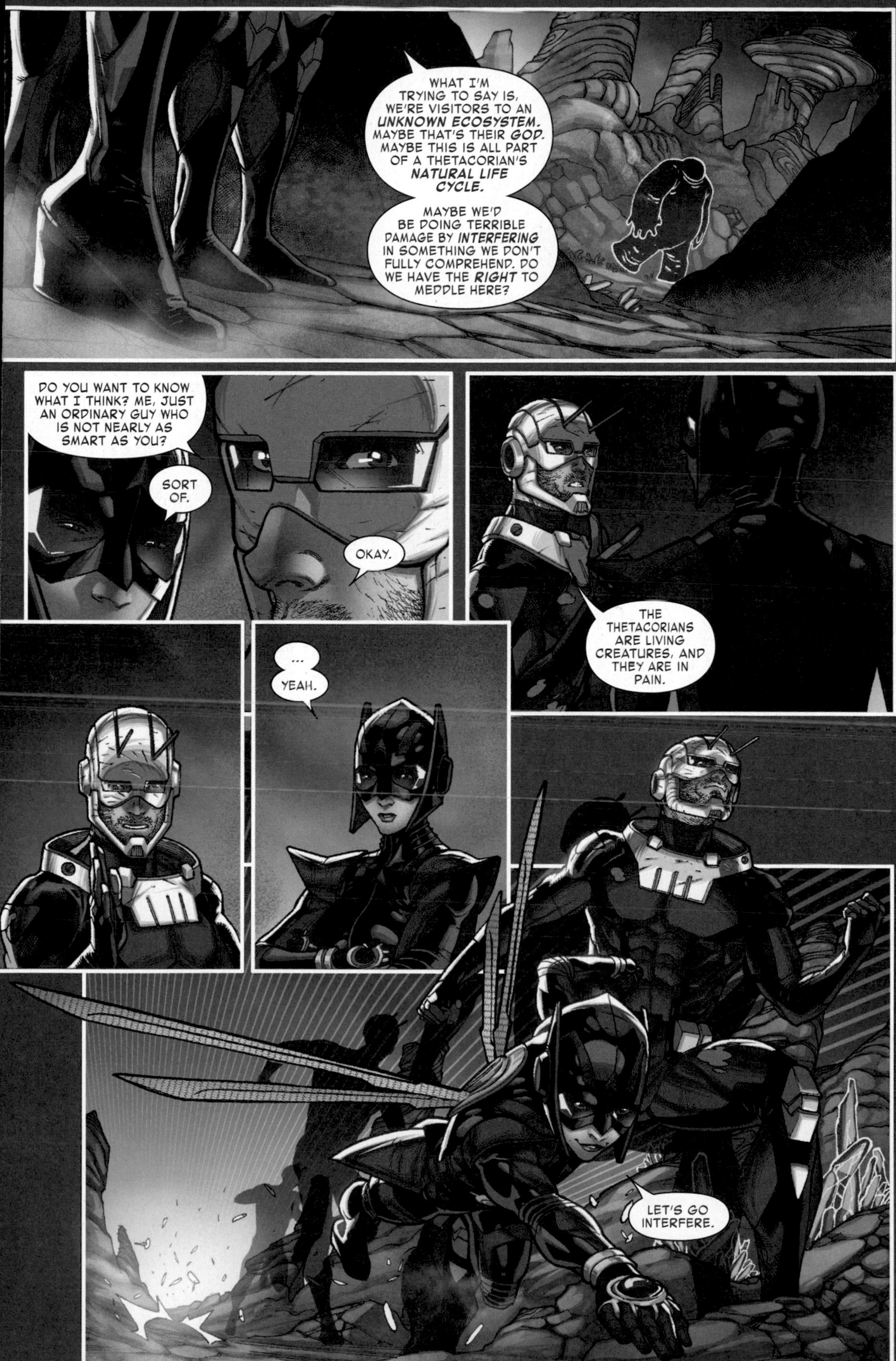
WHAT I'M TRYING TO SAY IS, WE'RE VISITORS TO AN UNKNOWN ECOSYSTEM. MAYBE THAT'S THEIR GOD. MAYBE THIS IS ALL PART OF A THETACORIAN'S NATURAL LIFE CYCLE.
MAYBE WE'D BE DOING TERRIBLE DAMAGE BY INTERFERING IN SOMETHING WE DON'T FULLY COMPREHEND. DO WE HAVE THE RIGHT TO MEDDLE HERE?
DO YOU WANT TO KNOW WHAT I THINK? ME, JUST AN ORDINARY GUY WHO IS NOT NEARLY AS SMART AS YOU?
SORT OF.
OKAY.
THE THETACORIANS ARE LIVING CREATURES, AND THEY ARE IN PAIN.
...
YEAH.
LET'S GO INTERFERE.

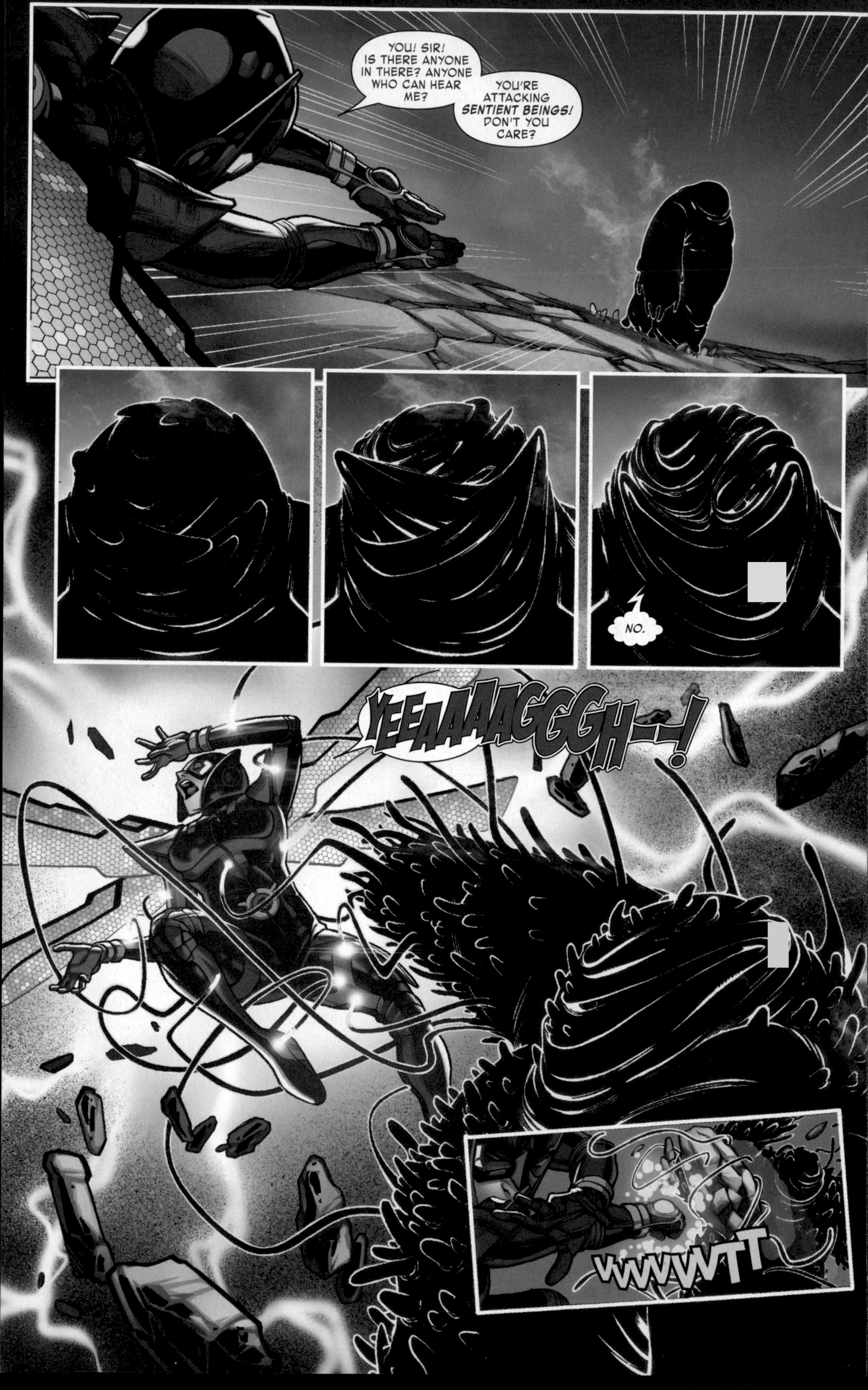
YOU! SIR! IS THERE ANYONE IN THERE? ANYONE WHO CAN HEAR ME?
YOU'RE ATTACKING **SENTIENT BEINGS!** DON'T YOU CARE?
NO.
YEEAAAAGGGH--!
VVVVVTT

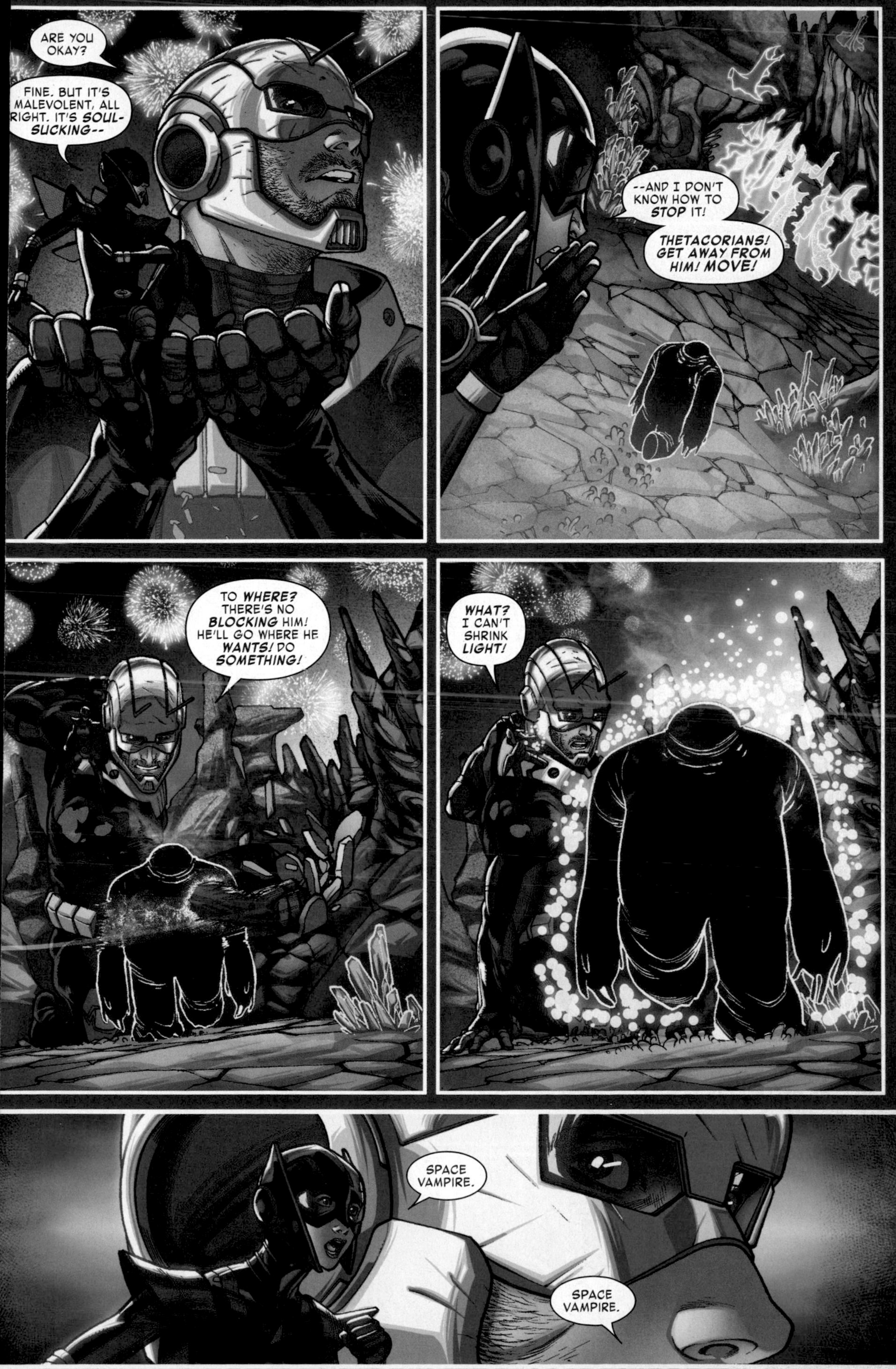
ARE YOU OKAY?
FINE. BUT IT'S MALEVOLENT, ALL RIGHT. IT'S SOUL-SUCKING--
--AND I DON'T KNOW HOW TO STOP IT!
THETACORIANS! GET AWAY FROM HIM! MOVE!
TO WHERE? THERE'S NO BLOCKING HIM! HE'LL GO WHERE HE WANTS! DO SOMETHING!
WHAT? I CAN'T SHRINK LIGHT!
SPACE VAMPIRE.
SPACE VAMPIRE.

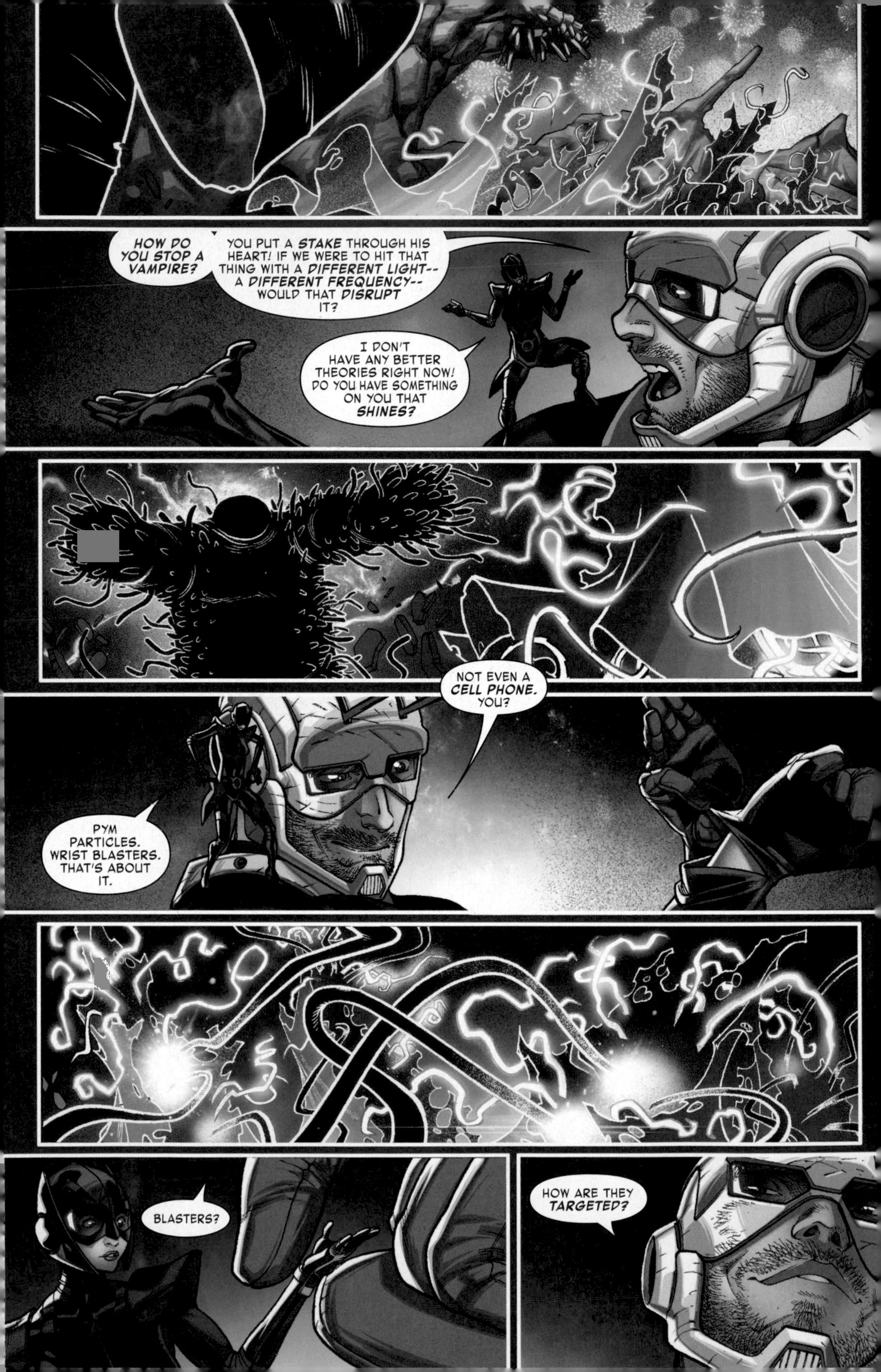
HOW DO YOU STOP A VAMPIRE?
YOU PUT A STAKE THROUGH HIS HEART! IF WE WERE TO HIT THAT THING WITH A DIFFERENT LIGHT-- A DIFFERENT FREQUENCY-- WOULD THAT DISRUPT IT?
I DON'T HAVE ANY BETTER THEORIES RIGHT NOW! DO YOU HAVE SOMETHING ON YOU THAT SHINES?
NOT EVEN A CELL PHONE. YOU?
PYM PARTICLES. WRIST BLASTERS. THAT'S ABOUT IT.
BLASTERS?
HOW ARE THEY TARGETED?

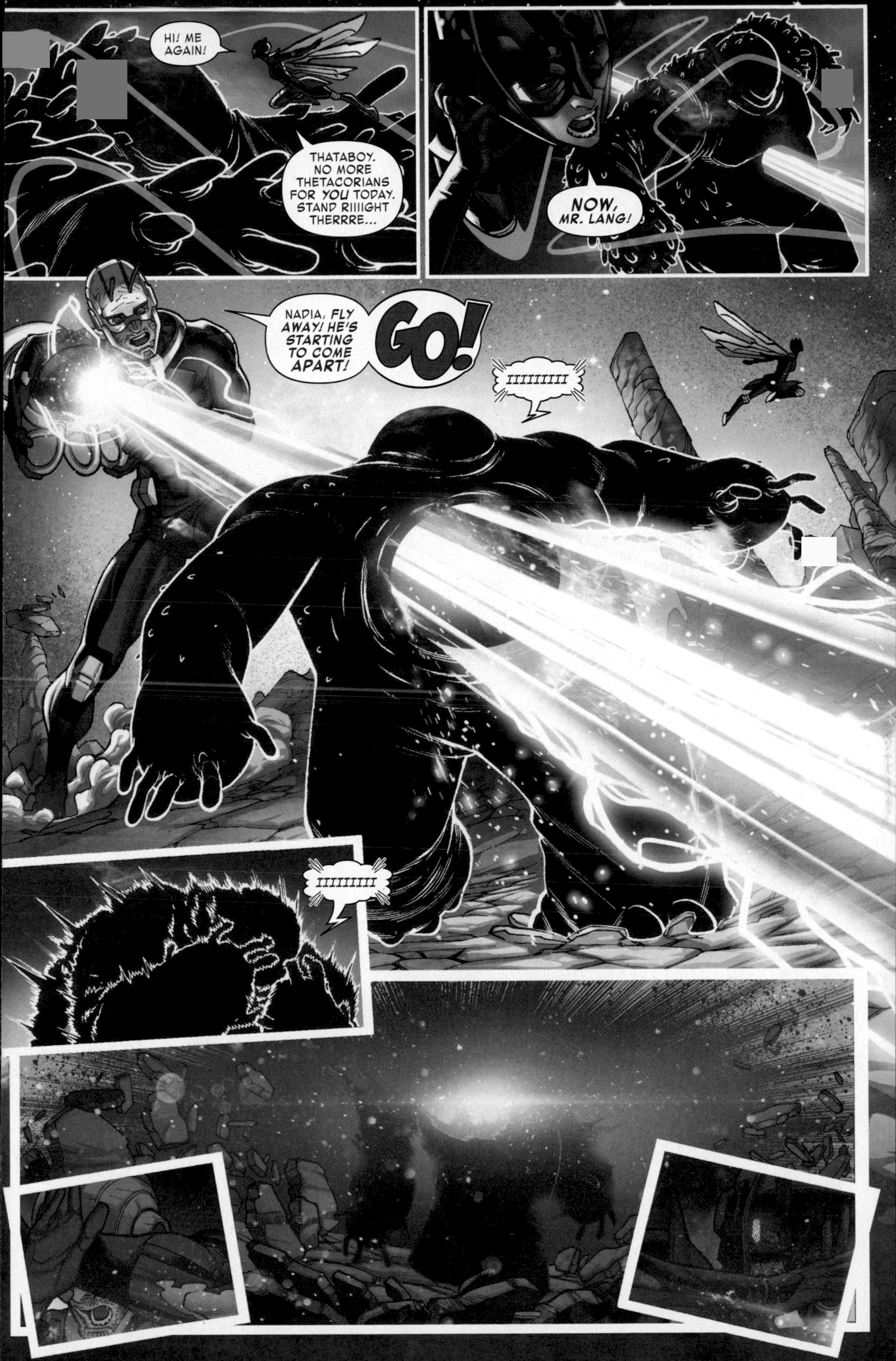
HI! ME AGAIN!
THATABOY. NO MORE THETACORIANS FOR YOU TODAY. STAND RIIIIGHT THERRRE...
NOW, MR. LANG!
NADIA, FLY AWAY! HE'S STARTING TO COME APART!
GO!
IIIIIIIII
IIIIIIIII

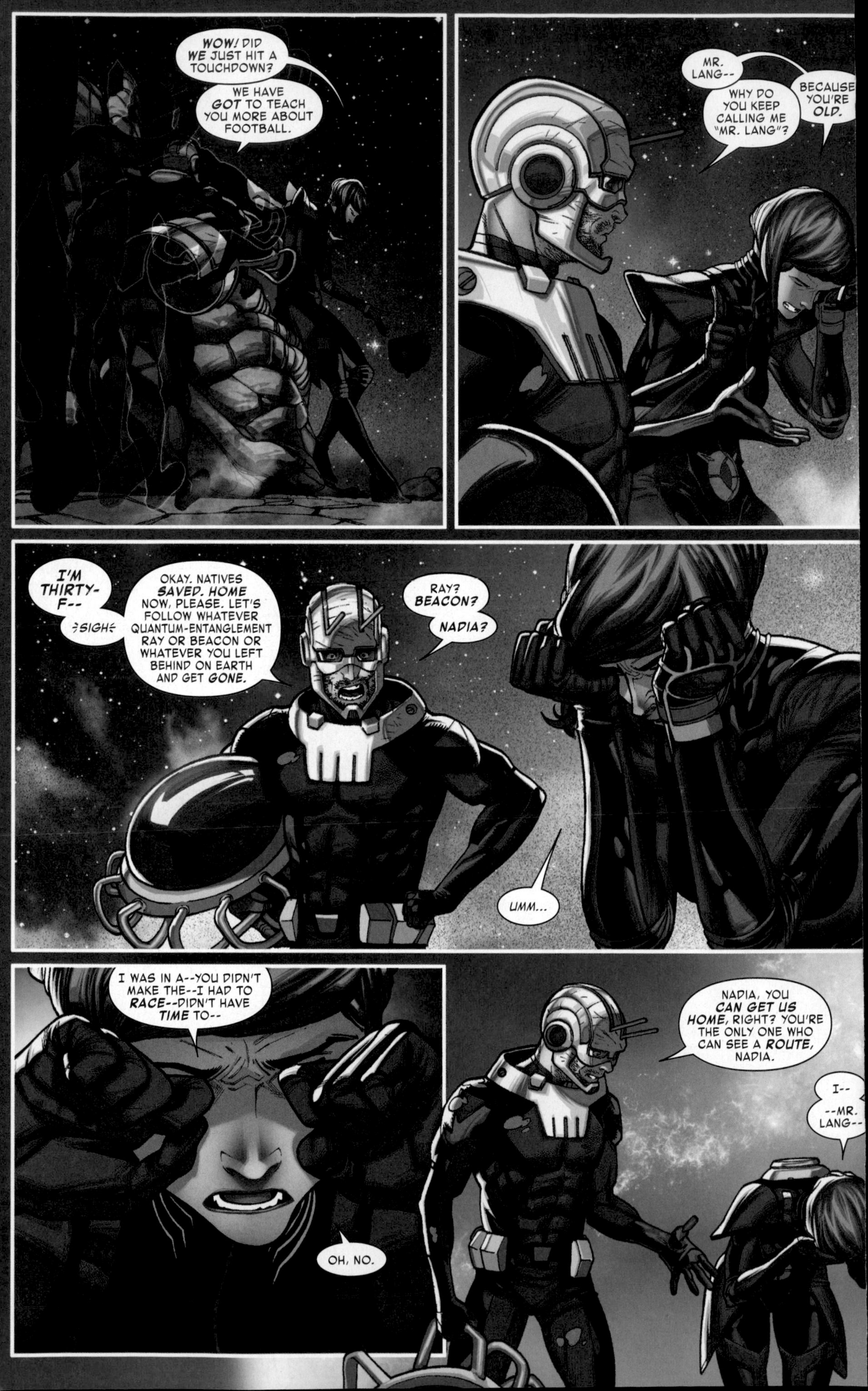
WOW! DID WE JUST HIT A TOUCHDOWN?
WE HAVE GOT TO TEACH YOU MORE ABOUT FOOTBALL.
MR. LANG--
WHY DO YOU KEEP CALLING ME "MR. LANG"?
BECAUSE YOU'RE OLD.
I'M THIRTY-F--
SIGH
OKAY. NATIVES SAVED. HOME NOW, PLEASE. LET'S FOLLOW WHATEVER QUANTUM-ENTANGLEMENT RAY OR BEACON OR WHATEVER YOU LEFT BEHIND ON EARTH AND GET GONE.
RAY? BEACON?
NADIA?
UMM...
I WAS IN A--YOU DIDN'T MAKE THE--I HAD TO RACE--DIDN'T HAVE TIME TO--
OH, NO.
NADIA, YOU CAN GET US HOME, RIGHT? YOU'RE THE ONLY ONE WHO CAN SEE A ROUTE, NADIA.
I--
--MR. LANG--

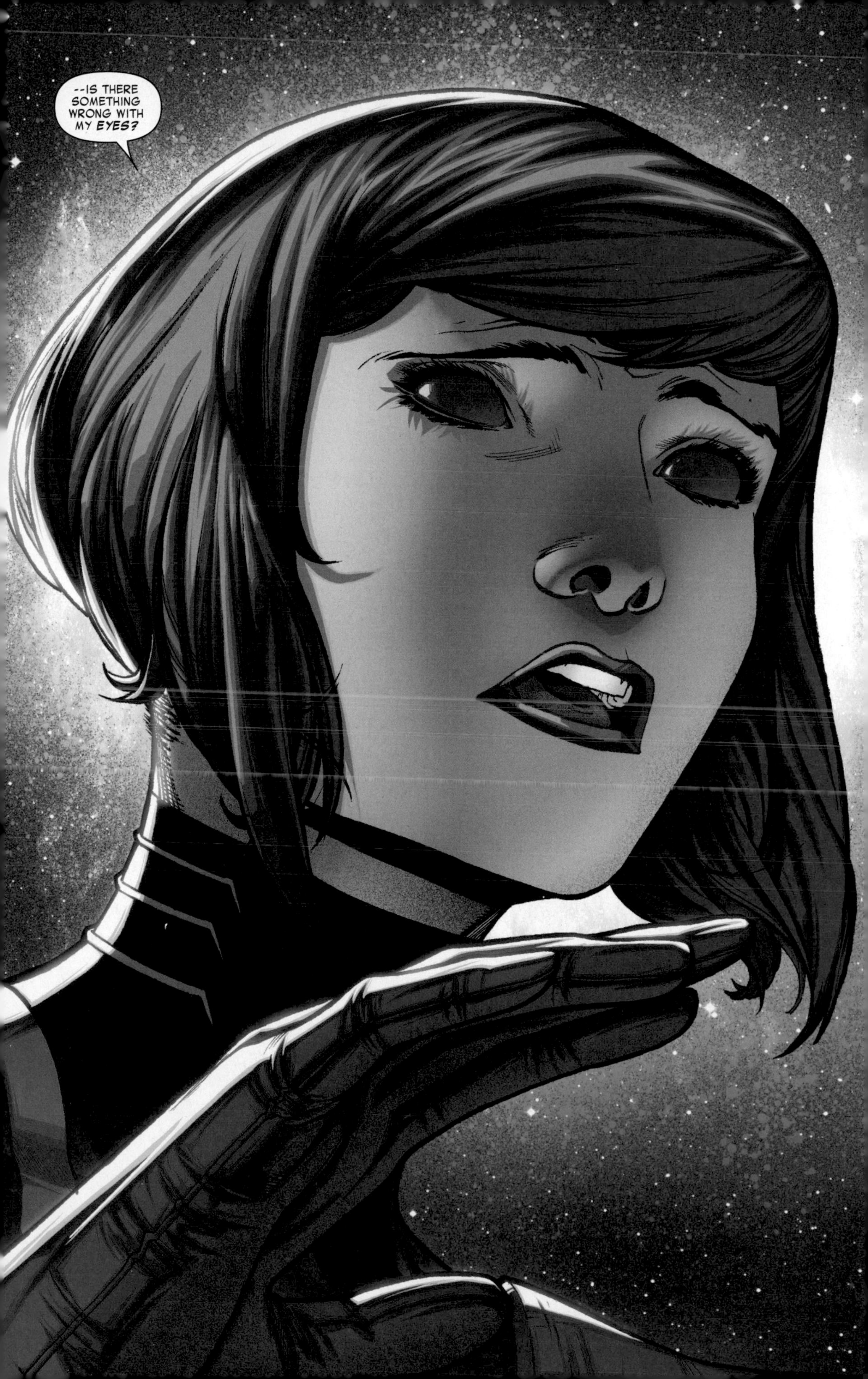
--IS THERE SOMETHING WRONG WITH MY EYES?

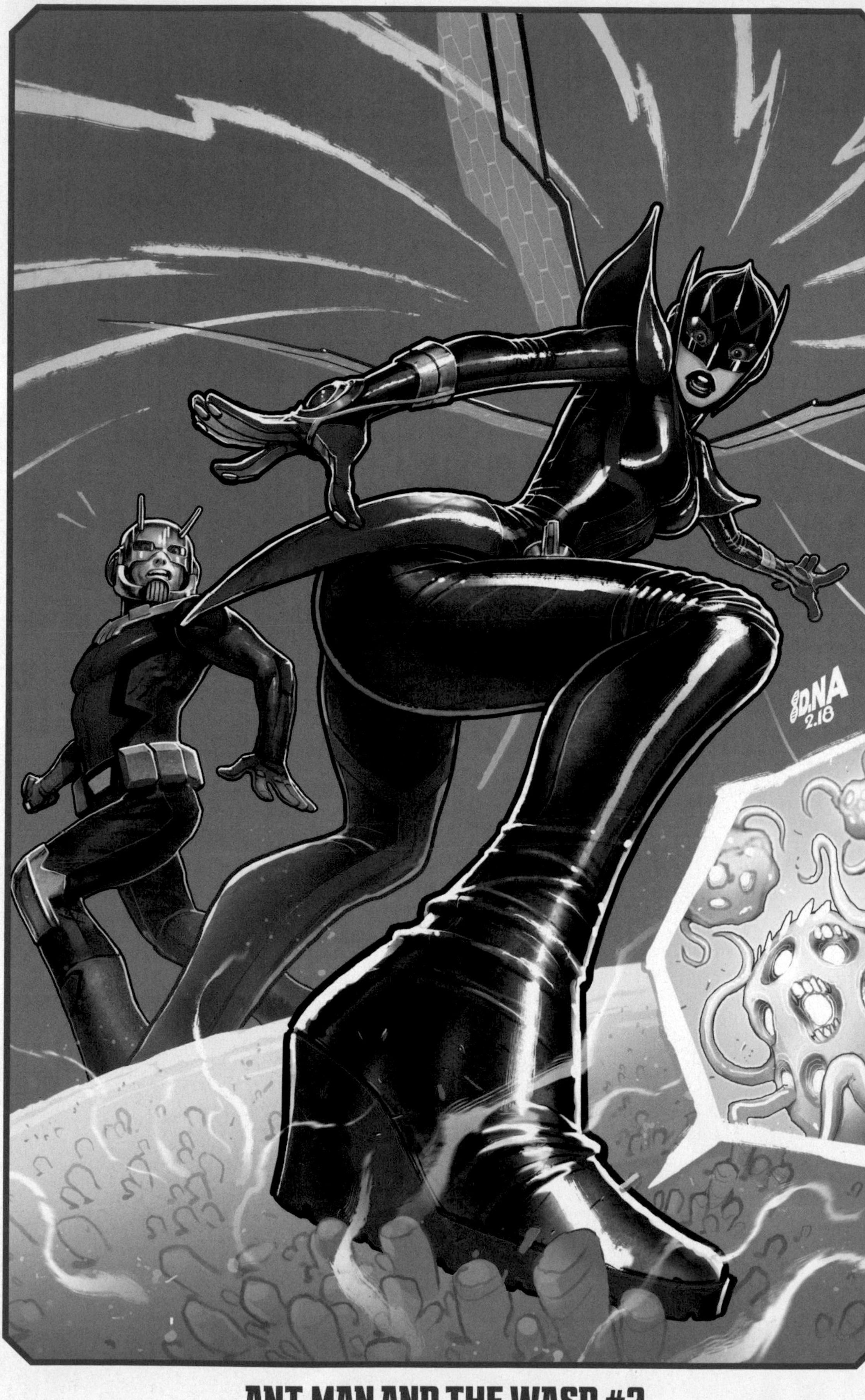
D.NA
2.18

ANT-MAN AND THE WASP #2

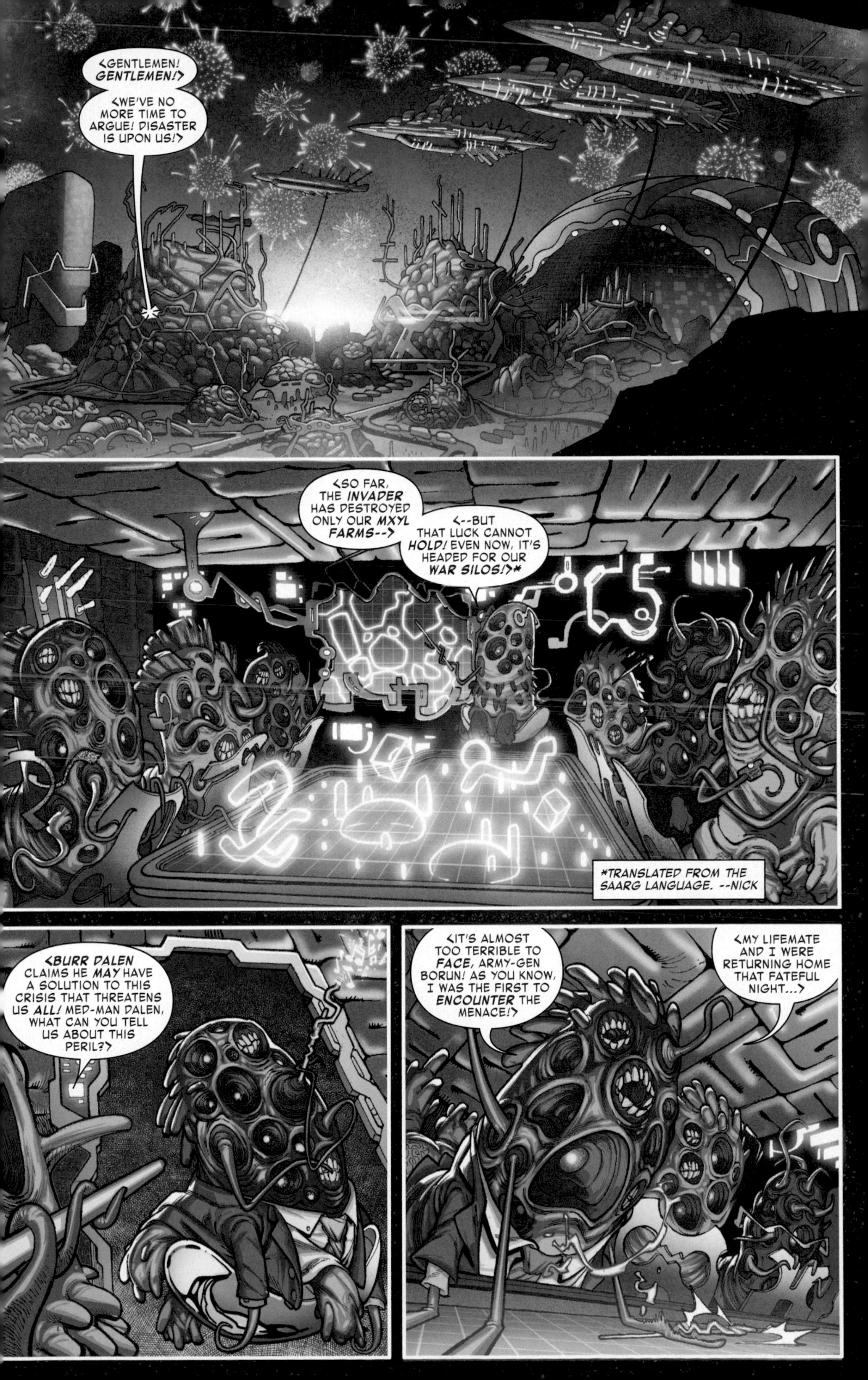

<GENTLEMEN! *GENTLEMEN!*>
<WE'VE NO MORE TIME TO ARGUE! DISASTER IS UPON US!>
<SO FAR, THE *INVADER* HAS DESTROYED ONLY OUR *MXYL FARMS*-->
<--BUT THAT LUCK CANNOT *HOLD!* EVEN NOW, IT'S HEADED FOR OUR *WAR SILOS!*>*
*TRANSLATED FROM THE SAARG LANGUAGE. --NICK
<*BURR DALEN* CLAIMS HE *MAY* HAVE A SOLUTION TO THIS CRISIS THAT THREATENS US *ALL!* MED-MAN DALEN, WHAT CAN YOU TELL US ABOUT THIS PERIL?>
<IT'S ALMOST TOO TERRIBLE TO *FACE,* ARMY-GEN BORUN! AS YOU KNOW, I WAS THE FIRST TO *ENCOUNTER* THE MENACE!>
<MY LIFEMATE AND I WERE RETURNING HOME THAT FATEFUL NIGHT...>

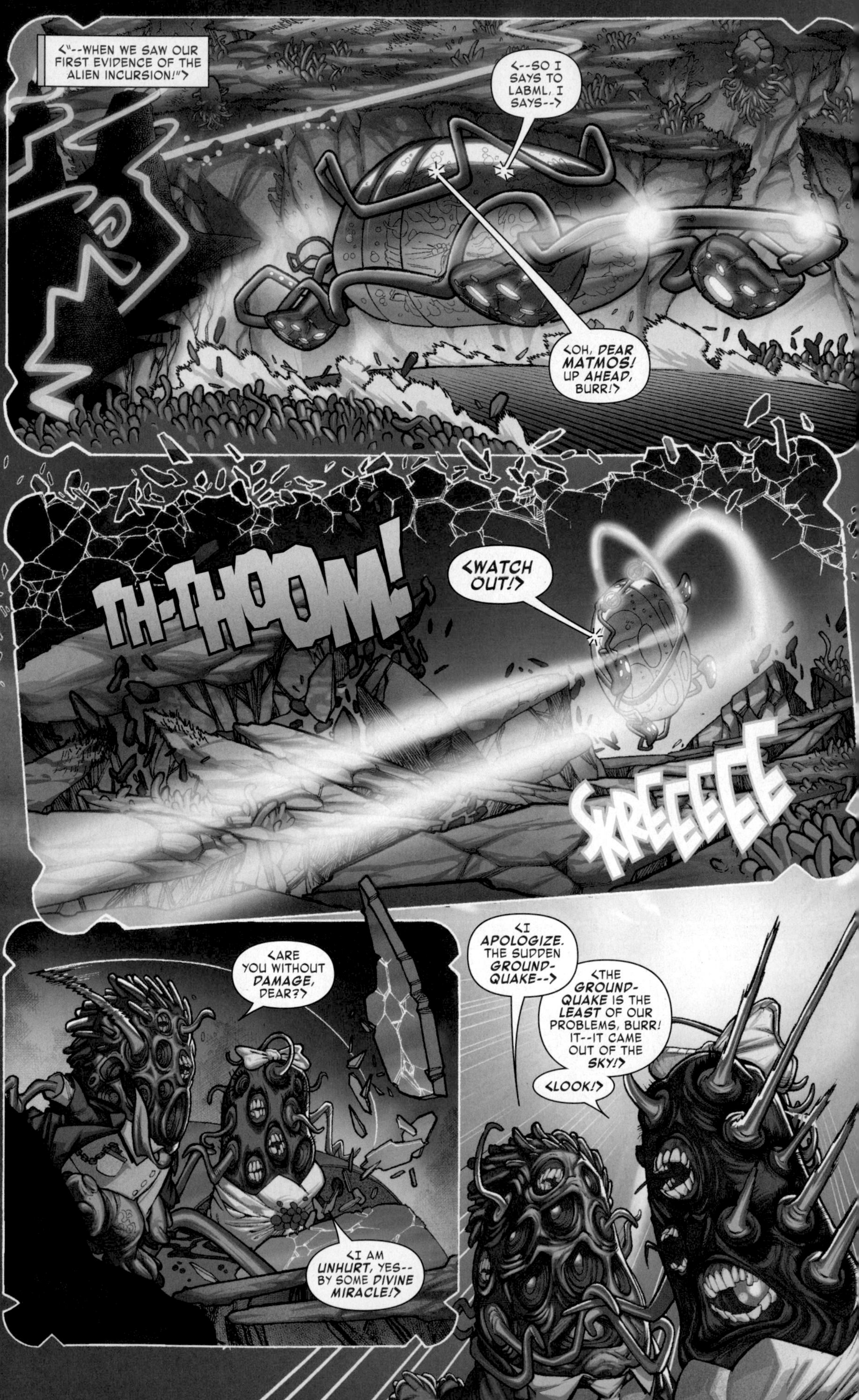
<"--WHEN WE SAW OUR FIRST EVIDENCE OF THE ALIEN INCURSION!">
<--SO I SAYS TO LABML, I SAYS-->
<OH, DEAR MATMOS! UP AHEAD, BURR!>
TH-THOOM!
<WATCH OUT!>
SKREEEEEE
<ARE YOU WITHOUT DAMAGE, DEAR?>
<I AM UNHURT, YES--BY SOME DIVINE MIRACLE!>
<I APOLOGIZE. THE SUDDEN GROUND-QUAKE-->
<THE GROUND-QUAKE IS THE LEAST OF OUR PROBLEMS, BURR! IT--IT CAME OUT OF THE SKY!>
<LOOK!>

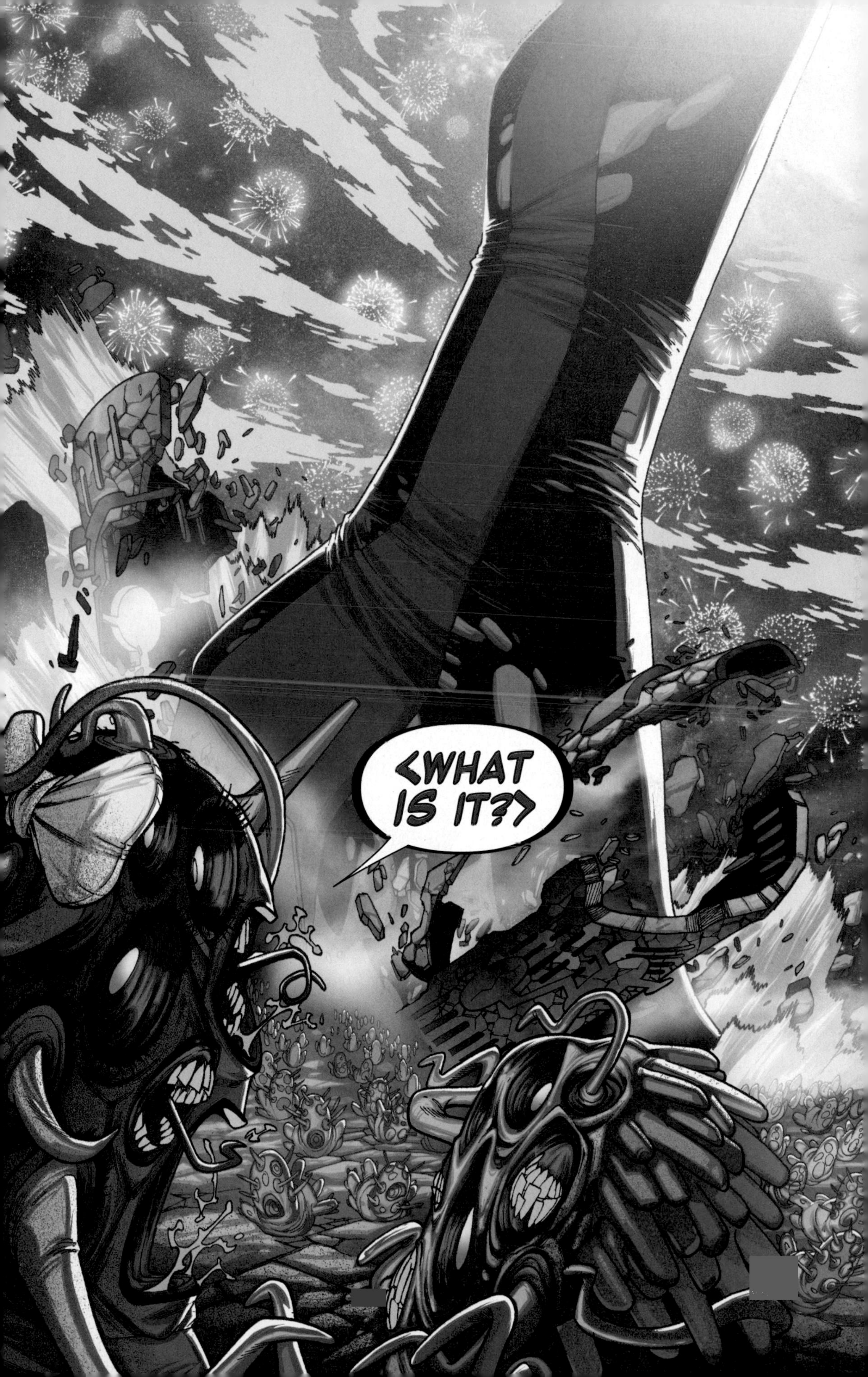
<WHAT IS IT?>

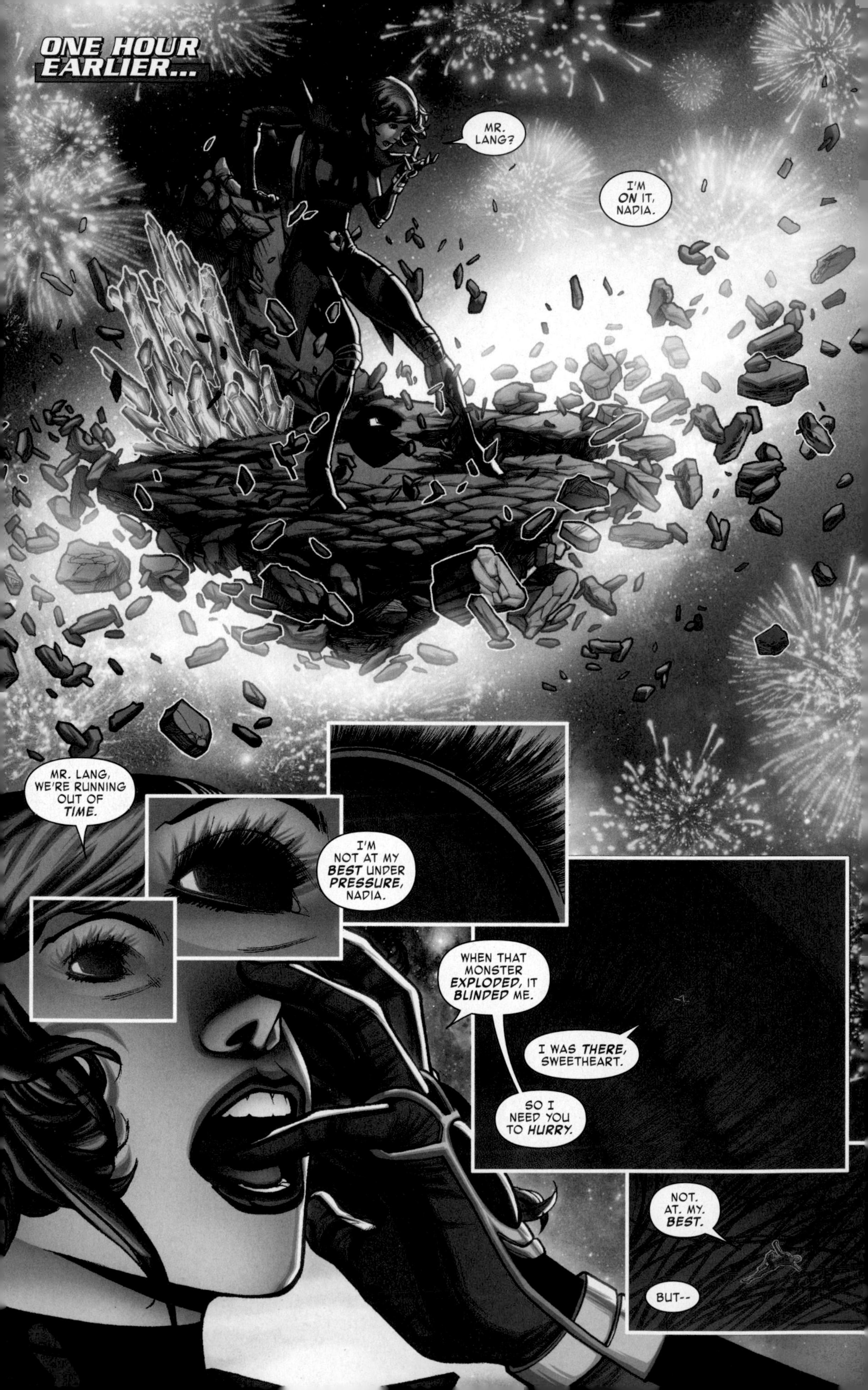
ONE HOUR EARLIER...
MR. LANG?
I'M ON IT, NADIA.
MR. LANG, WE'RE RUNNING OUT OF TIME.
I'M NOT AT MY BEST UNDER PRESSURE, NADIA.
WHEN THAT MONSTER EXPLODED, IT BLINDED ME.
I WAS THERE, SWEETHEART.
SO I NEED YOU TO HURRY.
NOT. AT. MY. BEST.
BUT--

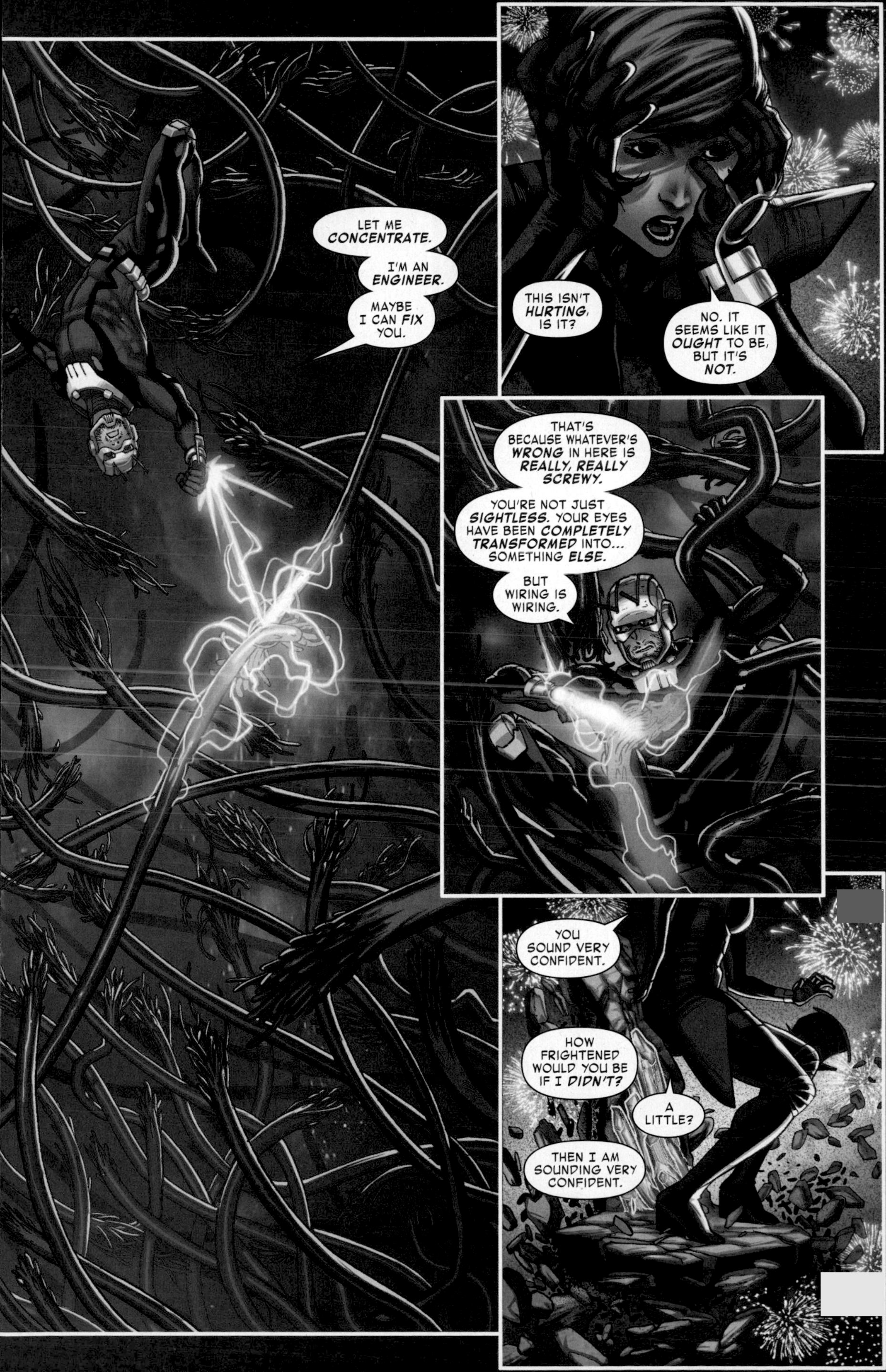
LET ME CONCENTRATE.
I'M AN ENGINEER.
MAYBE I CAN FIX YOU.
THIS ISN'T HURTING, IS IT?
NO. IT SEEMS LIKE IT OUGHT TO BE, BUT IT'S NOT.
THAT'S BECAUSE WHATEVER'S WRONG IN HERE IS REALLY, REALLY SCREWY.
YOU'RE NOT JUST SIGHTLESS. YOUR EYES HAVE BEEN COMPLETELY TRANSFORMED INTO... SOMETHING ELSE.
BUT WIRING IS WIRING.
YOU SOUND VERY CONFIDENT.
HOW FRIGHTENED WOULD YOU BE IF I DIDN'T?
A LITTLE?
THEN I AM SOUNDING VERY CONFIDENT.

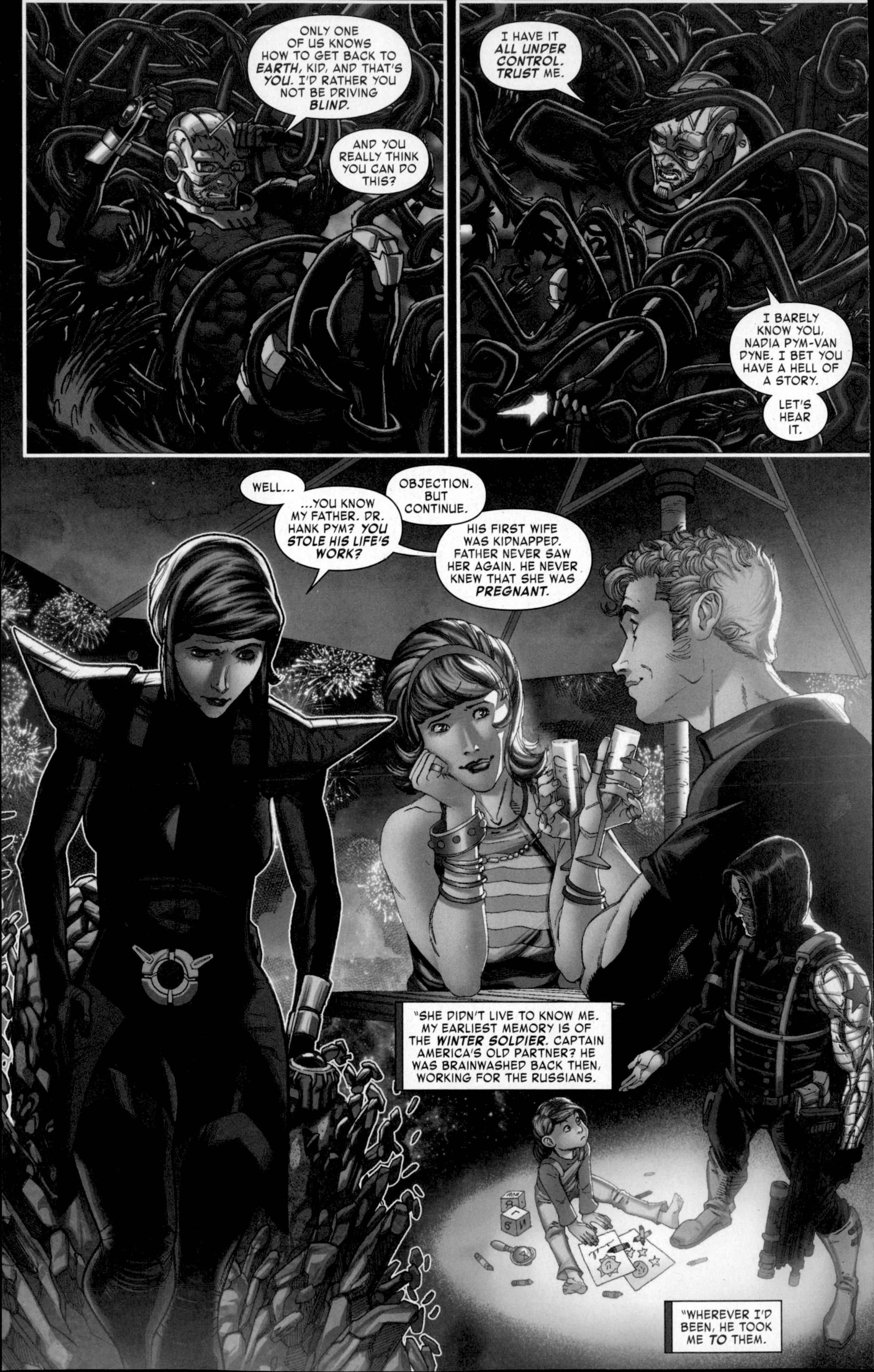
ONLY ONE OF US KNOWS HOW TO GET BACK TO EARTH, KID, AND THAT'S YOU. I'D RATHER YOU NOT BE DRIVING BLIND.
AND YOU REALLY THINK YOU CAN DO THIS?
I HAVE IT ALL UNDER CONTROL. TRUST ME.
I BARELY KNOW YOU, NADIA PYM-VAN DYNE. I BET YOU HAVE A HELL OF A STORY.
LET'S HEAR IT.
WELL...
...YOU KNOW MY FATHER. DR. HANK PYM? YOU STOLE HIS LIFE'S WORK?
OBJECTION. BUT CONTINUE.
HIS FIRST WIFE WAS KIDNAPPED. FATHER NEVER SAW HER AGAIN. HE NEVER KNEW THAT SHE WAS PREGNANT.
"SHE DIDN'T LIVE TO KNOW ME. MY EARLIEST MEMORY IS OF THE WINTER SOLDIER. CAPTAIN AMERICA'S OLD PARTNER? HE WAS BRAINWASHED BACK THEN, WORKING FOR THE RUSSIANS.
"WHEREVER I'D BEEN, HE TOOK ME TO THEM.

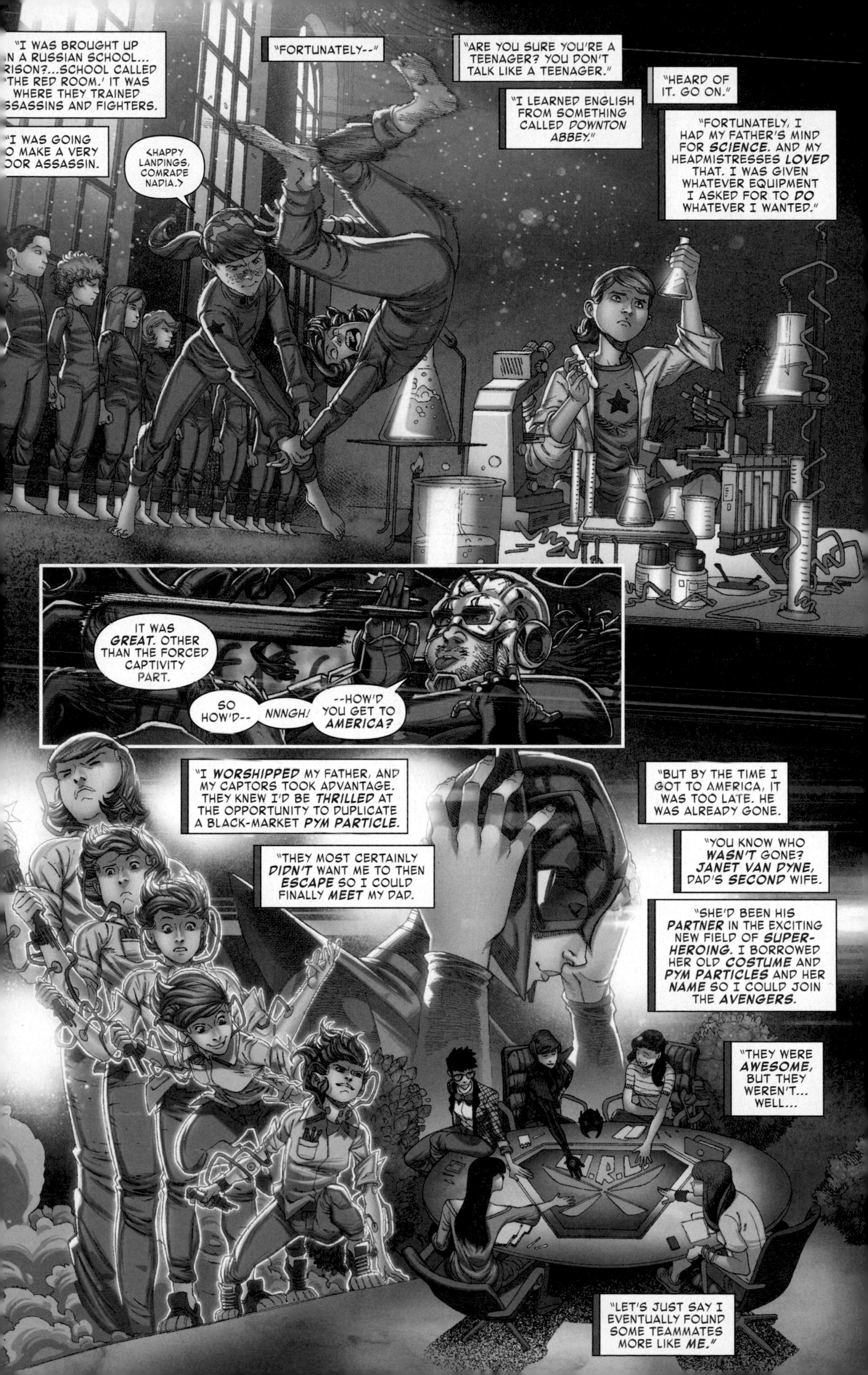
"I WAS BROUGHT UP
N A RUSSIAN SCHOOL...
RISON?...SCHOOL CALLED
THE RED ROOM.' IT WAS
WHERE THEY TRAINED
SSASSINS AND FIGHTERS.
"I WAS GOING
O MAKE A VERY
OOR ASSASSIN.
<HAPPY LANDINGS, COMRADE NADIA.>
"FORTUNATELY--"
"ARE YOU SURE YOU'RE A TEENAGER? YOU DON'T TALK LIKE A TEENAGER."
"I LEARNED ENGLISH FROM SOMETHING CALLED DOWNTON ABBEY."
"HEARD OF IT. GO ON."
"FORTUNATELY, I HAD MY FATHER'S MIND FOR SCIENCE. AND MY HEADMISTRESSES LOVED THAT. I WAS GIVEN WHATEVER EQUIPMENT I ASKED FOR TO DO WHATEVER I WANTED."
IT WAS GREAT. OTHER THAN THE FORCED CAPTIVITY PART.
SO HOW'D--
NNNGH!
--HOW'D YOU GET TO AMERICA?
"I WORSHIPPED MY FATHER, AND MY CAPTORS TOOK ADVANTAGE. THEY KNEW I'D BE THRILLED AT THE OPPORTUNITY TO DUPLICATE A BLACK-MARKET PYM PARTICLE.
"THEY MOST CERTAINLY DIDN'T WANT ME TO THEN ESCAPE SO I COULD FINALLY MEET MY DAD.
"BUT BY THE TIME I GOT TO AMERICA, IT WAS TOO LATE. HE WAS ALREADY GONE.
"YOU KNOW WHO WASN'T GONE? JANET VAN DYNE, DAD'S SECOND WIFE.
"SHE'D BEEN HIS PARTNER IN THE EXCITING NEW FIELD OF SUPER-HEROING. I BORROWED HER OLD COSTUME AND PYM PARTICLES AND HER NAME SO I COULD JOIN THE AVENGERS.
"THEY WERE AWESOME, BUT THEY WEREN'T... WELL...
"LET'S JUST SAY I EVENTUALLY FOUND SOME TEAMMATES MORE LIKE ME."

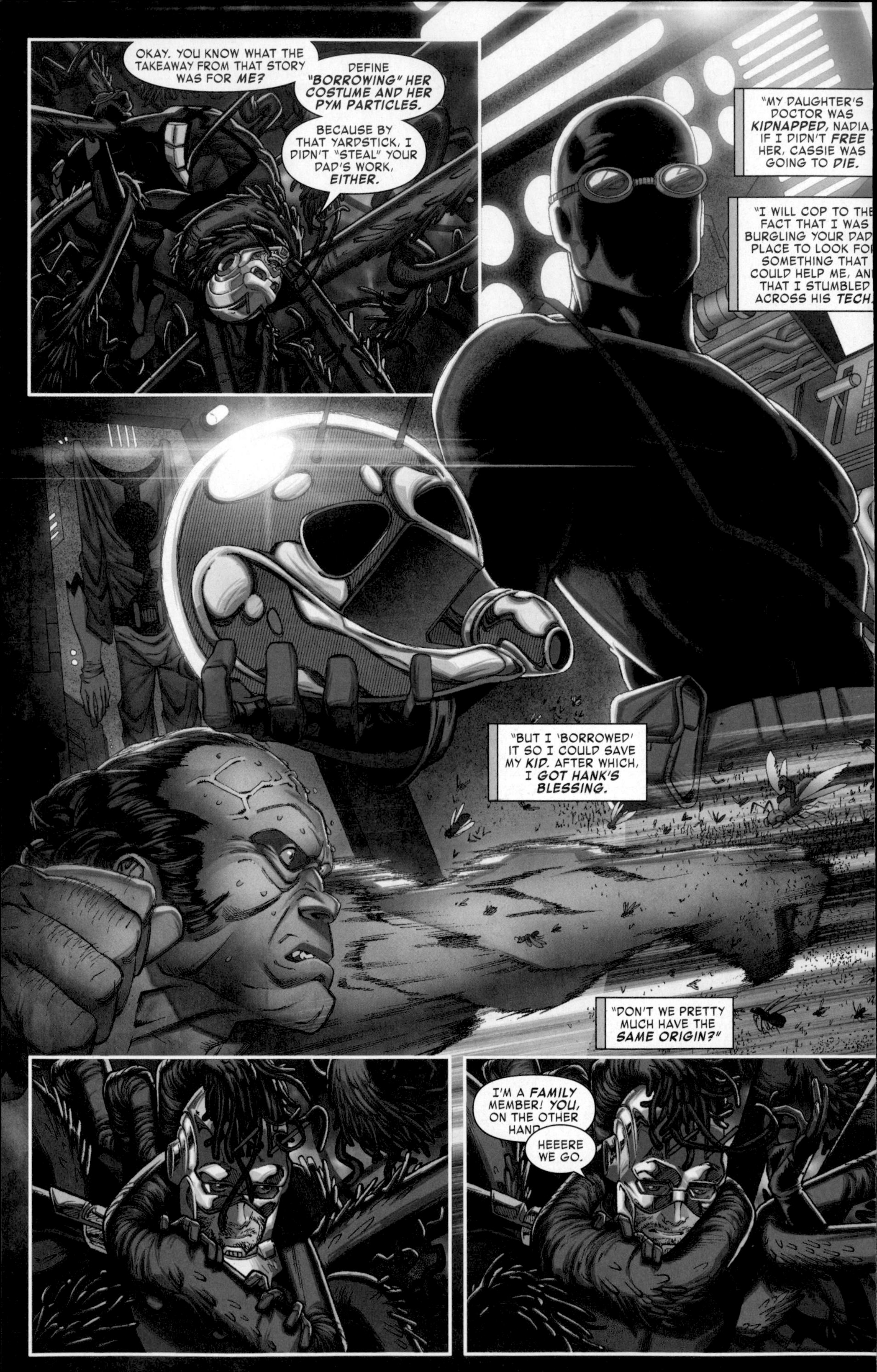

OKAY. YOU KNOW WHAT THE TAKEAWAY FROM THAT STORY WAS FOR ME?
DEFINE "BORROWING" HER COSTUME AND HER PYM PARTICLES.
BECAUSE BY THAT YARDSTICK, I DIDN'T "STEAL" YOUR DAD'S WORK, EITHER.
"MY DAUGHTER'S DOCTOR WAS KIDNAPPED, NADIA. IF I DIDN'T FREE HER, CASSIE WAS GOING TO DIE.
"I WILL COP TO THE FACT THAT I WAS BURGLING YOUR DAD'S PLACE TO LOOK FOR SOMETHING THAT COULD HELP ME, AND THAT I STUMBLED ACROSS HIS TECH.
"BUT I 'BORROWED' IT SO I COULD SAVE MY KID. AFTER WHICH, I GOT HANK'S BLESSING.
"DON'T WE PRETTY MUCH HAVE THE SAME ORIGIN?"
I'M A FAMILY MEMBER! YOU, ON THE OTHER HAND--
HEEERE WE GO.

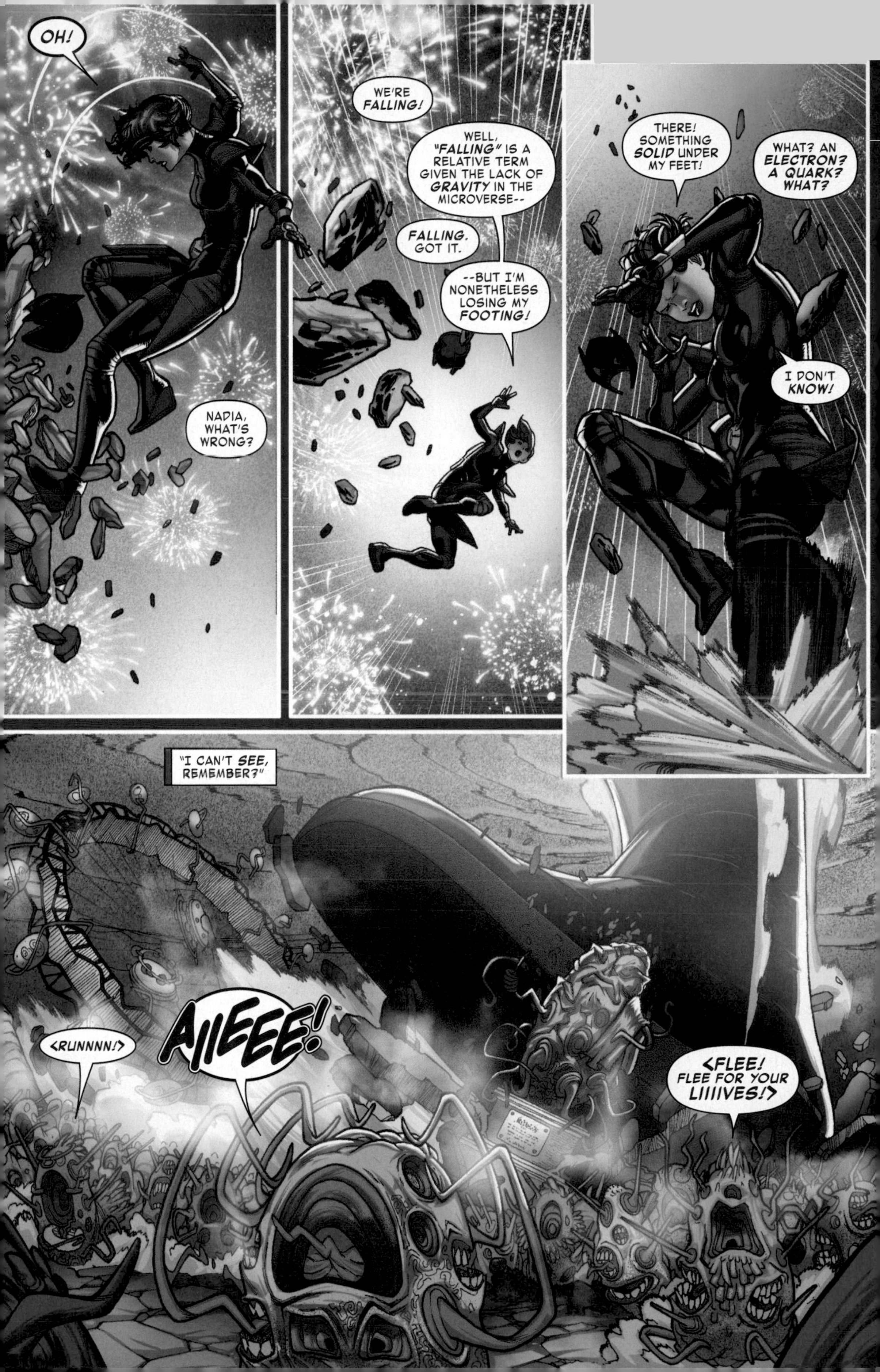
OH!
NADIA, WHAT'S WRONG?
WE'RE FALLING!
WELL, "FALLING" IS A RELATIVE TERM GIVEN THE LACK OF GRAVITY IN THE MICROVERSE--
FALLING. GOT IT.
--BUT I'M NONETHELESS LOSING MY FOOTING!
THERE! SOMETHING SOLID UNDER MY FEET!
WHAT? AN ELECTRON? A QUARK? WHAT?
I DON'T KNOW!
"I CAN'T SEE, REMEMBER?"
AIIEEE!
<RUNNNN!>
<FLEE! FLEE FOR YOUR LIIIIVES!>

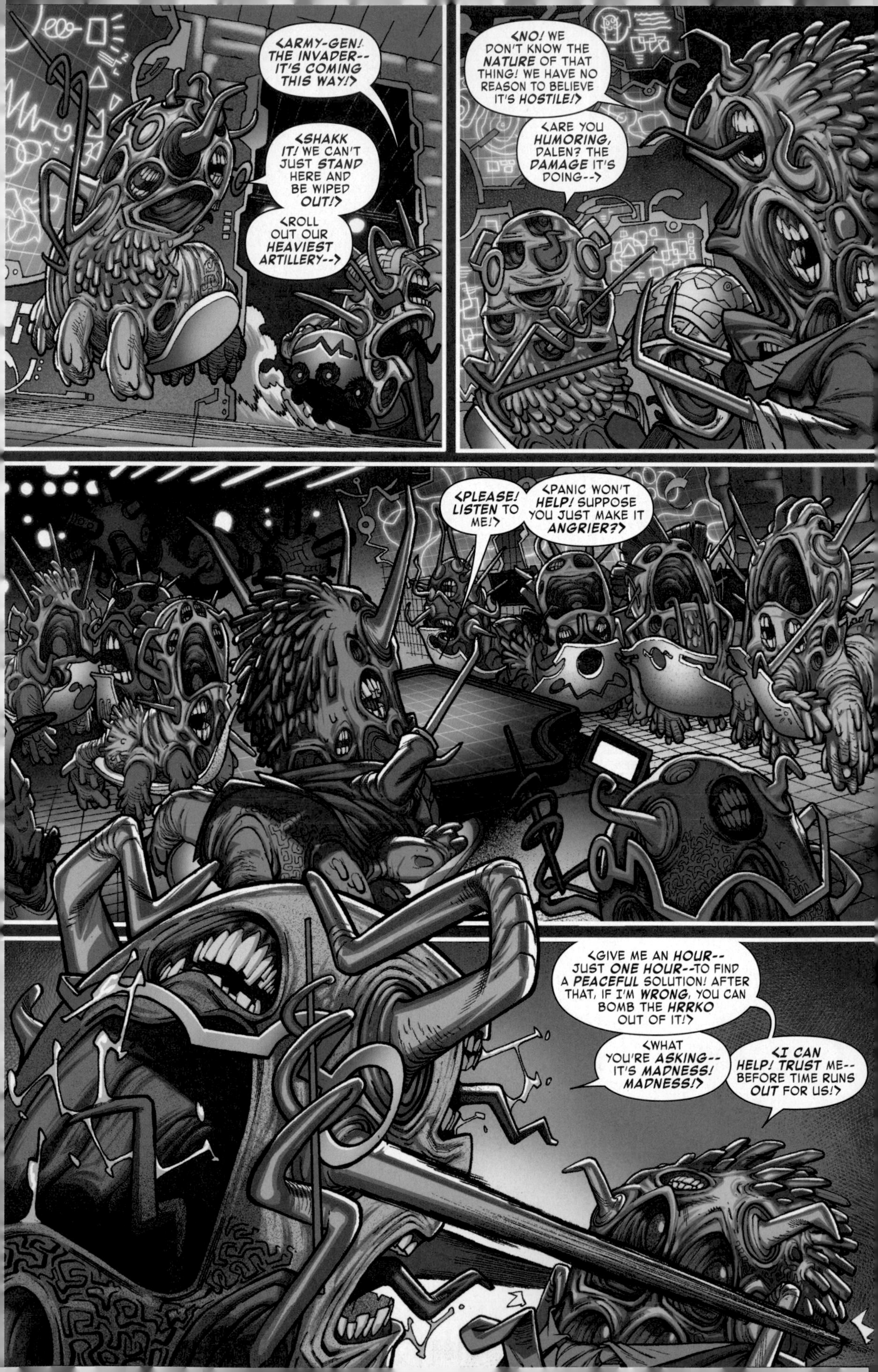
<ARMY-GEN! THE INVADER-- IT'S COMING THIS WAY!>
<SHAKK IT! WE CAN'T JUST STAND HERE AND BE WIPED OUT!>
<ROLL OUT OUR HEAVIEST ARTILLERY-->
<NO! WE DON'T KNOW THE NATURE OF THAT THING! WE HAVE NO REASON TO BELIEVE IT'S HOSTILE!>
<ARE YOU HUMORING, DALEN? THE DAMAGE IT'S DOING-->
<PLEASE! LISTEN TO ME!>
<PANIC WON'T HELP! SUPPOSE YOU JUST MAKE IT ANGRIER?>
<GIVE ME AN HOUR-- JUST ONE HOUR--TO FIND A PEACEFUL SOLUTION! AFTER THAT, IF I'M WRONG, YOU CAN BOMB THE HRRKO OUT OF IT!>
<WHAT YOU'RE ASKING-- IT'S MADNESS! MADNESS!>
<I CAN HELP! TRUST ME-- BEFORE TIME RUNS OUT FOR US!>

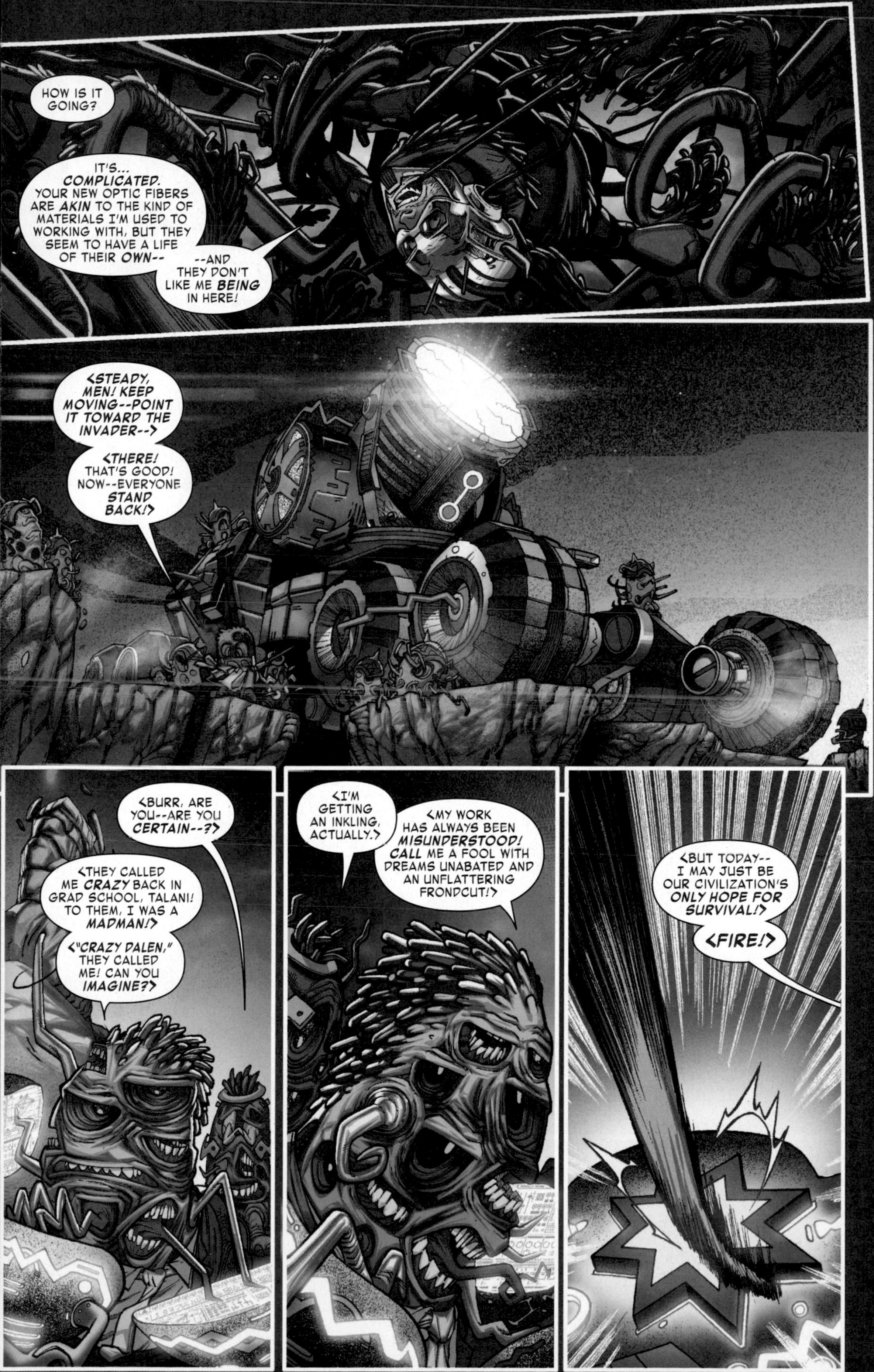
HOW IS IT GOING?
IT'S... COMPLICATED. YOUR NEW OPTIC FIBERS ARE AKIN TO THE KIND OF MATERIALS I'M USED TO WORKING WITH, BUT THEY SEEM TO HAVE A LIFE OF THEIR OWN--
--AND THEY DON'T LIKE ME BEING IN HERE!
<STEADY, MEN! KEEP MOVING--POINT IT TOWARD THE INVADER-->
<THERE! THAT'S GOOD! NOW--EVERYONE STAND BACK!>
<BURR, ARE YOU--ARE YOU CERTAIN--?>
<THEY CALLED ME CRAZY BACK IN GRAD SCHOOL, TALANI! TO THEM, I WAS A MADMAN!>
<"CRAZY DALEN," THEY CALLED ME! CAN YOU IMAGINE?>
<I'M GETTING AN INKLING, ACTUALLY.>
<MY WORK HAS ALWAYS BEEN MISUNDERSTOOD! CALL ME A FOOL WITH DREAMS UNABATED AND AN UNFLATTERING FRONDCUT!>
<BUT TODAY-- I MAY JUST BE OUR CIVILIZATION'S ONLY HOPE FOR SURVIVAL!>
<FIRE!>

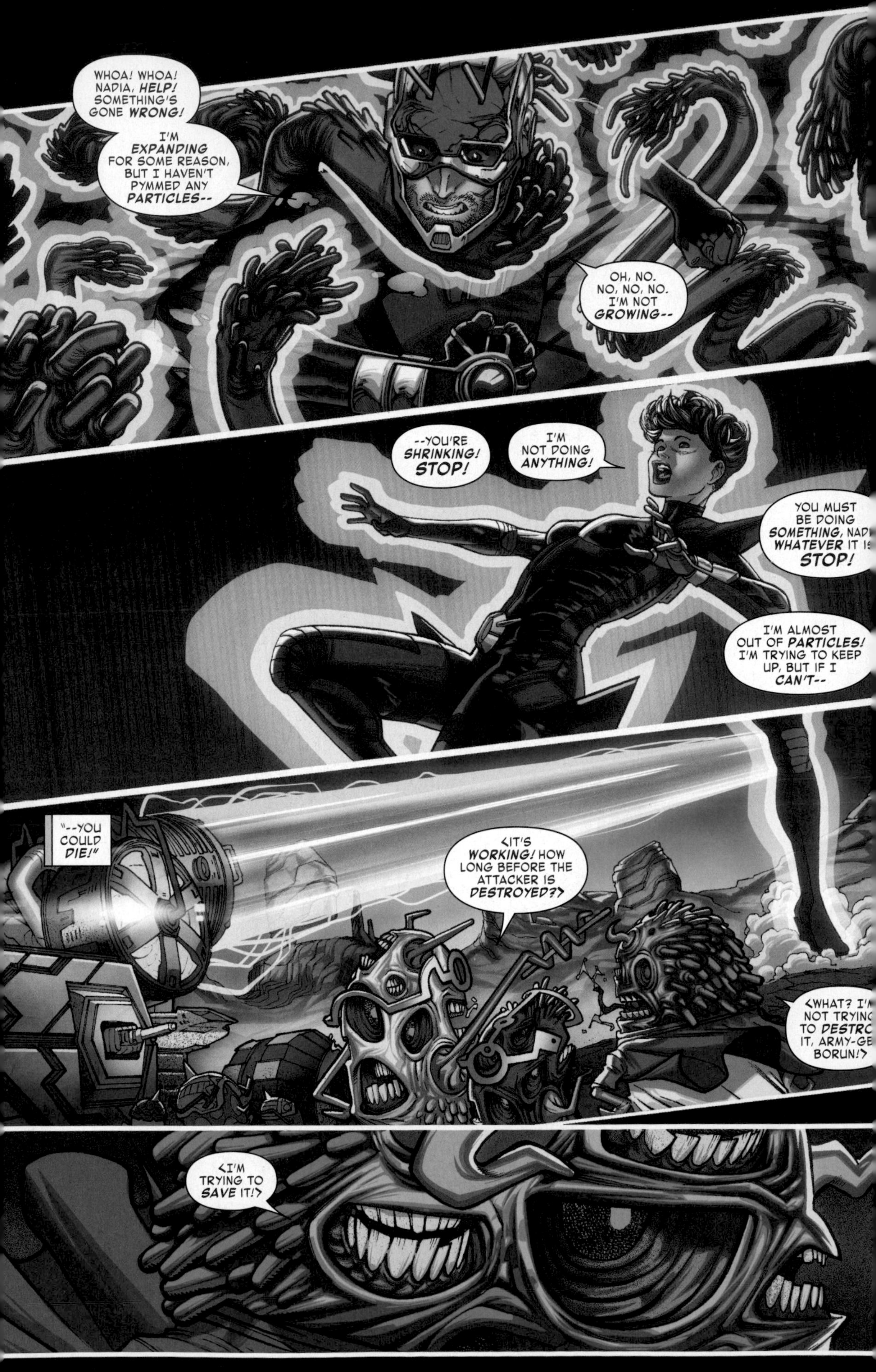
WHOA! WHOA! NADIA, HELP! SOMETHING'S GONE WRONG!
I'M EXPANDING FOR SOME REASON, BUT I HAVEN'T PYMMED ANY PARTICLES--
OH, NO. NO, NO, NO. I'M NOT GROWING--
--YOU'RE SHRINKING! STOP!
I'M NOT DOING ANYTHING!
YOU MUST BE DOING SOMETHING, NAD WHATEVER IT IS STOP!
I'M ALMOST OUT OF PARTICLES! I'M TRYING TO KEEP UP, BUT IF I CAN'T--
"--YOU COULD DIE!"
<IT'S WORKING! HOW LONG BEFORE THE ATTACKER IS DESTROYED?>
<WHAT? I'M NOT TRYING TO DESTRO IT, ARMY-GE BORUN!>
<I'M TRYING TO SAVE IT!>

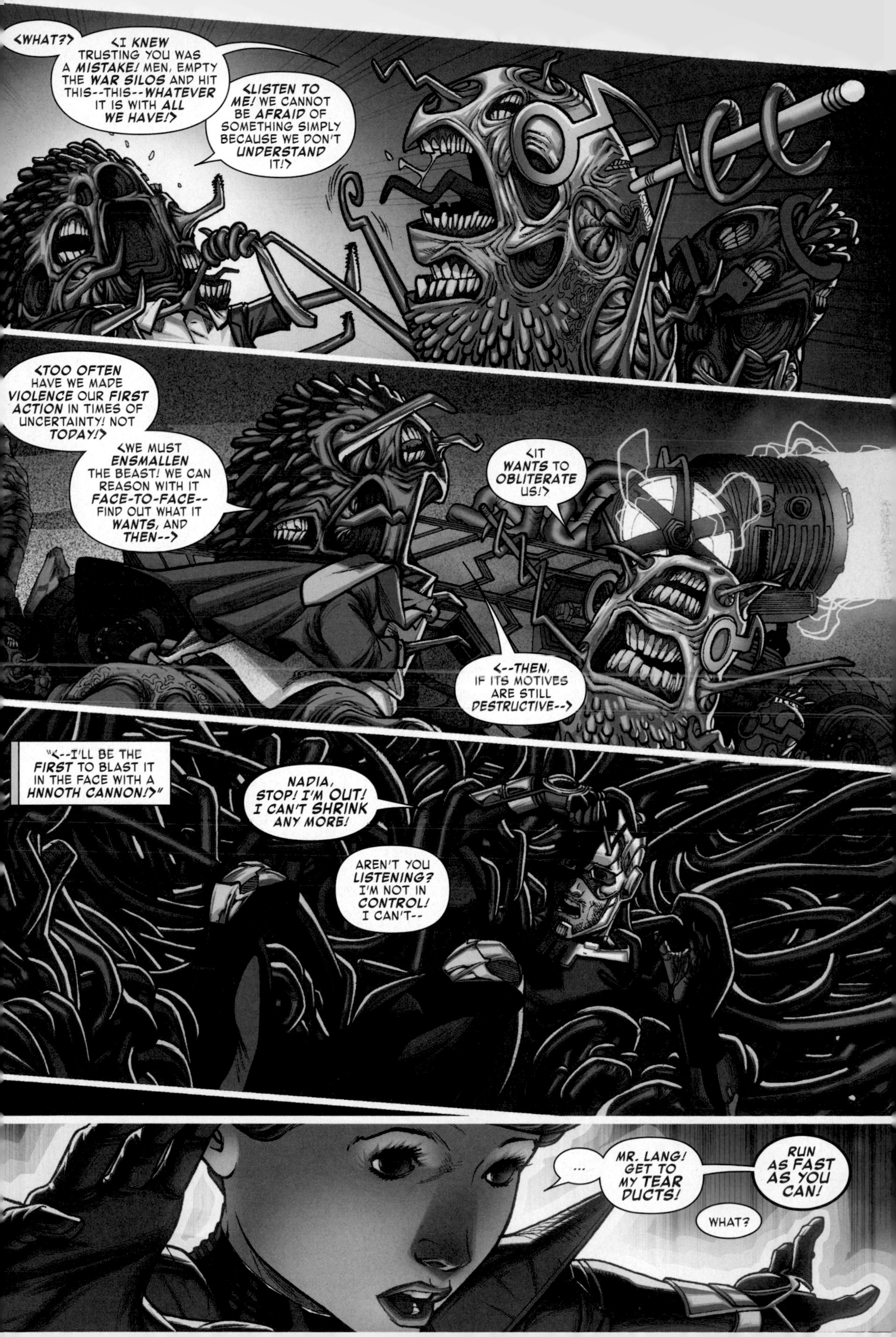
<WHAT?>
<I KNEW TRUSTING YOU WAS A MISTAKE! MEN, EMPTY THE WAR SILOS AND HIT THIS--THIS--WHATEVER IT IS WITH ALL WE HAVE!>
<LISTEN TO ME! WE CANNOT BE AFRAID OF SOMETHING SIMPLY BECAUSE WE DON'T UNDERSTAND IT!>
<TOO OFTEN HAVE WE MADE VIOLENCE OUR FIRST ACTION IN TIMES OF UNCERTAINTY! NOT TODAY!>
<WE MUST ENSMALLEN THE BEAST! WE CAN REASON WITH IT FACE-TO-FACE-- FIND OUT WHAT IT WANTS, AND THEN-->
<IT WANTS TO OBLITERATE US!>
<--THEN, IF ITS MOTIVES ARE STILL DESTRUCTIVE-->
"<--I'LL BE THE FIRST TO BLAST IT IN THE FACE WITH A HNNOTH CANNON!>"
NADIA, STOP! I'M OUT! I CAN'T SHRINK ANY MORE!
AREN'T YOU LISTENING? I'M NOT IN CONTROL! I CAN'T--
...
MR. LANG! GET TO MY TEAR DUCTS!
RUN AS FAST AS YOU CAN!
WHAT?

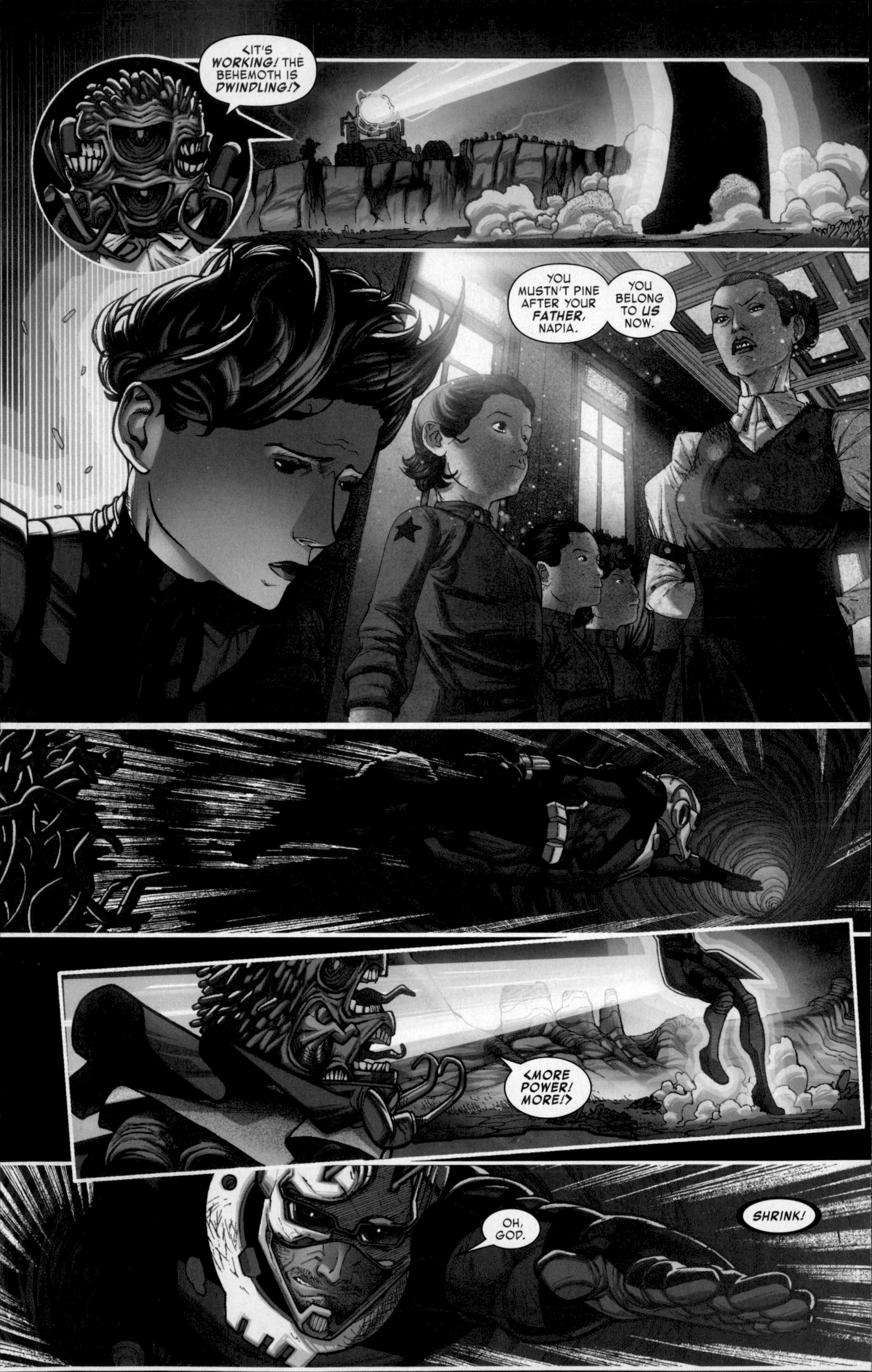
<IT'S WORKING! THE BEHEMOTH IS DWINDLING!>
YOU MUSTN'T PINE AFTER YOUR FATHER, NADIA.
YOU BELONG TO US NOW.
<MORE POWER! MORE!>
OH, GOD.
SHRINK!

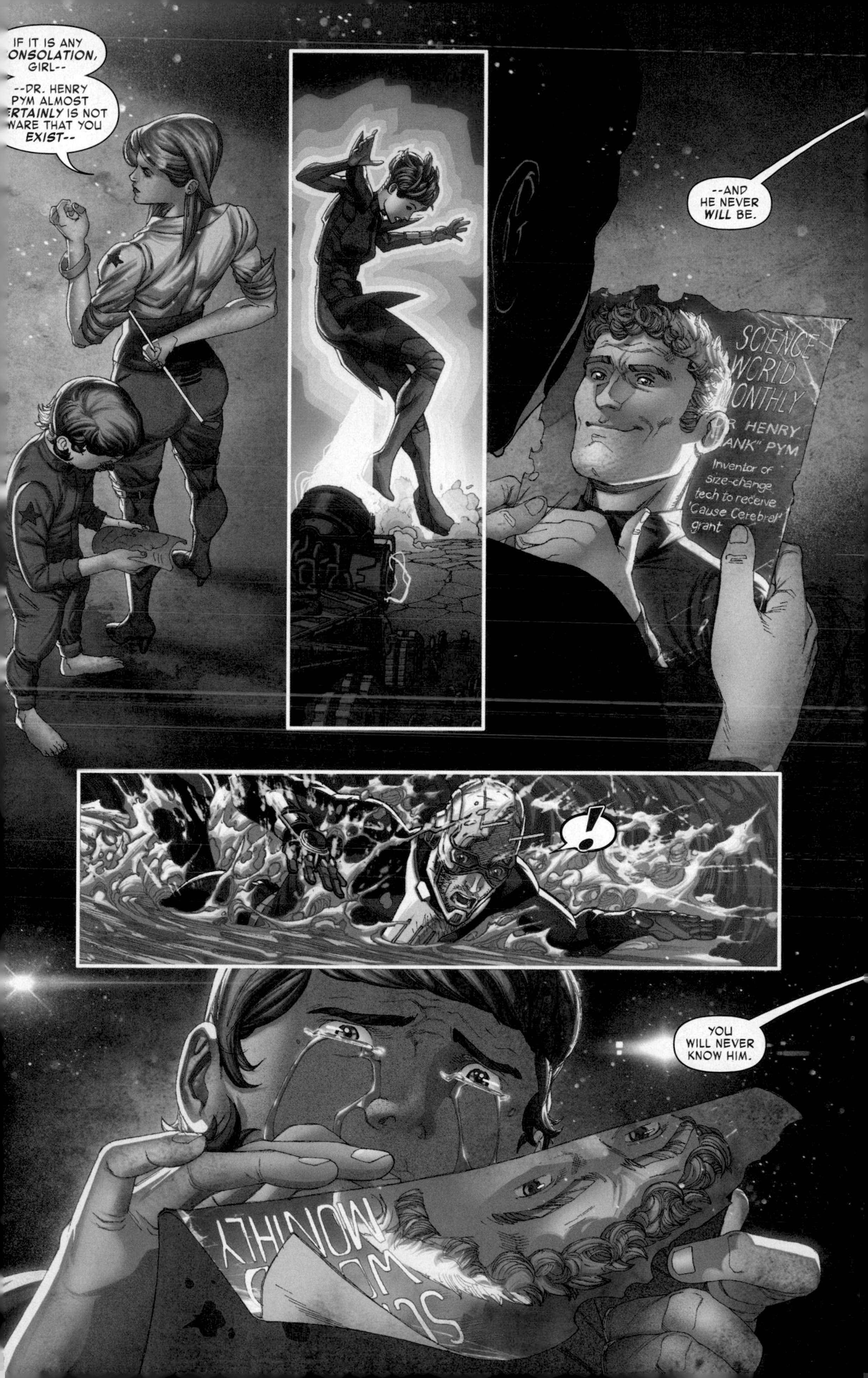
IF IT IS ANY ONSOLATION, GIRL--
--DR. HENRY PYM ALMOST ERTAINLY IS NOT WARE THAT YOU EXIST--
--AND HE NEVER WILL BE.
SCIENCE WORLD MONTHLY
R HENRY ANK" PYM
Inventor of size-change tech to receive 'Cause Celebral' grant
!
YOU WILL NEVER KNOW HIM.

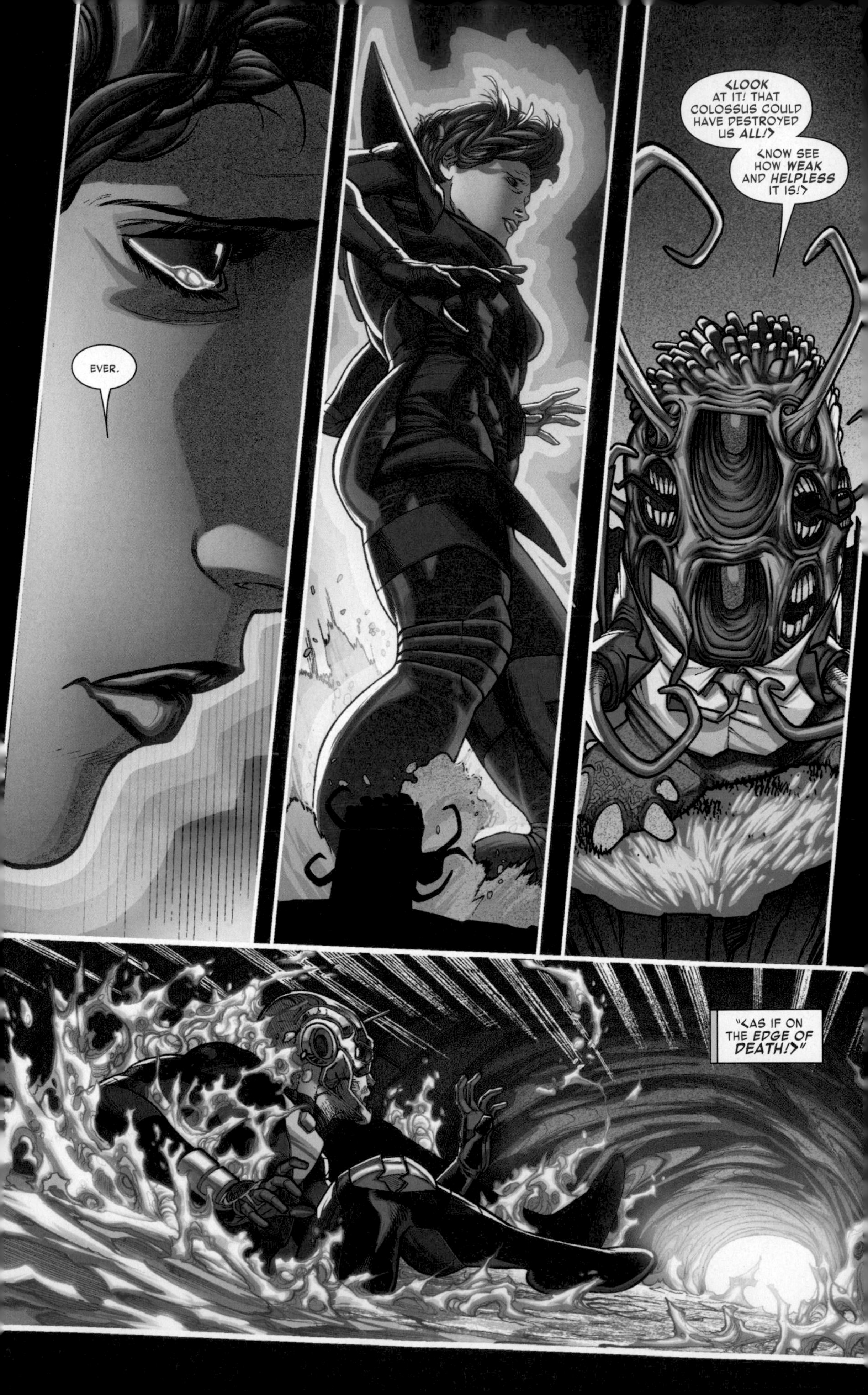
EVER.
<LOOK AT IT! THAT COLOSSUS COULD HAVE DESTROYED US ALL!>
<NOW SEE HOW WEAK AND HELPLESS IT IS!>
"<AS IF ON THE EDGE OF DEATH!>"

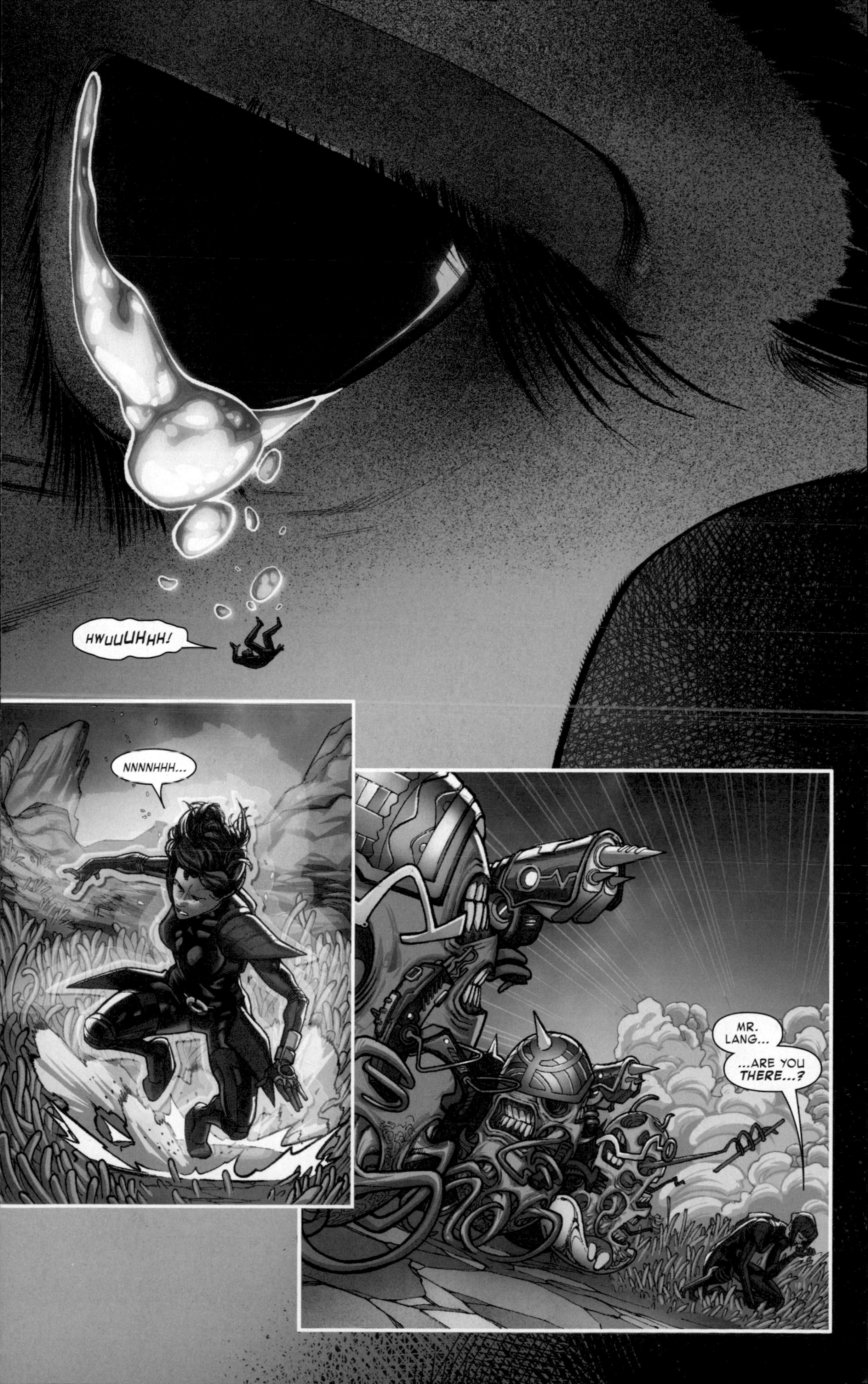
HWUUUHHH!
NNNNHHH...
MR. LANG...
...ARE YOU THERE...?

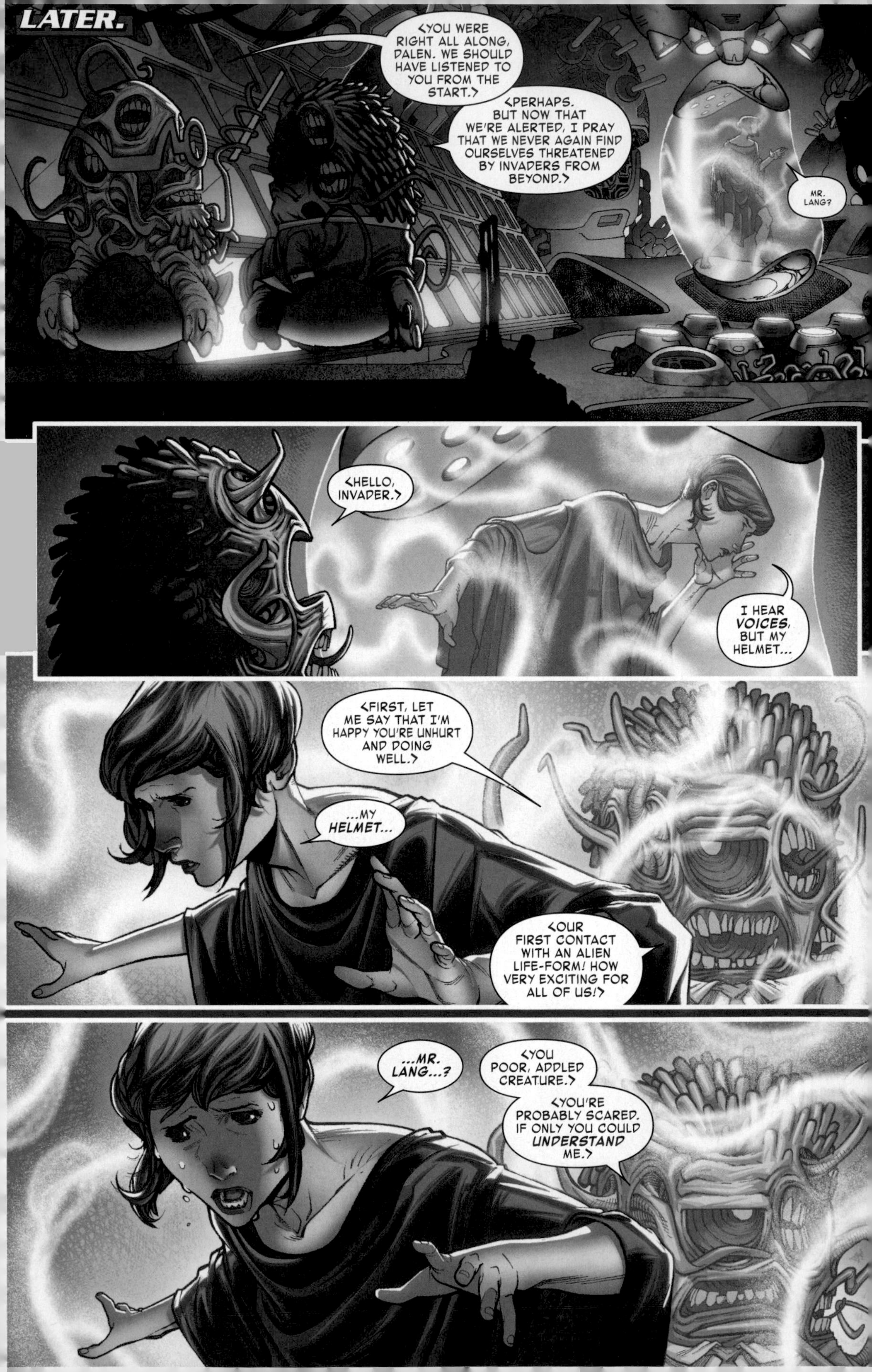
LATER.
<YOU WERE RIGHT ALL ALONG, DALEN. WE SHOULD HAVE LISTENED TO YOU FROM THE START.>
<PERHAPS. BUT NOW THAT WE'RE ALERTED, I PRAY THAT WE NEVER AGAIN FIND OURSELVES THREATENED BY INVADERS FROM BEYOND.>
MR. LANG?
<HELLO, INVADER.>
I HEAR VOICES, BUT MY HELMET...
<FIRST, LET ME SAY THAT I'M HAPPY YOU'RE UNHURT AND DOING WELL.>
...MY HELMET...
<OUR FIRST CONTACT WITH AN ALIEN LIFE-FORM! HOW VERY EXCITING FOR ALL OF US!>
...MR. LANG...?
<YOU POOR, ADDLED CREATURE.>
<YOU'RE PROBABLY SCARED. IF ONLY YOU COULD UNDERSTAND ME.>

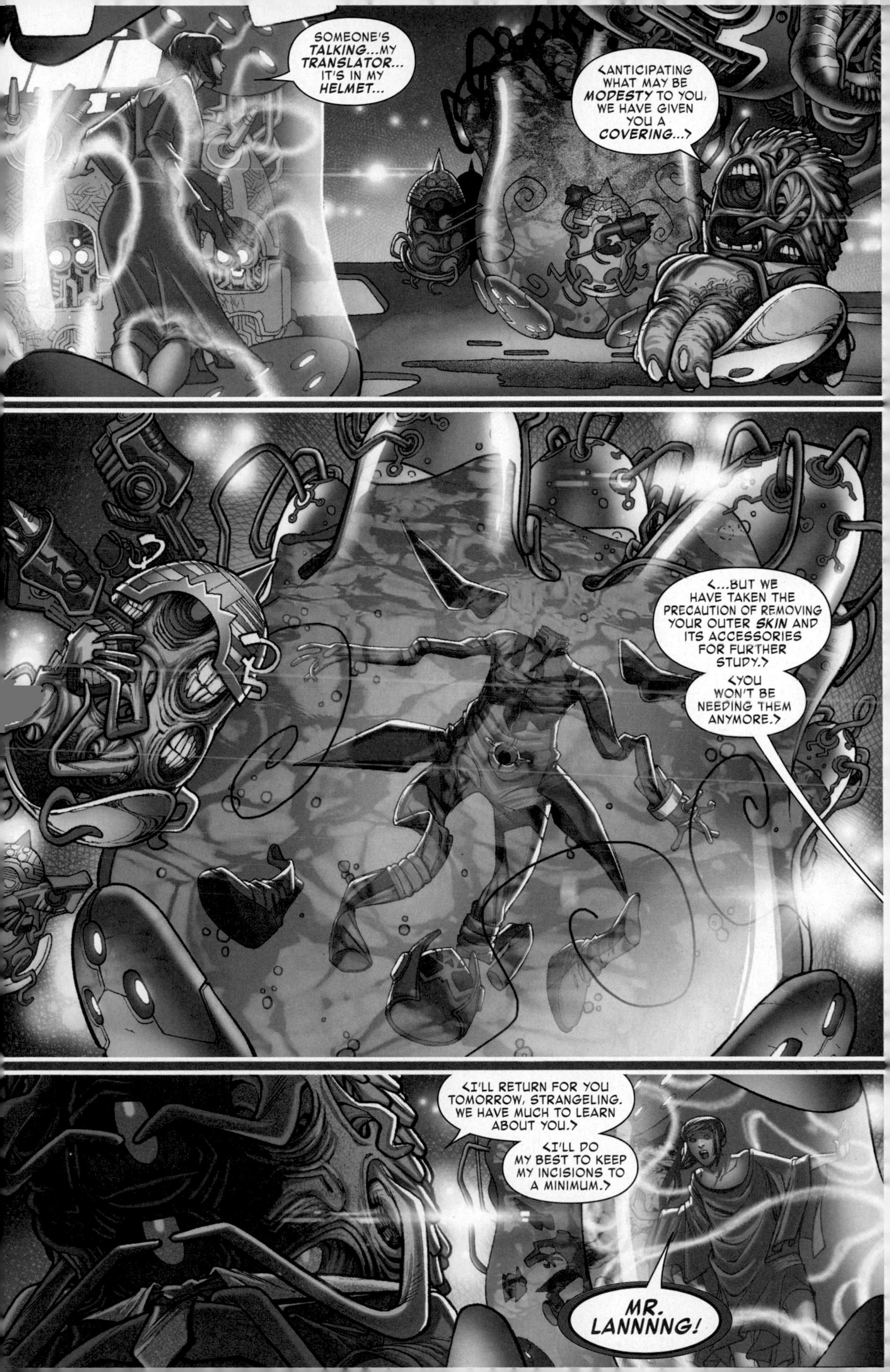
SOMEONE'S TALKING...MY TRANSLATOR... IT'S IN MY HELMET...
<ANTICIPATING WHAT MAY BE MODESTY TO YOU, WE HAVE GIVEN YOU A COVERING...>
<...BUT WE HAVE TAKEN THE PRECAUTION OF REMOVING YOUR OUTER SKIN AND ITS ACCESSORIES FOR FURTHER STUDY.>
<YOU WON'T BE NEEDING THEM ANYMORE.>
<I'LL RETURN FOR YOU TOMORROW, STRANGELING. WE HAVE MUCH TO LEARN ABOUT YOU.>
<I'LL DO MY BEST TO KEEP MY INCISIONS TO A MINIMUM.>
MR. LANNNNG!

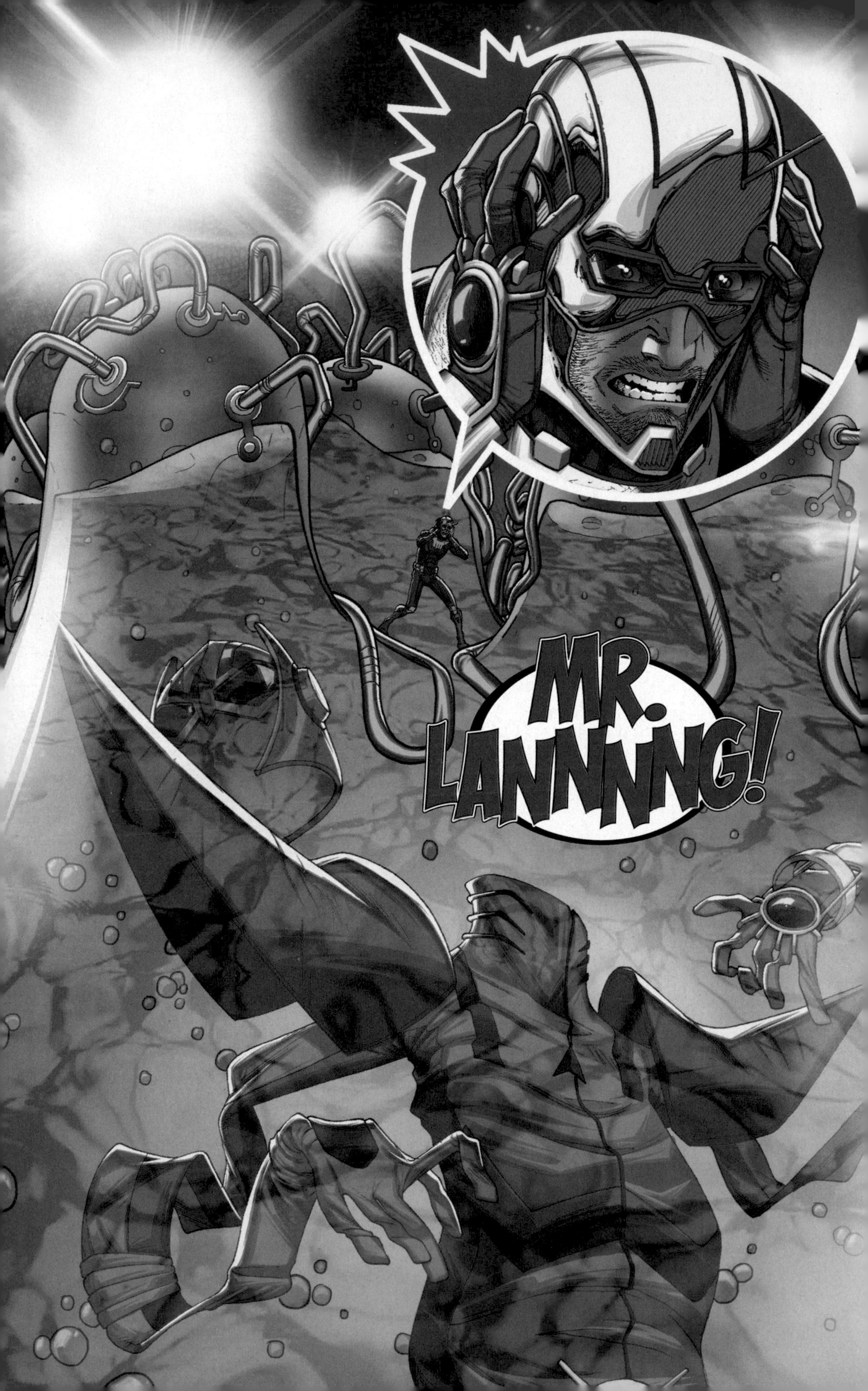
MR. LANNNNG!

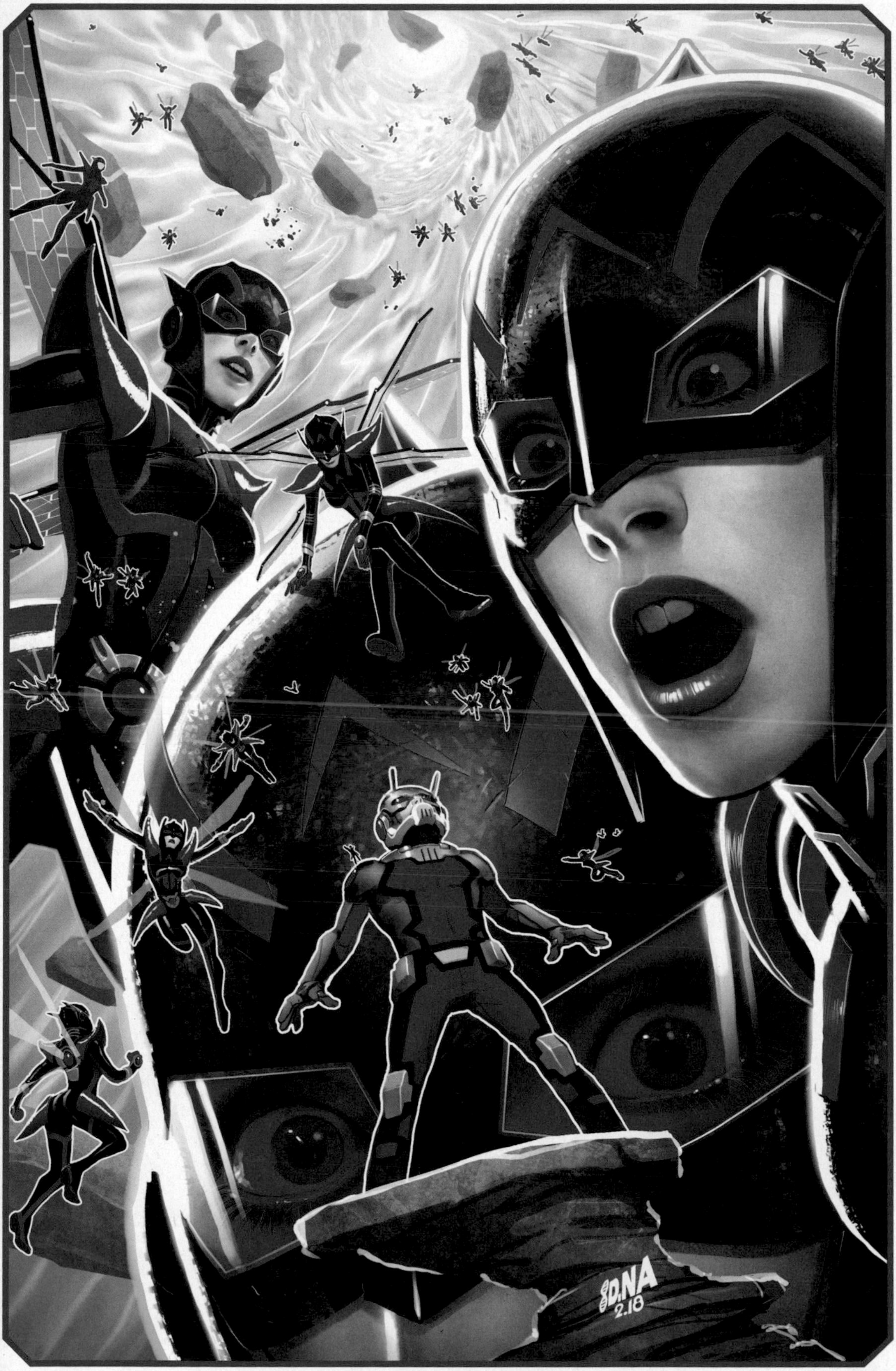
D.NA
2.18

ANT-MAN AND THE WASP #3

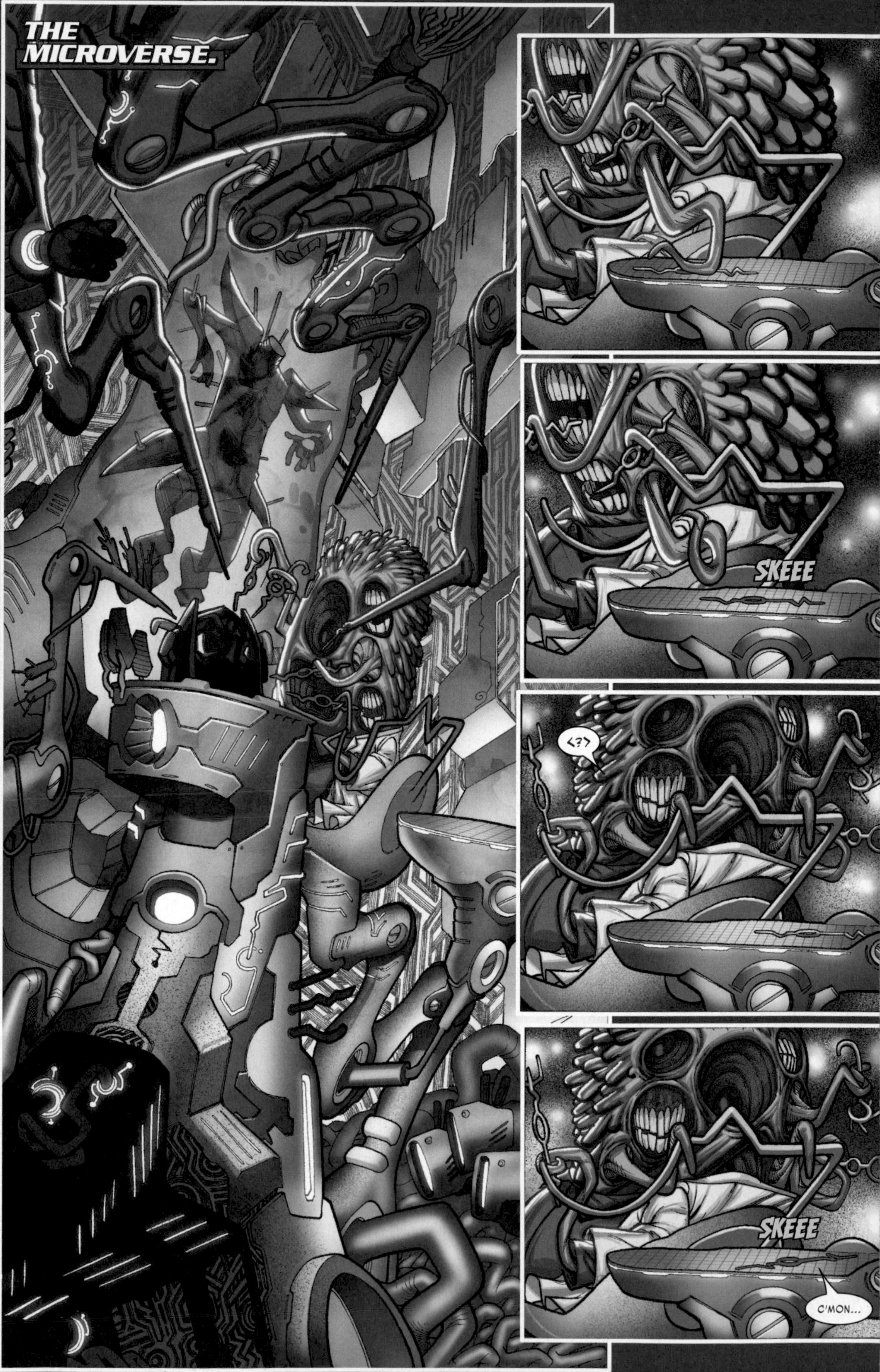
THE MICROVERSE.
SKEEE
<?>
SKEEE
C'MON...

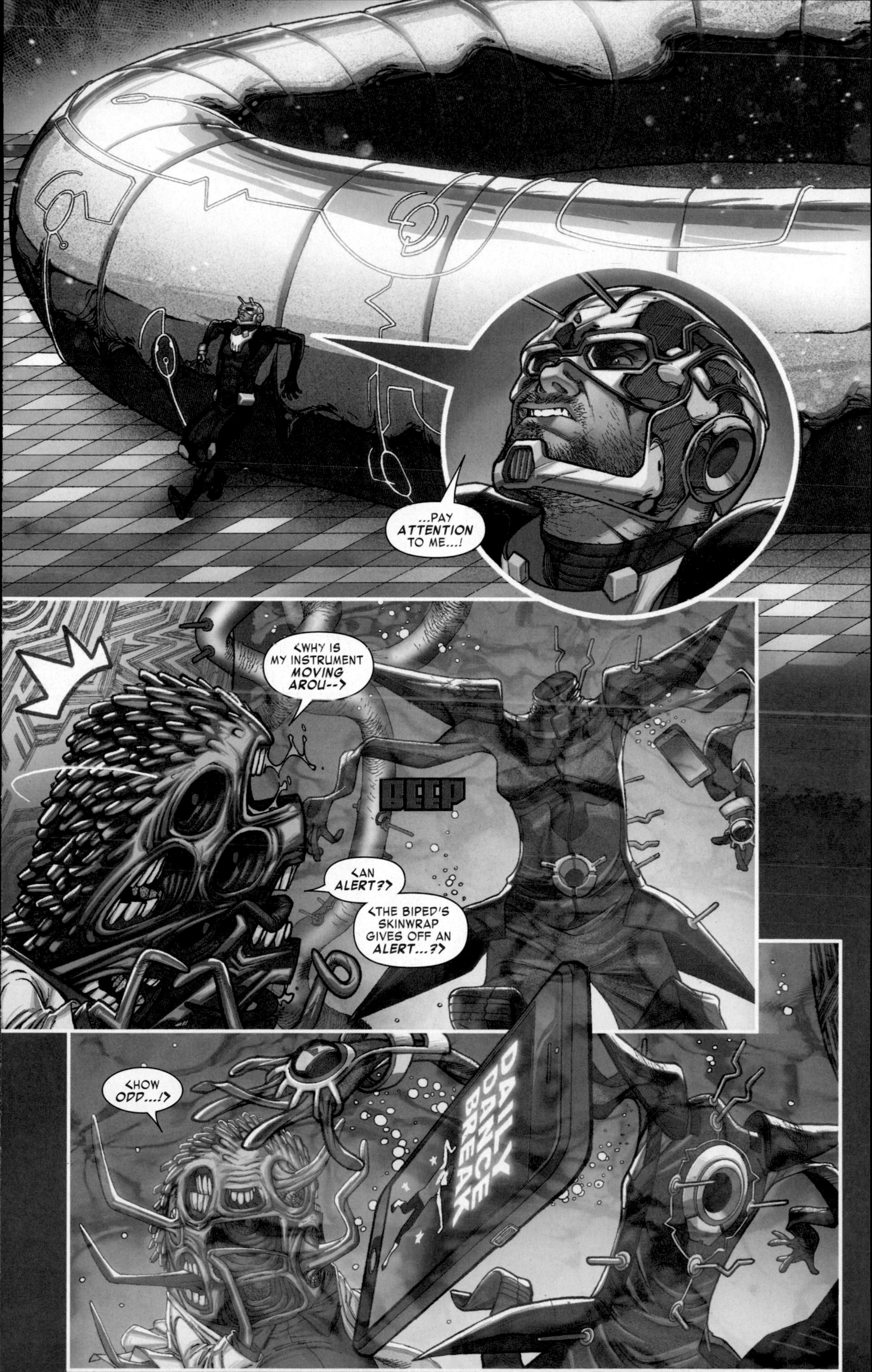
...PAY ATTENTION TO ME...!
<WHY IS MY INSTRUMENT MOVING AROU-->
BEEP
<AN ALERT?>
<THE BIPED'S SKINWRAP GIVES OFF AN ALERT...?>
<HOW ODD...!>
DAILY DANCE BREAK

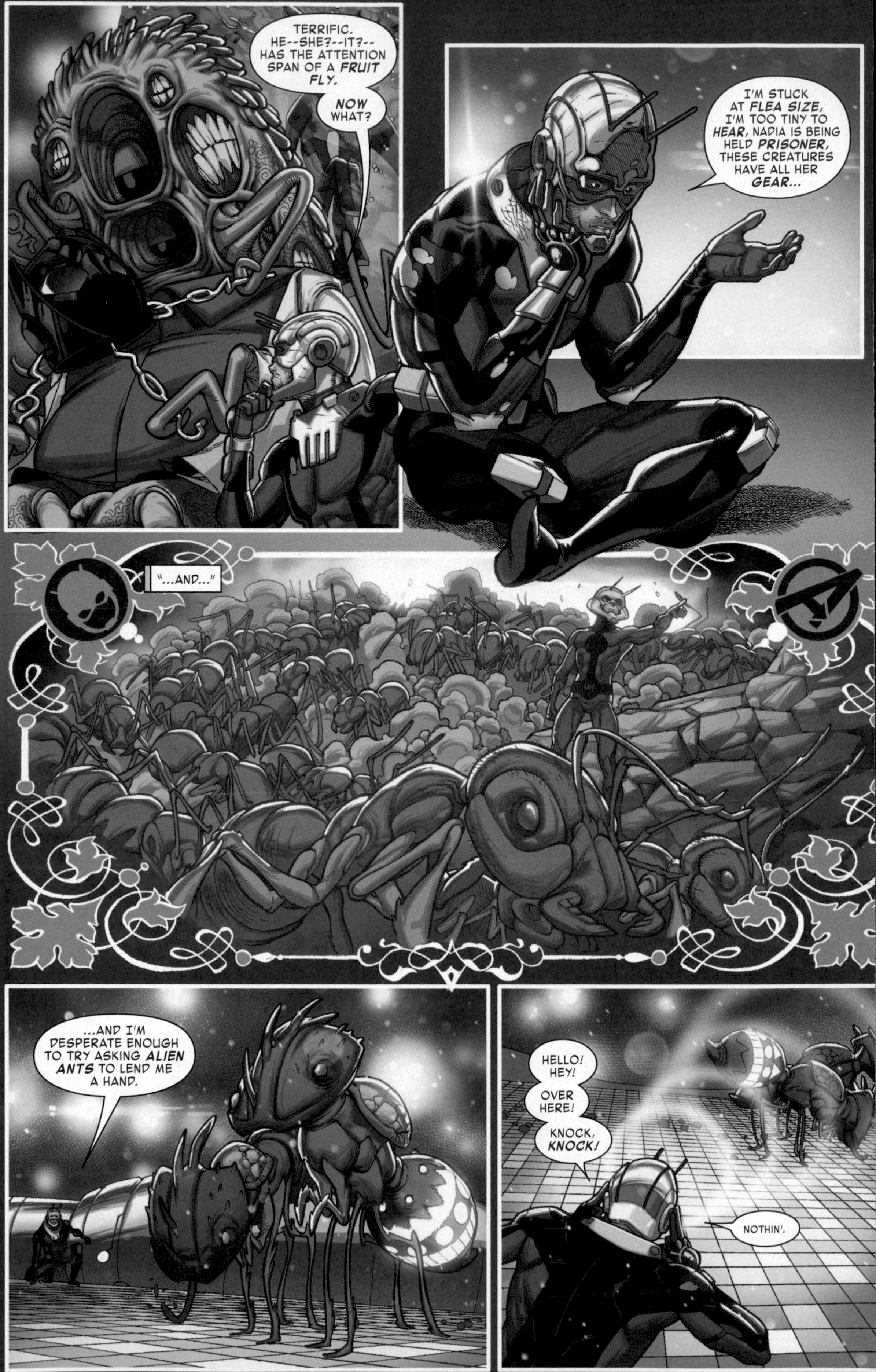
TERRIFIC. HE--SHE?--IT?--HAS THE ATTENTION SPAN OF A FRUIT FLY.
NOW WHAT?
I'M STUCK AT FLEA SIZE, I'M TOO TINY TO HEAR, NADIA IS BEING HELD PRISONER, THESE CREATURES HAVE ALL HER GEAR...
"...AND..."
...AND I'M DESPERATE ENOUGH TO TRY ASKING ALIEN ANTS TO LEND ME A HAND.
HELLO! HEY!
OVER HERE!
KNOCK, KNOCK!
NOTHIN'.

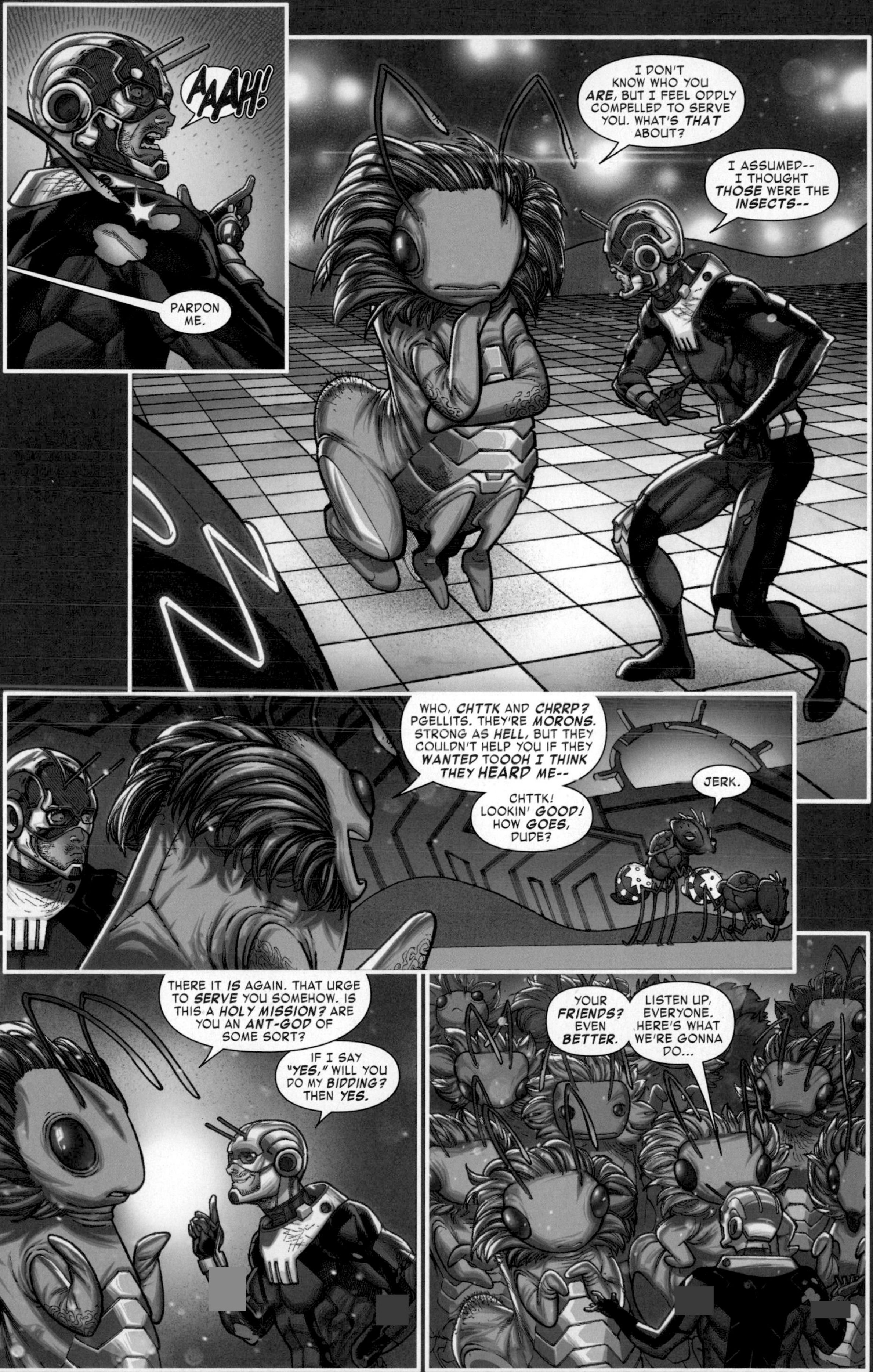
AAAH!
PARDON ME.
I DON'T KNOW WHO YOU ARE, BUT I FEEL ODDLY COMPELLED TO SERVE YOU. WHAT'S THAT ABOUT?
I ASSUMED-- I THOUGHT THOSE WERE THE INSECTS--
WHO, CHTTK AND CHRRP? PGELLITS. THEY'RE MORONS. STRONG AS HELL, BUT THEY COULDN'T HELP YOU IF THEY WANTED TOOOH I THINK THEY HEARD ME--
CHTTK! LOOKIN' GOOD! HOW GOES, DUDE?
JERK.
THERE IT IS AGAIN. THAT URGE TO SERVE YOU SOMEHOW. IS THIS A HOLY MISSION? ARE YOU AN ANT-GOD OF SOME SORT?
IF I SAY "YES," WILL YOU DO MY BIDDING? THEN YES.
YOUR FRIENDS? EVEN BETTER.
LISTEN UP, EVERYONE. HERE'S WHAT WE'RE GONNA DO...

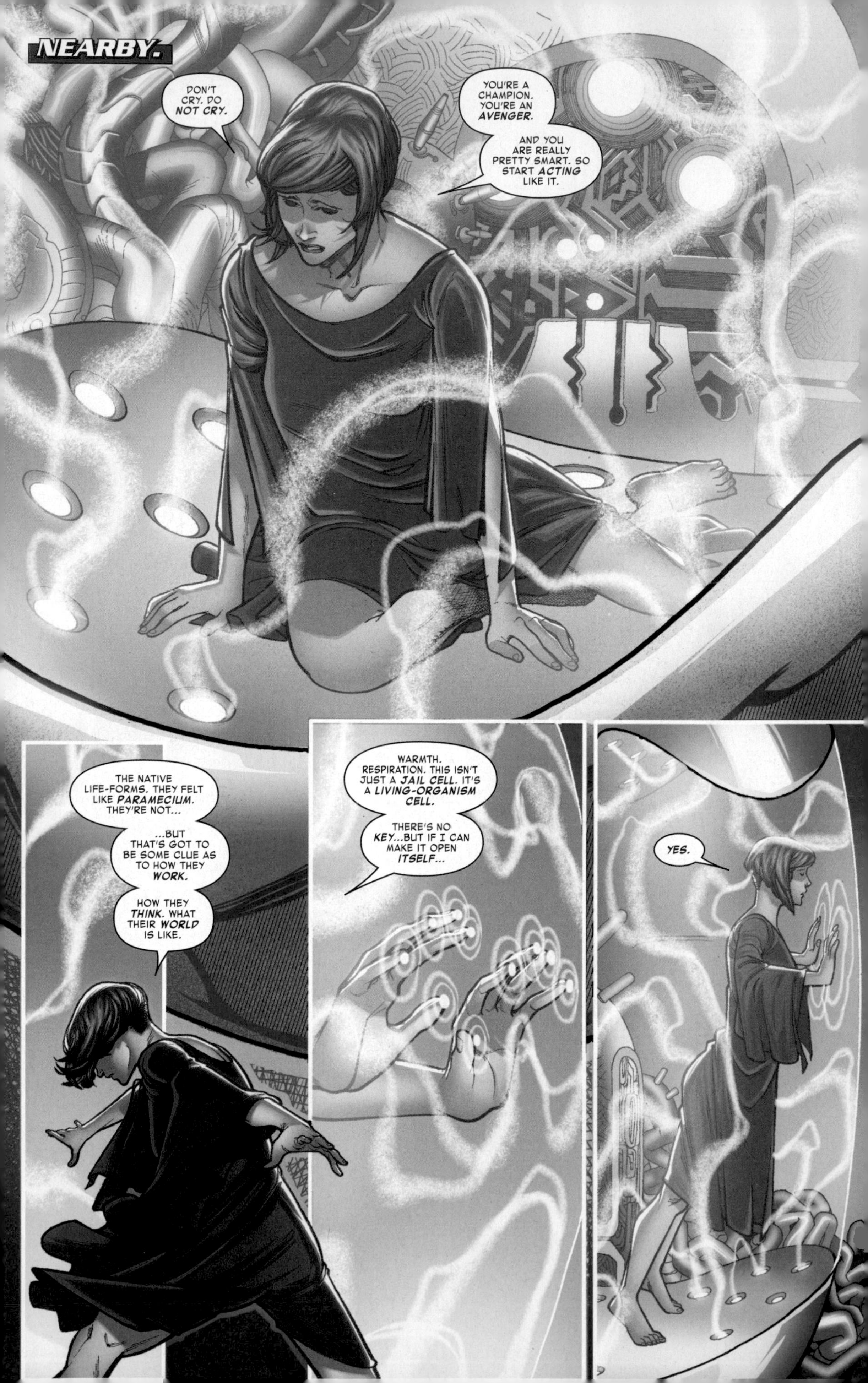
NEARBY.
DON'T CRY. DO NOT CRY.
YOU'RE A CHAMPION. YOU'RE AN AVENGER.
AND YOU ARE REALLY PRETTY SMART. SO START ACTING LIKE IT.
THE NATIVE LIFE-FORMS. THEY FELT LIKE PARAMECIUM. THEY'RE NOT...
...BUT THAT'S GOT TO BE SOME CLUE AS TO HOW THEY WORK.
HOW THEY THINK. WHAT THEIR WORLD IS LIKE.
WARMTH. RESPIRATION. THIS ISN'T JUST A JAIL CELL. IT'S A LIVING-ORGANISM CELL.
THERE'S NO KEY...BUT IF I CAN MAKE IT OPEN ITSELF...
YES.

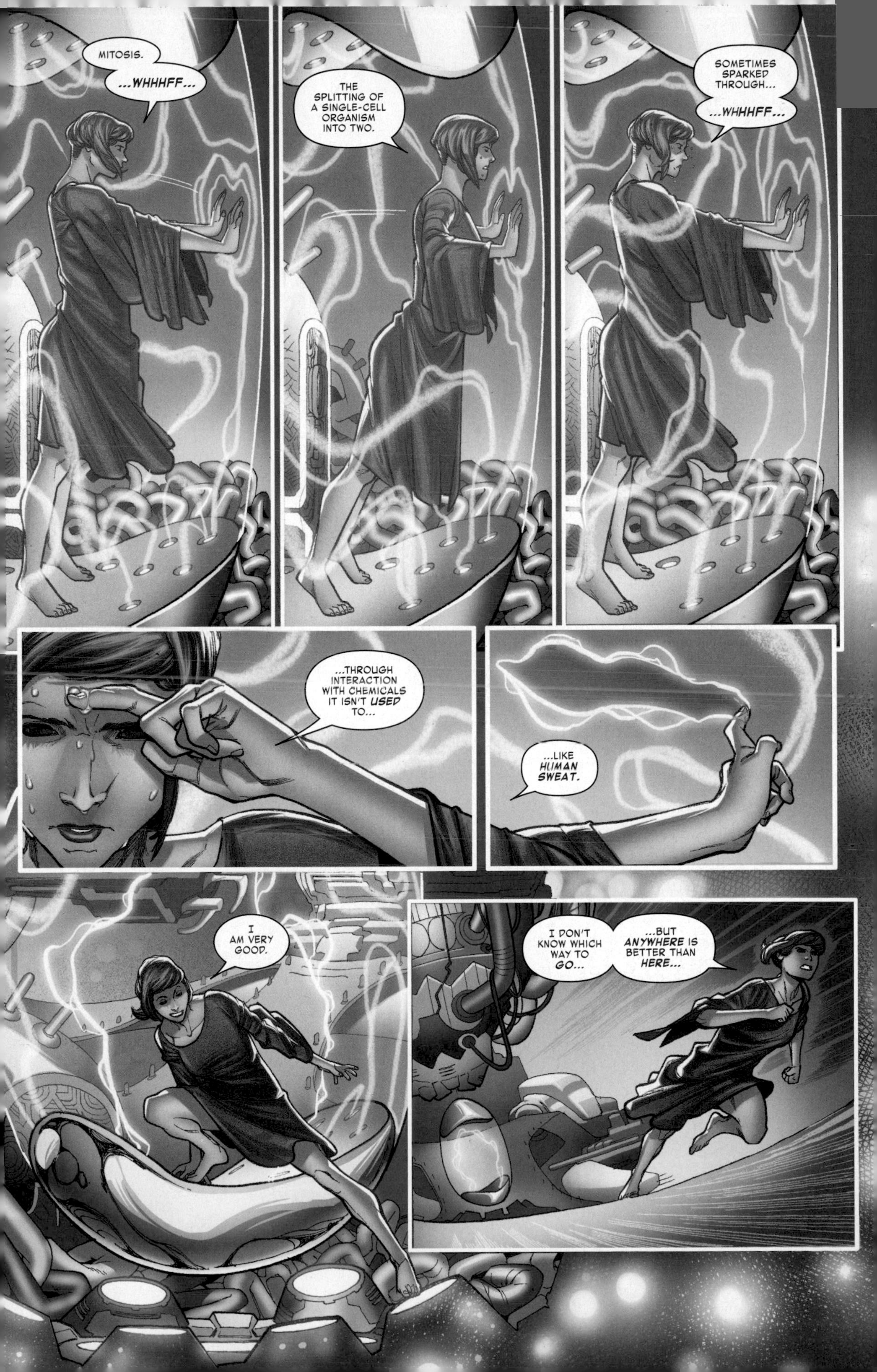
MITOSIS.
...WHHHFF...
THE SPLITTING OF A SINGLE-CELL ORGANISM INTO TWO.
SOMETIMES SPARKED THROUGH...
...WHHHFF...
...THROUGH INTERACTION WITH CHEMICALS IT ISN'T USED TO...
...LIKE HUMAN SWEAT.
I AM VERY GOOD.
I DON'T KNOW WHICH WAY TO GO...
...BUT ANYWHERE IS BETTER THAN HERE...

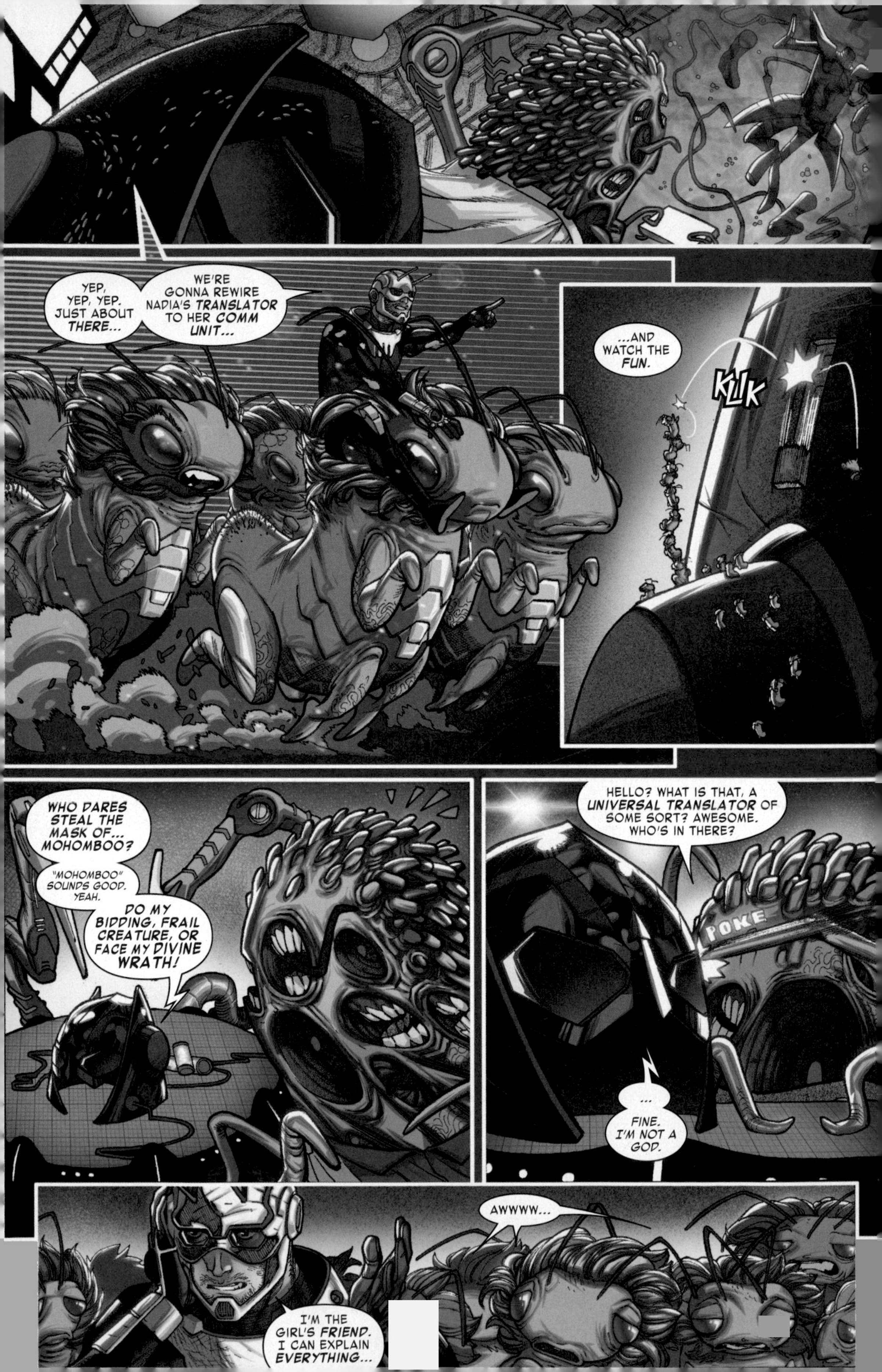
YEP, YEP, YEP. JUST ABOUT THERE...
WE'RE GONNA REWIRE NADIA'S TRANSLATOR TO HER COMM UNIT...
...AND WATCH THE FUN.
KLIK
WHO DARES STEAL THE MASK OF... MOHOMBOO?
"MOHOMBOO" SOUNDS GOOD. YEAH.
DO MY BIDDING, FRAIL CREATURE, OR FACE MY DIVINE WRATH!
HELLO? WHAT IS THAT, A UNIVERSAL TRANSLATOR OF SOME SORT? AWESOME. WHO'S IN THERE?
POKE
...
FINE. I'M NOT A GOD.
AWWWW...
I'M THE GIRL'S FRIEND. I CAN EXPLAIN EVERYTHING...

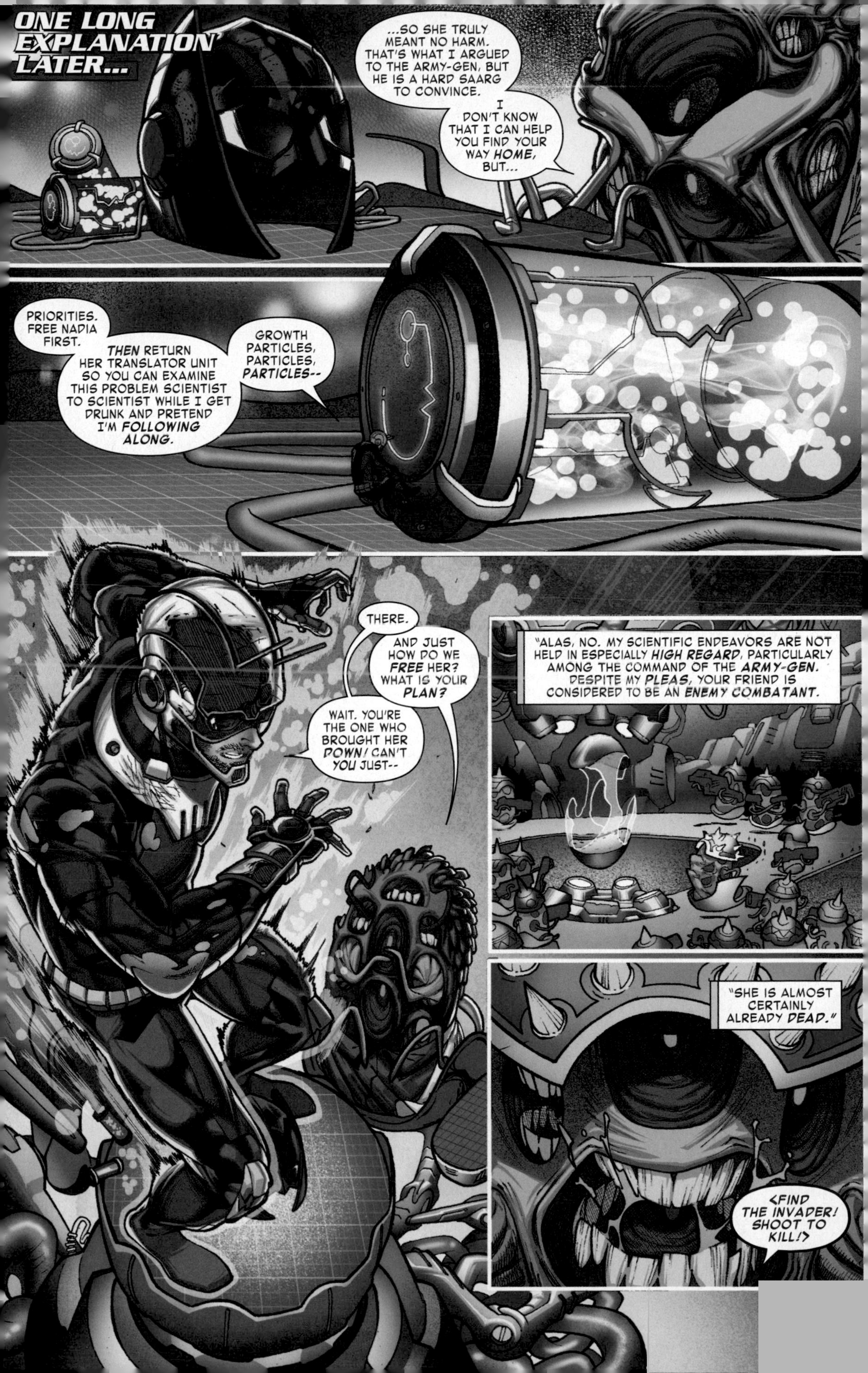
ONE LONG EXPLANATION LATER...
...SO SHE TRULY MEANT NO HARM. THAT'S WHAT I ARGUED TO THE ARMY-GEN, BUT HE IS A HARD SAARG TO CONVINCE.
I DON'T KNOW THAT I CAN HELP YOU FIND YOUR WAY HOME, BUT...
PRIORITIES. FREE NADIA FIRST.
THEN RETURN HER TRANSLATOR UNIT SO YOU CAN EXAMINE THIS PROBLEM SCIENTIST TO SCIENTIST WHILE I GET DRUNK AND PRETEND I'M FOLLOWING ALONG.
GROWTH PARTICLES, PARTICLES, PARTICLES--
THERE.
AND JUST HOW DO WE FREE HER? WHAT IS YOUR PLAN?
WAIT. YOU'RE THE ONE WHO BROUGHT HER DOWN! CAN'T YOU JUST--
"ALAS, NO. MY SCIENTIFIC ENDEAVORS ARE NOT HELD IN ESPECIALLY HIGH REGARD, PARTICULARLY AMONG THE COMMAND OF THE ARMY-GEN. DESPITE MY PLEAS, YOUR FRIEND IS CONSIDERED TO BE AN ENEMY COMBATANT.
"SHE IS ALMOST CERTAINLY ALREADY DEAD."
<FIND THE INVADER! SHOOT TO KILL!>

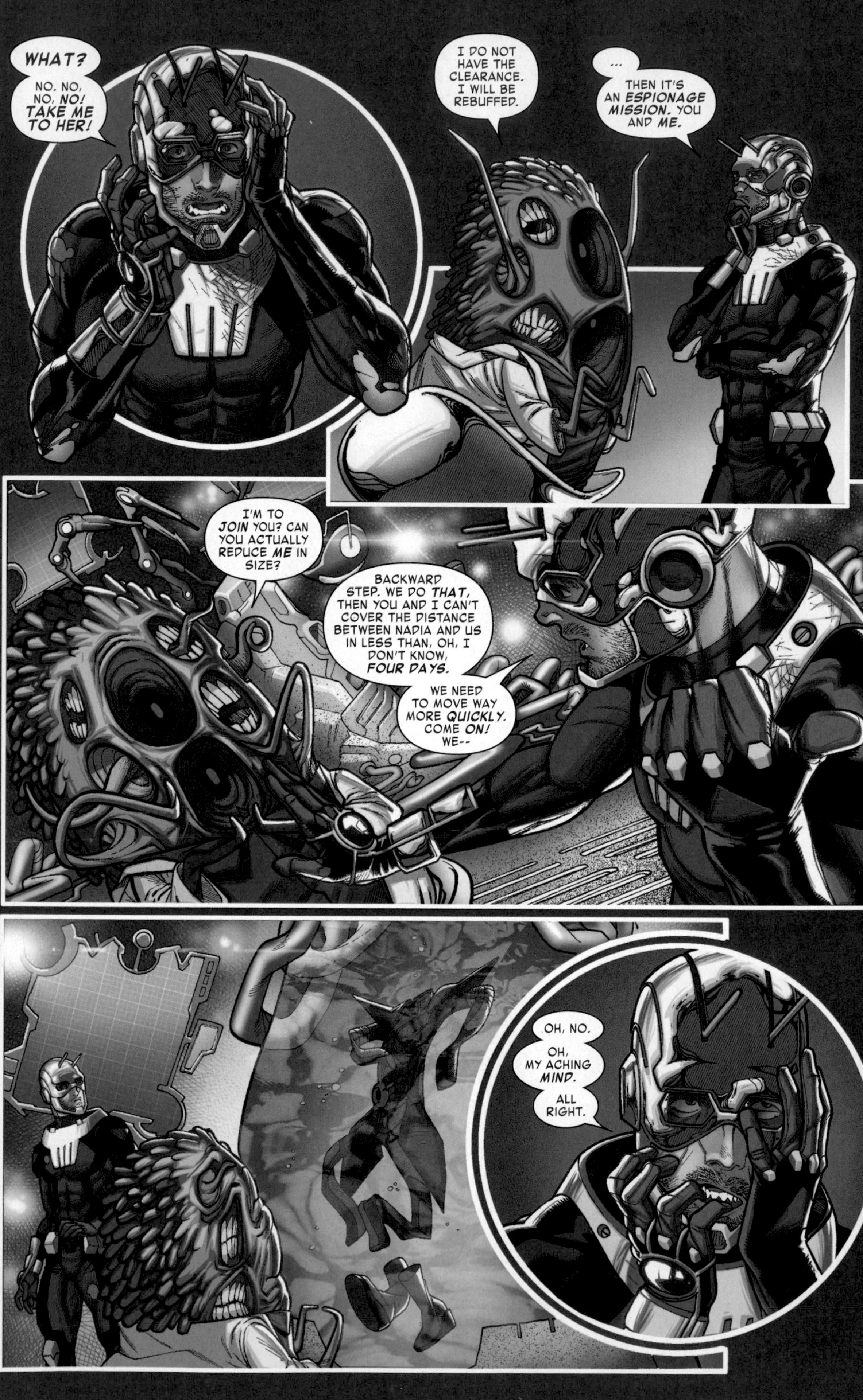
WHAT?
NO. NO, NO, NO! TAKE ME TO HER!
I DO NOT HAVE THE CLEARANCE. I WILL BE REBUFFED.
...
THEN IT'S AN ESPIONAGE MISSION. YOU AND ME.
I'M TO JOIN YOU? CAN YOU ACTUALLY REDUCE ME IN SIZE?
BACKWARD STEP. WE DO THAT, THEN YOU AND I CAN'T COVER THE DISTANCE BETWEEN NADIA AND US IN LESS THAN, OH, I DON'T KNOW, FOUR DAYS.
WE NEED TO MOVE WAY MORE QUICKLY. COME ON! WE--
OH, NO.
OH, MY ACHING MIND.
ALL RIGHT.

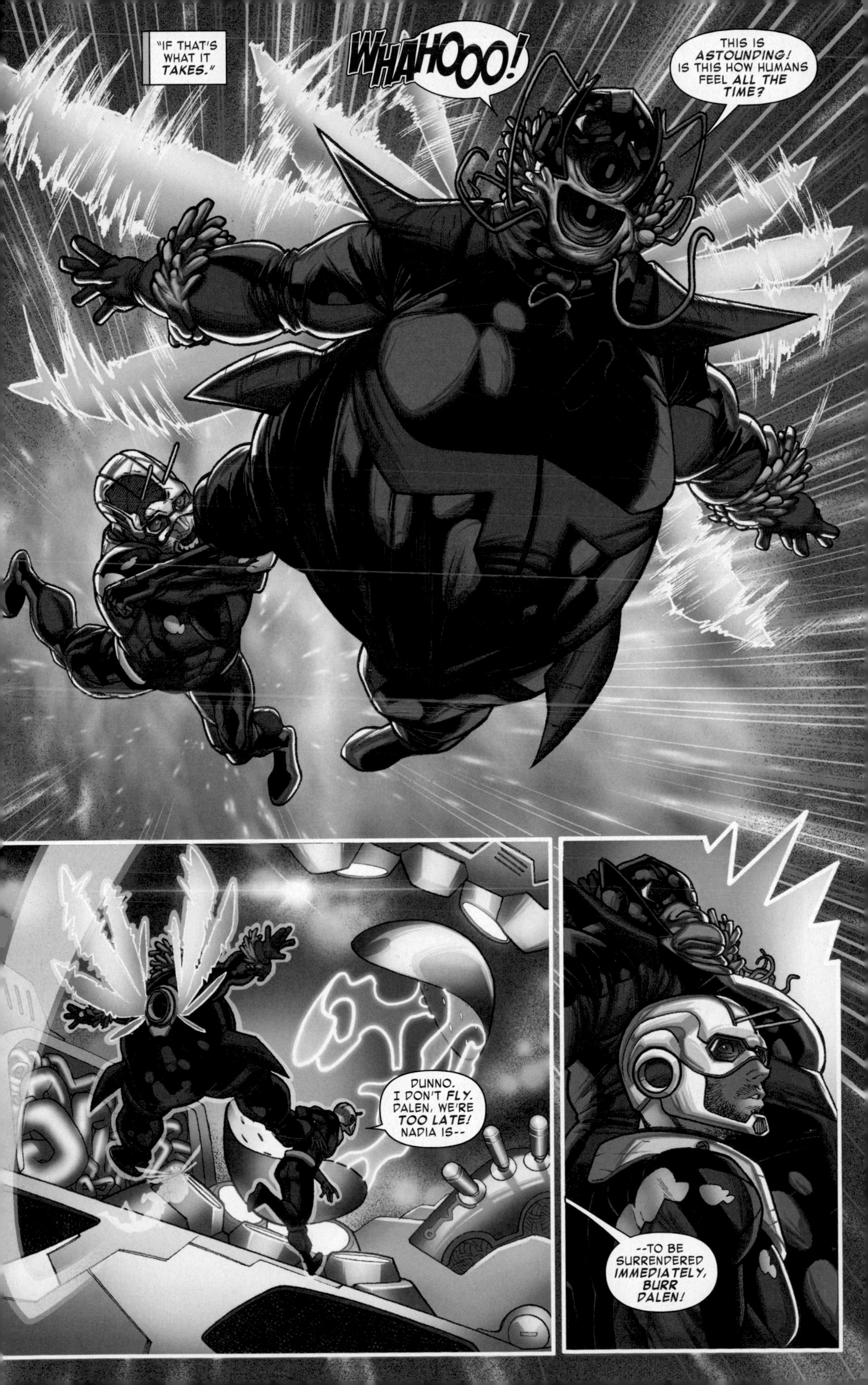
"IF THAT'S WHAT IT TAKES."
WHAHOOO!
THIS IS ASTOUNDING! IS THIS HOW HUMANS FEEL ALL THE TIME?
DUNNO. I DON'T FLY. DALEN, WE'RE TOO LATE! NADIA IS--
--TO BE SURRENDERED IMMEDIATELY, BURR DALEN!

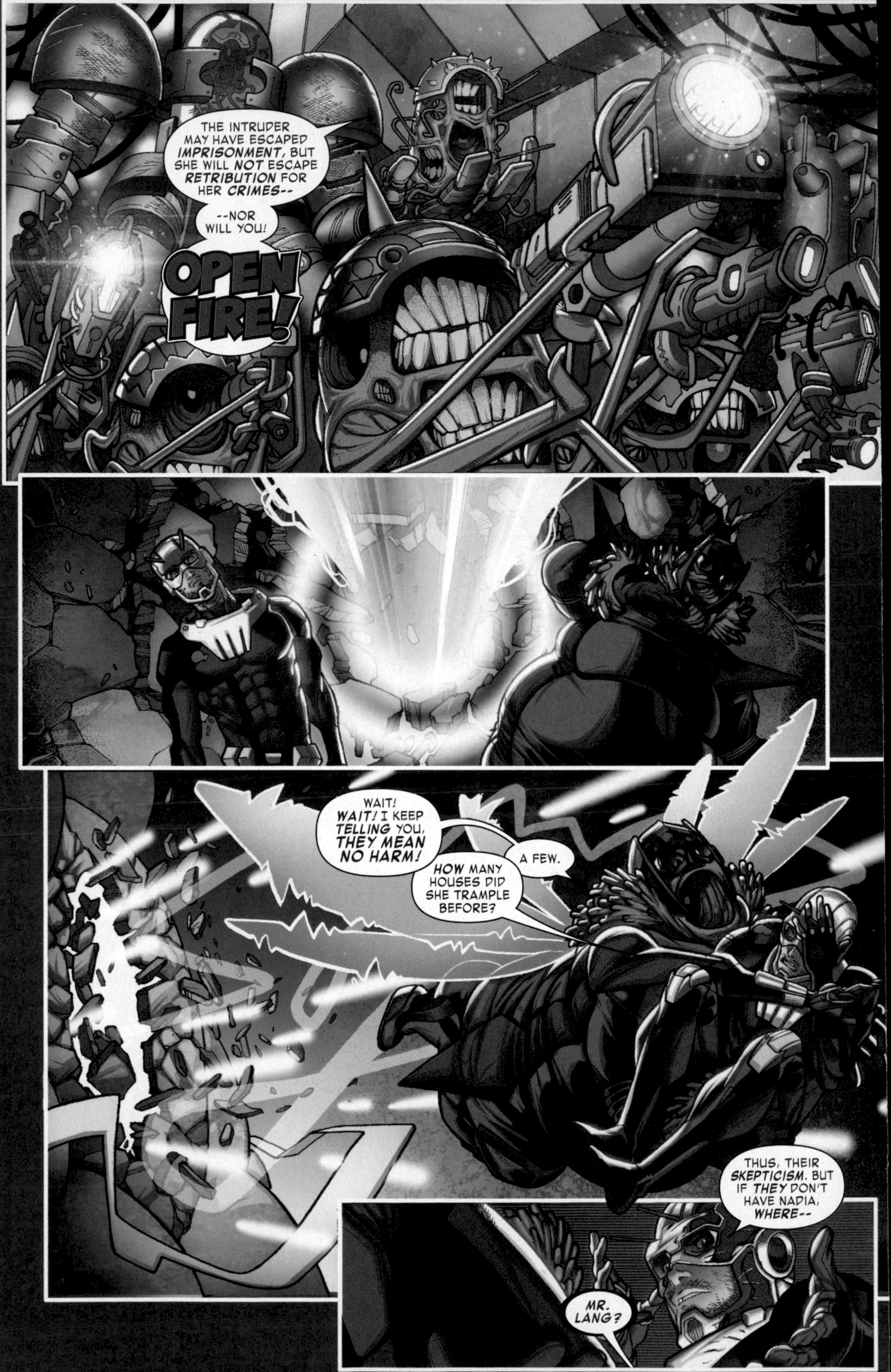
THE INTRUDER MAY HAVE ESCAPED IMPRISONMENT, BUT SHE WILL NOT ESCAPE RETRIBUTION FOR HER CRIMES--
--NOR WILL YOU!
OPEN FIRE!
WAIT! WAIT! I KEEP TELLING YOU, THEY MEAN NO HARM!
HOW MANY HOUSES DID SHE TRAMPLE BEFORE?
A FEW.
THUS, THEIR SKEPTICISM. BUT IF THEY DON'T HAVE NADIA, WHERE--
MR. LANG?

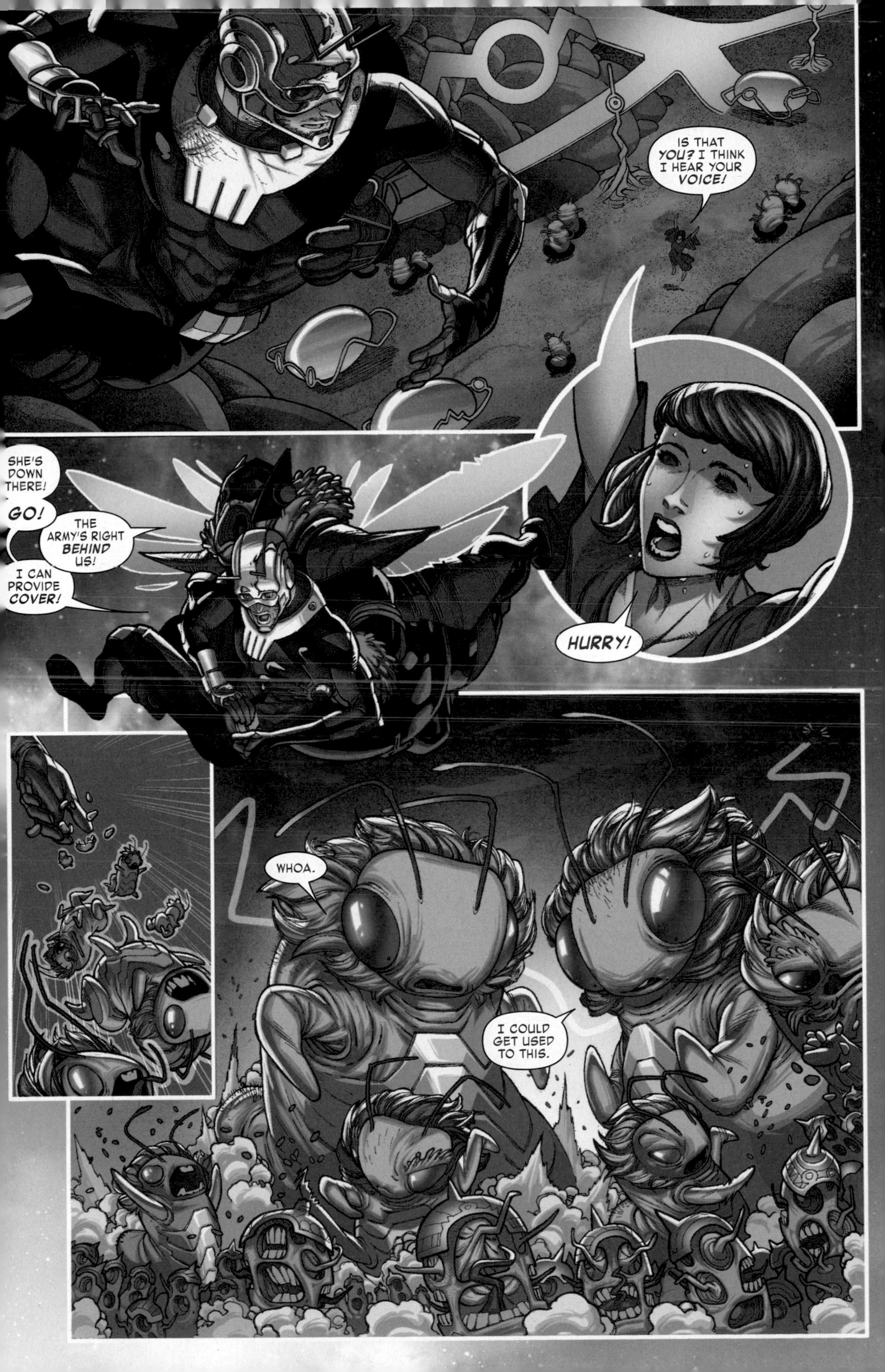
IS THAT YOU? I THINK I HEAR YOUR VOICE!
HURRY!
SHE'S DOWN THERE!
GO!
THE ARMY'S RIGHT BEHIND US!
I CAN PROVIDE COVER!
WHOA.
I COULD GET USED TO THIS.

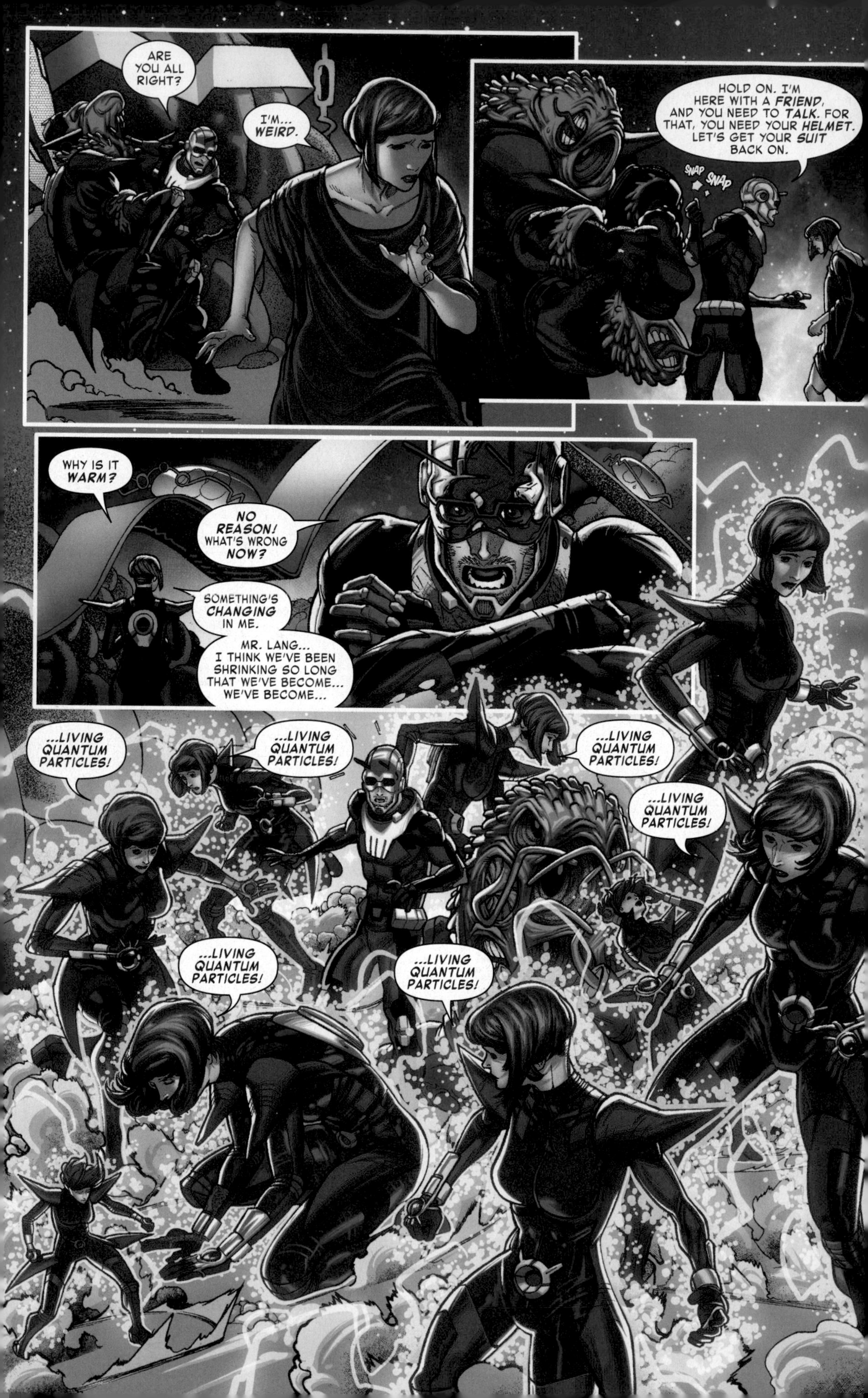
ARE YOU ALL RIGHT?
I'M... WEIRD.
HOLD ON. I'M HERE WITH A FRIEND, AND YOU NEED TO TALK. FOR THAT, YOU NEED YOUR HELMET. LET'S GET YOUR SUIT BACK ON.
SNAP SNAP
WHY IS IT WARM?
NO REASON! WHAT'S WRONG NOW?
SOMETHING'S CHANGING IN ME.
MR. LANG... I THINK WE'VE BEEN SHRINKING SO LONG THAT WE'VE BECOME... WE'VE BECOME...
...LIVING QUANTUM PARTICLES!
...LIVING QUANTUM PARTICLES!
...LIVING QUANTUM PARTICLES!
...LIVING QUANTUM PARTICLES!
...LIVING QUANTUM PARTICLES!
...LIVING QUANTUM PARTICLES!

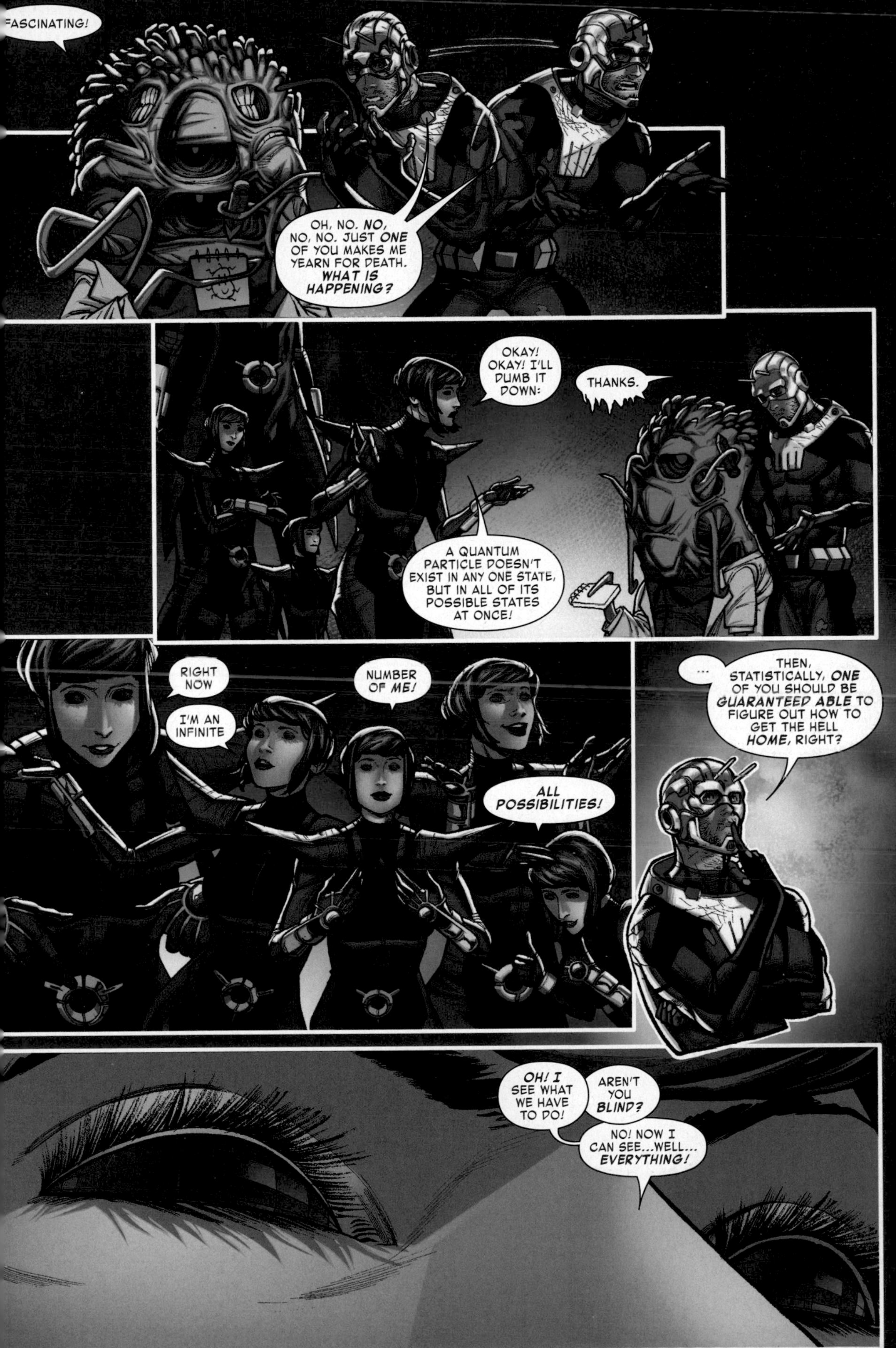
FASCINATING!
OH, NO. NO, NO, NO. JUST ONE OF YOU MAKES ME YEARN FOR DEATH. WHAT IS HAPPENING?
OKAY! OKAY! I'LL DUMB IT DOWN:
THANKS.
A QUANTUM PARTICLE DOESN'T EXIST IN ANY ONE STATE, BUT IN ALL OF ITS POSSIBLE STATES AT ONCE!
RIGHT NOW
I'M AN INFINITE
NUMBER OF ME!
ALL POSSIBILITIES!
...
THEN, STATISTICALLY, ONE OF YOU SHOULD BE GUARANTEED ABLE TO FIGURE OUT HOW TO GET THE HELL HOME, RIGHT?
OH! I SEE WHAT WE HAVE TO DO!
AREN'T YOU BLIND?
NO! NOW I CAN SEE...WELL... EVERYTHING!

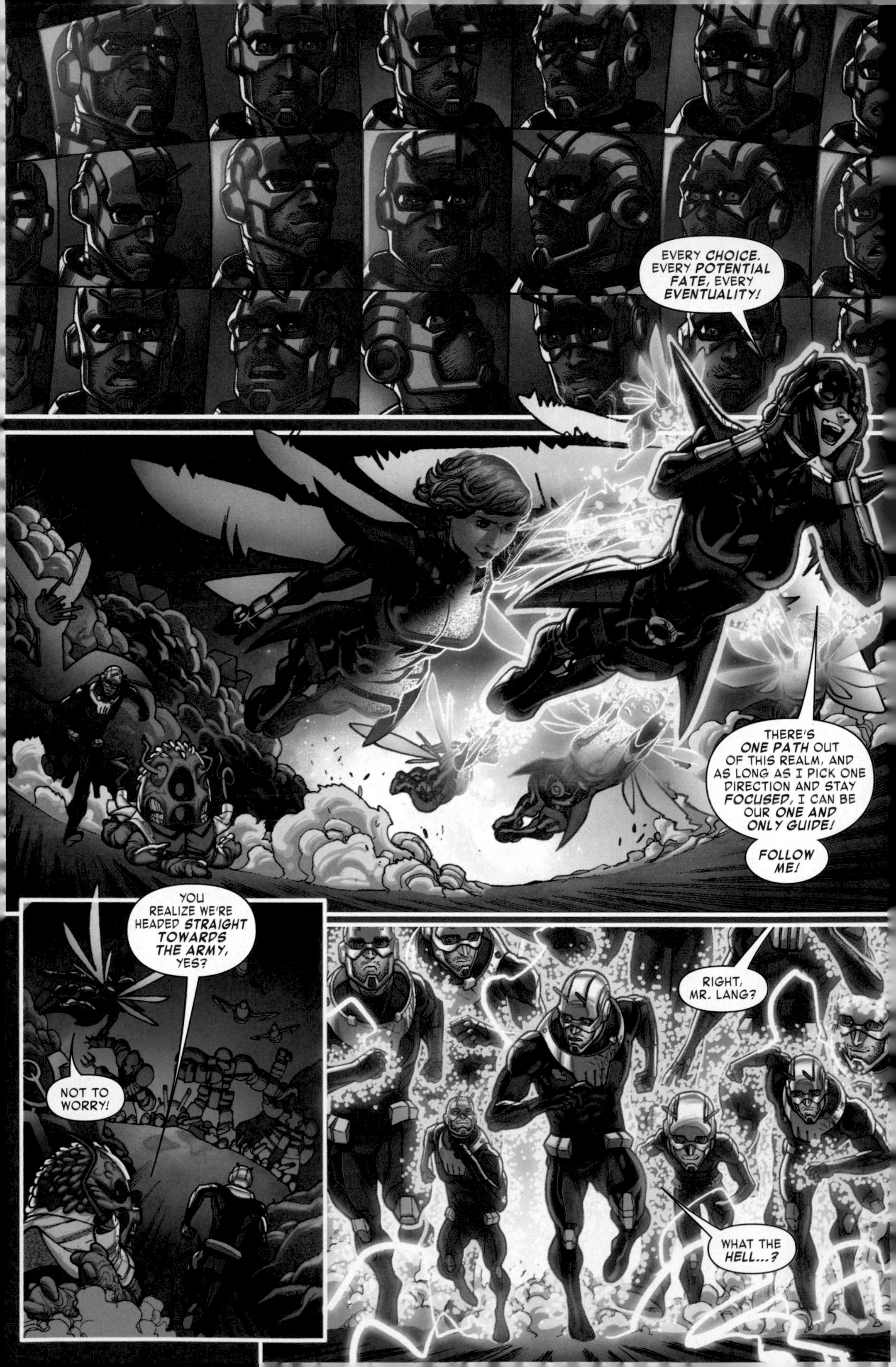
EVERY CHOICE. EVERY POTENTIAL FATE, EVERY EVENTUALITY!
THERE'S ONE PATH OUT OF THIS REALM, AND AS LONG AS I PICK ONE DIRECTION AND STAY FOCUSED, I CAN BE OUR ONE AND ONLY GUIDE!
FOLLOW ME!
YOU REALIZE WE'RE HEADED STRAIGHT TOWARDS THE ARMY, YES?
NOT TO WORRY!
RIGHT, MR. LANG?
WHAT THE HELL...?

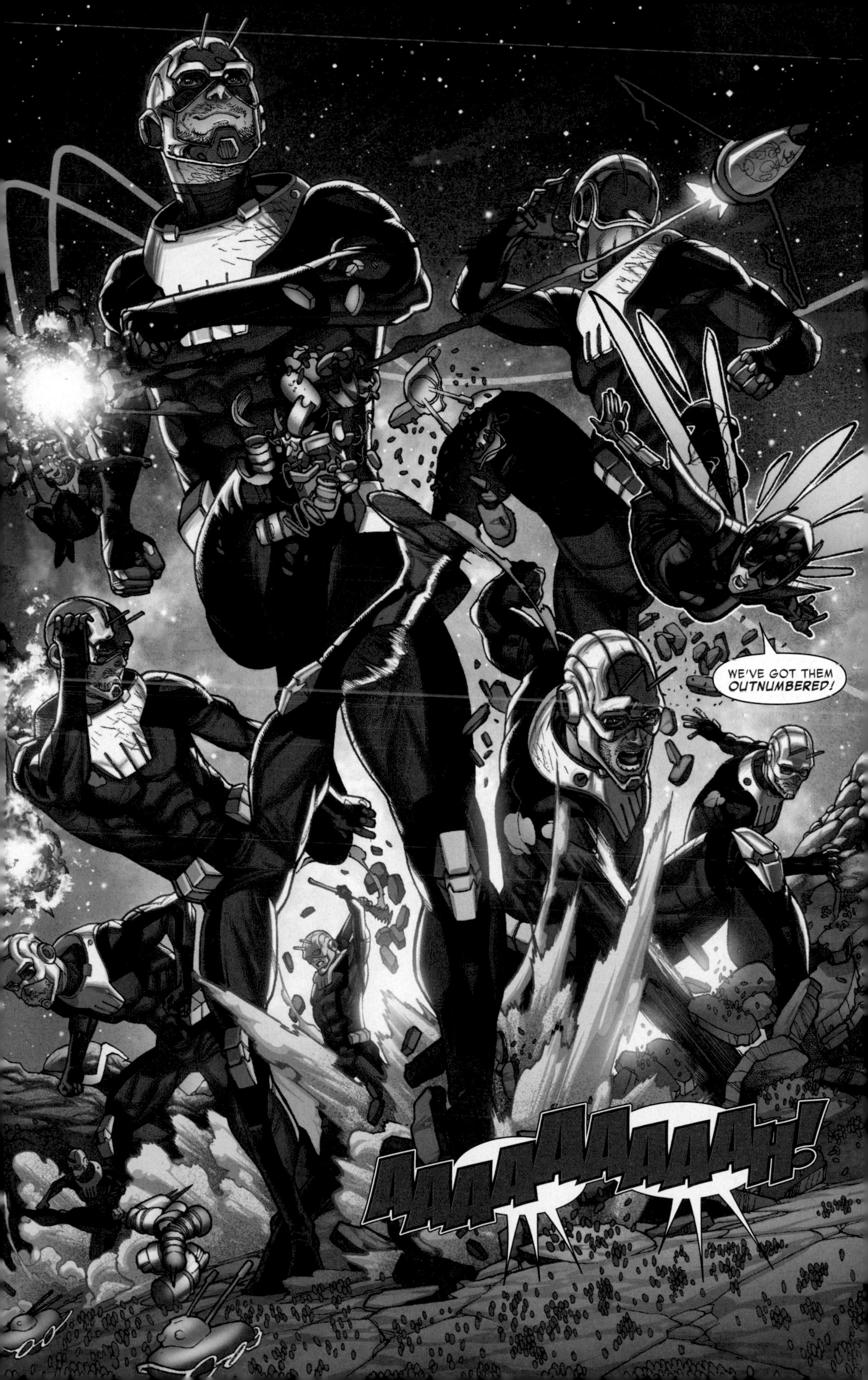
WE'VE GOT THEM OUTNUMBERED!
AAAAAAAAAAAH!

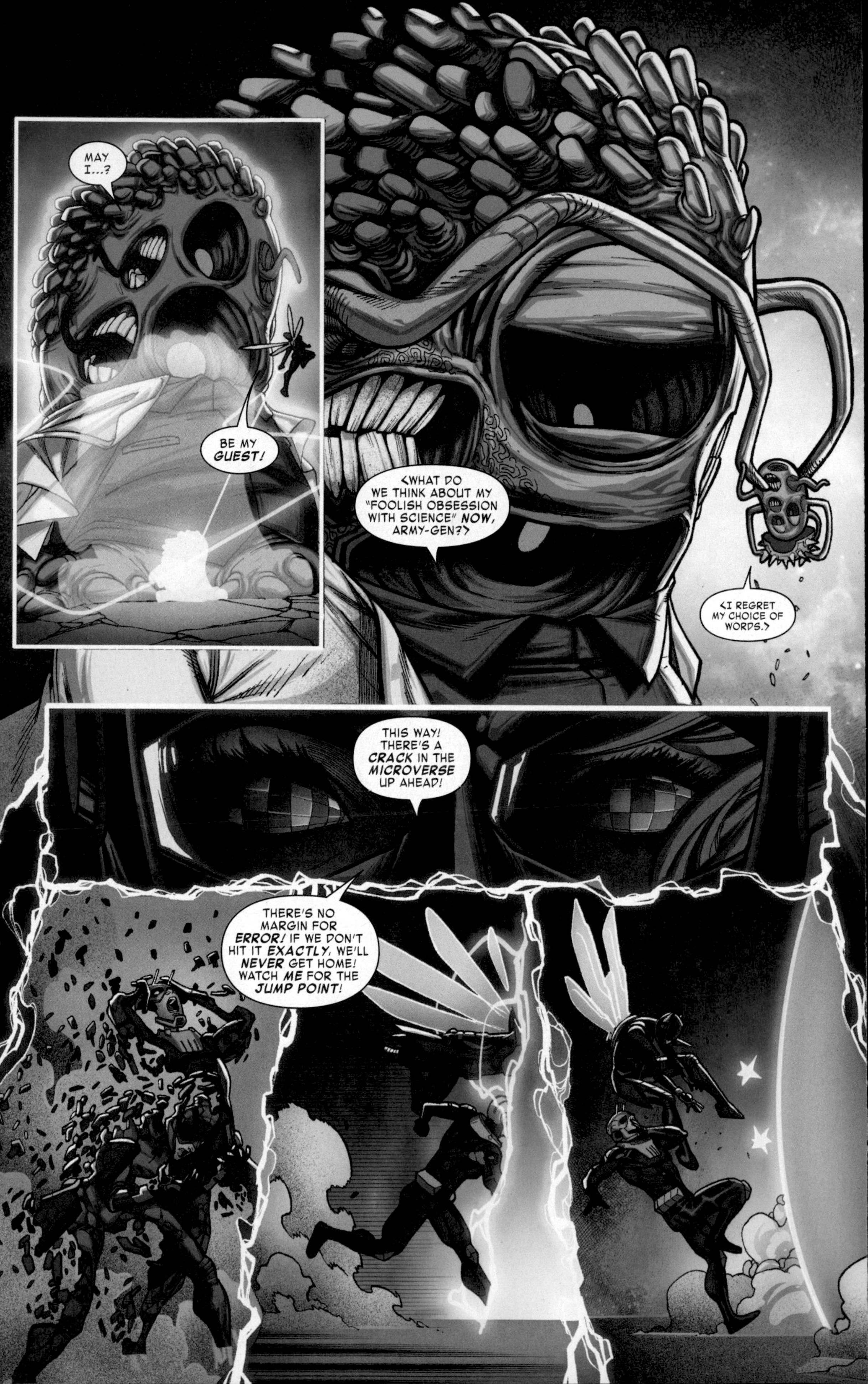
MAY I...?
BE MY GUEST!
<WHAT DO WE THINK ABOUT MY "FOOLISH OBSESSION WITH SCIENCE" NOW, ARMY-GEN?>
<I REGRET MY CHOICE OF WORDS.>
THIS WAY! THERE'S A CRACK IN THE MICROVERSE UP AHEAD!
THERE'S NO MARGIN FOR ERROR! IF WE DON'T HIT IT EXACTLY, WE'LL NEVER GET HOME! WATCH ME FOR THE JUMP POINT!

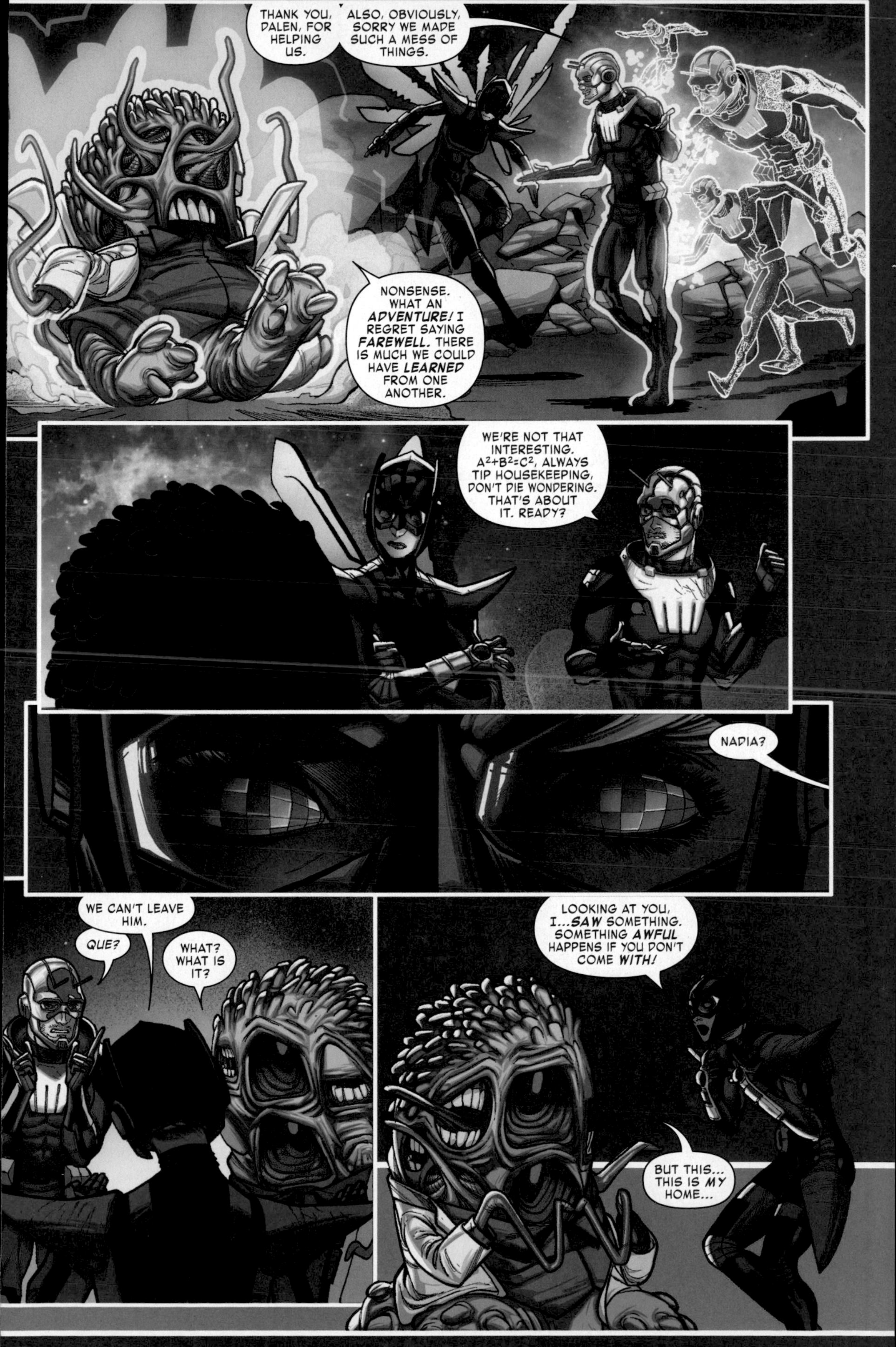
THANK YOU, DALEN, FOR HELPING US.
ALSO, OBVIOUSLY, SORRY WE MADE SUCH A MESS OF THINGS.
NONSENSE. WHAT AN ADVENTURE! I REGRET SAYING FAREWELL. THERE IS MUCH WE COULD HAVE LEARNED FROM ONE ANOTHER.
WE'RE NOT THAT INTERESTING. $A^2+B^2=C^2$, ALWAYS TIP HOUSEKEEPING, DON'T DIE WONDERING. THAT'S ABOUT IT. READY?
NADIA?
WE CAN'T LEAVE HIM.
QUE?
WHAT? WHAT IS IT?
LOOKING AT YOU, I...SAW SOMETHING. SOMETHING AWFUL HAPPENS IF YOU DON'T COME WITH!
BUT THIS... THIS IS MY HOME...

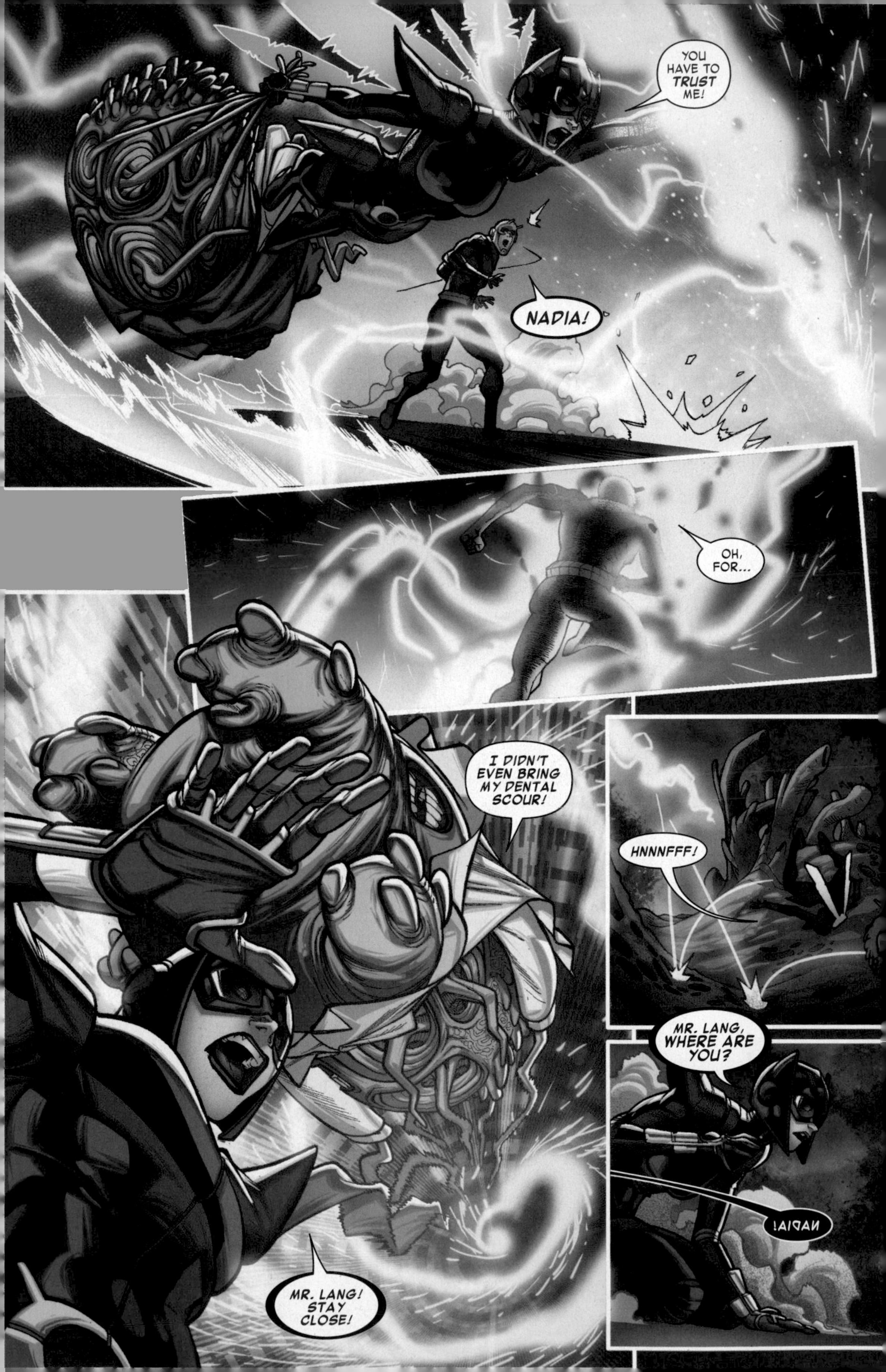
YOU HAVE TO TRUST ME!
NADIA!
OH, FOR...
I DIDN'T EVEN BRING MY DENTAL SCOUR!
MR. LANG! STAY CLOSE!
HNNNFFF!
MR. LANG, WHERE ARE YOU?
NADIA!

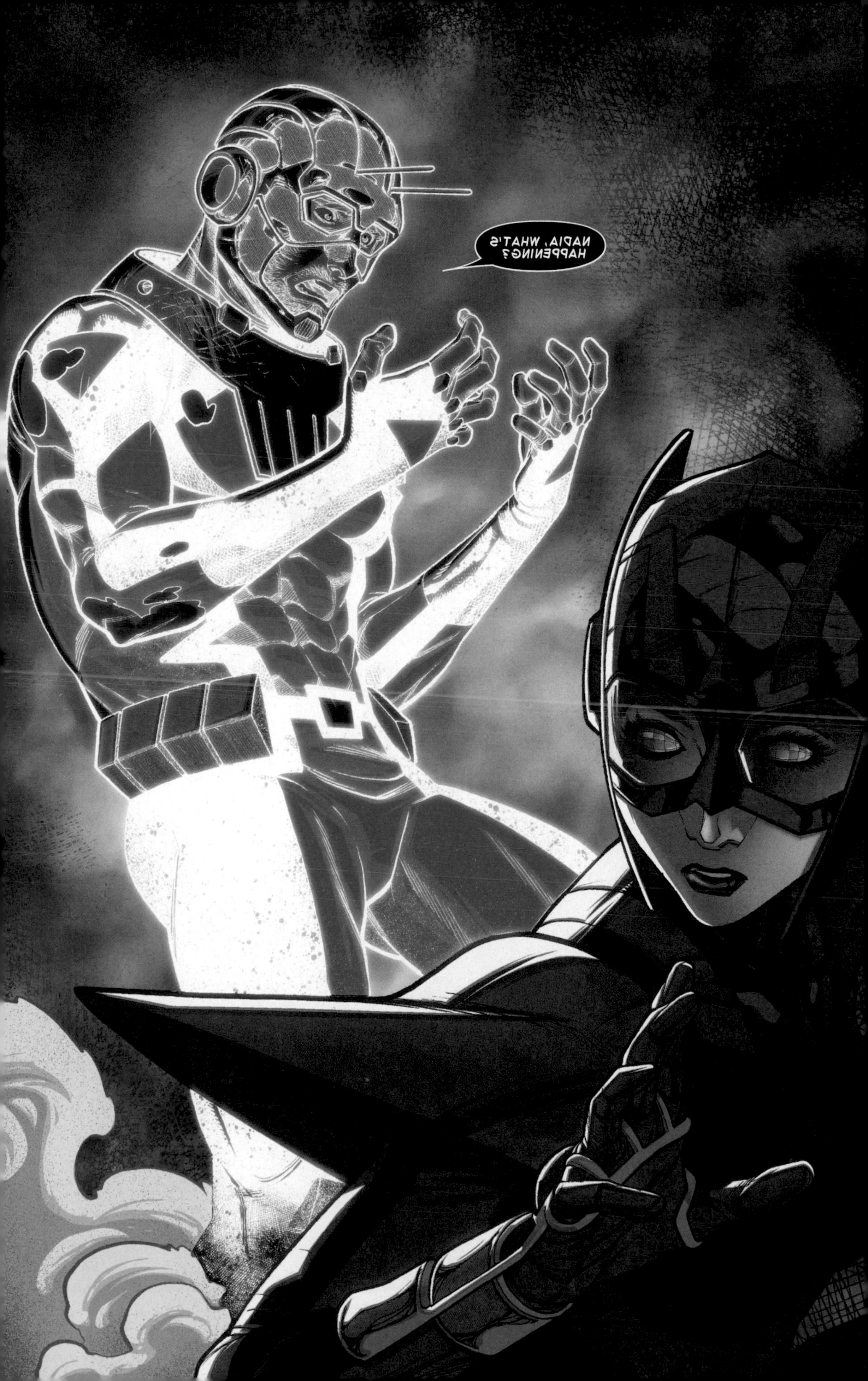
NADIA, WHAT'S HAPPENING?

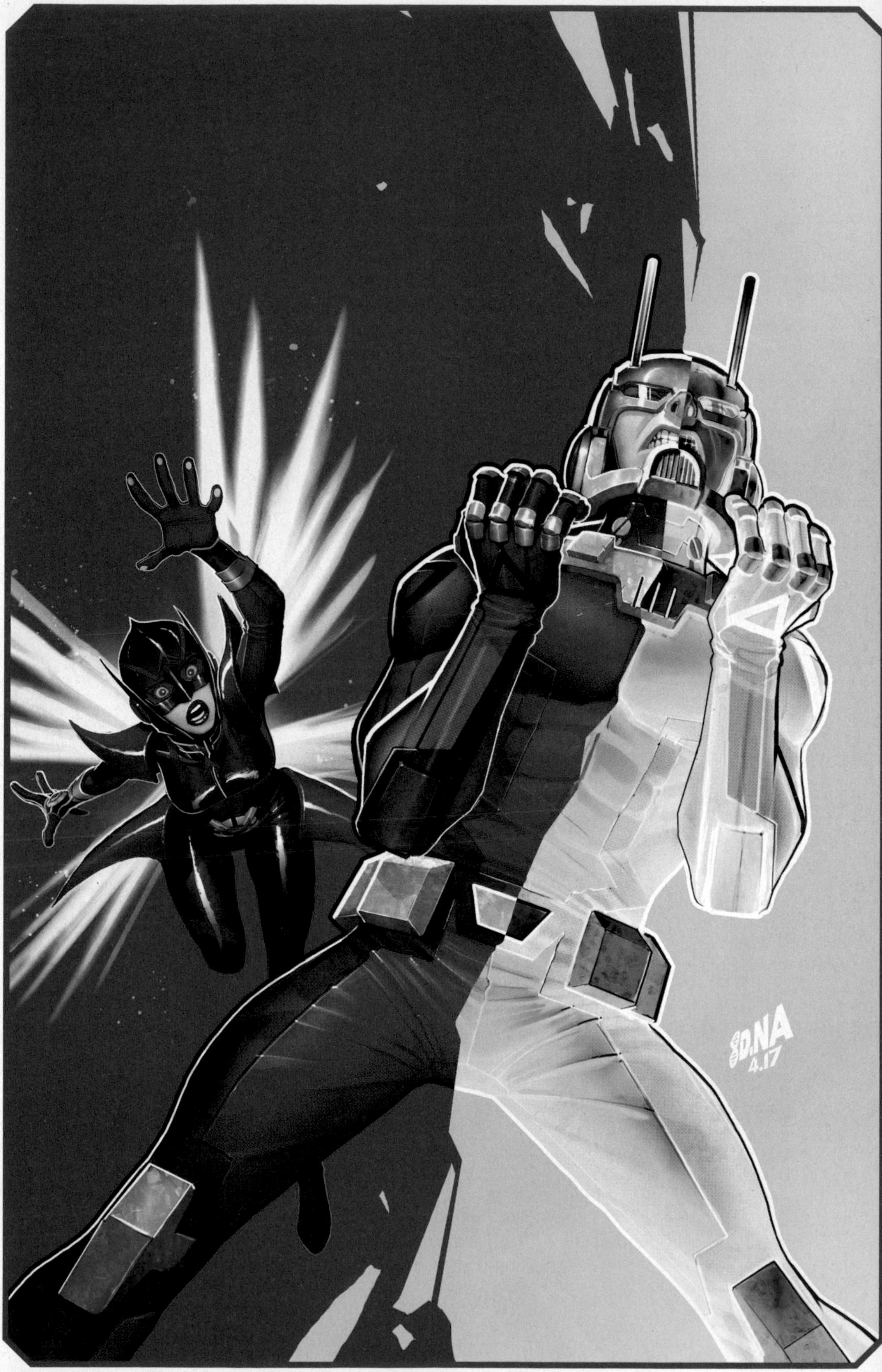
D.NA
4.17

ANT-MAN AND THE WASP #4

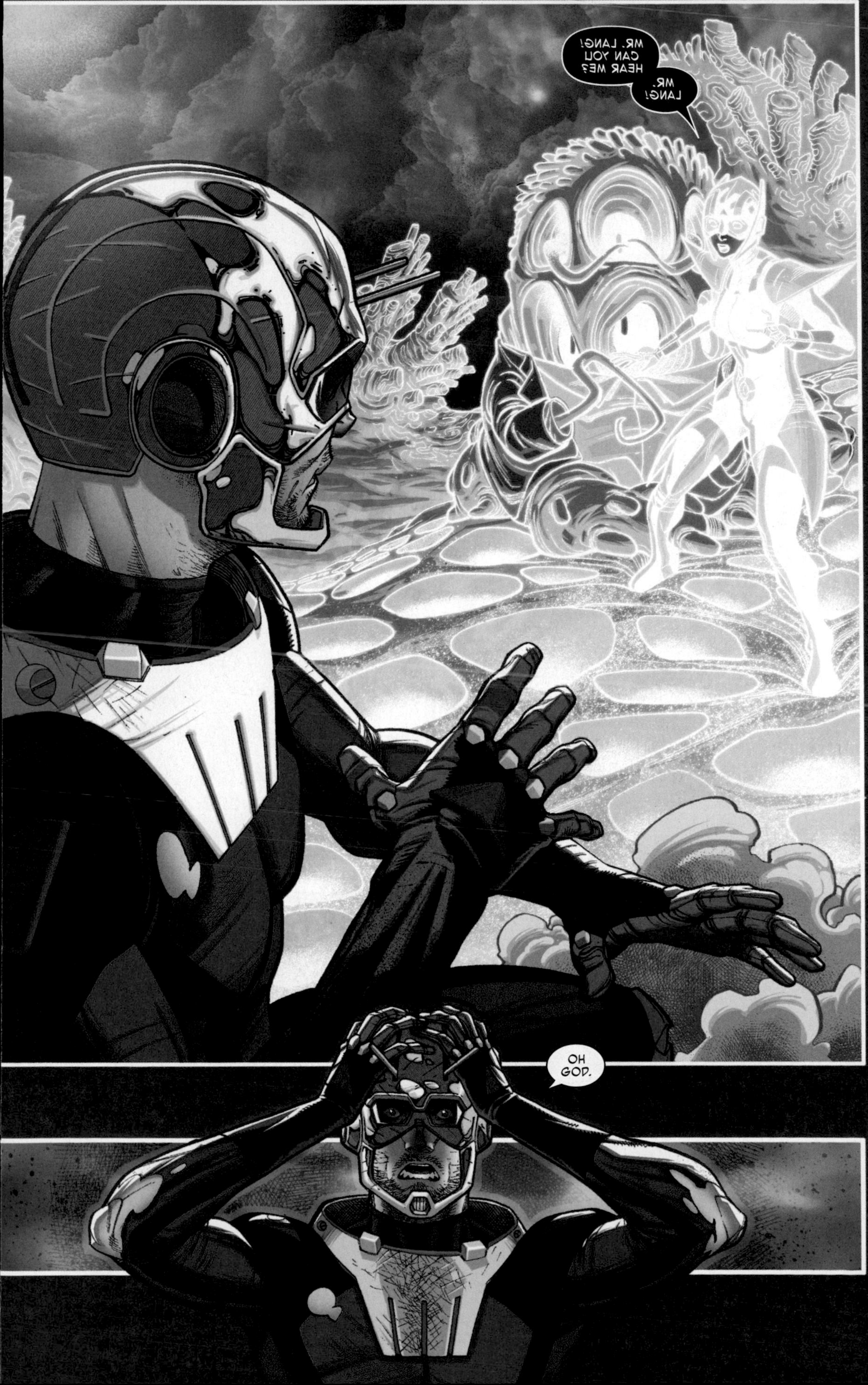

MR. LANG! CAN YOU HEAR ME?
MR. LANG!
OH GOD.

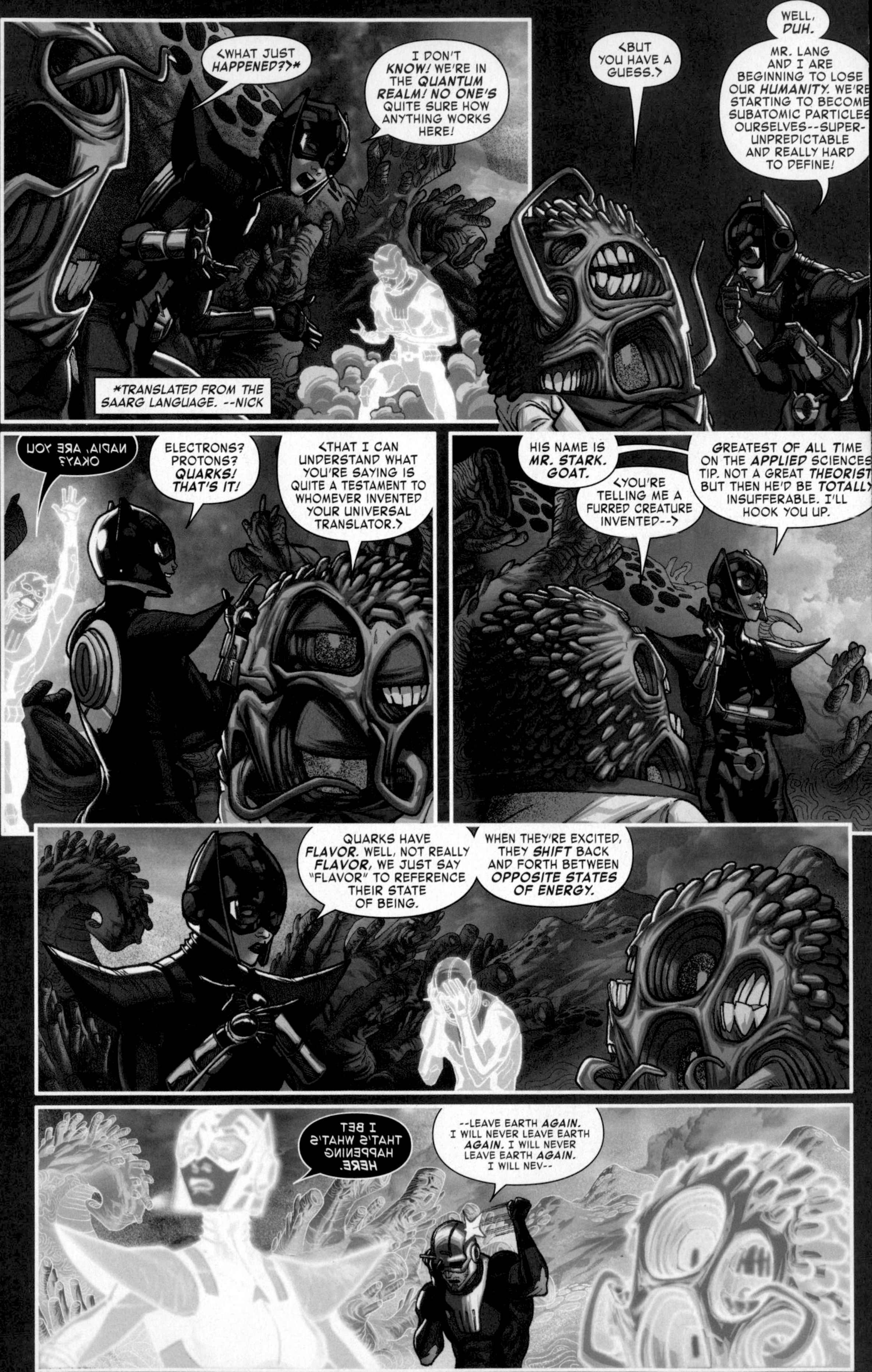

<WHAT JUST HAPPENED?>*
I DON'T KNOW! WE'RE IN THE QUANTUM REALM! NO ONE'S QUITE SURE HOW ANYTHING WORKS HERE!
*TRANSLATED FROM THE SAARG LANGUAGE. --NICK
<BUT YOU HAVE A GUESS.>
WELL, DUH.
MR. LANG AND I ARE BEGINNING TO LOSE OUR HUMANITY. WE'RE STARTING TO BECOME SUBATOMIC PARTICLES OURSELVES--SUPER-UNPREDICTABLE AND REALLY HARD TO DEFINE!
NADIA, ARE YOU OKAY?
ELECTRONS? PROTONS? QUARKS! THAT'S IT!
<THAT I CAN UNDERSTAND WHAT YOU'RE SAYING IS QUITE A TESTAMENT TO WHOMEVER INVENTED YOUR UNIVERSAL TRANSLATOR.>
HIS NAME IS MR. STARK. GOAT.
<YOU'RE TELLING ME A FURRED CREATURE INVENTED-->
GREATEST OF ALL TIME ON THE APPLIED SCIENCES TIP. NOT A GREAT THEORIST, BUT THEN HE'D BE TOTALLY INSUFFERABLE. I'LL HOOK YOU UP.
QUARKS HAVE FLAVOR. WELL, NOT REALLY FLAVOR, WE JUST SAY "FLAVOR" TO REFERENCE THEIR STATE OF BEING.
WHEN THEY'RE EXCITED, THEY SHIFT BACK AND FORTH BETWEEN OPPOSITE STATES OF ENERGY.
I BET THAT'S WHAT'S HAPPENING HERE.
--LEAVE EARTH AGAIN. I WILL NEVER LEAVE EARTH AGAIN. I WILL NEVER LEAVE EARTH AGAIN. I WILL NEV--

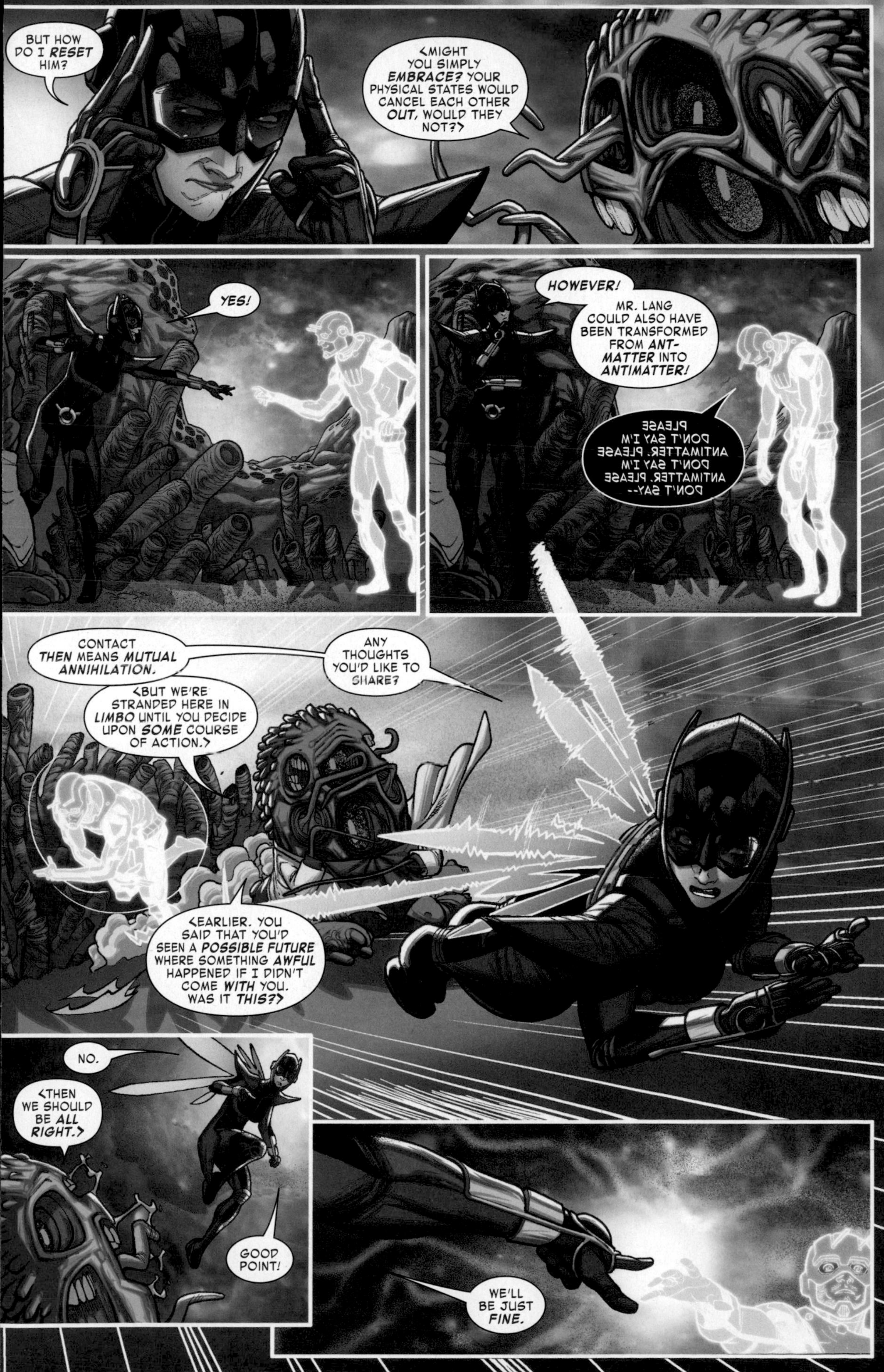
BUT HOW DO I *RESET* HIM?
<MIGHT YOU SIMPLY *EMBRACE?* YOUR PHYSICAL STATES WOULD CANCEL EACH OTHER *OUT,* WOULD THEY NOT?>
YES!
HOWEVER!
MR. LANG COULD ALSO HAVE BEEN TRANSFORMED FROM *ANT-MATTER* INTO *ANTIMATTER!*
PLEASE DON'T SAY I'M ANTIMATTER. PLEASE DON'T SAY I'M ANTIMATTER. PLEASE DON'T SAY--
CONTACT *THEN* MEANS *MUTUAL ANNIHILATION.*
ANY THOUGHTS YOU'D LIKE TO *SHARE?*
<BUT WE'RE STRANDED HERE IN *LIMBO* UNTIL YOU DECIDE UPON *SOME* COURSE OF ACTION.>
<EARLIER. YOU SAID THAT YOU'D SEEN A *POSSIBLE FUTURE* WHERE SOMETHING *AWFUL* HAPPENED IF I DIDN'T COME *WITH* YOU. WAS IT *THIS?*>
NO.
<THEN WE SHOULD BE *ALL RIGHT.*>
GOOD POINT!
WE'LL BE JUST *FINE.*

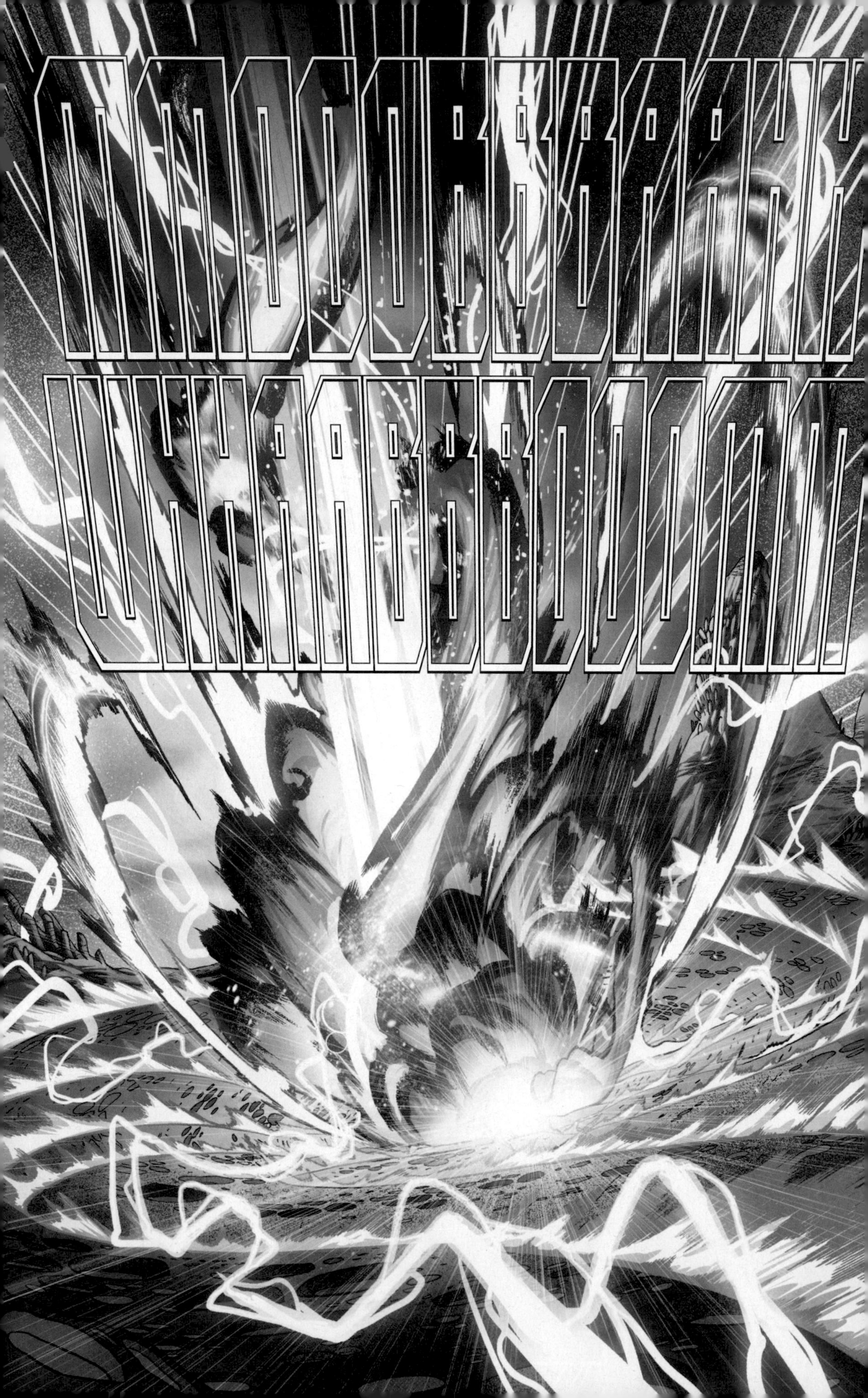

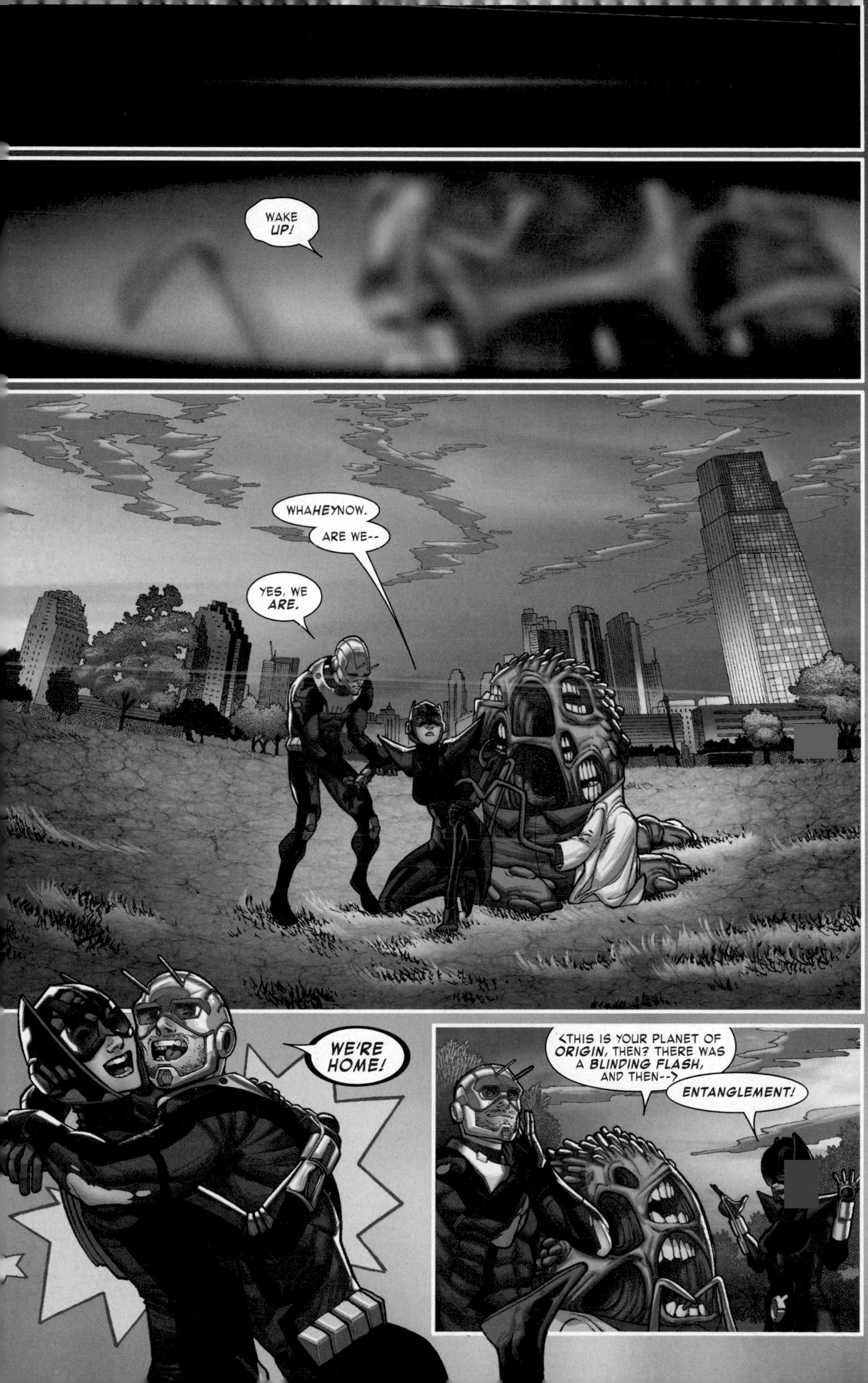
WAKE UP!
WHAHEYNOW.
ARE WE--
YES, WE ARE.
WE'RE HOME!
<THIS IS YOUR PLANET OF ORIGIN, THEN? THERE WAS A BLINDING FLASH, AND THEN-->
ENTANGLEMENT!

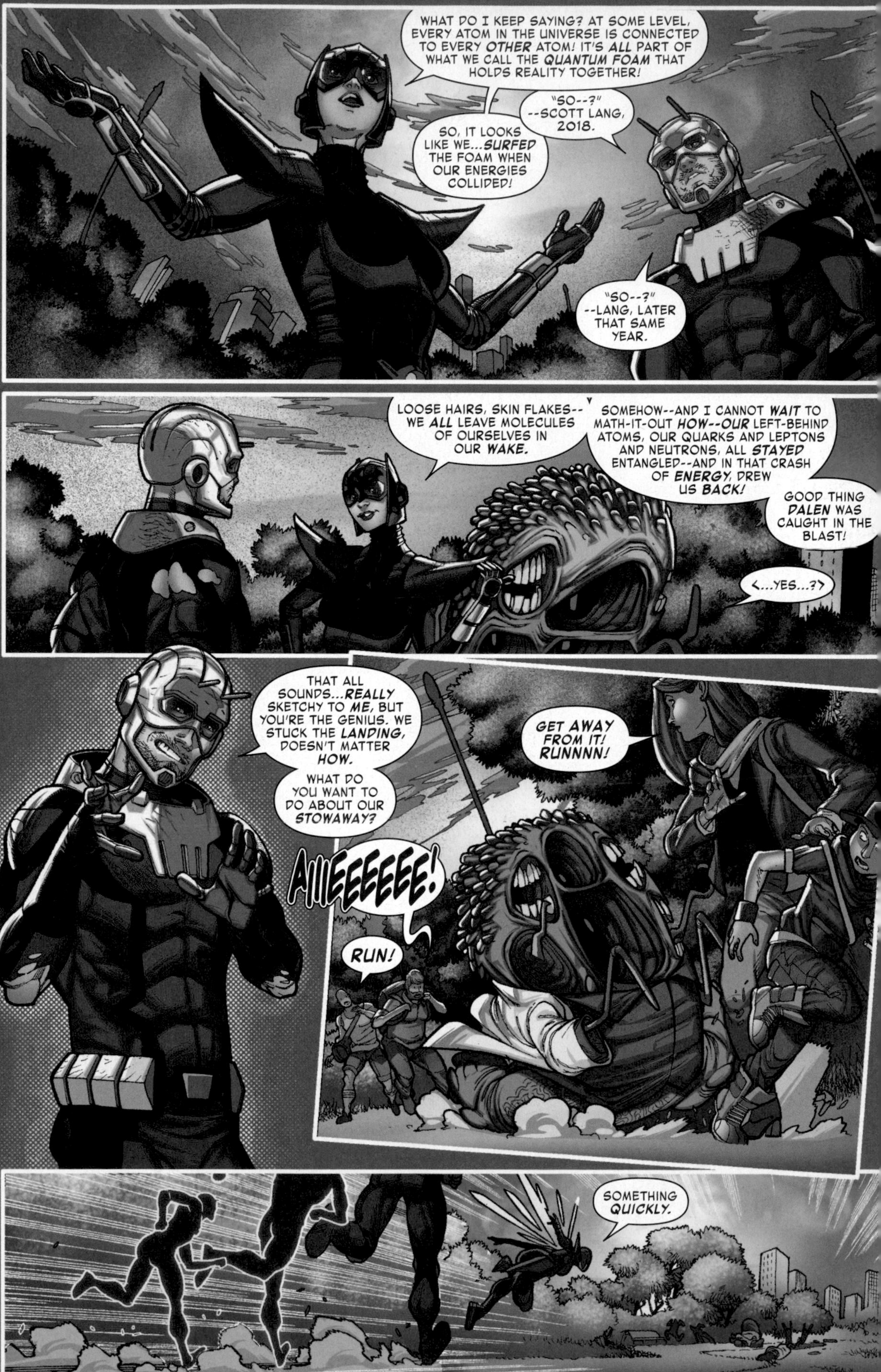
WHAT DO I KEEP SAYING? AT SOME LEVEL, EVERY ATOM IN THE UNIVERSE IS CONNECTED TO EVERY OTHER ATOM! IT'S ALL PART OF WHAT WE CALL THE QUANTUM FOAM THAT HOLDS REALITY TOGETHER!
SO, IT LOOKS LIKE WE...SURFED THE FOAM WHEN OUR ENERGIES COLLIDED!
"SO--?" --SCOTT LANG, 2018.
"SO--?" --LANG, LATER THAT SAME YEAR.
LOOSE HAIRS, SKIN FLAKES-- WE ALL LEAVE MOLECULES OF OURSELVES IN OUR WAKE.
SOMEHOW--AND I CANNOT WAIT TO MATH-IT-OUT HOW--OUR LEFT-BEHIND ATOMS, OUR QUARKS AND LEPTONS AND NEUTRONS, ALL STAYED ENTANGLED--AND IN THAT CRASH OF ENERGY, DREW US BACK!
GOOD THING DALEN WAS CAUGHT IN THE BLAST!
<...YES...?>
THAT ALL SOUNDS...REALLY SKETCHY TO ME, BUT YOU'RE THE GENIUS. WE STUCK THE LANDING, DOESN'T MATTER HOW.
WHAT DO YOU WANT TO DO ABOUT OUR STOWAWAY?
GET AWAY FROM IT! RUNNNN!
AIIIEEEEEE!
RUN!
SOMETHING QUICKLY.

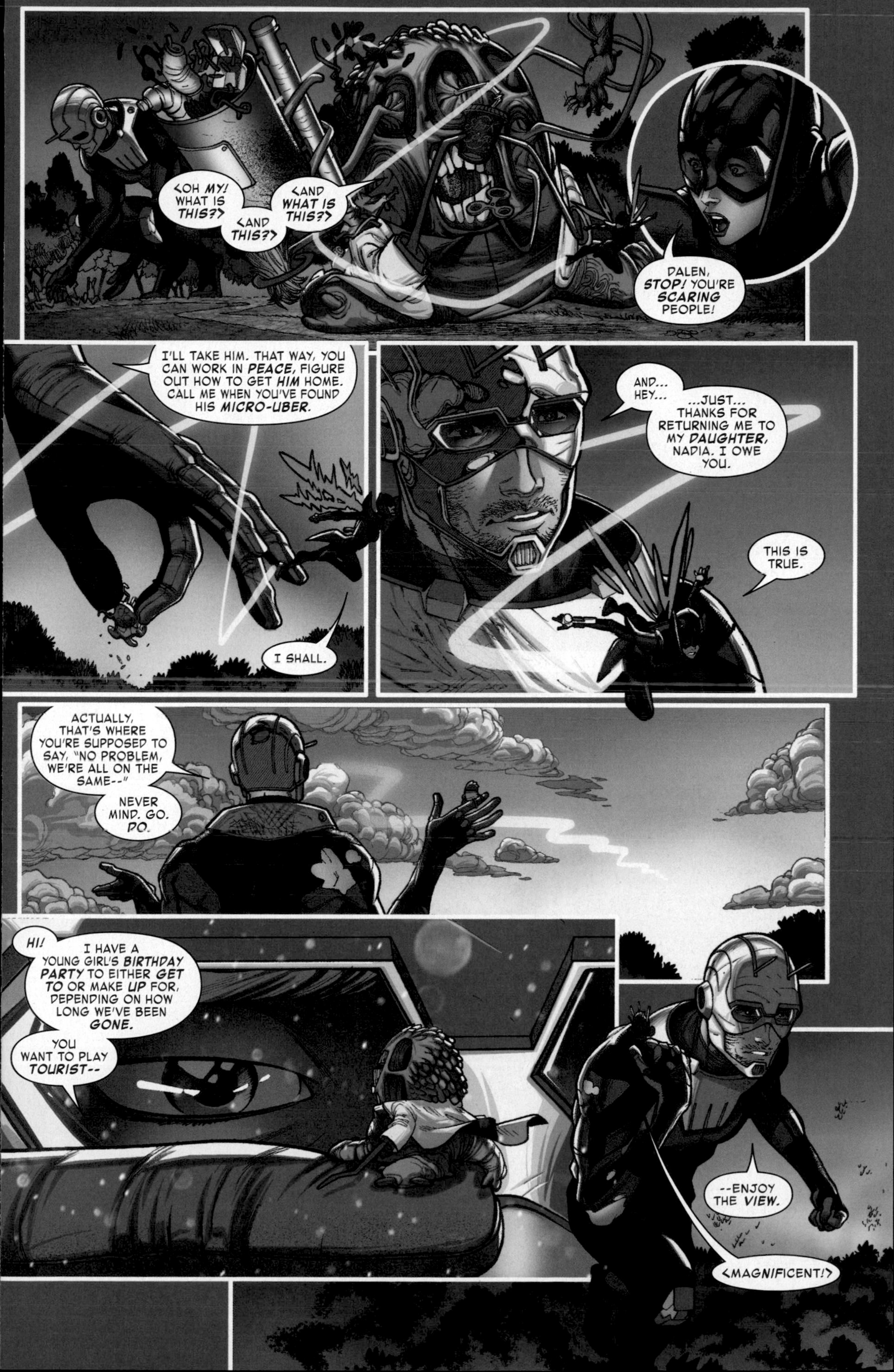
<OH MY! WHAT IS THIS?>
<AND THIS?>
<AND WHAT IS THIS?>
DALEN, STOP! YOU'RE SCARING PEOPLE!
I'LL TAKE HIM. THAT WAY, YOU CAN WORK IN PEACE, FIGURE OUT HOW TO GET HIM HOME. CALL ME WHEN YOU'VE FOUND HIS MICRO-UBER.
I SHALL.
AND... HEY...
...JUST... THANKS FOR RETURNING ME TO MY DAUGHTER, NADIA. I OWE YOU.
THIS IS TRUE.
ACTUALLY, THAT'S WHERE YOU'RE SUPPOSED TO SAY, "NO PROBLEM, WE'RE ALL ON THE SAME--"
NEVER MIND. GO. DO.
HI!
I HAVE A YOUNG GIRL'S BIRTHDAY PARTY TO EITHER GET TO OR MAKE UP FOR, DEPENDING ON HOW LONG WE'VE BEEN GONE.
YOU WANT TO PLAY TOURIST--
--ENJOY THE VIEW.
<MAGNIFICENT!>

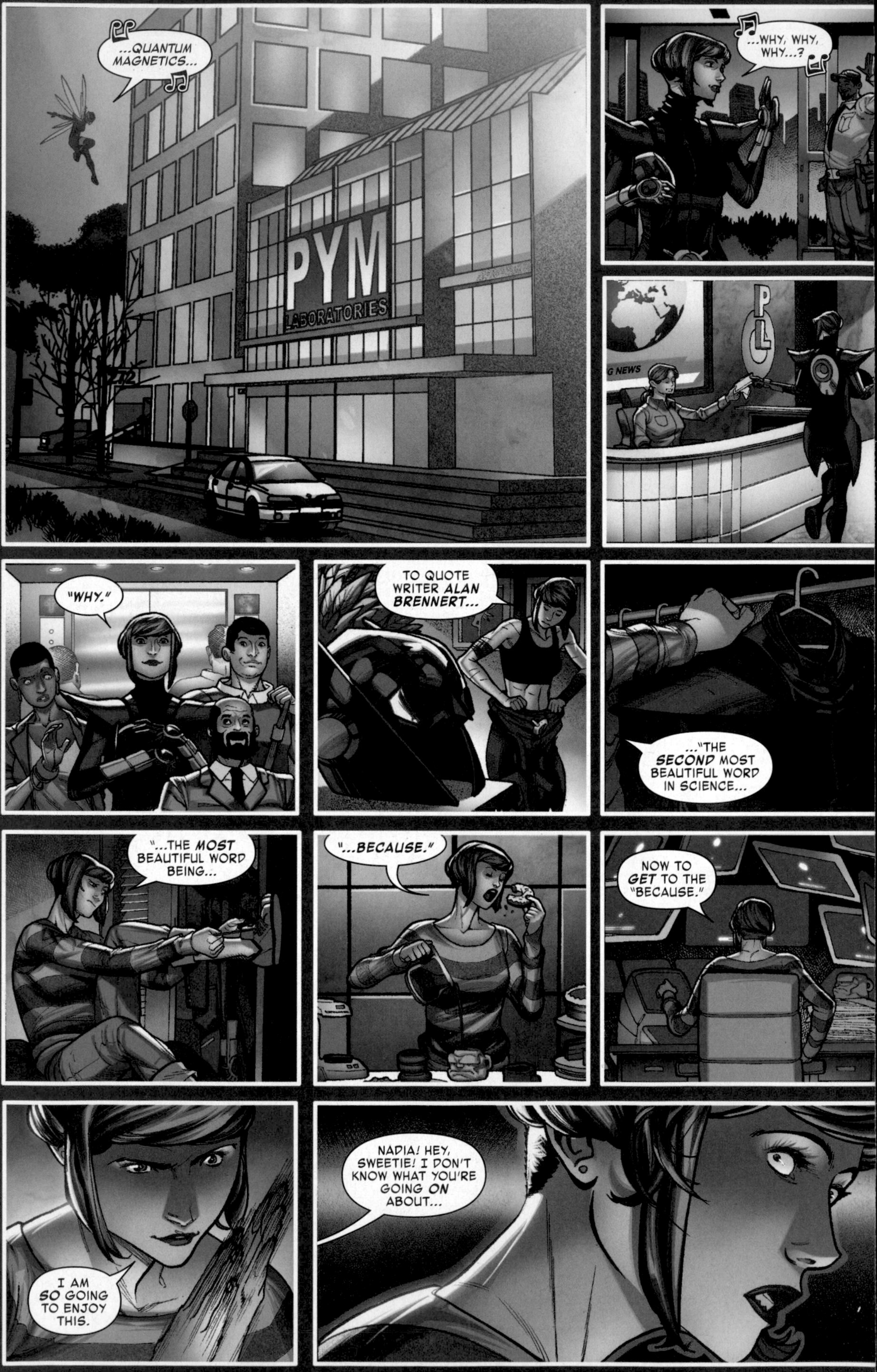

...QUANTUM MAGNETICS...
PYM LABORATORIES
...WHY, WHY, WHY...?
"WHY."
TO QUOTE WRITER ALAN BRENNERT...
..."THE SECOND MOST BEAUTIFUL WORD IN SCIENCE...
"...THE MOST BEAUTIFUL WORD BEING...
"...BECAUSE."
NOW TO GET TO THE "BECAUSE."
I AM SO GOING TO ENJOY THIS.
NADIA! HEY, SWEETIE! I DON'T KNOW WHAT YOU'RE GOING ON ABOUT...

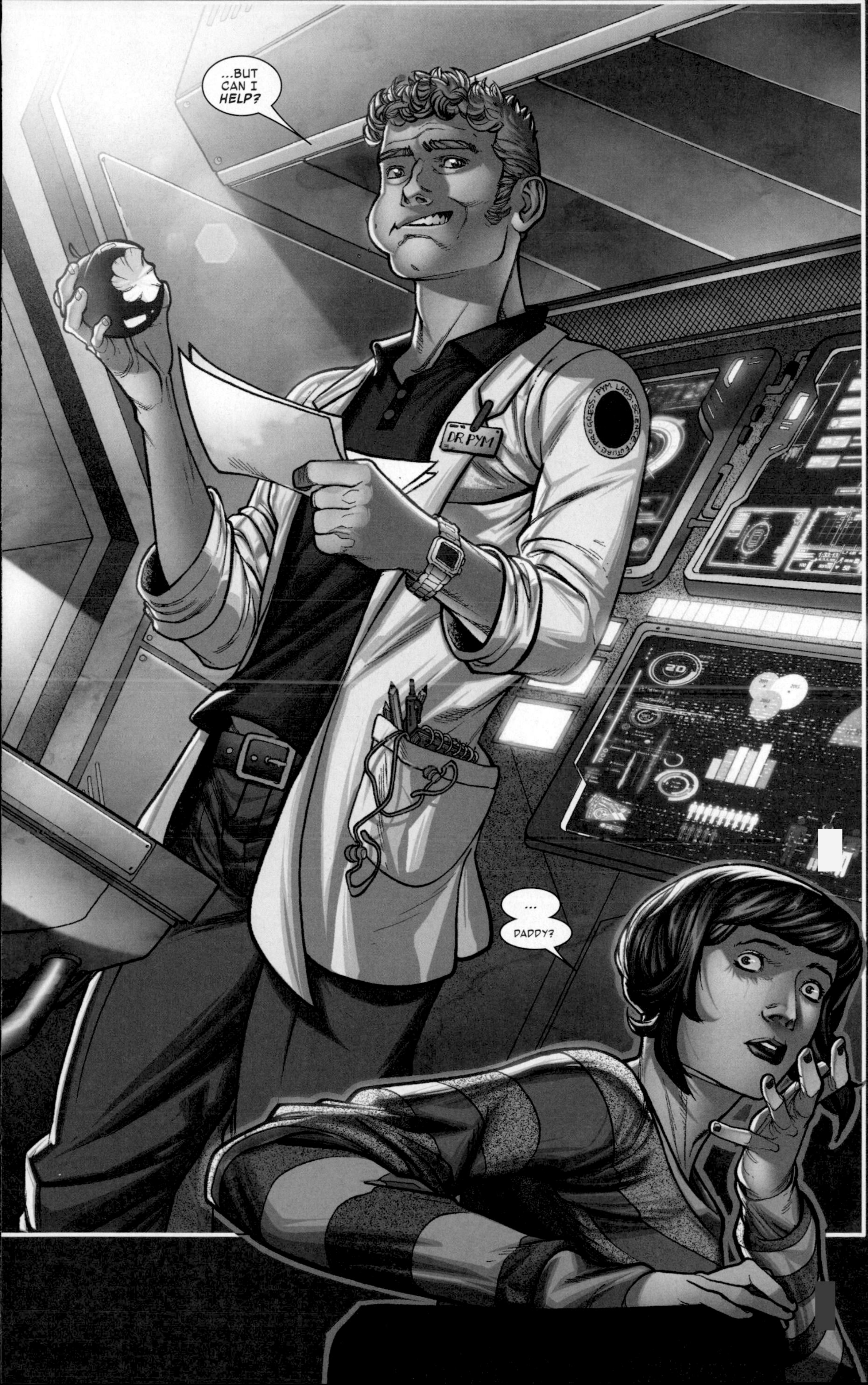
...BUT CAN I HELP?
... DADDY?

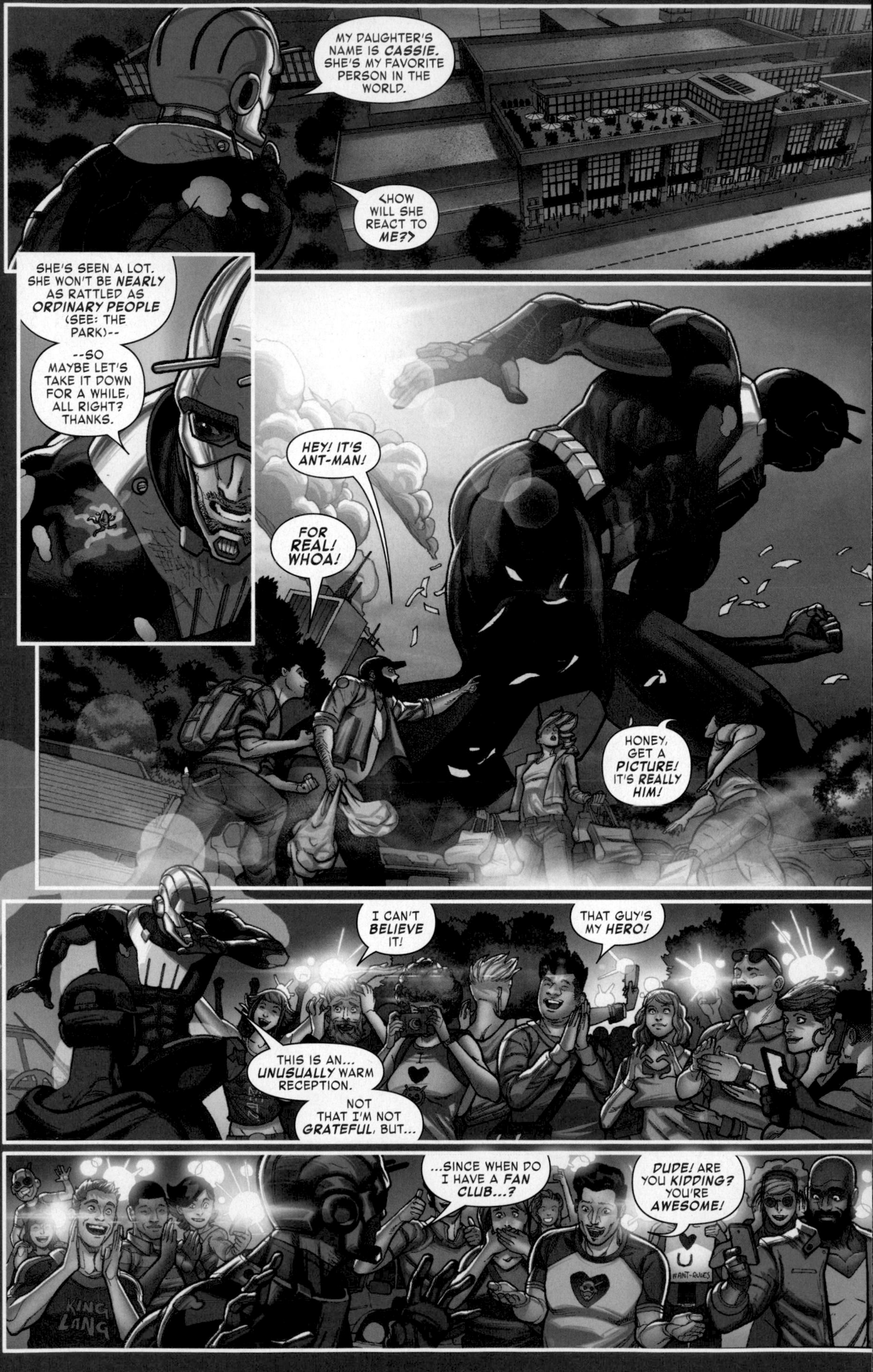
MY DAUGHTER'S NAME IS CASSIE. SHE'S MY FAVORITE PERSON IN THE WORLD.
<HOW WILL SHE REACT TO ME?>
SHE'S SEEN A LOT. SHE WON'T BE NEARLY AS RATTLED AS ORDINARY PEOPLE (SEE: THE PARK)--
--SO MAYBE LET'S TAKE IT DOWN FOR A WHILE, ALL RIGHT? THANKS.
HEY! IT'S ANT-MAN!
FOR REAL! WHOA!
HONEY, GET A PICTURE! IT'S REALLY HIM!
I CAN'T BELIEVE IT!
THAT GUY'S MY HERO!
THIS IS AN... UNUSUALLY WARM RECEPTION.
NOT THAT I'M NOT GRATEFUL, BUT...
...SINCE WHEN DO I HAVE A FAN CLUB...?
DUDE! ARE YOU KIDDING? YOU'RE AWESOME!
KING LANG
#ANT-RULES

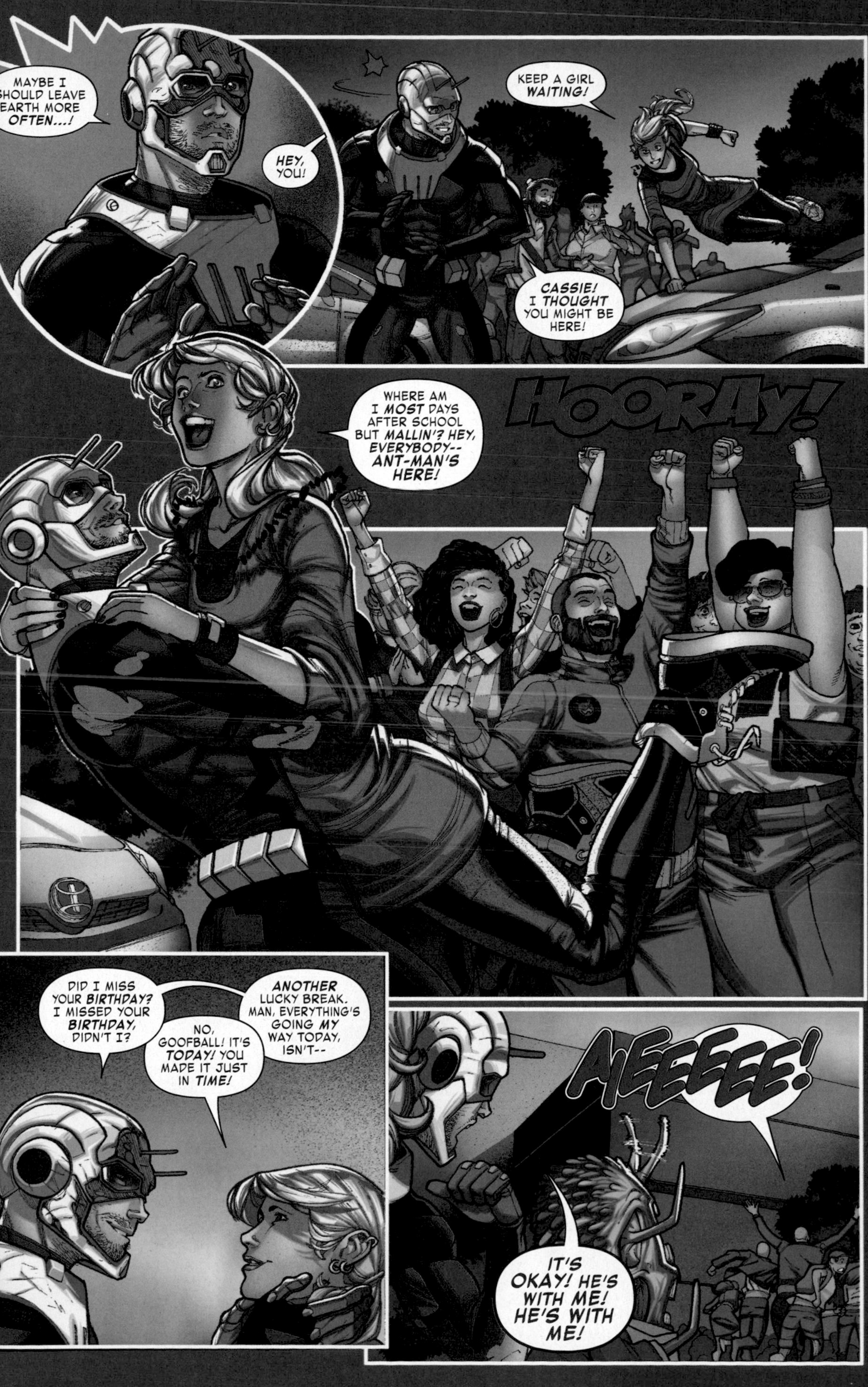
MAYBE I SHOULD LEAVE EARTH MORE OFTEN...!
HEY, YOU!
KEEP A GIRL WAITING!
CASSIE! I THOUGHT YOU MIGHT BE HERE!
WHERE AM I MOST DAYS AFTER SCHOOL BUT MALLIN'? HEY, EVERYBODY-- ANT-MAN'S HERE!
HOORAY!
DID I MISS YOUR BIRTHDAY? I MISSED YOUR BIRTHDAY, DIDN'T I?
NO, GOOFBALL! IT'S TODAY! YOU MADE IT JUST IN TIME!
ANOTHER LUCKY BREAK. MAN, EVERYTHING'S GOING MY WAY TODAY, ISN'T--
AIEEEEE!
IT'S OKAY! HE'S WITH ME! HE'S WITH ME!

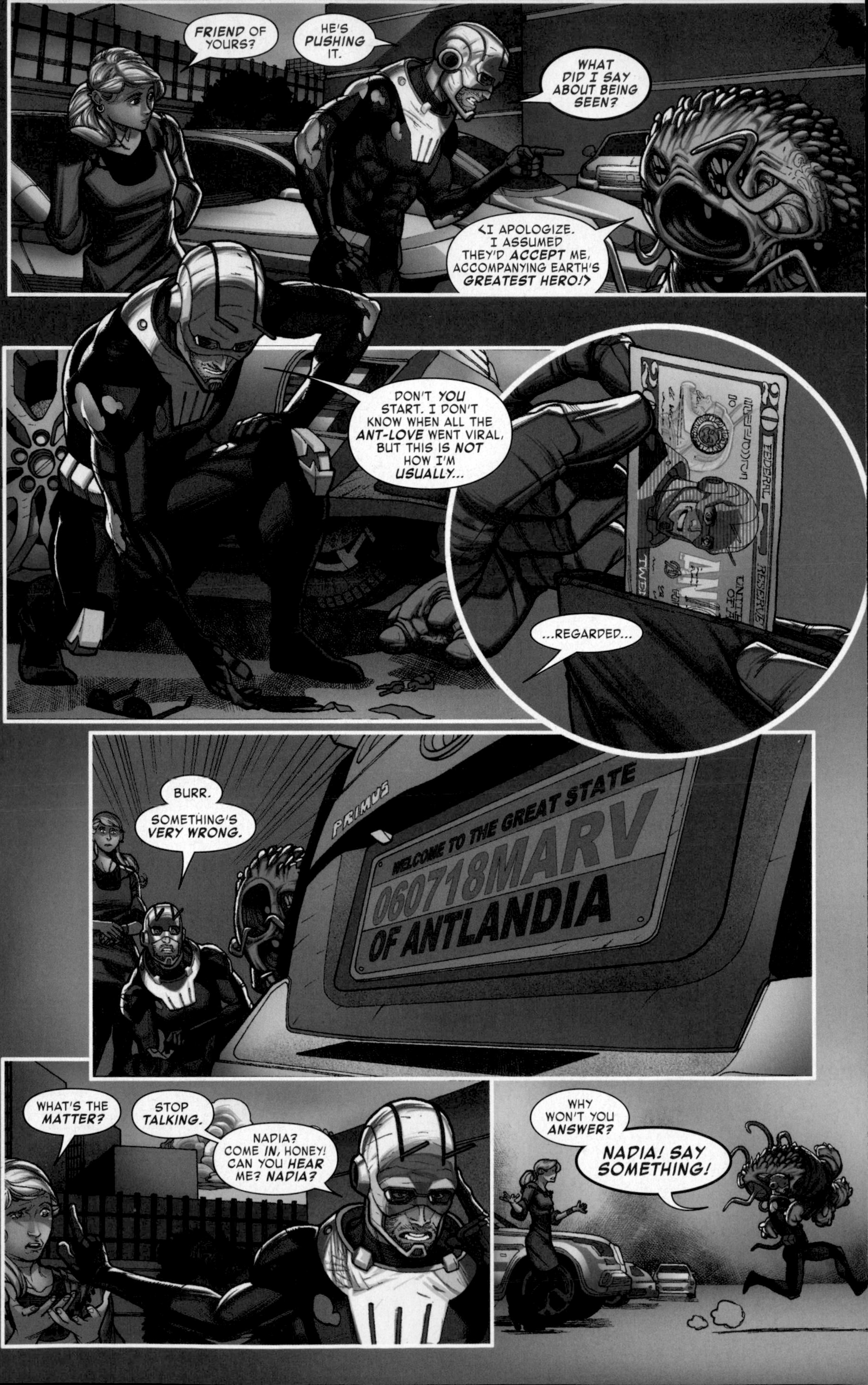
FRIEND OF YOURS?
HE'S PUSHING IT.
WHAT DID I SAY ABOUT BEING SEEN?
<I APOLOGIZE. I ASSUMED THEY'D ACCEPT ME, ACCOMPANYING EARTH'S GREATEST HERO!>
DON'T YOU START. I DON'T KNOW WHEN ALL THE ANT-LOVE WENT VIRAL, BUT THIS IS NOT HOW I'M USUALLY...
...REGARDED...
BURR.
SOMETHING'S VERY WRONG.
PRIMUS
WELCOME TO THE GREAT STATE
060718MARV
OF ANTLANDIA
WHAT'S THE MATTER?
STOP TALKING.
NADIA? COME IN, HONEY! CAN YOU HEAR ME? NADIA?
WHY WON'T YOU ANSWER?
NADIA! SAY SOMETHING!

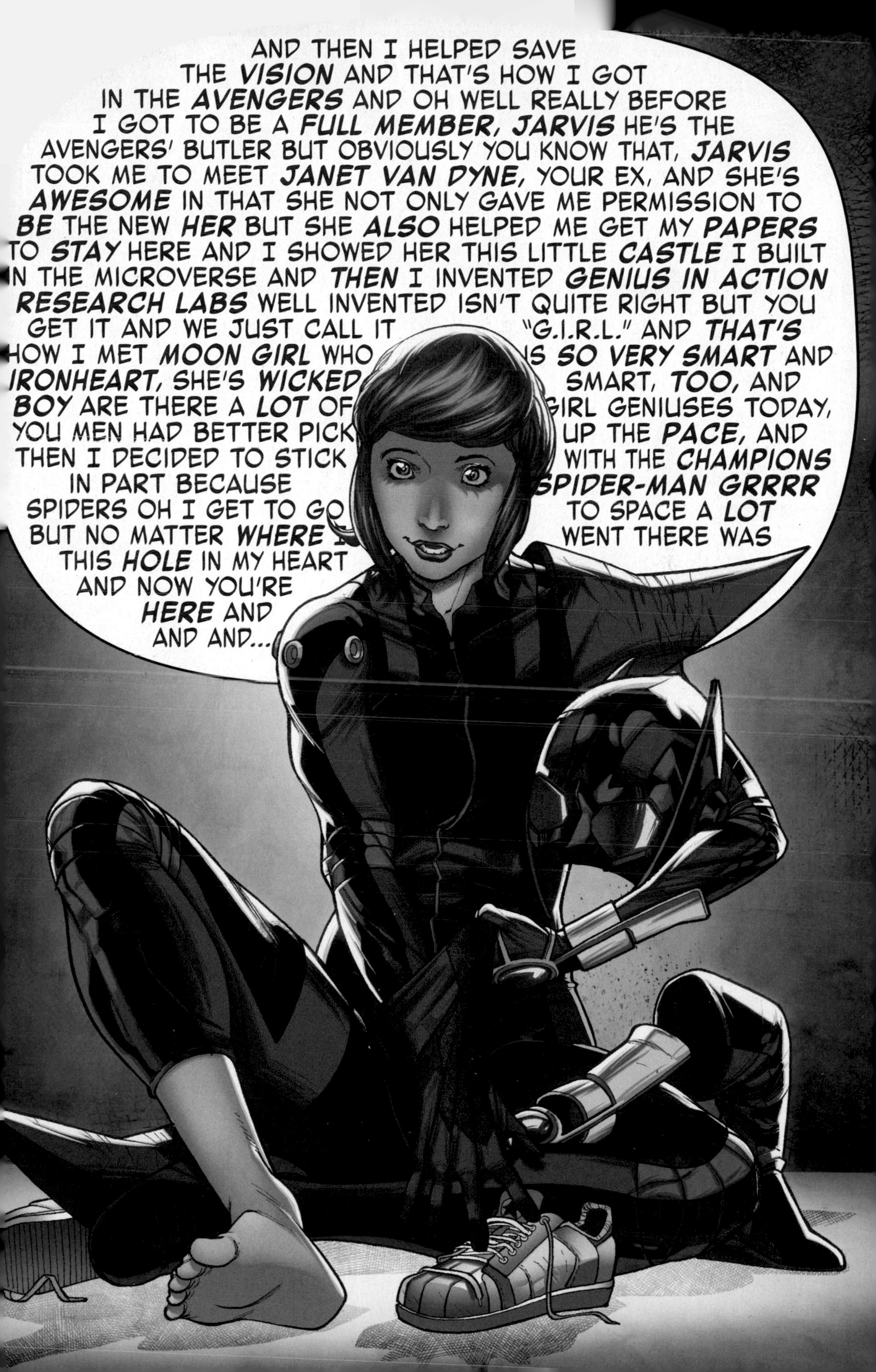
AND THEN I HELPED SAVE THE VISION AND THAT'S HOW I GOT IN THE AVENGERS AND OH WELL REALLY BEFORE I GOT TO BE A FULL MEMBER, JARVIS HE'S THE AVENGERS' BUTLER BUT OBVIOUSLY YOU KNOW THAT, JARVIS TOOK ME TO MEET JANET VAN DYNE, YOUR EX, AND SHE'S AWESOME IN THAT SHE NOT ONLY GAVE ME PERMISSION TO BE THE NEW HER BUT SHE ALSO HELPED ME GET MY PAPERS TO STAY HERE AND I SHOWED HER THIS LITTLE CASTLE I BUILT IN THE MICROVERSE AND THEN I INVENTED GENIUS IN ACTION RESEARCH LABS WELL INVENTED ISN'T QUITE RIGHT BUT YOU GET IT AND WE JUST CALL IT "G.I.R.L." AND THAT'S HOW I MET MOON GIRL WHO IS SO VERY SMART AND IRONHEART, SHE'S WICKED SMART, TOO, AND BOY ARE THERE A LOT OF GIRL GENIUSES TODAY, YOU MEN HAD BETTER PICK UP THE PACE, AND THEN I DECIDED TO STICK WITH THE CHAMPIONS IN PART BECAUSE SPIDER-MAN GRRRR SPIDERS OH I GET TO GO TO SPACE A LOT BUT NO MATTER WHERE I WENT THERE WAS THIS HOLE IN MY HEART AND NOW YOU'RE HERE AND AND AND...

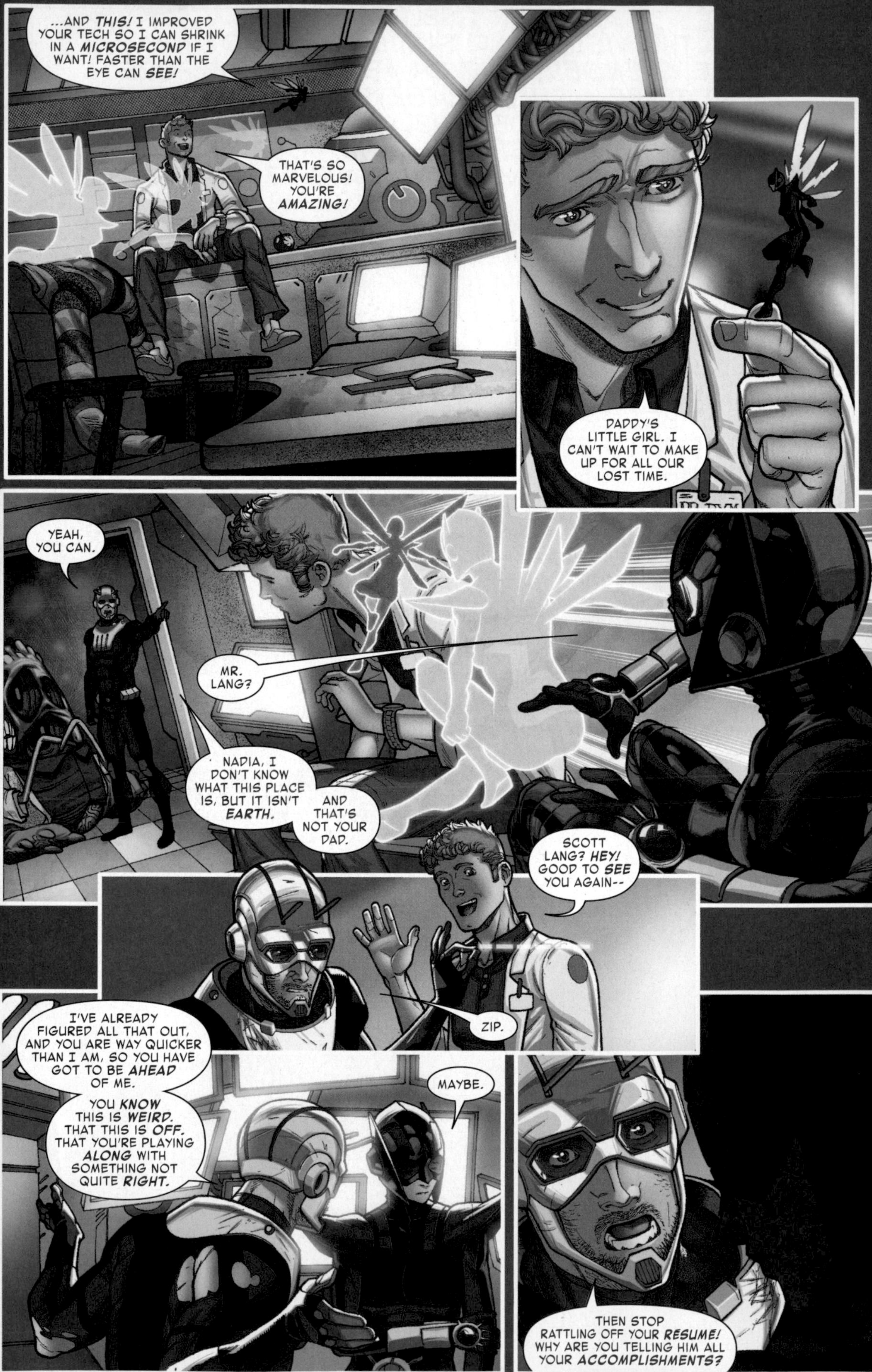
...AND THIS! I IMPROVED YOUR TECH SO I CAN SHRINK IN A MICROSECOND IF I WANT! FASTER THAN THE EYE CAN SEE!
THAT'S SO MARVELOUS! YOU'RE AMAZING!
DADDY'S LITTLE GIRL. I CAN'T WAIT TO MAKE UP FOR ALL OUR LOST TIME.
YEAH, YOU CAN.
MR. LANG?
NADIA, I DON'T KNOW WHAT THIS PLACE IS, BUT IT ISN'T EARTH.
AND THAT'S NOT YOUR DAD.
SCOTT LANG? HEY! GOOD TO SEE YOU AGAIN--
ZIP.
I'VE ALREADY FIGURED ALL THAT OUT, AND YOU ARE WAY QUICKER THAN I AM, SO YOU HAVE GOT TO BE AHEAD OF ME.
YOU KNOW THIS IS WEIRD. THAT THIS IS OFF. THAT YOU'RE PLAYING ALONG WITH SOMETHING NOT QUITE RIGHT.
MAYBE.
THEN STOP RATTLING OFF YOUR RESUME! WHY ARE YOU TELLING HIM ALL YOUR ACCOMPLISHMENTS?

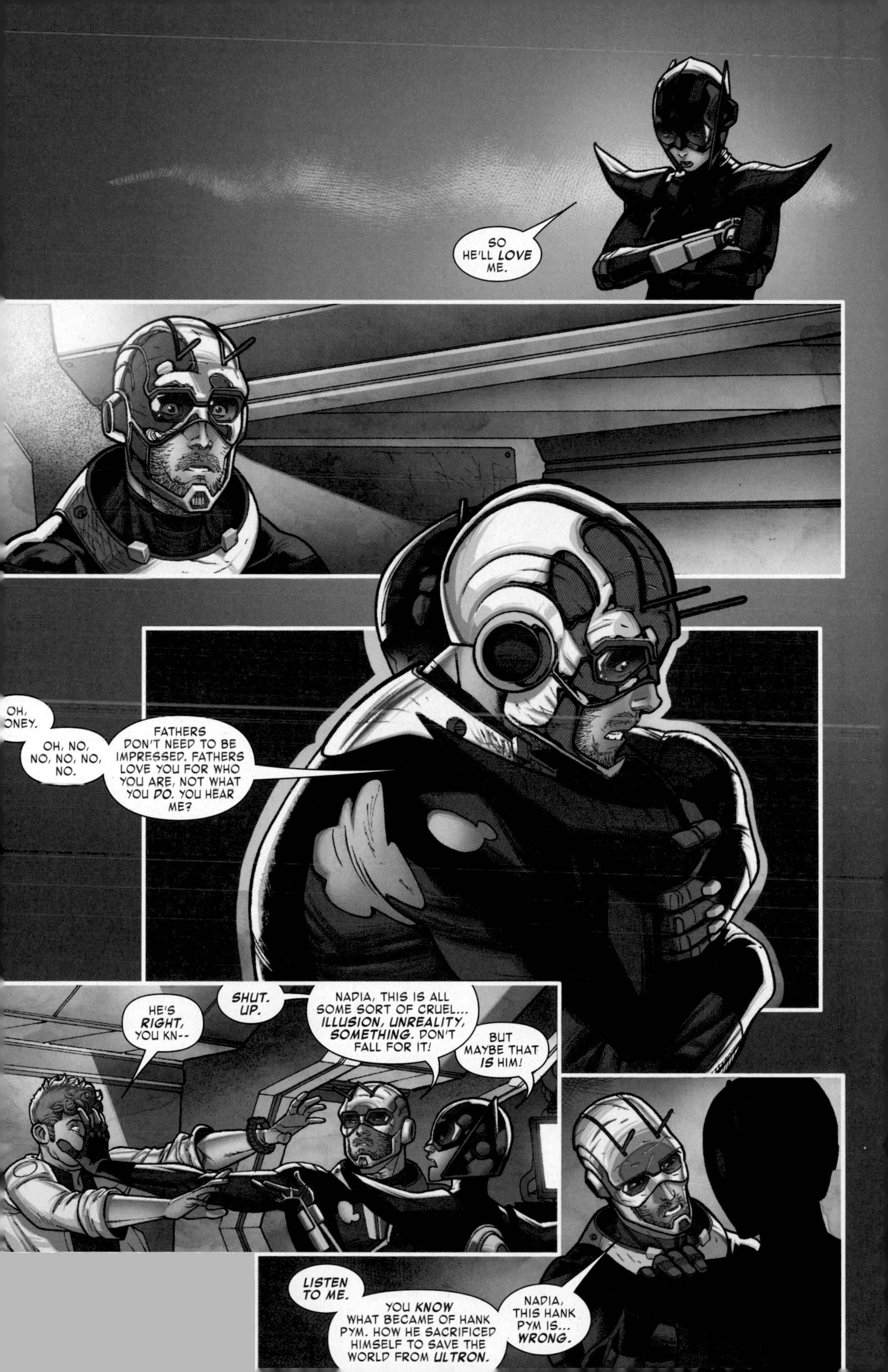
SO HE'LL ***LOVE*** ME.
OH, ONEY.
OH, NO, NO, NO, NO, NO.
FATHERS DON'T NEED TO BE IMPRESSED. FATHERS LOVE YOU FOR WHO YOU ARE, NOT WHAT YOU *DO*. YOU HEAR ME?
HE'S ***RIGHT***, YOU KN--
SHUT. UP.
NADIA, THIS IS ALL SOME SORT OF CRUEL... ***ILLUSION, UNREALITY, SOMETHING.*** DON'T FALL FOR IT!
BUT MAYBE THAT ***IS*** HIM!
LISTEN TO ME.
YOU ***KNOW*** WHAT BECAME OF HANK PYM. HOW HE SACRIFICED HIMSELF TO SAVE THE WORLD FROM **ULTRON**.
NADIA, THIS HANK PYM IS... ***WRONG.***

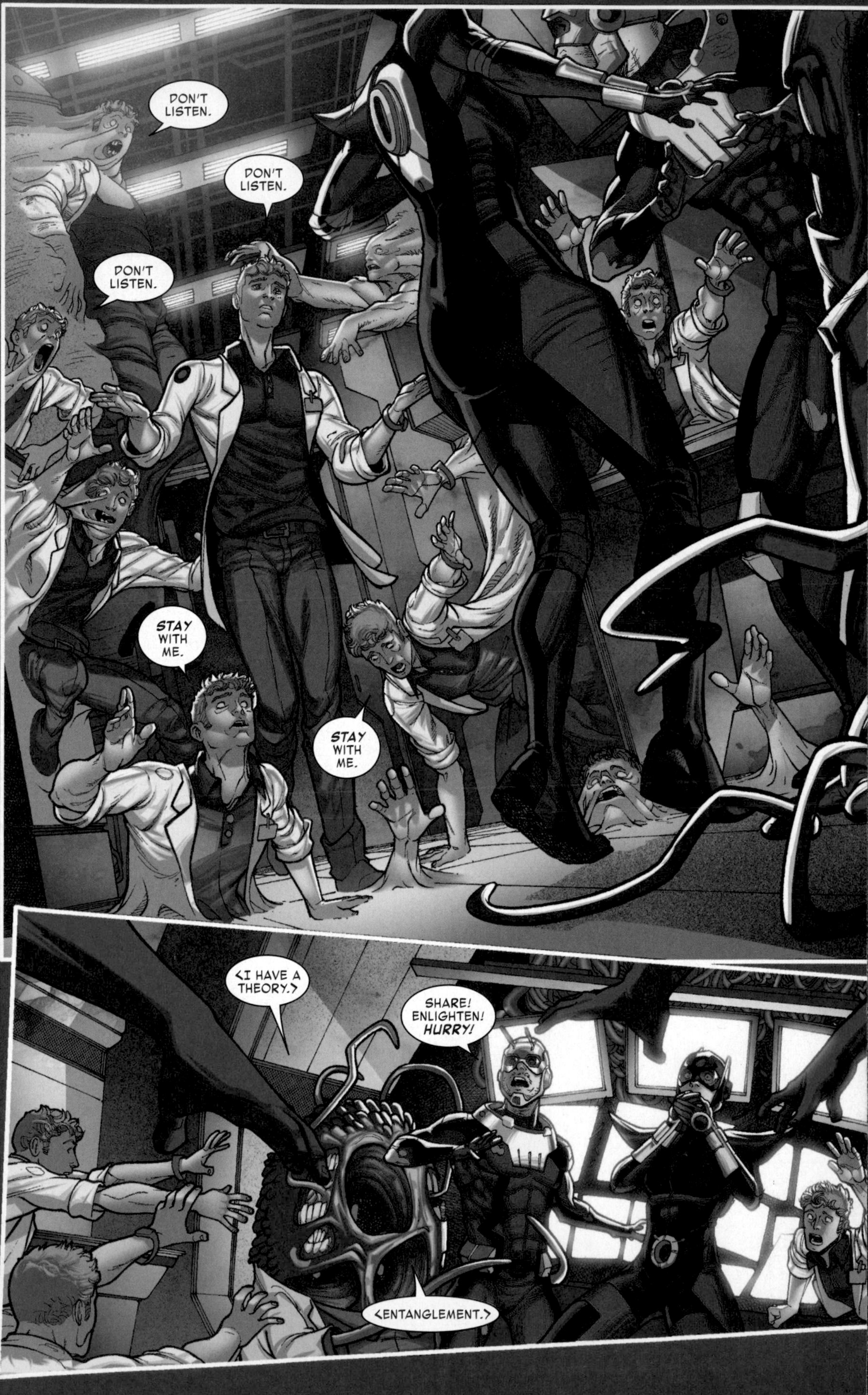
DON'T LISTEN.
DON'T LISTEN.
DON'T LISTEN.
STAY WITH ME.
STAY WITH ME.
<I HAVE A THEORY.>
SHARE! ENLIGHTEN! HURRY!
<ENTANGLEMENT.>

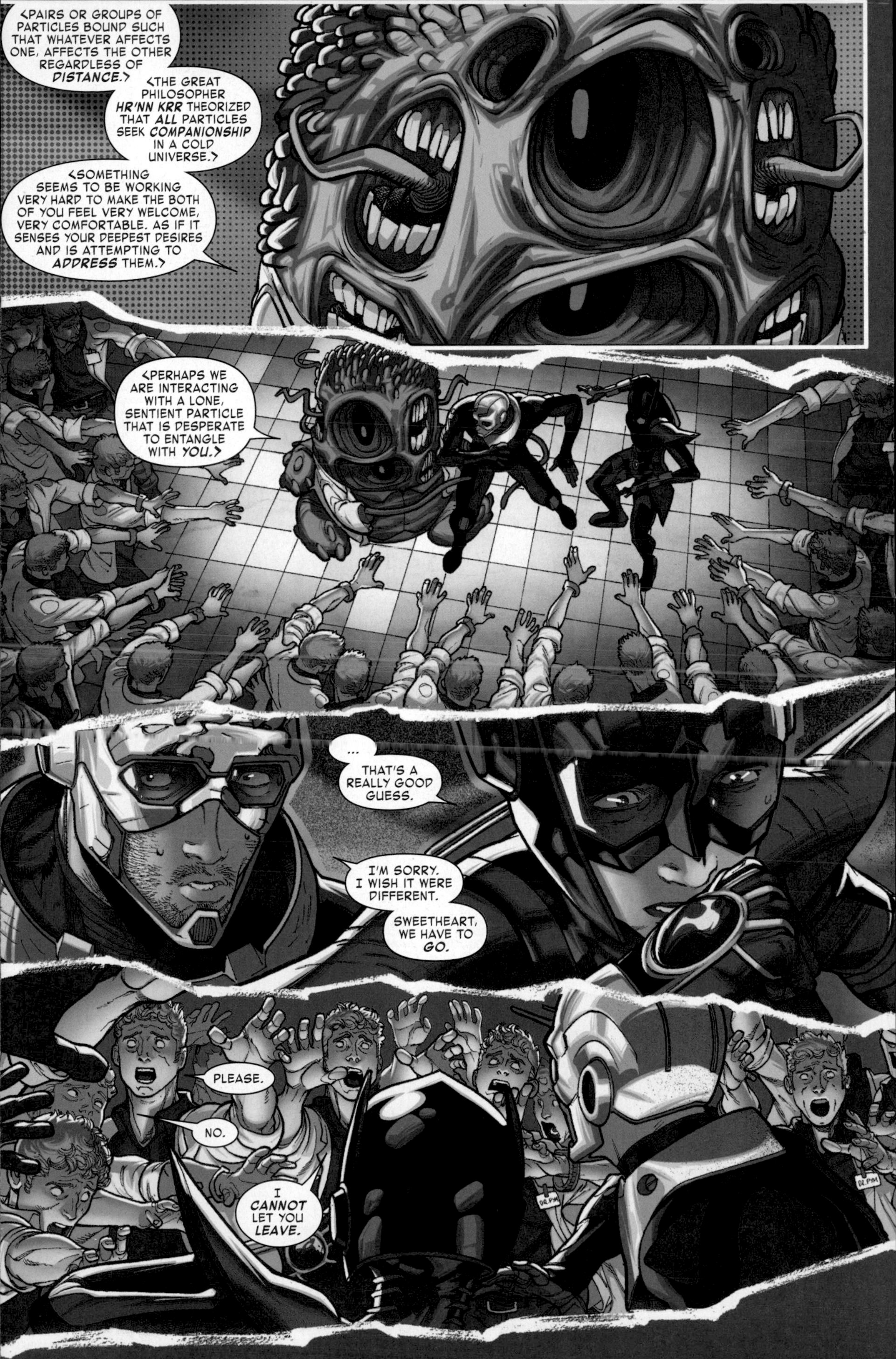
<PAIRS OR GROUPS OF PARTICLES BOUND SUCH THAT WHATEVER AFFECTS ONE, AFFECTS THE OTHER REGARDLESS OF DISTANCE.>
<THE GREAT PHILOSOPHER HR'NN KRR THEORIZED THAT ALL PARTICLES SEEK COMPANIONSHIP IN A COLD UNIVERSE.>
<SOMETHING SEEMS TO BE WORKING VERY HARD TO MAKE THE BOTH OF YOU FEEL VERY WELCOME, VERY COMFORTABLE. AS IF IT SENSES YOUR DEEPEST DESIRES AND IS ATTEMPTING TO ADDRESS THEM.>
<PERHAPS WE ARE INTERACTING WITH A LONE, SENTIENT PARTICLE THAT IS DESPERATE TO ENTANGLE WITH YOU.>
...
THAT'S A REALLY GOOD GUESS.
I'M SORRY. I WISH IT WERE DIFFERENT.
SWEETHEART, WE HAVE TO GO.
PLEASE.
NO.
I CANNOT LET YOU LEAVE.

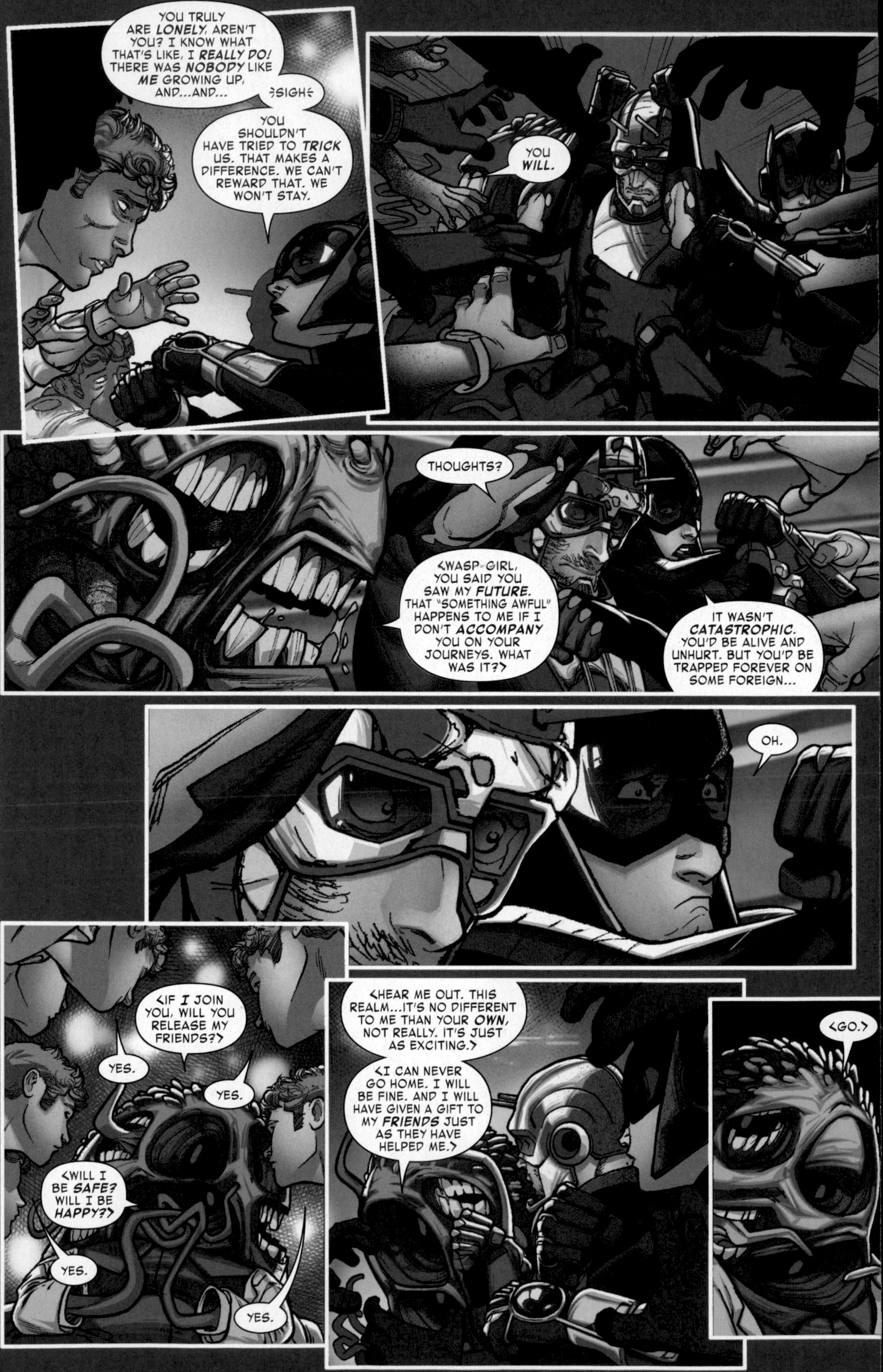
YOU TRULY ARE LONELY, AREN'T YOU? I KNOW WHAT THAT'S LIKE, I REALLY DO! THERE WAS NOBODY LIKE ME GROWING UP, AND...AND...
SIGH
YOU SHOULDN'T HAVE TRIED TO TRICK US. THAT MAKES A DIFFERENCE. WE CAN'T REWARD THAT. WE WON'T STAY.
YOU WILL.
THOUGHTS?
<WASP-GIRL, YOU SAID YOU SAW MY FUTURE. THAT "SOMETHING AWFUL" HAPPENS TO ME IF I DON'T ACCOMPANY YOU ON YOUR JOURNEYS. WHAT WAS IT?>
IT WASN'T CATASTROPHIC. YOU'D BE ALIVE AND UNHURT. BUT YOU'D BE TRAPPED FOREVER ON SOME FOREIGN...
OH.
<IF I JOIN YOU, WILL YOU RELEASE MY FRIENDS?>
YES.
YES.
<WILL I BE SAFE? WILL I BE HAPPY?>
YES.
YES.
<HEAR ME OUT. THIS REALM...IT'S NO DIFFERENT TO ME THAN YOUR OWN, NOT REALLY. IT'S JUST AS EXCITING.>
<I CAN NEVER GO HOME. I WILL BE FINE. AND I WILL HAVE GIVEN A GIFT TO MY FRIENDS JUST AS THEY HAVE HELPED ME.>
<GO.>

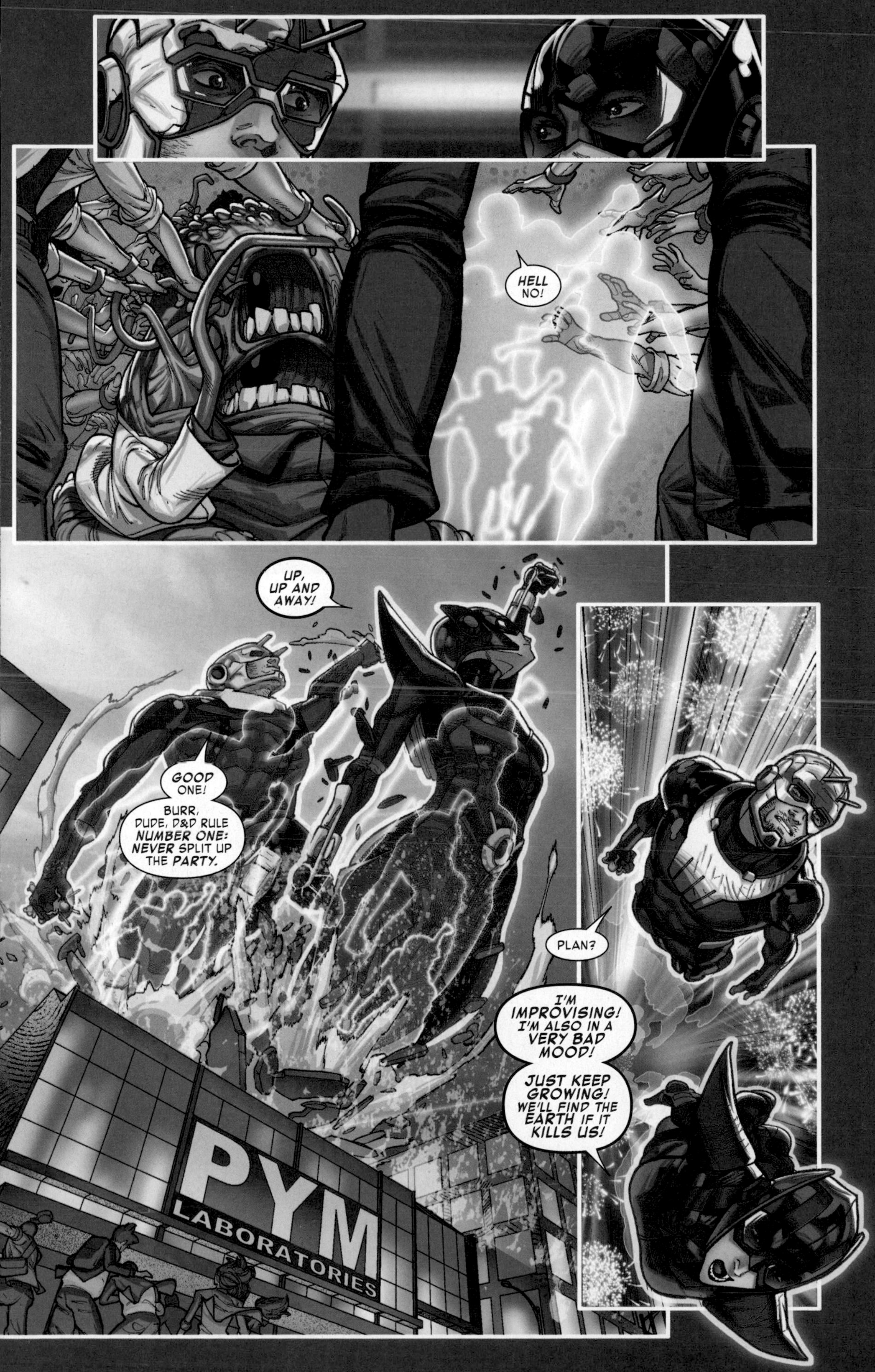
HELL NO!
UP, UP AND AWAY!
GOOD ONE!
BURR, DUDE, D&D RULE NUMBER ONE: NEVER SPLIT UP THE PARTY.
PYM LABORATORIES
PLAN?
I'M IMPROVISING! I'M ALSO IN A VERY BAD MOOD!
JUST KEEP GROWING! WE'LL FIND THE EARTH IF IT KILLS US!

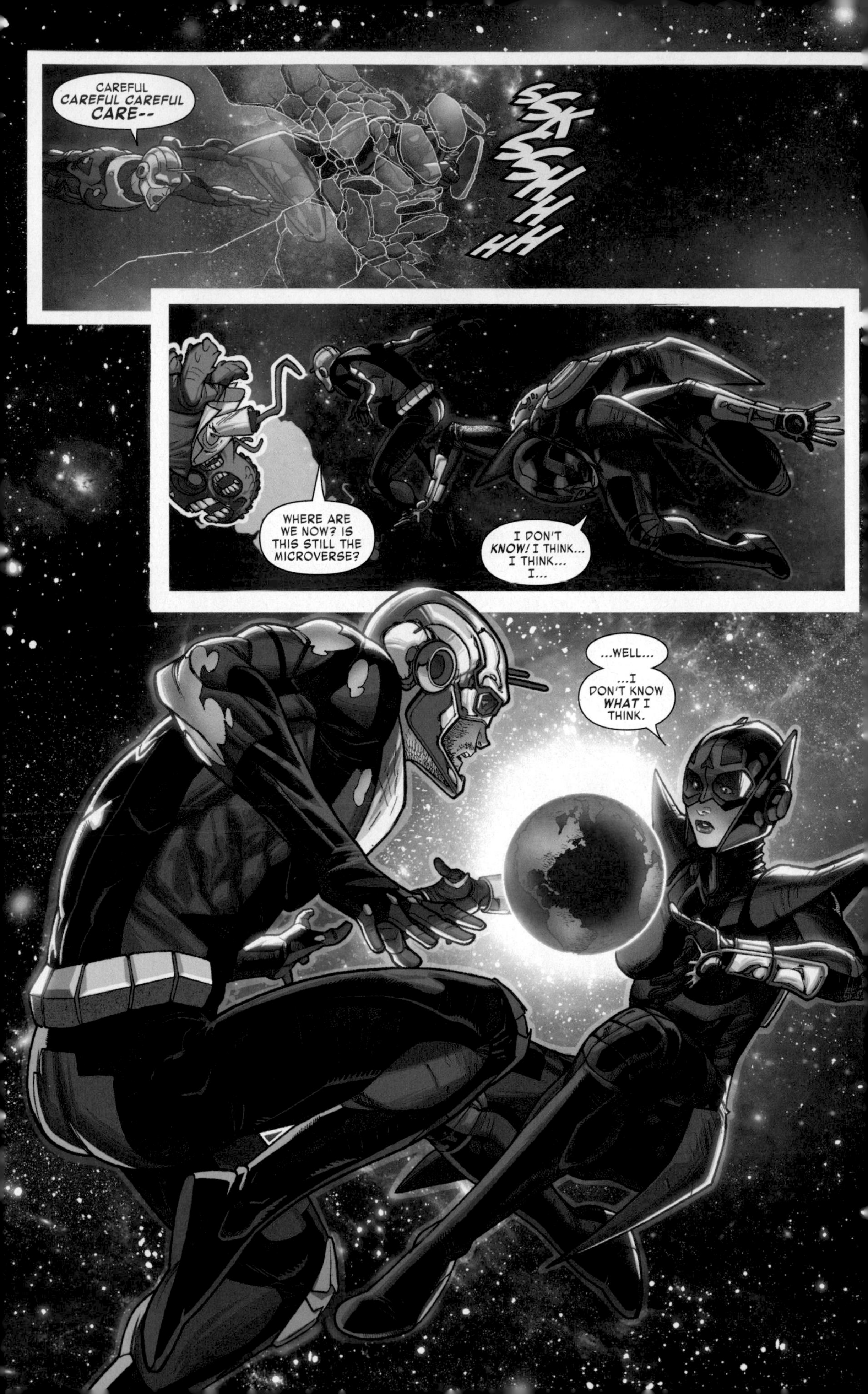
CAREFUL CAREFUL CAREFUL CARE--
SSKSSHHHH
WHERE ARE WE NOW? IS THIS STILL THE MICROVERSE?
I DON'T KNOW! I THINK... I THINK... I...
...WELL...
...I DON'T KNOW WHAT I THINK.

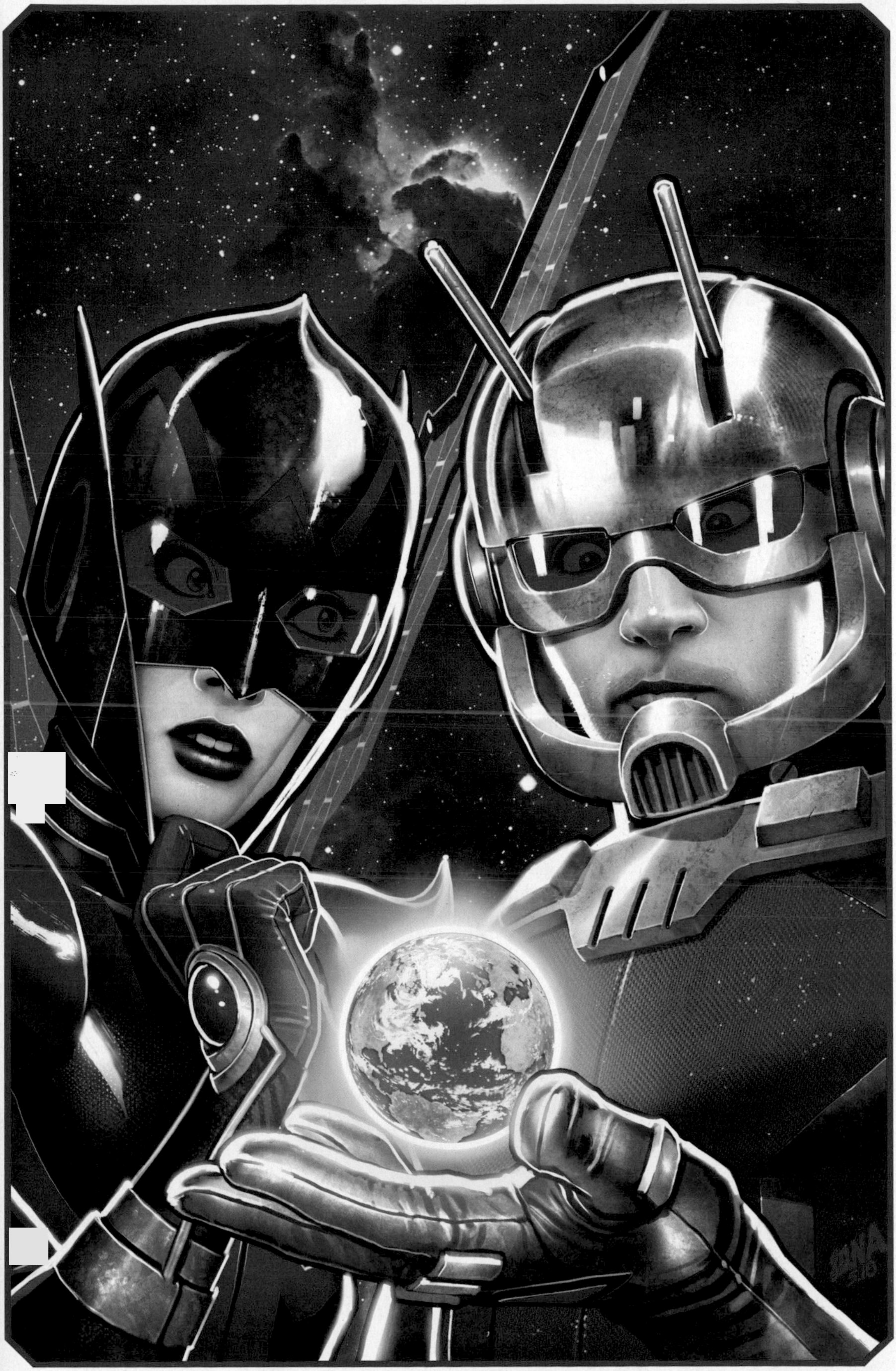

ANT-MAN AND THE WASP #5

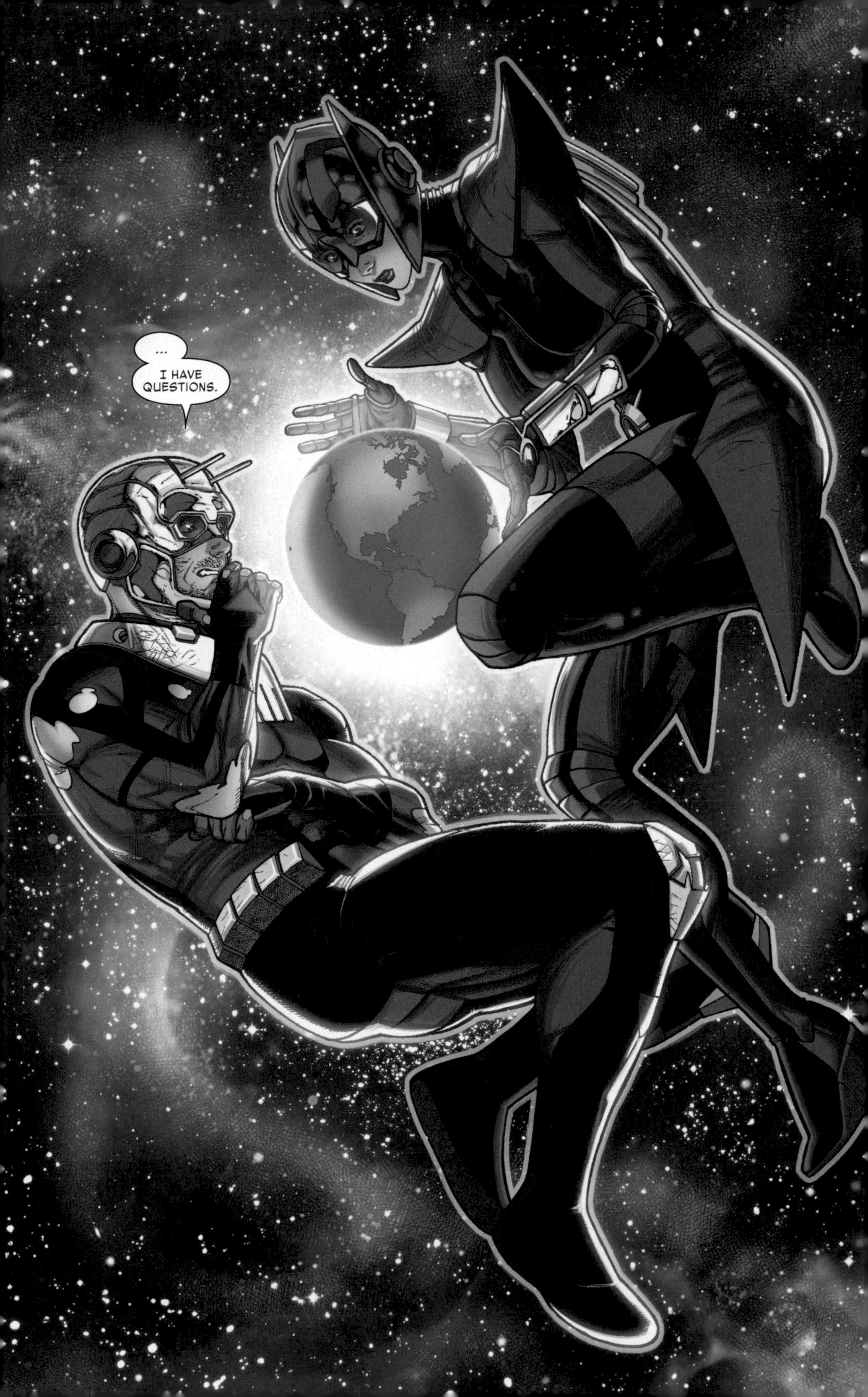
...
I HAVE QUESTIONS.

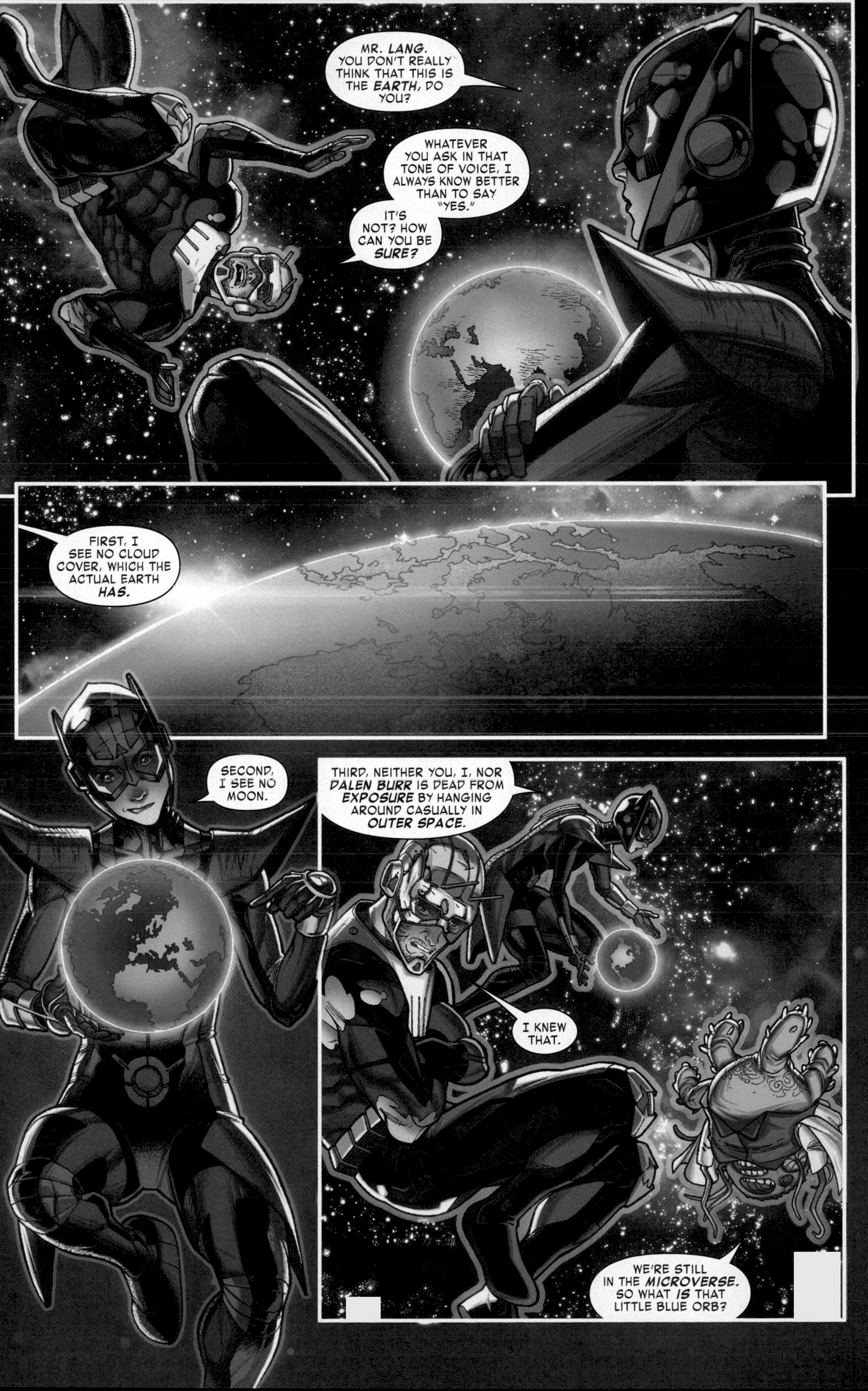
MR. LANG. YOU DON'T REALLY THINK THAT THIS IS THE EARTH, DO YOU?
WHATEVER YOU ASK IN THAT TONE OF VOICE, I ALWAYS KNOW BETTER THAN TO SAY "YES."
IT'S NOT? HOW CAN YOU BE SURE?
FIRST, I SEE NO CLOUD COVER, WHICH THE ACTUAL EARTH HAS.
SECOND, I SEE NO MOON.
THIRD, NEITHER YOU, I, NOR DALEN BURR IS DEAD FROM EXPOSURE BY HANGING AROUND CASUALLY IN OUTER SPACE.
I KNEW THAT.
WE'RE STILL IN THE MICROVERSE. SO WHAT IS THAT LITTLE BLUE ORB?

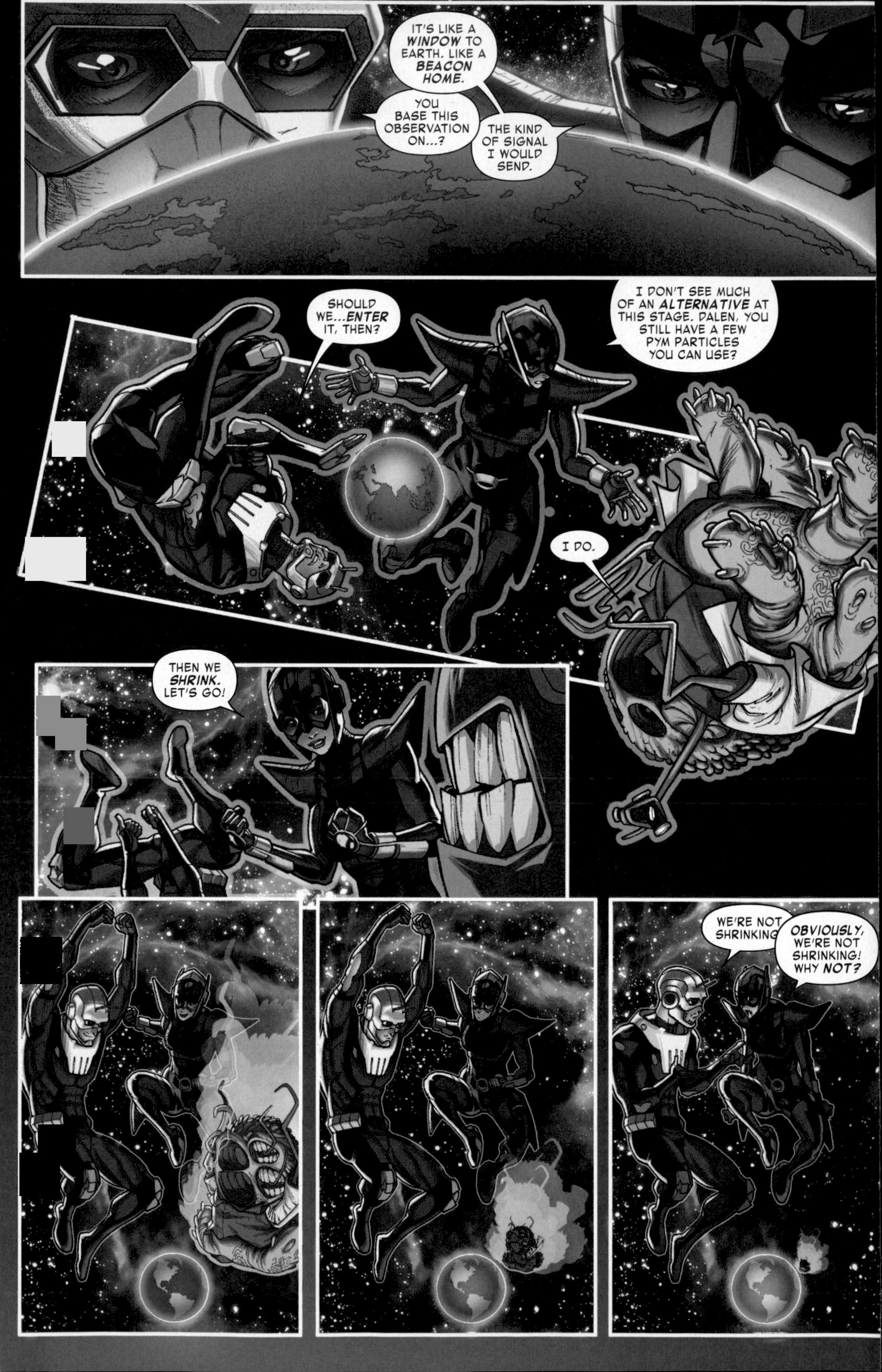
IT'S LIKE A WINDOW TO EARTH. LIKE A BEACON HOME.
YOU BASE THIS OBSERVATION ON...?
THE KIND OF SIGNAL I WOULD SEND.
SHOULD WE...ENTER IT, THEN?
I DON'T SEE MUCH OF AN ALTERNATIVE AT THIS STAGE. DALEN, YOU STILL HAVE A FEW PYM PARTICLES YOU CAN USE?
I DO.
THEN WE SHRINK. LET'S GO!
WE'RE NOT SHRINKING
OBVIOUSLY, WE'RE NOT SHRINKING! WHY NOT?

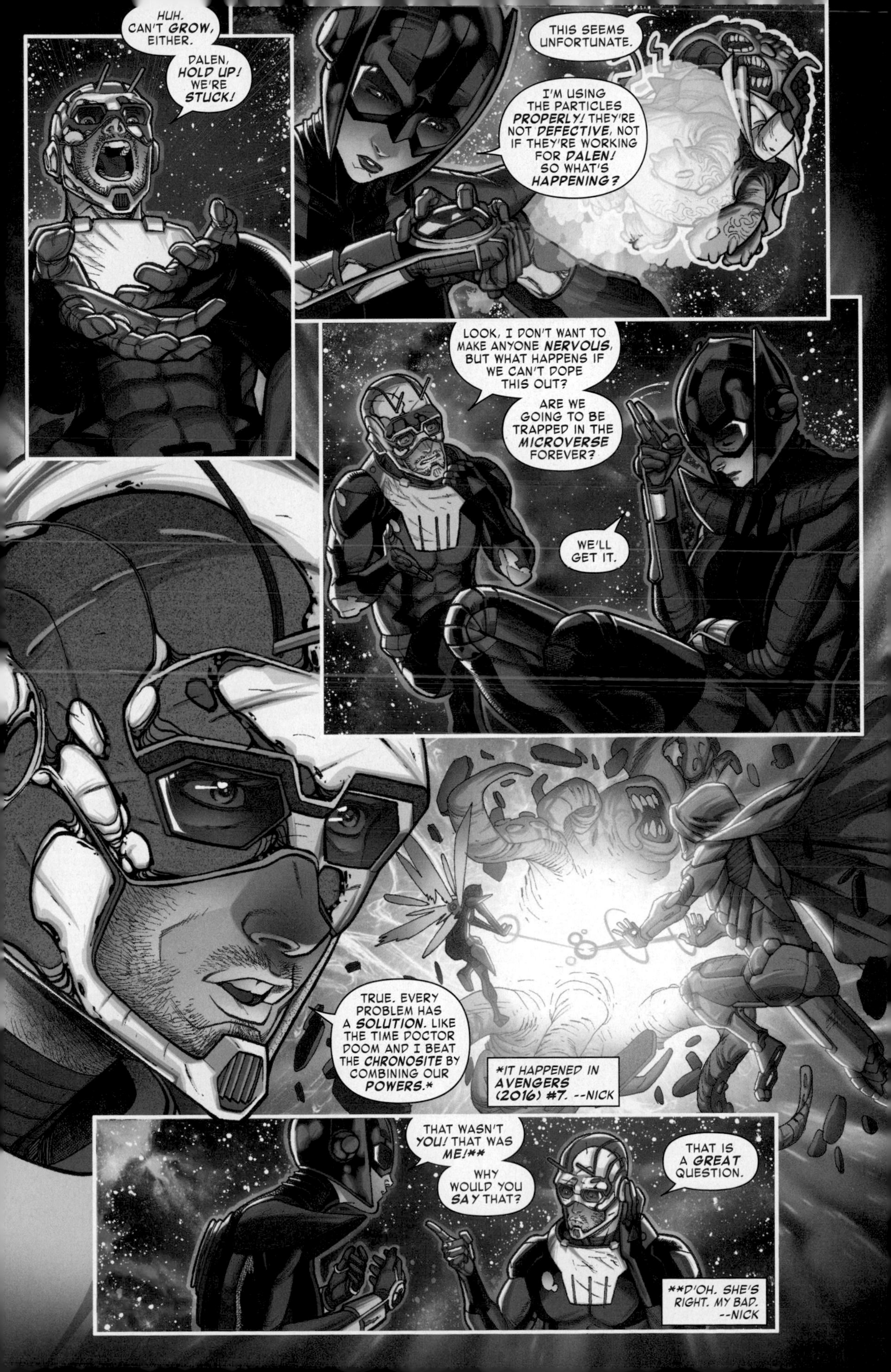
HUH. CAN'T GROW, EITHER.
DALEN, HOLD UP! WE'RE STUCK!
THIS SEEMS UNFORTUNATE.
I'M USING THE PARTICLES PROPERLY! THEY'RE NOT DEFECTIVE, NOT IF THEY'RE WORKING FOR DALEN! SO WHAT'S HAPPENING?
LOOK, I DON'T WANT TO MAKE ANYONE NERVOUS, BUT WHAT HAPPENS IF WE CAN'T DOPE THIS OUT?
ARE WE GOING TO BE TRAPPED IN THE MICROVERSE FOREVER?
WE'LL GET IT.
TRUE. EVERY PROBLEM HAS A SOLUTION. LIKE THE TIME DOCTOR DOOM AND I BEAT THE CHRONOSITE BY COMBINING OUR POWERS.*
*IT HAPPENED IN AVENGERS (2016) #7. --NICK
THAT WASN'T YOU! THAT WAS ME!**
WHY WOULD YOU SAY THAT?
THAT IS A GREAT QUESTION.
**D'OH. SHE'S RIGHT. MY BAD. --NICK

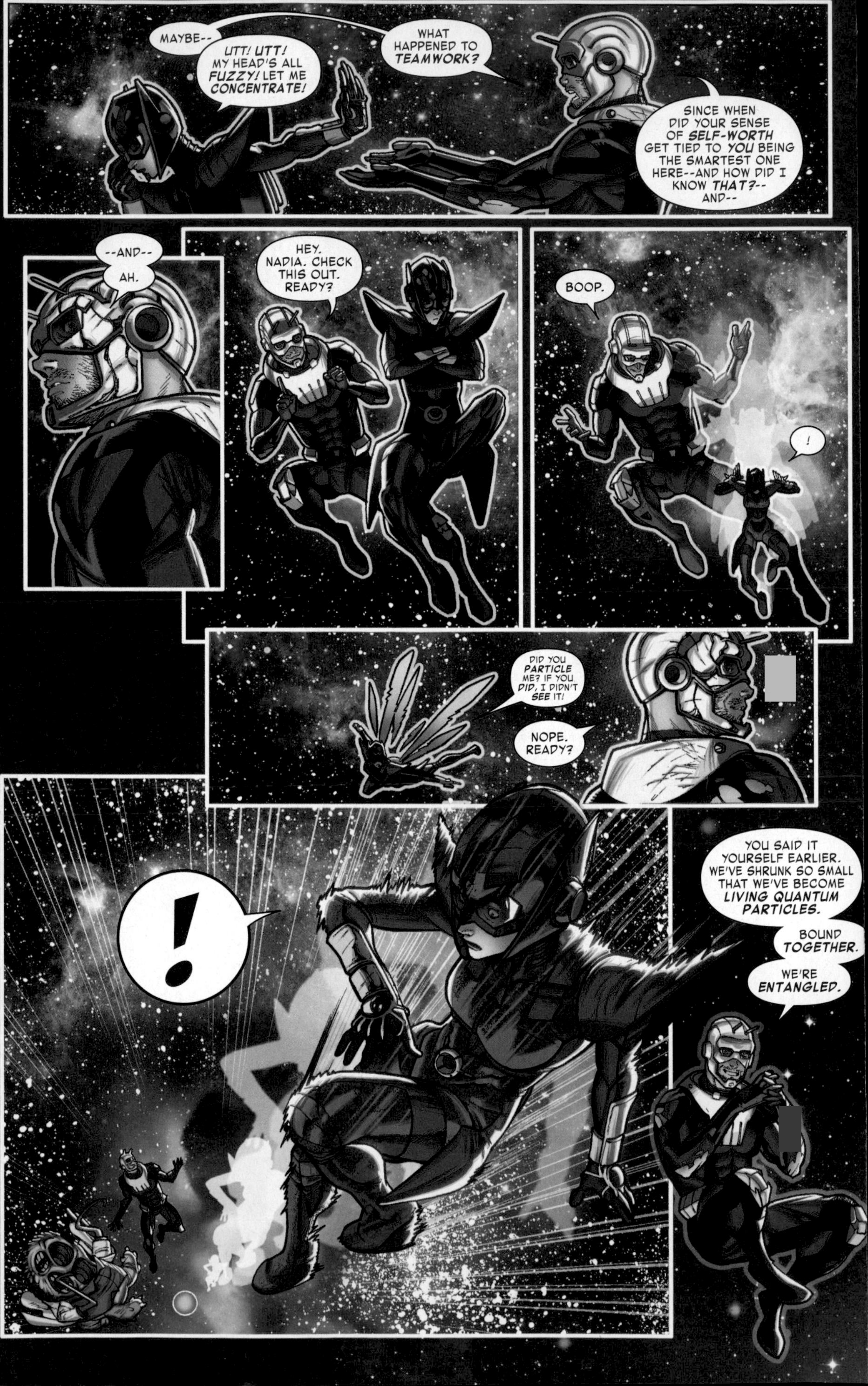
MAYBE--
UTT! UTT! MY HEAD'S ALL FUZZY! LET ME CONCENTRATE!
WHAT HAPPENED TO TEAMWORK?
SINCE WHEN DID YOUR SENSE OF SELF-WORTH GET TIED TO YOU BEING THE SMARTEST ONE HERE--AND HOW DID I KNOW THAT?-- AND--
--AND--
AH.
HEY. NADIA. CHECK THIS OUT. READY?
BOOP.
!
DID YOU PARTICLE ME? IF YOU DID, I DIDN'T SEE IT!
NOPE. READY?
!
YOU SAID IT YOURSELF EARLIER. WE'VE SHRUNK SO SMALL THAT WE'VE BECOME LIVING QUANTUM PARTICLES.
BOUND TOGETHER.
WE'RE ENTANGLED.

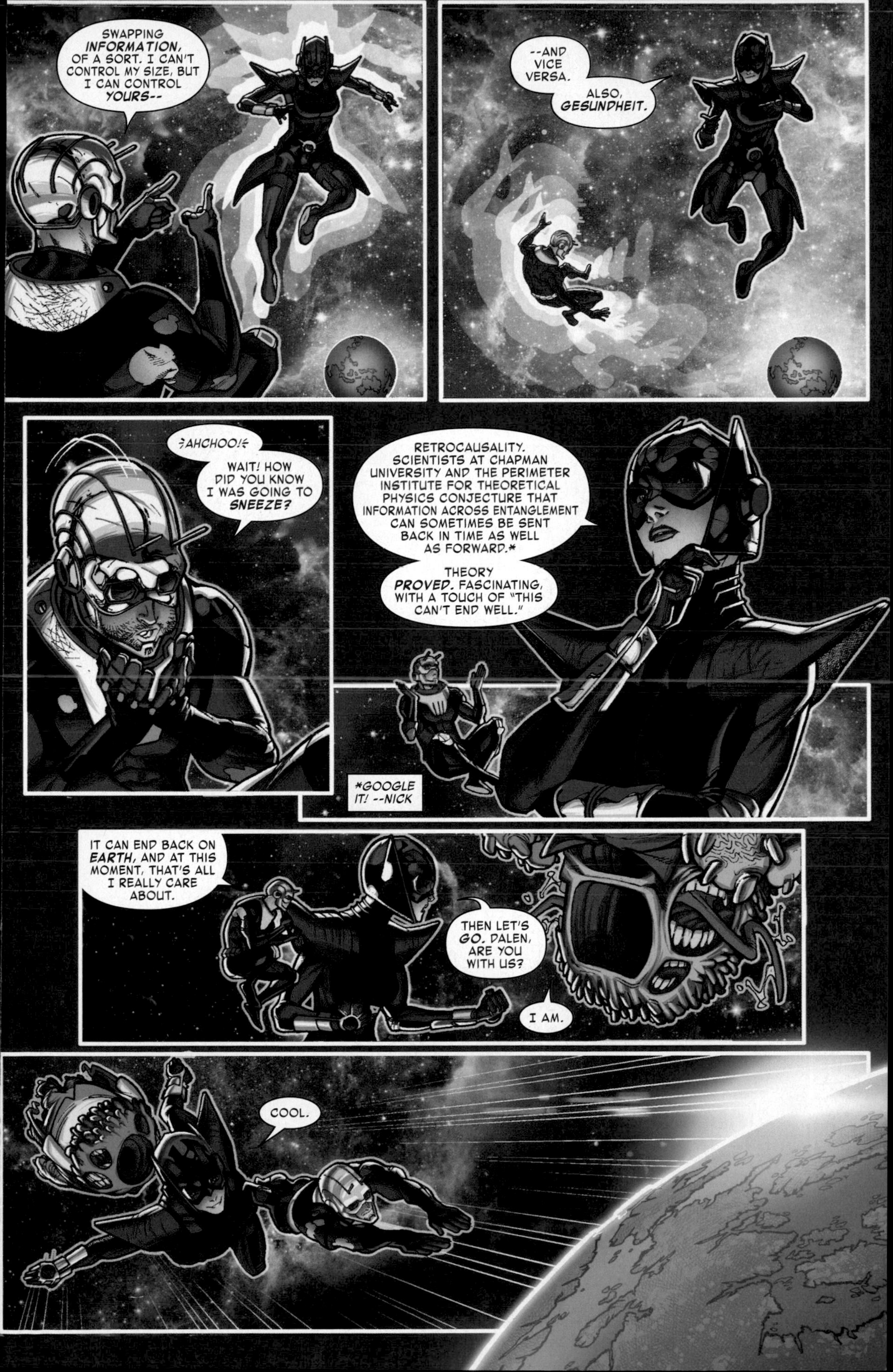
SWAPPING INFORMATION, OF A SORT. I CAN'T CONTROL MY SIZE, BUT I CAN CONTROL YOURS--
--AND VICE VERSA.
ALSO, GESUNDHEIT.
AHCHOO!
WAIT! HOW DID YOU KNOW I WAS GOING TO SNEEZE?
RETROCAUSALITY. SCIENTISTS AT CHAPMAN UNIVERSITY AND THE PERIMETER INSTITUTE FOR THEORETICAL PHYSICS CONJECTURE THAT INFORMATION ACROSS ENTANGLEMENT CAN SOMETIMES BE SENT BACK IN TIME AS WELL AS FORWARD.*
THEORY PROVED. FASCINATING, WITH A TOUCH OF "THIS CAN'T END WELL."
*GOOGLE IT! --NICK
IT CAN END BACK ON EARTH, AND AT THIS MOMENT, THAT'S ALL I REALLY CARE ABOUT.
THEN LET'S GO. DALEN, ARE YOU WITH US?
I AM.
COOL.

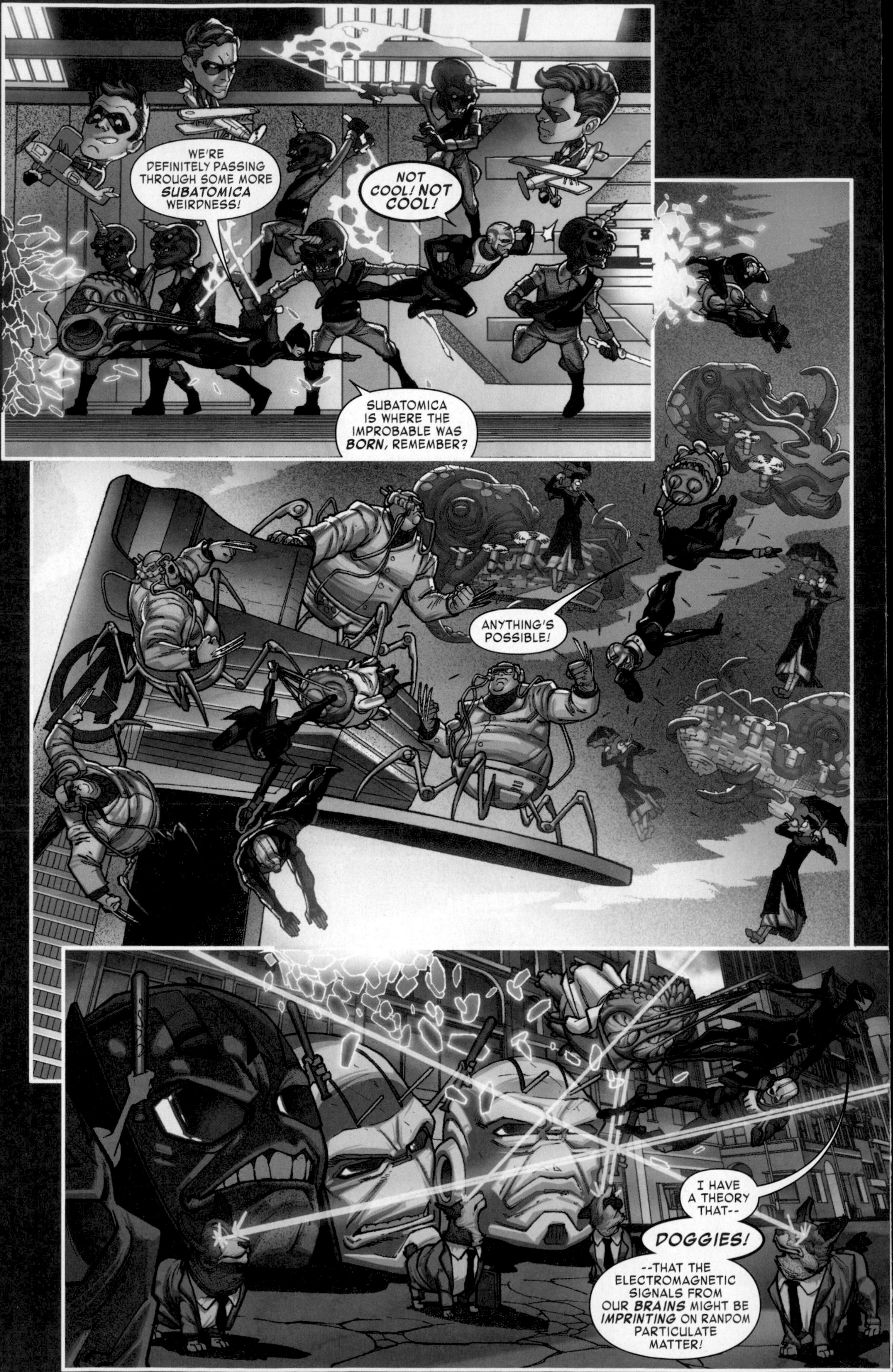

WE'RE DEFINITELY PASSING THROUGH SOME MORE SUBATOMICA WEIRDNESS!
NOT COOL! NOT COOL!
SUBATOMICA IS WHERE THE IMPROBABLE WAS BORN, REMEMBER?
ANYTHING'S POSSIBLE!
I HAVE A THEORY THAT--
DOGGIES!
--THAT THE ELECTROMAGNETIC SIGNALS FROM OUR BRAINS MIGHT BE IMPRINTING ON RANDOM PARTICULATE MATTER!

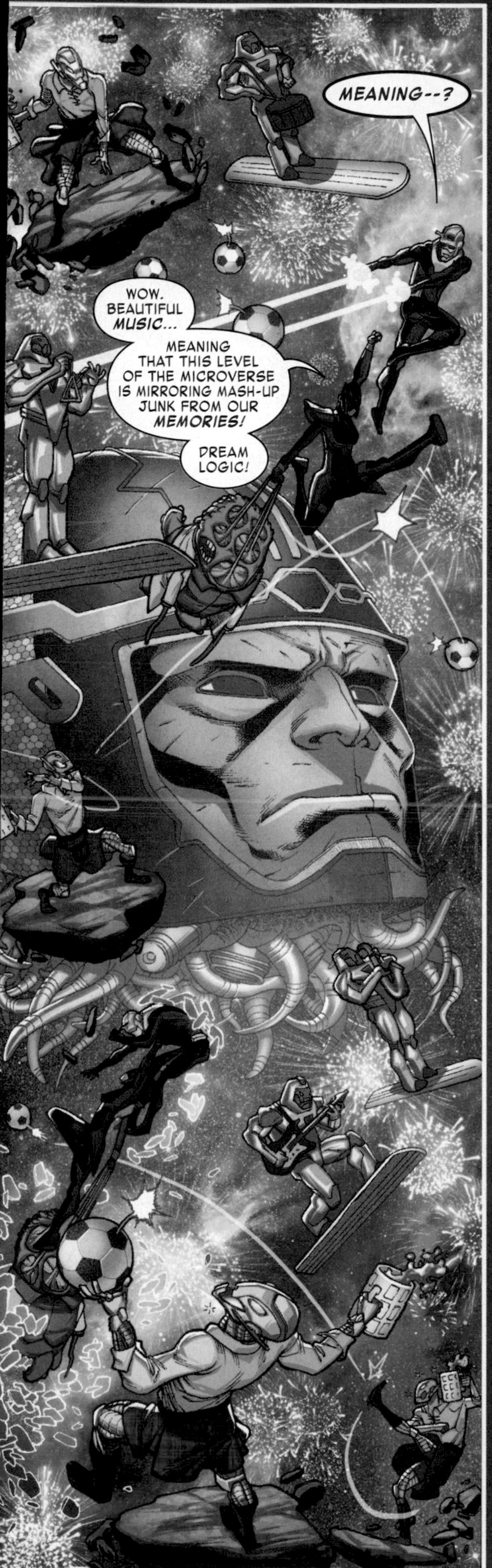
MEANING--?
WOW. BEAUTIFUL MUSIC...
MEANING THAT THIS LEVEL OF THE MICROVERSE IS MIRRORING MASH-UP JUNK FROM OUR MEMORIES!
DREAM LOGIC!

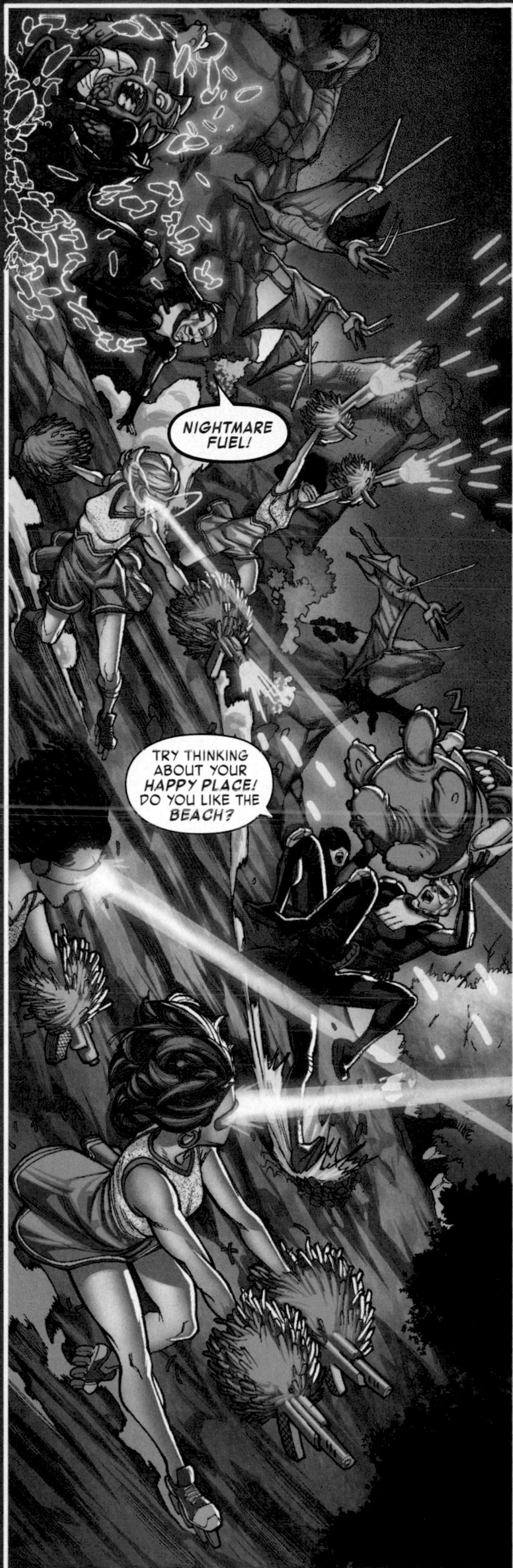
NIGHTMARE FUEL!
TRY THINKING ABOUT YOUR HAPPY PLACE! DO YOU LIKE THE BEACH?

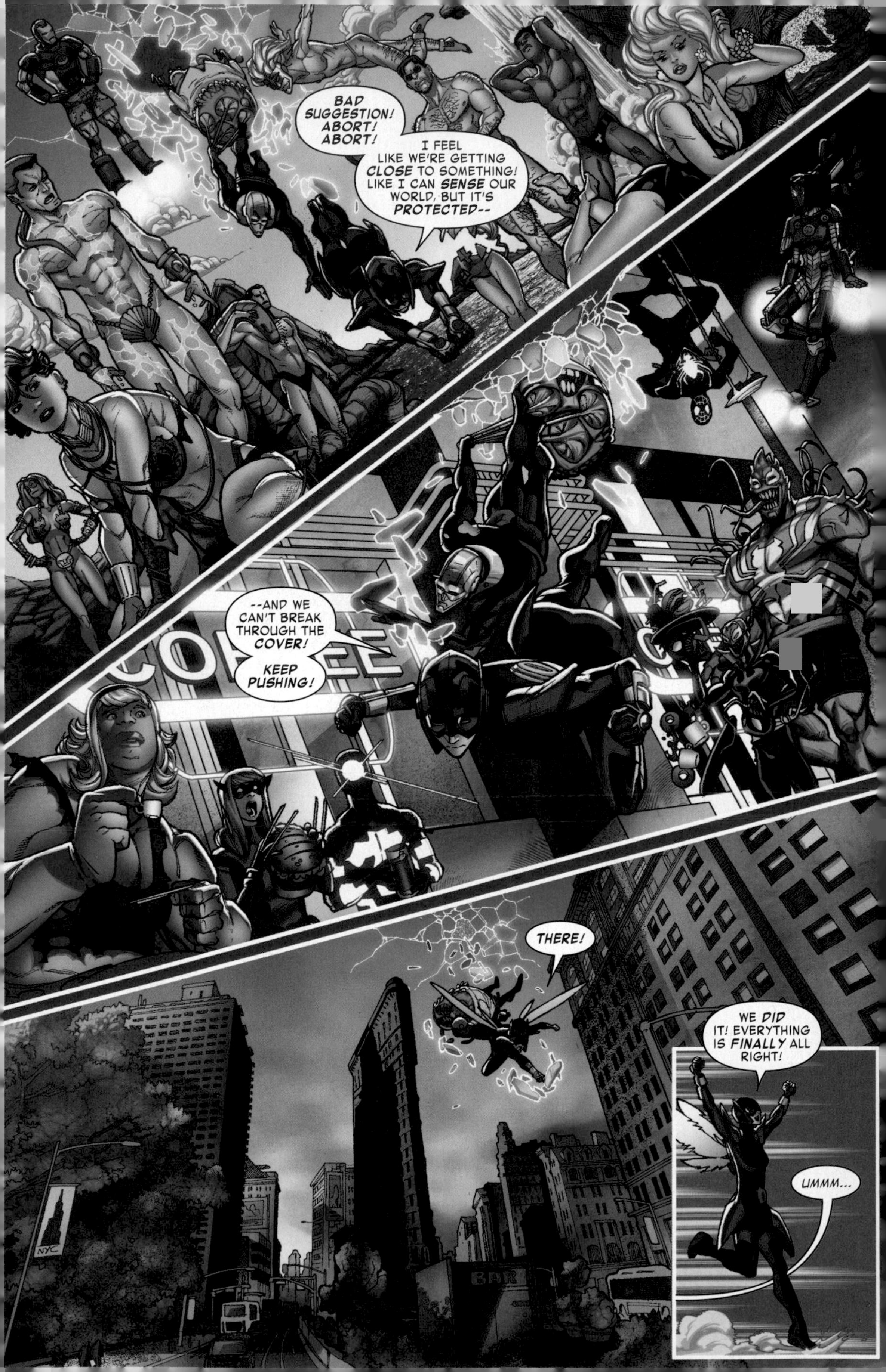
BAD SUGGESTION! ABORT! ABORT!
I FEEL LIKE WE'RE GETTING CLOSE TO SOMETHING! LIKE I CAN SENSE OUR WORLD, BUT IT'S PROTECTED--
--AND WE CAN'T BREAK THROUGH THE COVER!
KEEP PUSHING!
THERE!
WE DID IT! EVERYTHING IS FINALLY ALL RIGHT!
UMMM...

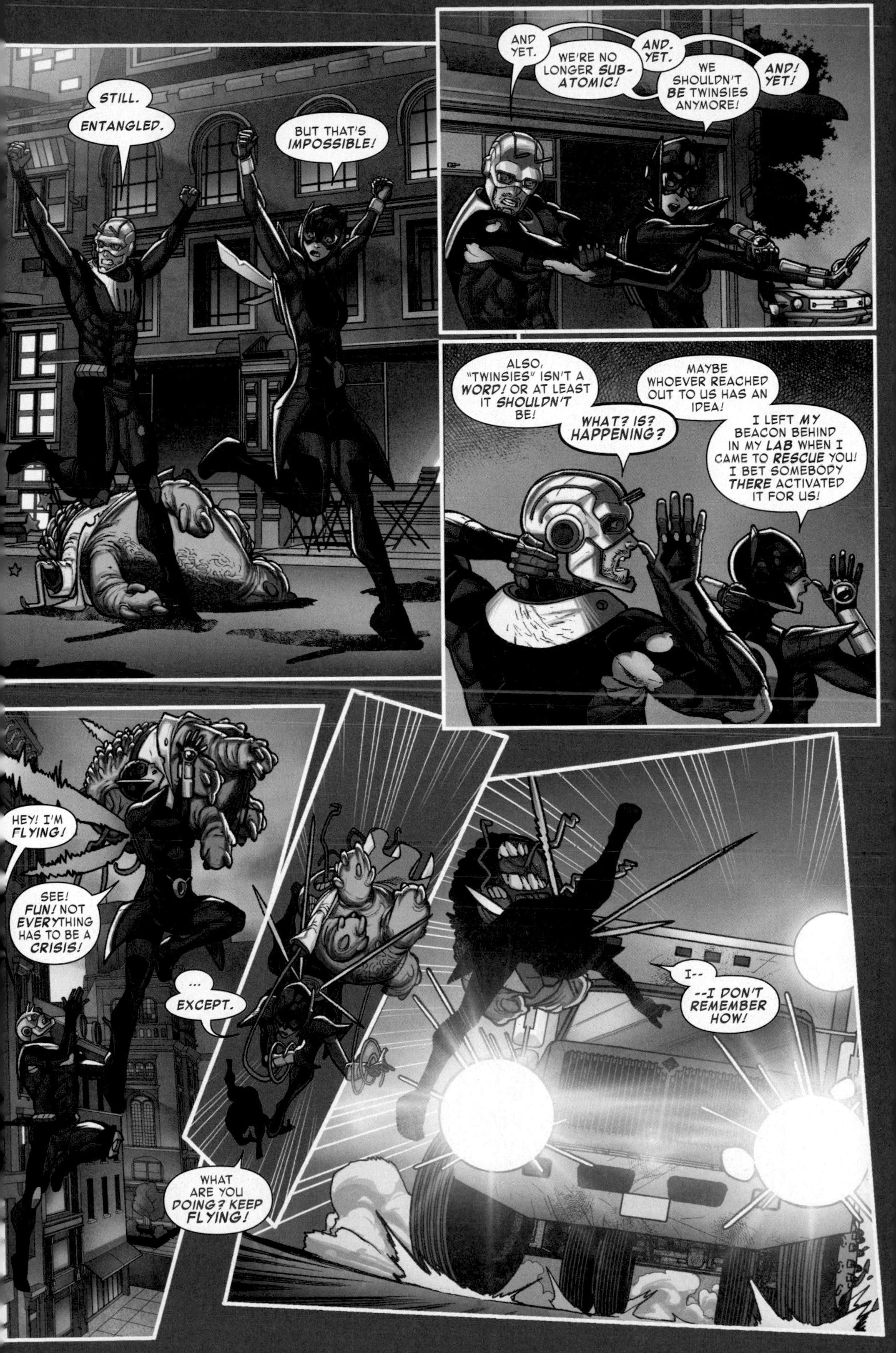
STILL.
ENTANGLED.
BUT THAT'S IMPOSSIBLE!
AND YET.
WE'RE NO LONGER SUB-ATOMIC!
AND. YET.
WE SHOULDN'T BE TWINSIES ANYMORE!
AND! YET!
ALSO, "TWINSIES" ISN'T A WORD! OR AT LEAST IT SHOULDN'T BE!
WHAT? IS? HAPPENING?
MAYBE WHOEVER REACHED OUT TO US HAS AN IDEA!
I LEFT MY BEACON BEHIND IN MY LAB WHEN I CAME TO RESCUE YOU! I BET SOMEBODY THERE ACTIVATED IT FOR US!
HEY! I'M FLYING!
SEE! FUN! NOT EVERYTHING HAS TO BE A CRISIS!
...
EXCEPT.
WHAT ARE YOU DOING? KEEP FLYING!
I--
--I DON'T REMEMBER HOW!

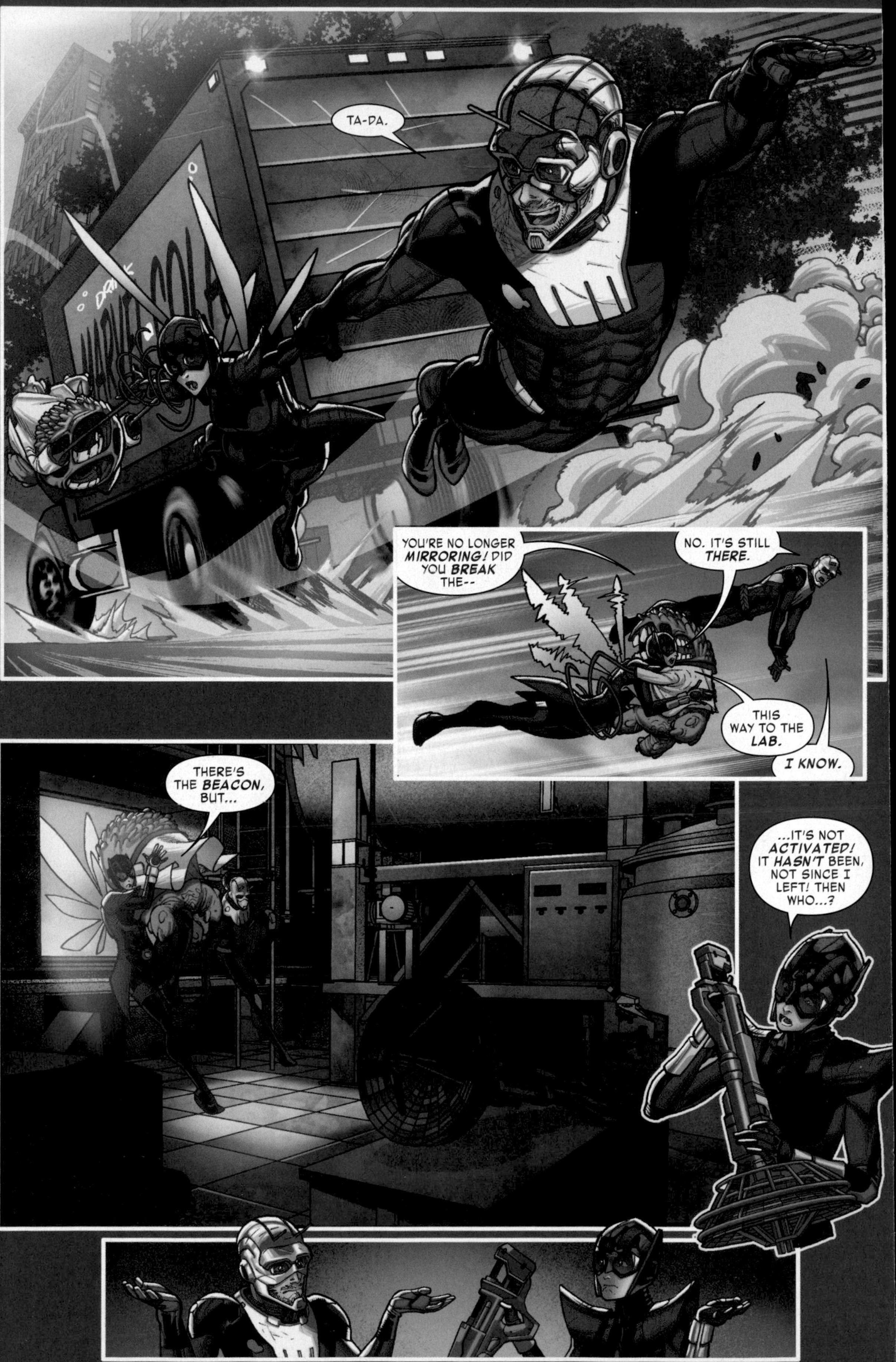
TA-DA.
YOU'RE NO LONGER MIRRORING! DID YOU BREAK THE--
NO. IT'S STILL THERE.
THIS WAY TO THE LAB.
I KNOW.
THERE'S THE BEACON, BUT...
...IT'S NOT ACTIVATED! IT HASN'T BEEN, NOT SINCE I LEFT! THEN WHO...?

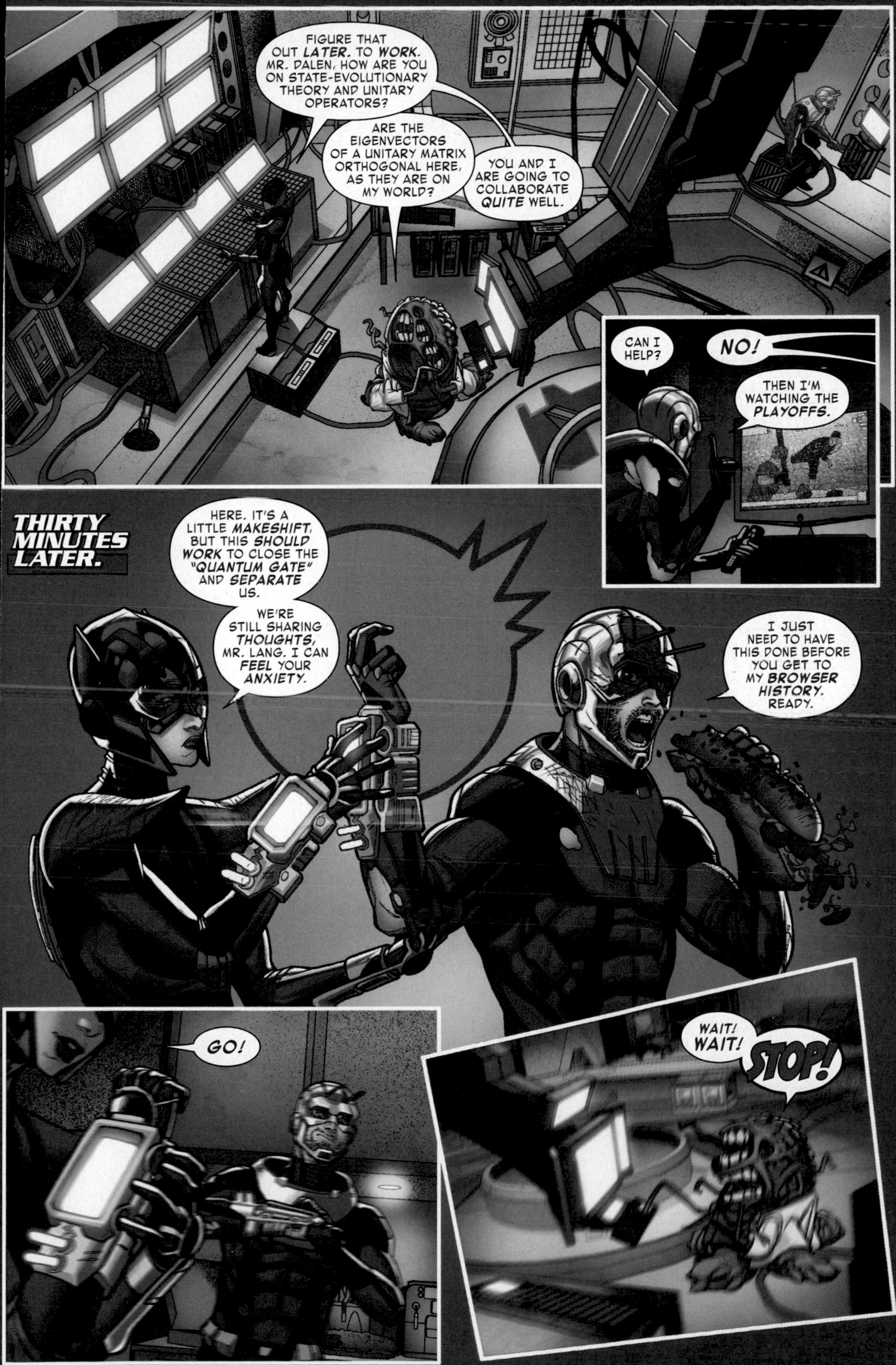
FIGURE THAT OUT LATER. TO WORK. MR. DALEN, HOW ARE YOU ON STATE-EVOLUTIONARY THEORY AND UNITARY OPERATORS?
ARE THE EIGENVECTORS OF A UNITARY MATRIX ORTHOGONAL HERE, AS THEY ARE ON MY WORLD?
YOU AND I ARE GOING TO COLLABORATE QUITE WELL.
CAN I HELP?
NO!
THEN I'M WATCHING THE PLAYOFFS.
THIRTY MINUTES LATER.
HERE. IT'S A LITTLE MAKESHIFT, BUT THIS SHOULD WORK TO CLOSE THE "QUANTUM GATE" AND SEPARATE US.
WE'RE STILL SHARING THOUGHTS, MR. LANG. I CAN FEEL YOUR ANXIETY.
I JUST NEED TO HAVE THIS DONE BEFORE YOU GET TO MY BROWSER HISTORY. READY.
GO!
WAIT! WAIT!
STOP!

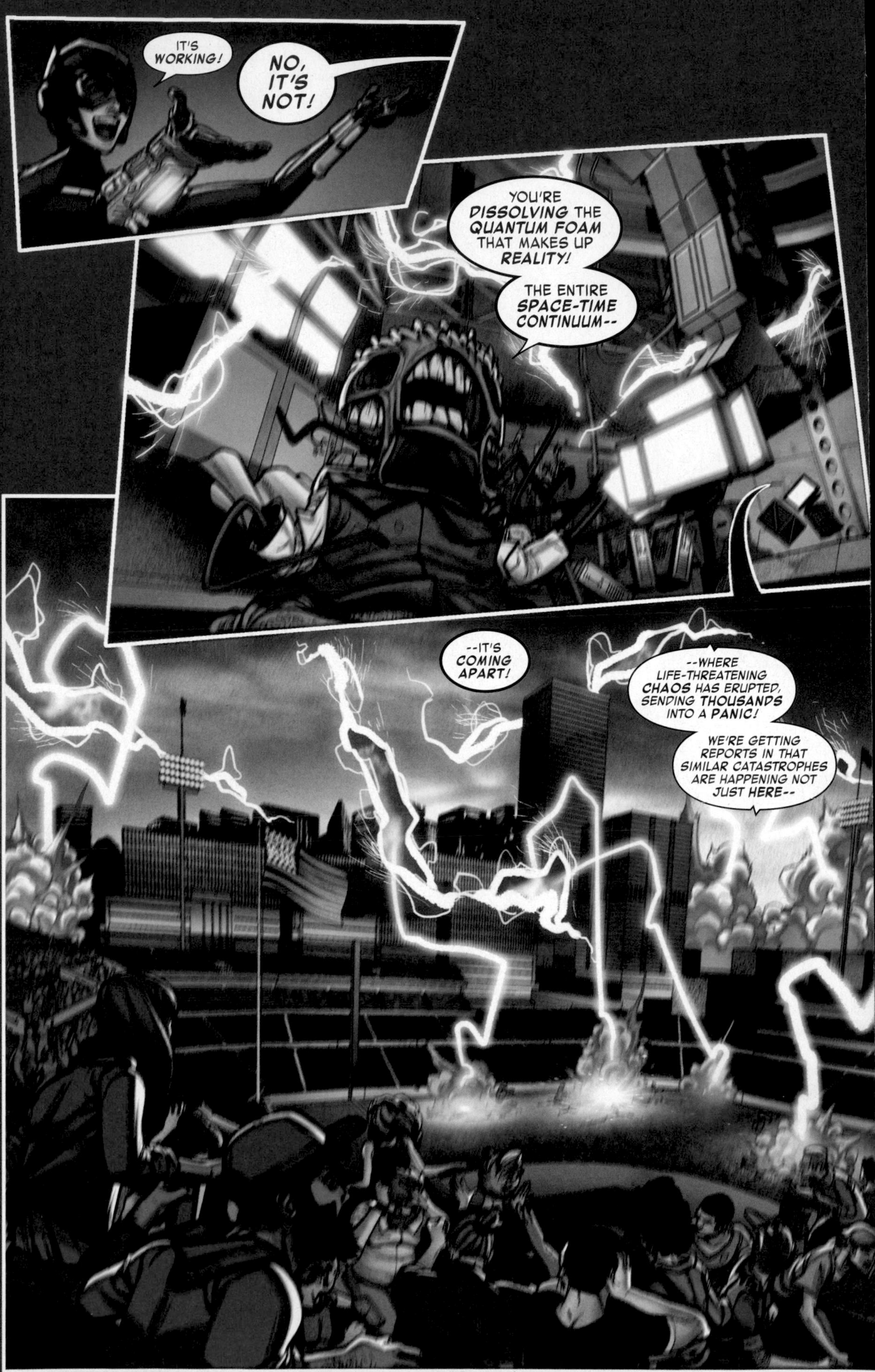
IT'S WORKING!
NO, IT'S NOT!
YOU'RE DISSOLVING THE QUANTUM FOAM THAT MAKES UP REALITY!
THE ENTIRE SPACE-TIME CONTINUUM--
--IT'S COMING APART!
--WHERE LIFE-THREATENING CHAOS HAS ERUPTED, SENDING THOUSANDS INTO A PANIC!
WE'RE GETTING REPORTS IN THAT SIMILAR CATASTROPHES ARE HAPPENING NOT JUST HERE--

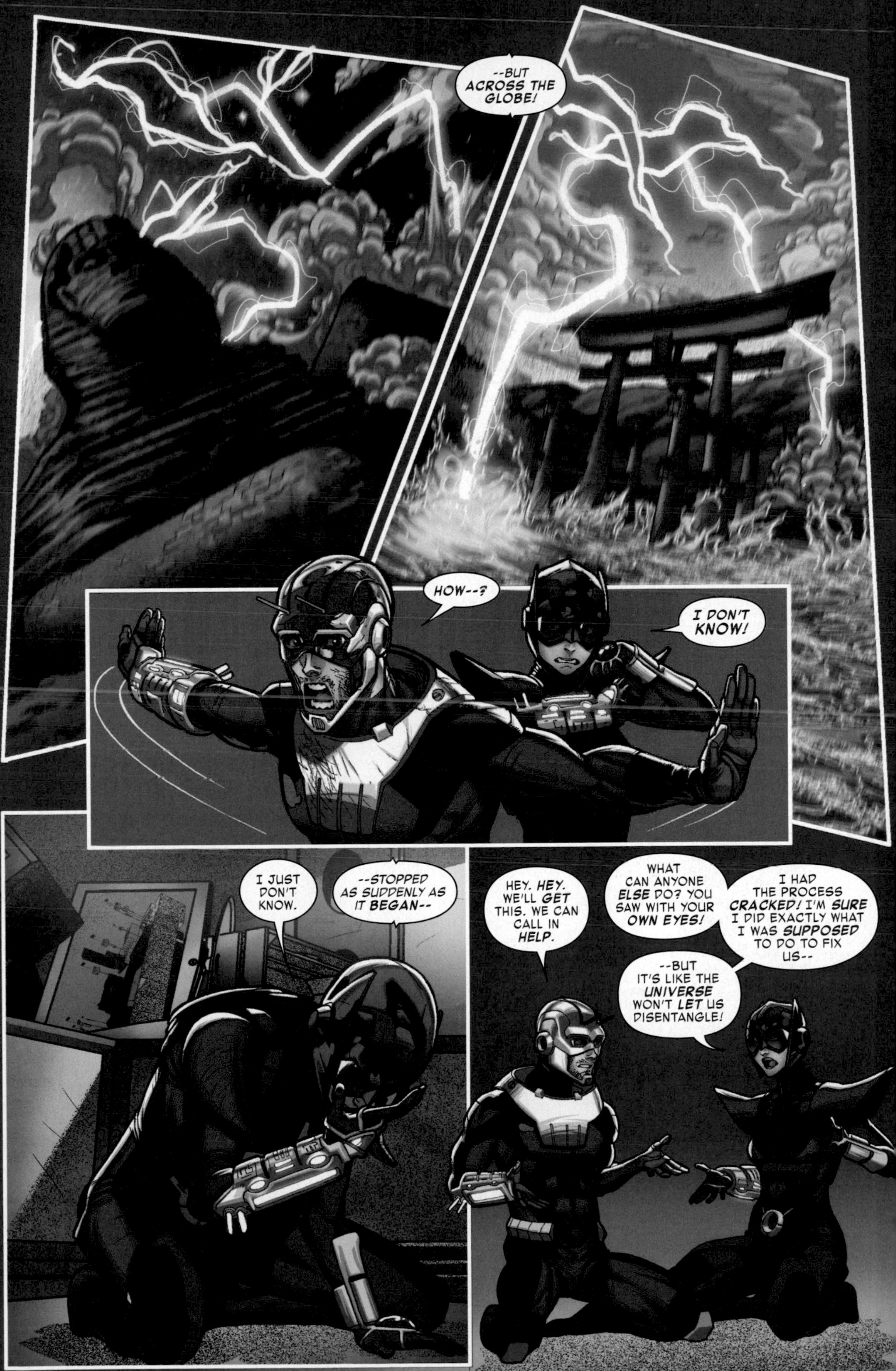
--BUT ACROSS THE GLOBE!
HOW--?
I DON'T KNOW!
I JUST DON'T KNOW.
--STOPPED AS SUDDENLY AS IT BEGAN--
HEY. HEY. WE'LL GET THIS. WE CAN CALL IN HELP.
WHAT CAN ANYONE ELSE DO? YOU SAW WITH YOUR OWN EYES!
I HAD THE PROCESS CRACKED! I'M SURE I DID EXACTLY WHAT I WAS SUPPOSED TO DO TO FIX US--
--BUT IT'S LIKE THE UNIVERSE WON'T LET US DISENTANGLE!

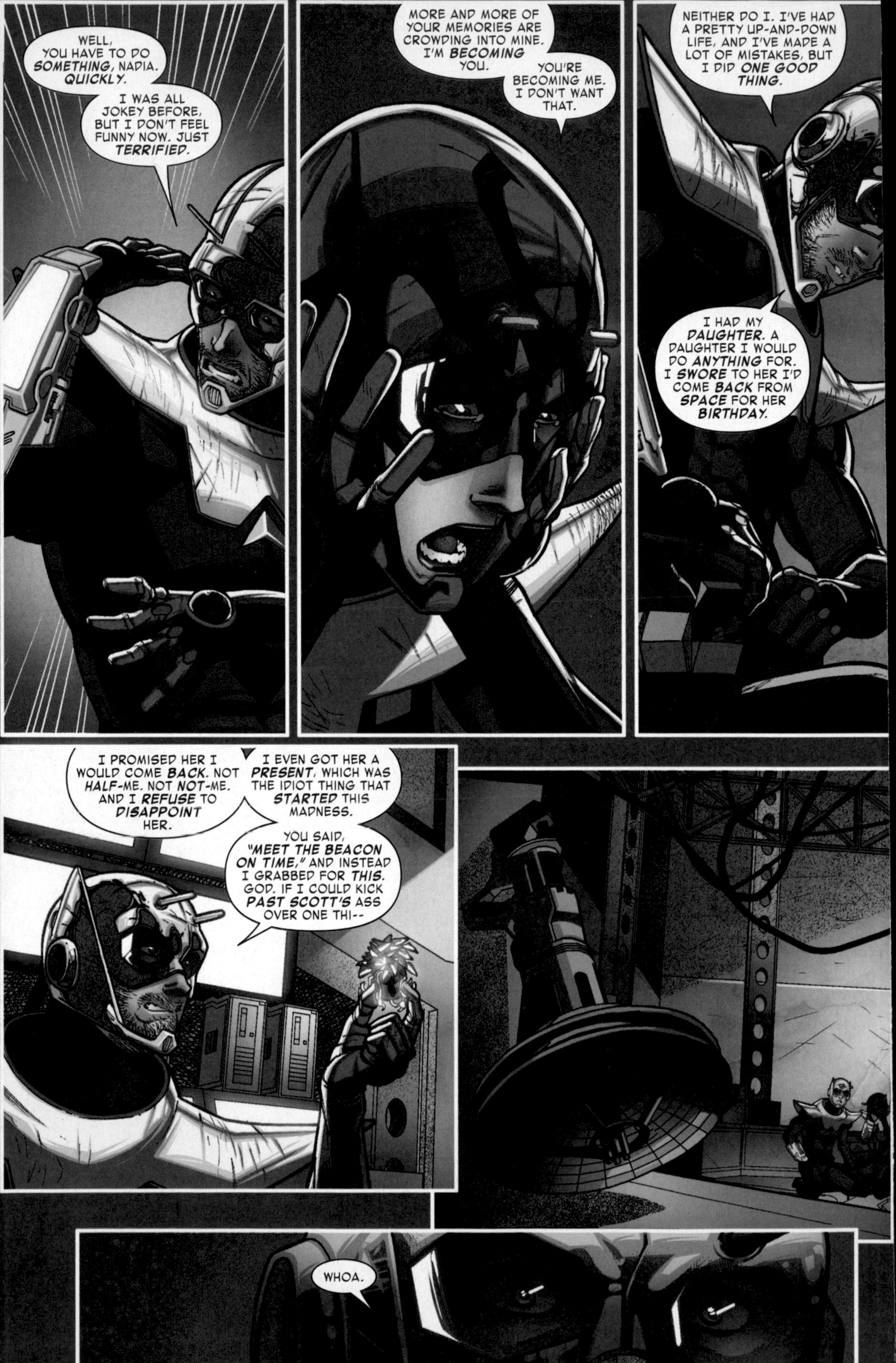
WELL, YOU HAVE TO DO SOMETHING, NADIA. QUICKLY.
I WAS ALL JOKEY BEFORE, BUT I DON'T FEEL FUNNY NOW. JUST TERRIFIED.
MORE AND MORE OF YOUR MEMORIES ARE CROWDING INTO MINE. I'M BECOMING YOU.
YOU'RE BECOMING ME. I DON'T WANT THAT.
NEITHER DO I. I'VE HAD A PRETTY UP-AND-DOWN LIFE, AND I'VE MADE A LOT OF MISTAKES, BUT I DID ONE GOOD THING.
I HAD MY DAUGHTER. A DAUGHTER I WOULD DO ANYTHING FOR. I SWORE TO HER I'D COME BACK FROM SPACE FOR HER BIRTHDAY.
I PROMISED HER I WOULD COME BACK. NOT HALF-ME. NOT NOT-ME. AND I REFUSE TO DISAPPOINT HER.
I EVEN GOT HER A PRESENT, WHICH WAS THE IDIOT THING THAT STARTED THIS MADNESS.
YOU SAID, "MEET THE BEACON ON TIME," AND INSTEAD I GRABBED FOR THIS. GOD. IF I COULD KICK PAST SCOTT'S ASS OVER ONE THI--
WHOA.

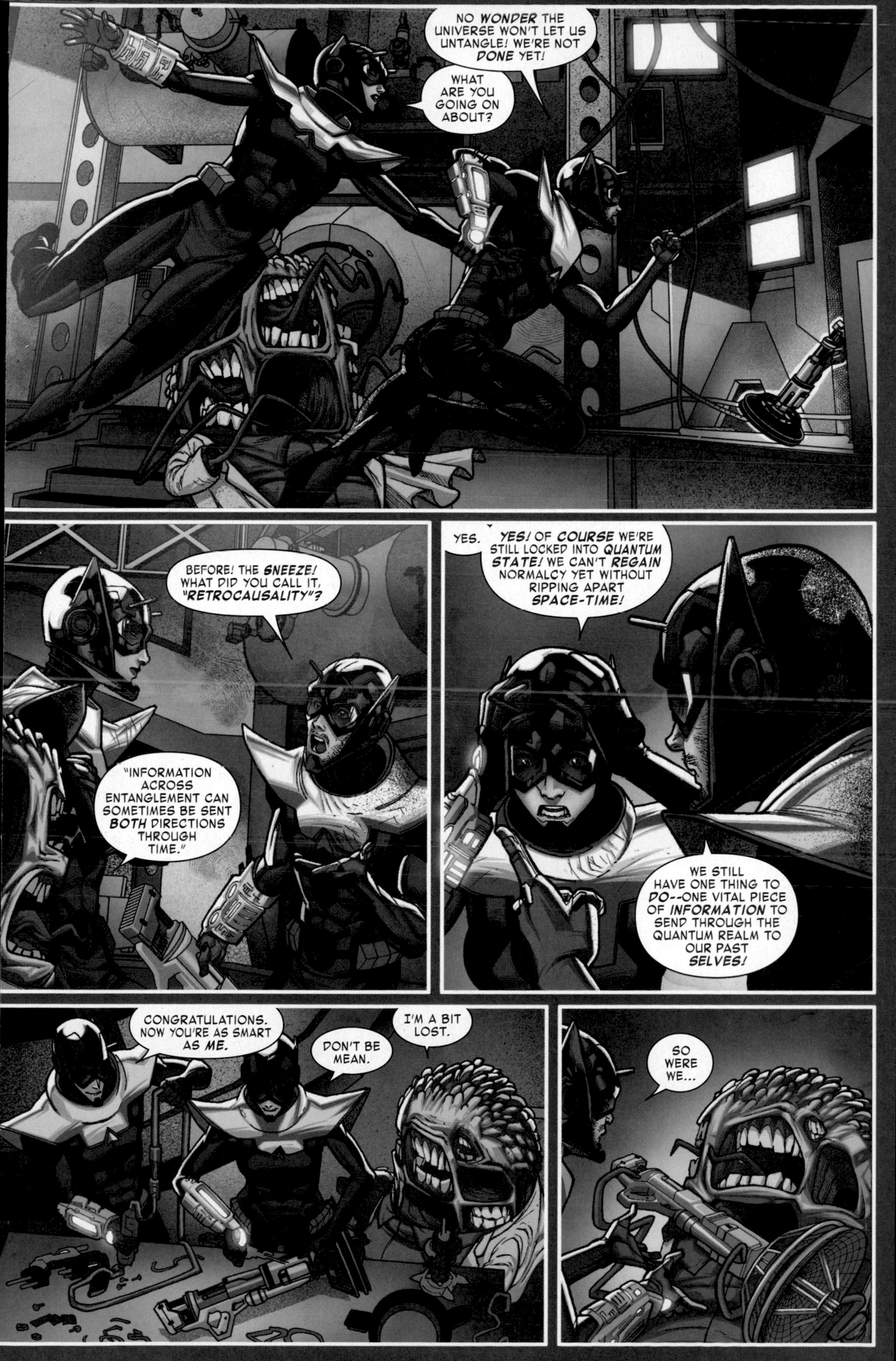
NO WONDER THE UNIVERSE WON'T LET US UNTANGLE! WE'RE NOT DONE YET!
WHAT ARE YOU GOING ON ABOUT?
BEFORE! THE SNEEZE! WHAT DID YOU CALL IT, "RETROCAUSALITY"?
"INFORMATION ACROSS ENTANGLEMENT CAN SOMETIMES BE SENT BOTH DIRECTIONS THROUGH TIME."
YES.
YES! OF COURSE WE'RE STILL LOCKED INTO QUANTUM STATE! WE CAN'T REGAIN NORMALCY YET WITHOUT RIPPING APART SPACE-TIME!
WE STILL HAVE ONE THING TO DO--ONE VITAL PIECE OF INFORMATION TO SEND THROUGH THE QUANTUM REALM TO OUR PAST SELVES!
CONGRATULATIONS. NOW YOU'RE AS SMART AS ME.
DON'T BE MEAN.
I'M A BIT LOST.
SO WERE WE...

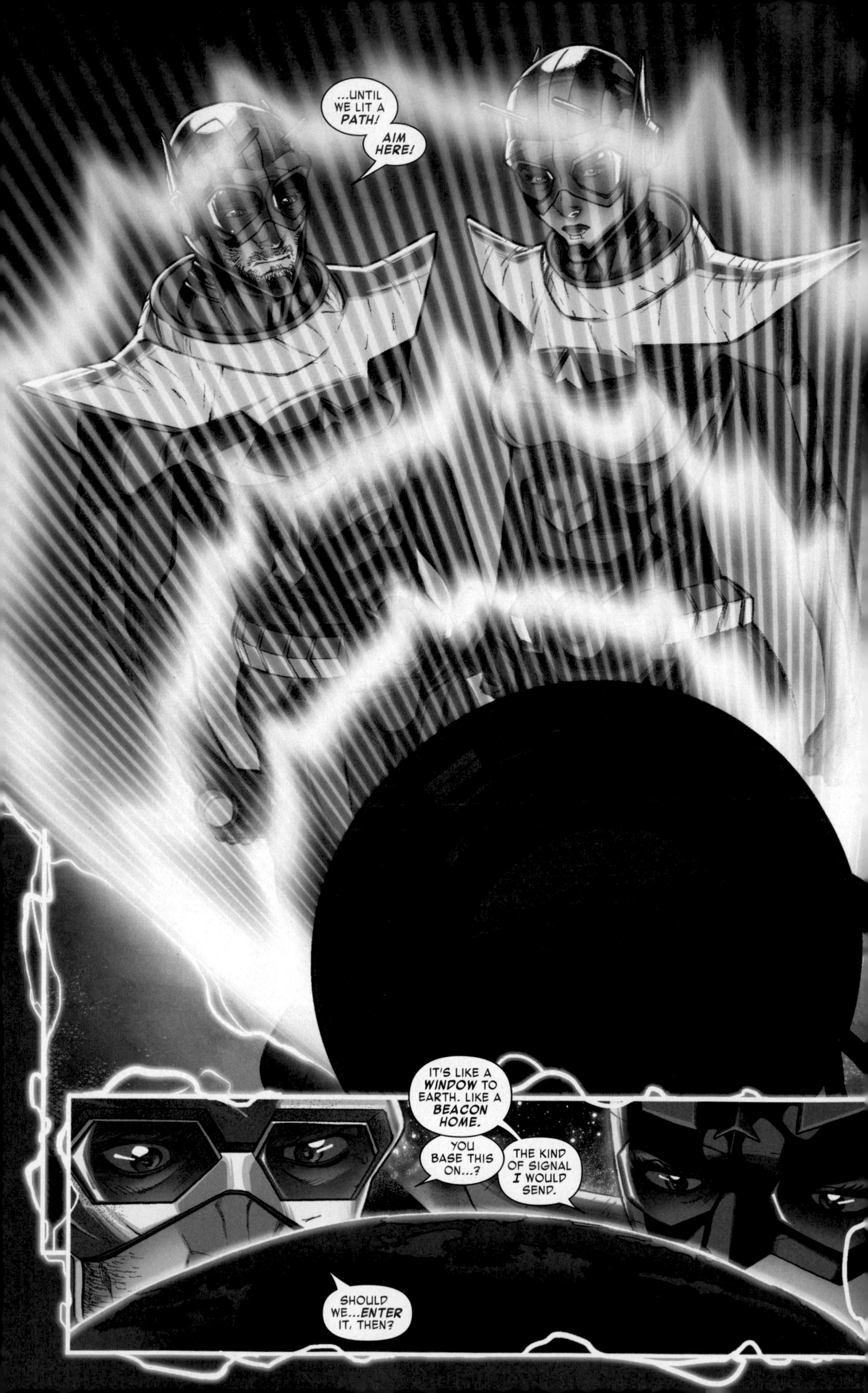
...UNTIL WE LIT A PATH!
AIM HERE!
IT'S LIKE A WINDOW TO EARTH. LIKE A BEACON HOME.
YOU BASE THIS ON...?
THE KIND OF SIGNAL I WOULD SEND.
SHOULD WE...ENTER IT, THEN?

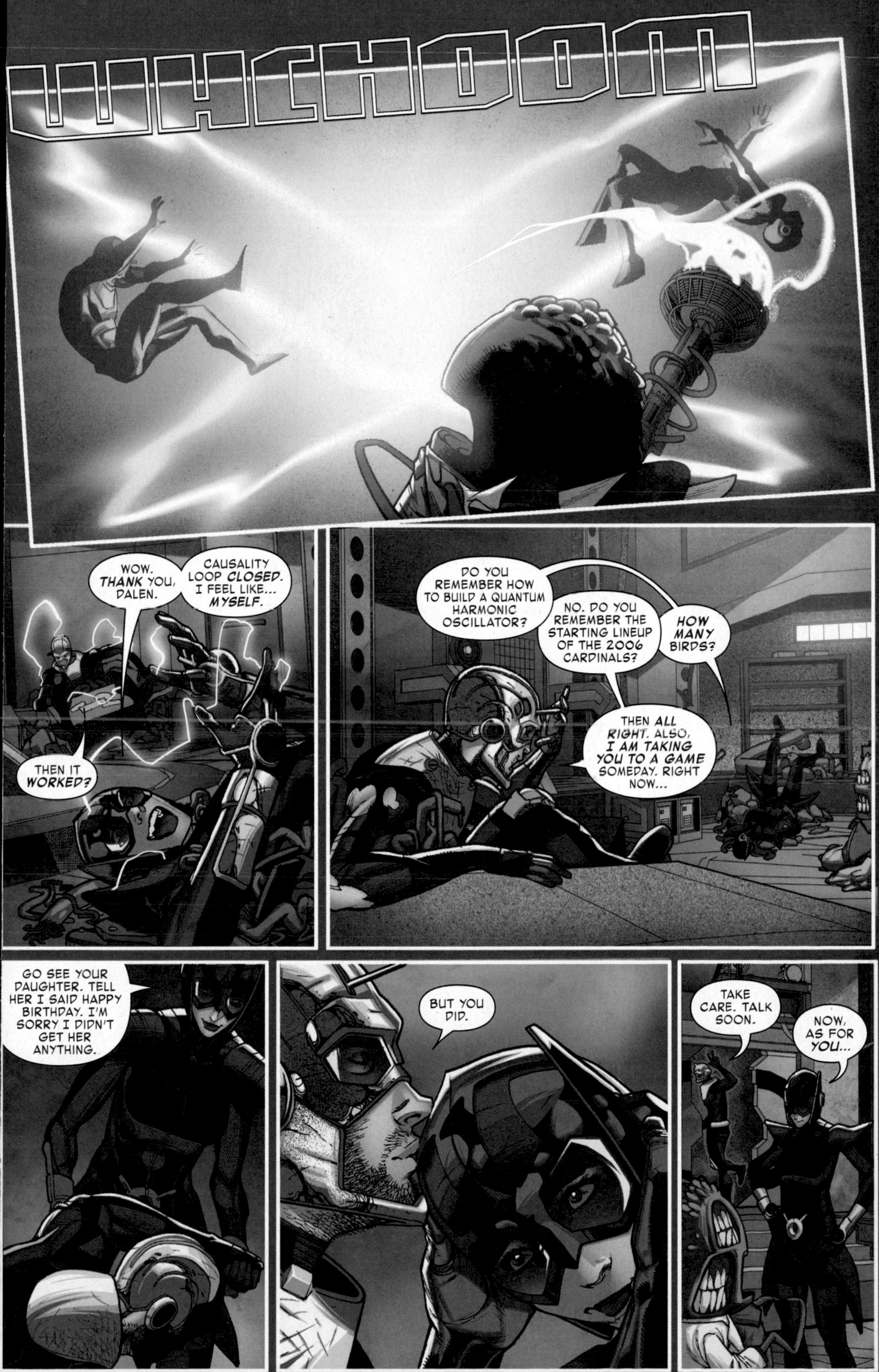
WHCHOOM
WOW. THANK YOU, DALEN.
CAUSALITY LOOP CLOSED. I FEEL LIKE... MYSELF.
THEN IT WORKED?
DO YOU REMEMBER HOW TO BUILD A QUANTUM HARMONIC OSCILLATOR?
NO. DO YOU REMEMBER THE STARTING LINEUP OF THE 2006 CARDINALS?
HOW MANY BIRDS?
THEN ALL RIGHT. ALSO, I AM TAKING YOU TO A GAME SOMEDAY. RIGHT NOW...
GO SEE YOUR DAUGHTER. TELL HER I SAID HAPPY BIRTHDAY. I'M SORRY I DIDN'T GET HER ANYTHING.
BUT YOU DID.
TAKE CARE. TALK SOON.
NOW, AS FOR YOU...

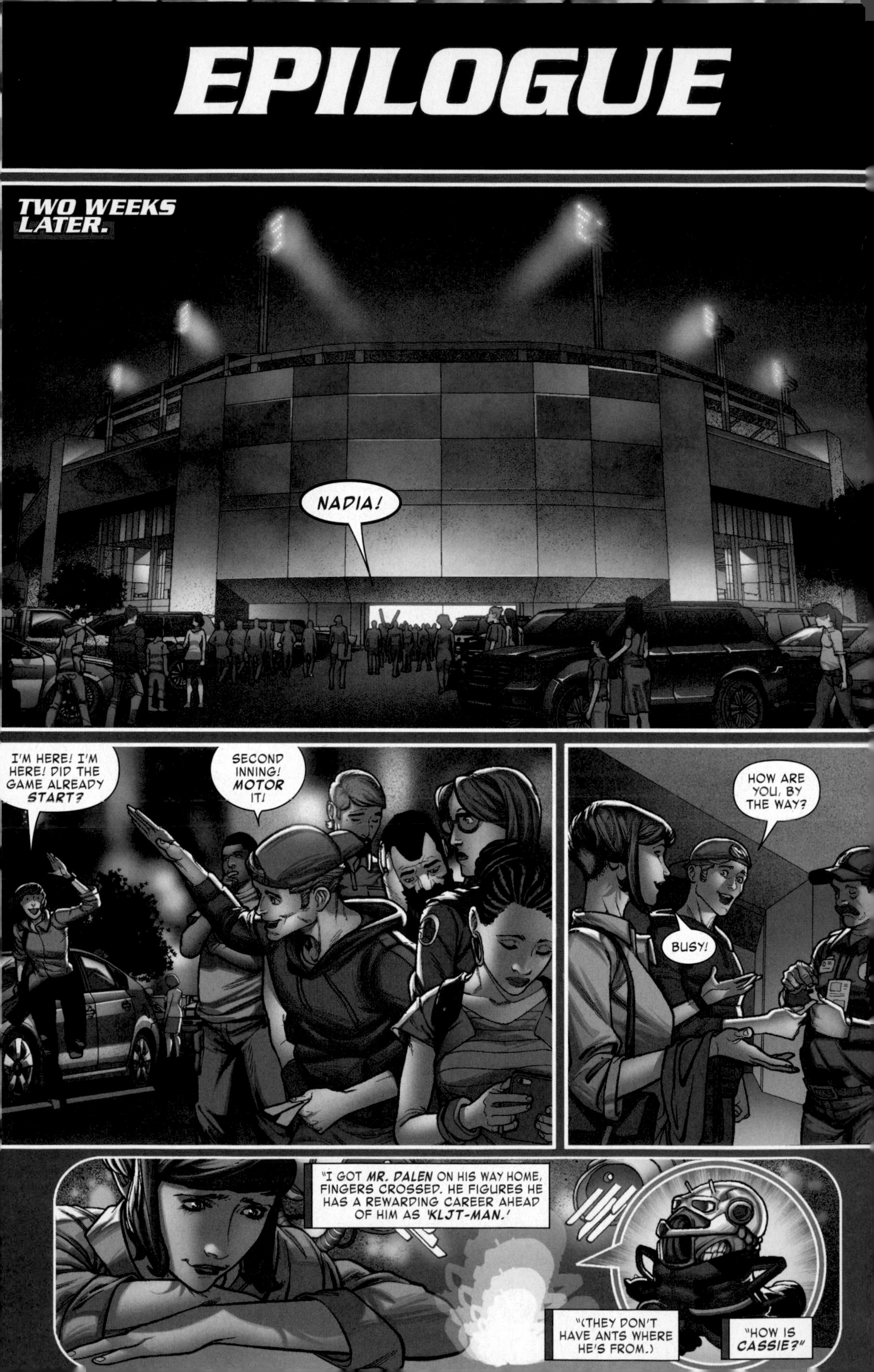
EPILOGUE
TWO WEEKS LATER.
NADIA!
I'M HERE! I'M HERE! DID THE GAME ALREADY START?
SECOND INNING! MOTOR IT!
HOW ARE YOU, BY THE WAY?
BUSY!
"I GOT MR. DALEN ON HIS WAY HOME, FINGERS CROSSED. HE FIGURES HE HAS A REWARDING CAREER AHEAD OF HIM AS 'KLJT-MAN.'
"(THEY DON'T HAVE ANTS WHERE HE'S FROM.)
"HOW IS CASSIE?"

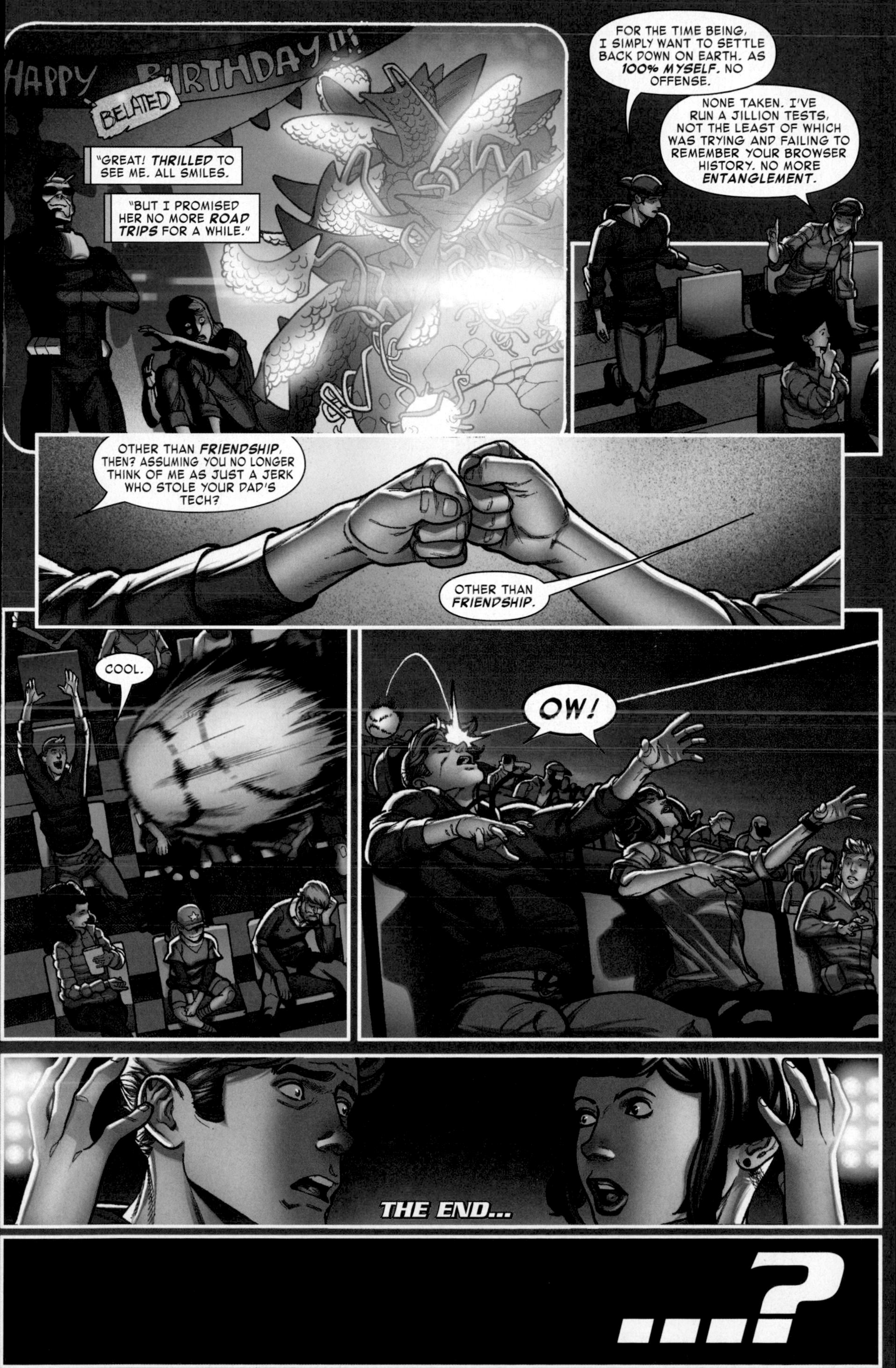
HAPPY BELATED BIRTHDAY!!!
"GREAT! THRILLED TO SEE ME. ALL SMILES.
"BUT I PROMISED HER NO MORE ROAD TRIPS FOR A WHILE."
FOR THE TIME BEING, I SIMPLY WANT TO SETTLE BACK DOWN ON EARTH. AS 100% MYSELF. NO OFFENSE.
NONE TAKEN. I'VE RUN A JILLION TESTS, NOT THE LEAST OF WHICH WAS TRYING AND FAILING TO REMEMBER YOUR BROWSER HISTORY. NO MORE ENTANGLEMENT.
OTHER THAN FRIENDSHIP, THEN? ASSUMING YOU NO LONGER THINK OF ME AS JUST A JERK WHO STOLE YOUR DAD'S TECH?
OTHER THAN FRIENDSHIP.
COOL.
OW!
THE END...
...?

The **WAR OF THE REALMS** has begun! After laying waste to nine of the Ten Realms, the **DARK ELF KING MALEKITH** and his powerful allies have brought their war to the last realm standing: Earth! Now, as the planet's heroes battle Malekith's forces, **LAUFEY**, king of the enormous beings known as Frost Giants, has claimed North America for his kin...

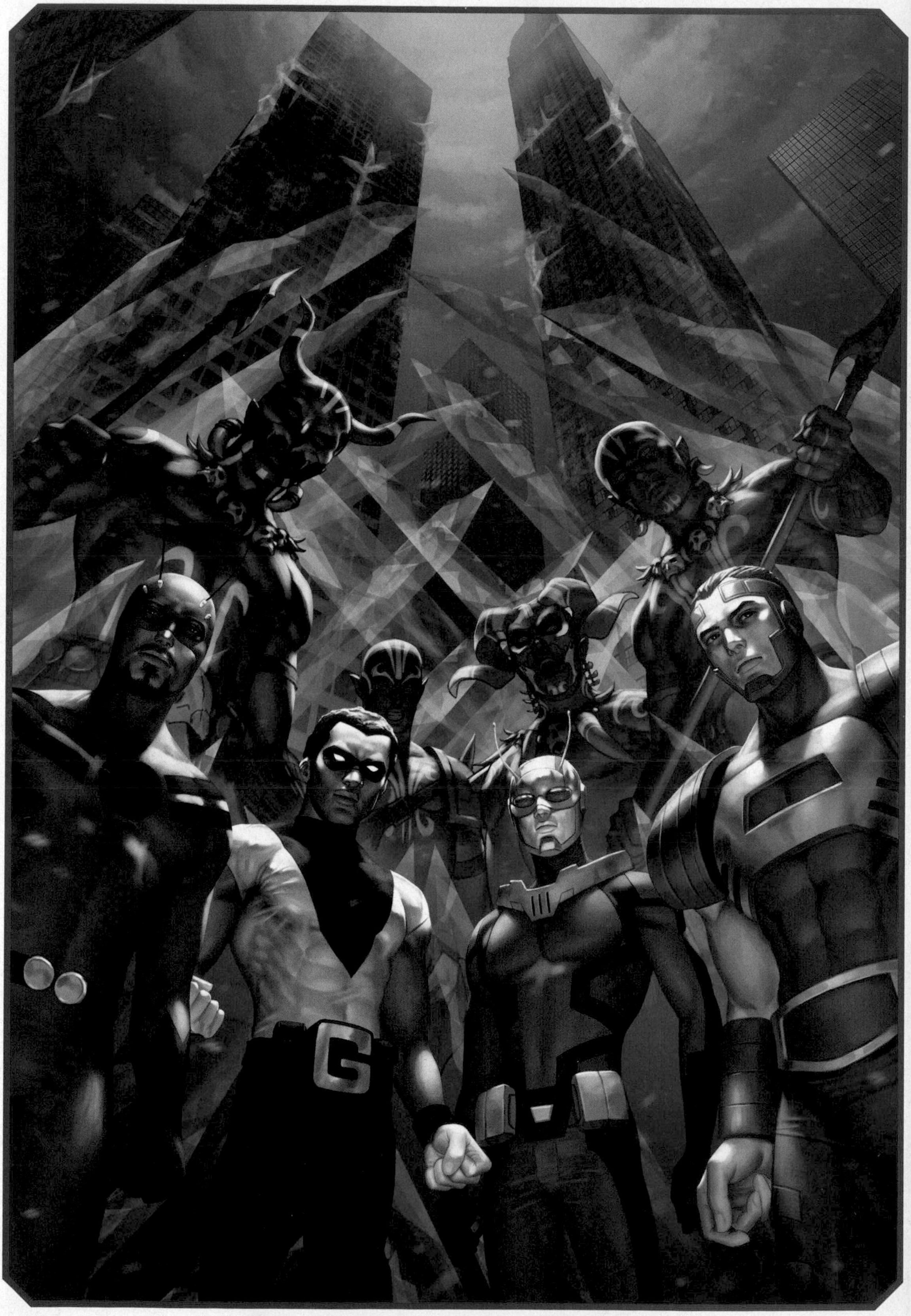

G

GIANT-MAN #1 "A FEW GIANT MEN"

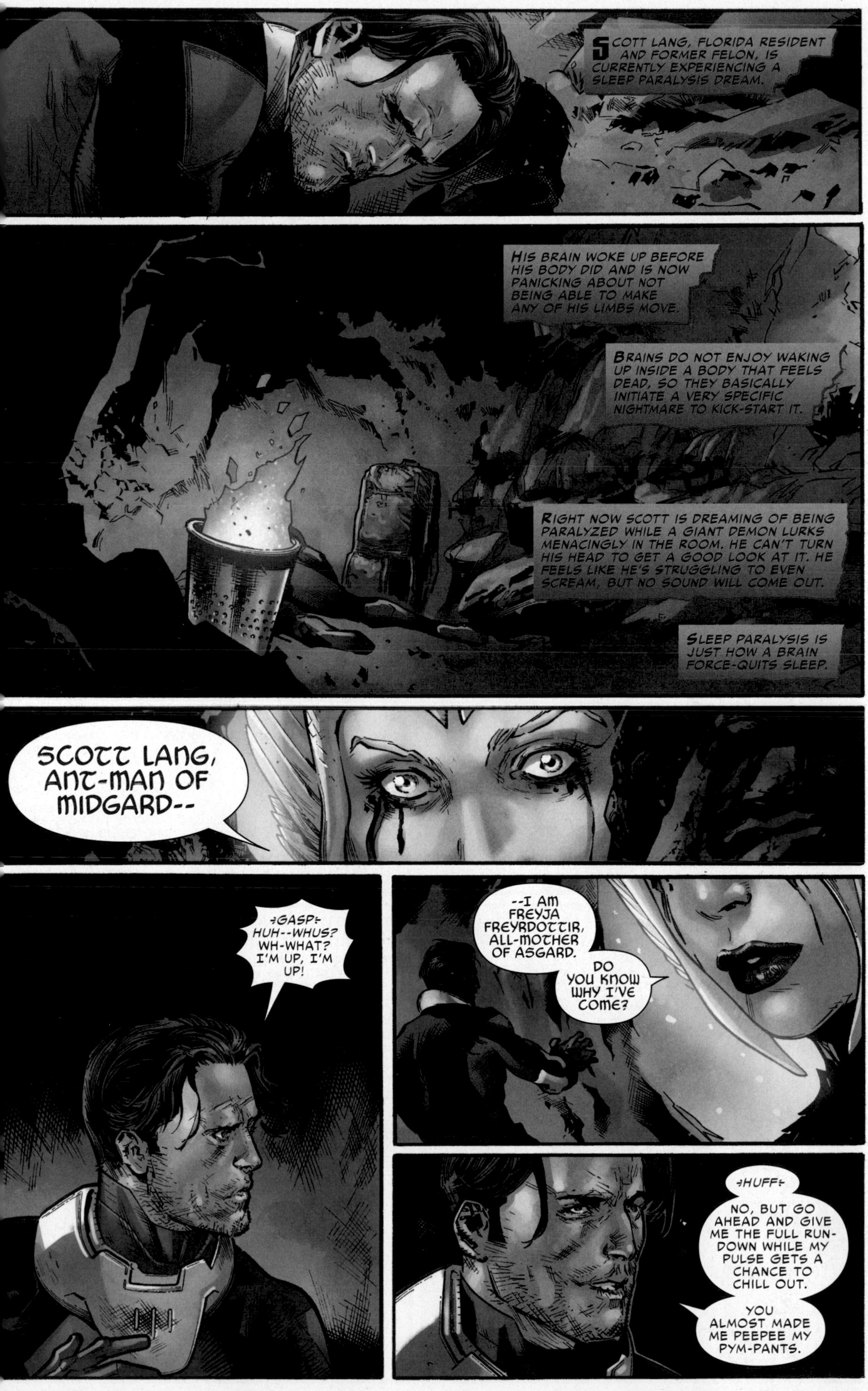
SCOTT LANG, FLORIDA RESIDENT AND FORMER FELON, IS CURRENTLY EXPERIENCING A SLEEP PARALYSIS DREAM.
HIS BRAIN WOKE UP BEFORE HIS BODY DID AND IS NOW PANICKING ABOUT NOT BEING ABLE TO MAKE ANY OF HIS LIMBS MOVE.
BRAINS DO NOT ENJOY WAKING UP INSIDE A BODY THAT FEELS DEAD, SO THEY BASICALLY INITIATE A VERY SPECIFIC NIGHTMARE TO KICK-START IT.
RIGHT NOW SCOTT IS DREAMING OF BEING PARALYZED WHILE A GIANT DEMON LURKS MENACINGLY IN THE ROOM. HE CAN'T TURN HIS HEAD TO GET A GOOD LOOK AT IT. HE FEELS LIKE HE'S STRUGGLING TO EVEN SCREAM, BUT NO SOUND WILL COME OUT.
SLEEP PARALYSIS IS JUST HOW A BRAIN FORCE-QUITS SLEEP.
SCOTT LANG, ANT-MAN OF MIDGARD--
÷GASP÷ HUH--WHUS? WH-WHAT? I'M UP, I'M UP!
--I AM FREYJA FREYRDOTTIR, ALL-MOTHER OF ASGARD.
DO YOU KNOW WHY I'VE COME?
÷HUFF÷
NO, BUT GO AHEAD AND GIVE ME THE FULL RUN-DOWN WHILE MY PULSE GETS A CHANCE TO CHILL OUT.
YOU ALMOST MADE ME PEEPEE MY PYM-PANTS.

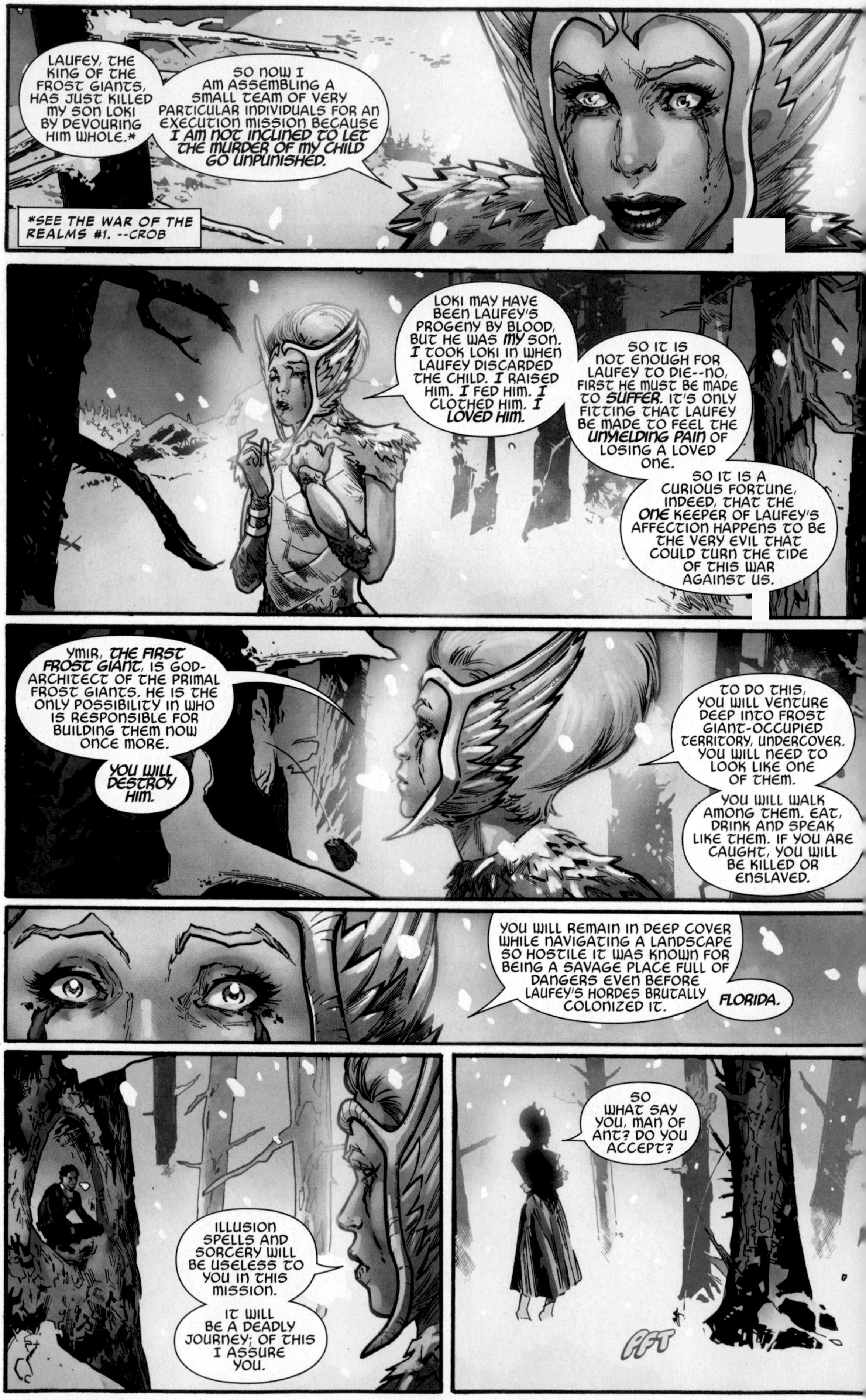
LAUFEY, THE KING OF THE FROST GIANTS, HAS JUST KILLED MY SON LOKI BY DEVOURING HIM WHOLE.*
SO NOW I AM ASSEMBLING A SMALL TEAM OF VERY PARTICULAR INDIVIDUALS FOR AN EXECUTION MISSION BECAUSE *I AM NOT INCLINED TO LET THE MURDER OF MY CHILD GO UNPUNISHED.*
*SEE THE WAR OF THE REALMS #1. --CROB
LOKI MAY HAVE BEEN LAUFEY'S PROGENY BY BLOOD, BUT HE WAS *MY* SON. *I* TOOK LOKI IN WHEN LAUFEY DISCARDED THE CHILD. *I* RAISED HIM. *I* FED HIM. *I* CLOTHED HIM. *I LOVED HIM.*
SO IT IS NOT ENOUGH FOR LAUFEY TO DIE--NO, FIRST HE MUST BE MADE TO *SUFFER*. IT'S ONLY FITTING THAT LAUFEY BE MADE TO FEEL THE *UNYIELDING PAIN* OF LOSING A LOVED ONE.
SO IT IS A CURIOUS FORTUNE, INDEED, THAT THE *ONE* KEEPER OF LAUFEY'S AFFECTION HAPPENS TO BE THE VERY EVIL THAT COULD TURN THE TIDE OF THIS WAR AGAINST US.
YMIR, *THE FIRST FROST GIANT*, IS GOD-ARCHITECT OF THE PRIMAL FROST GIANTS. HE IS THE ONLY POSSIBILITY IN WHO IS RESPONSIBLE FOR BUILDING THEM NOW ONCE MORE.
YOU WILL DESTROY HIM.
TO DO THIS, YOU WILL VENTURE DEEP INTO FROST GIANT-OCCUPIED TERRITORY, UNDERCOVER. YOU WILL NEED TO LOOK LIKE ONE OF THEM.
YOU WILL WALK AMONG THEM. EAT, DRINK AND SPEAK LIKE THEM. IF YOU ARE CAUGHT, YOU WILL BE KILLED OR ENSLAVED.
YOU WILL REMAIN IN DEEP COVER WHILE NAVIGATING A LANDSCAPE SO HOSTILE IT WAS KNOWN FOR BEING A SAVAGE PLACE FULL OF DANGERS EVEN BEFORE LAUFEY'S HORDES BRUTALLY COLONIZED IT.
FLORIDA.
ILLUSION SPELLS AND SORCERY WILL BE USELESS TO YOU IN THIS MISSION.
IT WILL BE A DEADLY JOURNEY; OF THIS I ASSURE YOU.
SO WHAT SAY YOU, MAN OF ANT? DO YOU ACCEPT?
PFT

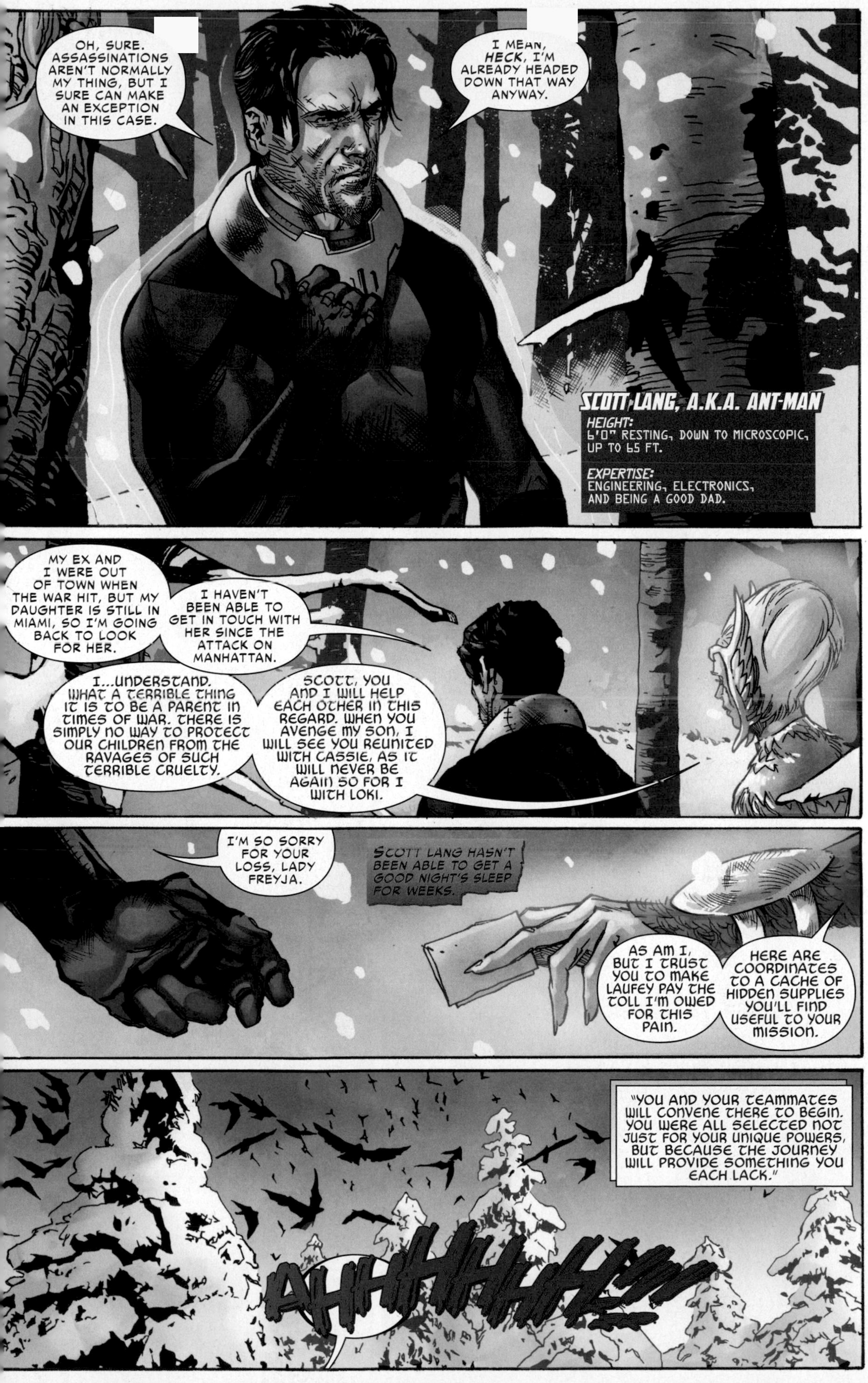
OH, SURE. ASSASSINATIONS AREN'T NORMALLY MY THING, BUT I SURE CAN MAKE AN EXCEPTION IN THIS CASE.
I MEAN, HECK, I'M ALREADY HEADED DOWN THAT WAY ANYWAY.
SCOTT LANG, A.K.A. ANT-MAN
HEIGHT: 6'0" RESTING, DOWN TO MICROSCOPIC, UP TO 65 FT.
EXPERTISE: ENGINEERING, ELECTRONICS, AND BEING A GOOD DAD.
MY EX AND I WERE OUT OF TOWN WHEN THE WAR HIT, BUT MY DAUGHTER IS STILL IN MIAMI, SO I'M GOING BACK TO LOOK FOR HER.
I HAVEN'T BEEN ABLE TO GET IN TOUCH WITH HER SINCE THE ATTACK ON MANHATTAN.
I...UNDERSTAND. WHAT A TERRIBLE THING IT IS TO BE A PARENT IN TIMES OF WAR. THERE IS SIMPLY NO WAY TO PROTECT OUR CHILDREN FROM THE RAVAGES OF SUCH TERRIBLE CRUELTY.
SCOTT, YOU AND I WILL HELP EACH OTHER IN THIS REGARD. WHEN YOU AVENGE MY SON, I WILL SEE YOU REUNITED WITH CASSIE, AS IT WILL NEVER BE AGAIN SO FOR I WITH LOKI.
I'M SO SORRY FOR YOUR LOSS, LADY FREYJA.
SCOTT LANG HASN'T BEEN ABLE TO GET A GOOD NIGHT'S SLEEP FOR WEEKS.
AS AM I, BUT I TRUST YOU TO MAKE LAUFEY PAY THE TOLL I'M OWED FOR THIS PAIN.
HERE ARE COORDINATES TO A CACHE OF HIDDEN SUPPLIES YOU'LL FIND USEFUL TO YOUR MISSION.
"YOU AND YOUR TEAMMATES WILL CONVENE THERE TO BEGIN. YOU WERE ALL SELECTED NOT JUST FOR YOUR UNIQUE POWERS, BUT BECAUSE THE JOURNEY WILL PROVIDE SOMETHING YOU EACH LACK."
AHHHHHHH!!!

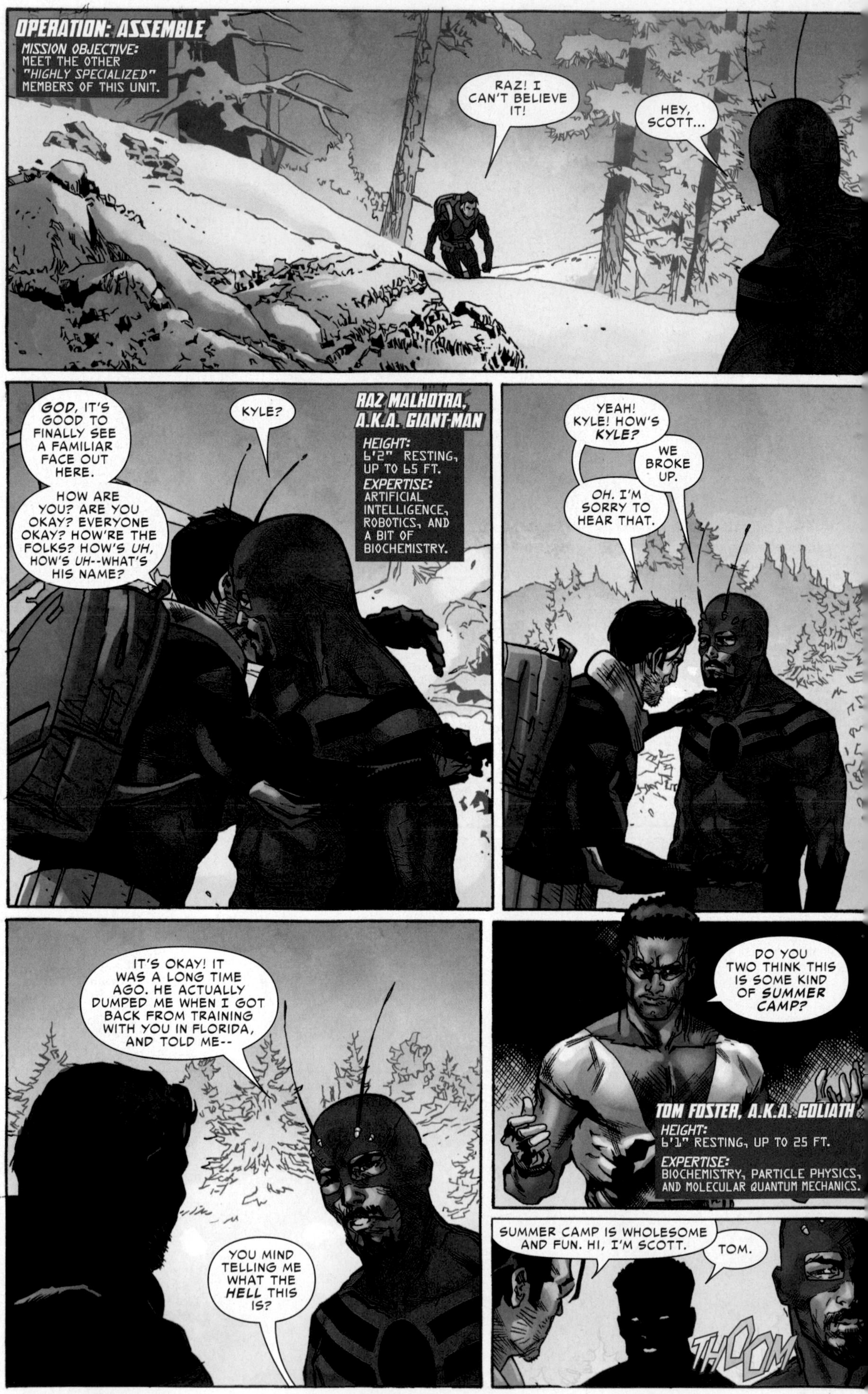
OPERATION: ASSEMBLE
MISSION OBJECTIVE: MEET THE OTHER "HIGHLY SPECIALIZED" MEMBERS OF THIS UNIT.
RAZ! I CAN'T BELIEVE IT!
HEY, SCOTT...
GOD, IT'S GOOD TO FINALLY SEE A FAMILIAR FACE OUT HERE.
HOW ARE YOU? ARE YOU OKAY? EVERYONE OKAY? HOW'RE THE FOLKS? HOW'S UH, HOW'S UH--WHAT'S HIS NAME?
KYLE?
RAZ MALHOTRA, A.K.A. GIANT-MAN
HEIGHT: 6'2" RESTING, UP TO 65 FT.
EXPERTISE: ARTIFICIAL INTELLIGENCE, ROBOTICS, AND A BIT OF BIOCHEMISTRY.
YEAH! KYLE! HOW'S KYLE?
WE BROKE UP.
OH. I'M SORRY TO HEAR THAT.
IT'S OKAY! IT WAS A LONG TIME AGO. HE ACTUALLY DUMPED ME WHEN I GOT BACK FROM TRAINING WITH YOU IN FLORIDA, AND TOLD ME--
YOU MIND TELLING ME WHAT THE HELL THIS IS?
DO YOU TWO THINK THIS IS SOME KIND OF SUMMER CAMP?
TOM FOSTER, A.K.A. GOLIATH
HEIGHT: 6'1" RESTING, UP TO 25 FT.
EXPERTISE: BIOCHEMISTRY, PARTICLE PHYSICS, AND MOLECULAR QUANTUM MECHANICS.
SUMMER CAMP IS WHOLESOME AND FUN. HI, I'M SCOTT.
TOM.
THOOM

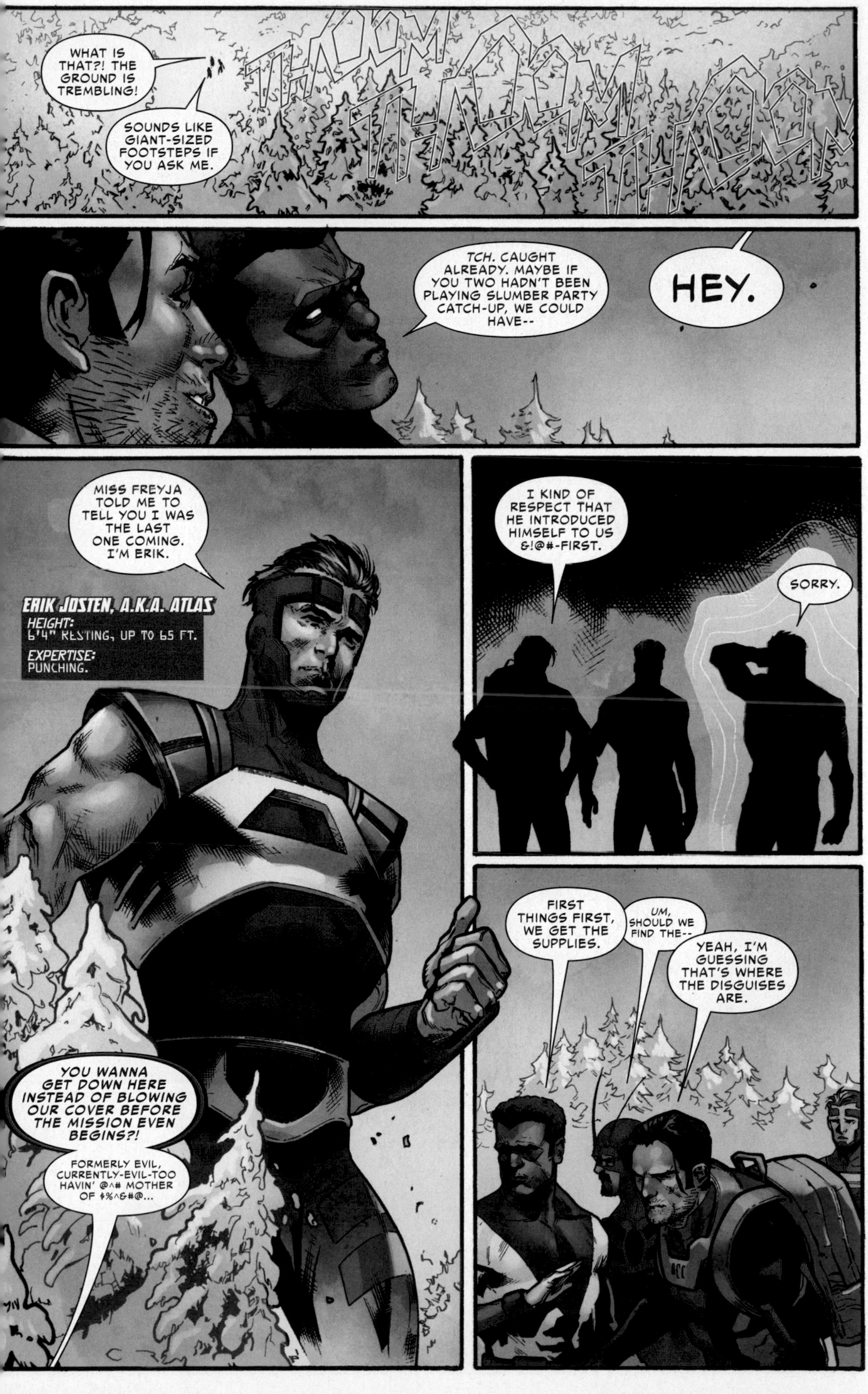
WHAT IS THAT?! THE GROUND IS TREMBLING!
SOUNDS LIKE GIANT-SIZED FOOTSTEPS IF YOU ASK ME.
THOOM THOOM THOOM THOOM
HEY.
TCH. CAUGHT ALREADY. MAYBE IF YOU TWO HADN'T BEEN PLAYING SLUMBER PARTY CATCH-UP, WE COULD HAVE--
MISS FREYJA TOLD ME TO TELL YOU I WAS THE LAST ONE COMING. I'M ERIK.
ERIK JOSTEN, A.K.A. ATLAS
HEIGHT:
6'4" RESTING, UP TO 65 FT.
EXPERTISE:
PUNCHING.
YOU WANNA GET DOWN HERE INSTEAD OF BLOWING OUR COVER BEFORE THE MISSION EVEN BEGINS?!
FORMERLY EVIL, CURRENTLY-EVIL-TOO HAVIN' @^# MOTHER OF $%^&#@...
I KIND OF RESPECT THAT HE INTRODUCED HIMSELF TO US &!@#-FIRST.
SORRY.
FIRST THINGS FIRST, WE GET THE SUPPLIES.
UM, SHOULD WE FIND THE--
YEAH, I'M GUESSING THAT'S WHERE THE DISGUISES ARE.

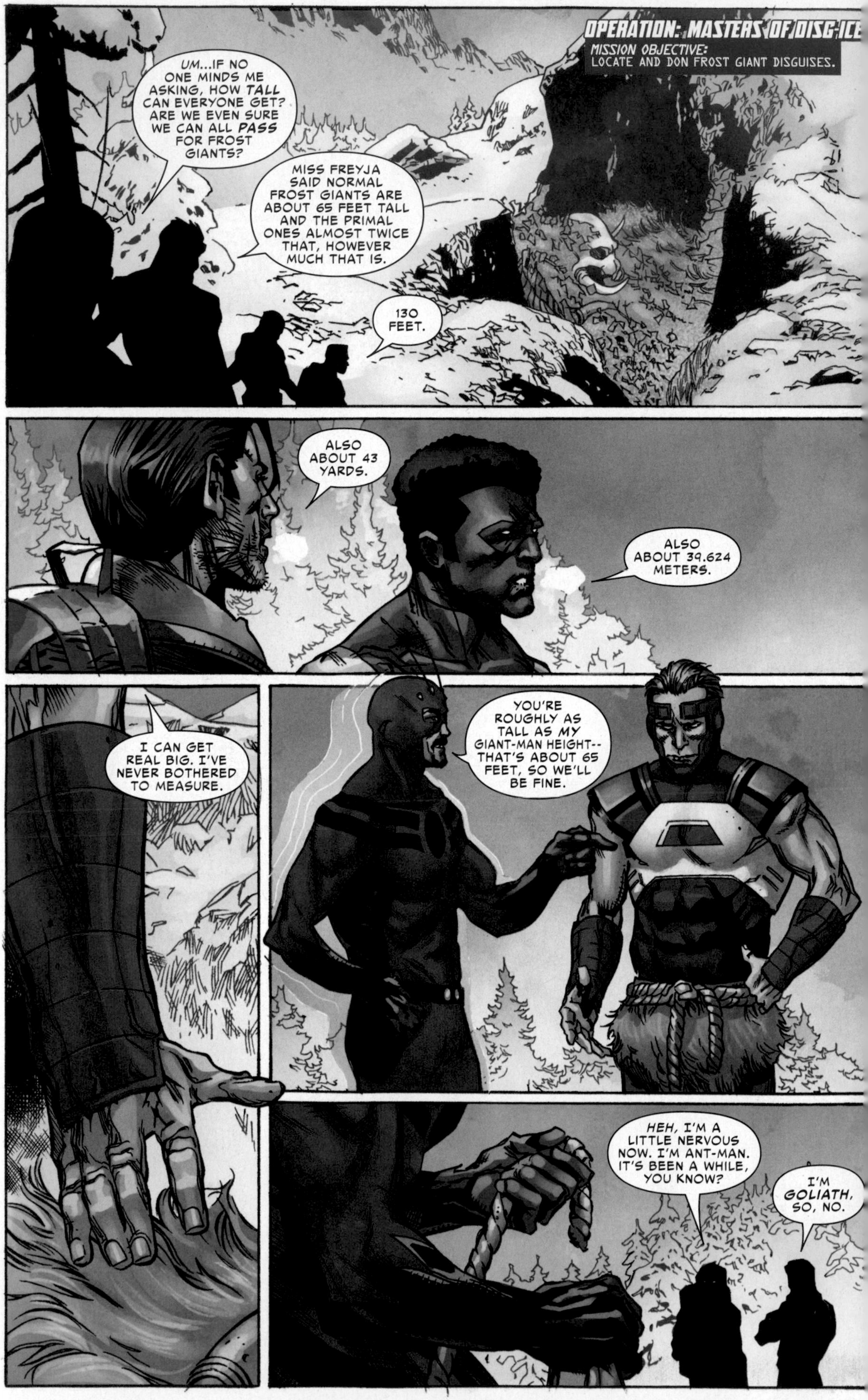
OPERATION: MASTERS OF DISG-ICE
MISSION OBJECTIVE: LOCATE AND DON FROST GIANT DISGUISES.
UM...IF NO ONE MINDS ME ASKING, HOW TALL CAN EVERYONE GET? ARE WE EVEN SURE WE CAN ALL PASS FOR FROST GIANTS?
MISS FREYJA SAID NORMAL FROST GIANTS ARE ABOUT 65 FEET TALL AND THE PRIMAL ONES ALMOST TWICE THAT, HOWEVER MUCH THAT IS.
130 FEET.
ALSO ABOUT 43 YARDS.
ALSO ABOUT 39.624 METERS.
I CAN GET REAL BIG. I'VE NEVER BOTHERED TO MEASURE.
YOU'RE ROUGHLY AS TALL AS MY GIANT-MAN HEIGHT-- THAT'S ABOUT 65 FEET, SO WE'LL BE FINE.
HEH, I'M A LITTLE NERVOUS NOW. I'M ANT-MAN. IT'S BEEN A WHILE, YOU KNOW?
I'M GOLIATH, SO, NO.

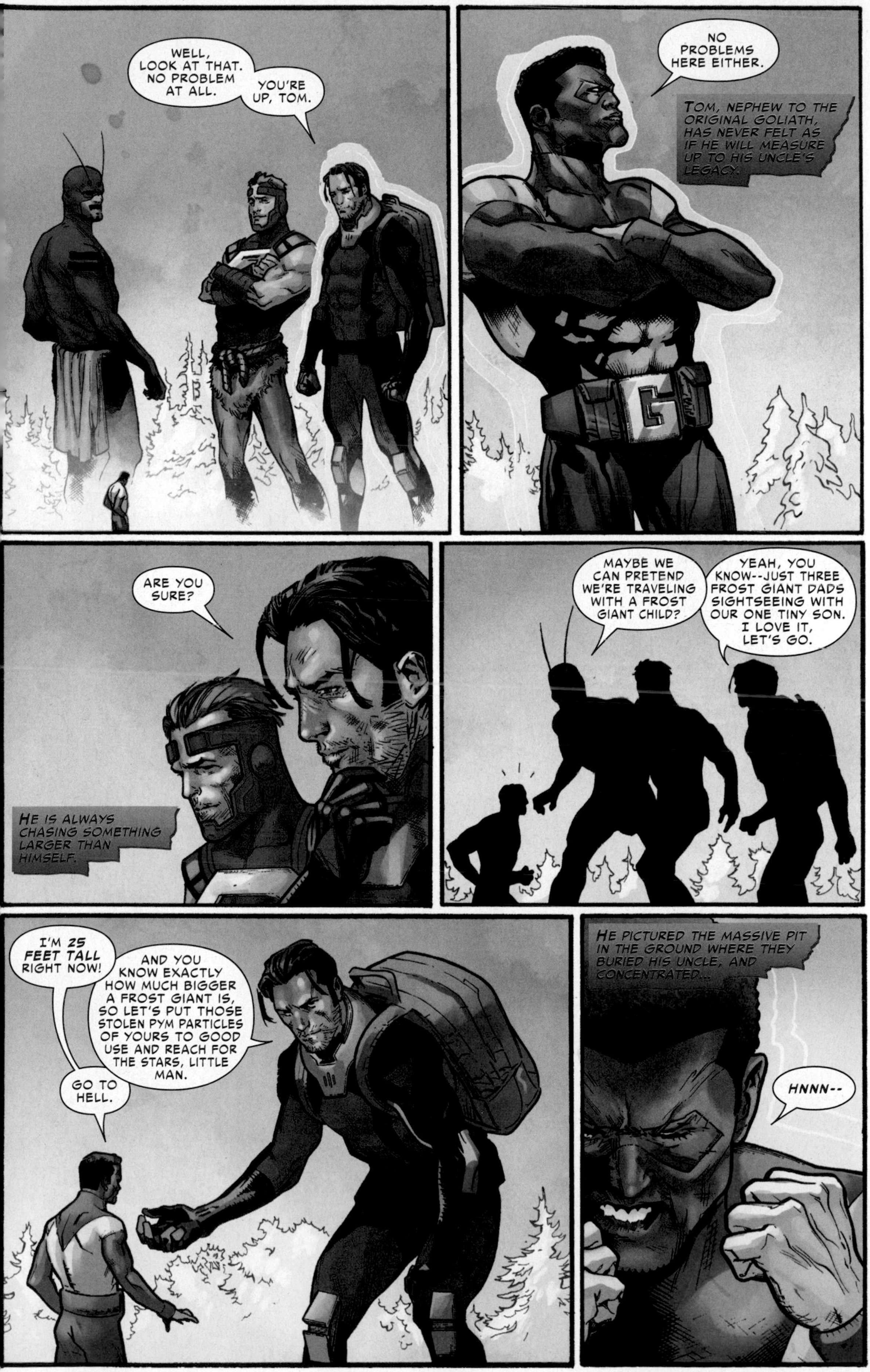

WELL, LOOK AT THAT. NO PROBLEM AT ALL.
YOU'RE UP, TOM.
NO PROBLEMS HERE EITHER.
TOM, NEPHEW TO THE ORIGINAL GOLIATH, HAS NEVER FELT AS IF HE WILL MEASURE UP TO HIS UNCLE'S LEGACY.
ARE YOU SURE?
HE IS ALWAYS CHASING SOMETHING LARGER THAN HIMSELF.
MAYBE WE CAN PRETEND WE'RE TRAVELING WITH A FROST GIANT CHILD?
YEAH, YOU KNOW--JUST THREE FROST GIANT DADS SIGHTSEEING WITH OUR ONE TINY SON. I LOVE IT, LET'S GO.
I'M 25 FEET TALL RIGHT NOW!
AND YOU KNOW EXACTLY HOW MUCH BIGGER A FROST GIANT IS, SO LET'S PUT THOSE STOLEN PYM PARTICLES OF YOURS TO GOOD USE AND REACH FOR THE STARS, LITTLE MAN.
GO TO HELL.
HE PICTURED THE MASSIVE PIT IN THE GROUND WHERE THEY BURIED HIS UNCLE, AND CONCENTRATED...
HNNN--

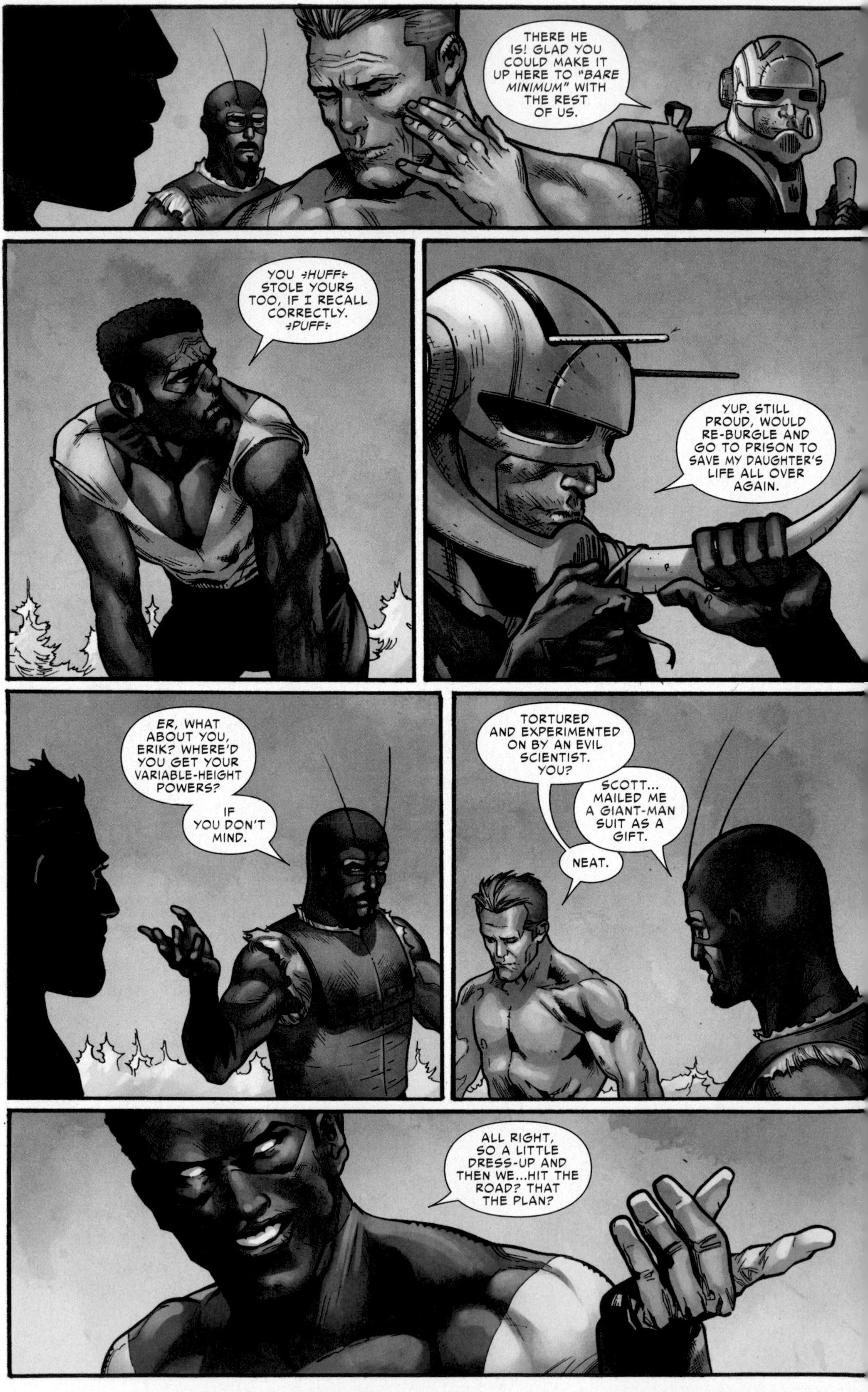
THERE HE IS! GLAD YOU COULD MAKE IT UP HERE TO "BARE MINIMUM" WITH THE REST OF US.
YOU -HUFF- STOLE YOURS TOO, IF I RECALL CORRECTLY. -PUFF-
YUP. STILL PROUD, WOULD RE-BURGLE AND GO TO PRISON TO SAVE MY DAUGHTER'S LIFE ALL OVER AGAIN.
ER, WHAT ABOUT YOU, ERIK? WHERE'D YOU GET YOUR VARIABLE-HEIGHT POWERS?
IF YOU DON'T MIND.
TORTURED AND EXPERIMENTED ON BY AN EVIL SCIENTIST. YOU?
SCOTT... MAILED ME A GIANT-MAN SUIT AS A GIFT.
NEAT.
ALL RIGHT, SO A LITTLE DRESS-UP AND THEN WE...HIT THE ROAD? THAT THE PLAN?

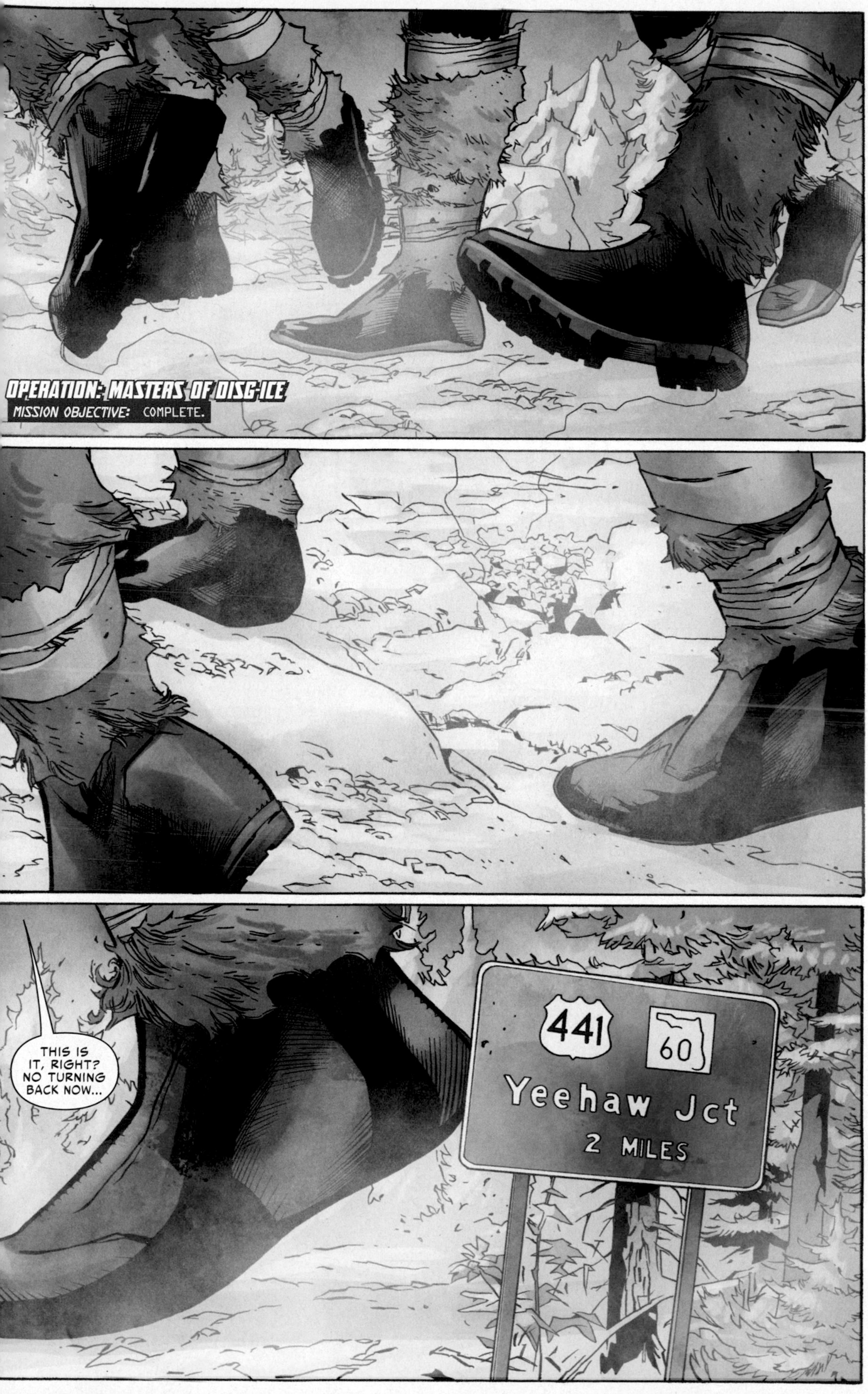
OPERATION: MASTERS OF DISG-ICE
MISSION OBJECTIVE: COMPLETE.
THIS IS IT, RIGHT? NO TURNING BACK NOW...
441
60
Yeehaw Jct
2 MILES

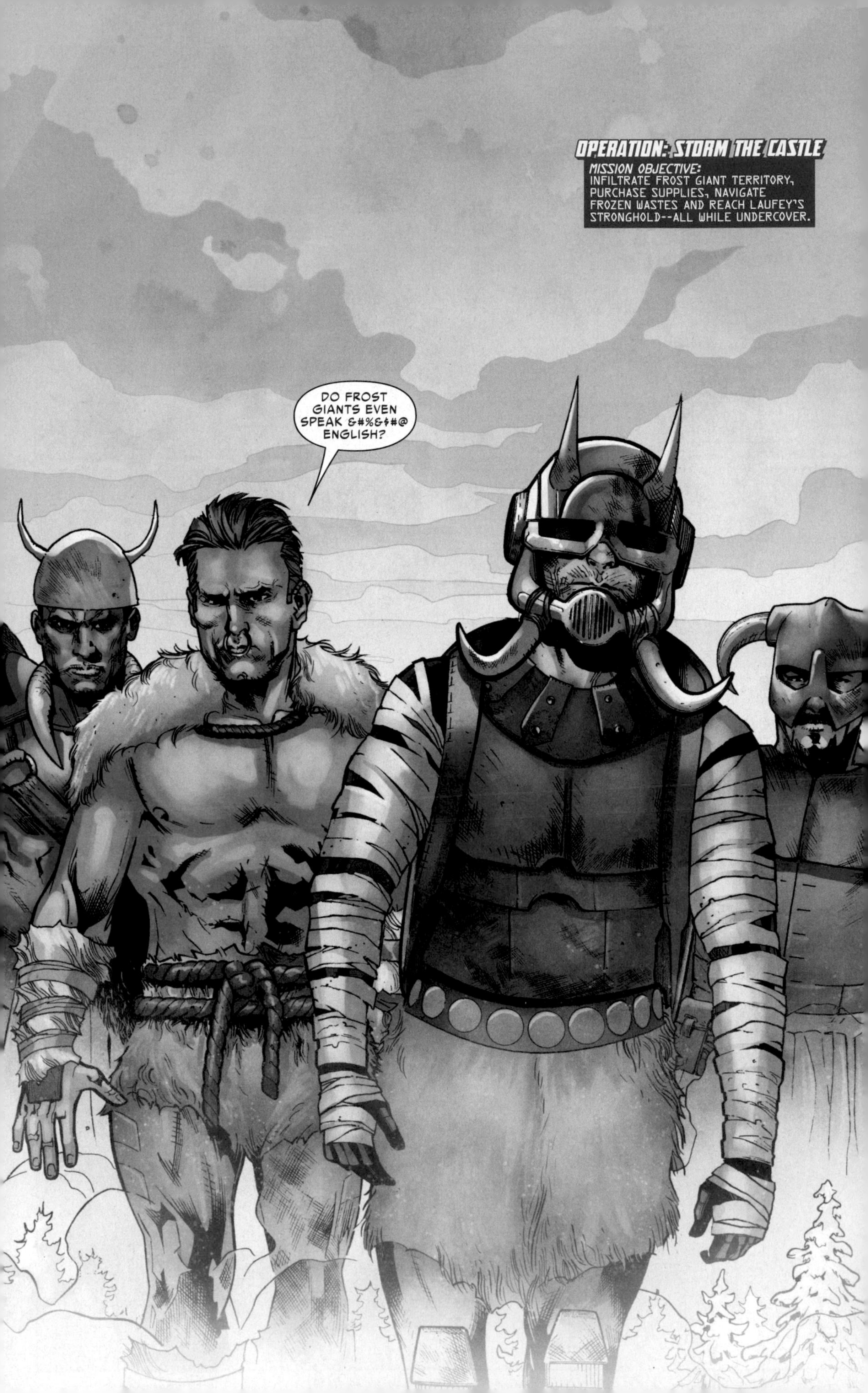
OPERATION: STORM THE CASTLE
MISSION OBJECTIVE: INFILTRATE FROST GIANT TERRITORY, PURCHASE SUPPLIES, NAVIGATE FROZEN WASTES AND REACH LAUFEY'S STRONGHOLD--ALL WHILE UNDERCOVER.
DO FROST GIANTS EVEN SPEAK &#%&$#@ ENGLISH?

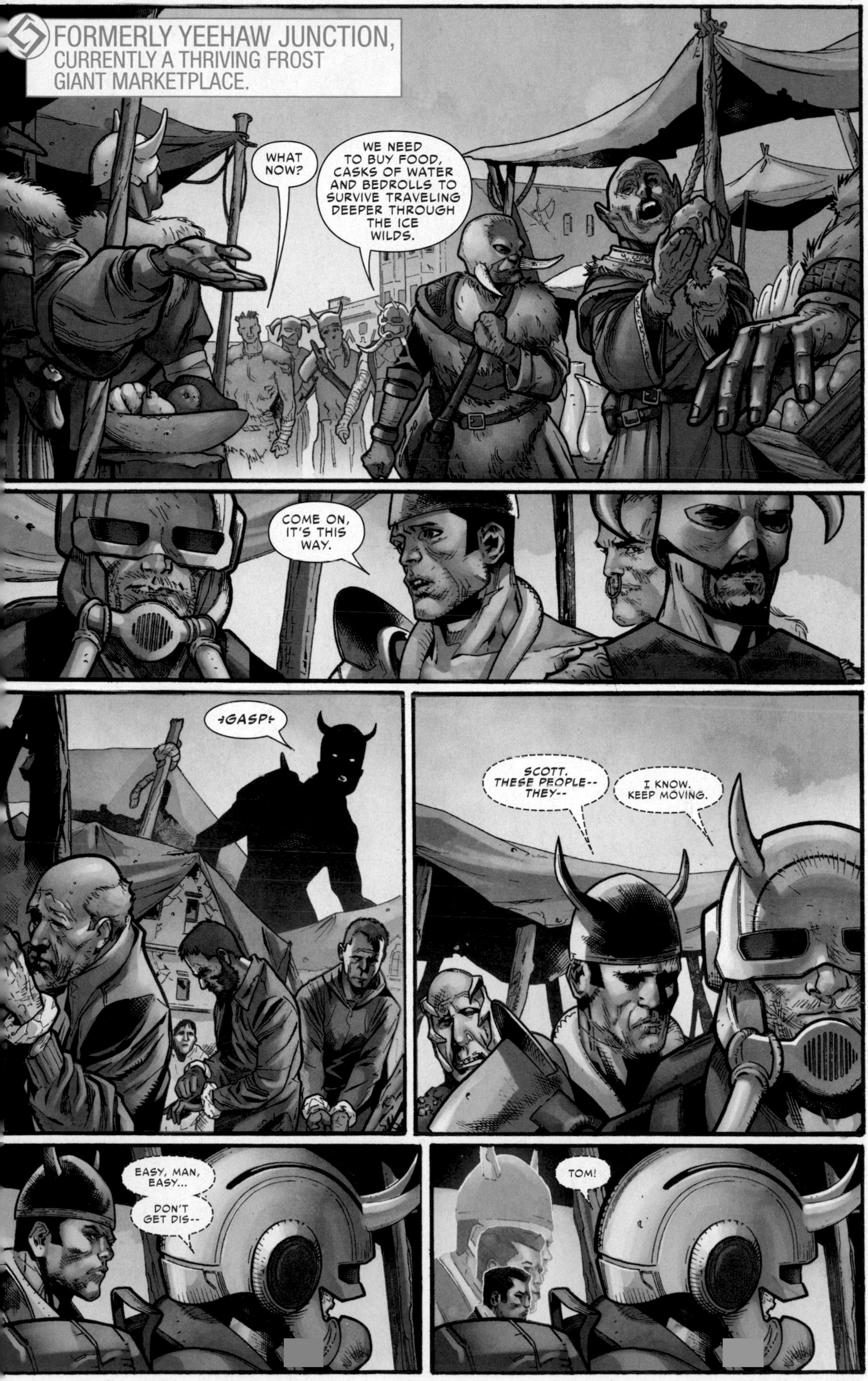
FORMERLY YEEHAW JUNCTION, CURRENTLY A THRIVING FROST GIANT MARKETPLACE.
WHAT NOW?
WE NEED TO BUY FOOD, CASKS OF WATER AND BEDROLLS TO SURVIVE TRAVELING DEEPER THROUGH THE ICE WILDS.
COME ON, IT'S THIS WAY.
GASP
SCOTT. THESE PEOPLE-- THEY--
I KNOW. KEEP MOVING.
EASY, MAN, EASY...
DON'T GET DIS--
TOM!

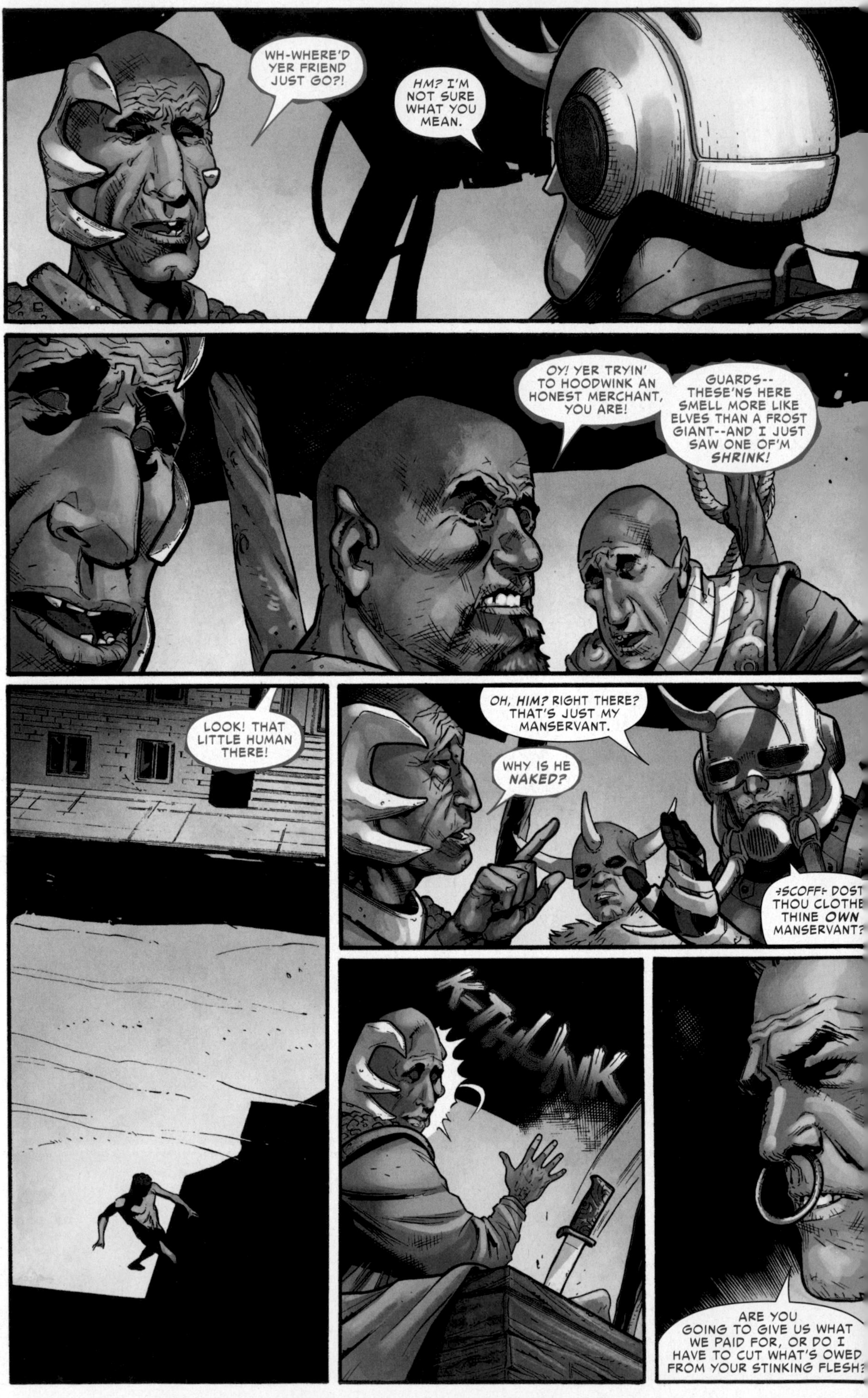
WH-WHERE'D YER FRIEND JUST GO?!
HM? I'M NOT SURE WHAT YOU MEAN.
OY! YER TRYIN' TO HOODWINK AN HONEST MERCHANT, YOU ARE!
GUARDS-- THESE'NS HERE SMELL MORE LIKE ELVES THAN A FROST GIANT--AND I JUST SAW ONE OF'M SHRINK!
LOOK! THAT LITTLE HUMAN THERE!
OH, HIM? RIGHT THERE? THAT'S JUST MY MANSERVANT.
WHY IS HE NAKED?
⸗SCOFF⸗ DOST THOU CLOTHE THINE OWN MANSERVANT?
K-THUNK
ARE YOU GOING TO GIVE US WHAT WE PAID FOR, OR DO I HAVE TO CUT WHAT'S OWED FROM YOUR STINKING FLESH?

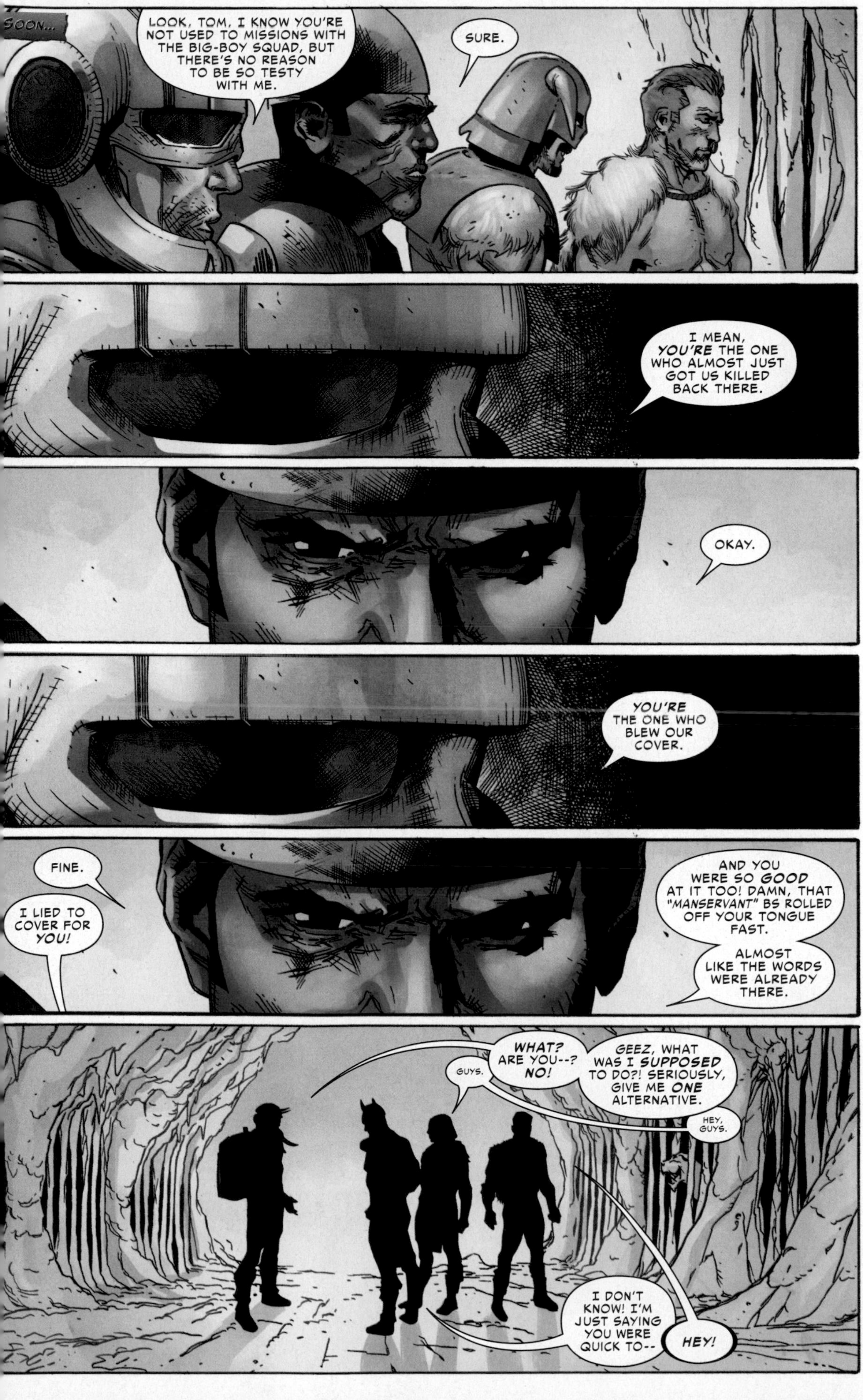
SOON...
LOOK, TOM, I KNOW YOU'RE NOT USED TO MISSIONS WITH THE BIG-BOY SQUAD, BUT THERE'S NO REASON TO BE SO TESTY WITH ME.
SURE.
I MEAN, YOU'RE THE ONE WHO ALMOST JUST GOT US KILLED BACK THERE.
OKAY.
YOU'RE THE ONE WHO BLEW OUR COVER.
FINE.
I LIED TO COVER FOR YOU!
AND YOU WERE SO GOOD AT IT TOO! DAMN, THAT "MANSERVANT" BS ROLLED OFF YOUR TONGUE FAST.
ALMOST LIKE THE WORDS WERE ALREADY THERE.
WHAT? ARE YOU--? NO!
GUYS.
GEEZ, WHAT WAS I SUPPOSED TO DO?! SERIOUSLY, GIVE ME ONE ALTERNATIVE.
HEY, GUYS.
I DON'T KNOW! I'M JUST SAYING YOU WERE QUICK TO--
HEY!

ARE THESE DOGS?

HI, DOGGY.

WE'RE IN FRONT OF KENNELS, YOU GUYS.

ARRRAAAARRRARARARRRARARARRAR!

AW.

ERIK. C'MON, MAN.

WHAT? BLAME THE OWNER, NOT THE BREED.

IT'S NOT HER FAULT SHE'S LIKE THIS. DOGS JUST MIRROR THEIR PEOPLE.

NOT DOGS--

THEY'RE NOT DOGS-- THEY'RE ICE HOUNDS.

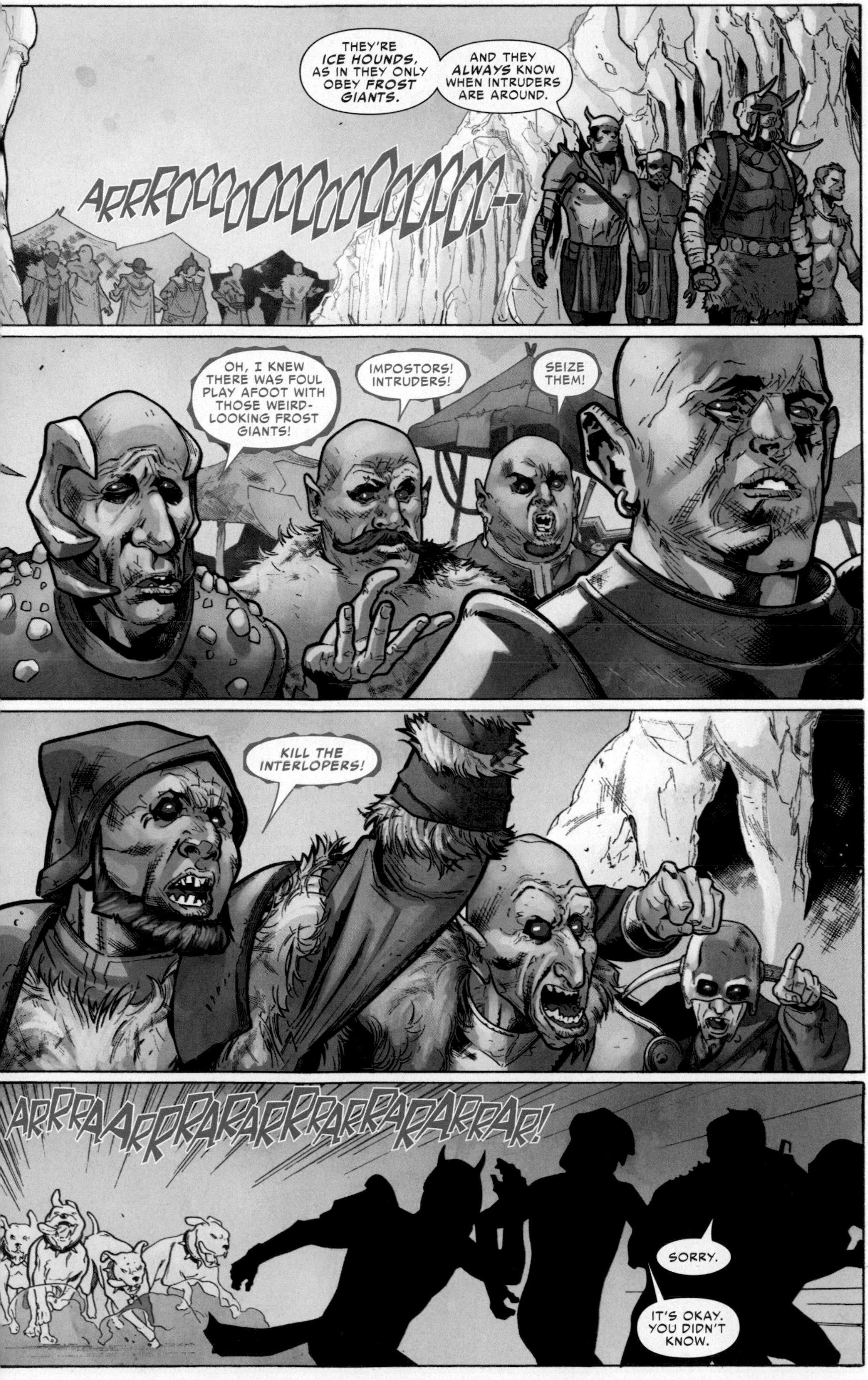
THEY'RE ICE HOUNDS, AS IN THEY ONLY OBEY FROST GIANTS.
AND THEY ALWAYS KNOW WHEN INTRUDERS ARE AROUND.
ARRROOOOOOOOOOOOOOOOOOO--
OH, I KNEW THERE WAS FOUL PLAY AFOOT WITH THOSE WEIRD-LOOKING FROST GIANTS!
IMPOSTORS! INTRUDERS!
SEIZE THEM!
KILL THE INTERLOPERS!
ARRRAARRRARARRRARRRARARRAR!
SORRY.
IT'S OKAY. YOU DIDN'T KNOW.

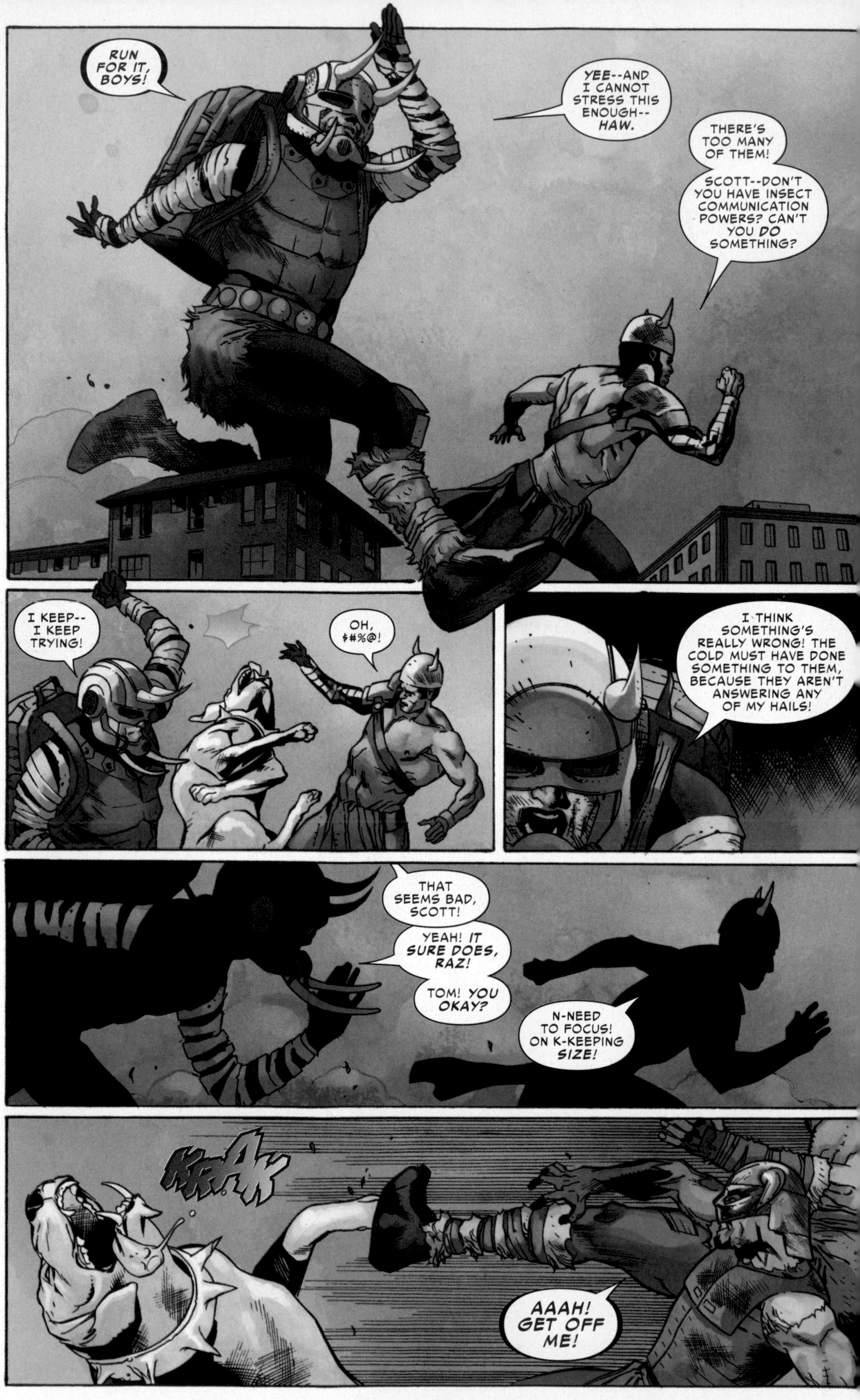
RUN FOR IT, BOYS!
YEE--AND I CANNOT STRESS THIS ENOUGH--HAW.
THERE'S TOO MANY OF THEM!
SCOTT--DON'T YOU HAVE INSECT COMMUNICATION POWERS? CAN'T YOU DO SOMETHING?
I KEEP-- I KEEP TRYING!
OH, $#%@!
I THINK SOMETHING'S REALLY WRONG! THE COLD MUST HAVE DONE SOMETHING TO THEM, BECAUSE THEY AREN'T ANSWERING ANY OF MY HAILS!
THAT SEEMS BAD, SCOTT!
YEAH! IT SURE DOES, RAZ!
TOM! YOU OKAY?
N-NEED TO FOCUS! ON K-KEEPING SIZE!
KRAK
AAAH! GET OFF ME!

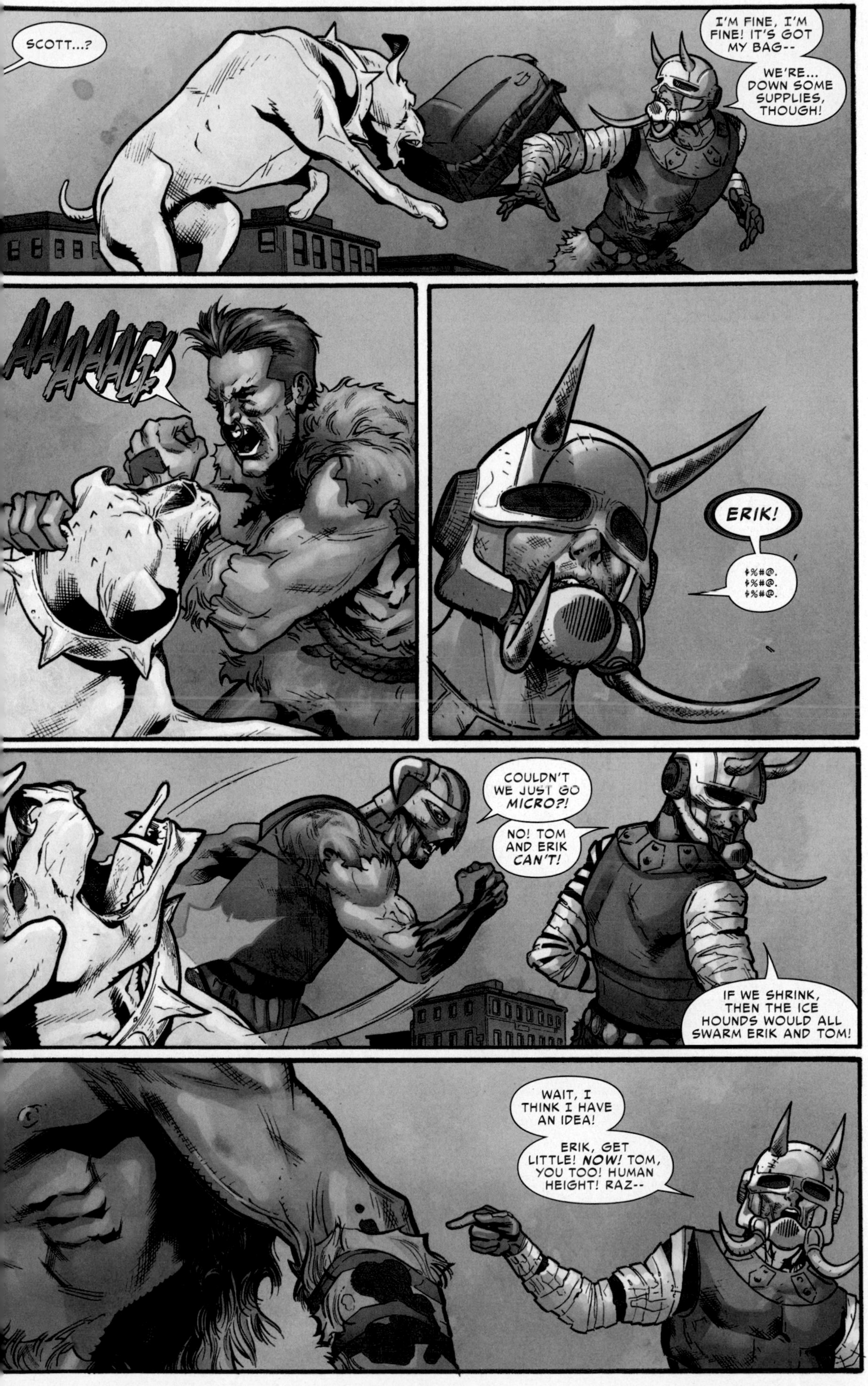
SCOTT...?
I'M FINE, I'M FINE! IT'S GOT MY BAG--
WE'RE... DOWN SOME SUPPLIES, THOUGH!
AAAAAAG!
ERIK!
$%#@. $%#@. $%#@.
COULDN'T WE JUST GO MICRO?!
NO! TOM AND ERIK CAN'T!
IF WE SHRINK, THEN THE ICE HOUNDS WOULD ALL SWARM ERIK AND TOM!
WAIT, I THINK I HAVE AN IDEA!
ERIK, GET LITTLE! NOW! TOM, YOU TOO! HUMAN HEIGHT! RAZ--

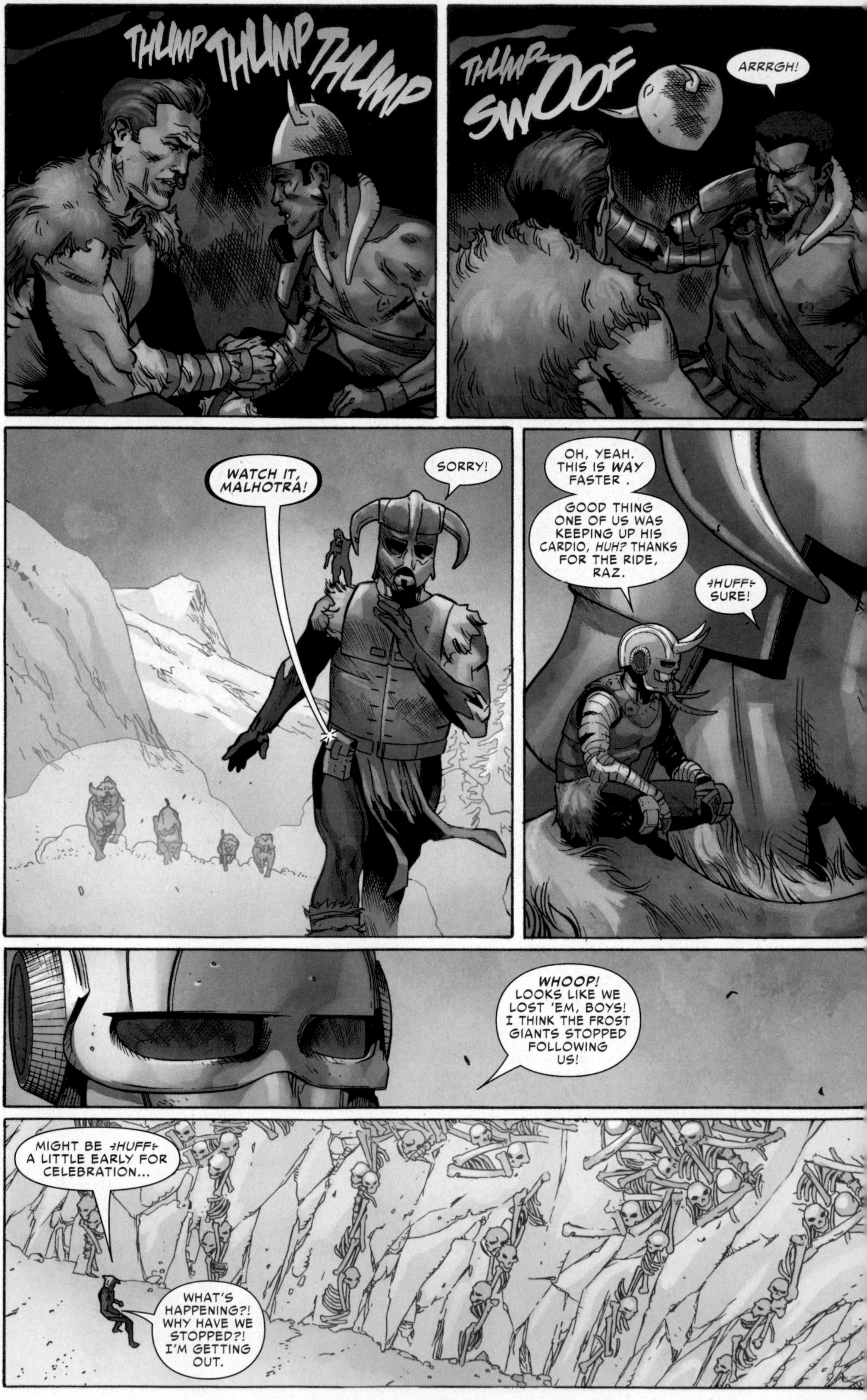
THUMP THUMP THUMP
THUMP SWOOF
ARRRGH!
WATCH IT, MALHOTRA!
SORRY!
OH, YEAH. THIS IS WAY FASTER .
GOOD THING ONE OF US WAS KEEPING UP HIS CARDIO, HUH? THANKS FOR THE RIDE, RAZ.
=HUFF= SURE!
WHOOP! LOOKS LIKE WE LOST 'EM, BOYS! I THINK THE FROST GIANTS STOPPED FOLLOWING US!
MIGHT BE =HUFF= A LITTLE EARLY FOR CELEBRATION...
WHAT'S HAPPENING?! WHY HAVE WE STOPPED?! I'M GETTING OUT.

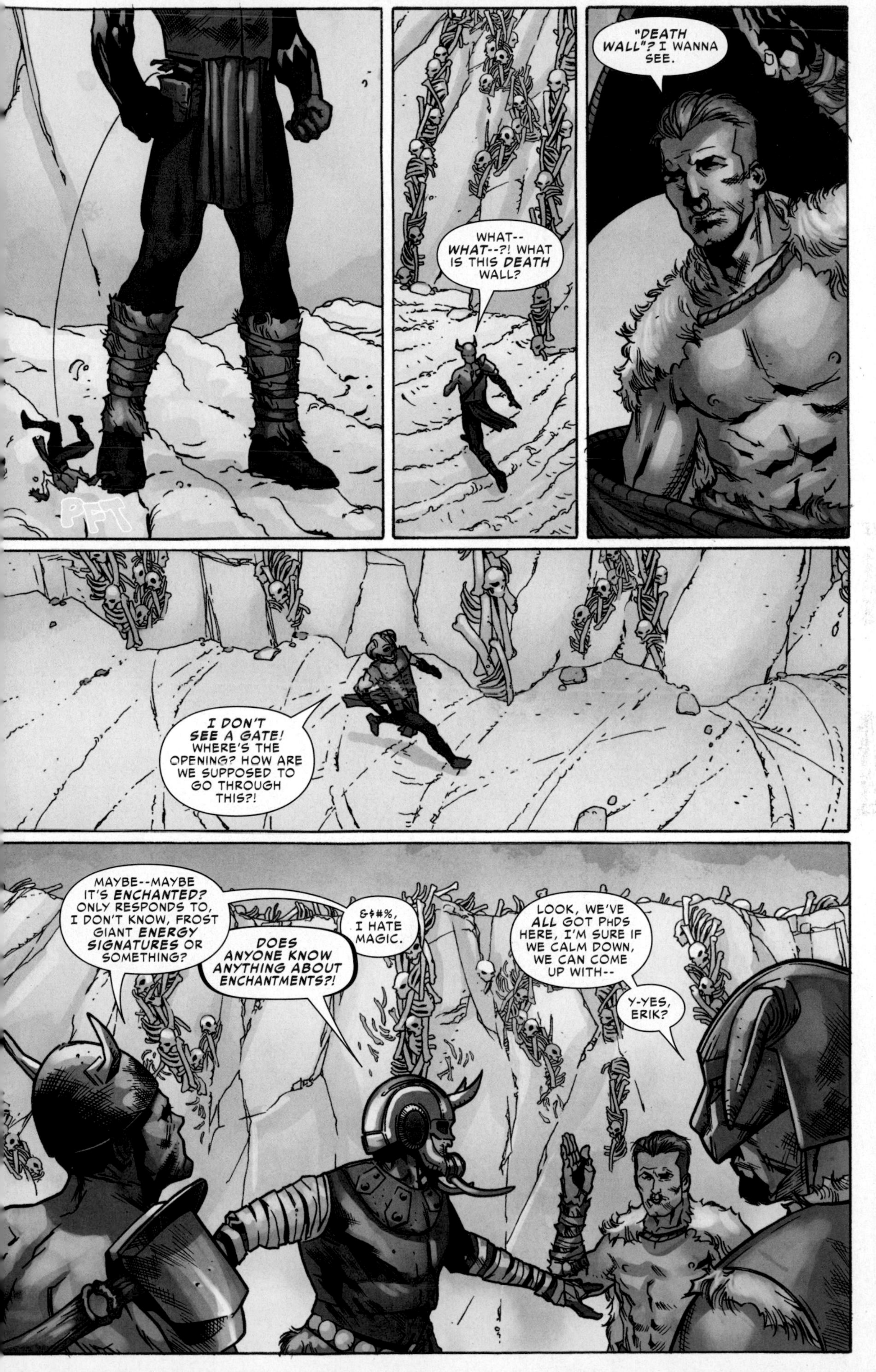
PFT
WHAT-- WHAT--?! WHAT IS THIS DEATH WALL?
"DEATH WALL"? I WANNA SEE.
I DON'T SEE A GATE! WHERE'S THE OPENING? HOW ARE WE SUPPOSED TO GO THROUGH THIS?!
MAYBE--MAYBE IT'S ENCHANTED? ONLY RESPONDS TO, I DON'T KNOW, FROST GIANT ENERGY SIGNATURES OR SOMETHING?
&$#%, I HATE MAGIC.
DOES ANYONE KNOW ANYTHING ABOUT ENCHANTMENTS?!
LOOK, WE'VE ALL GOT PHDS HERE, I'M SURE IF WE CALM DOWN, WE CAN COME UP WITH--
Y-YES, ERIK?

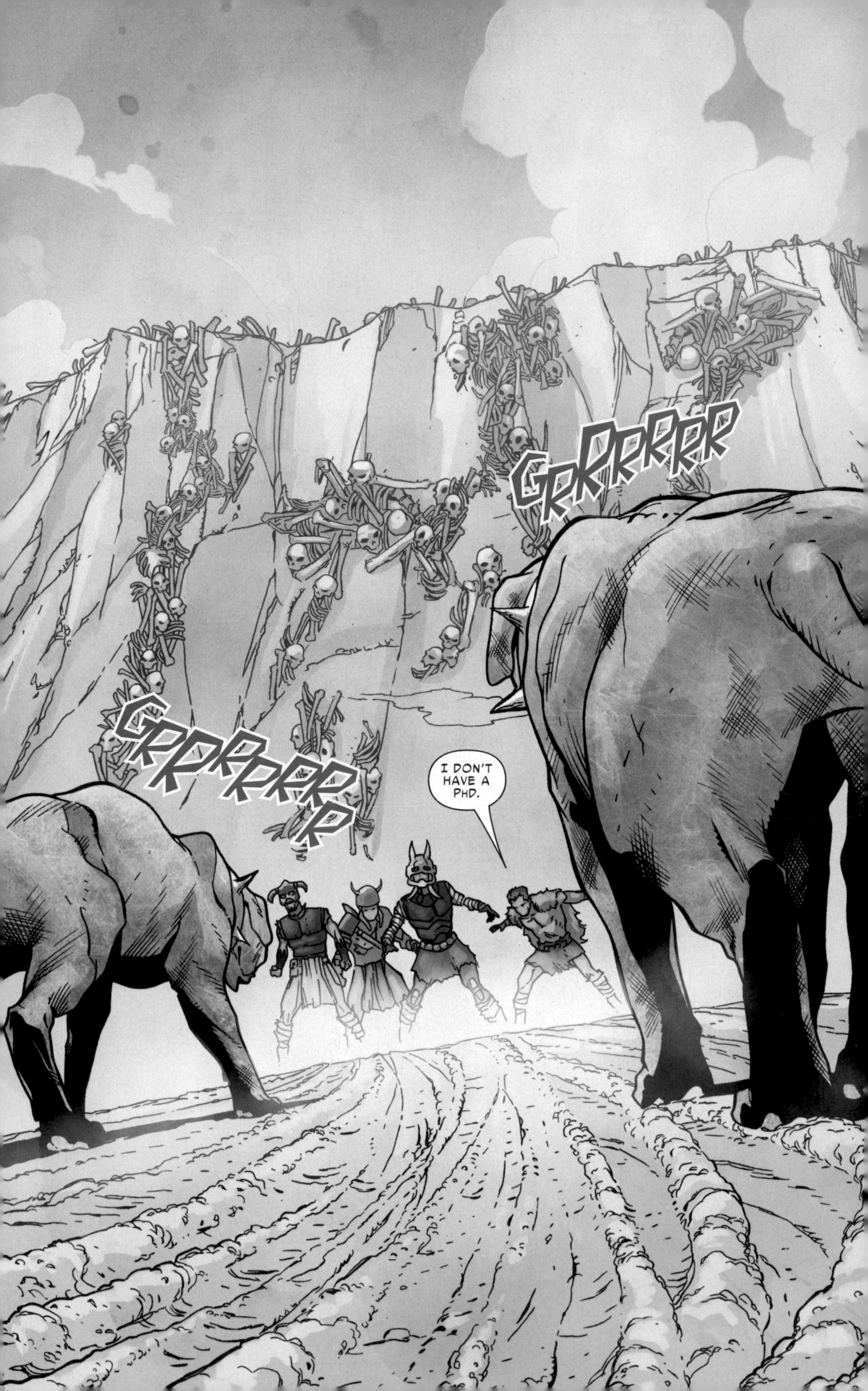
GRRRRRR
GRRRRRRRR
I DON'T HAVE A PHD.

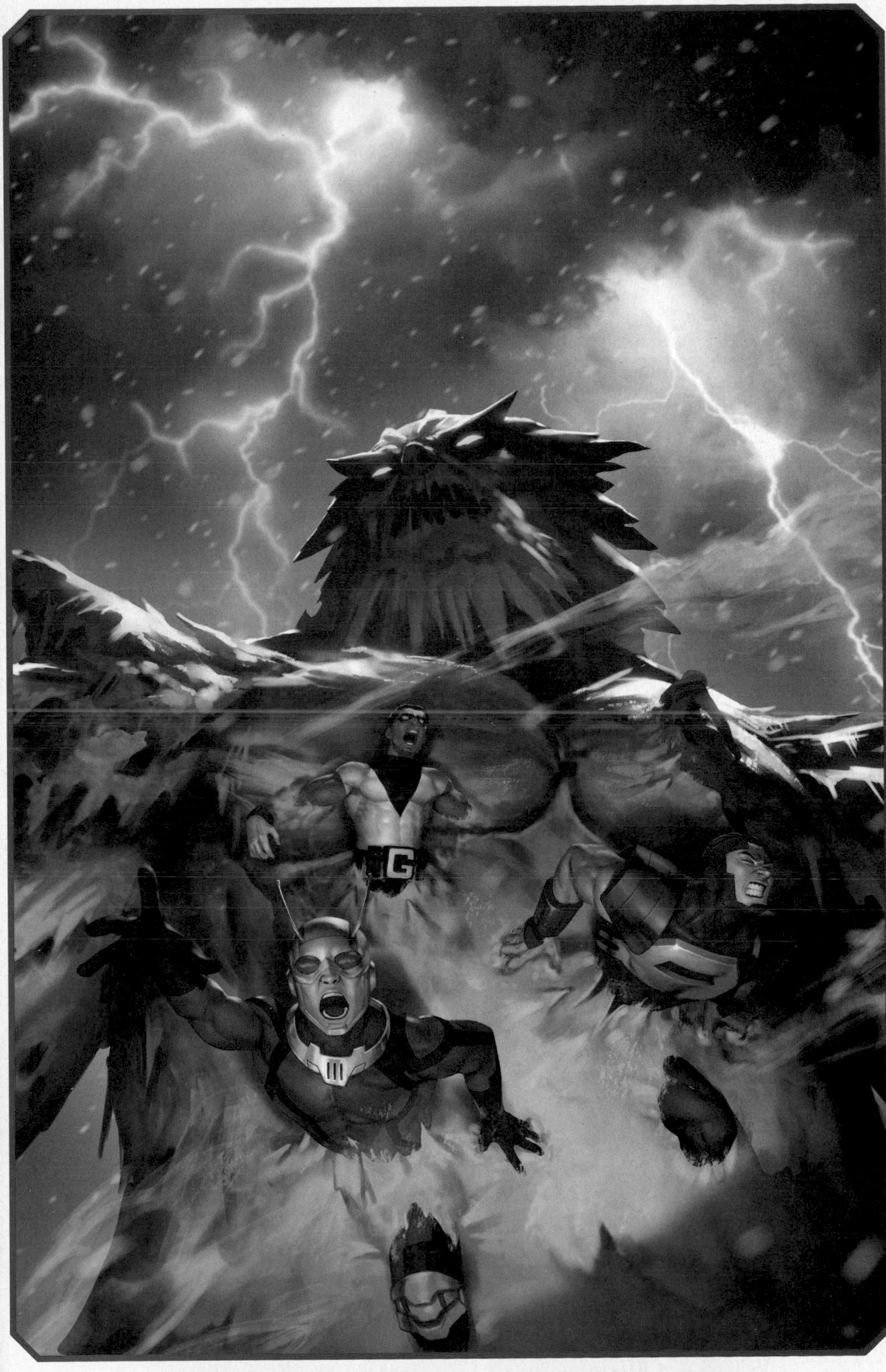

GIANT-MAN #2 "A FEW MORE GIANT MEN"

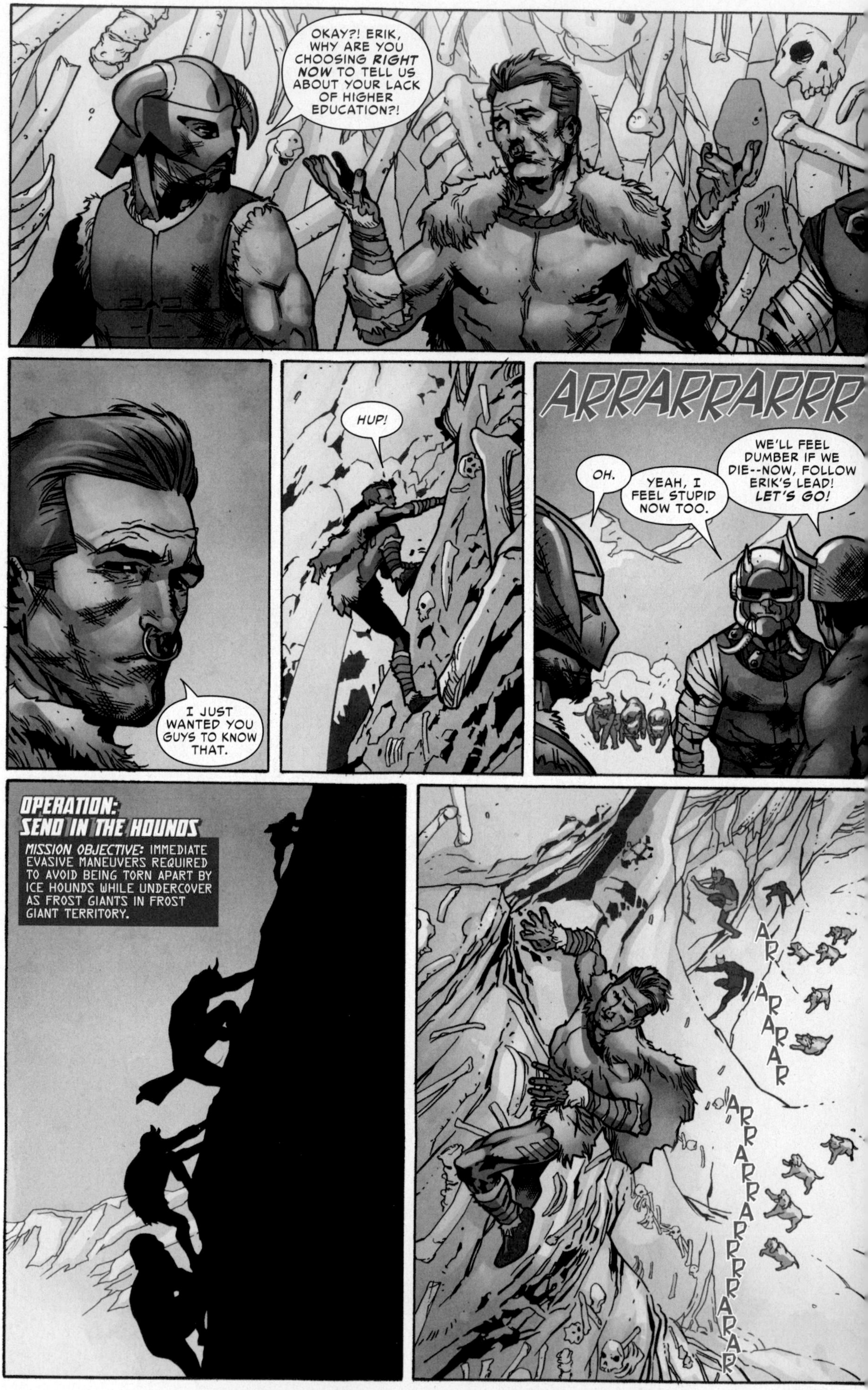
OKAY?! ERIK, WHY ARE YOU CHOOSING RIGHT NOW TO TELL US ABOUT YOUR LACK OF HIGHER EDUCATION?!
I JUST WANTED YOU GUYS TO KNOW THAT.
HUP!
ARRARRARRR
OH.
YEAH, I FEEL STUPID NOW TOO.
WE'LL FEEL DUMBER IF WE DIE--NOW, FOLLOW ERIK'S LEAD! LET'S GO!
OPERATION: SEND IN THE HOUNDS
MISSION OBJECTIVE: IMMEDIATE EVASIVE MANEUVERS REQUIRED TO AVOID BEING TORN APART BY ICE HOUNDS WHILE UNDERCOVER AS FROST GIANTS IN FROST GIANT TERRITORY.
ARARARARAR
ARRARRARRRARAR

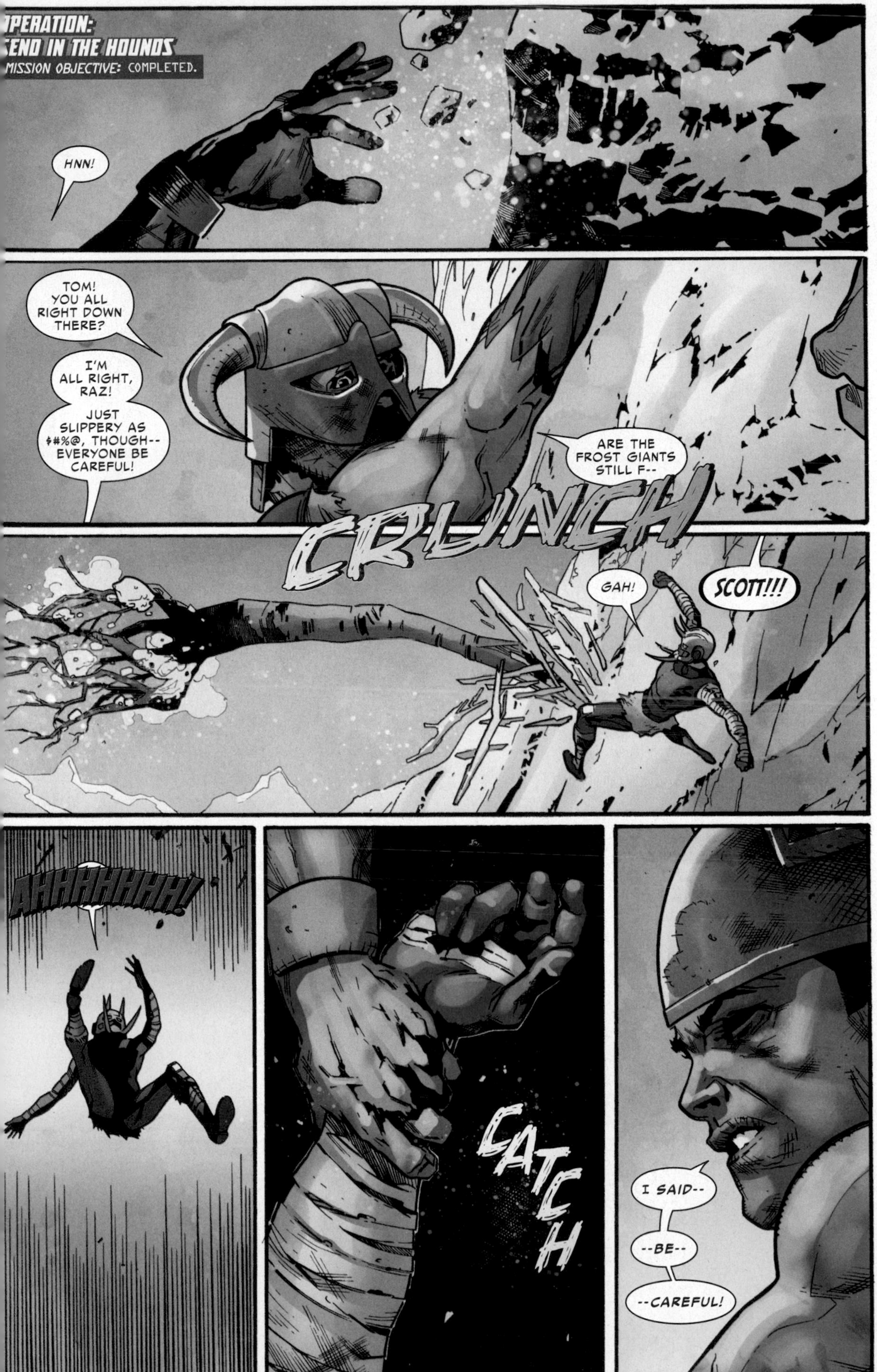
OPERATION:
SEND IN THE HOUNDS
MISSION OBJECTIVE: COMPLETED.
HNN!
TOM! YOU ALL RIGHT DOWN THERE?
I'M ALL RIGHT, RAZ!
JUST SLIPPERY AS $#%@, THOUGH-- EVERYONE BE CAREFUL!
ARE THE FROST GIANTS STILL F--
CRUNCH
GAH!
SCOTT!!!
AHHHHHHH!
CATCH
I SAID--
--BE--
--CAREFUL!

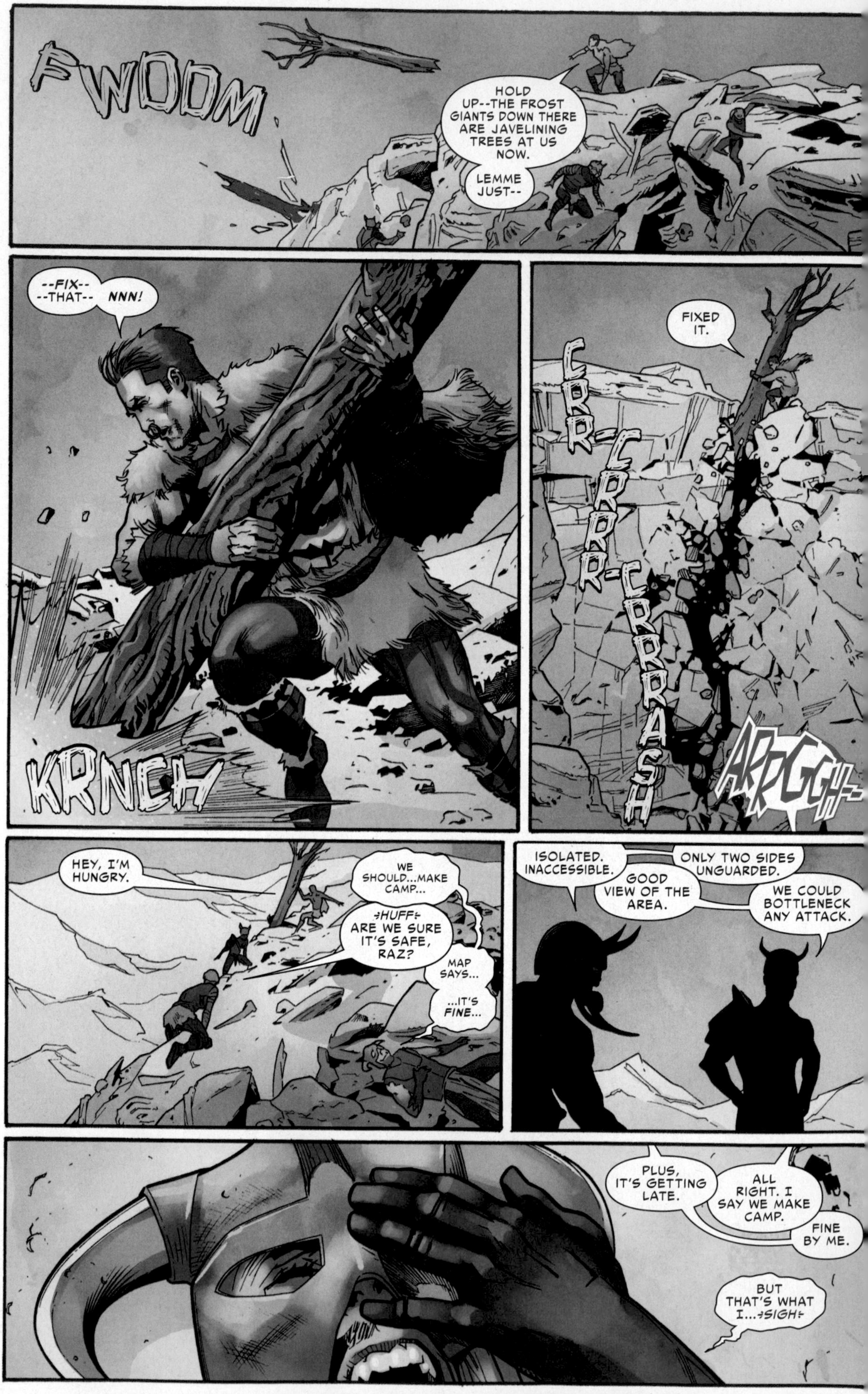
FWOOM
HOLD UP--THE FROST GIANTS DOWN THERE ARE JAVELINING TREES AT US NOW.
LEMME JUST--
--FIX-- --THAT-- NNN!
KRNCH
FIXED IT.
CRR-CRRR-CRRRASH
ARRGGH--
HEY, I'M HUNGRY.
WE SHOULD...MAKE CAMP...
HUFF ARE WE SURE IT'S SAFE, RAZ?
MAP SAYS...
...IT'S FINE...
ISOLATED. INACCESSIBLE.
ONLY TWO SIDES UNGUARDED.
GOOD VIEW OF THE AREA.
WE COULD BOTTLENECK ANY ATTACK.
PLUS, IT'S GETTING LATE.
ALL RIGHT. I SAY WE MAKE CAMP.
FINE BY ME.
BUT THAT'S WHAT I... SIGH

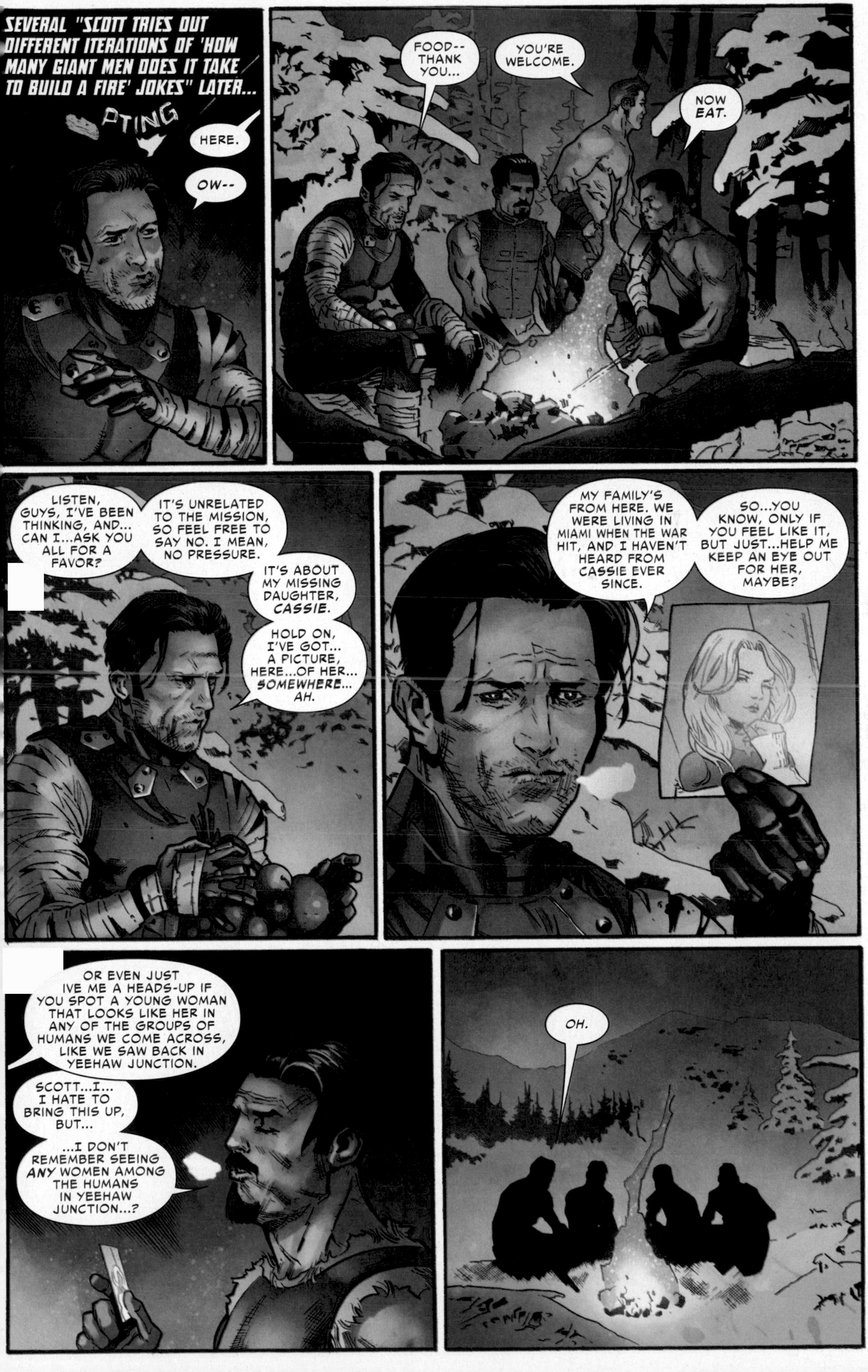

SEVERAL "SCOTT TRIES OUT DIFFERENT ITERATIONS OF 'HOW MANY GIANT MEN DOES IT TAKE TO BUILD A FIRE' JOKES" LATER...
PTING
HERE.
OW--
FOOD-- THANK YOU...
YOU'RE WELCOME.
NOW EAT.
LISTEN, GUYS, I'VE BEEN THINKING, AND... CAN I...ASK YOU ALL FOR A FAVOR?
IT'S UNRELATED TO THE MISSION, SO FEEL FREE TO SAY NO. I MEAN, NO PRESSURE.
IT'S ABOUT MY MISSING DAUGHTER, CASSIE.
HOLD ON, I'VE GOT... A PICTURE, HERE...OF HER... SOMEWHERE... AH.
MY FAMILY'S FROM HERE. WE WERE LIVING IN MIAMI WHEN THE WAR HIT, AND I HAVEN'T HEARD FROM CASSIE EVER SINCE.
SO...YOU KNOW, ONLY IF YOU FEEL LIKE IT, BUT JUST...HELP ME KEEP AN EYE OUT FOR HER, MAYBE?
OR EVEN JUST IVE ME A HEADS-UP IF YOU SPOT A YOUNG WOMAN THAT LOOKS LIKE HER IN ANY OF THE GROUPS OF HUMANS WE COME ACROSS, LIKE WE SAW BACK IN YEEHAW JUNCTION.
SCOTT...I... I HATE TO BRING THIS UP, BUT...
...I DON'T REMEMBER SEEING ANY WOMEN AMONG THE HUMANS IN YEEHAW JUNCTION...?
OH.

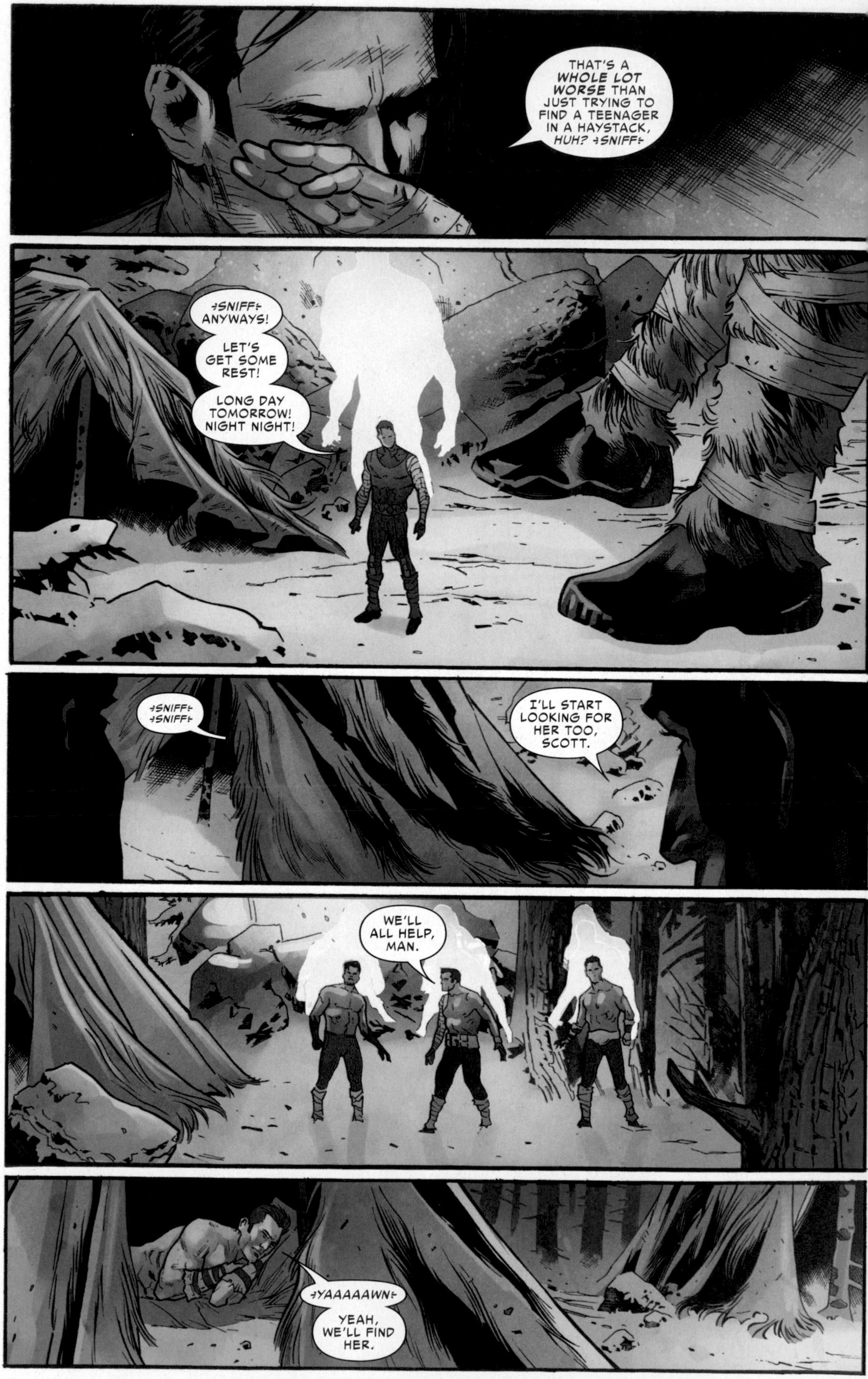
THAT'S A WHOLE LOT WORSE THAN JUST TRYING TO FIND A TEENAGER IN A HAYSTACK, HUH? ⸗SNIFF⸗
⸗SNIFF⸗ ANYWAYS!
LET'S GET SOME REST!
LONG DAY TOMORROW! NIGHT NIGHT!
⸗SNIFF⸗ ⸗SNIFF⸗
I'LL START LOOKING FOR HER TOO, SCOTT.
WE'LL ALL HELP, MAN.
⸗YAAAAAWN⸗
YEAH, WE'LL FIND HER.

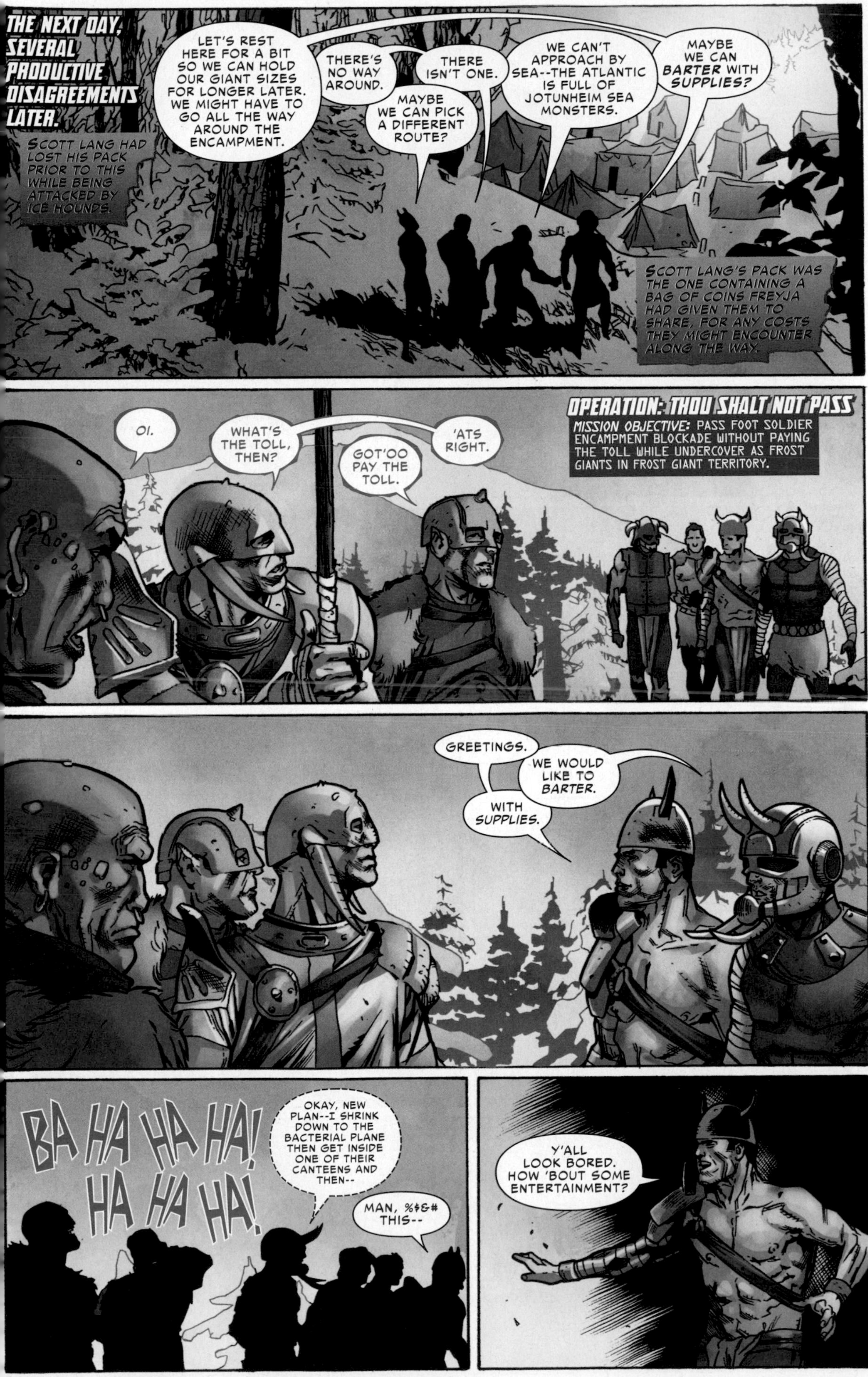
THE NEXT DAY, SEVERAL PRODUCTIVE DISAGREEMENTS LATER.
SCOTT LANG HAD LOST HIS PACK PRIOR TO THIS WHILE BEING ATTACKED BY ICE HOUNDS.
LET'S REST HERE FOR A BIT SO WE CAN HOLD OUR GIANT SIZES FOR LONGER LATER. WE MIGHT HAVE TO GO ALL THE WAY AROUND THE ENCAMPMENT.
THERE'S NO WAY AROUND.
THERE ISN'T ONE.
MAYBE WE CAN PICK A DIFFERENT ROUTE?
WE CAN'T APPROACH BY SEA--THE ATLANTIC IS FULL OF JOTUNHEIM SEA MONSTERS.
MAYBE WE CAN BARTER WITH SUPPLIES?
SCOTT LANG'S PACK WAS THE ONE CONTAINING A BAG OF COINS FREYJA HAD GIVEN THEM TO SHARE, FOR ANY COSTS THEY MIGHT ENCOUNTER ALONG THE WAY.
OPERATION: THOU SHALT NOT PASS
MISSION OBJECTIVE: PASS FOOT SOLDIER ENCAMPMENT BLOCKADE WITHOUT PAYING THE TOLL WHILE UNDERCOVER AS FROST GIANTS IN FROST GIANT TERRITORY.
OI.
WHAT'S THE TOLL, THEN?
GOT'OO PAY THE TOLL.
'ATS RIGHT.
GREETINGS.
WE WOULD LIKE TO BARTER.
WITH SUPPLIES.
BA HA HA HA! HA HA HA!
OKAY, NEW PLAN--I SHRINK DOWN TO THE BACTERIAL PLANE THEN GET INSIDE ONE OF THEIR CANTEENS AND THEN--
MAN, %$&# THIS--
Y'ALL LOOK BORED. HOW 'BOUT SOME ENTERTAINMENT?

TOM HAS NEVER BELIEVED IN GOD.

BUT HE HAS ALSO NEVER FELT TALLER THAN WHEN HE WAS A CHILD SINGING IN A CHURCH CHOIR.

IS THAT "JOLENE"?

HA HA HA HA HA! HA HA HA HA!

MAN, %$&# THEM! DOLLY PARTON IS AMAZING.

TRUTH.

RIGHT, SO I GET INSIDE THE CANTEEN--

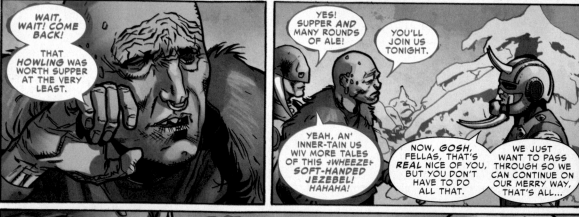

WAIT, WAIT! COME BACK!

THAT HOWLING WAS WORTH SUPPER AT THE VERY LEAST.

YES! SUPPER AND MANY ROUNDS OF ALE!

YOU'LL JOIN US TONIGHT.

YEAH, AN' INNER-TAIN US WIV MORE TALES OF THIS ＊WHEEZE＊ SOFT-HANDED JEZEBEL! HAHAHA!

NOW, GOSH, FELLAS, THAT'S REAL NICE OF YOU, BUT YOU DON'T HAVE TO DO ALL THAT.

WE JUST WANT TO PASS THROUGH SO WE CAN CONTINUE ON OUR MERRY WAY, THAT'S ALL...

WOT'OO GOT ON THE OTHER SIDE OF THIS ROAD, THEN, THAT'S SO IMPORTANT?

YEAH. NOTHIN' PAST US EXCEPT YMIR'S STRONGHOLD, INNIT?

YEAH. WOT'OO GOT BUSINESS WITH YMIR FER?

AN' LAST-LIKE-- WHAT KIND OF SELF-RESPECTIN' FROST GIANT TURNS DOWN AN OFFER OF FREE ALE?

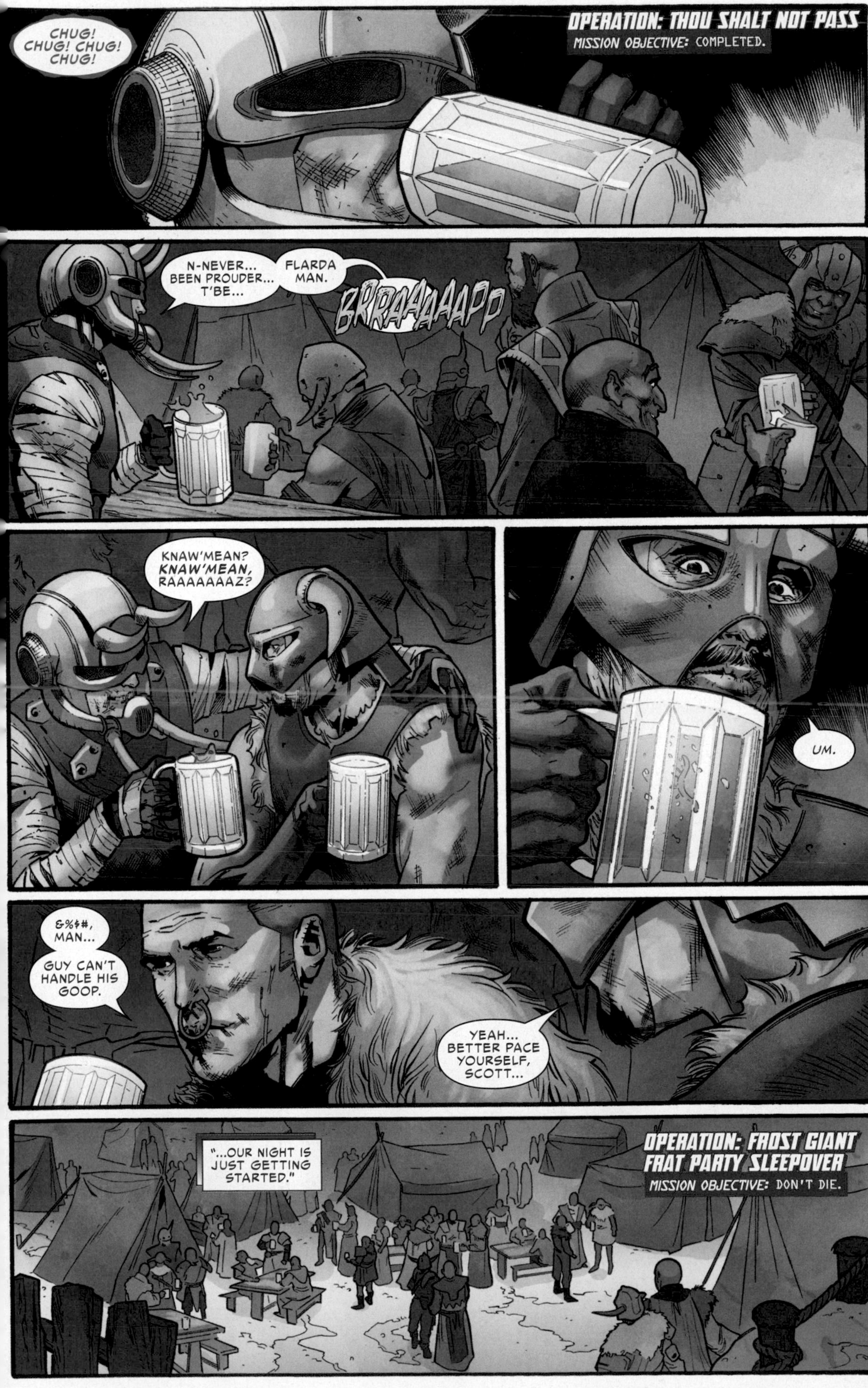
CHUG! CHUG! CHUG! CHUG!
OPERATION: THOU SHALT NOT PASS
MISSION OBJECTIVE: COMPLETED.
N-NEVER... BEEN PROUDER... T'BE...
FLARDA MAN.
BRRAAAAAPP
KNAW'MEAN? KNAW'MEAN, RAAAAAAAZ?
UM.
&%$#, MAN...
GUY CAN'T HANDLE HIS GOOP.
YEAH... BETTER PACE YOURSELF, SCOTT...
"...OUR NIGHT IS JUST GETTING STARTED."
OPERATION: FROST GIANT FRAT PARTY SLEEPOVER
MISSION OBJECTIVE: DON'T DIE.

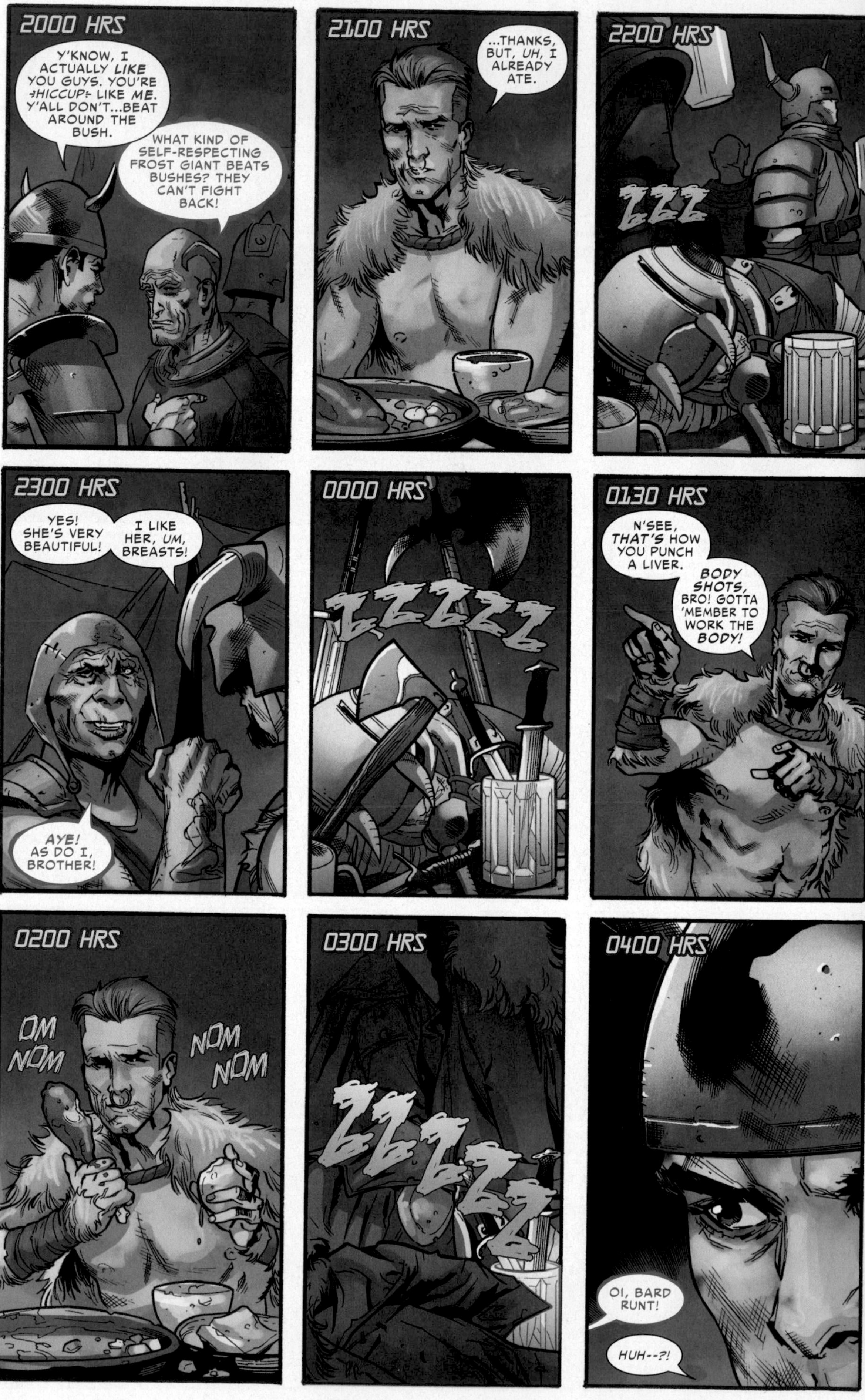
2000 HRS
Y'KNOW, I ACTUALLY LIKE YOU GUYS. YOU'RE *HICCUP* LIKE ME. Y'ALL DON'T...BEAT AROUND THE BUSH.
WHAT KIND OF SELF-RESPECTING FROST GIANT BEATS BUSHES? THEY CAN'T FIGHT BACK!
2100 HRS
...THANKS, BUT, UH, I ALREADY ATE.
2200 HRS
ZZZ
2300 HRS
YES! SHE'S VERY BEAUTIFUL!
I LIKE HER, UM, BREASTS!
AYE! AS DO I, BROTHER!
0000 HRS
ZZZZZZ
0130 HRS
N'SEE, THAT'S HOW YOU PUNCH A LIVER.
BODY SHOTS, BRO! GOTTA 'MEMBER TO WORK THE BODY!
0200 HRS
OM NOM
NOM NOM
0300 HRS
ZZZZZ
0400 HRS
OI, BARD RUNT!
HUH--?!

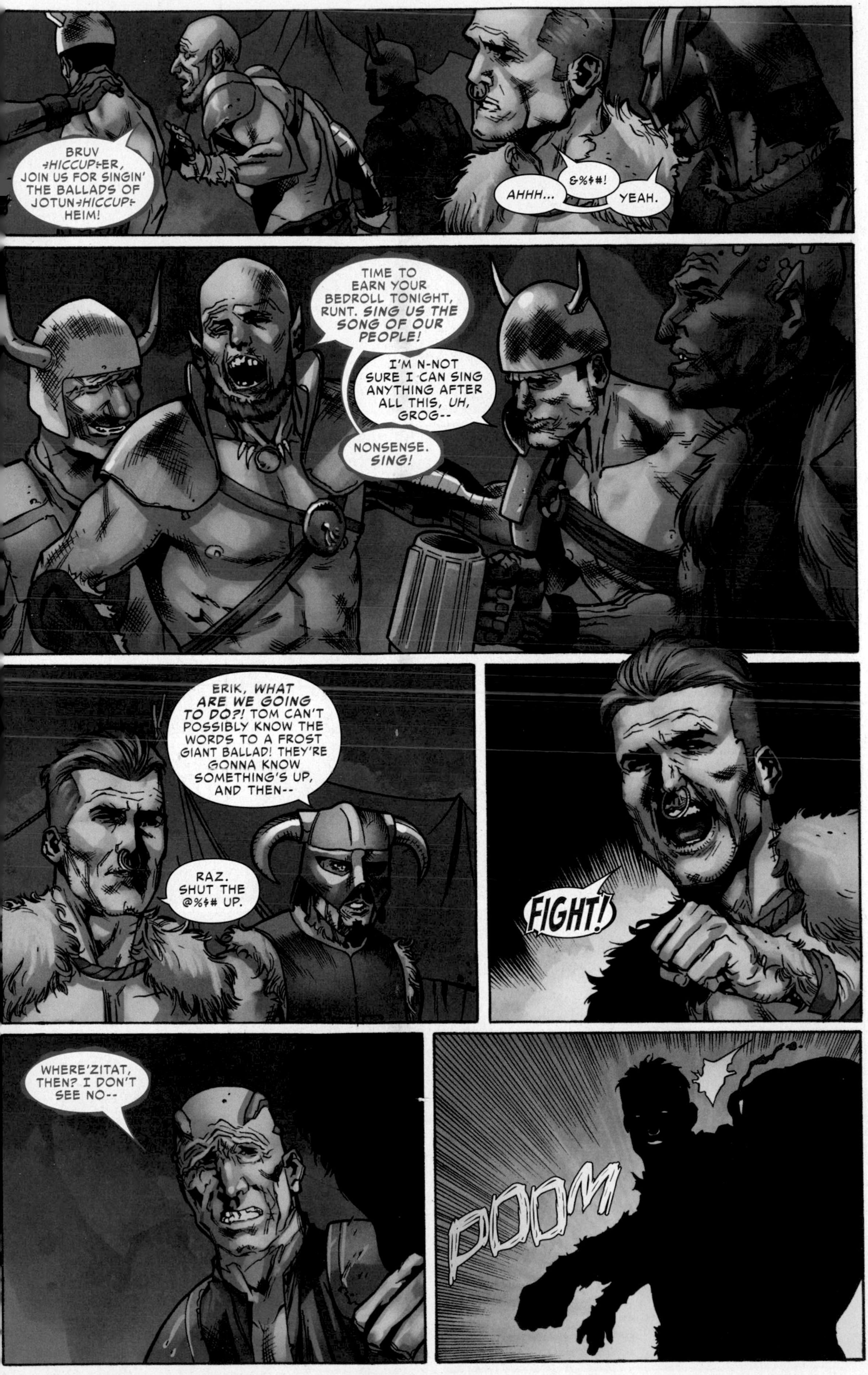

BRUV ⸗HICCUP⸗ER, JOIN US FOR SINGIN' THE BALLADS OF JOTUN⸗HICCUP⸗HEIM!
AHHH...
&%$#!
YEAH.
TIME TO EARN YOUR BEDROLL TONIGHT, RUNT. SING US THE SONG OF OUR PEOPLE!
I'M N-NOT SURE I CAN SING ANYTHING AFTER ALL THIS, UH, GROG--
NONSENSE. SING!
ERIK, WHAT ARE WE GOING TO DO?! TOM CAN'T POSSIBLY KNOW THE WORDS TO A FROST GIANT BALLAD! THEY'RE GONNA KNOW SOMETHING'S UP, AND THEN--
RAZ. SHUT THE @%$# UP.
FIGHT!
WHERE'ZITAT, THEN? I DON'T SEE NO--
DOOM

RAaAAAAAAR!

GRRRASH

I'M AWAKE! I'M UP! WHAT'S-- WHAT'RE WE--

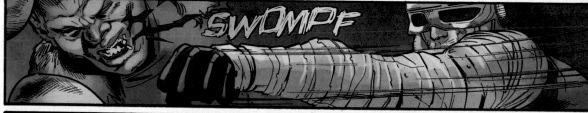

SWOMPF

THAT OUGHTA KEEP THEM DISTRACTED FOR A WHILE.

WHERE'S TOM...?

≠YAWN≠ THAT WAS THE BEST SLEEP I'VE GOTTEN IN WEEKS.

HEY, SCOTT.

HI! WHERE'S TOM?

♪ LONG THE DAWN OF FROST GIANT MORN, T'WAS FATHER GOD YMIR WHO BIRTHED US TRUE... ♪

I... LOVE YOU GUYS...

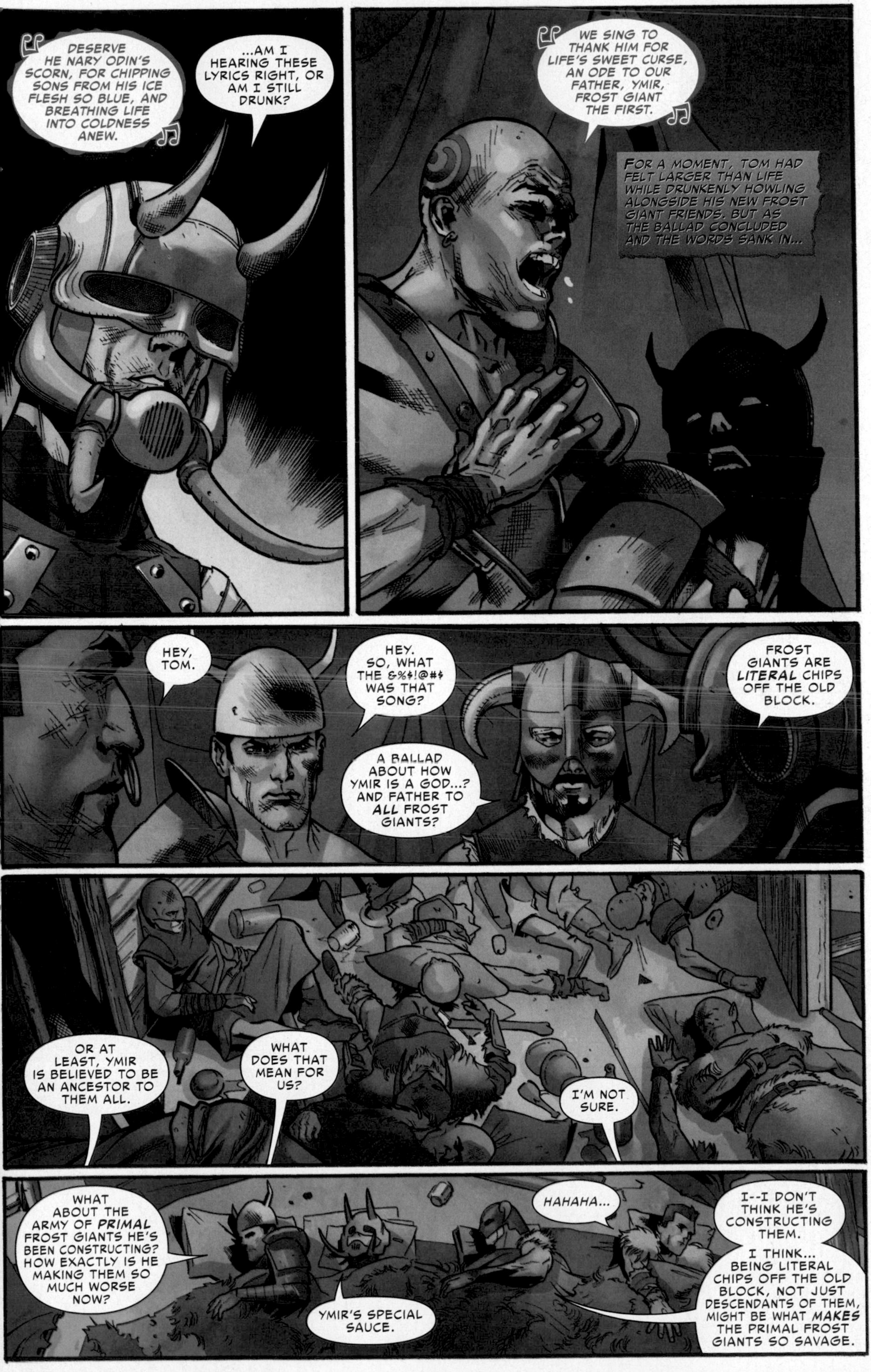

DESERVE HE NARY ODIN'S SCORN, FOR CHIPPING SONS FROM HIS ICE FLESH SO BLUE, AND BREATHING LIFE INTO COLDNESS ANEW.
...AM I HEARING THESE LYRICS RIGHT, OR AM I STILL DRUNK?
WE SING TO THANK HIM FOR LIFE'S SWEET CURSE, AN ODE TO OUR FATHER, YMIR, FROST GIANT THE FIRST.
FOR A MOMENT, TOM HAD FELT LARGER THAN LIFE WHILE DRUNKENLY HOWLING ALONGSIDE HIS NEW FROST GIANT FRIENDS. BUT AS THE BALLAD CONCLUDED AND THE WORDS SANK IN...
HEY, TOM.
HEY. SO, WHAT THE &%$!@#$ WAS THAT SONG?
A BALLAD ABOUT HOW YMIR IS A GOD...? AND FATHER TO ALL FROST GIANTS?
FROST GIANTS ARE LITERAL CHIPS OFF THE OLD BLOCK.
OR AT LEAST, YMIR IS BELIEVED TO BE AN ANCESTOR TO THEM ALL.
WHAT DOES THAT MEAN FOR US?
I'M NOT SURE.
WHAT ABOUT THE ARMY OF PRIMAL FROST GIANTS HE'S BEEN CONSTRUCTING? HOW EXACTLY IS HE MAKING THEM SO MUCH WORSE NOW?
YMIR'S SPECIAL SAUCE.
HAHAHA...
I--I DON'T THINK HE'S CONSTRUCTING THEM.
I THINK... BEING LITERAL CHIPS OFF THE OLD BLOCK, NOT JUST DESCENDANTS OF THEM, MIGHT BE WHAT MAKES THE PRIMAL FROST GIANTS SO SAVAGE.

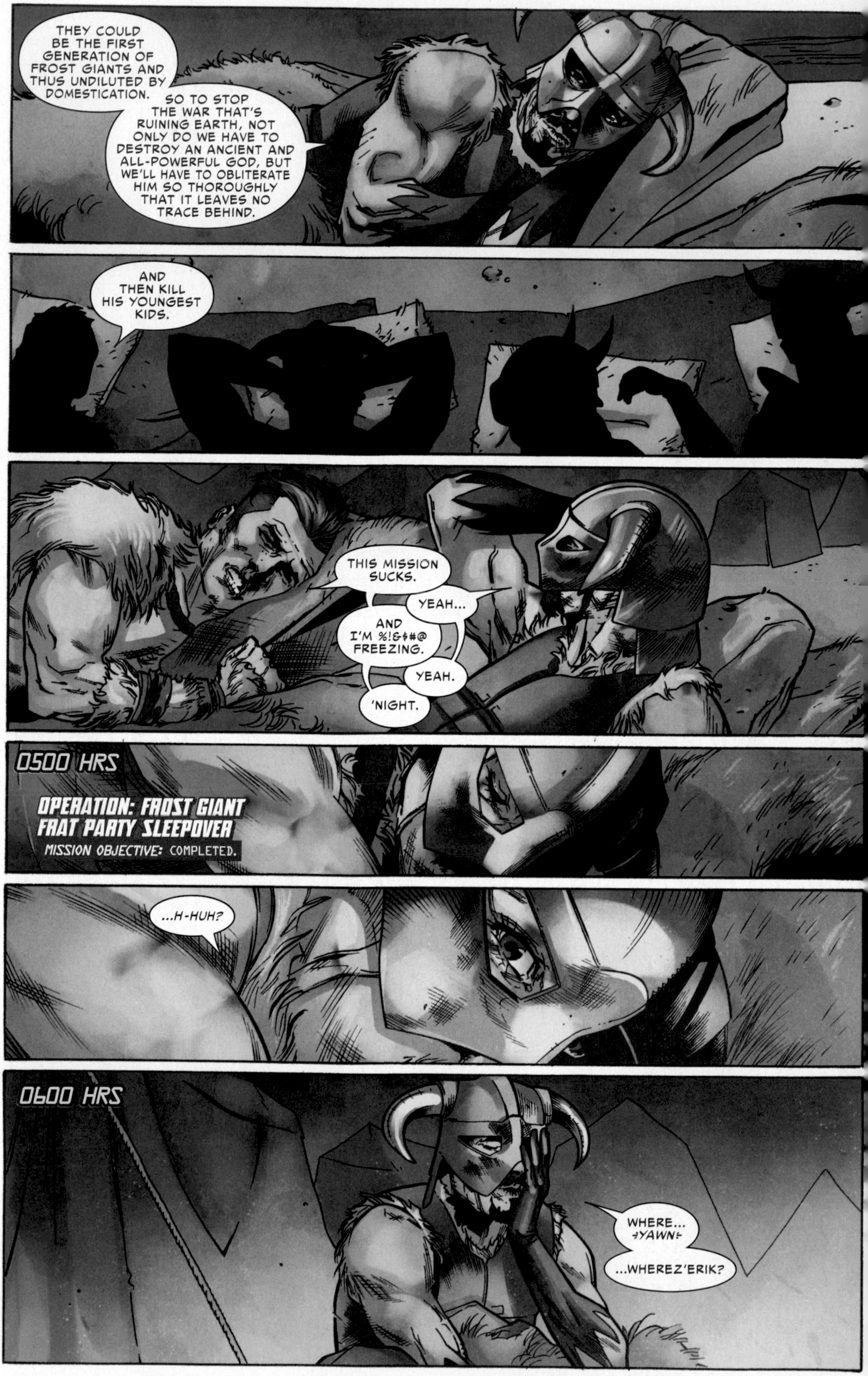
THEY COULD BE THE FIRST GENERATION OF FROST GIANTS AND THUS UNDILUTED BY DOMESTICATION.
SO TO STOP THE WAR THAT'S RUINING EARTH, NOT ONLY DO WE HAVE TO DESTROY AN ANCIENT AND ALL-POWERFUL GOD, BUT WE'LL HAVE TO OBLITERATE HIM SO THOROUGHLY THAT IT LEAVES NO TRACE BEHIND.
AND THEN KILL HIS YOUNGEST KIDS.
THIS MISSION SUCKS.
YEAH...
AND I'M %!&$#@ FREEZING.
YEAH.
'NIGHT.
0500 HRS
OPERATION: FROST GIANT FRAT PARTY SLEEPOVER
MISSION OBJECTIVE: COMPLETED.
...H-HUH?
0600 HRS
WHERE... ⸗YAWN⸗
...WHEREZ'ERIK?

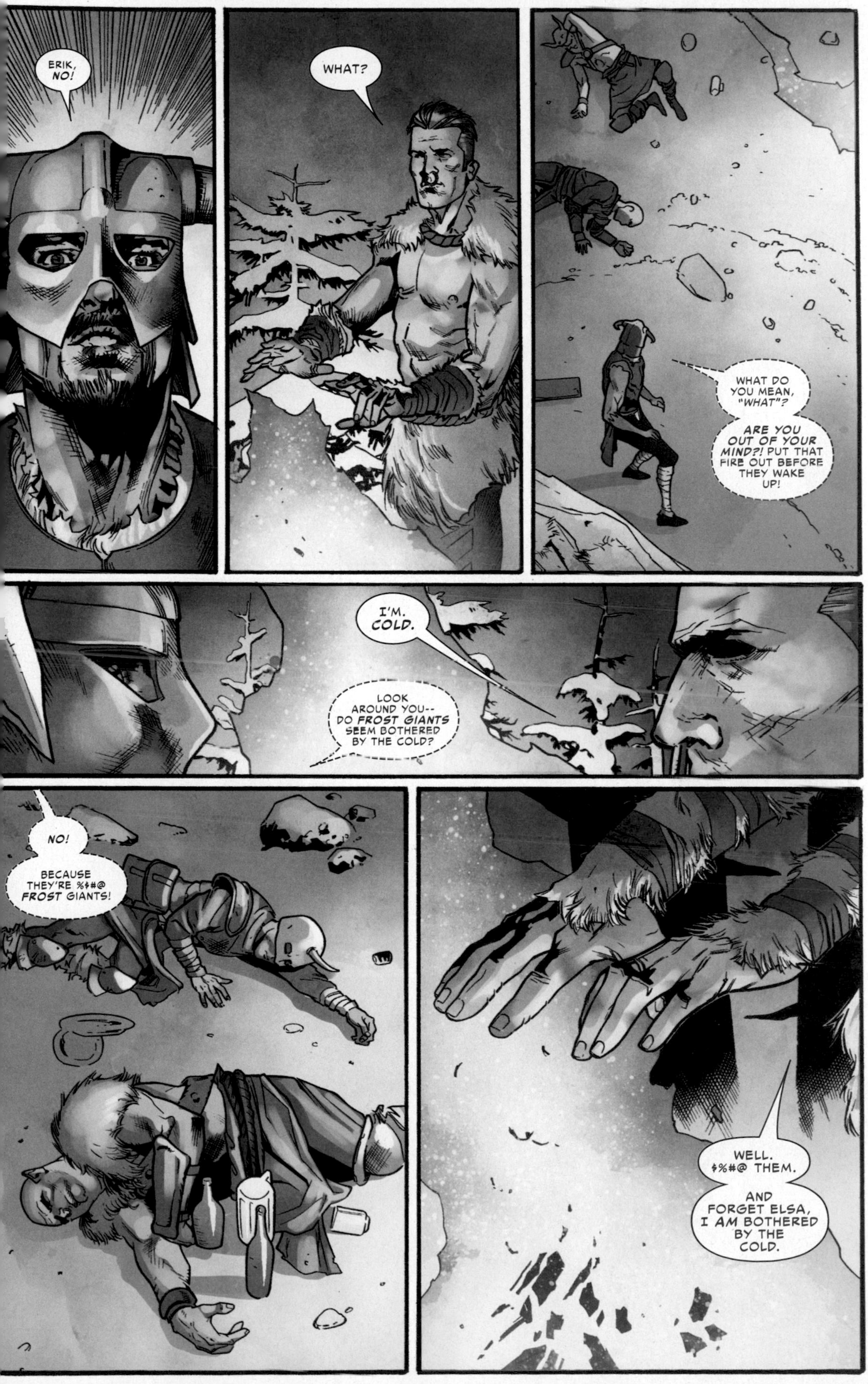
ERIK, NO!
WHAT?
WHAT DO YOU MEAN, "WHAT"?
ARE YOU OUT OF YOUR MIND?! PUT THAT FIRE OUT BEFORE THEY WAKE UP!
I'M. COLD.
LOOK AROUND YOU-- DO FROST GIANTS SEEM BOTHERED BY THE COLD?
NO!
BECAUSE THEY'RE %$#@ FROST GIANTS!
WELL. $%#@ THEM.
AND FORGET ELSA, I AM BOTHERED BY THE COLD.

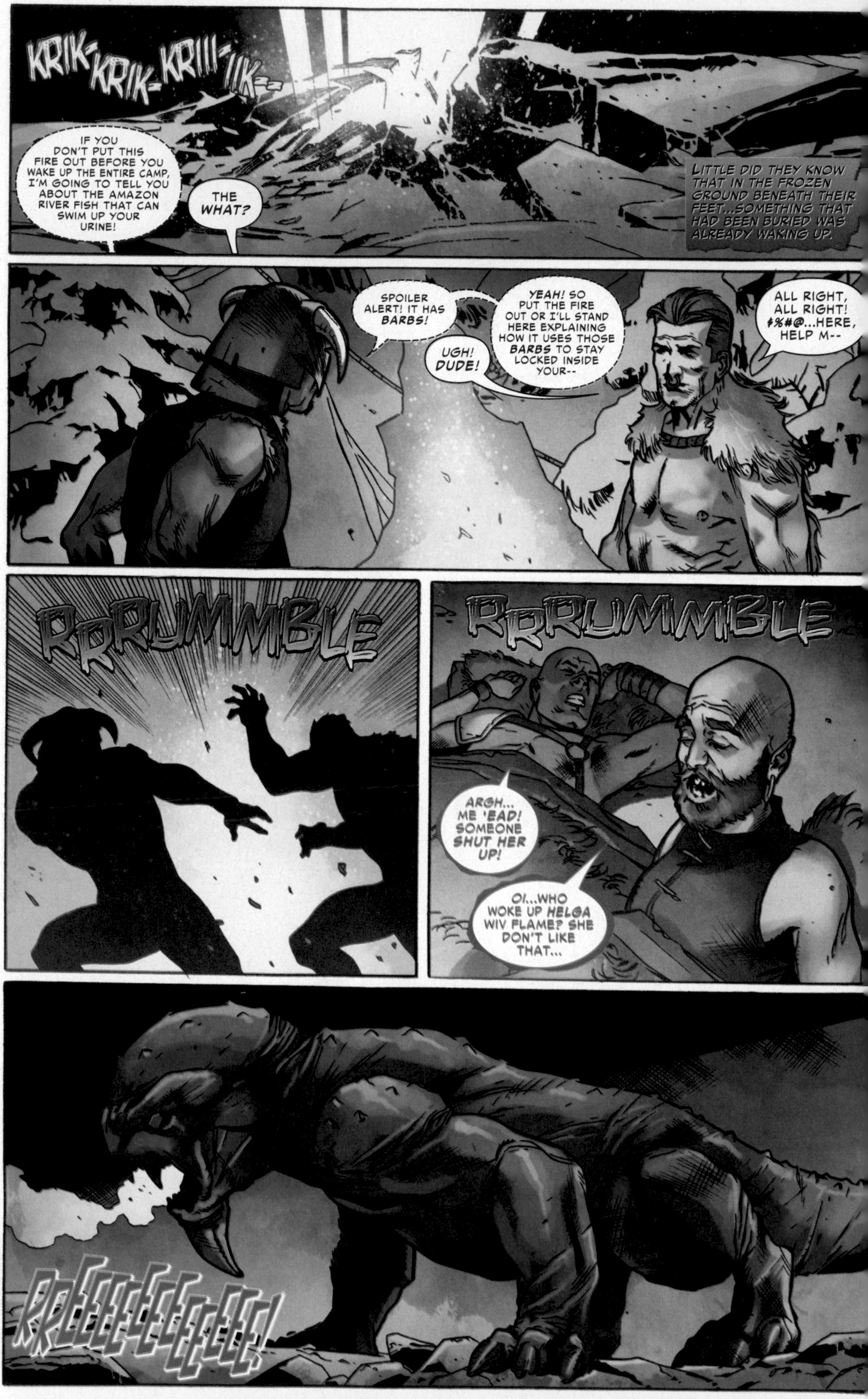
KRIK-KRIK-KRIII-IIK--
IF YOU DON'T PUT THIS FIRE OUT BEFORE YOU WAKE UP THE ENTIRE CAMP, I'M GOING TO TELL YOU ABOUT THE AMAZON RIVER FISH THAT CAN SWIM UP YOUR URINE!
THE WHAT?
LITTLE DID THEY KNOW THAT IN THE FROZEN GROUND BENEATH THEIR FEET...SOMETHING THAT HAD BEEN BURIED WAS ALREADY WAKING UP.
SPOILER ALERT! IT HAS BARBS!
UGH! DUDE!
YEAH! SO PUT THE FIRE OUT OR I'LL STAND HERE EXPLAINING HOW IT USES THOSE BARBS TO STAY LOCKED INSIDE YOUR--
ALL RIGHT, ALL RIGHT! $%#@...HERE, HELP M--
RRRUMMBLE
RRRUMMBLE
ARGH... ME 'EAD! SOMEONE SHUT HER UP!
OI...WHO WOKE UP HELGA WIV FLAME? SHE DON'T LIKE THAT...
KREEEEEEEEEEEE!

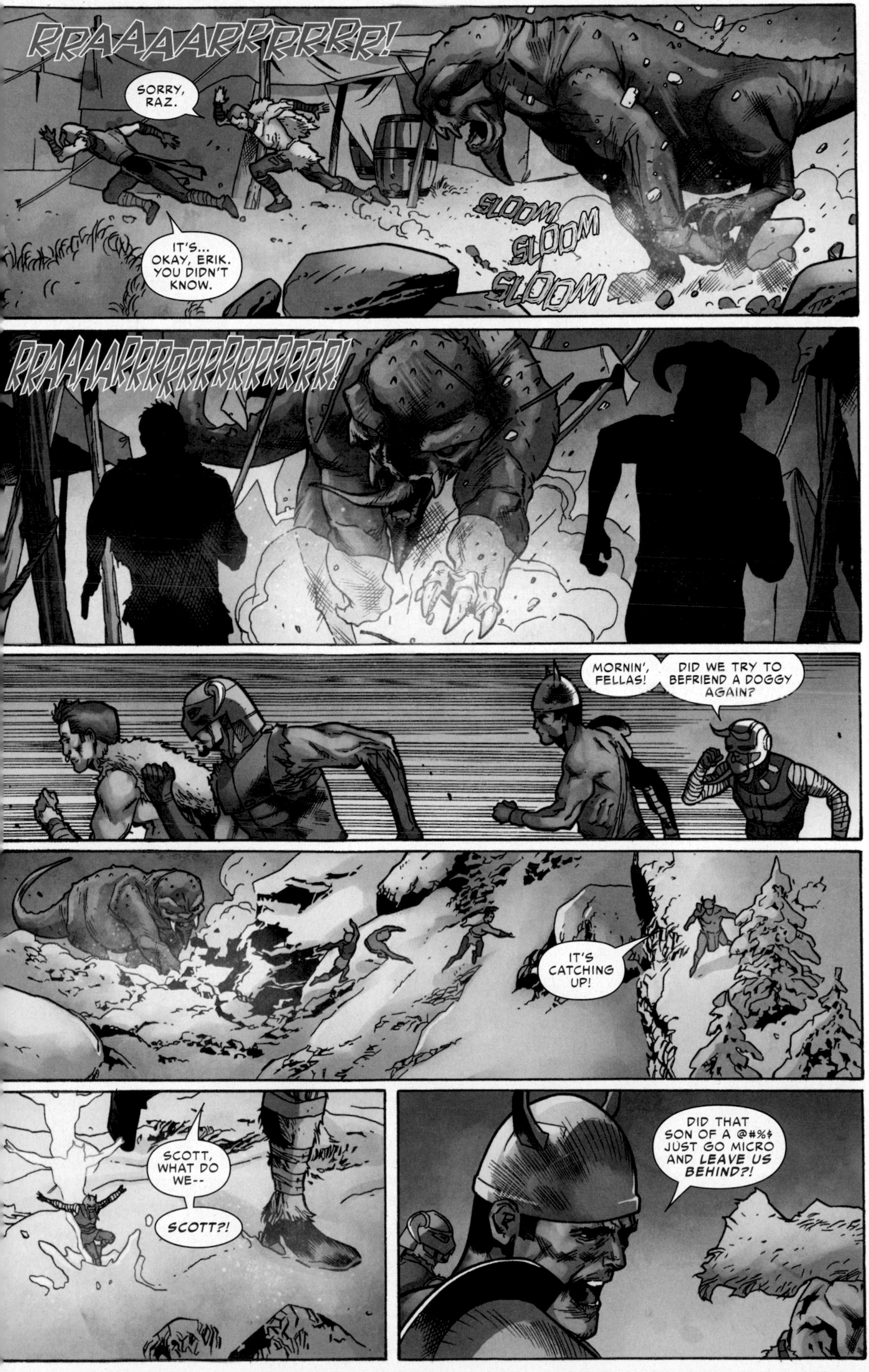
RRAAAAARRRRRR!
SORRY, RAZ.
IT'S... OKAY, ERIK. YOU DIDN'T KNOW.
SLOOM SLOOM SLOOM
RRAAAARRRRRRRRRRRRR!
MORNIN', FELLAS!
DID WE TRY TO BEFRIEND A DOGGY AGAIN?
IT'S CATCHING UP!
SCOTT, WHAT DO WE--
SCOTT?!
DID THAT SON OF A @#%$ JUST GO MICRO AND LEAVE US BEHIND?!

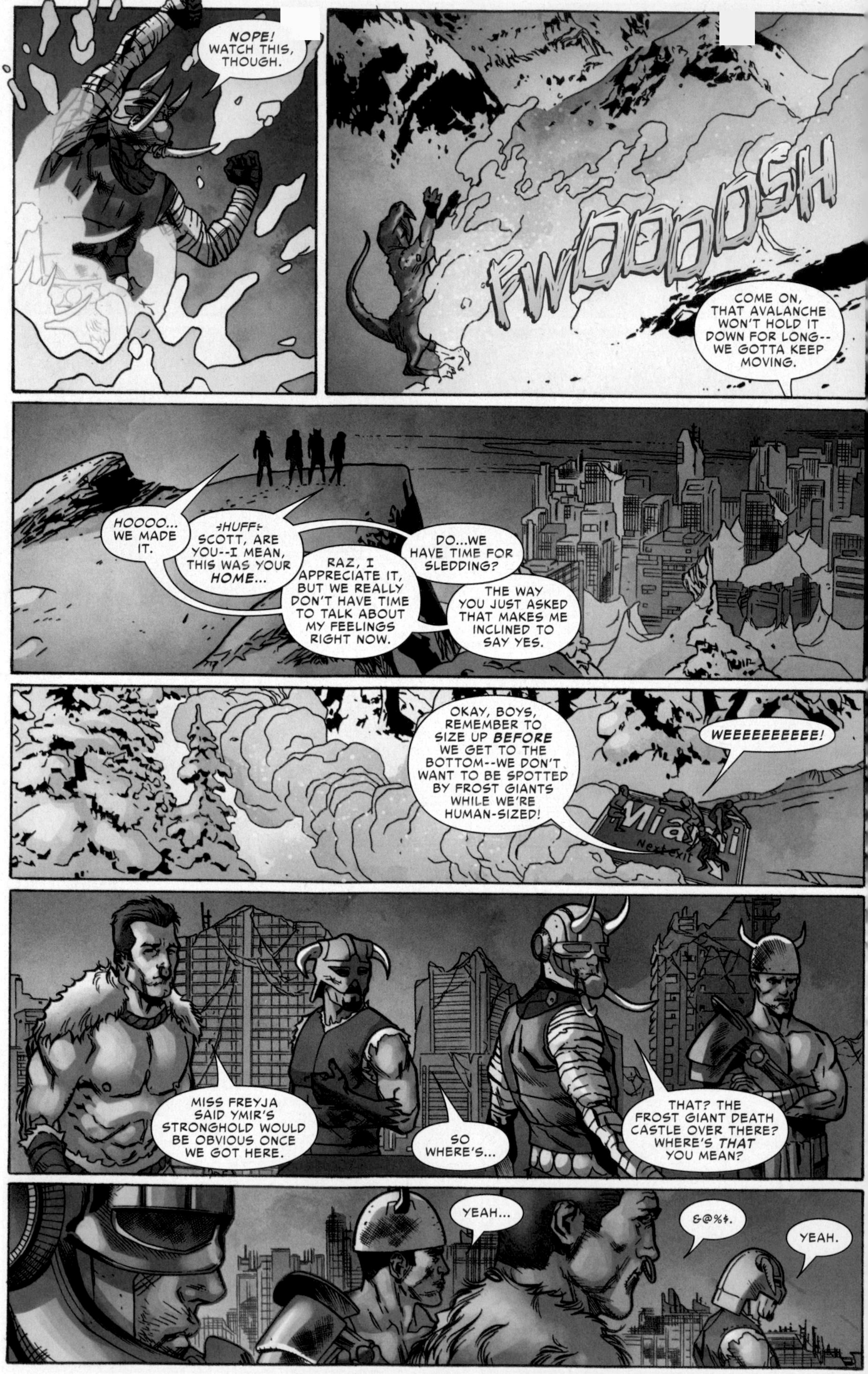
NOPE! WATCH THIS, THOUGH.
FWOOOOOSH
COME ON, THAT AVALANCHE WON'T HOLD IT DOWN FOR LONG-- WE GOTTA KEEP MOVING.
HOOOO... WE MADE IT.
HUFF SCOTT, ARE YOU--I MEAN, THIS WAS YOUR HOME...
RAZ, I APPRECIATE IT, BUT WE REALLY DON'T HAVE TIME TO TALK ABOUT MY FEELINGS RIGHT NOW.
DO...WE HAVE TIME FOR SLEDDING?
THE WAY YOU JUST ASKED THAT MAKES ME INCLINED TO SAY YES.
OKAY, BOYS, REMEMBER TO SIZE UP BEFORE WE GET TO THE BOTTOM--WE DON'T WANT TO BE SPOTTED BY FROST GIANTS WHILE WE'RE HUMAN-SIZED!
WEEEEEEEEEE!
Miami
Next Exit
MISS FREYJA SAID YMIR'S STRONGHOLD WOULD BE OBVIOUS ONCE WE GOT HERE.
SO WHERE'S...
THAT? THE FROST GIANT DEATH CASTLE OVER THERE? WHERE'S THAT YOU MEAN?
YEAH...
&@%$.
YEAH.

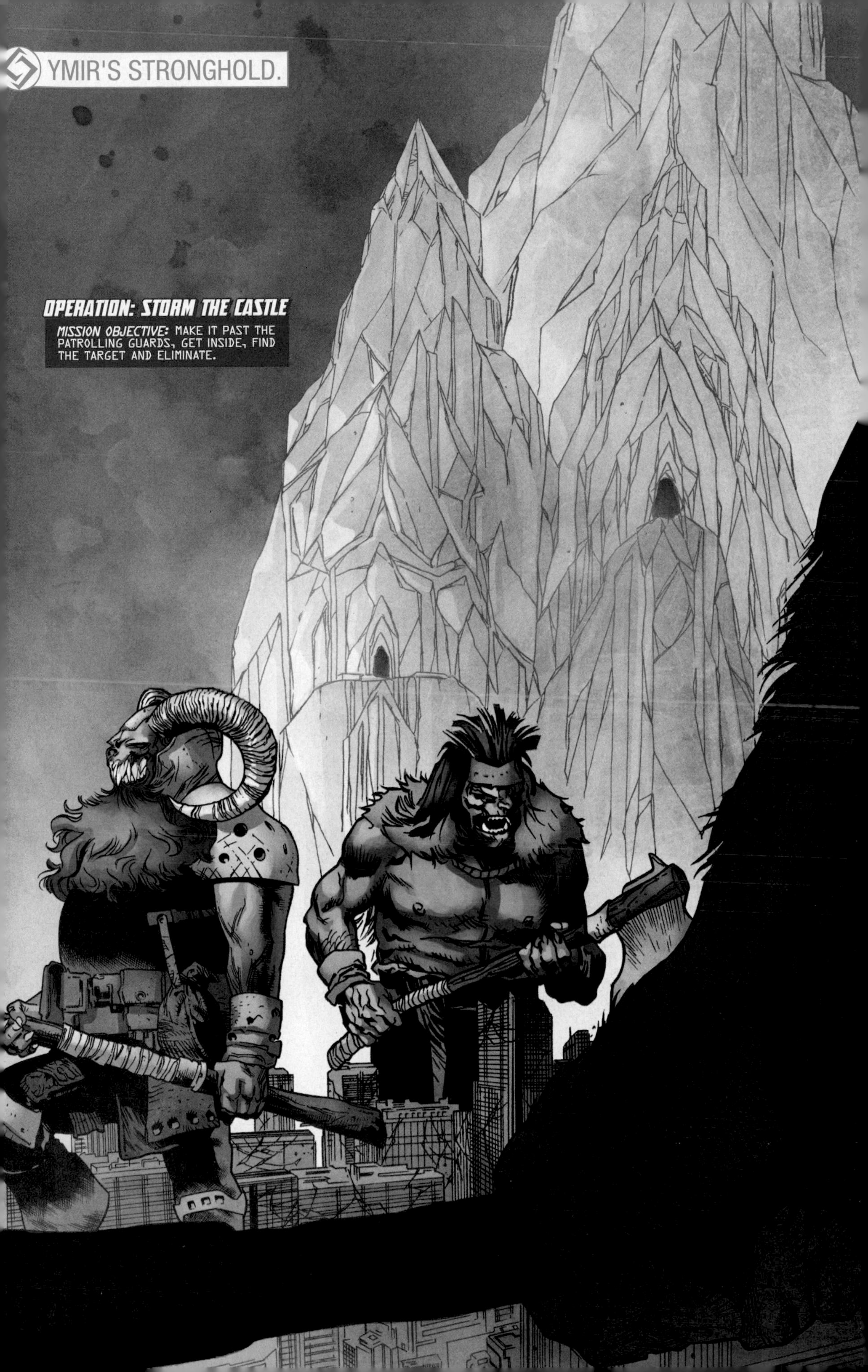
YMIR'S STRONGHOLD.
OPERATION: STORM THE CASTLE
MISSION OBJECTIVE: MAKE IT PAST THE PATROLLING GUARDS, GET INSIDE, FIND THE TARGET AND ELIMINATE.

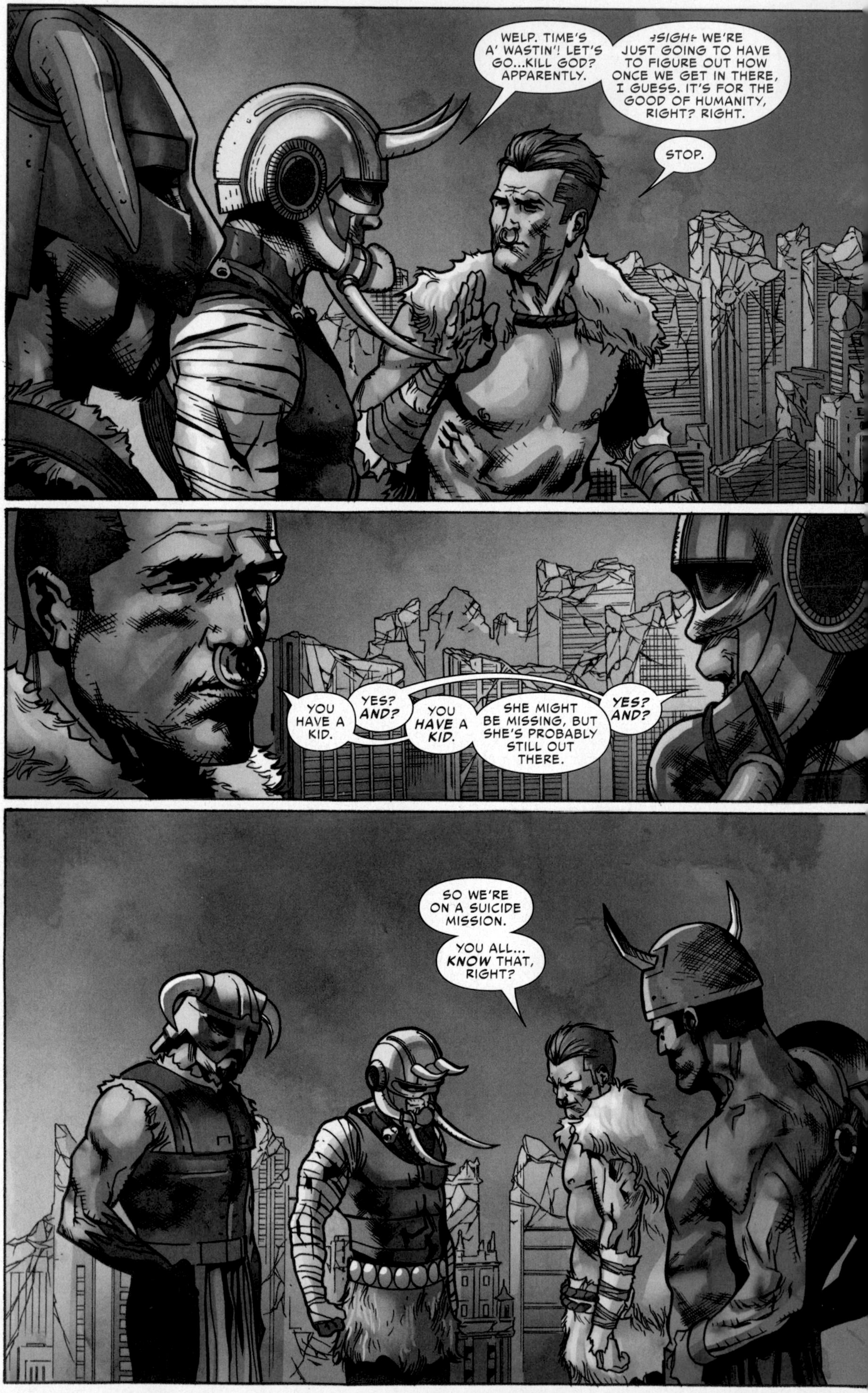
WELP. TIME'S A' WASTIN'! LET'S GO...KILL GOD? APPARENTLY.
-SIGH- WE'RE JUST GOING TO HAVE TO FIGURE OUT HOW ONCE WE GET IN THERE, I GUESS. IT'S FOR THE GOOD OF HUMANITY, RIGHT? RIGHT.
STOP.
YOU HAVE A KID.
YES? AND?
YOU HAVE A KID.
SHE MIGHT BE MISSING, BUT SHE'S PROBABLY STILL OUT THERE.
YES? AND?
SO WE'RE ON A SUICIDE MISSION.
YOU ALL... KNOW THAT, RIGHT?

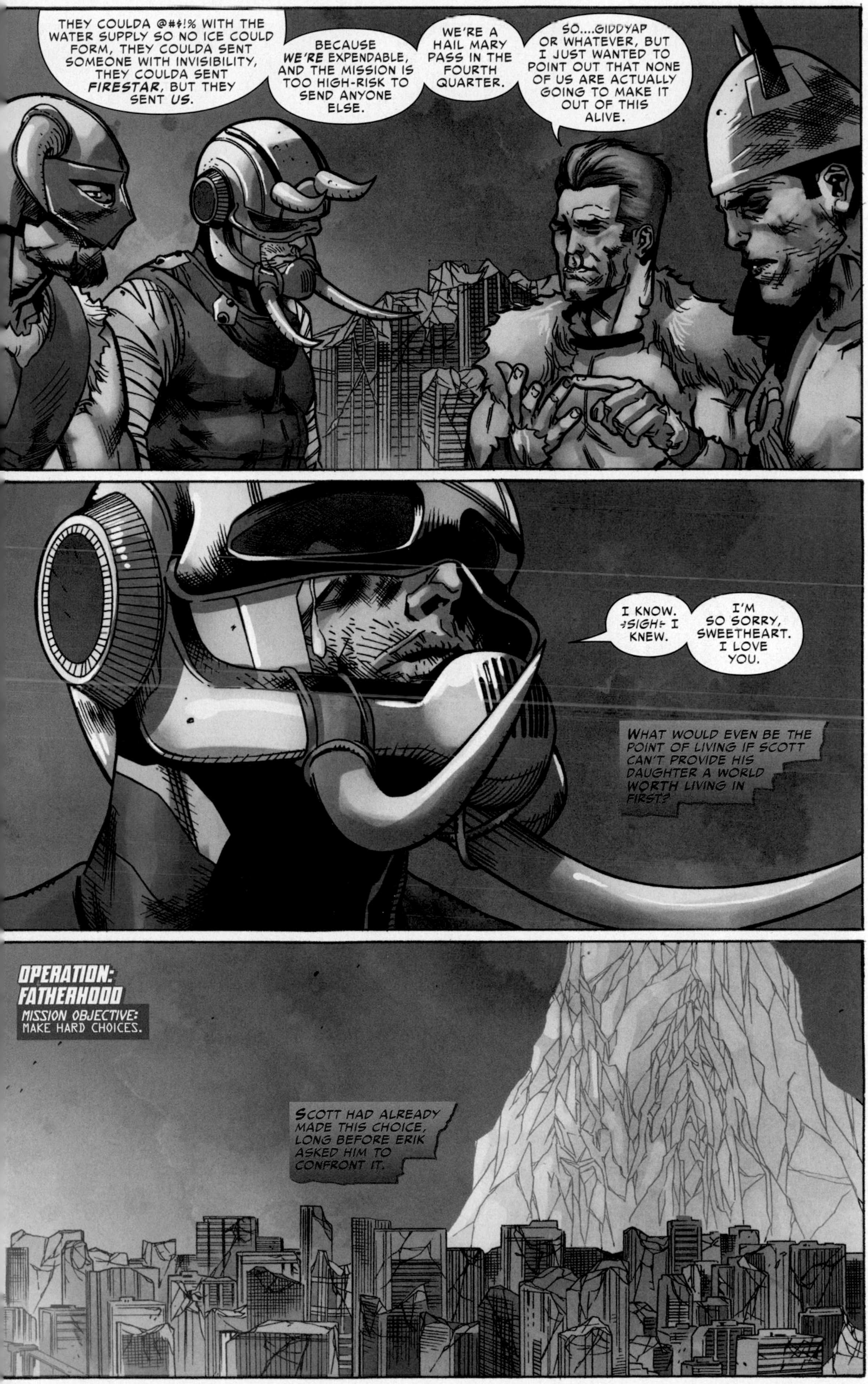
THEY COULDA @#$!% WITH THE WATER SUPPLY SO NO ICE COULD FORM, THEY COULDA SENT SOMEONE WITH INVISIBILITY, THEY COULDA SENT FIRESTAR, BUT THEY SENT US.
BECAUSE WE'RE EXPENDABLE, AND THE MISSION IS TOO HIGH-RISK TO SEND ANYONE ELSE.
WE'RE A HAIL MARY PASS IN THE FOURTH QUARTER.
SO....GIDDYAP OR WHATEVER, BUT I JUST WANTED TO POINT OUT THAT NONE OF US ARE ACTUALLY GOING TO MAKE IT OUT OF THIS ALIVE.
I KNOW. -SIGH- I KNEW.
I'M SO SORRY, SWEETHEART. I LOVE YOU.
WHAT WOULD EVEN BE THE POINT OF LIVING IF SCOTT CAN'T PROVIDE HIS DAUGHTER A WORLD WORTH LIVING IN FIRST?
OPERATION: FATHERHOOD
MISSION OBJECTIVE: MAKE HARD CHOICES.
SCOTT HAD ALREADY MADE THIS CHOICE, LONG BEFORE ERIK ASKED HIM TO CONFRONT IT.

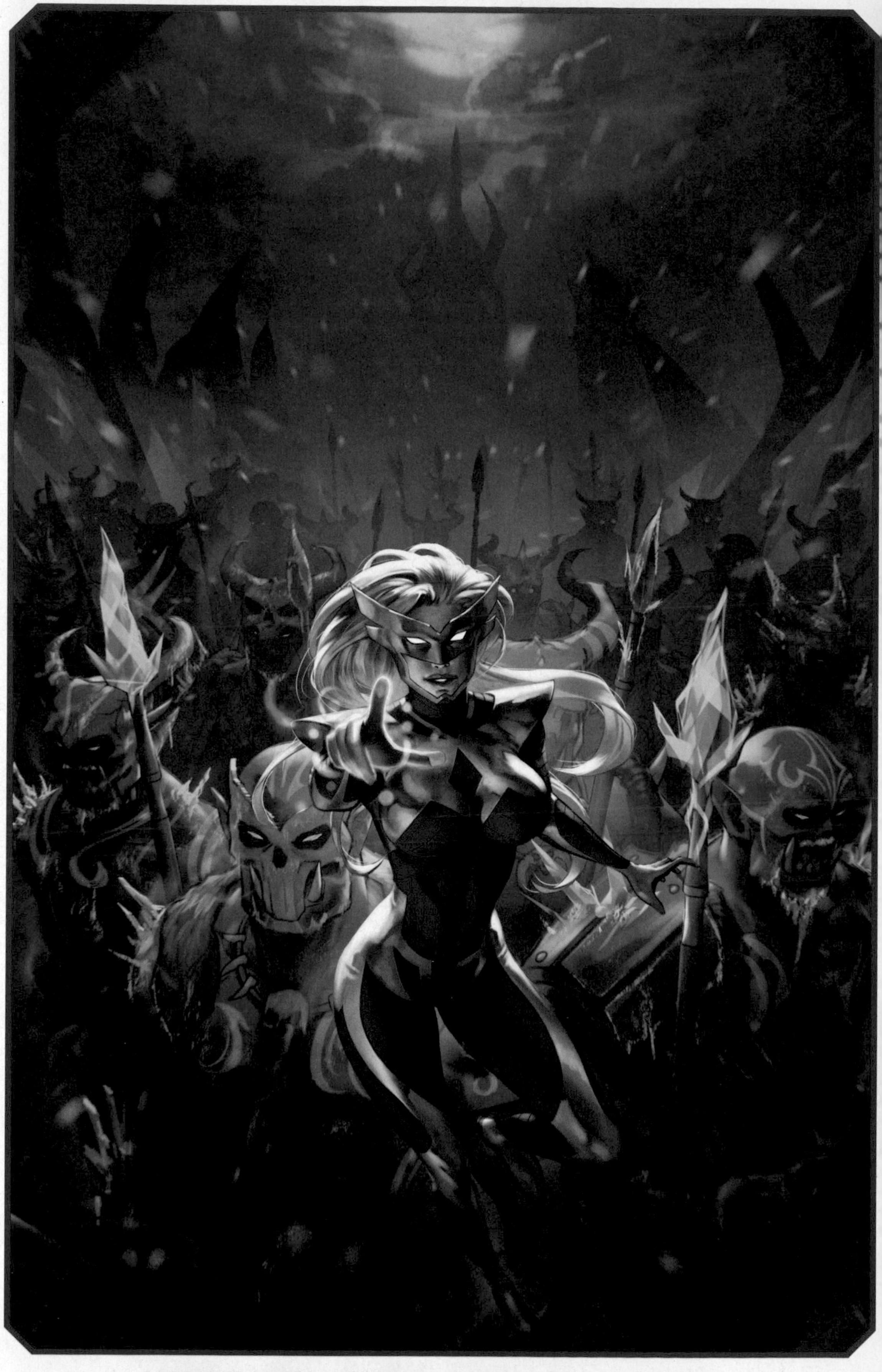

GIANT-MAN #3 "AND SOME LITTLE LADIES"

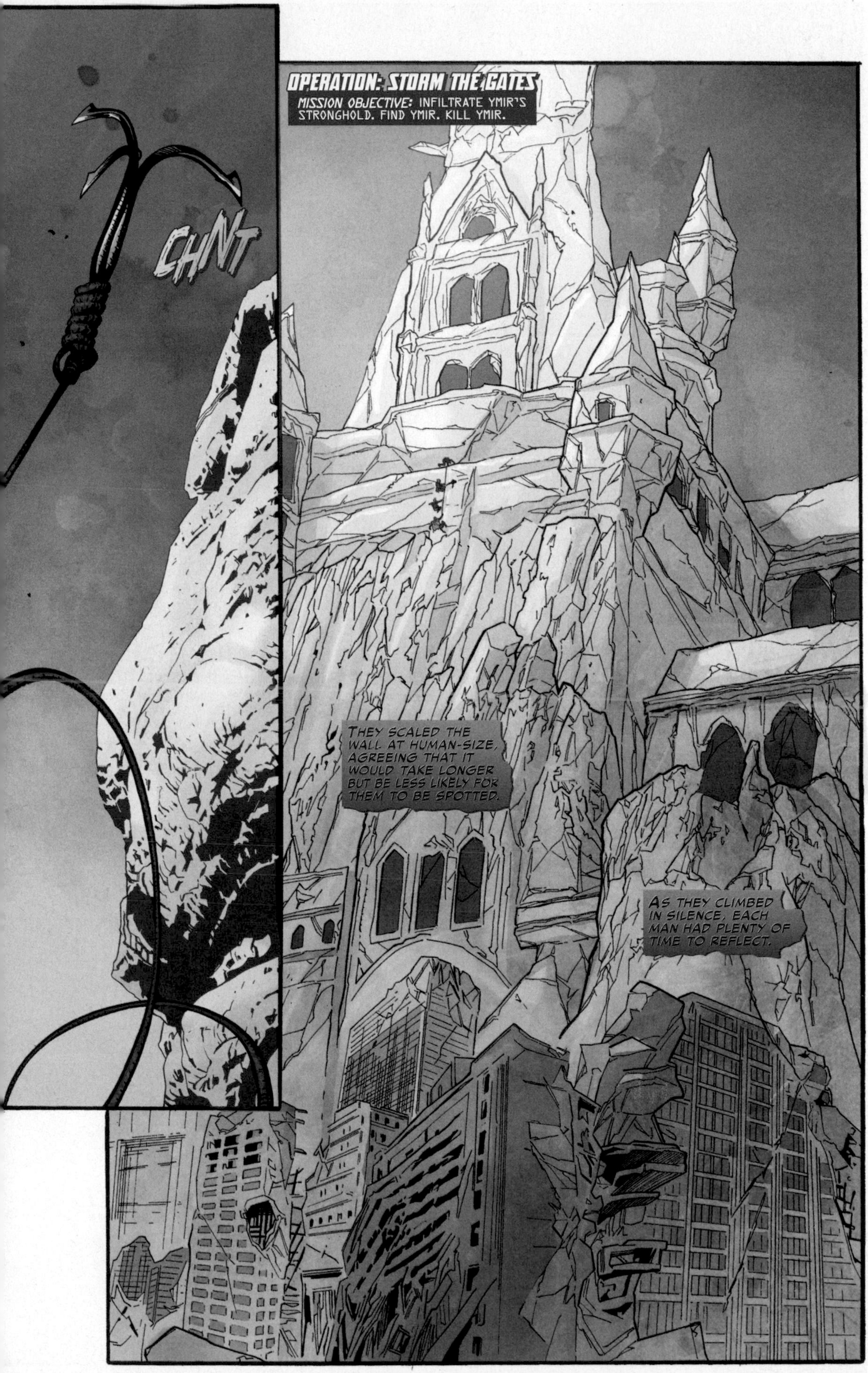
CHNT
OPERATION: STORM THE GATES
MISSION OBJECTIVE: INFILTRATE YMIR'S STRONGHOLD. FIND YMIR. KILL YMIR.
THEY SCALED THE WALL AT HUMAN-SIZE, AGREEING THAT IT WOULD TAKE LONGER BUT BE LESS LIKELY FOR THEM TO BE SPOTTED.
AS THEY CLIMBED IN SILENCE, EACH MAN HAD PLENTY OF TIME TO REFLECT.

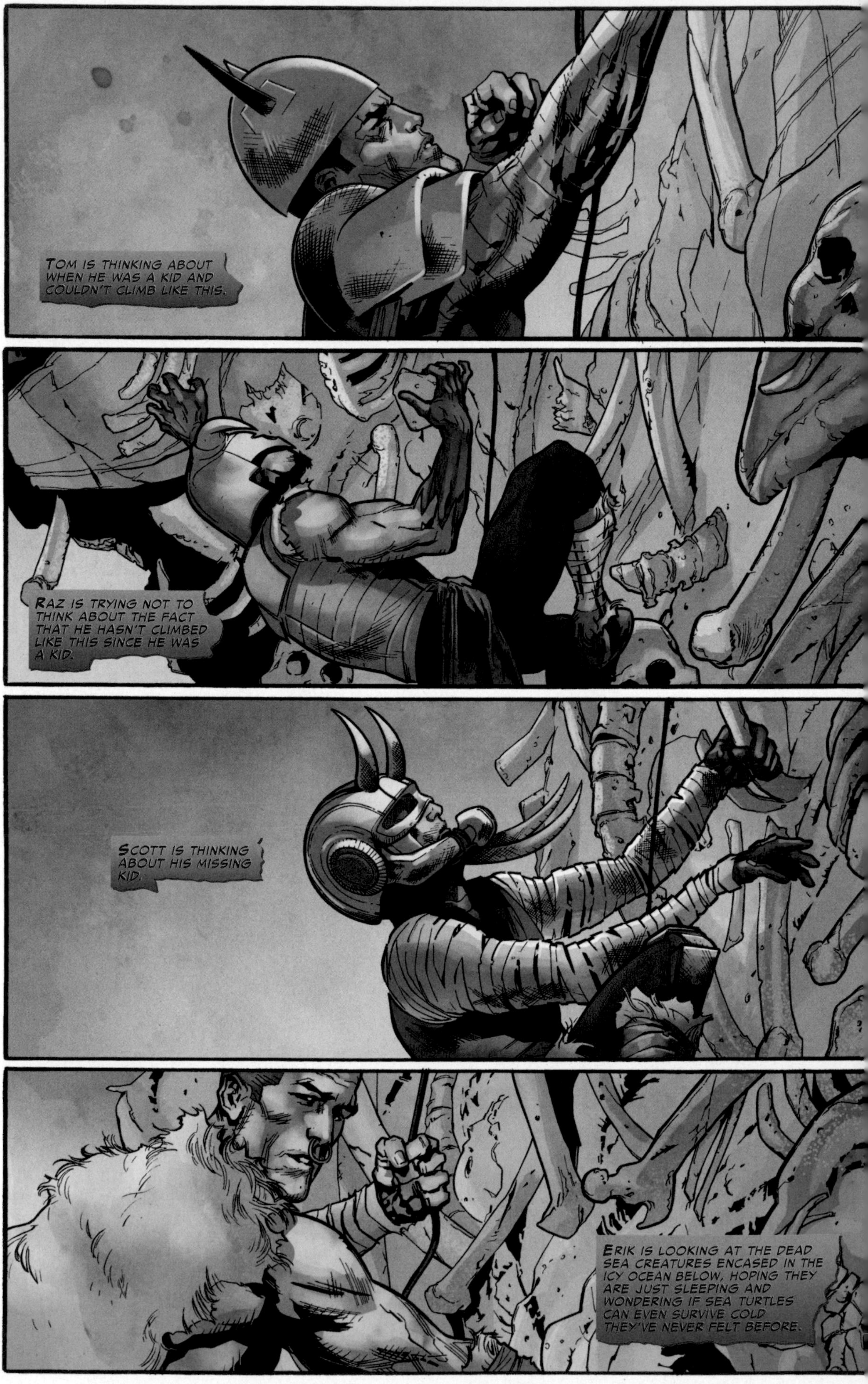
TOM IS THINKING ABOUT WHEN HE WAS A KID AND COULDN'T CLIMB LIKE THIS.
RAZ IS TRYING NOT TO THINK ABOUT THE FACT THAT HE HASN'T CLIMBED LIKE THIS SINCE HE WAS A KID.
SCOTT IS THINKING ABOUT HIS MISSING KID.
ERIK IS LOOKING AT THE DEAD SEA CREATURES ENCASED IN THE ICY OCEAN BELOW, HOPING THEY ARE JUST SLEEPING AND WONDERING IF SEA TURTLES CAN EVEN SURVIVE COLD THEY'VE NEVER FELT BEFORE.

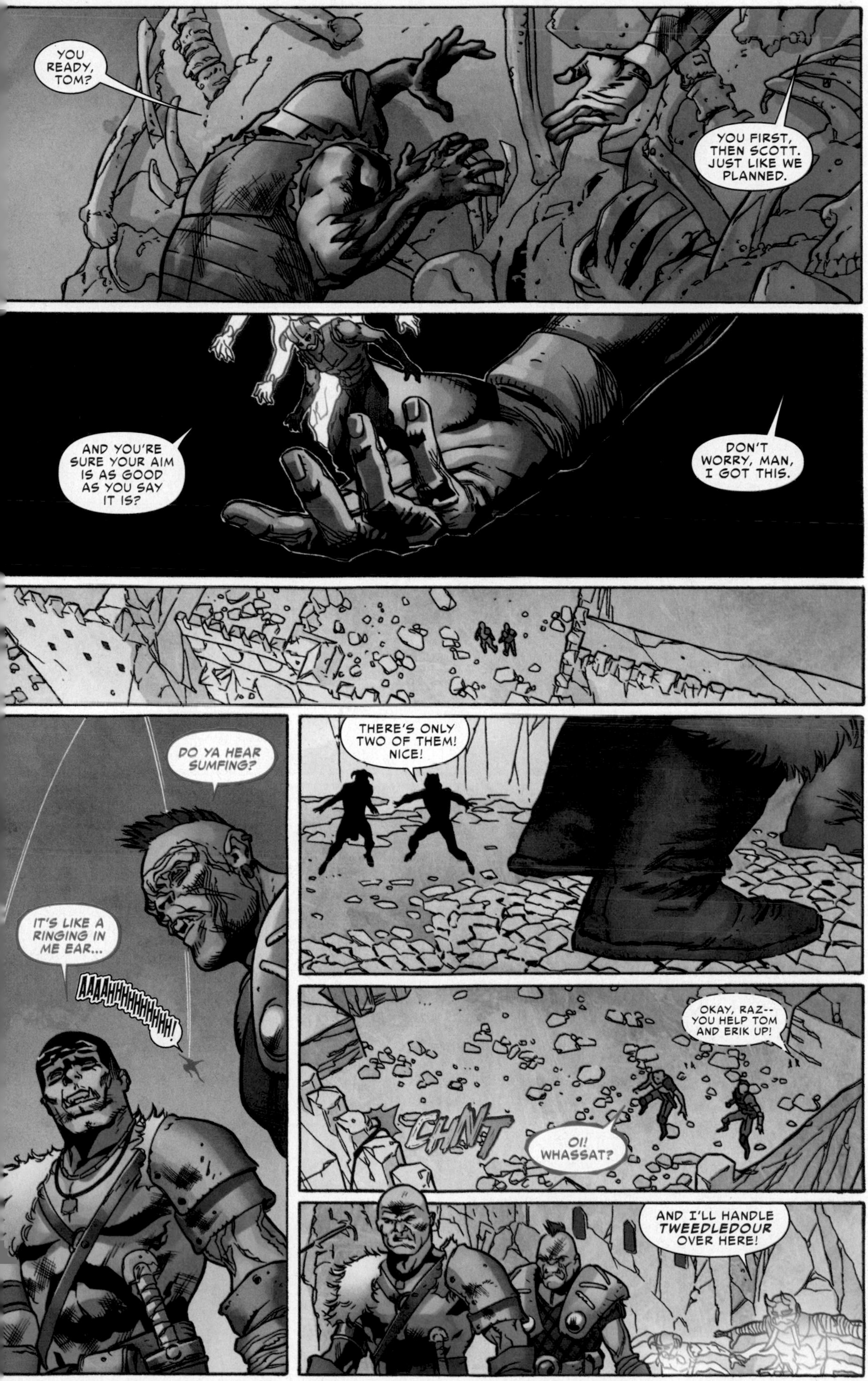
YOU READY, TOM?
YOU FIRST, THEN SCOTT. JUST LIKE WE PLANNED.
AND YOU'RE SURE YOUR AIM IS AS GOOD AS YOU SAY IT IS?
DON'T WORRY, MAN, I GOT THIS.
DO YA HEAR SUMFING?
IT'S LIKE A RINGING IN ME EAR...
AAAAHHHHHHHHHH!
THERE'S ONLY TWO OF THEM! NICE!
OKAY, RAZ-- YOU HELP TOM AND ERIK UP!
CHNT
OI! WHASSAT?
AND I'LL HANDLE *TWEEDLEDOUR* OVER HERE!

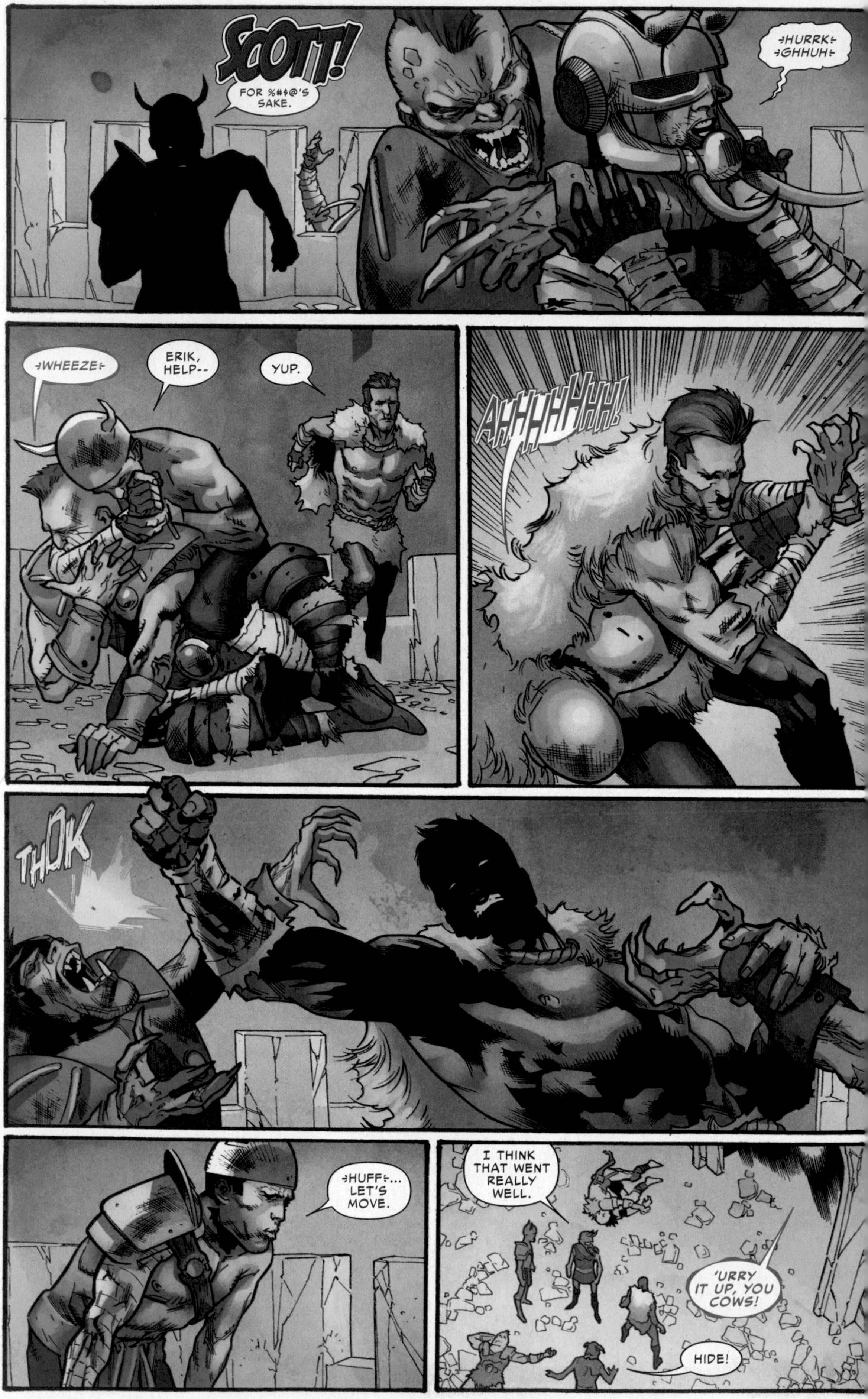
SCOTT!
FOR %#$@'S SAKE.
HURRK GHHUH
WHEEZE
ERIK, HELP--
YUP.
AHHHHHHH!
THOK
HUFF... LET'S MOVE.
I THINK THAT WENT REALLY WELL.
'URRY IT UP, YOU COWS!
HIDE!

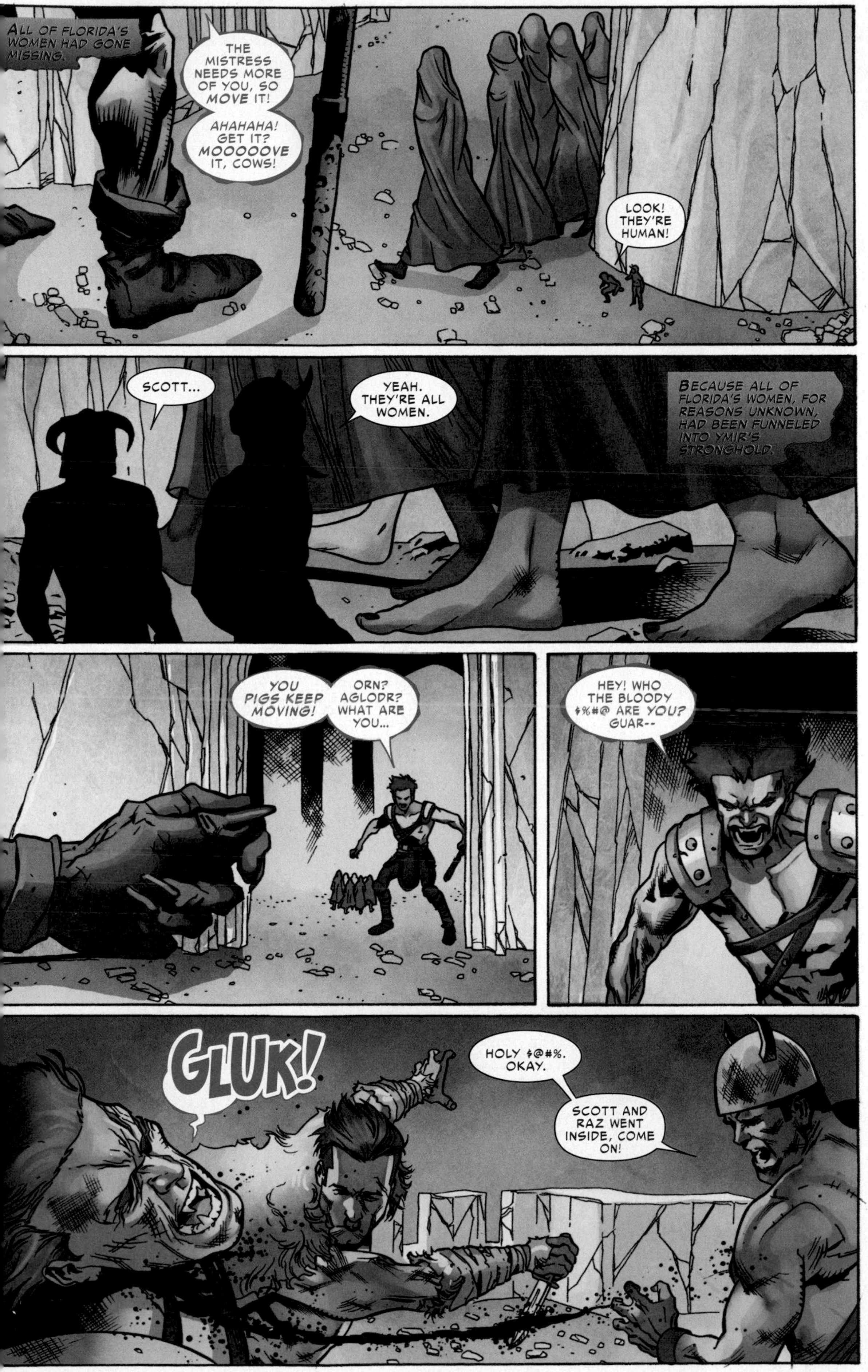
ALL OF FLORIDA'S WOMEN HAD GONE MISSING.
THE MISTRESS NEEDS MORE OF YOU, SO MOVE IT!
AHAHAHA! GET IT? MOOOOOVE IT, COWS!
LOOK! THEY'RE HUMAN!
SCOTT...
YEAH. THEY'RE ALL WOMEN.
BECAUSE ALL OF FLORIDA'S WOMEN, FOR REASONS UNKNOWN, HAD BEEN FUNNELED INTO YMIR'S STRONGHOLD.
YOU PIGS KEEP MOVING!
ORN? AGLODR? WHAT ARE YOU...
HEY! WHO THE BLOODY $%#@ ARE YOU? GUAR--
GLUK!
HOLY $@#%. OKAY.
SCOTT AND RAZ WENT INSIDE, COME ON!

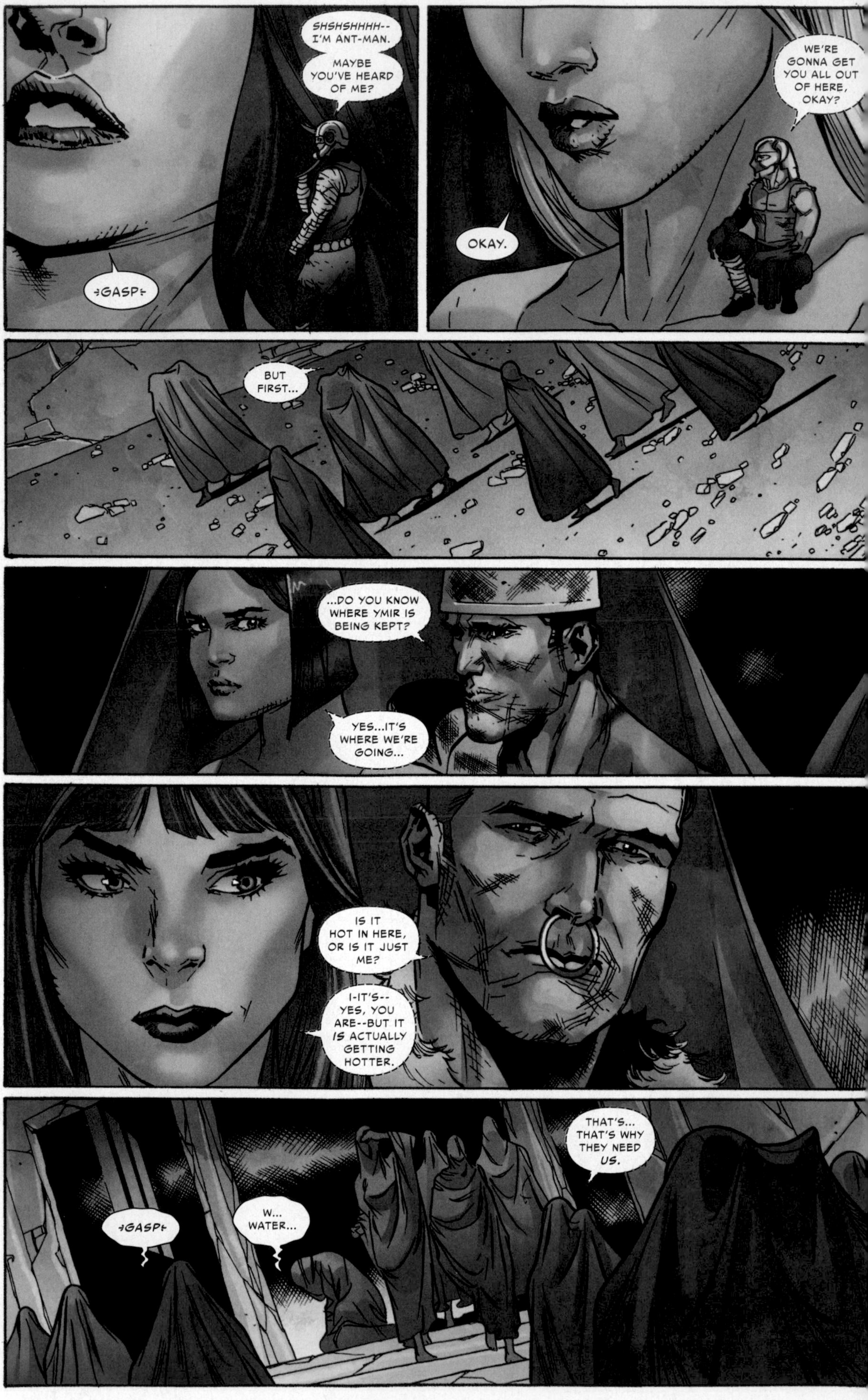
SHSHSHHHH--
I'M ANT-MAN.
MAYBE YOU'VE HEARD OF ME?
GASP
WE'RE GONNA GET YOU ALL OUT OF HERE, OKAY?
OKAY.
BUT FIRST...
...DO YOU KNOW WHERE YMIR IS BEING KEPT?
YES...IT'S WHERE WE'RE GOING...
IS IT HOT IN HERE, OR IS IT JUST ME?
I-IT'S-- YES, YOU ARE--BUT IT IS ACTUALLY GETTING HOTTER.
THAT'S... THAT'S WHY THEY NEED US.
GASP
W... WATER...

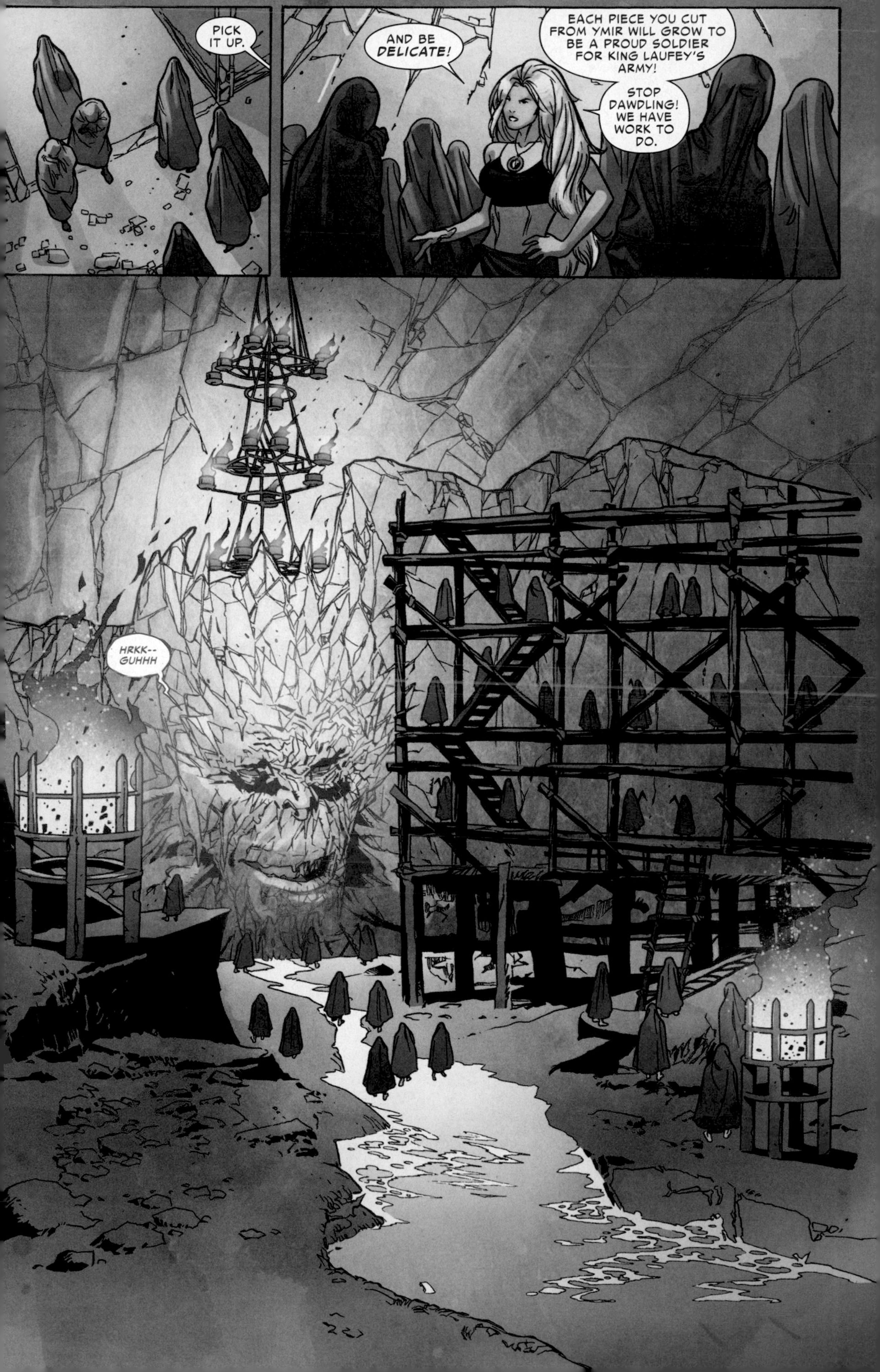
PICK IT UP.
AND BE DELICATE!
EACH PIECE YOU CUT FROM YMIR WILL GROW TO BE A PROUD SOLDIER FOR KING LAUFEY'S ARMY!
STOP DAWDLING! WE HAVE WORK TO DO.
HRKK-- GUHHH

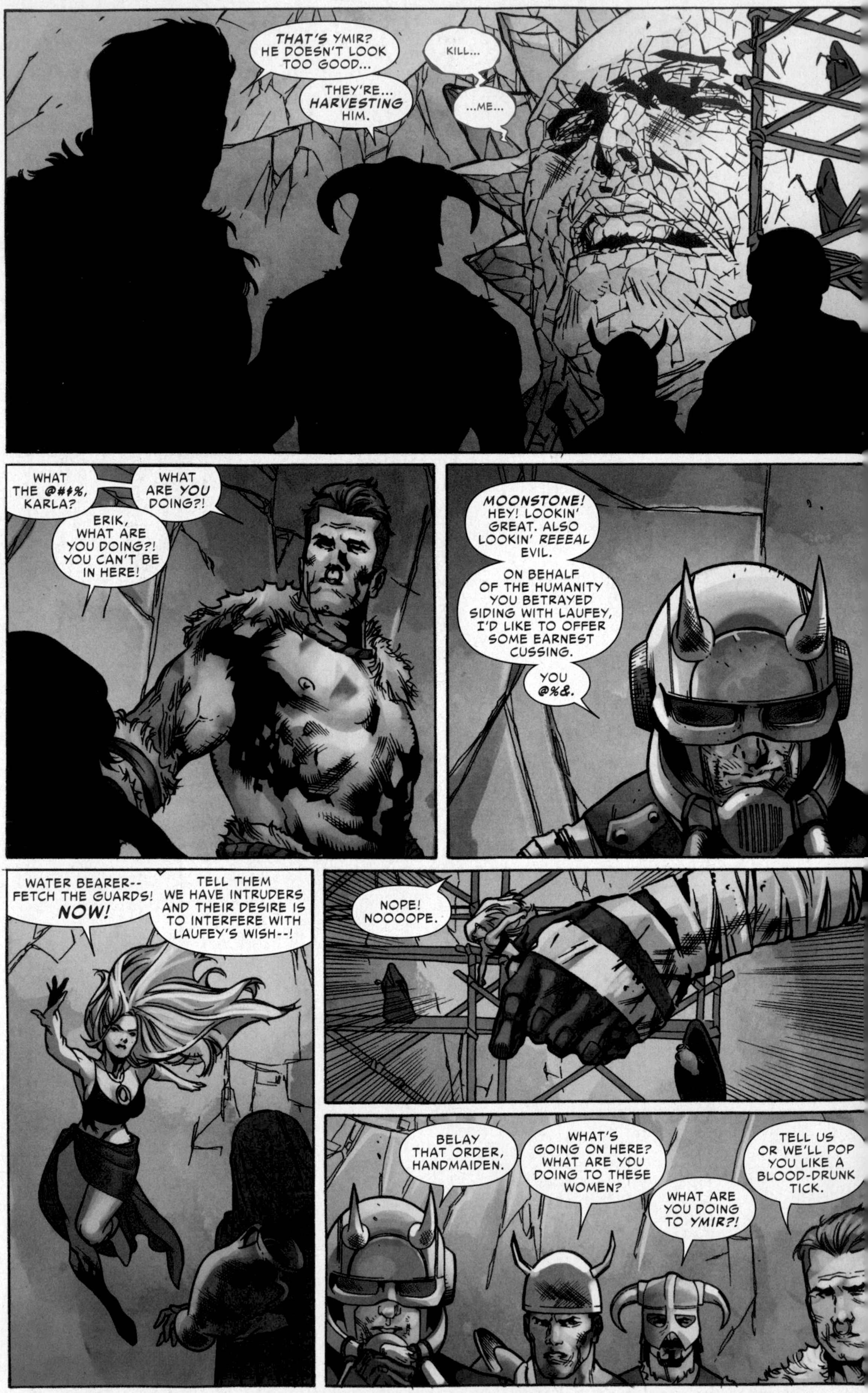
THAT'S YMIR? HE DOESN'T LOOK TOO GOOD...
THEY'RE... HARVESTING HIM.
KILL...
...ME...
WHAT THE @#$%, KARLA?
WHAT ARE YOU DOING?!
ERIK, WHAT ARE YOU DOING?! YOU CAN'T BE IN HERE!
MOONSTONE! HEY! LOOKIN' GREAT. ALSO LOOKIN' REEEAL EVIL.
ON BEHALF OF THE HUMANITY YOU BETRAYED SIDING WITH LAUFEY, I'D LIKE TO OFFER SOME EARNEST CUSSING.
YOU @%&.
WATER BEARER-- FETCH THE GUARDS! NOW!
TELL THEM WE HAVE INTRUDERS AND THEIR DESIRE IS TO INTERFERE WITH LAUFEY'S WISH--!
NOPE! NOOOOPE.
BELAY THAT ORDER, HANDMAIDEN.
WHAT'S GOING ON HERE? WHAT ARE YOU DOING TO THESE WOMEN?
WHAT ARE YOU DOING TO YMIR?!
TELL US OR WE'LL POP YOU LIKE A BLOOD-DRUNK TICK.

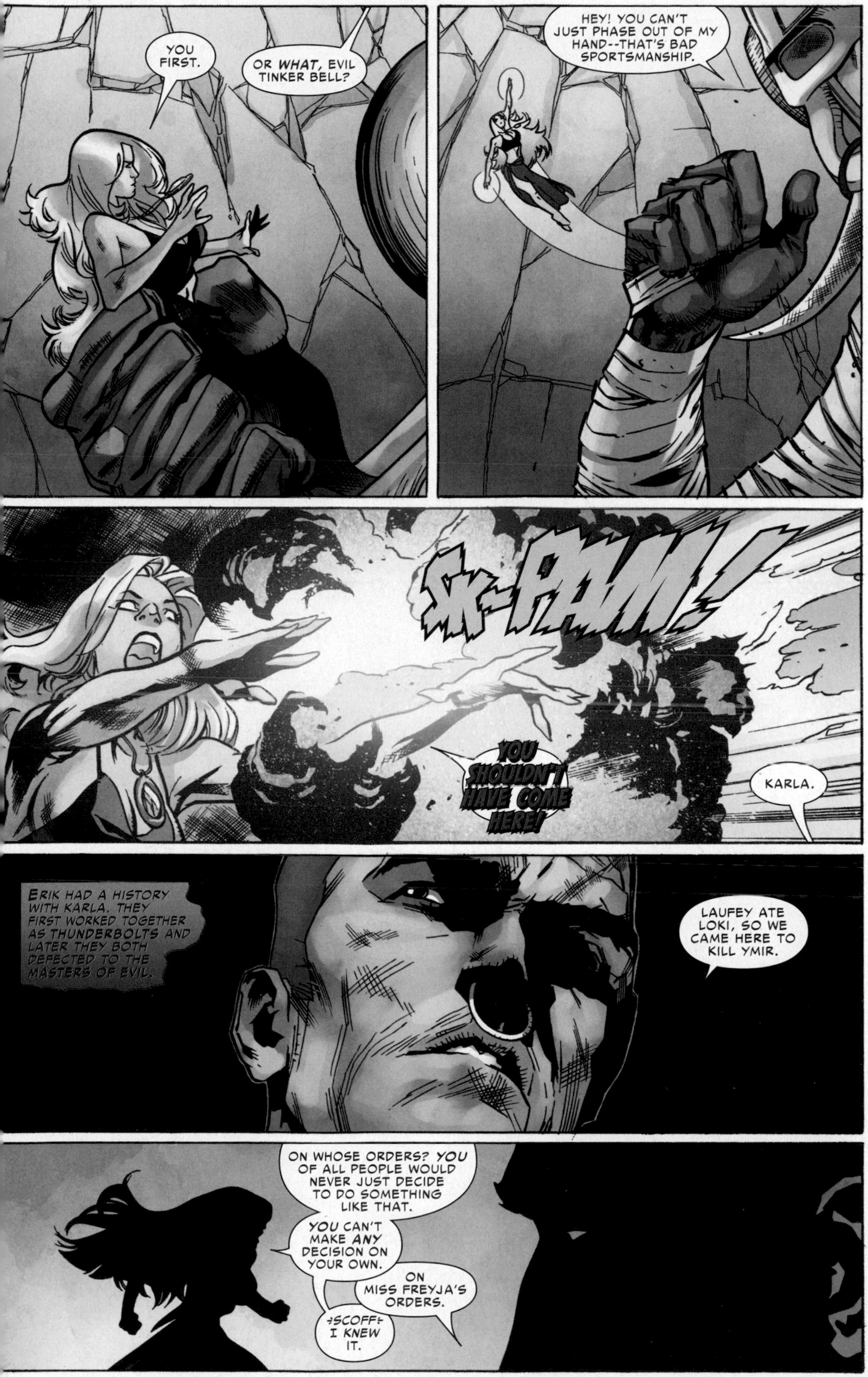
YOU FIRST.
OR *WHAT,* EVIL TINKER BELL?
HEY! YOU CAN'T JUST PHASE OUT OF MY HAND--THAT'S BAD SPORTSMANSHIP.
SK-PAM!
YOU SHOULDN'T HAVE COME HERE!
KARLA.
ERIK HAD A HISTORY WITH KARLA. THEY FIRST WORKED TOGETHER AS THUNDERBOLTS AND LATER THEY BOTH DEFECTED TO THE MASTERS OF EVIL.
LAUFEY ATE LOKI, SO WE CAME HERE TO KILL YMIR.
ON WHOSE ORDERS? *YOU* OF ALL PEOPLE WOULD NEVER JUST DECIDE TO DO SOMETHING LIKE THAT.
YOU CAN'T MAKE *ANY* DECISION ON YOUR OWN.
ON MISS FREYJA'S ORDERS.
=SCOFF= I KNEW IT.

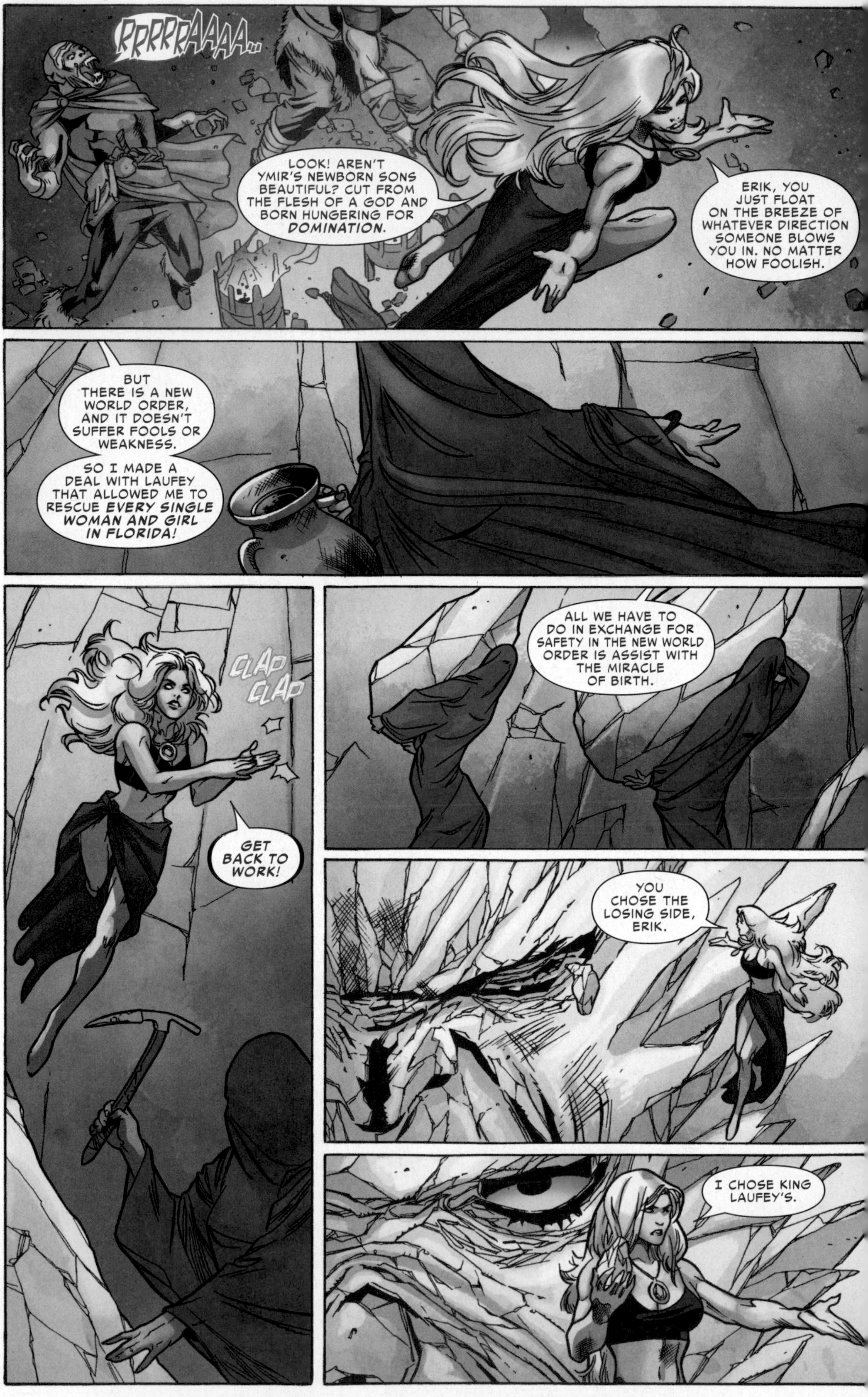
RRRRRAAAA..
LOOK! AREN'T YMIR'S NEWBORN SONS BEAUTIFUL? CUT FROM THE FLESH OF A GOD AND BORN HUNGERING FOR DOMINATION.
ERIK, YOU JUST FLOAT ON THE BREEZE OF WHATEVER DIRECTION SOMEONE BLOWS YOU IN. NO MATTER HOW FOOLISH.
BUT THERE IS A NEW WORLD ORDER, AND IT DOESN'T SUFFER FOOLS OR WEAKNESS.
SO I MADE A DEAL WITH LAUFEY THAT ALLOWED ME TO RESCUE EVERY SINGLE WOMAN AND GIRL IN FLORIDA!
CLAP CLAP
GET BACK TO WORK!
ALL WE HAVE TO DO IN EXCHANGE FOR SAFETY IN THE NEW WORLD ORDER IS ASSIST WITH THE MIRACLE OF BIRTH.
YOU CHOSE THE LOSING SIDE, ERIK.
I CHOSE KING LAUFEY'S.

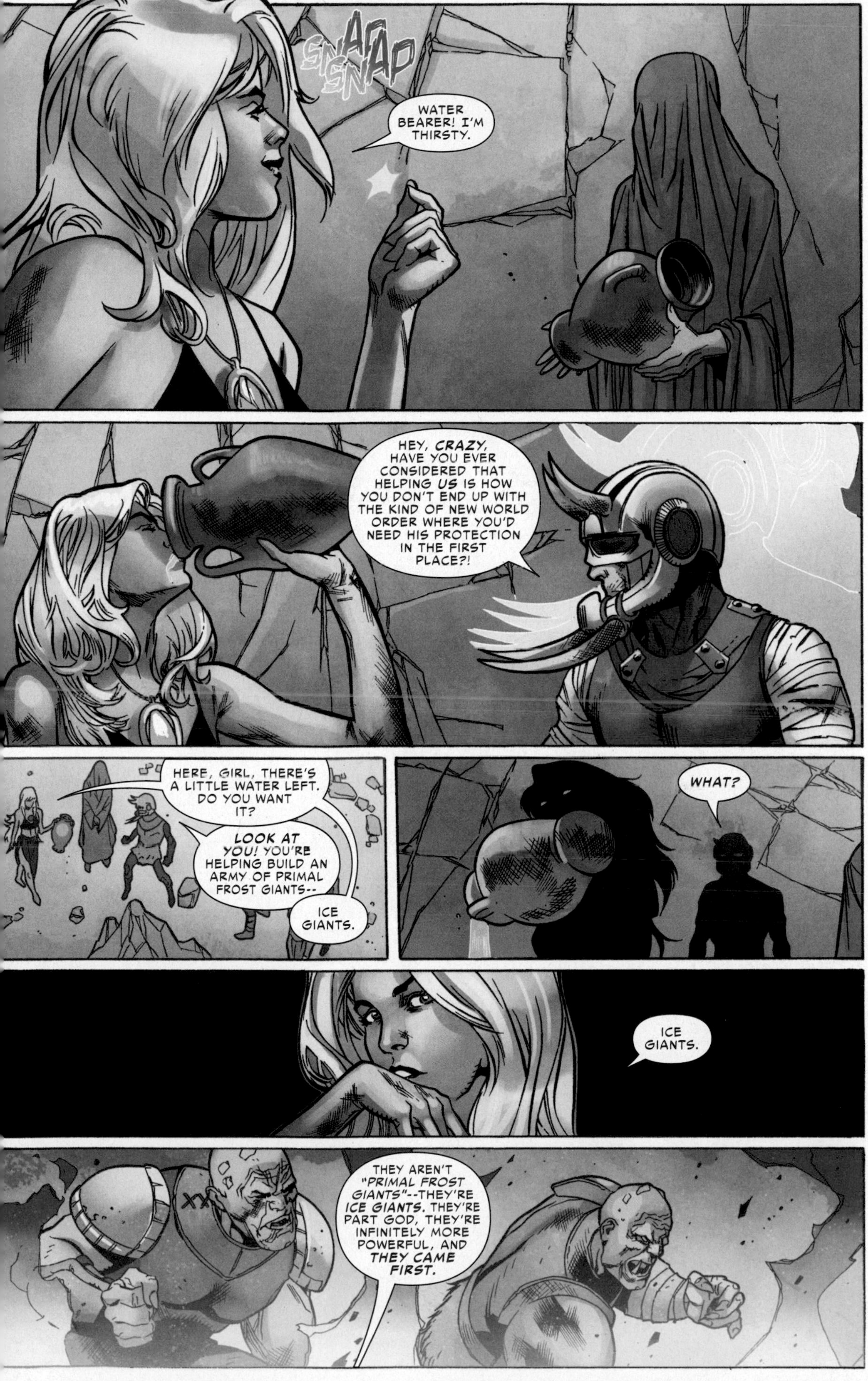
SNAP SNAP
WATER BEARER! I'M THIRSTY.
HEY, CRAZY, HAVE YOU EVER CONSIDERED THAT HELPING US IS HOW YOU DON'T END UP WITH THE KIND OF NEW WORLD ORDER WHERE YOU'D NEED HIS PROTECTION IN THE FIRST PLACE?!
HERE, GIRL, THERE'S A LITTLE WATER LEFT. DO YOU WANT IT?
LOOK AT YOU! YOU'RE HELPING BUILD AN ARMY OF PRIMAL FROST GIANTS--
ICE GIANTS.
WHAT?
ICE GIANTS.
THEY AREN'T "PRIMAL FROST GIANTS"--THEY'RE ICE GIANTS. THEY'RE PART GOD, THEY'RE INFINITELY MORE POWERFUL, AND THEY CAME FIRST.

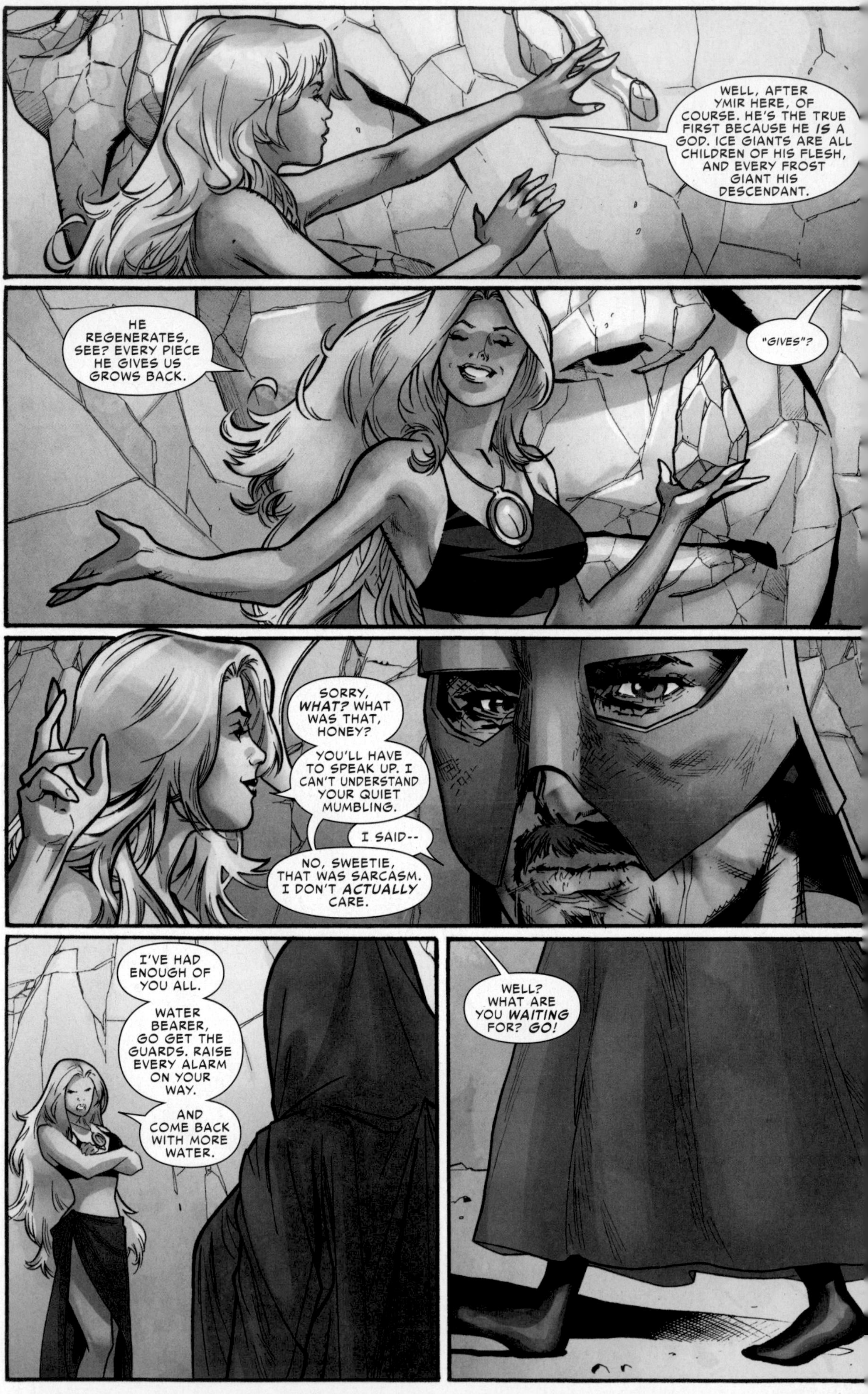
WELL, AFTER YMIR HERE, OF COURSE. HE'S THE TRUE FIRST BECAUSE HE *IS* A GOD. ICE GIANTS ARE ALL CHILDREN OF HIS FLESH, AND EVERY FROST GIANT HIS DESCENDANT.
HE REGENERATES, SEE? EVERY PIECE HE GIVES US GROWS BACK.
"GIVES"?
SORRY, *WHAT?* WHAT WAS THAT, HONEY?
YOU'LL HAVE TO SPEAK UP. I CAN'T UNDERSTAND YOUR QUIET MUMBLING.
I SAID--
NO, SWEETIE, THAT WAS SARCASM. I DON'T *ACTUALLY* CARE.
I'VE HAD ENOUGH OF YOU ALL.
WATER BEARER, GO GET THE GUARDS. RAISE EVERY ALARM ON YOUR WAY.
AND COME BACK WITH MORE WATER.
WELL? WHAT ARE YOU *WAITING* FOR? *GO!*

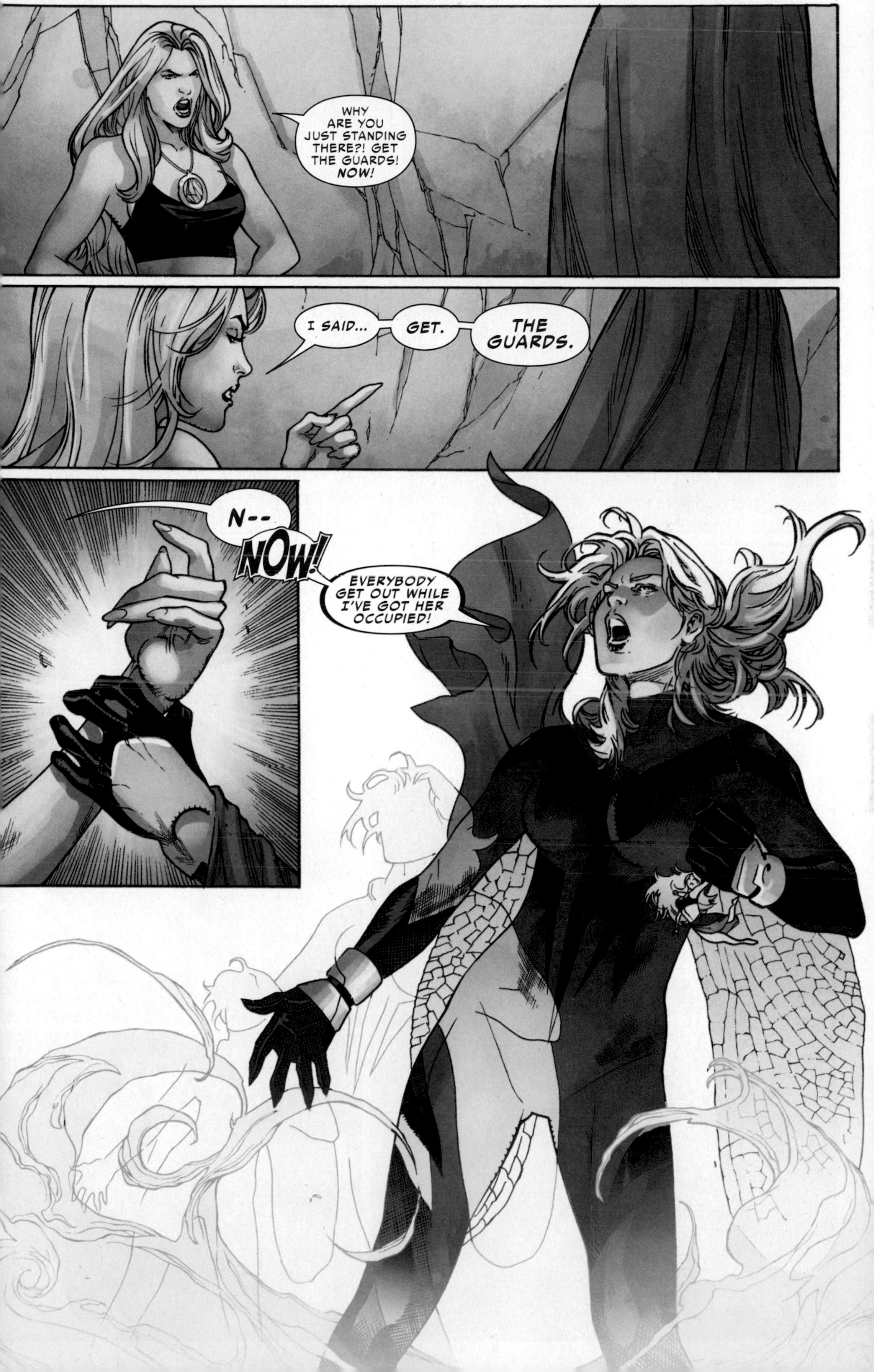
WHY ARE YOU JUST STANDING THERE?! GET THE GUARDS! NOW!
I SAID...
GET.
THE GUARDS.
N--
NOW!
EVERYBODY GET OUT WHILE I'VE GOT HER OCCUPIED!

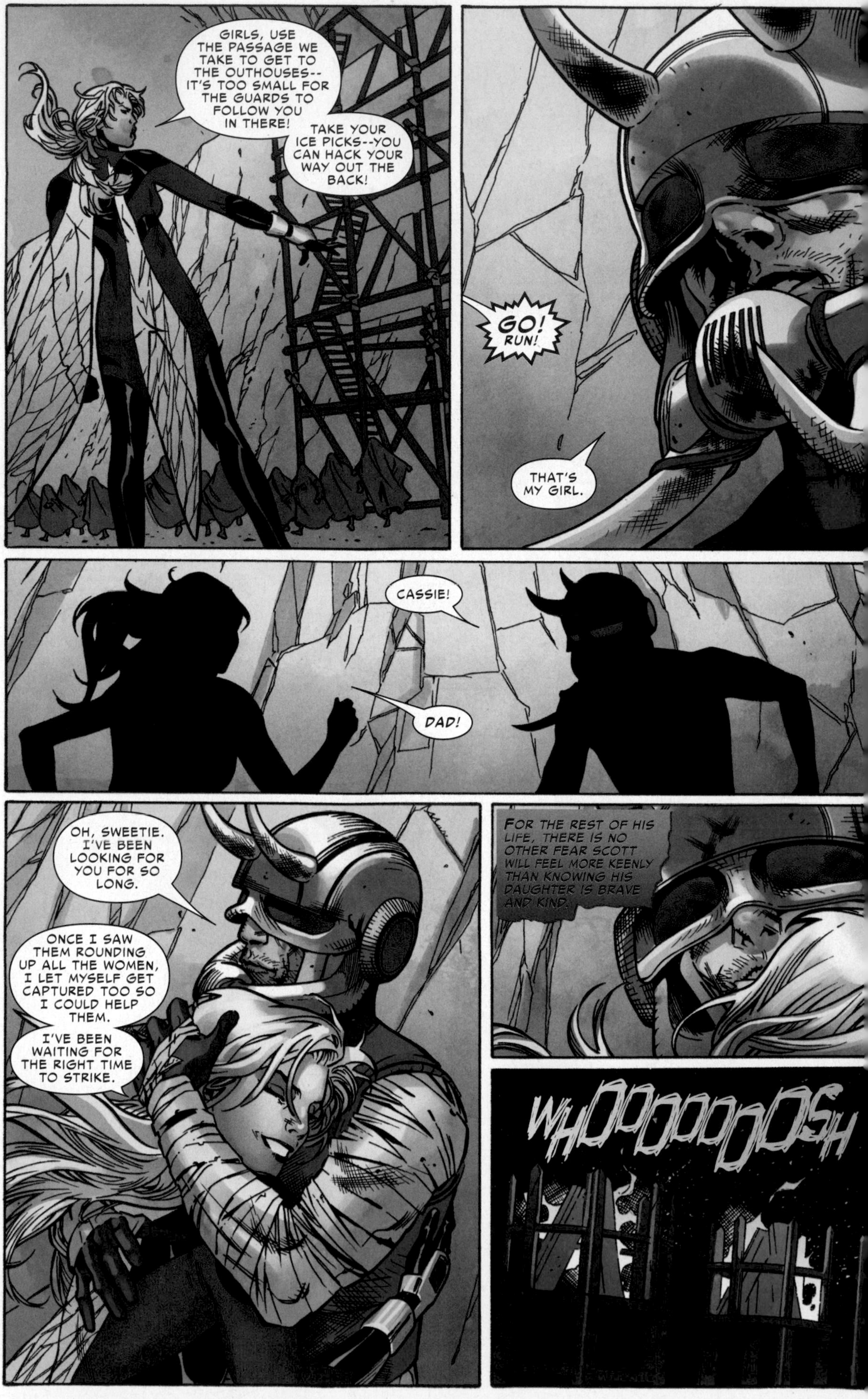
GIRLS, USE THE PASSAGE WE TAKE TO GET TO THE OUTHOUSES-- IT'S TOO SMALL FOR THE GUARDS TO FOLLOW YOU IN THERE!
TAKE YOUR ICE PICKS--YOU CAN HACK YOUR WAY OUT THE BACK!
GO! RUN!
THAT'S MY GIRL.
CASSIE!
DAD!
OH, SWEETIE. I'VE BEEN LOOKING FOR YOU FOR SO LONG.
ONCE I SAW THEM ROUNDING UP ALL THE WOMEN, I LET MYSELF GET CAPTURED TOO SO I COULD HELP THEM.
I'VE BEEN WAITING FOR THE RIGHT TIME TO STRIKE.
FOR THE REST OF HIS LIFE, THERE IS NO OTHER FEAR SCOTT WILL FEEL MORE KEENLY THAN KNOWING HIS DAUGHTER IS BRAVE AND KIND.
WHOOOOOOOOSH

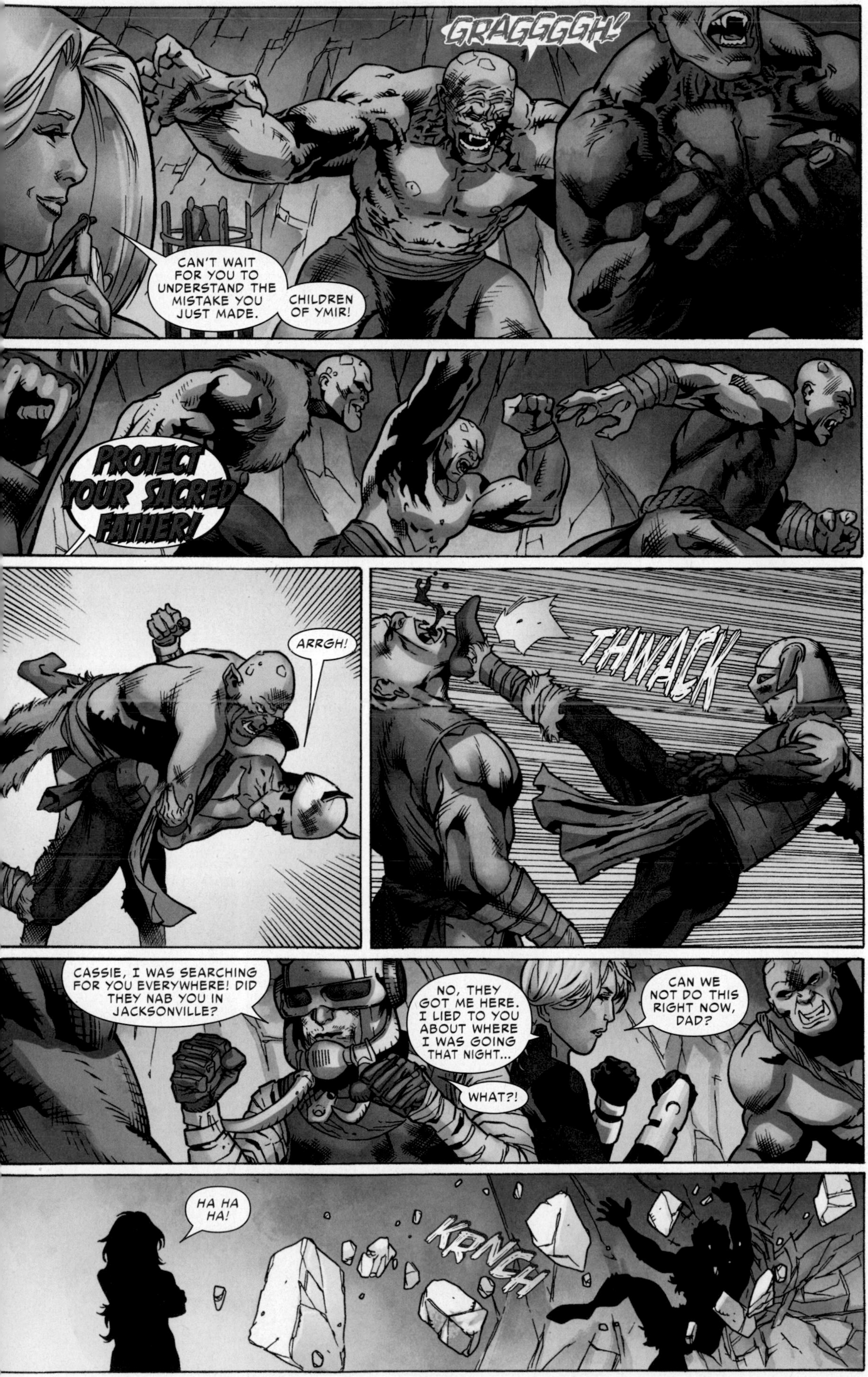
GRAGGGGH!
CAN'T WAIT FOR YOU TO UNDERSTAND THE MISTAKE YOU JUST MADE.
CHILDREN OF YMIR!
PROTECT YOUR SACRED FATHER!
ARRGH!
THWACK
CASSIE, I WAS SEARCHING FOR YOU EVERYWHERE! DID THEY NAB YOU IN JACKSONVILLE?
NO, THEY GOT ME HERE. I LIED TO YOU ABOUT WHERE I WAS GOING THAT NIGHT...
CAN WE NOT DO THIS RIGHT NOW, DAD?
WHAT?!
HA HA HA!
KRNCH

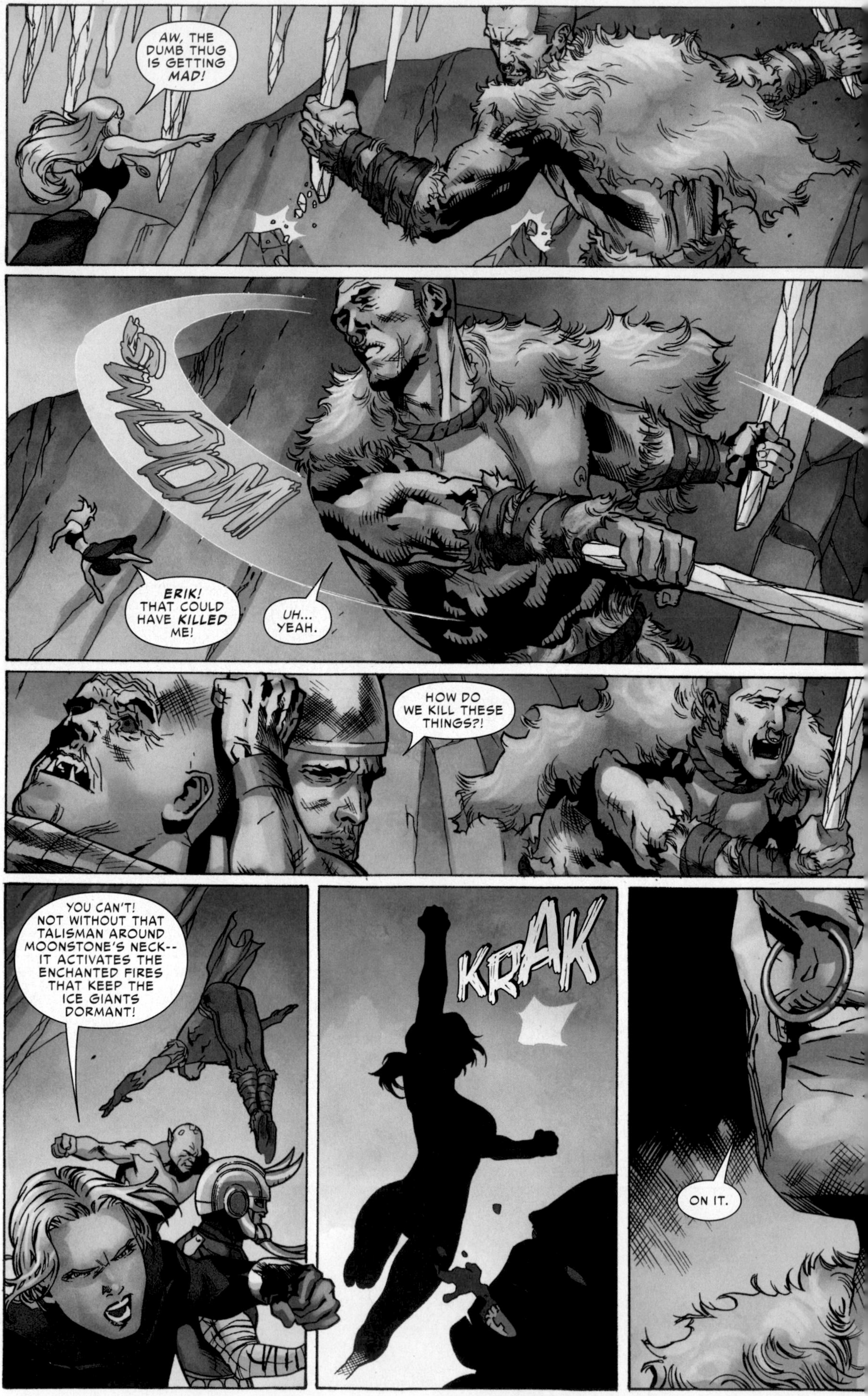
AW, THE DUMB THUG IS GETTING MAD!
SWOOM
ERIK! THAT COULD HAVE KILLED ME!
UH... YEAH.
HOW DO WE KILL THESE THINGS?!
YOU CAN'T! NOT WITHOUT THAT TALISMAN AROUND MOONSTONE'S NECK-- IT ACTIVATES THE ENCHANTED FIRES THAT KEEP THE ICE GIANTS DORMANT!
KRAK
ON IT.

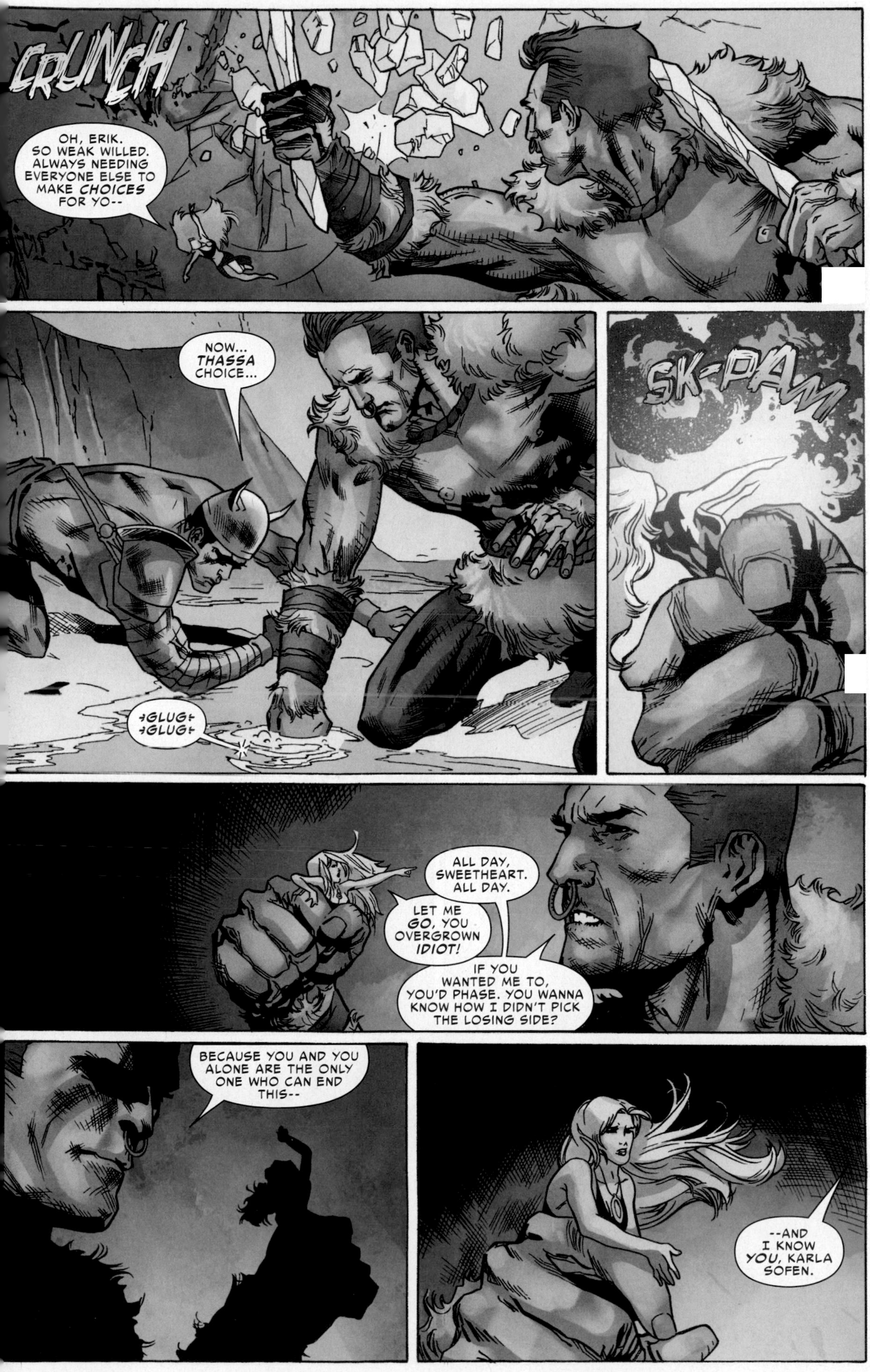
CRUNCH
OH, ERIK. SO WEAK WILLED. ALWAYS NEEDING EVERYONE ELSE TO MAKE CHOICES FOR YO--
NOW... THASSA CHOICE...
GLUG GLUG
SK-PAM
ALL DAY, SWEETHEART. ALL DAY.
LET ME GO, YOU OVERGROWN IDIOT!
IF YOU WANTED ME TO, YOU'D PHASE. YOU WANNA KNOW HOW I DIDN'T PICK THE LOSING SIDE?
BECAUSE YOU AND YOU ALONE ARE THE ONLY ONE WHO CAN END THIS--
--AND I KNOW YOU, KARLA SOFEN.

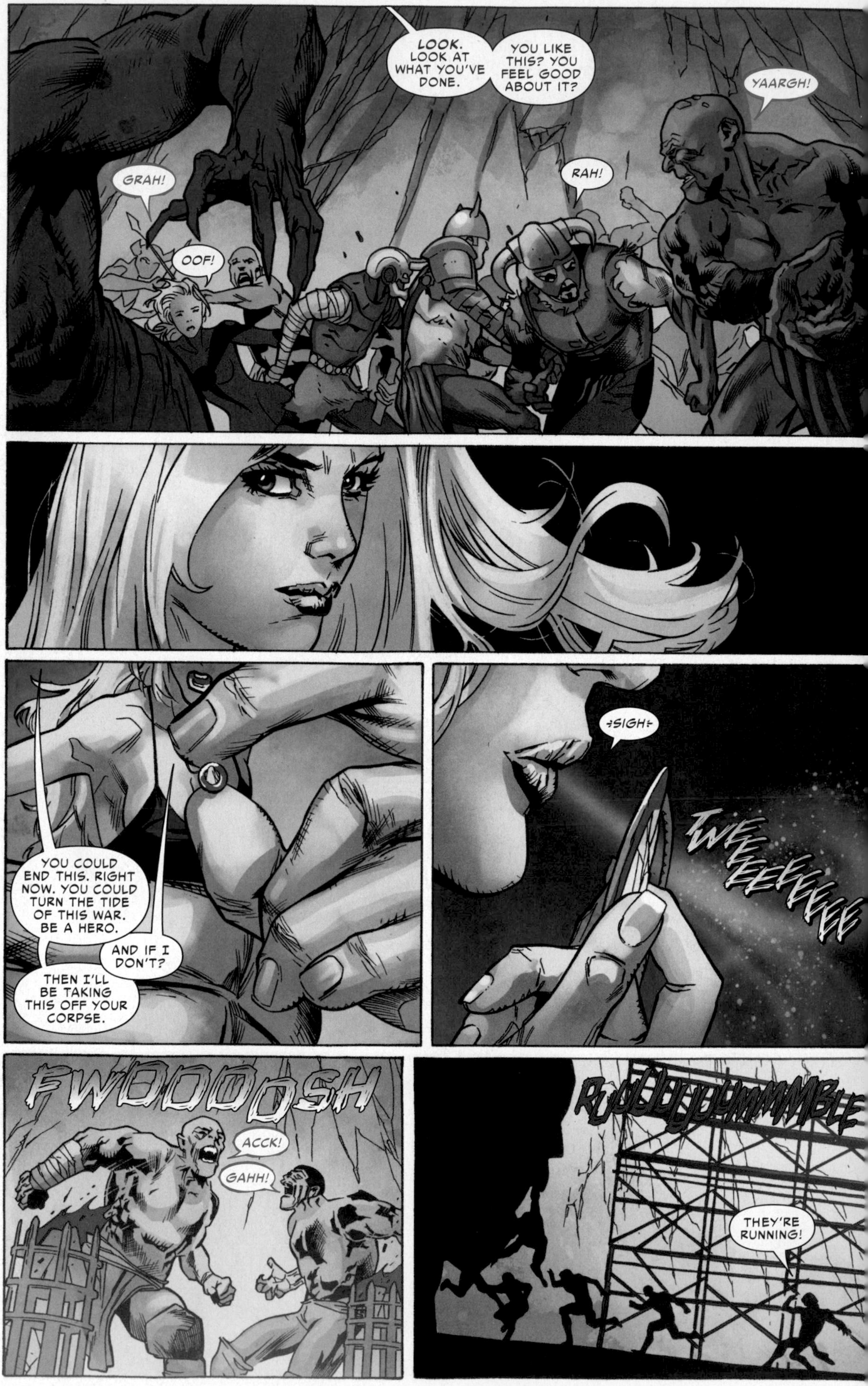
LOOK. LOOK AT WHAT YOU'VE DONE.
YOU LIKE THIS? YOU FEEL GOOD ABOUT IT?
YAARGH!
GRAH!
RAH!
OOF!
YOU COULD END THIS. RIGHT NOW. YOU COULD TURN THE TIDE OF THIS WAR. BE A HERO.
AND IF I DON'T?
THEN I'LL BE TAKING THIS OFF YOUR CORPSE.
SIGH
TWEEEEEEEEEE
FWOOOOSH
ACCK!
GAHH!
RUUUUUMMMBLE
THEY'RE RUNNING!

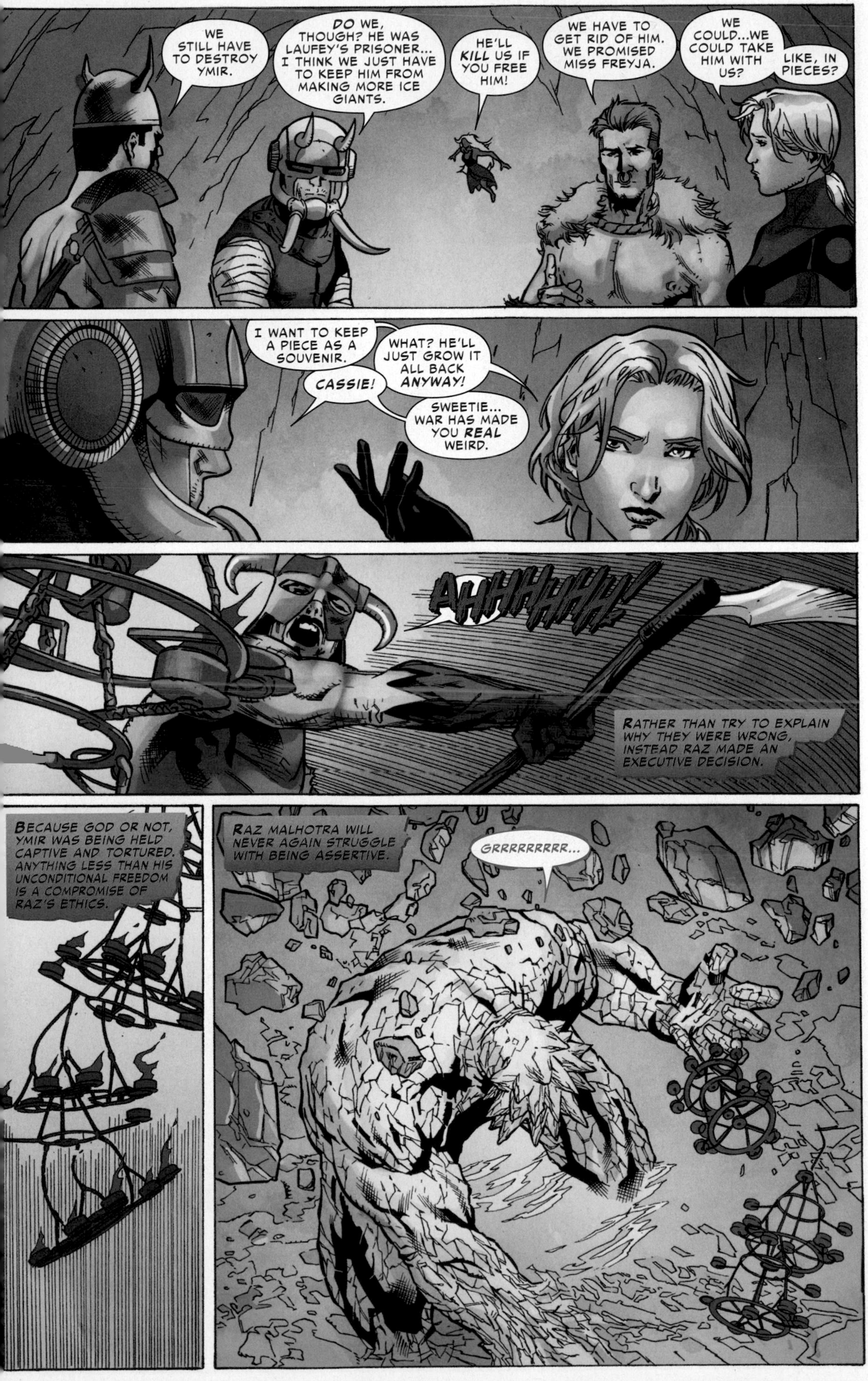
WE STILL HAVE TO DESTROY YMIR.
DO WE, THOUGH? HE WAS LAUFEY'S PRISONER... I THINK WE JUST HAVE TO KEEP HIM FROM MAKING MORE ICE GIANTS.
HE'LL KILL US IF YOU FREE HIM!
WE HAVE TO GET RID OF HIM. WE PROMISED MISS FREYJA.
WE COULD...WE COULD TAKE HIM WITH US?
LIKE, IN PIECES?
I WANT TO KEEP A PIECE AS A SOUVENIR.
CASSIE!
WHAT? HE'LL JUST GROW IT ALL BACK ANYWAY!
SWEETIE... WAR HAS MADE YOU REAL WEIRD.
AHHHHHH!
RATHER THAN TRY TO EXPLAIN WHY THEY WERE WRONG, INSTEAD RAZ MADE AN EXECUTIVE DECISION.
BECAUSE GOD OR NOT, YMIR WAS BEING HELD CAPTIVE AND TORTURED. ANYTHING LESS THAN HIS UNCONDITIONAL FREEDOM IS A COMPROMISE OF RAZ'S ETHICS.
RAZ MALHOTRA WILL NEVER AGAIN STRUGGLE WITH BEING ASSERTIVE.
GRRRRRRRRR...

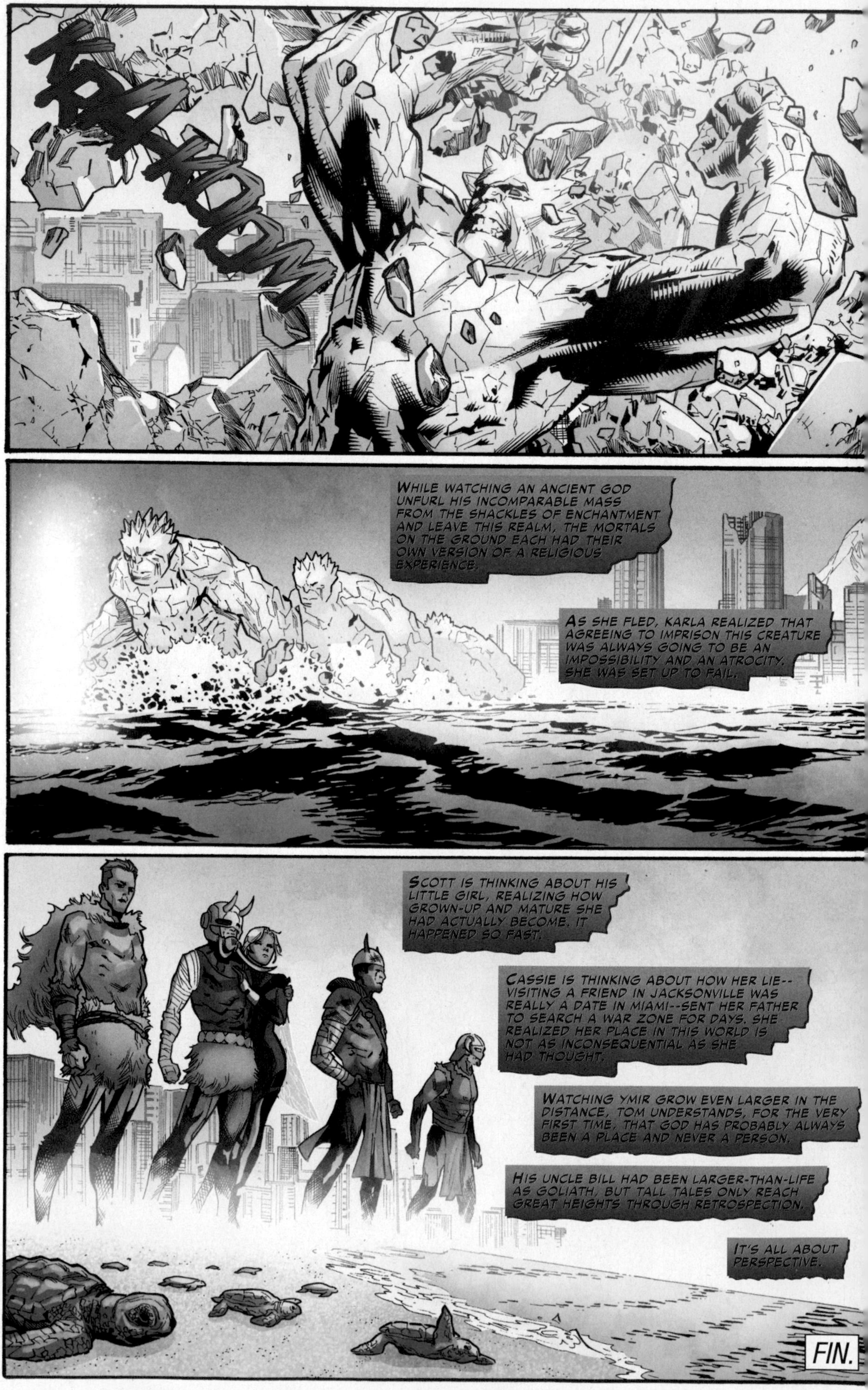
While watching an ancient god unfurl his incomparable mass from the shackles of enchantment and leave this realm, the mortals on the ground each had their own version of a religious experience.
As she fled, Karla realized that agreeing to imprison this creature was always going to be an impossibility and an atrocity. She was set up to fail.
Scott is thinking about his little girl, realizing how grown-up and mature she had actually become. It happened so fast.
Cassie is thinking about how her lie--visiting a friend in Jacksonville was really a date in Miami--sent her father to search a war zone for days. She realized her place in this world is not as inconsequential as she had thought.
Watching Ymir grow even larger in the distance, Tom understands, for the very first time, that God has probably always been a place and never a person.
His uncle Bill had been larger-than-life as Goliath, but tall tales only reach great heights through retrospection.
It's all about perspective.
FIN.

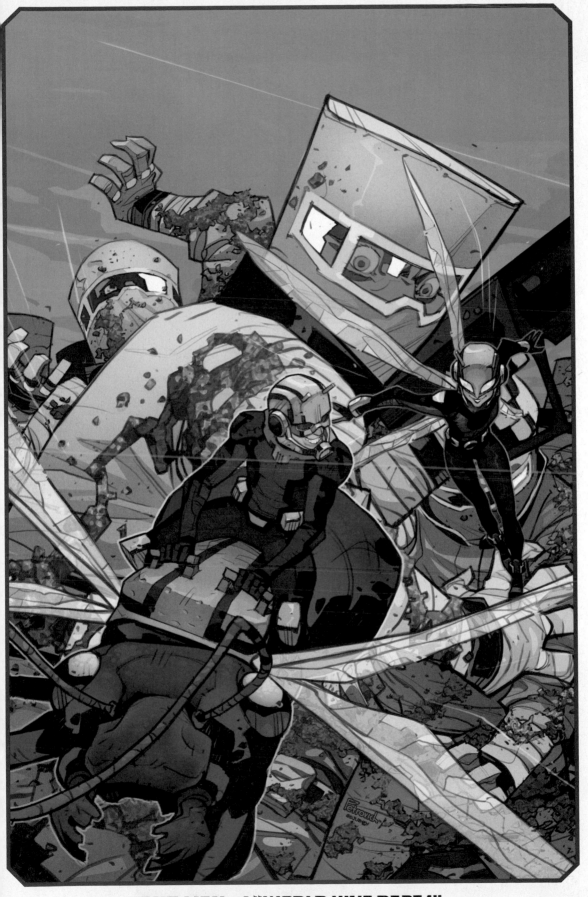

ANT-MAN #1 "WORLD HIVE PART 1"

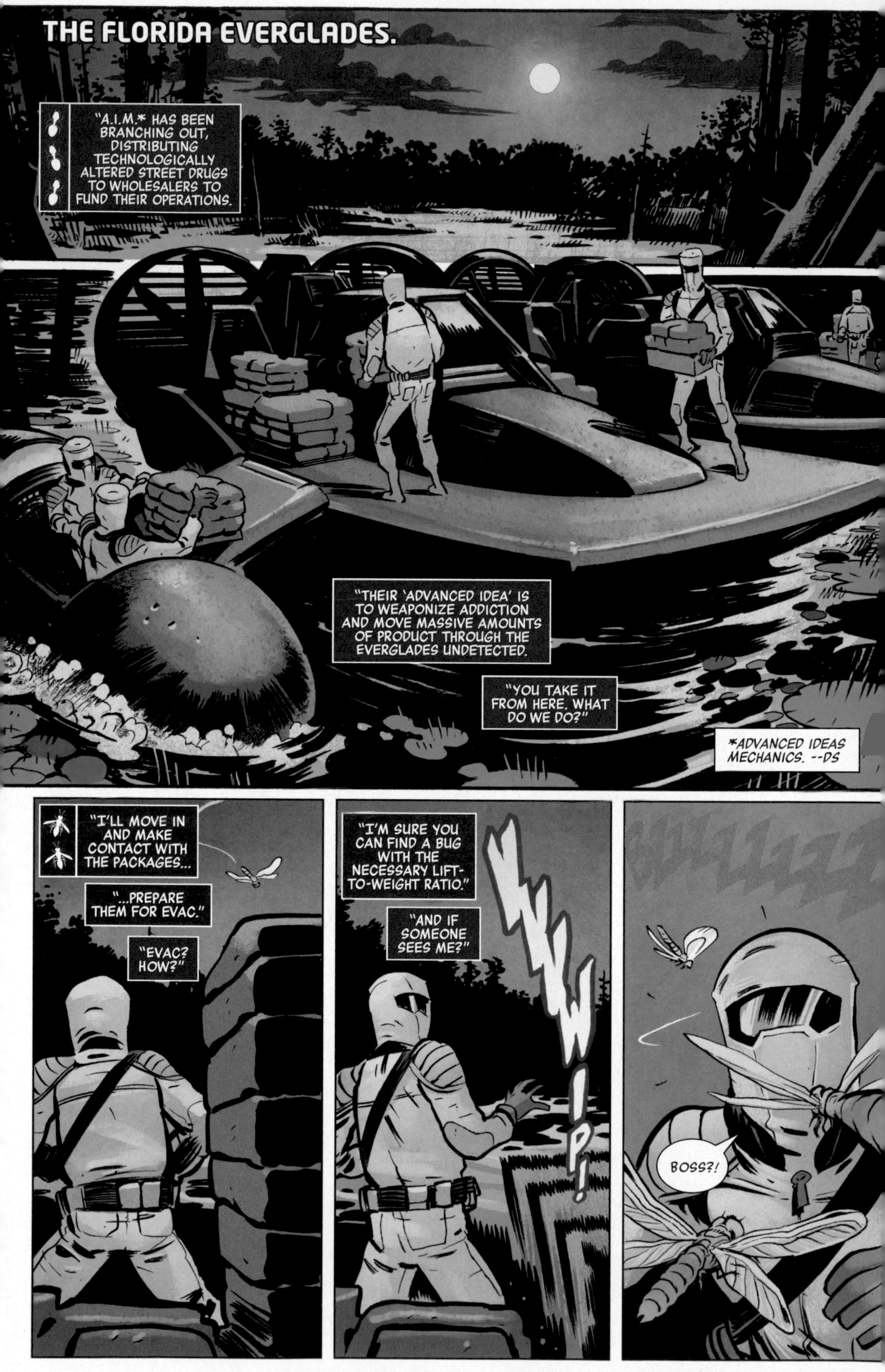
THE FLORIDA EVERGLADES.
"A.I.M.* HAS BEEN BRANCHING OUT, DISTRIBUTING TECHNOLOGICALLY ALTERED STREET DRUGS TO WHOLESALERS TO FUND THEIR OPERATIONS.
"THEIR 'ADVANCED IDEA' IS TO WEAPONIZE ADDICTION AND MOVE MASSIVE AMOUNTS OF PRODUCT THROUGH THE EVERGLADES UNDETECTED.
"YOU TAKE IT FROM HERE. WHAT DO WE DO?"
*ADVANCED IDEAS MECHANICS. --DS
"I'LL MOVE IN AND MAKE CONTACT WITH THE PACKAGES...
"...PREPARE THEM FOR EVAC."
"EVAC? HOW?"
"I'M SURE YOU CAN FIND A BUG WITH THE NECESSARY LIFT-TO-WEIGHT RATIO."
"AND IF SOMEONE SEES ME?"
WHWIP!
BOSS?!

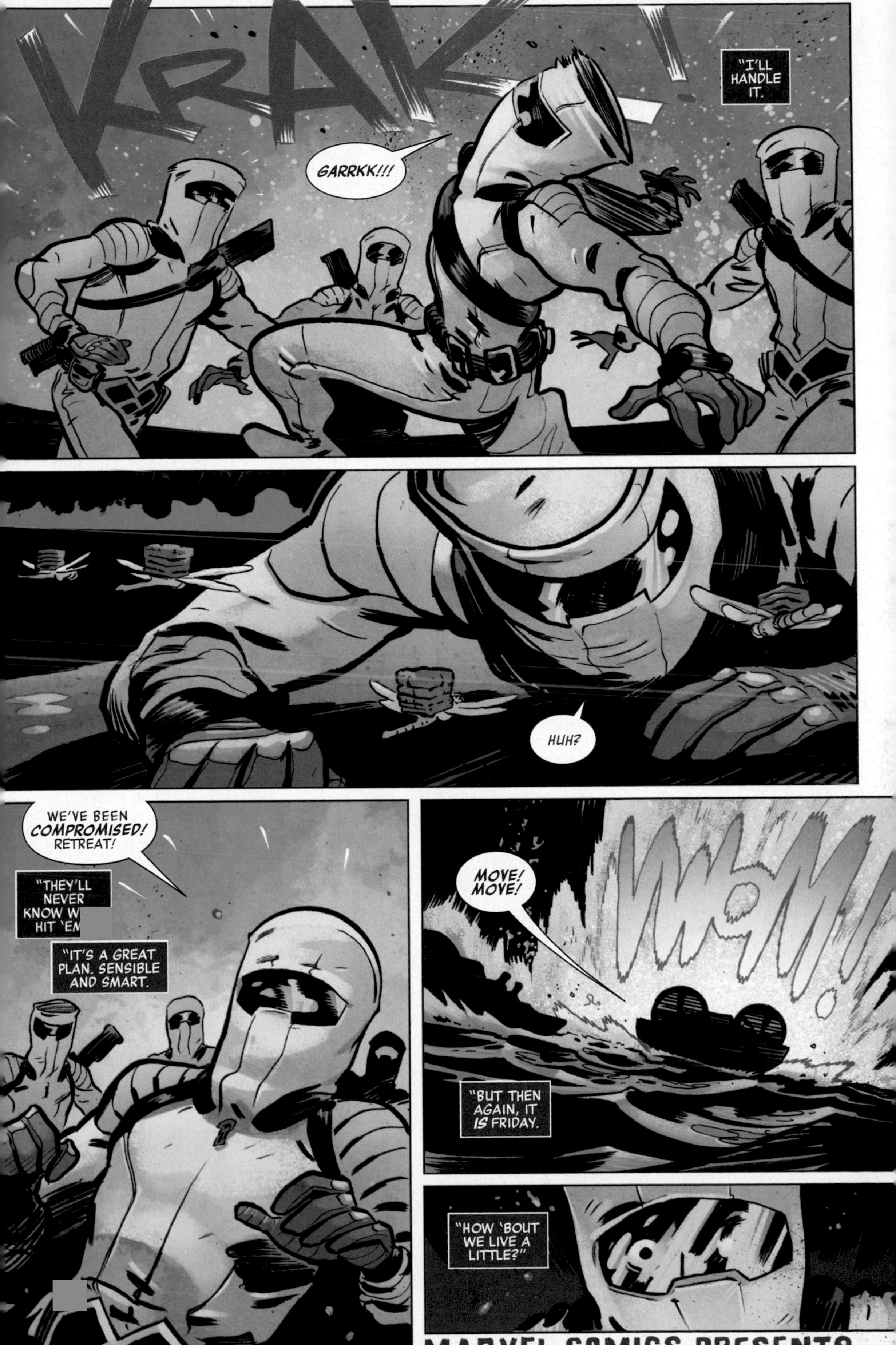

KRAK!
"I'LL HANDLE IT.
GARRKK!!!
HUH?
WE'VE BEEN COMPROMISED! RETREAT!
"THEY'LL NEVER KNOW W HIT 'EM
"IT'S A GREAT PLAN. SENSIBLE AND SMART.
MOVE! MOVE!
"BUT THEN AGAIN, IT *IS* FRIDAY.
"HOW 'BOUT WE LIVE A LITTLE?"

MARVEL COMICS PRESENTS...

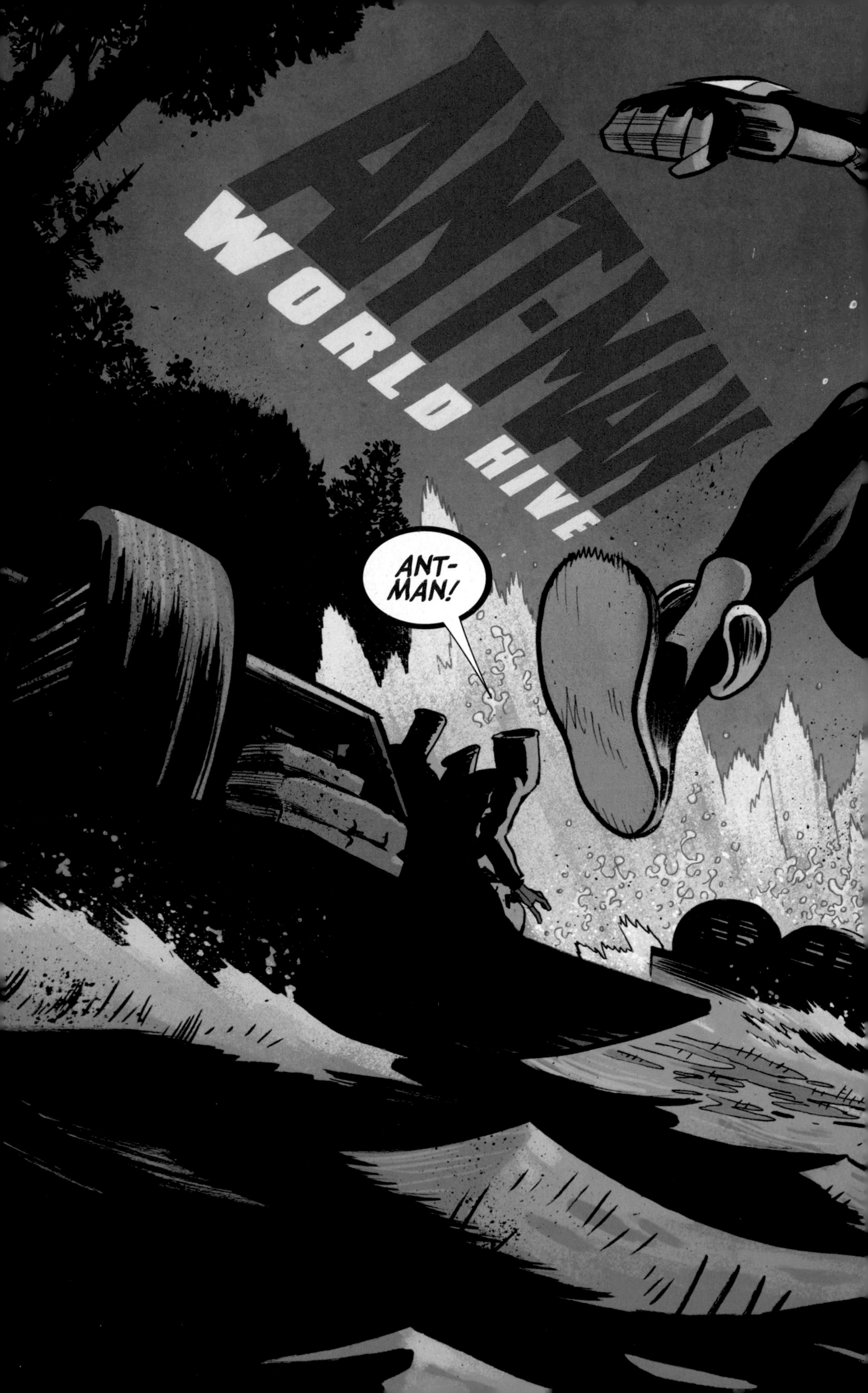
ANT-MAN
WORLD HIVE
ANT-MAN!

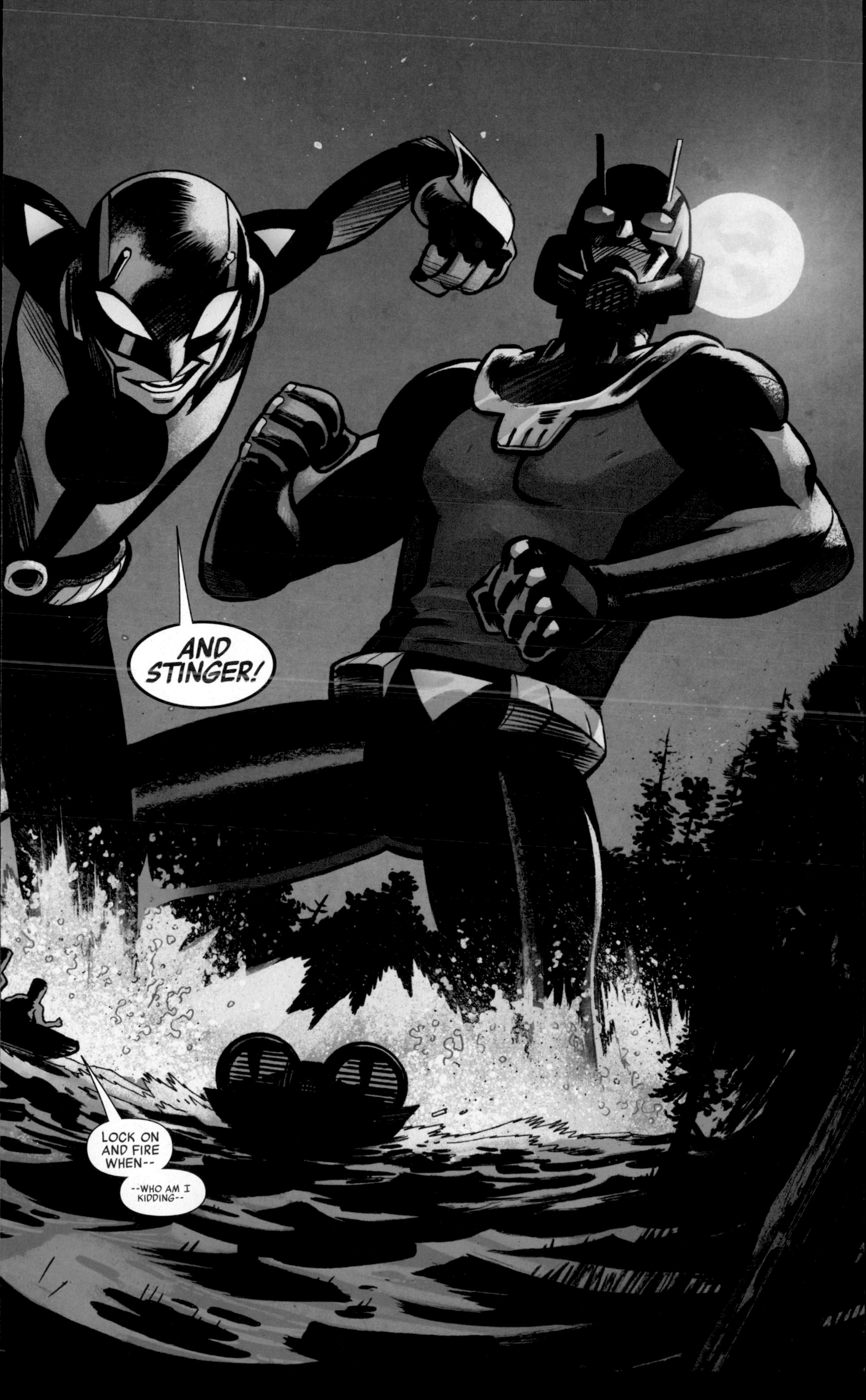
AND STINGER!
LOCK ON AND FIRE WHEN--
--WHO AM I KIDDING--

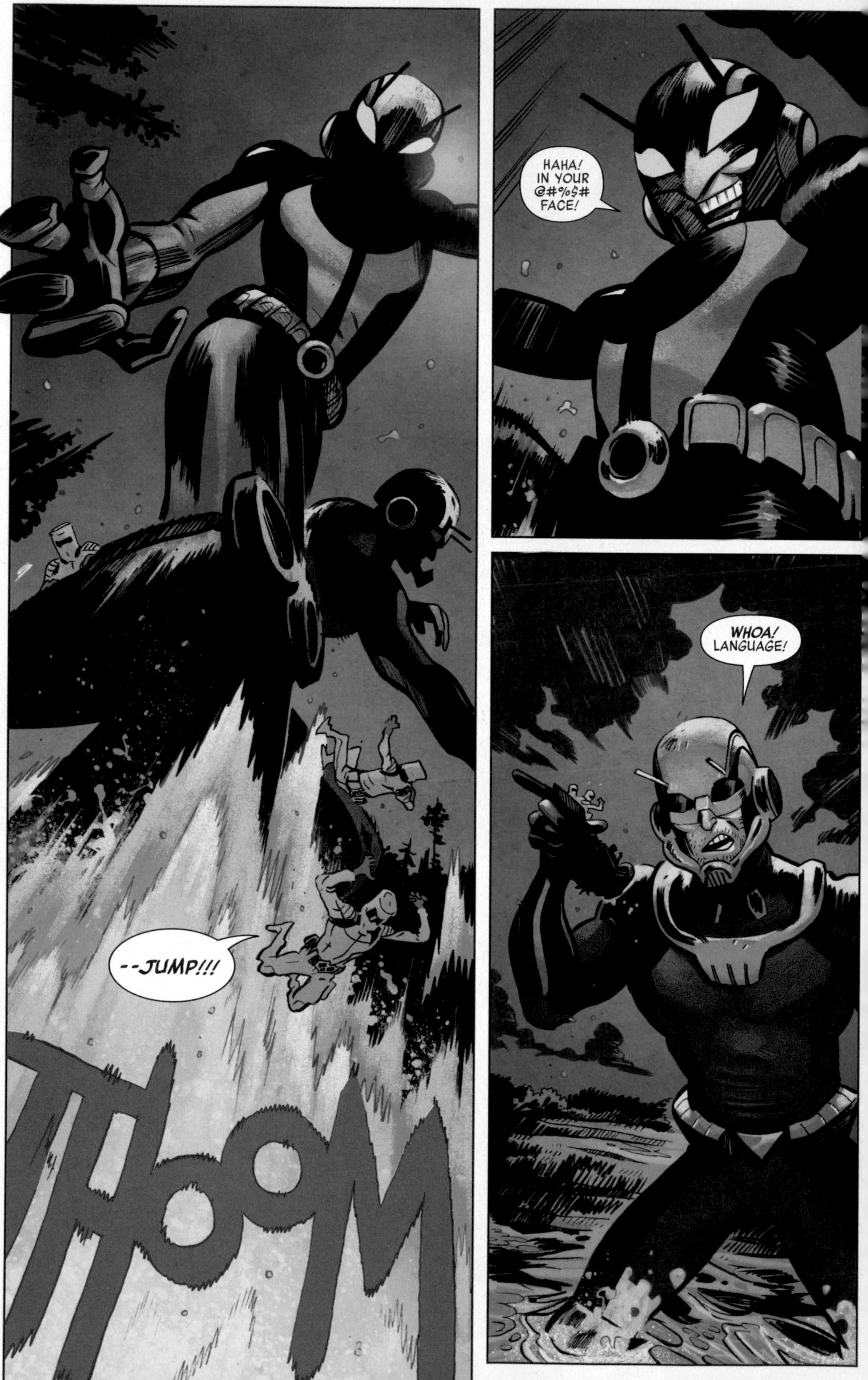
--JUMP!!!
THOOM
HAHA! IN YOUR @#%$# FACE!
WHOA! LANGUAGE!

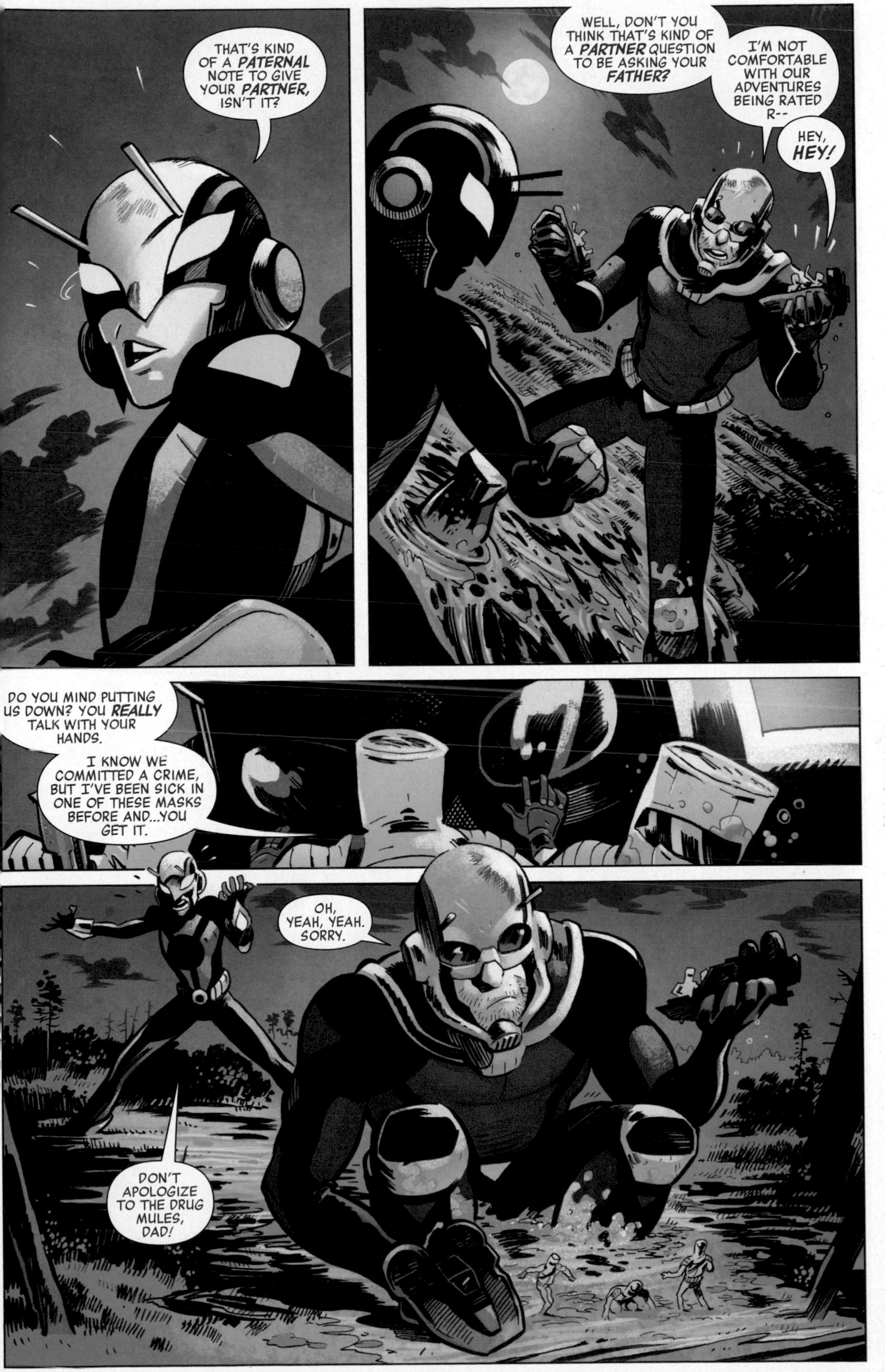

THAT'S KIND OF A PATERNAL NOTE TO GIVE YOUR PARTNER, ISN'T IT?
WELL, DON'T YOU THINK THAT'S KIND OF A PARTNER QUESTION TO BE ASKING YOUR FATHER?
I'M NOT COMFORTABLE WITH OUR ADVENTURES BEING RATED R--
HEY, HEY!
DO YOU MIND PUTTING US DOWN? YOU REALLY TALK WITH YOUR HANDS.
I KNOW WE COMMITTED A CRIME, BUT I'VE BEEN SICK IN ONE OF THESE MASKS BEFORE AND...YOU GET IT.
OH, YEAH, YEAH. SORRY.
DON'T APOLOGIZE TO THE DRUG MULES, DAD!

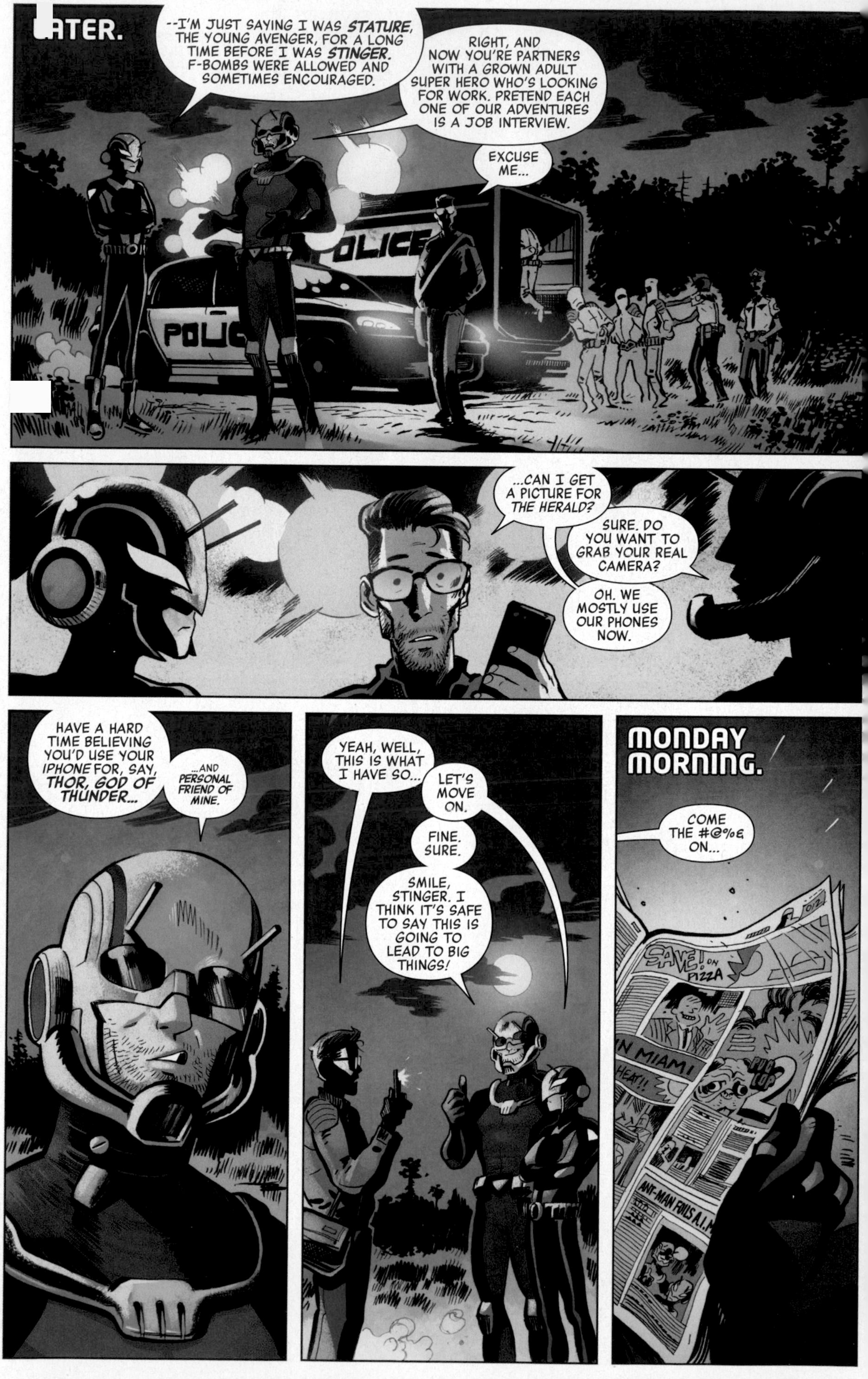
LATER.
--I'M JUST SAYING I WAS STATURE, THE YOUNG AVENGER, FOR A LONG TIME BEFORE I WAS STINGER. F-BOMBS WERE ALLOWED AND SOMETIMES ENCOURAGED.
RIGHT, AND NOW YOU'RE PARTNERS WITH A GROWN ADULT SUPER HERO WHO'S LOOKING FOR WORK. PRETEND EACH ONE OF OUR ADVENTURES IS A JOB INTERVIEW.
EXCUSE ME...
POLICE
POLICE
...CAN I GET A PICTURE FOR THE HERALD?
SURE. DO YOU WANT TO GRAB YOUR REAL CAMERA?
OH. WE MOSTLY USE OUR PHONES NOW.
HAVE A HARD TIME BELIEVING YOU'D USE YOUR IPHONE FOR, SAY, THOR, GOD OF THUNDER...
...AND PERSONAL FRIEND OF MINE.
YEAH, WELL, THIS IS WHAT I HAVE SO...
LET'S MOVE ON.
FINE. SURE.
SMILE, STINGER. I THINK IT'S SAFE TO SAY THIS IS GOING TO LEAD TO BIG THINGS!
MONDAY MORNING.
COME THE #@%& ON...
SAVE! ON PIZZA
IN MIAMI
HEAT!!
ANT-MAN FOILS A.I.M.

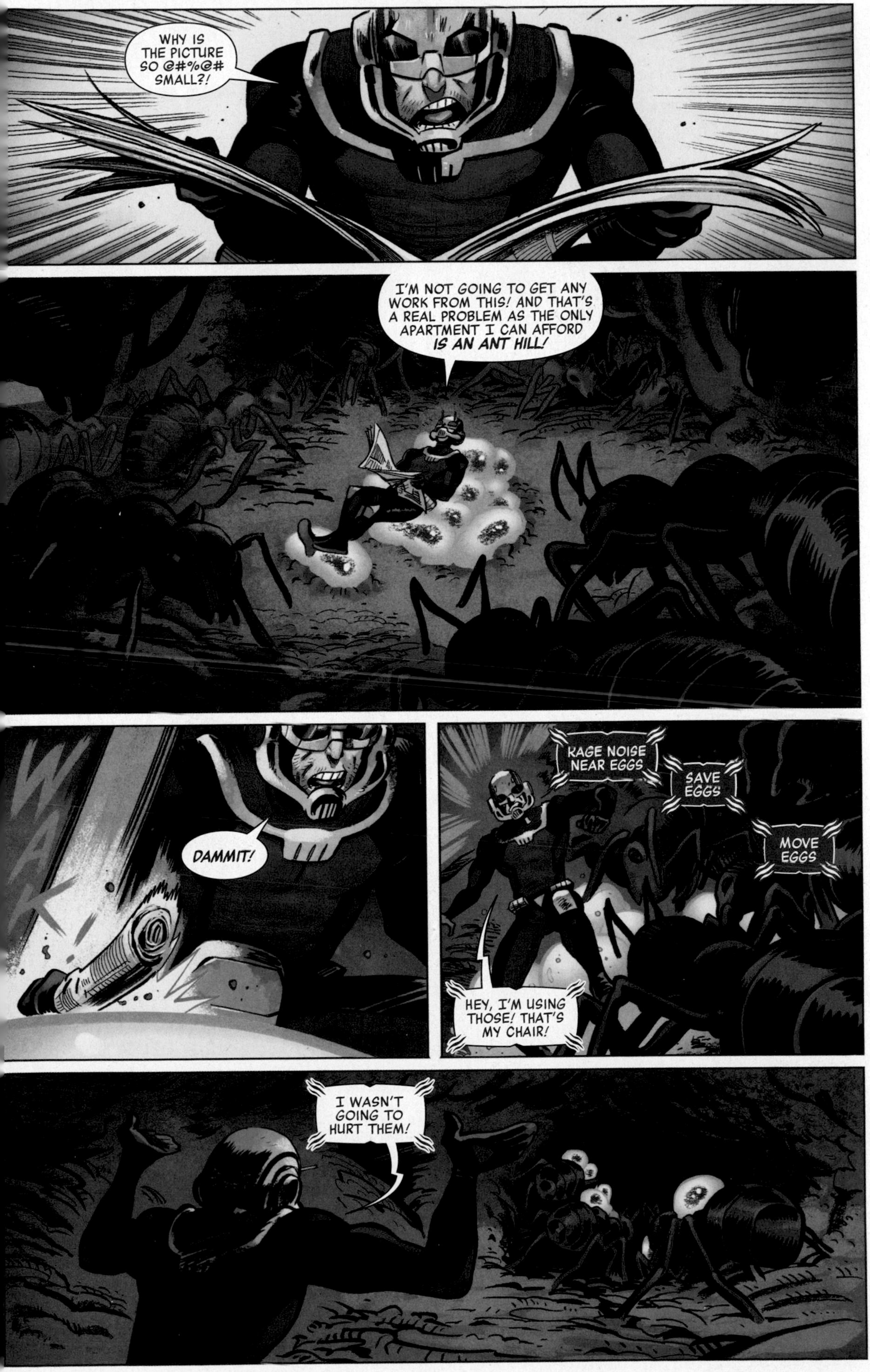
WHY IS THE PICTURE SO @#%@# SMALL?!
I'M NOT GOING TO GET ANY WORK FROM THIS! AND THAT'S A REAL PROBLEM AS THE ONLY APARTMENT I CAN AFFORD **IS AN ANT HILL!**
DAMMIT!
RAGE NOISE NEAR EGGS
SAVE EGGS
MOVE EGGS
HEY, I'M USING THOSE! THAT'S MY CHAIR!
I WASN'T GOING TO HURT THEM!

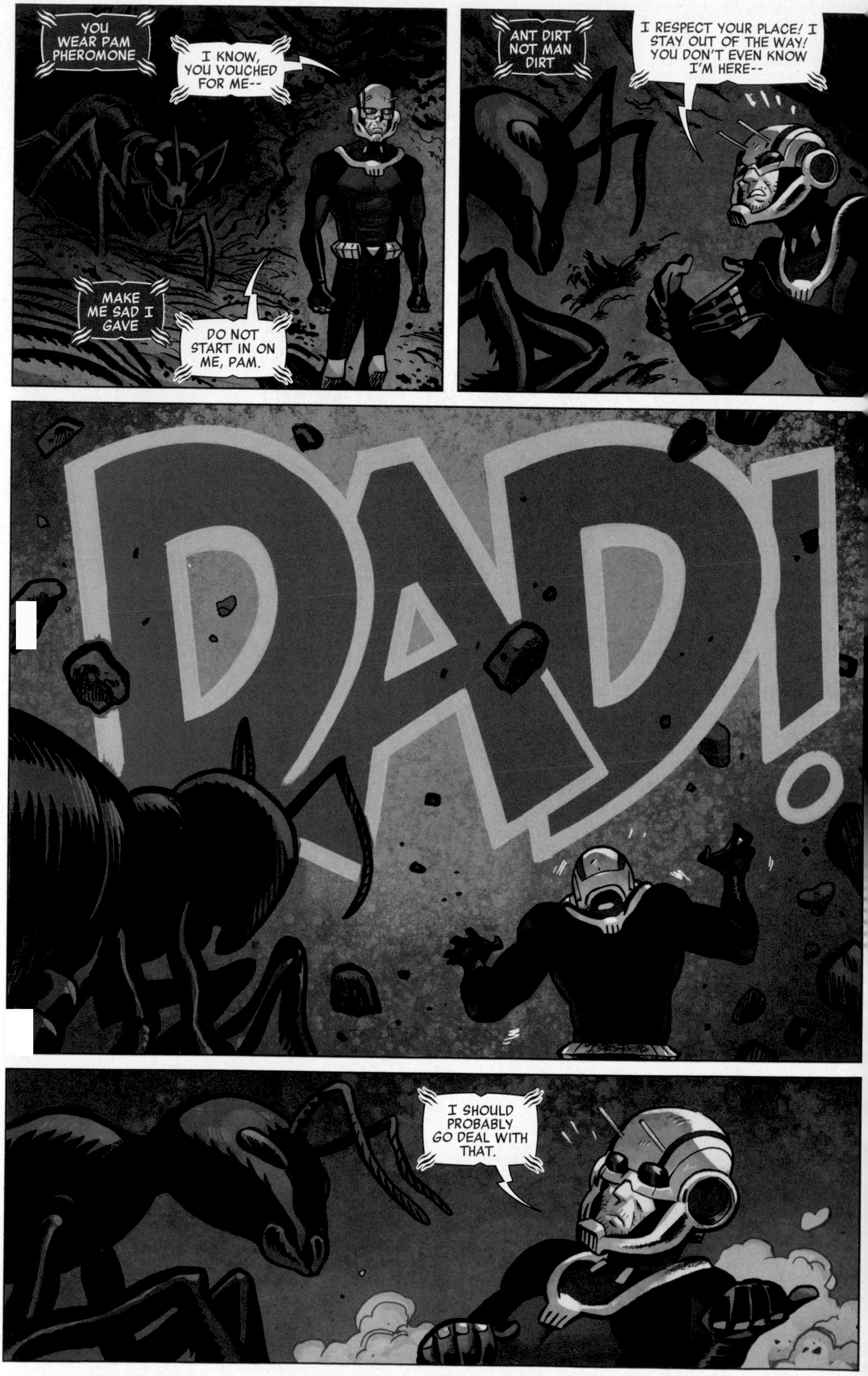
YOU WEAR PAM PHEROMONE
I KNOW, YOU VOUCHED FOR ME--
MAKE ME SAD I GAVE
DO NOT START IN ON ME, PAM.
ANT DIRT NOT MAN DIRT
I RESPECT YOUR PLACE! I STAY OUT OF THE WAY! YOU DON'T EVEN KNOW I'M HERE--
DAD!
I SHOULD PROBABLY GO DEAL WITH THAT.

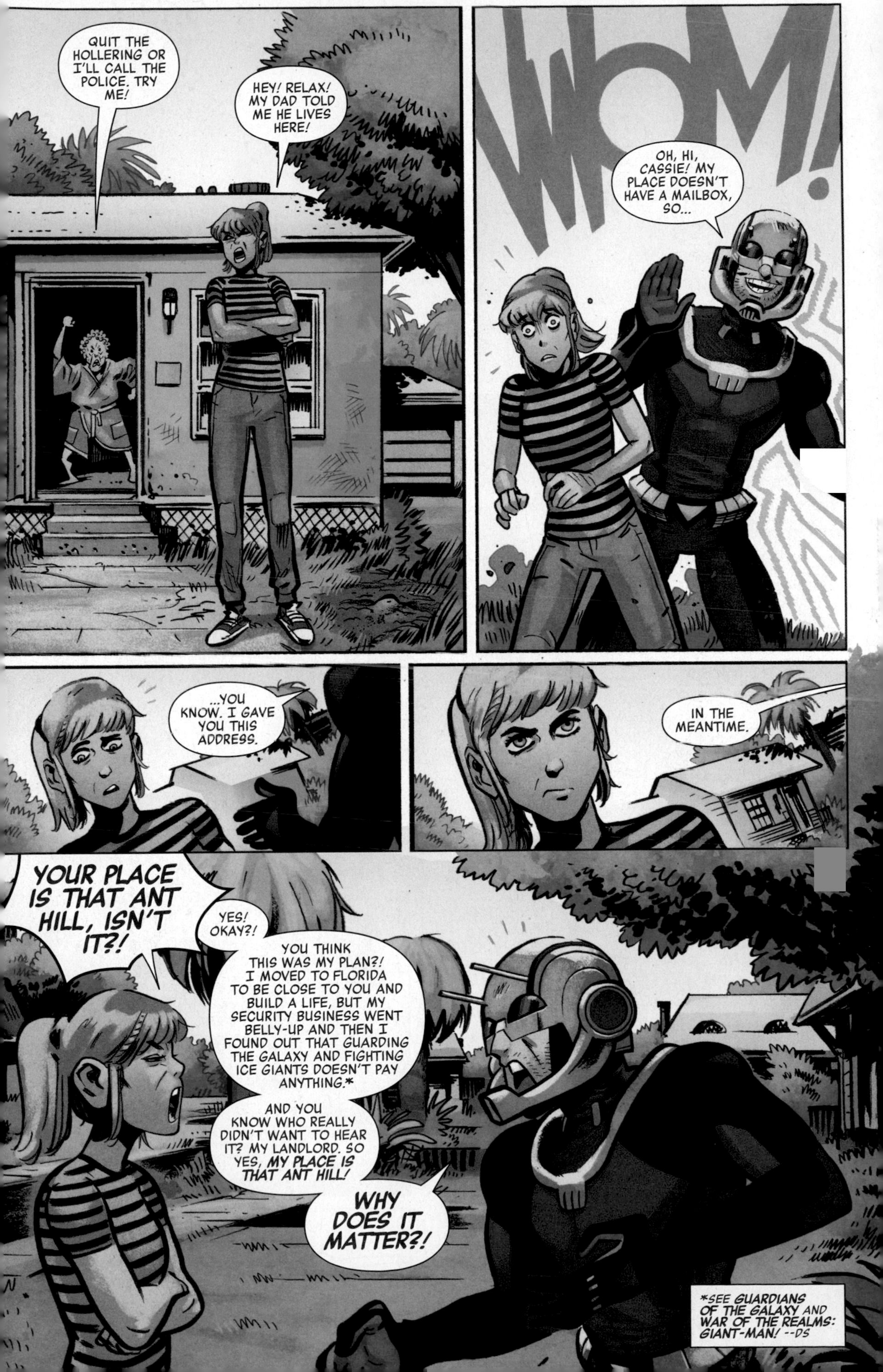
QUIT THE HOLLERING OR I'LL CALL THE POLICE. TRY ME!
HEY! RELAX! MY DAD TOLD ME HE LIVES HERE!
WOOM!
OH, HI, CASSIE! MY PLACE DOESN'T HAVE A MAILBOX, SO...
...YOU KNOW. I GAVE YOU THIS ADDRESS.
IN THE MEANTIME.
YOUR PLACE IS THAT ANT HILL, ISN'T IT?!
YES! OKAY?!
YOU THINK THIS WAS MY PLAN?! I MOVED TO FLORIDA TO BE CLOSE TO YOU AND BUILD A LIFE, BUT MY SECURITY BUSINESS WENT BELLY-UP AND THEN I FOUND OUT THAT GUARDING THE GALAXY AND FIGHTING ICE GIANTS DOESN'T PAY ANYTHING.*
AND YOU KNOW WHO REALLY DIDN'T WANT TO HEAR IT? MY LANDLORD. SO YES, MY PLACE IS THAT ANT HILL!
WHY DOES IT MATTER?!
*SEE GUARDIANS OF THE GALAXY AND WAR OF THE REALMS: GIANT-MAN! --DS

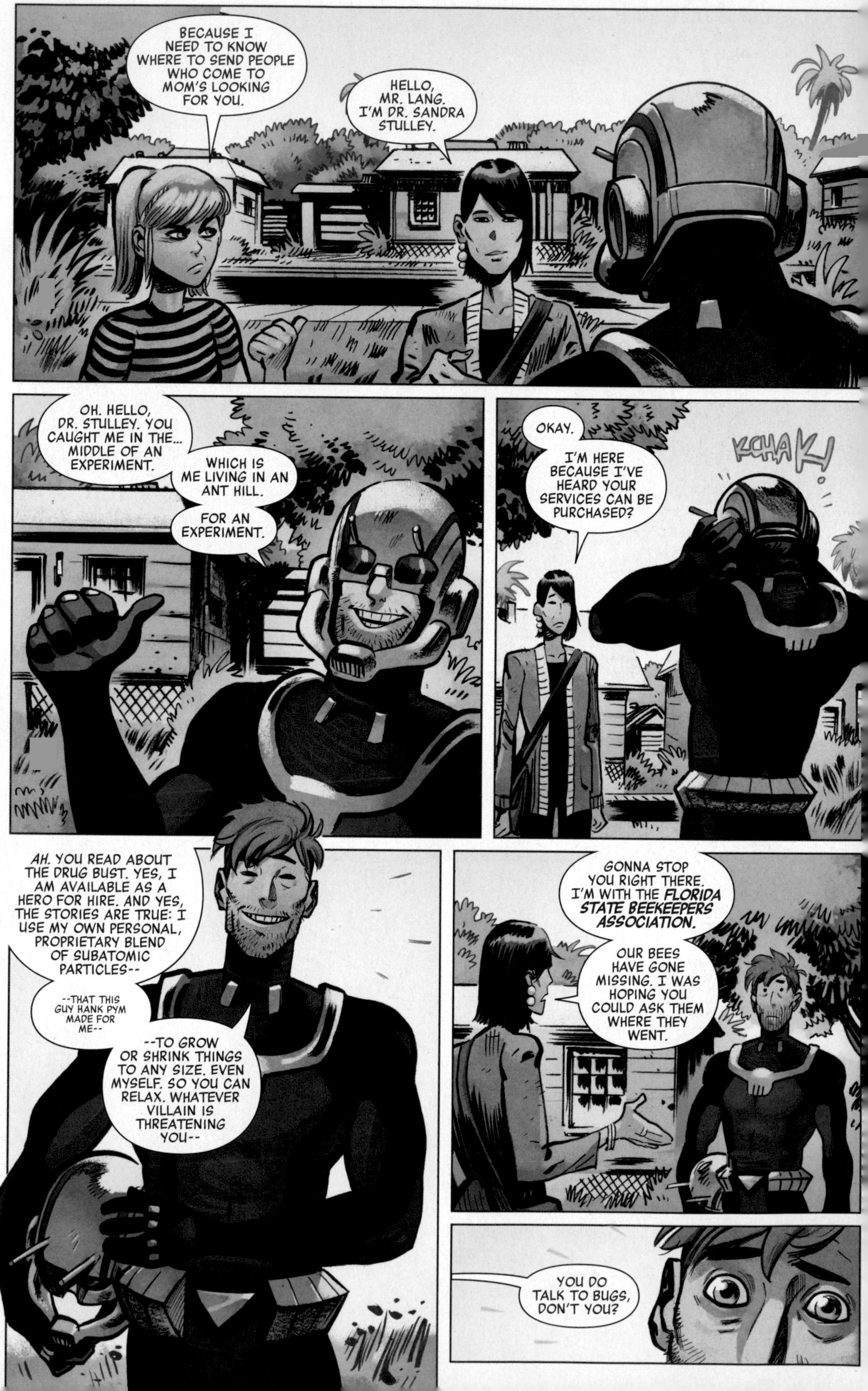
BECAUSE I NEED TO KNOW WHERE TO SEND PEOPLE WHO COME TO MOM'S LOOKING FOR YOU.
HELLO, MR. LANG. I'M DR. SANDRA STULLEY.
OH. HELLO, DR. STULLEY. YOU CAUGHT ME IN THE... MIDDLE OF AN EXPERIMENT.
WHICH IS ME LIVING IN AN ANT HILL.
FOR AN EXPERIMENT.
OKAY.
I'M HERE BECAUSE I'VE HEARD YOUR SERVICES CAN BE PURCHASED?
KCHAK!
AH. YOU READ ABOUT THE DRUG BUST. YES, I AM AVAILABLE AS A HERO FOR HIRE. AND YES, THE STORIES ARE TRUE: I USE MY OWN PERSONAL, PROPRIETARY BLEND OF SUBATOMIC PARTICLES--
--THAT THIS GUY HANK PYM MADE FOR ME--
--TO GROW OR SHRINK THINGS TO ANY SIZE. EVEN MYSELF. SO YOU CAN RELAX. WHATEVER VILLAIN IS THREATENING YOU--
GONNA STOP YOU RIGHT THERE. I'M WITH THE FLORIDA STATE BEEKEEPERS ASSOCIATION.
OUR BEES HAVE GONE MISSING. I WAS HOPING YOU COULD ASK THEM WHERE THEY WENT.
YOU DO TALK TO BUGS, DON'T YOU?

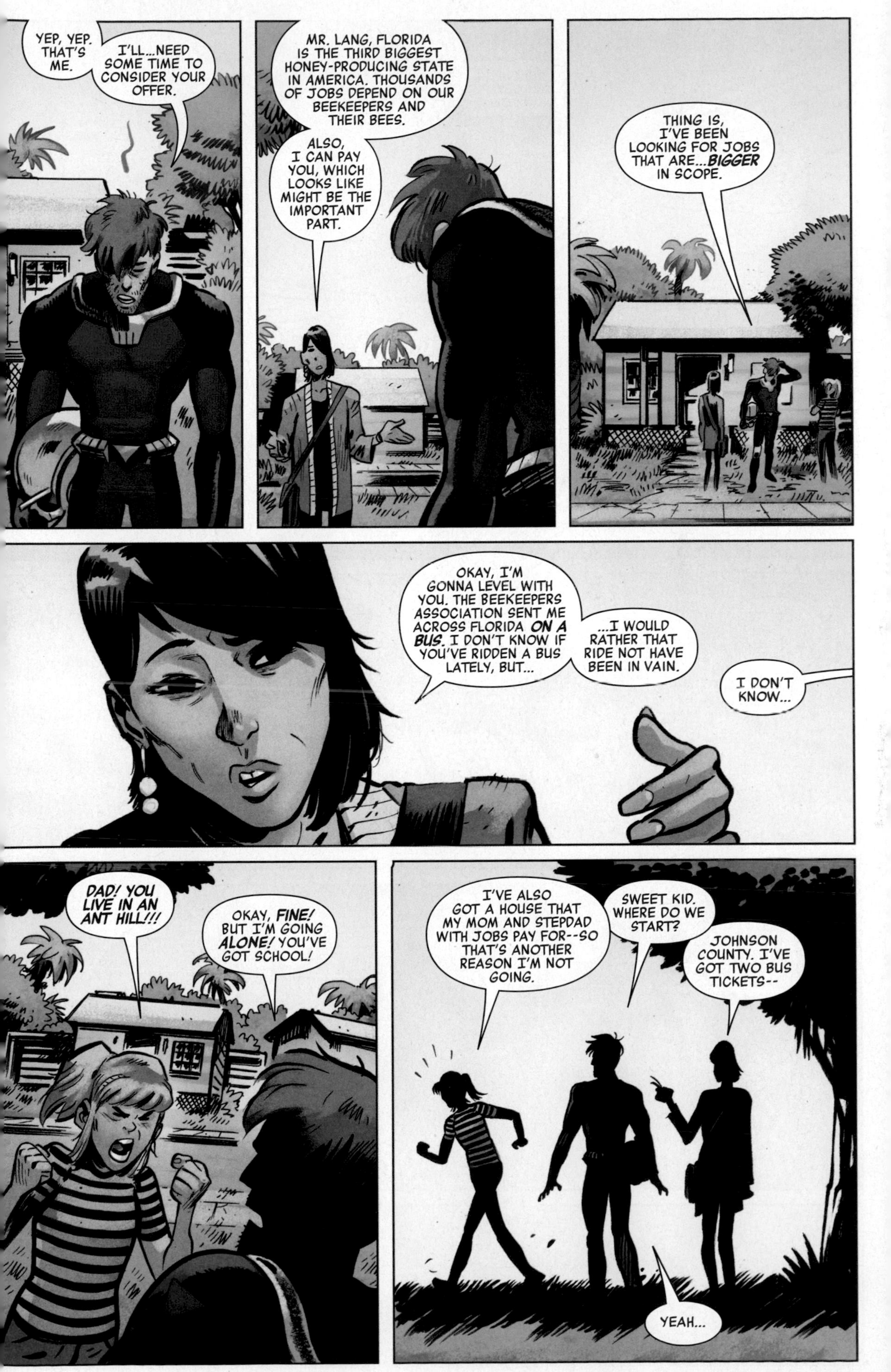
YEP, YEP. THAT'S ME.
I'LL...NEED SOME TIME TO CONSIDER YOUR OFFER.
MR. LANG, FLORIDA IS THE THIRD BIGGEST HONEY-PRODUCING STATE IN AMERICA. THOUSANDS OF JOBS DEPEND ON OUR BEEKEEPERS AND THEIR BEES.
ALSO, I CAN PAY YOU, WHICH LOOKS LIKE MIGHT BE THE IMPORTANT PART.
THING IS, I'VE BEEN LOOKING FOR JOBS THAT ARE...**BIGGER** IN SCOPE.
OKAY, I'M GONNA LEVEL WITH YOU. THE BEEKEEPERS ASSOCIATION SENT ME ACROSS FLORIDA ***ON A BUS.*** I DON'T KNOW IF YOU'VE RIDDEN A BUS LATELY, BUT...
...I WOULD RATHER THAT RIDE NOT HAVE BEEN IN VAIN.
I DON'T KNOW...
DAD! YOU LIVE IN AN ANT HILL!!!
OKAY, **FINE!** BUT I'M GOING ***ALONE!*** YOU'VE GOT SCHOOL!
I'VE ALSO GOT A HOUSE THAT MY MOM AND STEPDAD WITH JOBS PAY FOR--SO THAT'S ANOTHER REASON I'M NOT GOING.
SWEET KID. WHERE DO WE START?
JOHNSON COUNTY. I'VE GOT TWO BUS TICKETS--
YEAH...

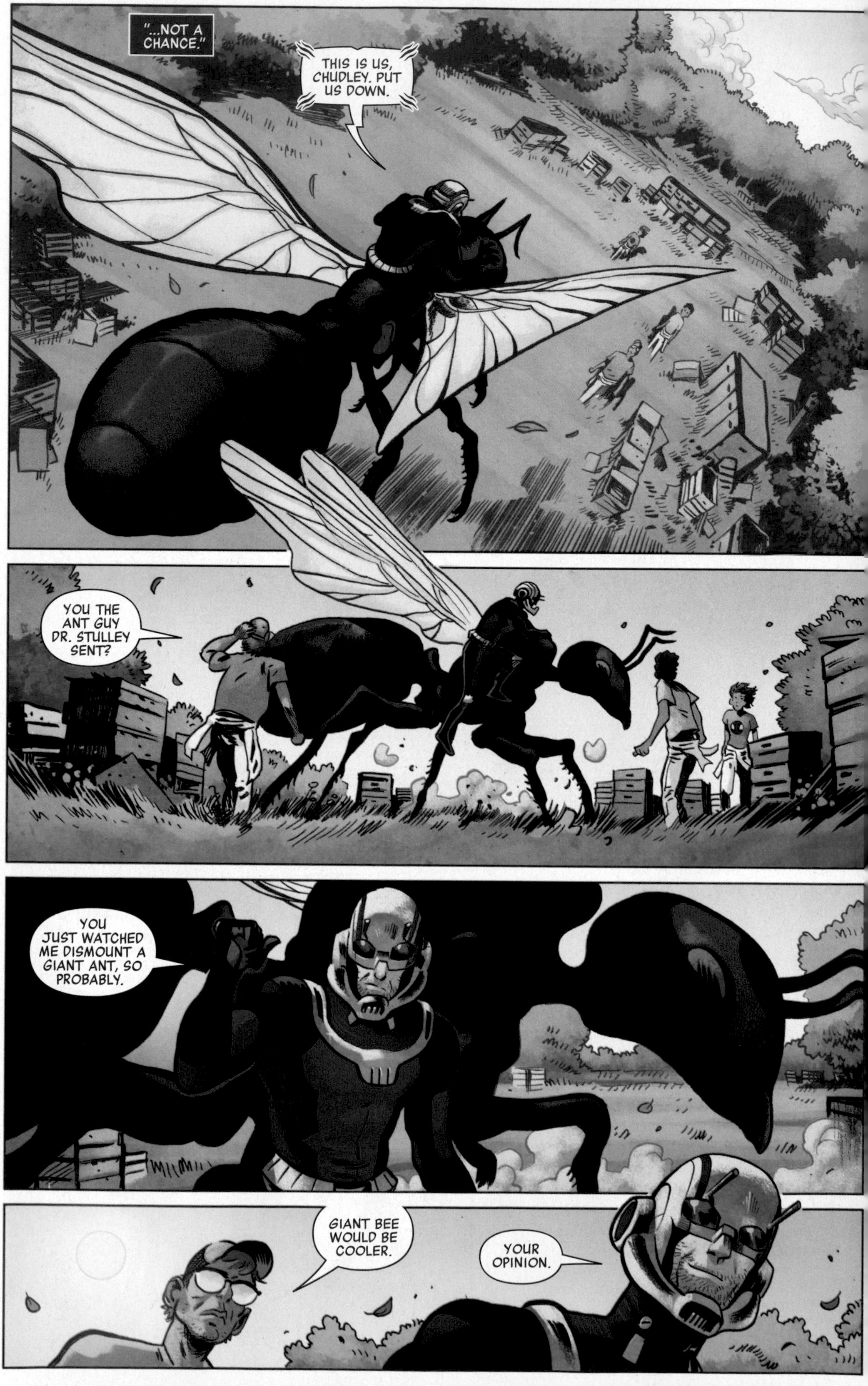
"...NOT A CHANCE."
THIS IS US, CHUDLEY. PUT US DOWN.
YOU THE ANT GUY DR. STULLEY SENT?
YOU JUST WATCHED ME DISMOUNT A GIANT ANT, SO PROBABLY.
GIANT BEE WOULD BE COOLER.
YOUR OPINION.

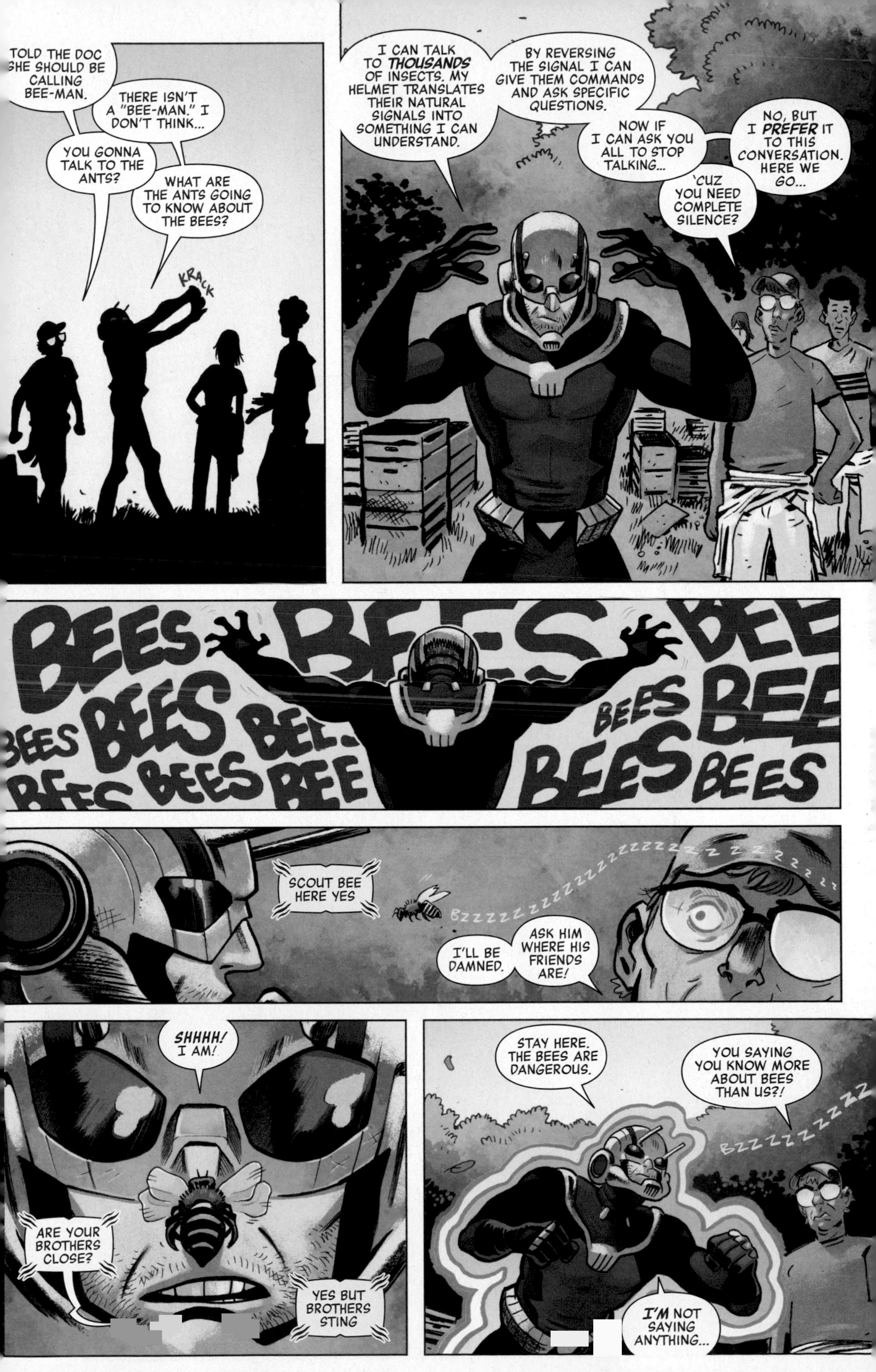
TOLD THE DOC SHE SHOULD BE CALLING BEE-MAN.
THERE ISN'T A "BEE-MAN." I DON'T THINK...
YOU GONNA TALK TO THE ANTS?
WHAT ARE THE ANTS GOING TO KNOW ABOUT THE BEES?
KRACK
I CAN TALK TO THOUSANDS OF INSECTS. MY HELMET TRANSLATES THEIR NATURAL SIGNALS INTO SOMETHING I CAN UNDERSTAND.
BY REVERSING THE SIGNAL I CAN GIVE THEM COMMANDS AND ASK SPECIFIC QUESTIONS.
NOW IF I CAN ASK YOU ALL TO STOP TALKING...
'CUZ YOU NEED COMPLETE SILENCE?
NO, BUT I PREFER IT TO THIS CONVERSATION. HERE WE GO...
BEES BEES BEES BEE
BEES BEES BEE. BEES BEE
BEES BEES BEE BEES BEES
SCOUT BEE HERE YES
BZZZZZ
I'LL BE DAMNED.
ASK HIM WHERE HIS FRIENDS ARE!
SHHHH! I AM!
ARE YOUR BROTHERS CLOSE?
YES BUT BROTHERS STING
STAY HERE. THE BEES ARE DANGEROUS.
YOU SAYING YOU KNOW MORE ABOUT BEES THAN US?!
BZZZZZZZZ
I'M NOT SAYING ANYTHING...

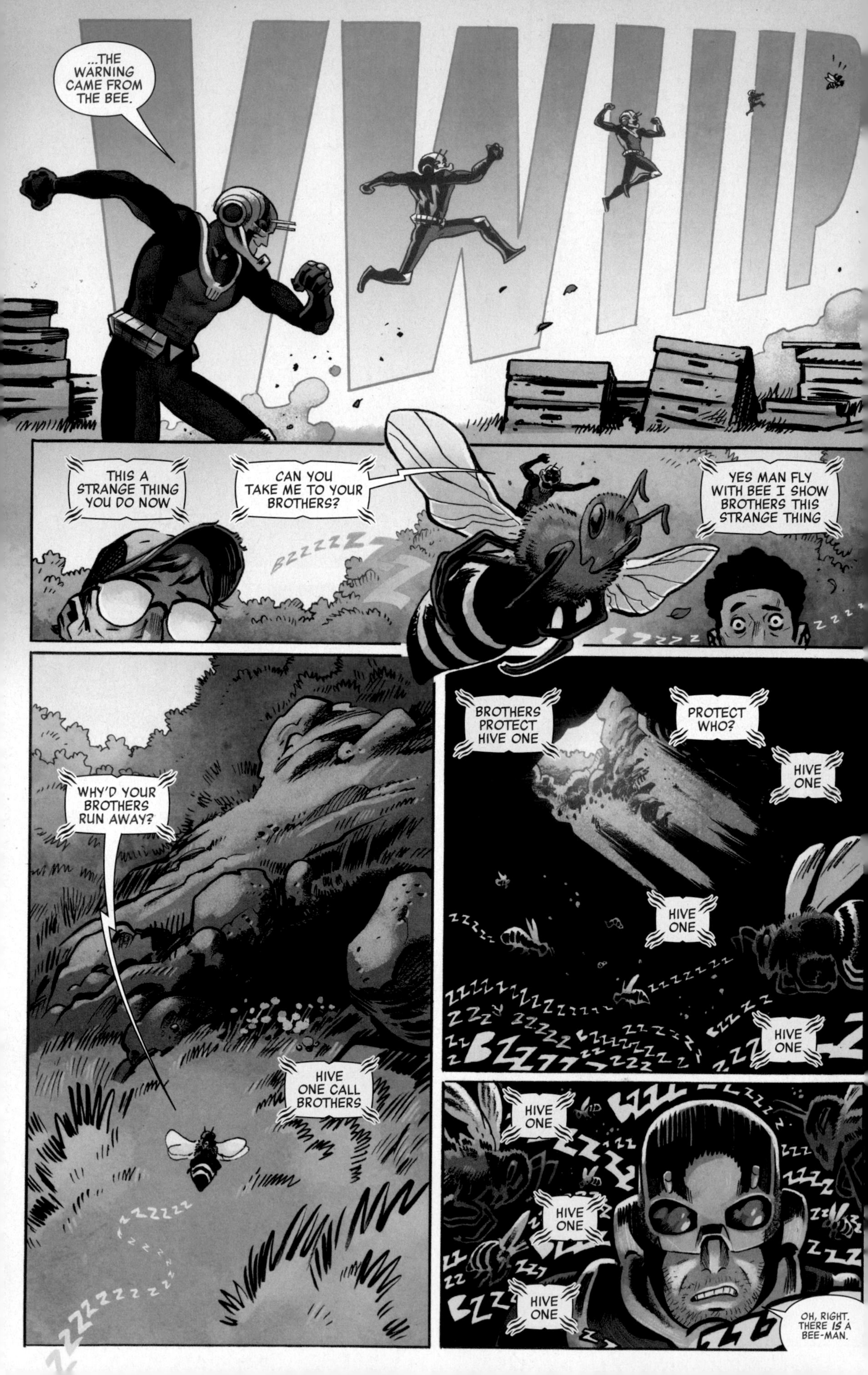

...THE WARNING CAME FROM THE BEE.
VWHIP
THIS A STRANGE THING YOU DO NOW
CAN YOU TAKE ME TO YOUR BROTHERS?
YES MAN FLY WITH BEE I SHOW BROTHERS THIS STRANGE THING
BZZZZZ
WHY'D YOUR BROTHERS RUN AWAY?
HIVE ONE CALL BROTHERS
BROTHERS PROTECT HIVE ONE
PROTECT WHO?
HIVE ONE
HIVE ONE
HIVE ONE
HIVE ONE
HIVE ONE
HIVE ONE
OH, RIGHT. THERE *IS* A BEE-MAN.

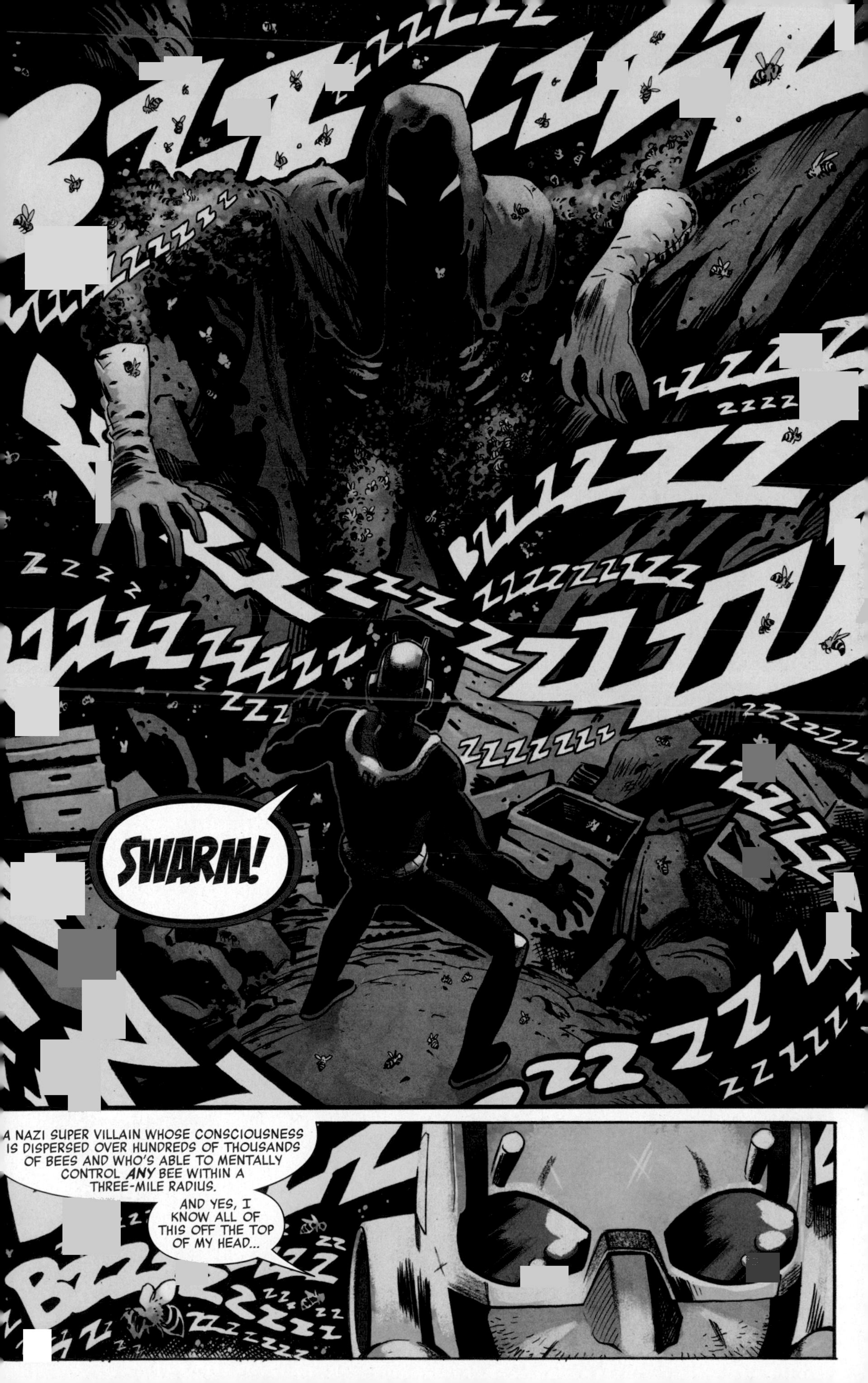
SWARM!
A NAZI SUPER VILLAIN WHOSE CONSCIOUSNESS IS DISPERSED OVER HUNDREDS OF THOUSANDS OF BEES AND WHO'S ABLE TO MENTALLY CONTROL *ANY* BEE WITHIN A THREE-MILE RADIUS.
AND YES, I KNOW ALL OF THIS OFF THE TOP OF MY HEAD...

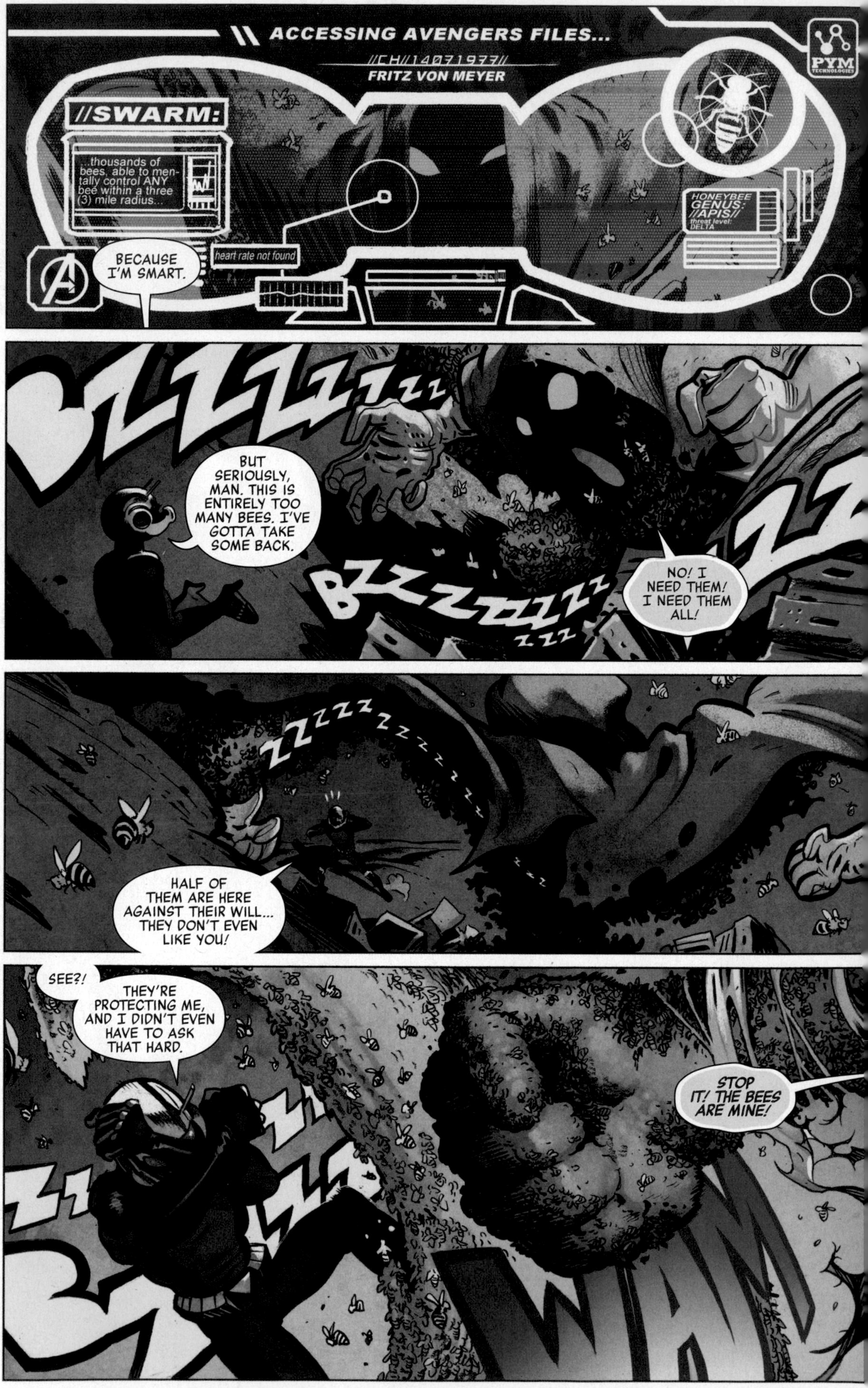
ACCESSING AVENGERS FILES...
//CH//14071977//
FRITZ VON MEYER
//SWARM:
...thousands of bees, able to mentally control ANY bee within a three (3) mile radius...
HONEYBEE GENUS: //APIS// threat level: DELTA
heart rate not found
BECAUSE I'M SMART.
BZZZZzzzz
BUT SERIOUSLY, MAN. THIS IS ENTIRELY TOO MANY BEES. I'VE GOTTA TAKE SOME BACK.
BZZZZzzzzz
NO! I NEED THEM! I NEED THEM ALL!
HALF OF THEM ARE HERE AGAINST THEIR WILL... THEY DON'T EVEN LIKE YOU!
SEE?!
THEY'RE PROTECTING ME, AND I DIDN'T EVEN HAVE TO ASK THAT HARD.
STOP IT! THE BEES ARE MINE!

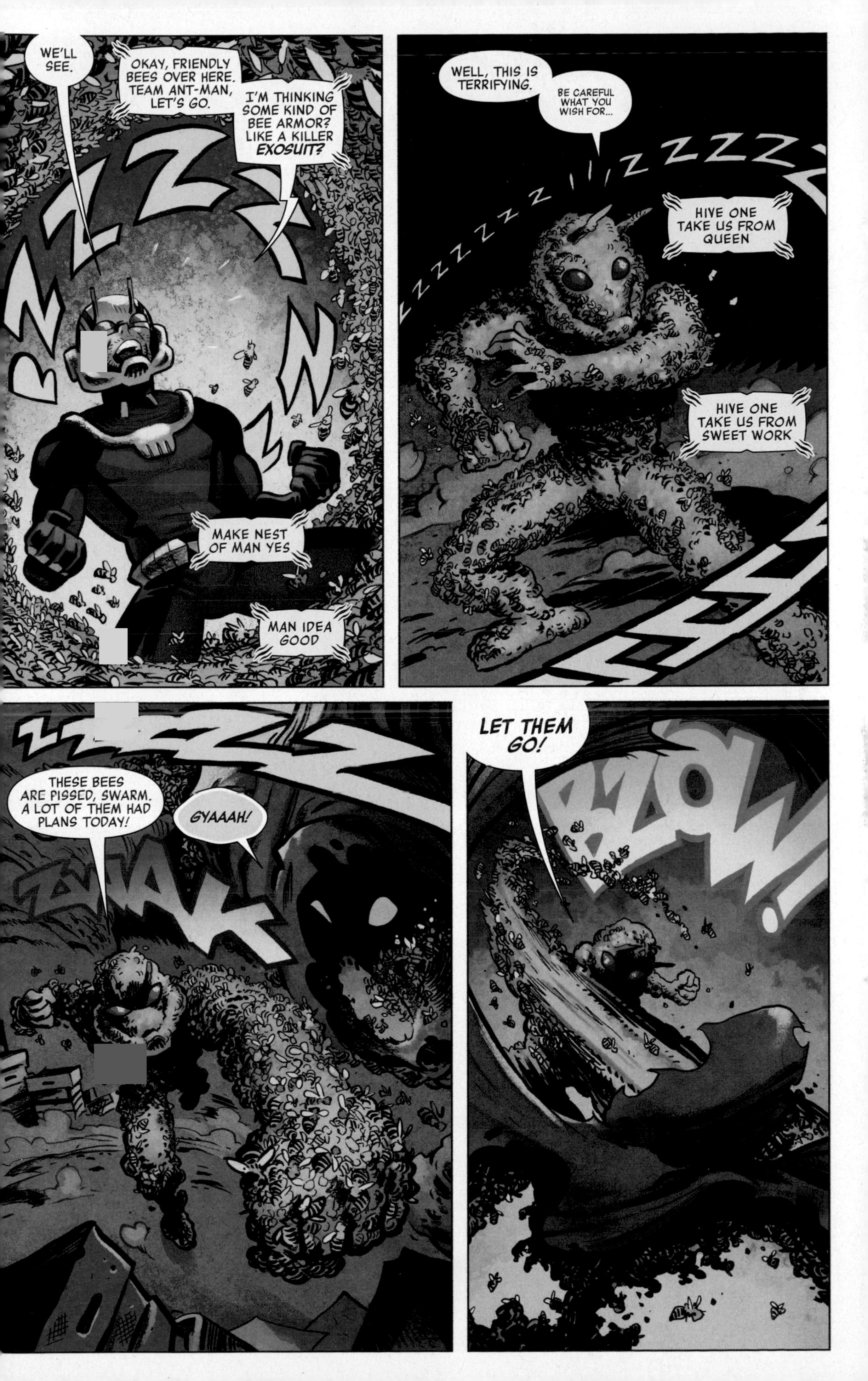
WE'LL SEE.
OKAY, FRIENDLY BEES OVER HERE. TEAM ANT-MAN, LET'S GO.
I'M THINKING SOME KIND OF BEE ARMOR? LIKE A KILLER EXOSUIT?
MAKE NEST OF MAN YES
MAN IDEA GOOD
WELL, THIS IS TERRIFYING.
BE CAREFUL WHAT YOU WISH FOR...
HIVE ONE TAKE US FROM QUEEN
HIVE ONE TAKE US FROM SWEET WORK
THESE BEES ARE PISSED, SWARM. A LOT OF THEM HAD PLANS TODAY!
GYAAAH!
LET THEM GO!

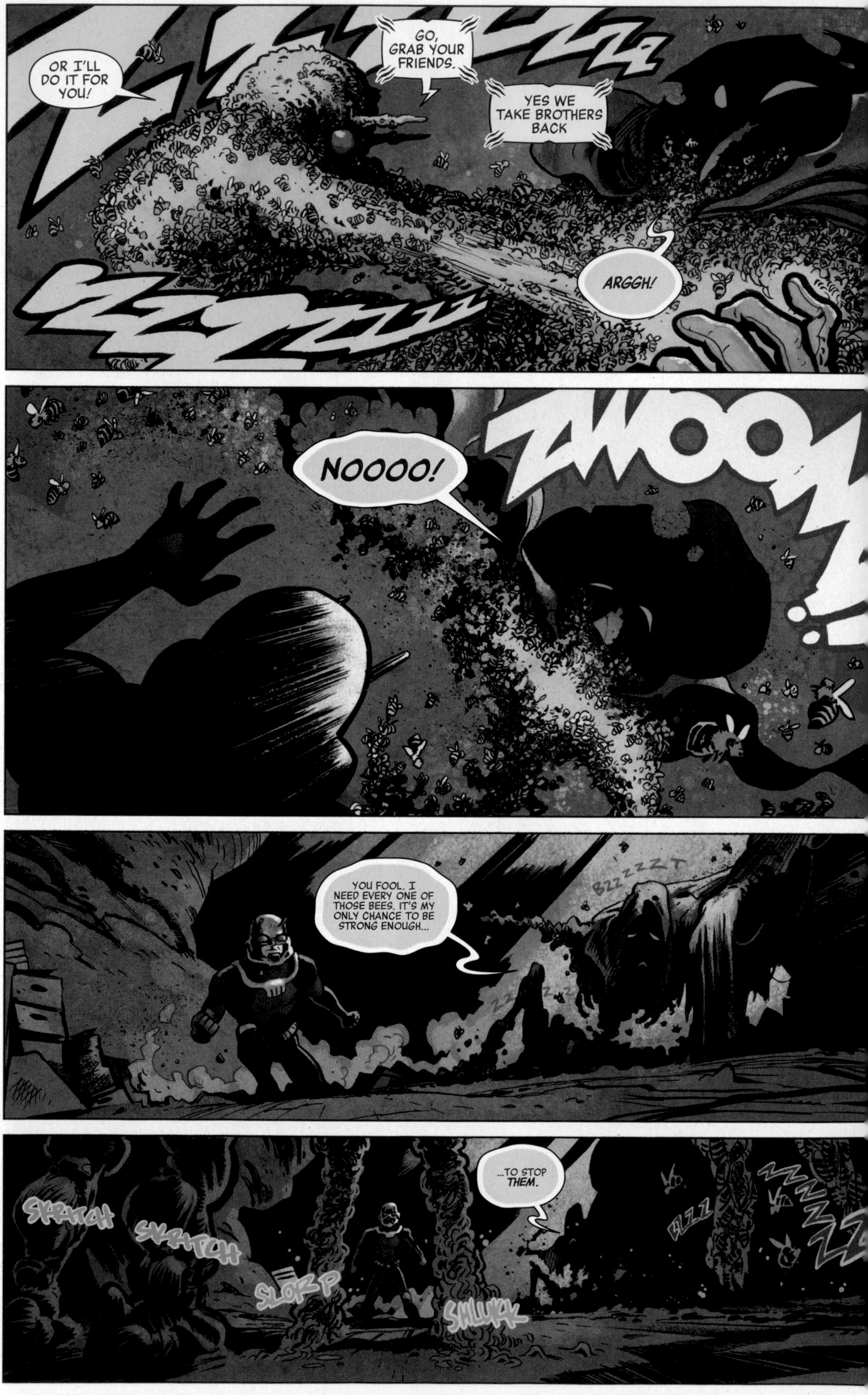

OR I'LL DO IT FOR YOU!
GO, GRAB YOUR FRIENDS.
YES WE TAKE BROTHERS BACK
ARGGH!
NOOOO!
ZWOO
YOU FOOL. I NEED EVERY ONE OF THOSE BEES. IT'S MY ONLY CHANCE TO BE STRONG ENOUGH...
...TO STOP THEM.
SKRITCH
SKRITCH
SLORP
SHLUKK

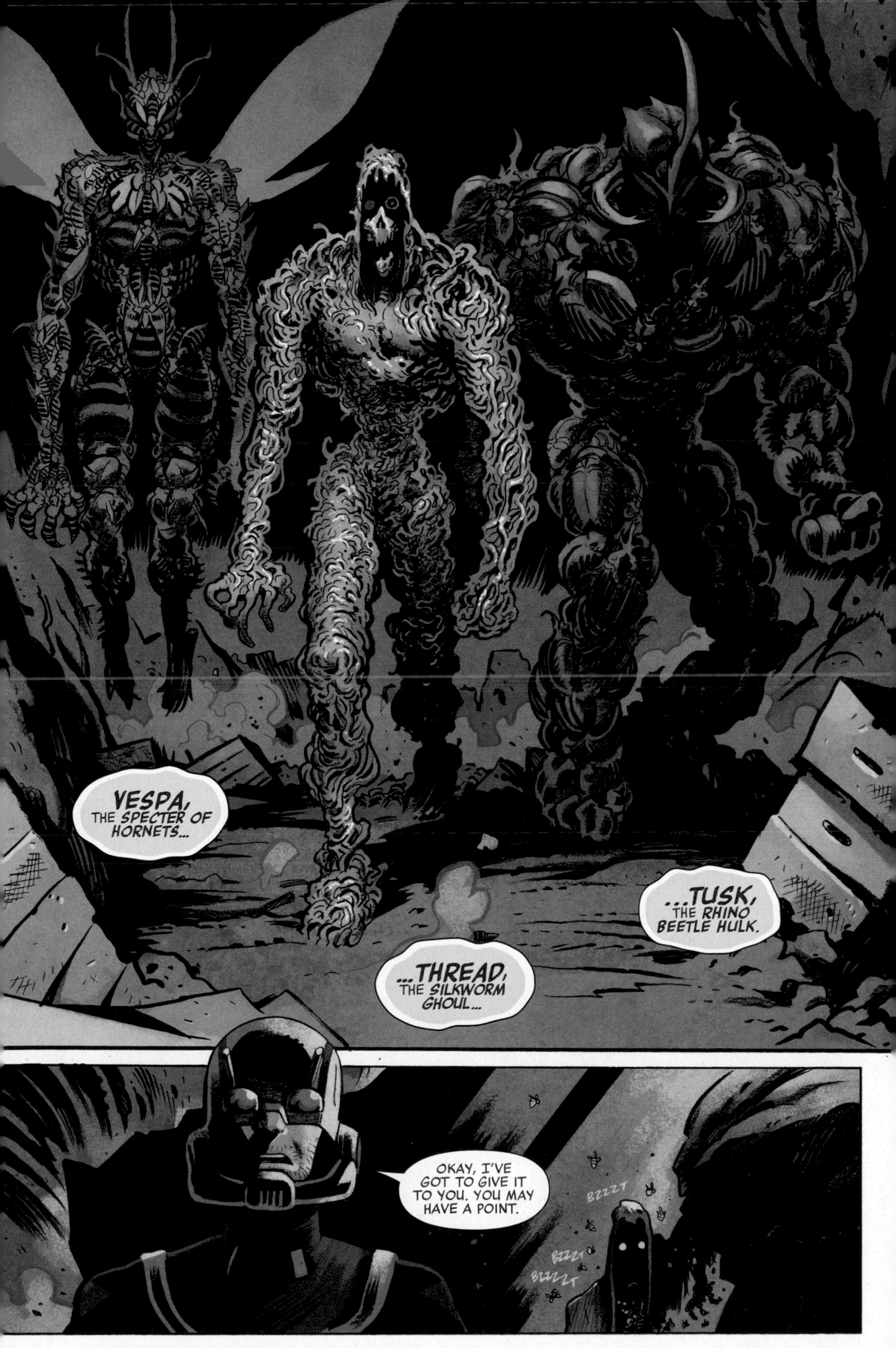
VESPA, THE SPECTER OF HORNETS...
...THREAD, THE SILKWORM GHOUL...
...TUSK, THE RHINO BEETLE HULK.
OKAY, I'VE GOT TO GIVE IT TO YOU. YOU MAY HAVE A POINT.
BZZZT
BZZZT
BZZZT

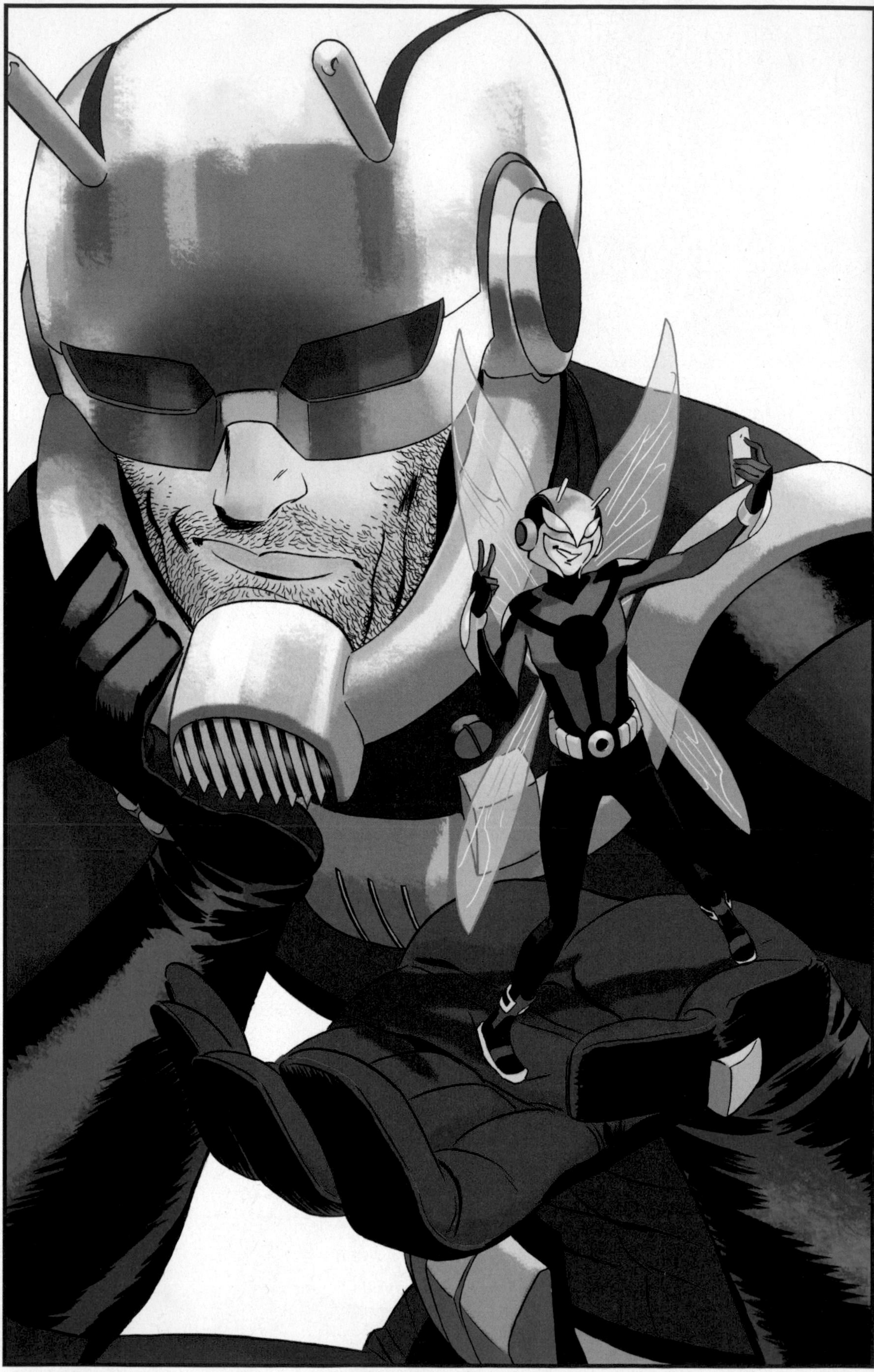

ANT-MAN #1 VARIANT BY **MARCOS MARTIN**

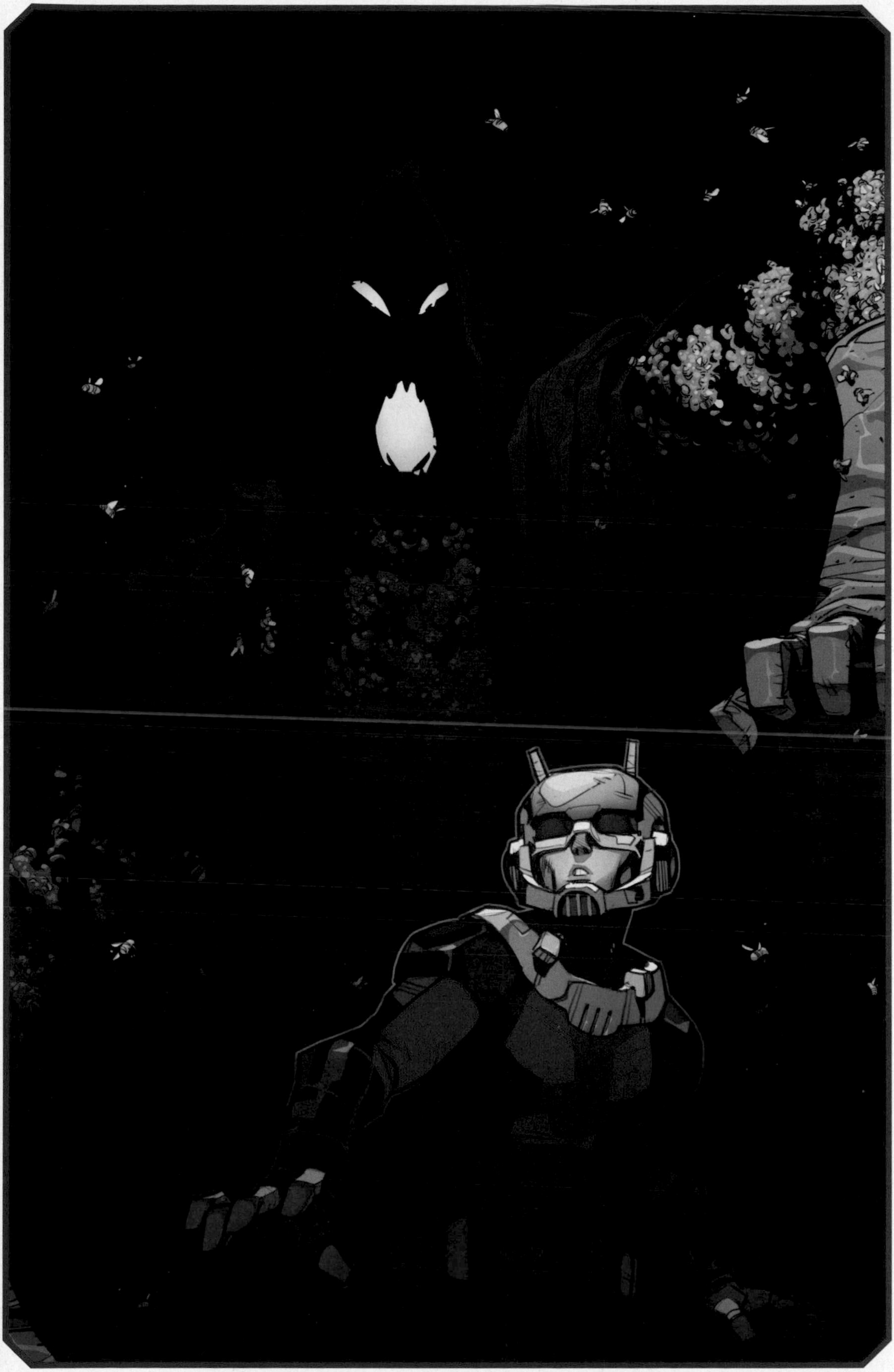

ANT-MAN #2 "WORLD HIVE PART 2"

HELLO
I AM PAMELA THE ANT
PAMELA AM LANDLORD OF ANT HILL THAT ANT-MAN LIVE IN
ANT-MAN WANT BE CLOSE TO DAUGHTER CASSIE BUT CASSIE NO RESPECT ANT-MAN FOR LIVING IN ANT HILL
PAMELA NOT INSULTED
FLORIDA BEE KEEPERS ASK ANT-MAN TO FIND LOST BEES
GOOD BEE LEAD ANT-MAN TO CAVE AND FIND EVIL MAN OF BEES CALLED SWARM
BUT SWARM RUN FROM ENEMIES MUCH MUCH WORSE

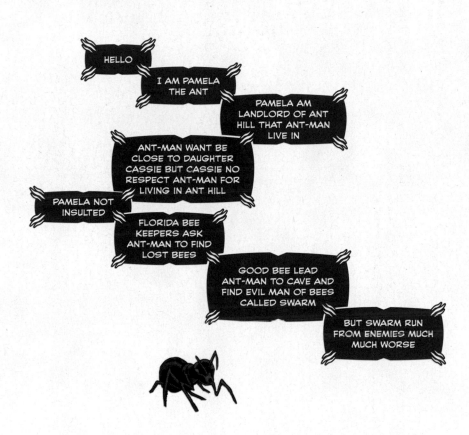

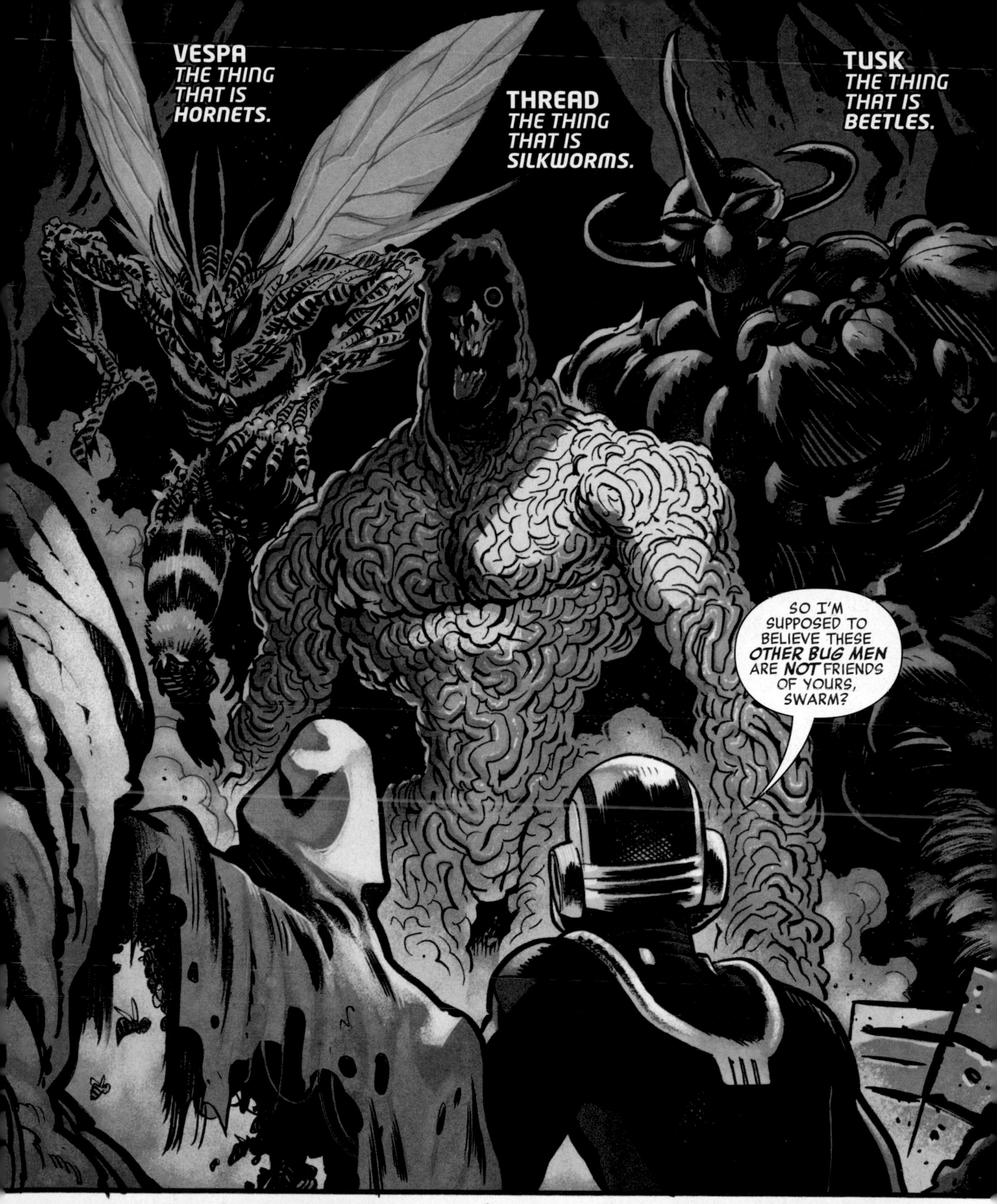
VESPA THE THING THAT IS HORNETS.
THREAD THE THING THAT IS SILKWORMS.
TUSK THE THING THAT IS BEETLES.
SO I'M SUPPOSED TO BELIEVE THESE OTHER BUG MEN ARE NOT FRIENDS OF YOURS, SWARM?

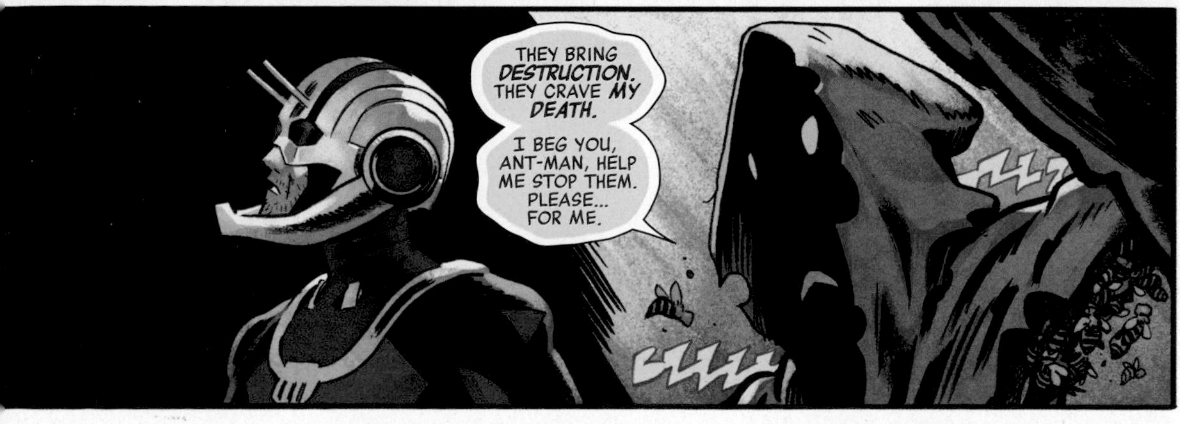
THEY BRING DESTRUCTION. THEY CRAVE MY DEATH.
I BEG YOU, ANT-MAN, HELP ME STOP THEM. PLEASE... FOR ME.

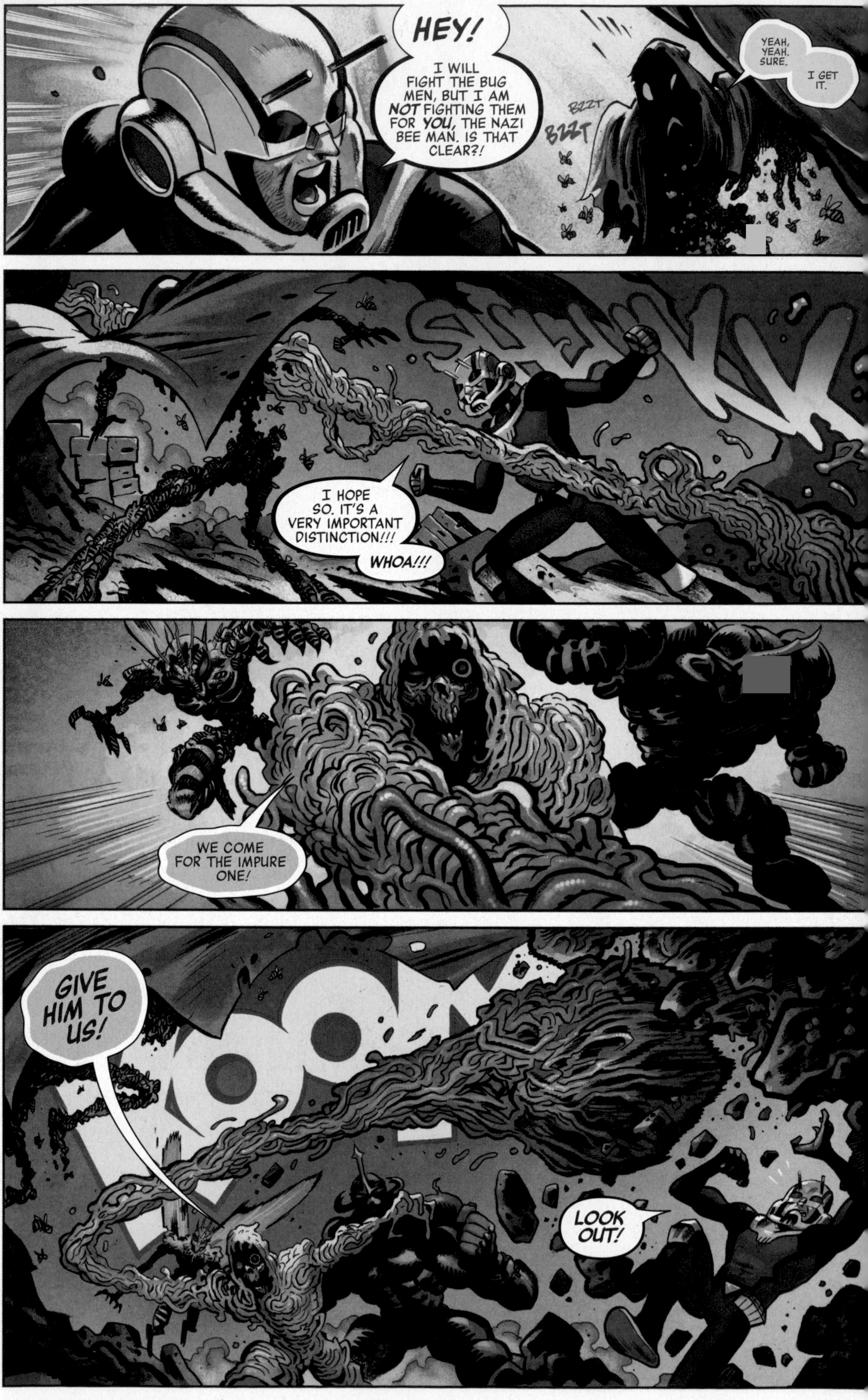
HEY!
I WILL FIGHT THE BUG MEN, BUT I AM NOT FIGHTING THEM FOR YOU, THE NAZI BEE MAN. IS THAT CLEAR?!
BZZT
BZZT
YEAH, YEAH. SURE.
I GET IT.
I HOPE SO. IT'S A VERY IMPORTANT DISTINCTION!!!
WHOA!!!
WE COME FOR THE IMPURE ONE!
GIVE HIM TO US!
LOOK OUT!

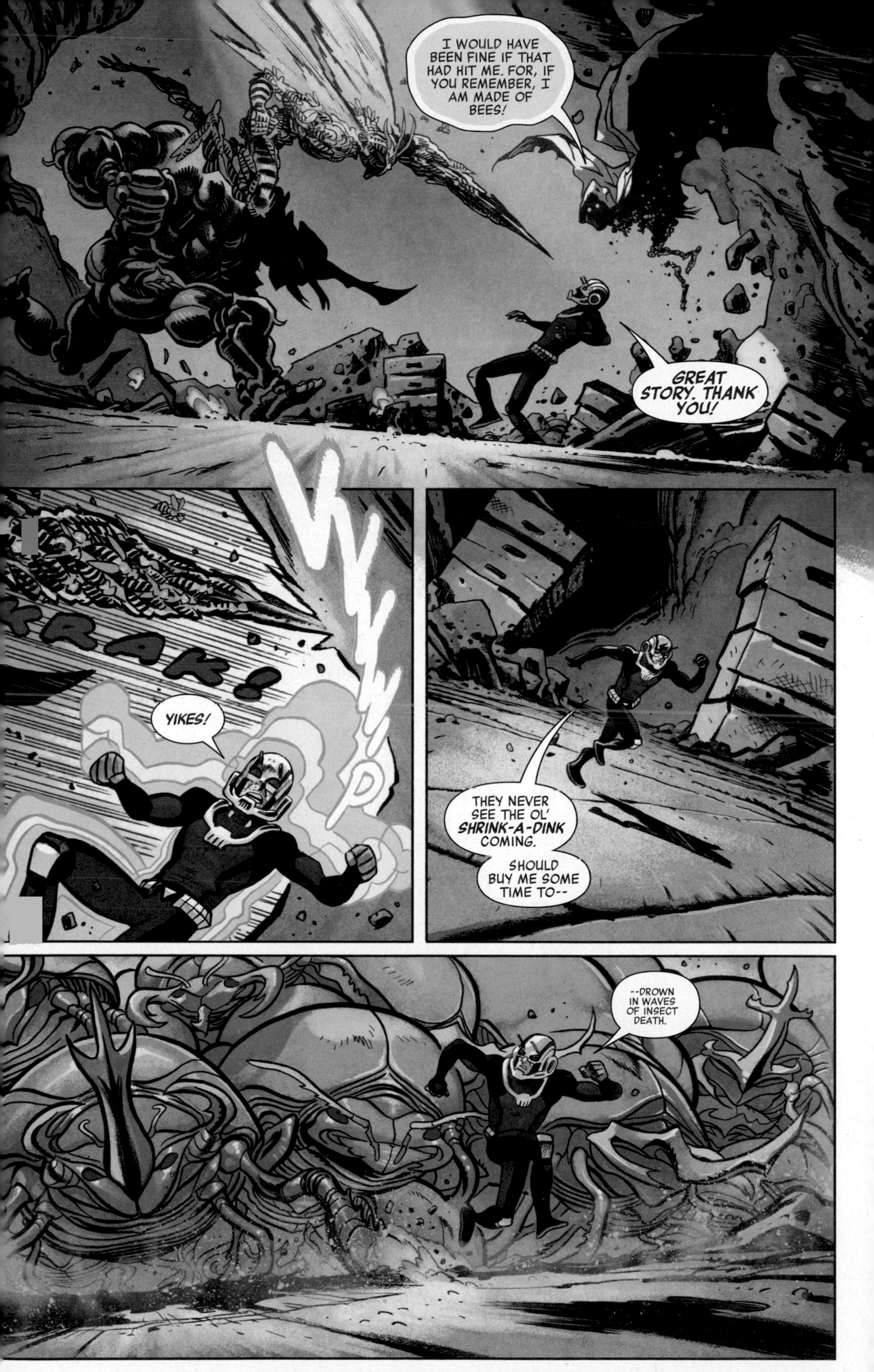
I WOULD HAVE BEEN FINE IF THAT HAD HIT ME. FOR, IF YOU REMEMBER, I AM MADE OF BEES!
GREAT STORY. THANK YOU!
RAK!
YIKES!
THEY NEVER SEE THE OL' SHRINK-A-DINK COMING.
SHOULD BUY ME SOME TIME TO--
--DROWN IN WAVES OF INSECT DEATH.

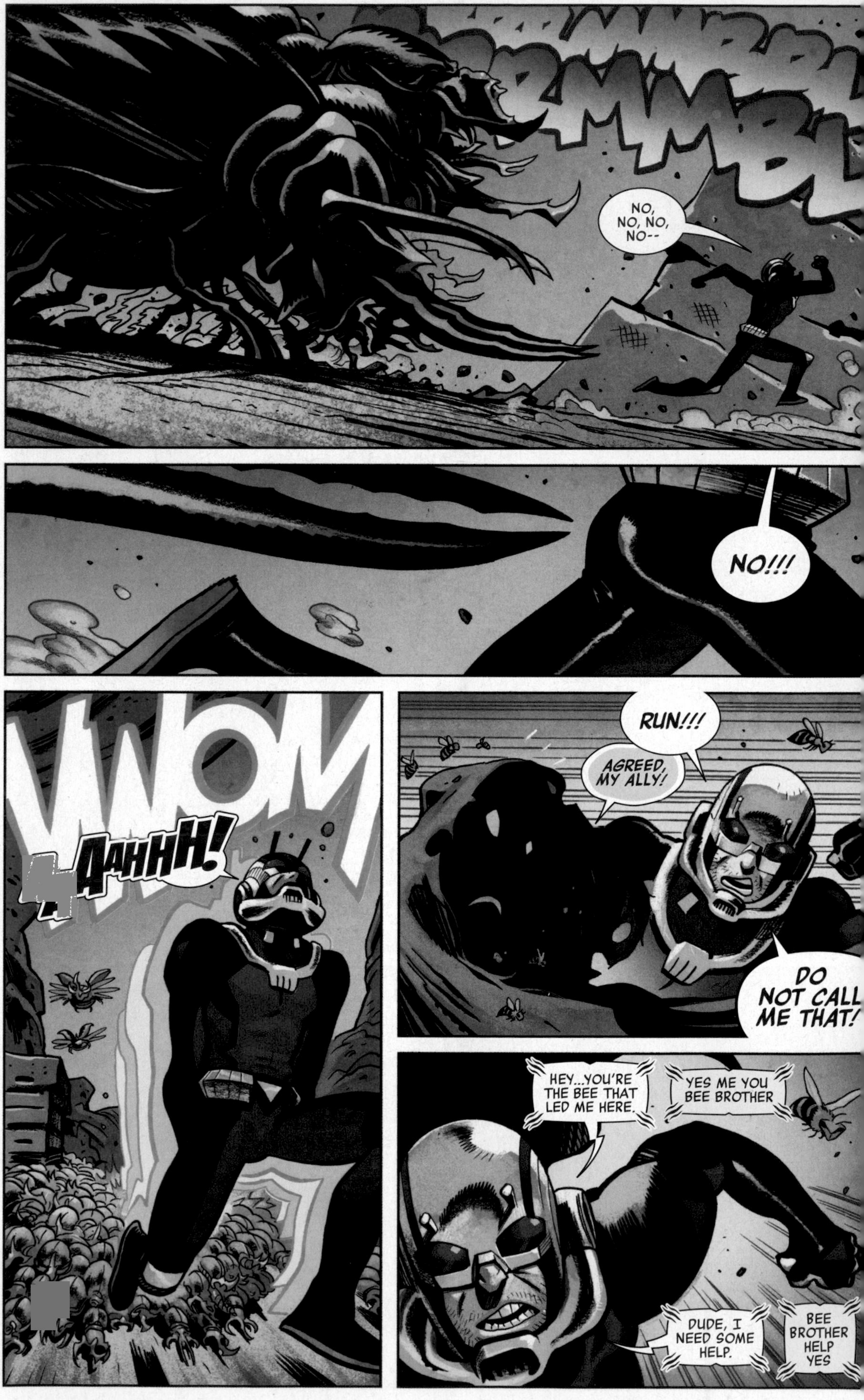
NO, NO, NO, NO--
NO!!!
VWOM
AHHH!
RUN!!!
AGREED, MY ALLY!
DO NOT CALL ME THAT!
HEY...YOU'RE THE BEE THAT LED ME HERE.
YES ME YOU BEE BROTHER
DUDE, I NEED SOME HELP.
BEE BROTHER HELP YES

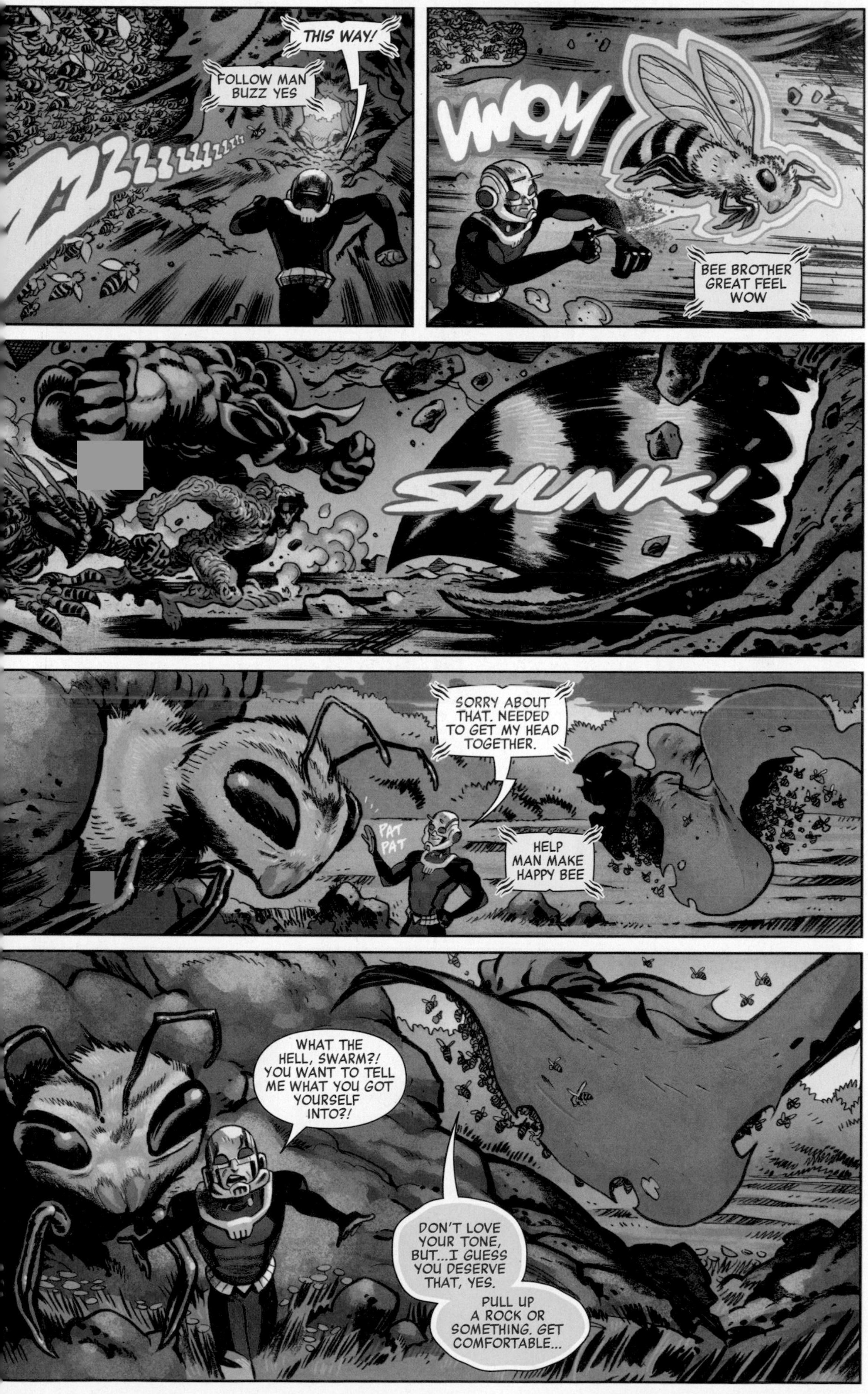
THIS WAY!
FOLLOW MAN BUZZ YES
WOM
BEE BROTHER GREAT FEEL WOW
SHUNK!
SORRY ABOUT THAT. NEEDED TO GET MY HEAD TOGETHER.
PAT PAT
HELP MAN MAKE HAPPY BEE
WHAT THE HELL, SWARM?! YOU WANT TO TELL ME WHAT YOU GOT YOURSELF INTO?!
DON'T LOVE YOUR TONE, BUT...I GUESS YOU DESERVE THAT, YES.
PULL UP A ROCK OR SOMETHING. GET COMFORTABLE...

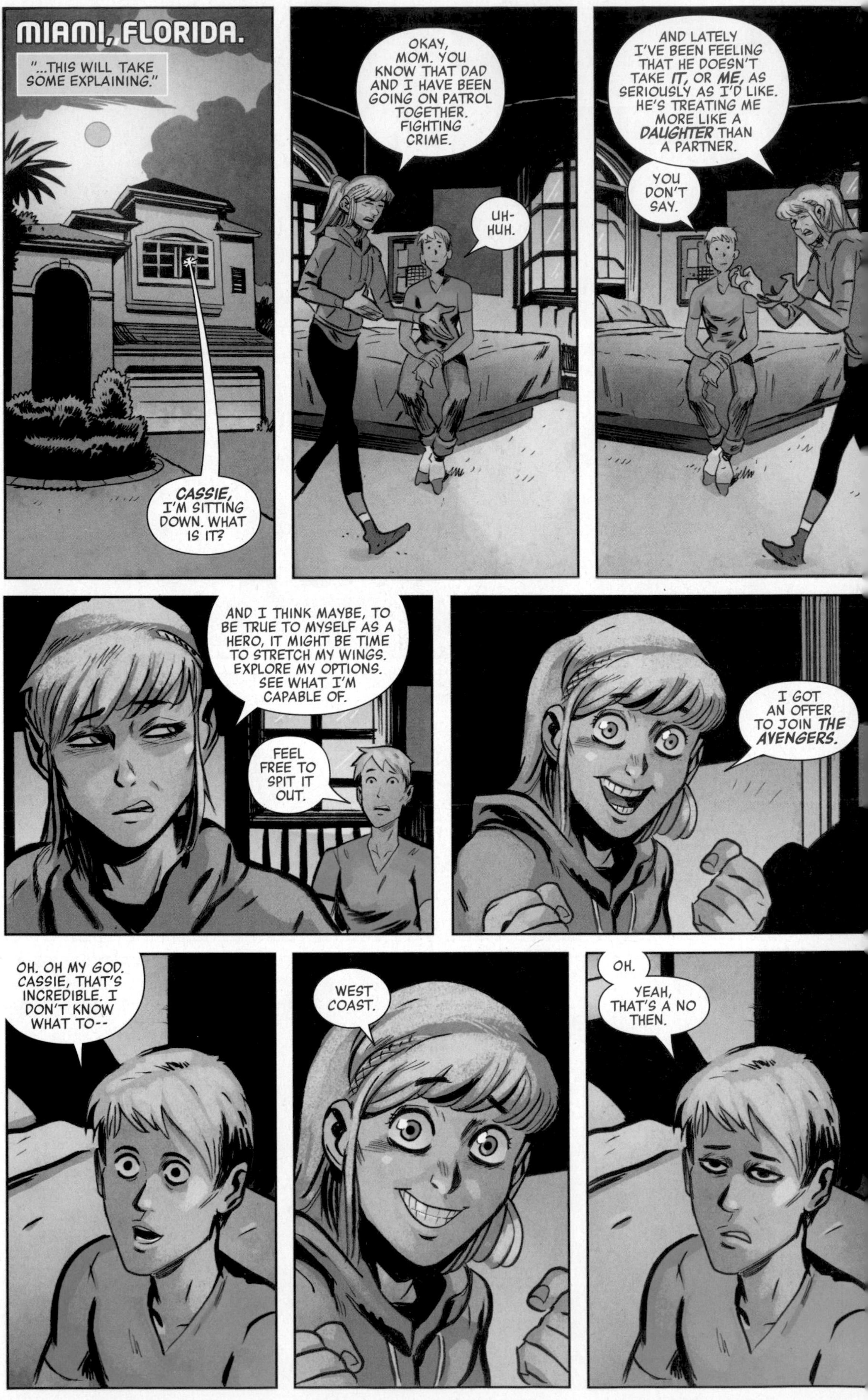
MIAMI, FLORIDA.
"...THIS WILL TAKE SOME EXPLAINING."
CASSIE, I'M SITTING DOWN. WHAT IS IT?
OKAY, MOM. YOU KNOW THAT DAD AND I HAVE BEEN GOING ON PATROL TOGETHER. FIGHTING CRIME.
UH-HUH.
AND LATELY I'VE BEEN FEELING THAT HE DOESN'T TAKE IT, OR ME, AS SERIOUSLY AS I'D LIKE. HE'S TREATING ME MORE LIKE A DAUGHTER THAN A PARTNER.
YOU DON'T SAY.
AND I THINK MAYBE, TO BE TRUE TO MYSELF AS A HERO, IT MIGHT BE TIME TO STRETCH MY WINGS. EXPLORE MY OPTIONS. SEE WHAT I'M CAPABLE OF.
FEEL FREE TO SPIT IT OUT.
I GOT AN OFFER TO JOIN THE AVENGERS.
OH. OH MY GOD. CASSIE, THAT'S INCREDIBLE. I DON'T KNOW WHAT TO--
WEST COAST.
OH.
YEAH, THAT'S A NO THEN.

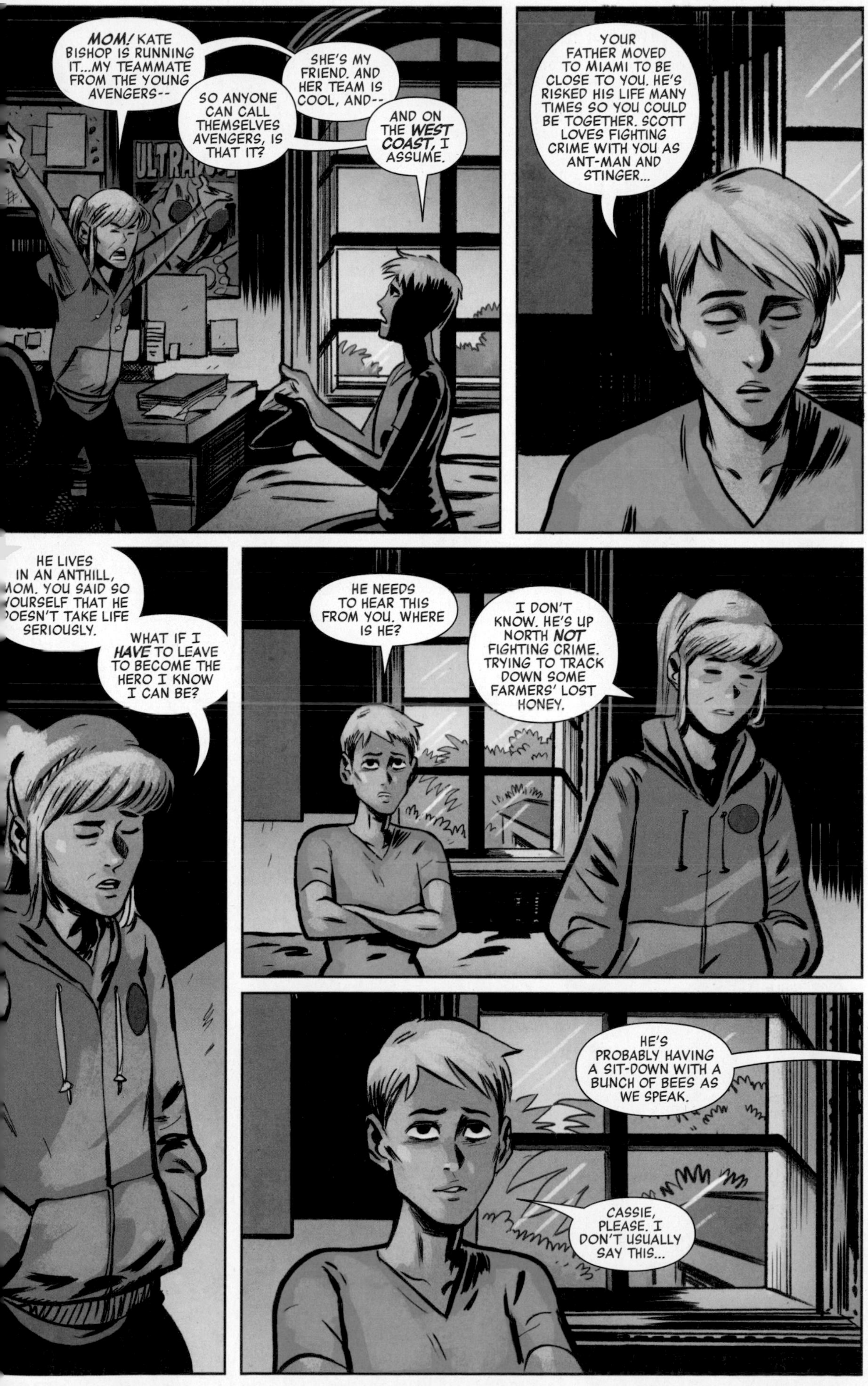
MOM! KATE BISHOP IS RUNNING IT...MY TEAMMATE FROM THE YOUNG AVENGERS--
SHE'S MY FRIEND. AND HER TEAM IS COOL, AND--
SO ANYONE CAN CALL THEMSELVES AVENGERS, IS THAT IT?
AND ON THE WEST COAST, I ASSUME.
YOUR FATHER MOVED TO MIAMI TO BE CLOSE TO YOU. HE'S RISKED HIS LIFE MANY TIMES SO YOU COULD BE TOGETHER. SCOTT LOVES FIGHTING CRIME WITH YOU AS ANT-MAN AND STINGER...
HE LIVES IN AN ANTHILL, MOM. YOU SAID SO YOURSELF THAT HE DOESN'T TAKE LIFE SERIOUSLY.
WHAT IF I HAVE TO LEAVE TO BECOME THE HERO I KNOW I CAN BE?
HE NEEDS TO HEAR THIS FROM YOU. WHERE IS HE?
I DON'T KNOW. HE'S UP NORTH NOT FIGHTING CRIME. TRYING TO TRACK DOWN SOME FARMERS' LOST HONEY.
HE'S PROBABLY HAVING A SIT-DOWN WITH A BUNCH OF BEES AS WE SPEAK.
CASSIE, PLEASE. I DON'T USUALLY SAY THIS...

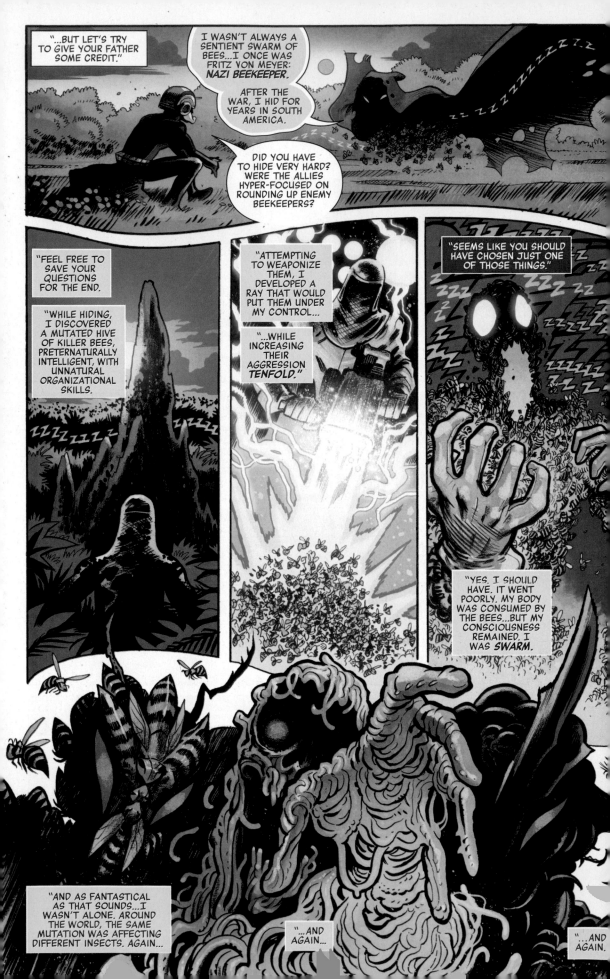

"...BUT LET'S TRY TO GIVE YOUR FATHER SOME CREDIT."

I WASN'T ALWAYS A SENTIENT SWARM OF BEES...I ONCE WAS FRITZ VON MEYER: *NAZI BEEKEEPER.*

AFTER THE WAR, I HID FOR YEARS IN SOUTH AMERICA.

DID YOU HAVE TO HIDE VERY HARD? WERE THE ALLIES HYPER-FOCUSED ON ROUNDING UP ENEMY BEEKEEPERS?

"FEEL FREE TO SAVE YOUR QUESTIONS FOR THE END.

"WHILE HIDING, I DISCOVERED A MUTATED HIVE OF KILLER BEES, PRETERNATURALLY INTELLIGENT, WITH UNNATURAL ORGANIZATIONAL SKILLS.

"ATTEMPTING TO WEAPONIZE THEM, I DEVELOPED A RAY THAT WOULD PUT THEM UNDER MY CONTROL...

"...WHILE INCREASING THEIR AGGRESSION *TENFOLD.*"

"SEEMS LIKE YOU SHOULD HAVE CHOSEN JUST ONE OF THOSE THINGS."

"YES, I SHOULD HAVE. IT WENT POORLY. MY BODY WAS CONSUMED BY THE BEES...BUT MY CONSCIOUSNESS REMAINED. I WAS *SWARM.*

"AND AS FANTASTICAL AS THAT SOUNDS...I WASN'T ALONE. AROUND THE WORLD, THE SAME MUTATION WAS AFFECTING DIFFERENT INSECTS. AGAIN...

"...AND AGAIN...

"...AND AGAIN.

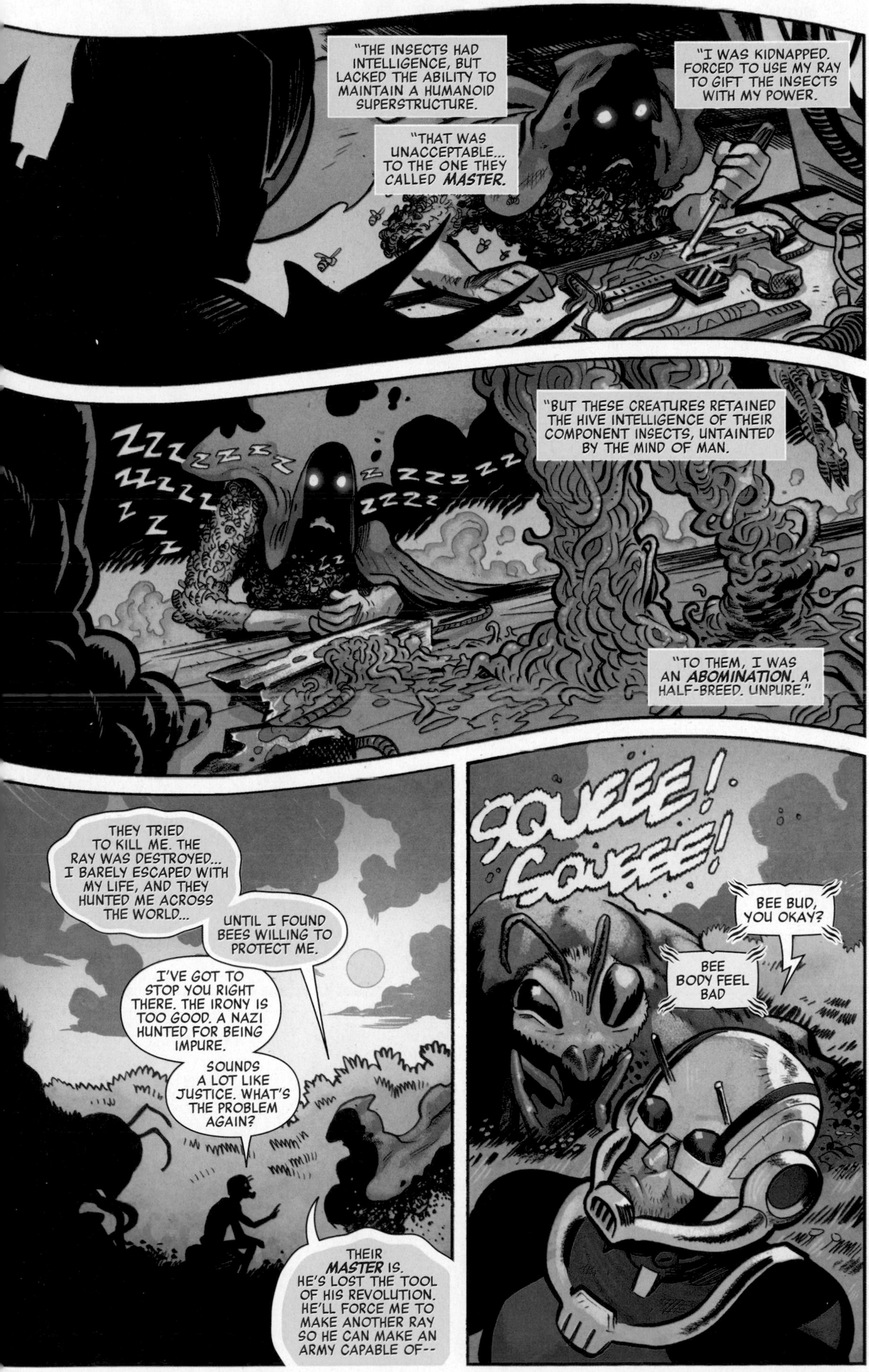
"THE INSECTS HAD INTELLIGENCE, BUT LACKED THE ABILITY TO MAINTAIN A HUMANOID SUPERSTRUCTURE.
"THAT WAS UNACCEPTABLE... TO THE ONE THEY CALLED MASTER.
"I WAS KIDNAPPED. FORCED TO USE MY RAY TO GIFT THE INSECTS WITH MY POWER.
ZZZZZZZZZ
"BUT THESE CREATURES RETAINED THE HIVE INTELLIGENCE OF THEIR COMPONENT INSECTS, UNTAINTED BY THE MIND OF MAN.
"TO THEM, I WAS AN ABOMINATION. A HALF-BREED. UNPURE."
THEY TRIED TO KILL ME. THE RAY WAS DESTROYED... I BARELY ESCAPED WITH MY LIFE, AND THEY HUNTED ME ACROSS THE WORLD...
UNTIL I FOUND BEES WILLING TO PROTECT ME.
I'VE GOT TO STOP YOU RIGHT THERE. THE IRONY IS TOO GOOD. A NAZI HUNTED FOR BEING IMPURE.
SOUNDS A LOT LIKE JUSTICE. WHAT'S THE PROBLEM AGAIN?
THEIR MASTER IS. HE'S LOST THE TOOL OF HIS REVOLUTION. HE'LL FORCE ME TO MAKE ANOTHER RAY SO HE CAN MAKE AN ARMY CAPABLE OF--
SQUEEE! SQUEEE!
BEE BUD, YOU OKAY?
BEE BODY FEEL BAD

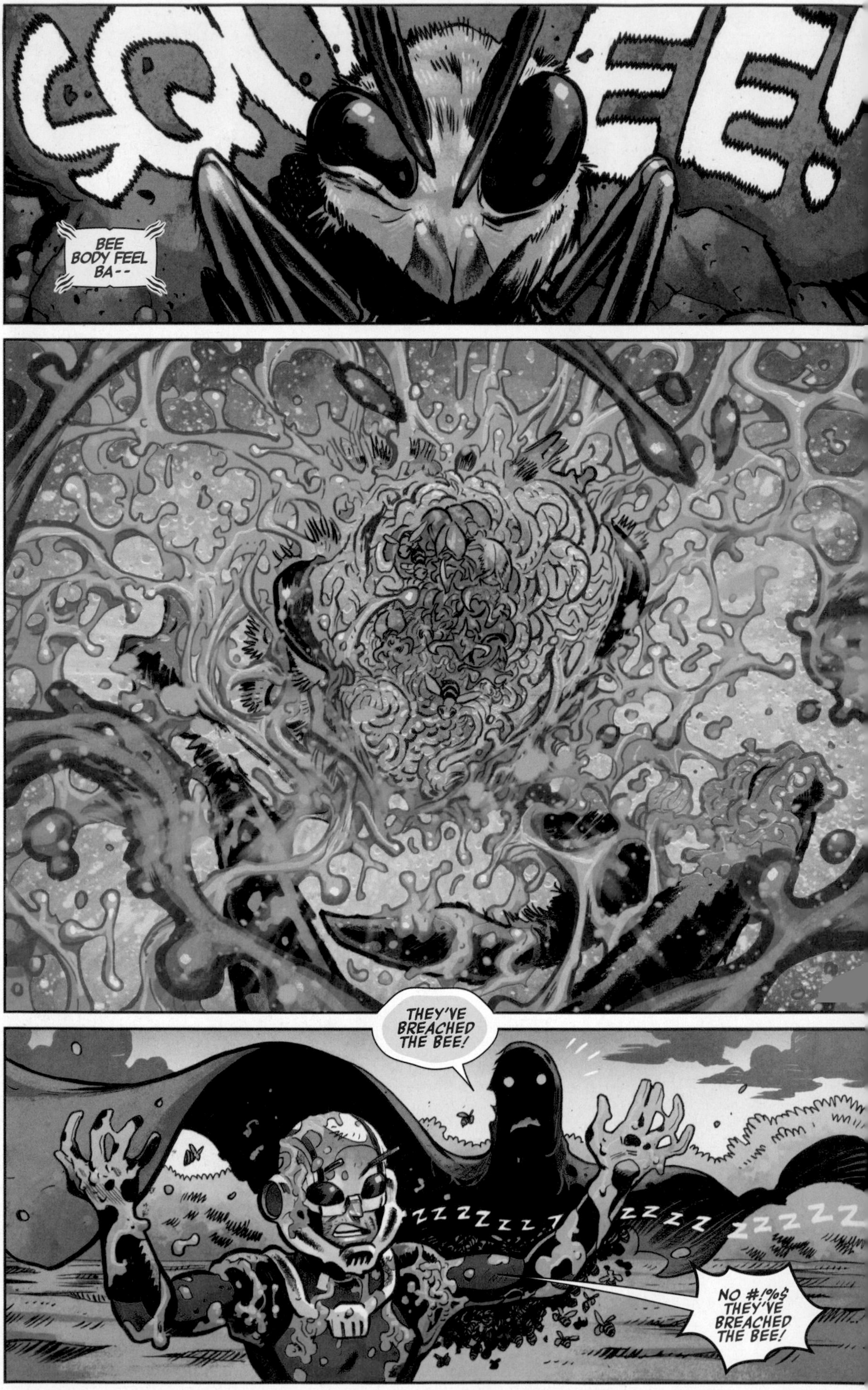
BEE BODY FEEL BA--
THEY'VE BREACHED THE BEE!
NO #!%$ THEY'VE BREACHED THE BEE!

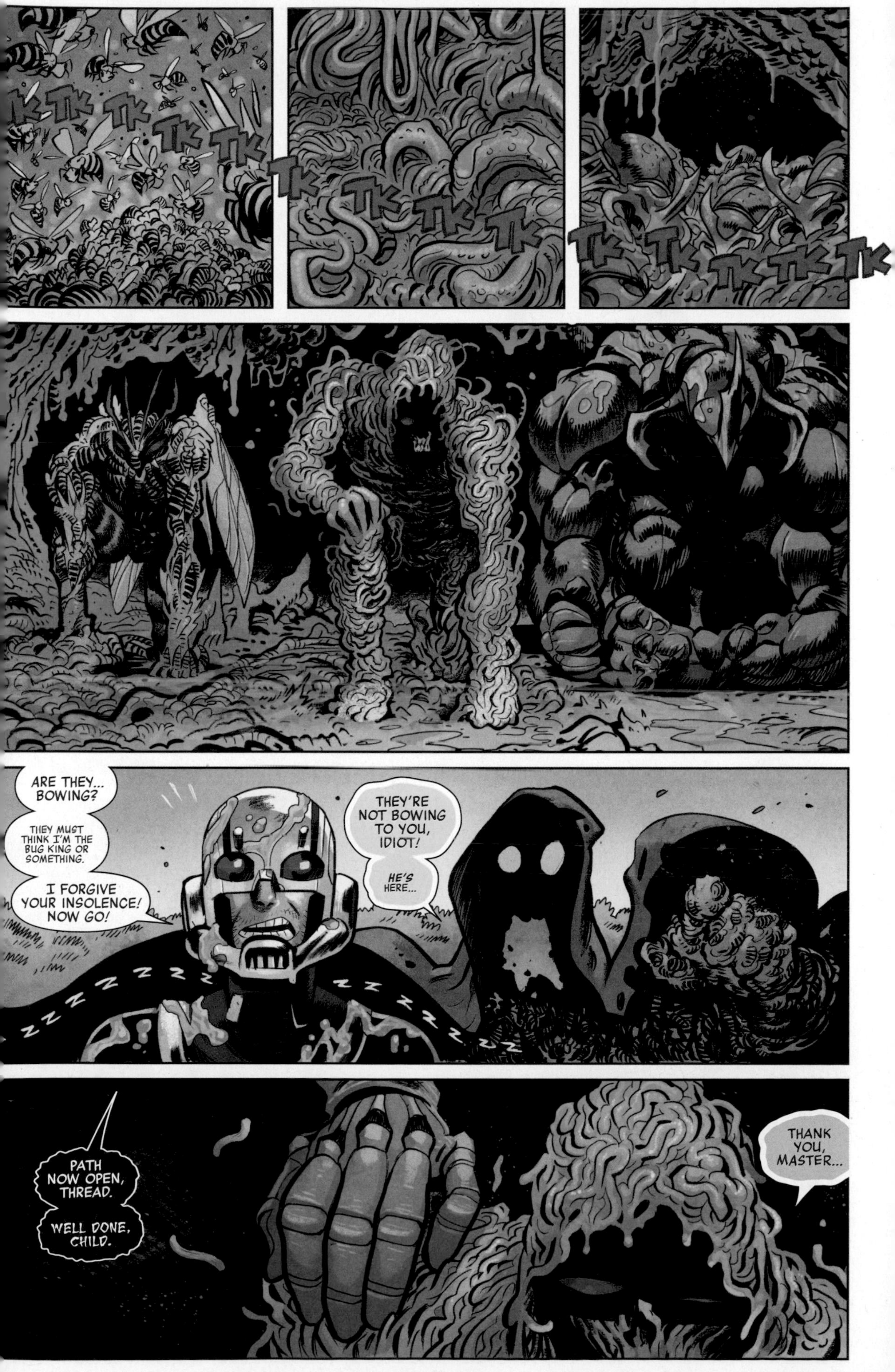
TK TK TK TK TK
TK TK TK TK
TK TK TK TK TK
ARE THEY... BOWING?
THEY MUST THINK I'M THE BUG KING OR SOMETHING.
I FORGIVE YOUR INSOLENCE! NOW GO!
THEY'RE NOT BOWING TO YOU, IDIOT!
HE'S HERE...
PATH NOW OPEN, THREAD.
WELL DONE, CHILD.
THANK YOU, MASTER...

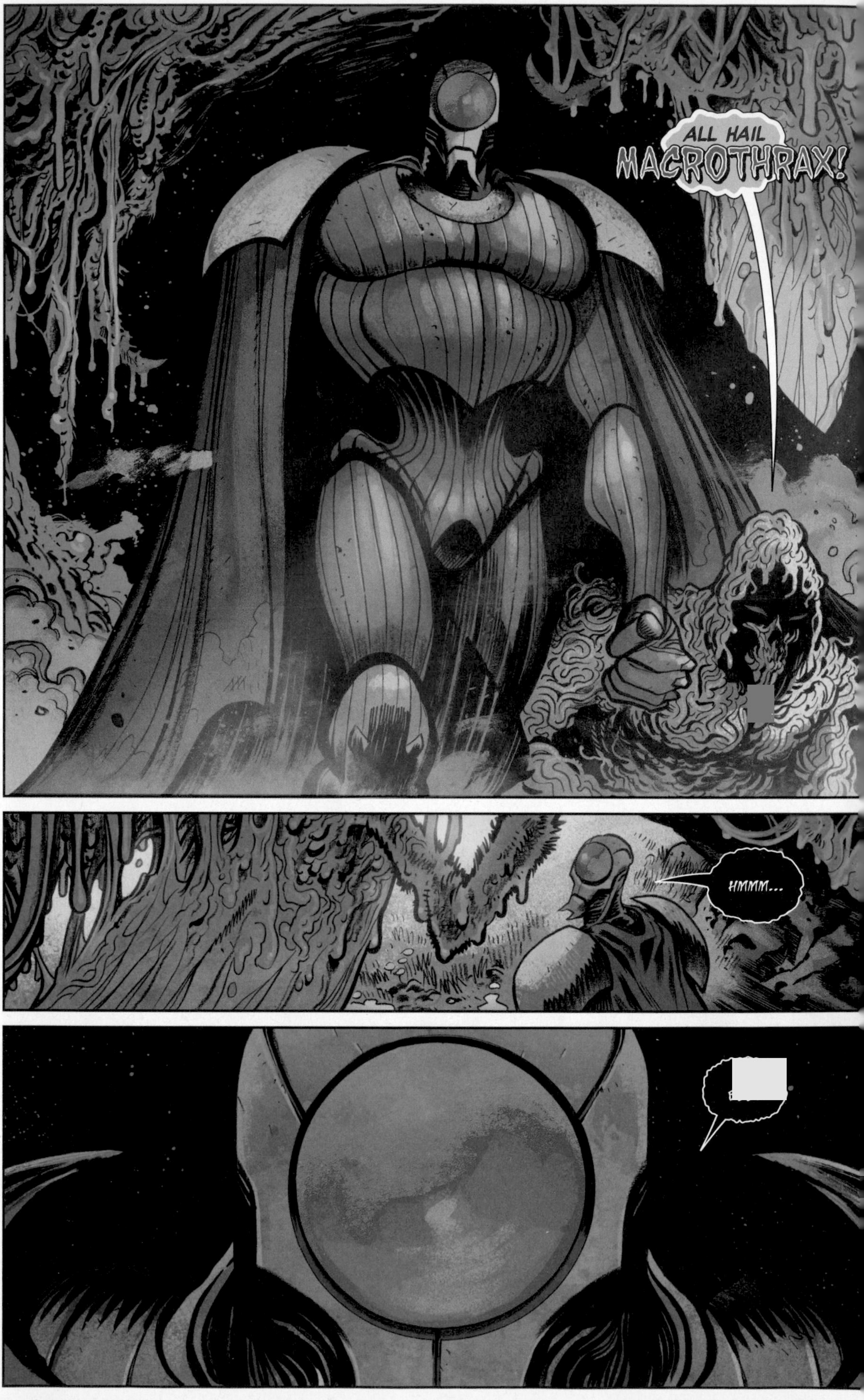
ALL HAIL MACROTHRAX!
HMMM...

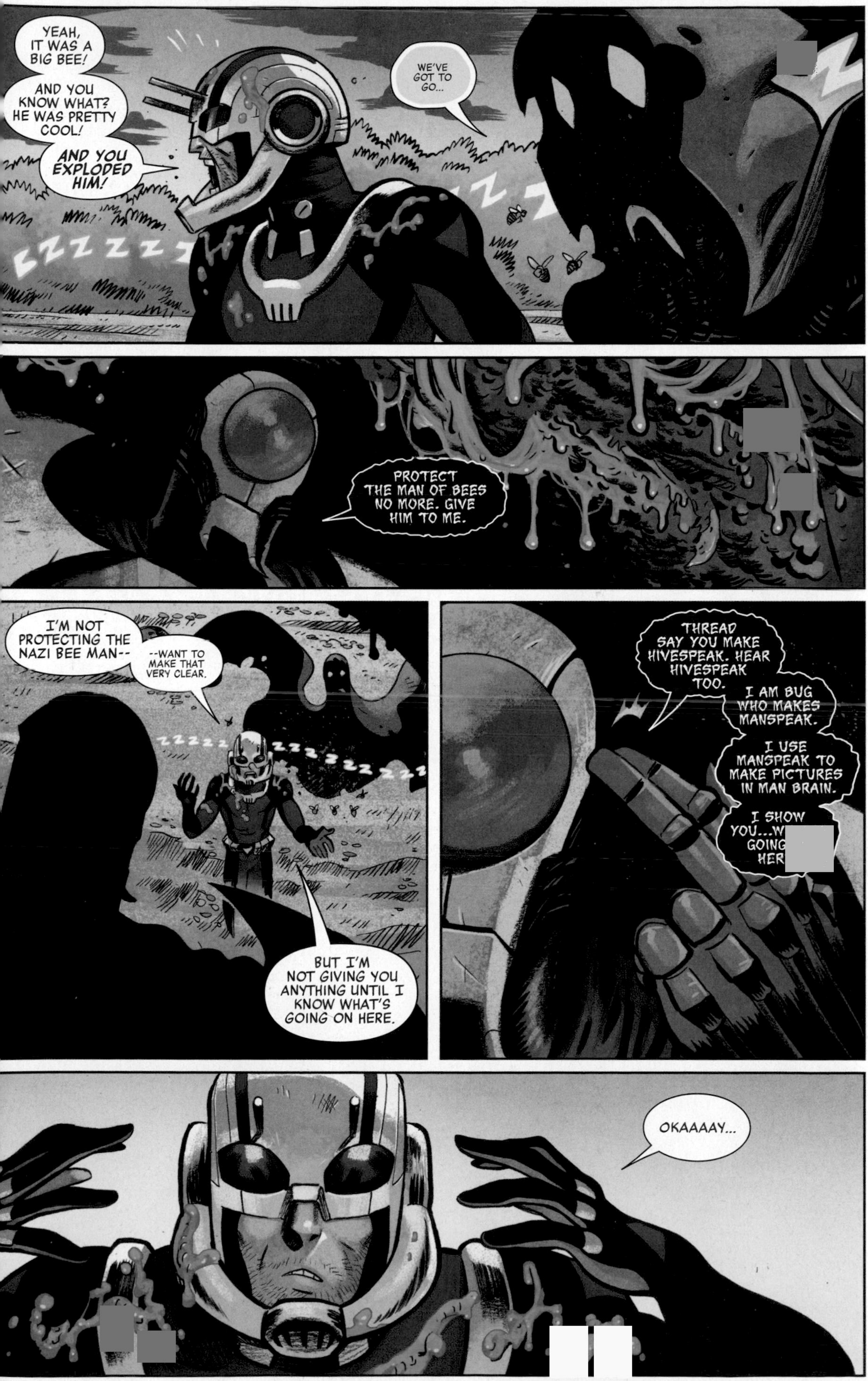

YEAH, IT WAS A BIG BEE!
AND YOU KNOW WHAT? HE WAS PRETTY COOL!
AND YOU EXPLODED HIM!
WE'VE GOT TO GO...
PROTECT THE MAN OF BEES NO MORE. GIVE HIM TO ME.
I'M NOT PROTECTING THE NAZI BEE MAN--
--WANT TO MAKE THAT VERY CLEAR.
BUT I'M NOT GIVING YOU ANYTHING UNTIL I KNOW WHAT'S GOING ON HERE.
THREAD SAY YOU MAKE HIVESPEAK. HEAR HIVESPEAK TOO.
I AM BUG WHO MAKES MANSPEAK.
I USE MANSPEAK TO MAKE PICTURES IN MAN BRAIN.
I SHOW YOU...W
GOING
HER
OKAAAAY...

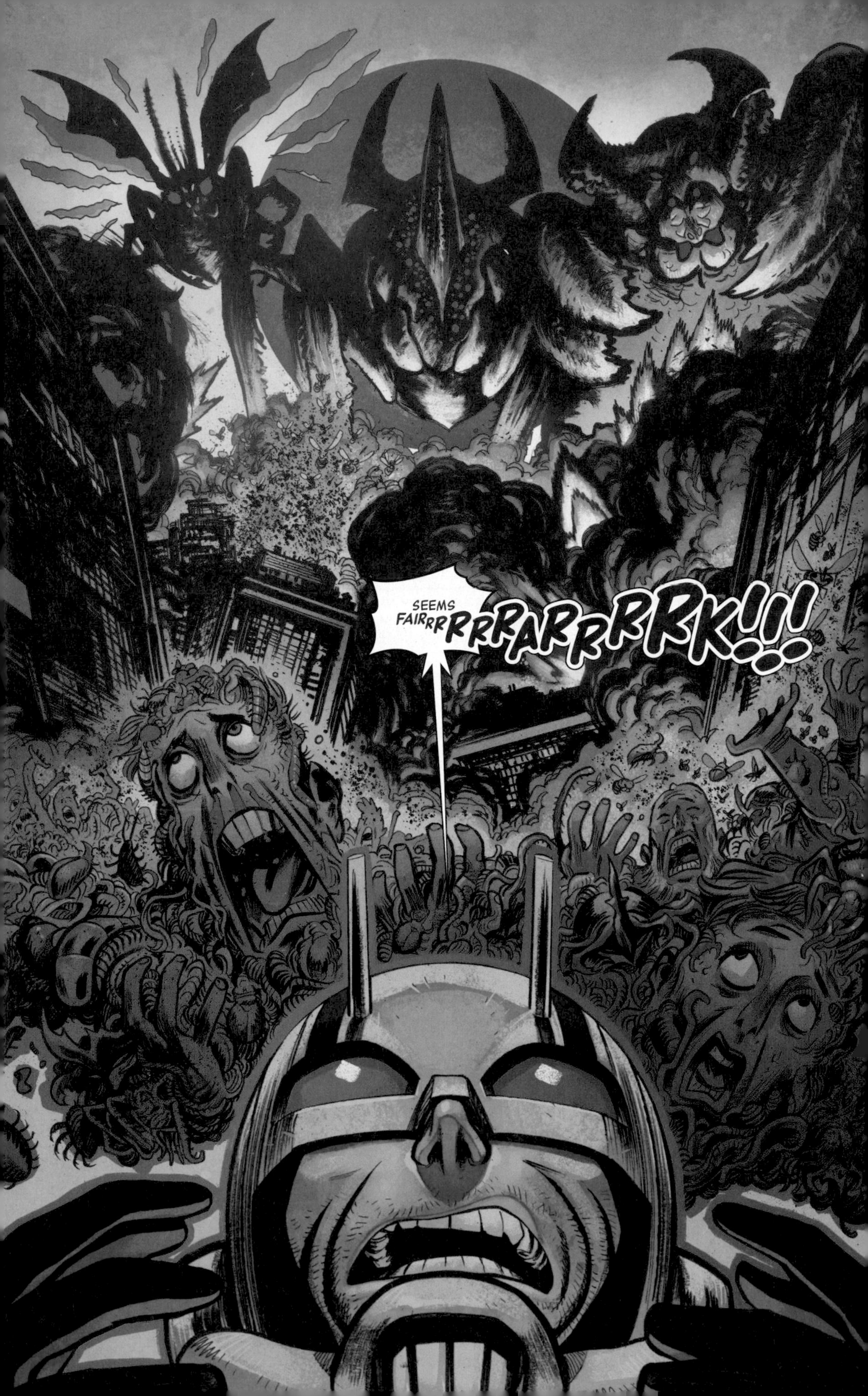
SEEMS FAIRRRRRRARRRRRK!!!

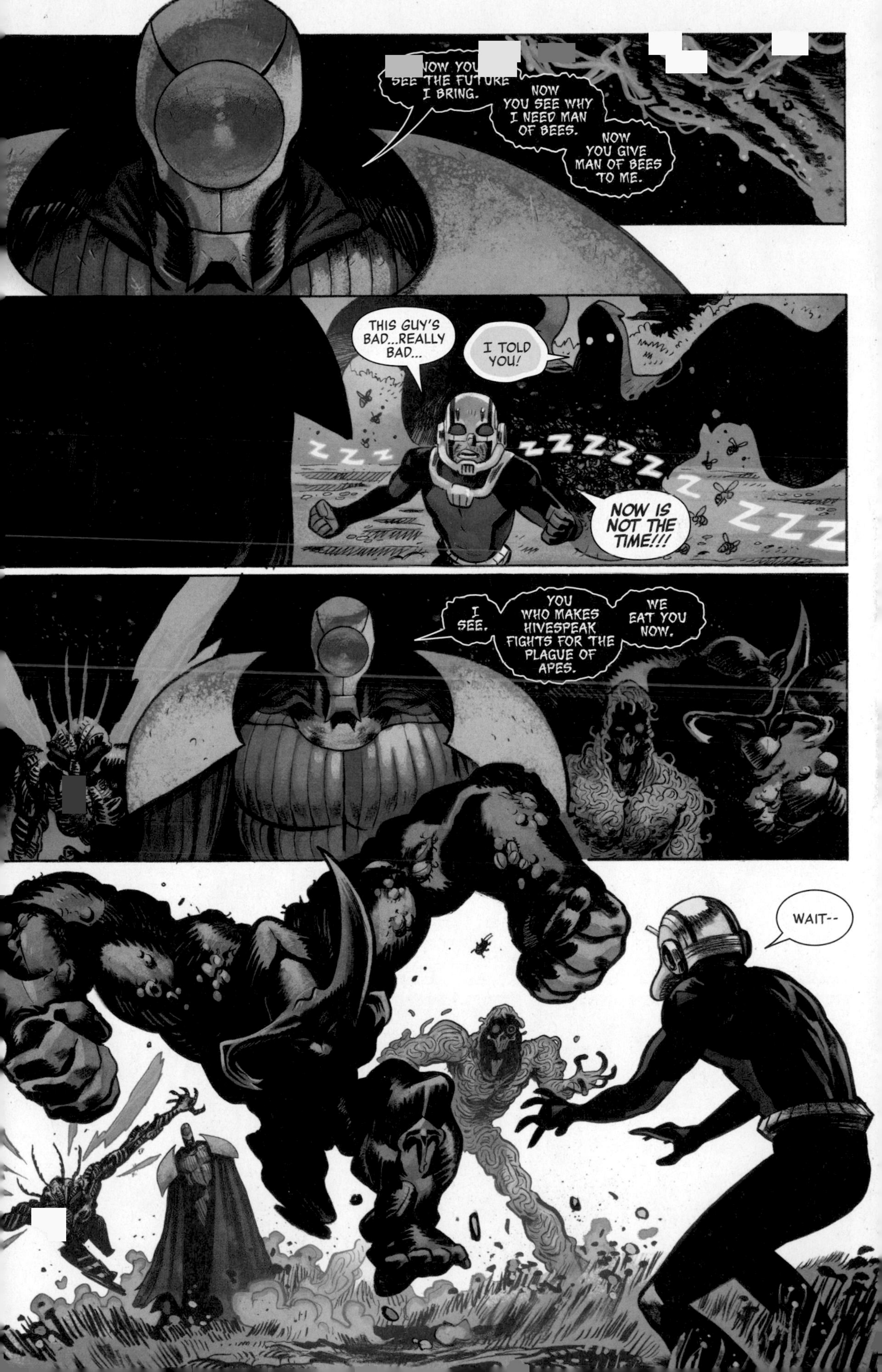
NOW YOU SEE THE FUTURE I BRING.
NOW YOU SEE WHY I NEED MAN OF BEES.
NOW YOU GIVE MAN OF BEES TO ME.
THIS GUY'S BAD...REALLY BAD...
I TOLD YOU!
ZZZZZZ
NOW IS NOT THE TIME!!!
I SEE.
YOU WHO MAKES HIVESPEAK FIGHTS FOR THE PLAGUE OF APES.
WE EAT YOU NOW.
WAIT--

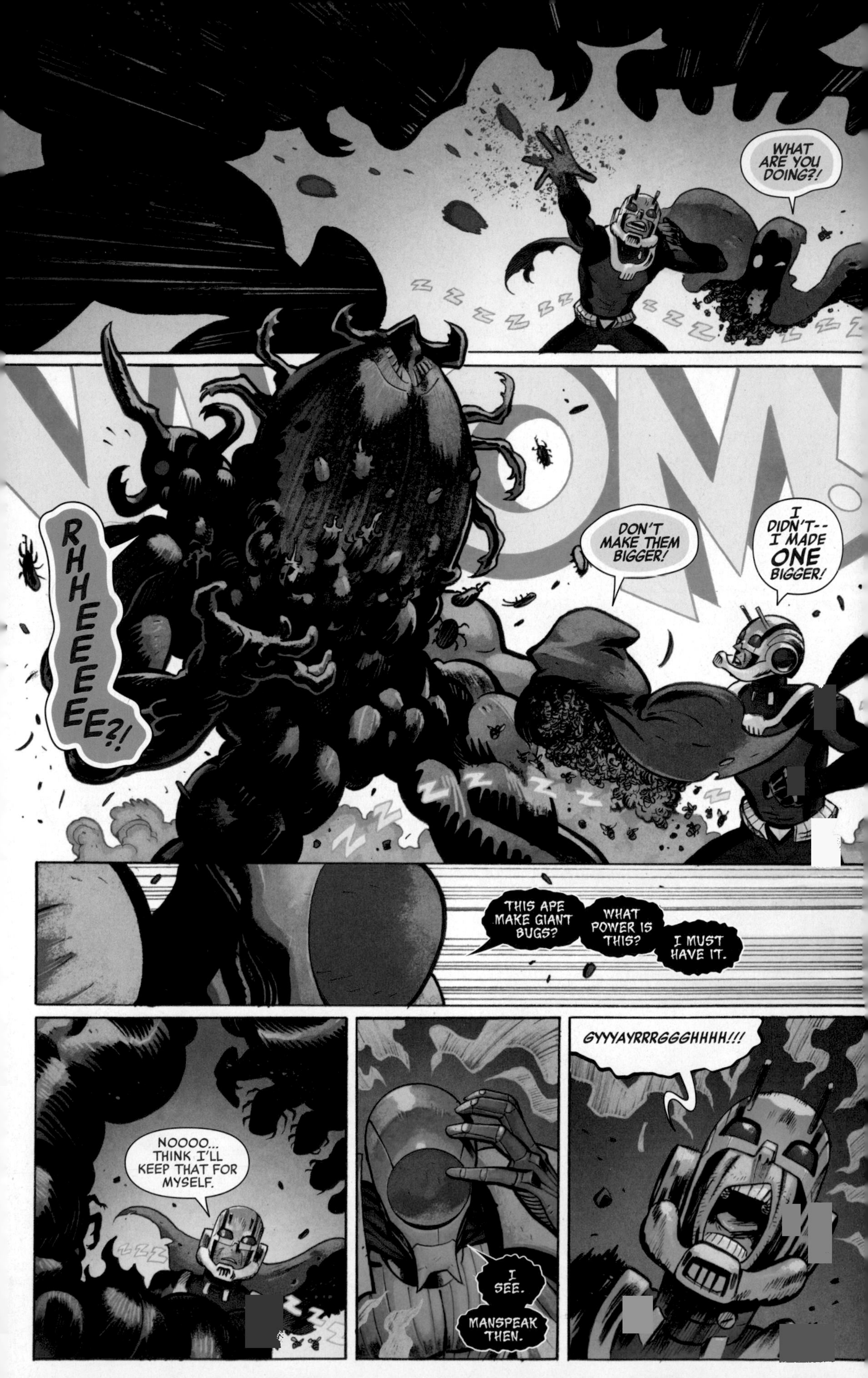

WHAT ARE YOU DOING?!
RHHEEEEEE?!
DON'T MAKE THEM BIGGER!
I DIDN'T-- I MADE ONE BIGGER!
THIS APE MAKE GIANT BUGS?
WHAT POWER IS THIS?
I MUST HAVE IT.
NOOOO... THINK I'LL KEEP THAT FOR MYSELF.
I SEE.
MANSPEAK THEN.
GYYYAYRRRGGGHHHH!!!

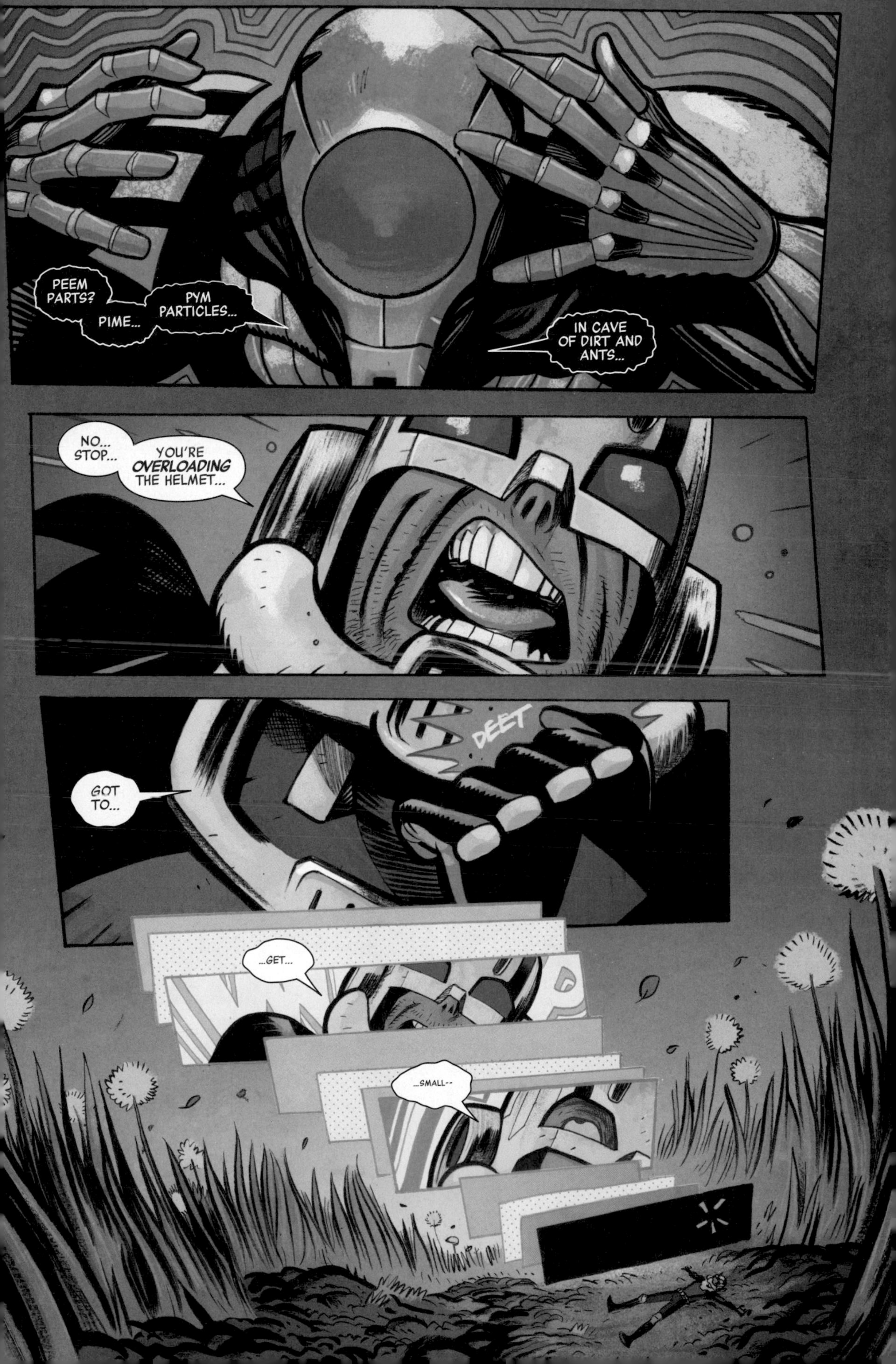
PEEM PARTS?
PIME...
PYM PARTICLES...
IN CAVE OF DIRT AND ANTS...
NO... STOP...
YOU'RE OVERLOADING THE HELMET...
DEET
GOT TO...
...GET...
...SMALL--

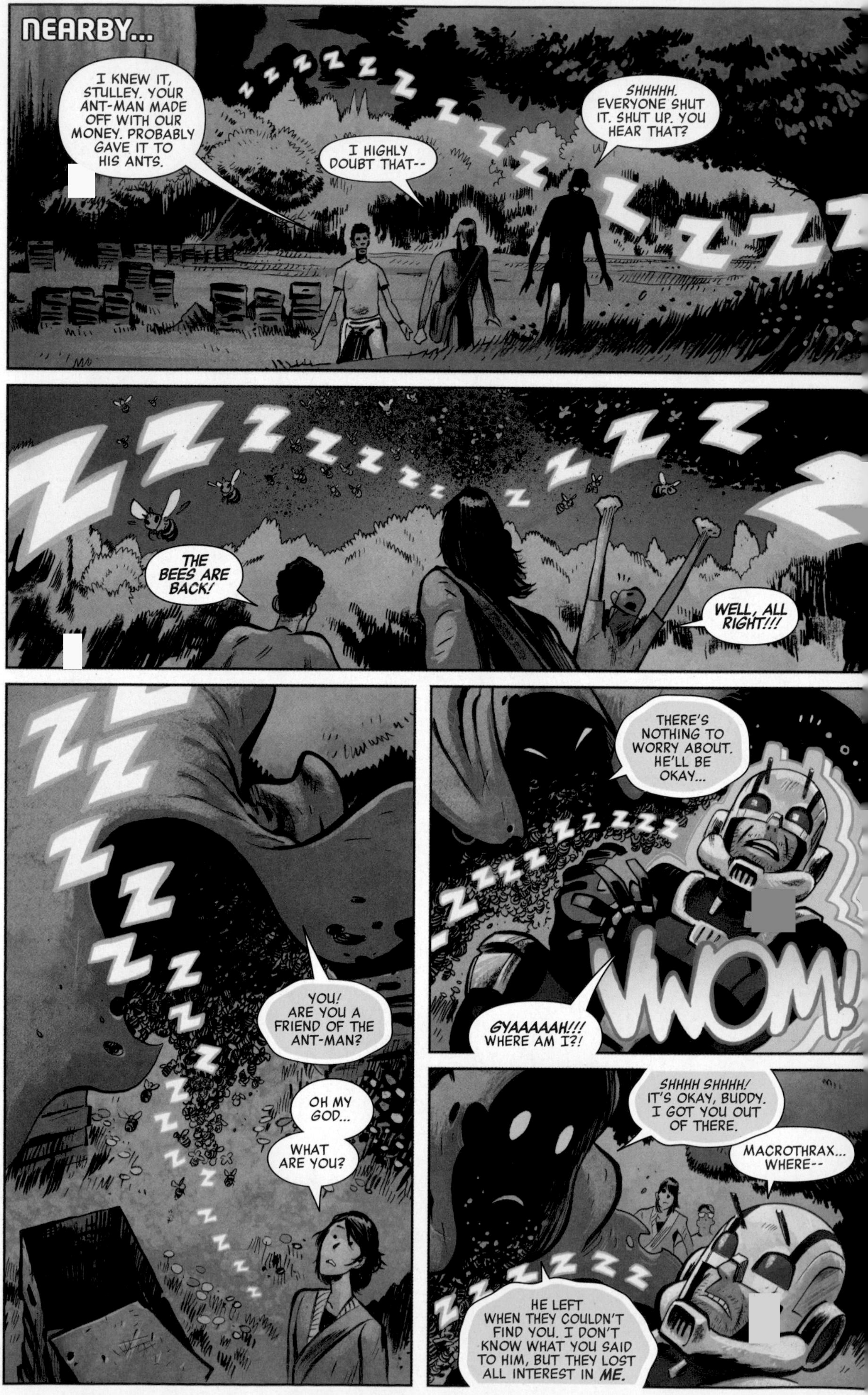
NEARBY...
I KNEW IT, STULLEY. YOUR ANT-MAN MADE OFF WITH OUR MONEY. PROBABLY GAVE IT TO HIS ANTS.
I HIGHLY DOUBT THAT--
SHHHHH. EVERYONE SHUT IT. SHUT UP. YOU HEAR THAT?
THE BEES ARE BACK!
WELL, ALL RIGHT!!!
YOU! ARE YOU A FRIEND OF THE ANT-MAN?
OH MY GOD...
WHAT ARE YOU?
THERE'S NOTHING TO WORRY ABOUT. HE'LL BE OKAY...
VWOM!
GYAAAAAH!!! WHERE AM I?!
SHHHH SHHHH! IT'S OKAY, BUDDY. I GOT YOU OUT OF THERE.
MACROTHRAX... WHERE--
HE LEFT WHEN THEY COULDN'T FIND YOU. I DON'T KNOW WHAT YOU SAID TO HIM, BUT THEY LOST ALL INTEREST IN ME.

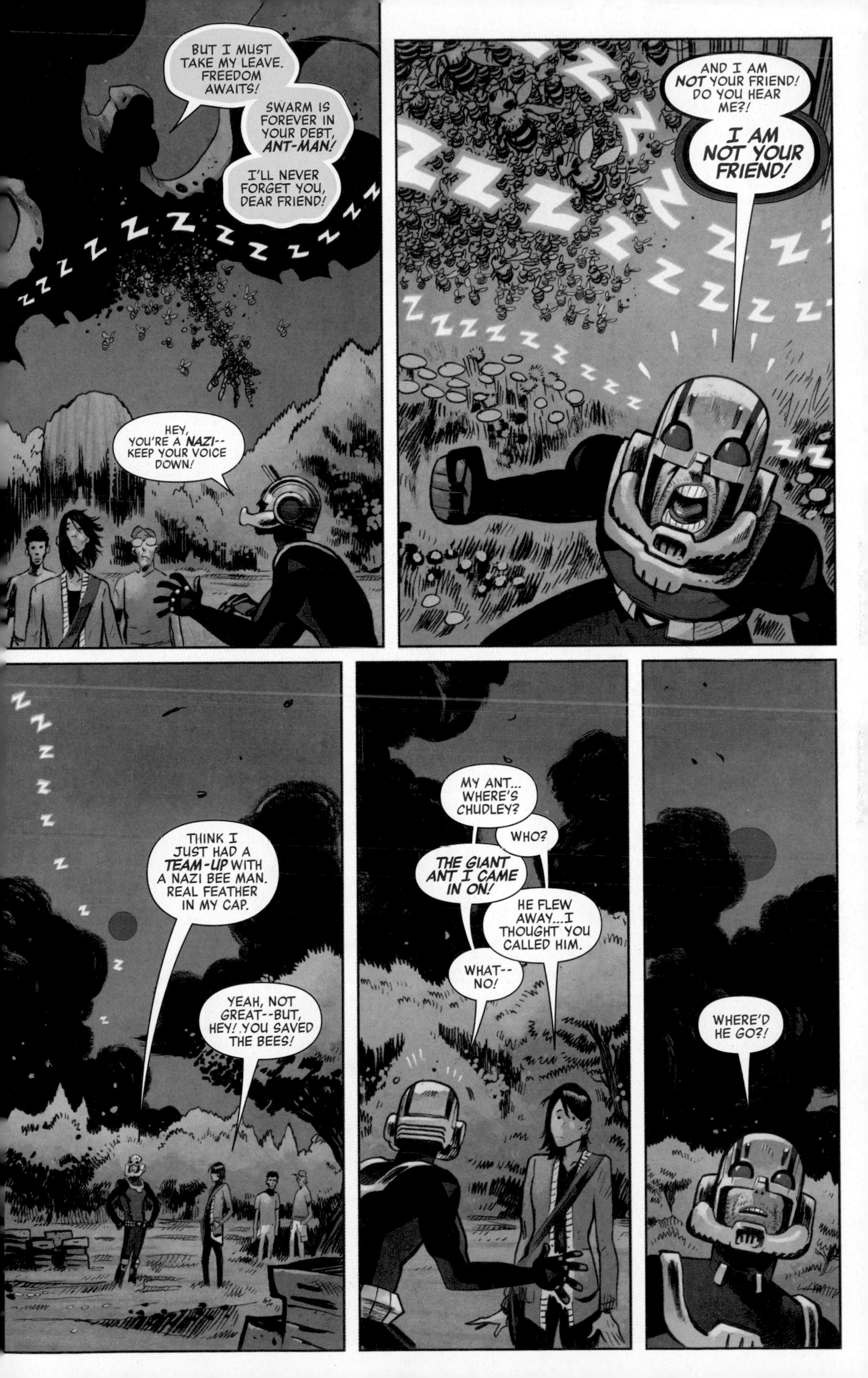

BUT I MUST TAKE MY LEAVE. FREEDOM AWAITS!
SWARM IS FOREVER IN YOUR DEBT, ANT-MAN!
I'LL NEVER FORGET YOU, DEAR FRIEND!
HEY, YOU'RE A NAZI-- KEEP YOUR VOICE DOWN!
AND I AM NOT YOUR FRIEND! DO YOU HEAR ME?!
I AM NOT YOUR FRIEND!
THINK I JUST HAD A TEAM-UP WITH A NAZI BEE MAN. REAL FEATHER IN MY CAP.
YEAH, NOT GREAT--BUT, HEY! YOU SAVED THE BEES!
MY ANT... WHERE'S CHUDLEY?
WHO?
THE GIANT ANT I CAME IN ON!
HE FLEW AWAY...I THOUGHT YOU CALLED HIM.
WHAT-- NO!
WHERE'D HE GO?!

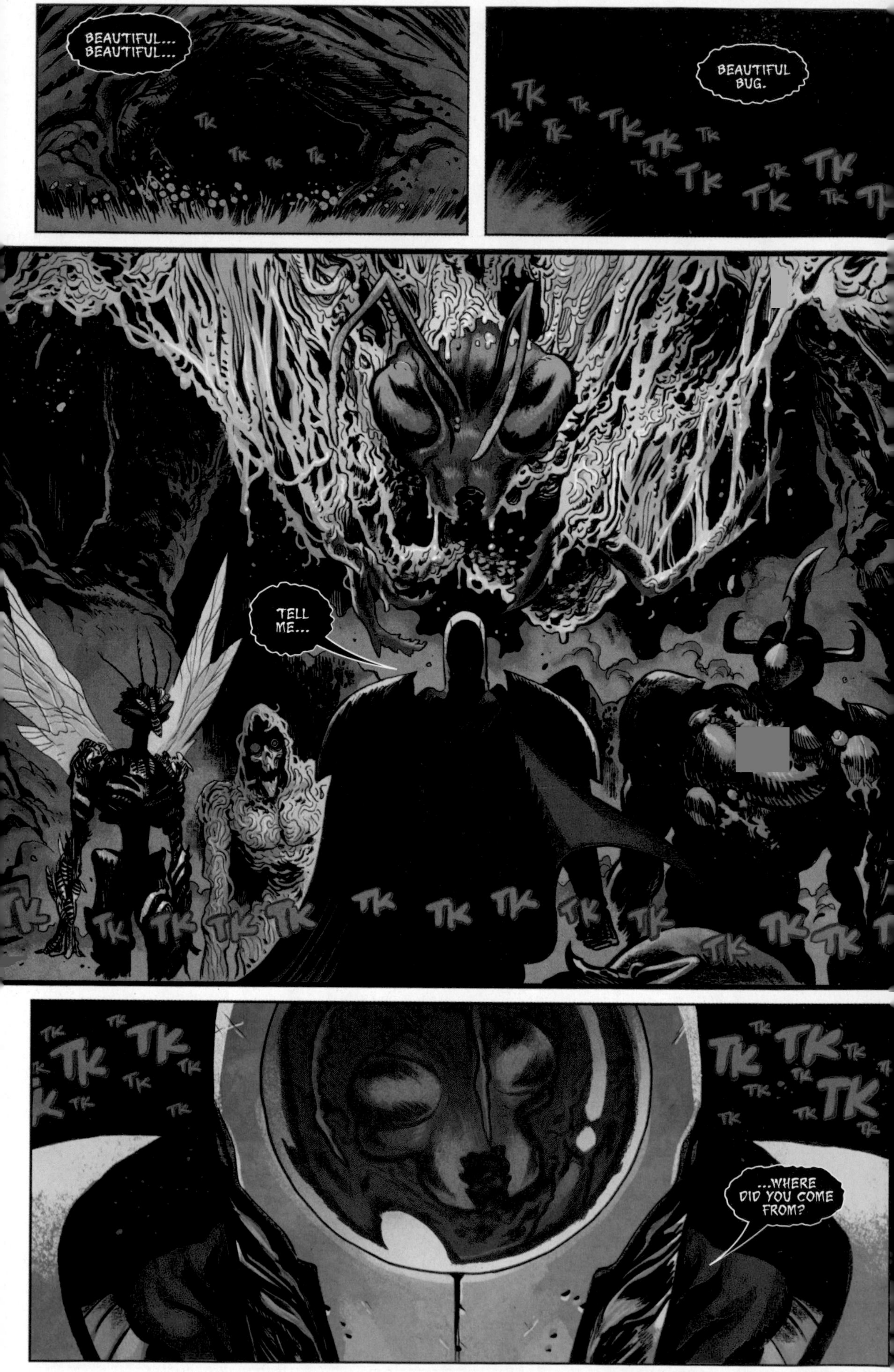
BEAUTIFUL... BEAUTIFUL...
TK TK TK TK
BEAUTIFUL BUG.
TK TK TK TK TK TK TK TK TK TK TK TK TK
TELL ME...
TK TK TK TK TK TK TK TK TK TK TK TK TK
TK TK TK TK TK TK TK TK TK TK TK TK TK
...WHERE DID YOU COME FROM?

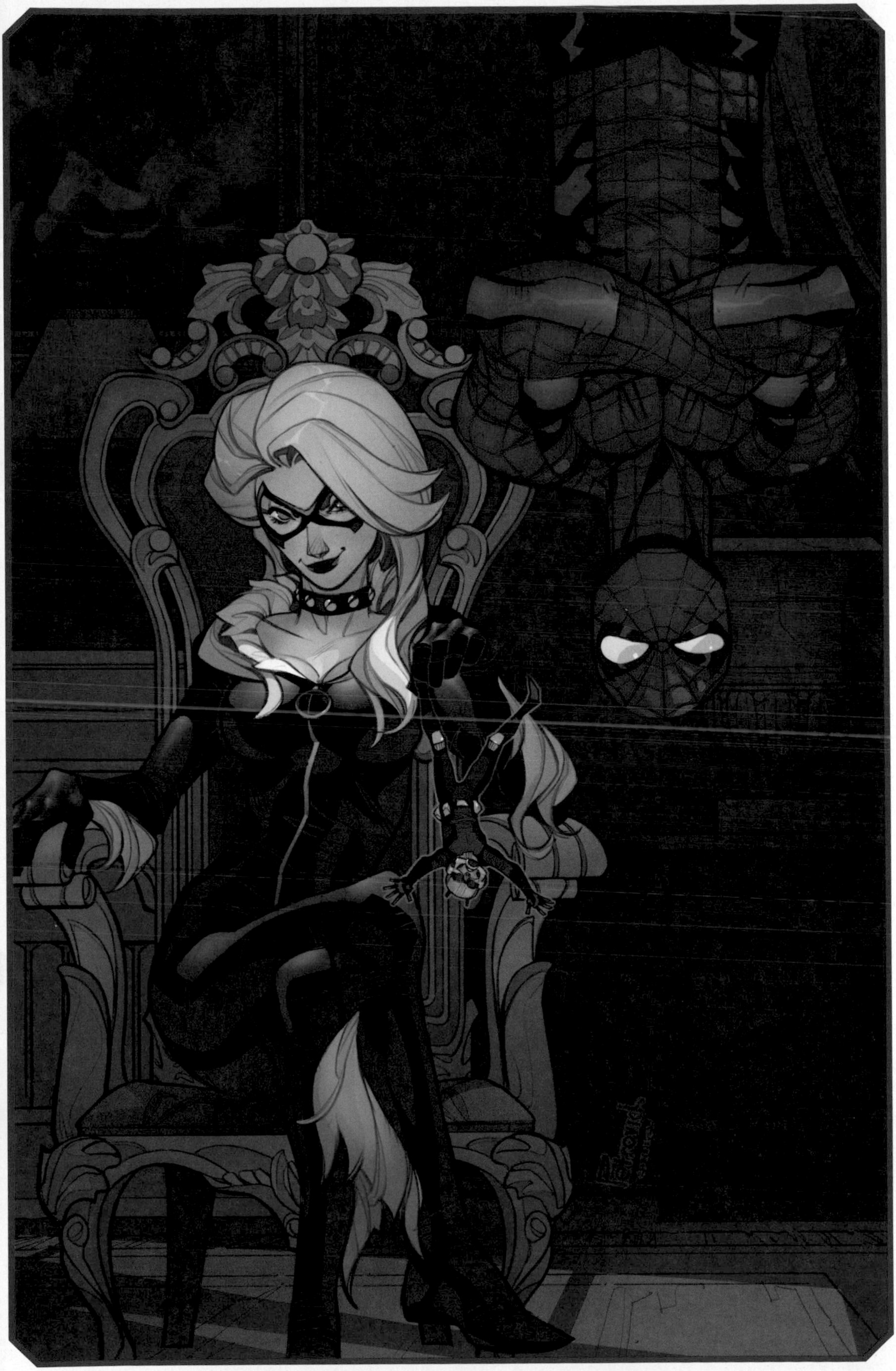

ANT-MAN #3 "WORLD HIVE PART 3"

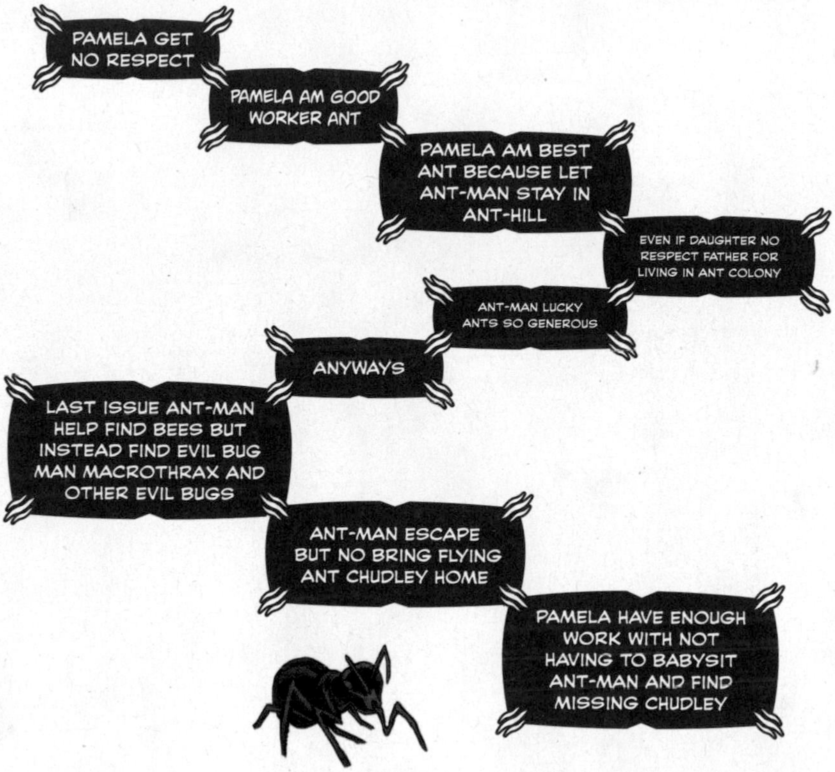
PAMELA GET NO RESPECT
PAMELA AM GOOD WORKER ANT
PAMELA AM BEST ANT BECAUSE LET ANT-MAN STAY IN ANT-HILL
EVEN IF DAUGHTER NO RESPECT FATHER FOR LIVING IN ANT COLONY
ANT-MAN LUCKY ANTS SO GENEROUS
ANYWAYS
LAST ISSUE ANT-MAN HELP FIND BEES BUT INSTEAD FIND EVIL BUG MAN MACROTHRAX AND OTHER EVIL BUGS
ANT-MAN ESCAPE BUT NO BRING FLYING ANT CHUDLEY HOME
PAMELA HAVE ENOUGH WORK WITH NOT HAVING TO BABYSIT ANT-MAN AND FIND MISSING CHUDLEY

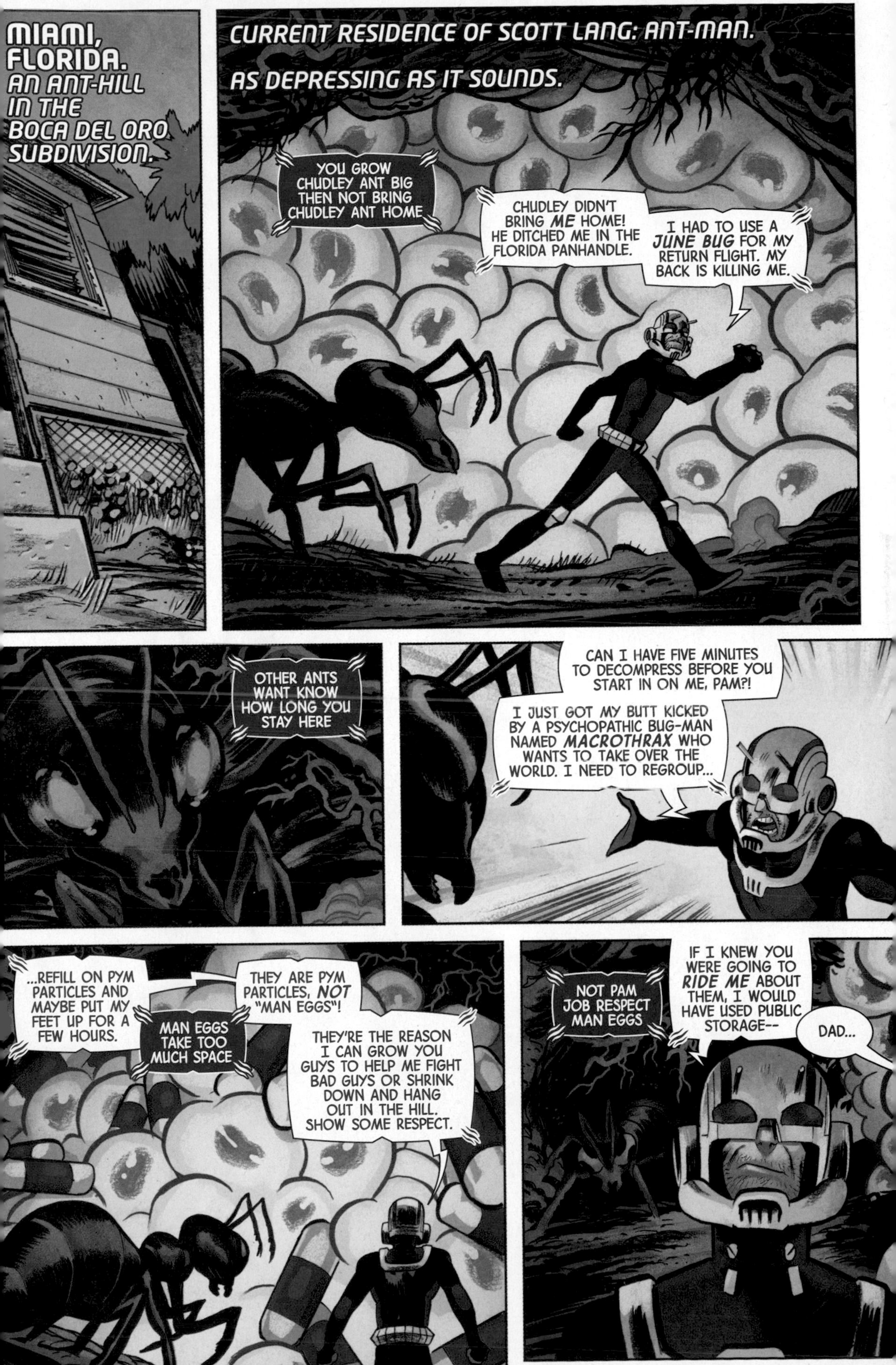
MIAMI, FLORIDA. AN ANT-HILL IN THE BOCA DEL ORO SUBDIVISION.
CURRENT RESIDENCE OF SCOTT LANG: ANT-MAN.
AS DEPRESSING AS IT SOUNDS.
YOU GROW CHUDLEY ANT BIG THEN NOT BRING CHUDLEY ANT HOME
CHUDLEY DIDN'T BRING ME HOME! HE DITCHED ME IN THE FLORIDA PANHANDLE.
I HAD TO USE A JUNE BUG FOR MY RETURN FLIGHT. MY BACK IS KILLING ME.
OTHER ANTS WANT KNOW HOW LONG YOU STAY HERE
CAN I HAVE FIVE MINUTES TO DECOMPRESS BEFORE YOU START IN ON ME, PAM?!
I JUST GOT MY BUTT KICKED BY A PSYCHOPATHIC BUG-MAN NAMED MACROTHRAX WHO WANTS TO TAKE OVER THE WORLD. I NEED TO REGROUP...
...REFILL ON PYM PARTICLES AND MAYBE PUT MY FEET UP FOR A FEW HOURS.
MAN EGGS TAKE TOO MUCH SPACE
THEY ARE PYM PARTICLES, NOT "MAN EGGS"!
THEY'RE THE REASON I CAN GROW YOU GUYS TO HELP ME FIGHT BAD GUYS OR SHRINK DOWN AND HANG OUT IN THE HILL. SHOW SOME RESPECT.
NOT PAM JOB RESPECT MAN EGGS
IF I KNEW YOU WERE GOING TO RIDE ME ABOUT THEM, I WOULD HAVE USED PUBLIC STORAGE--
DAD...

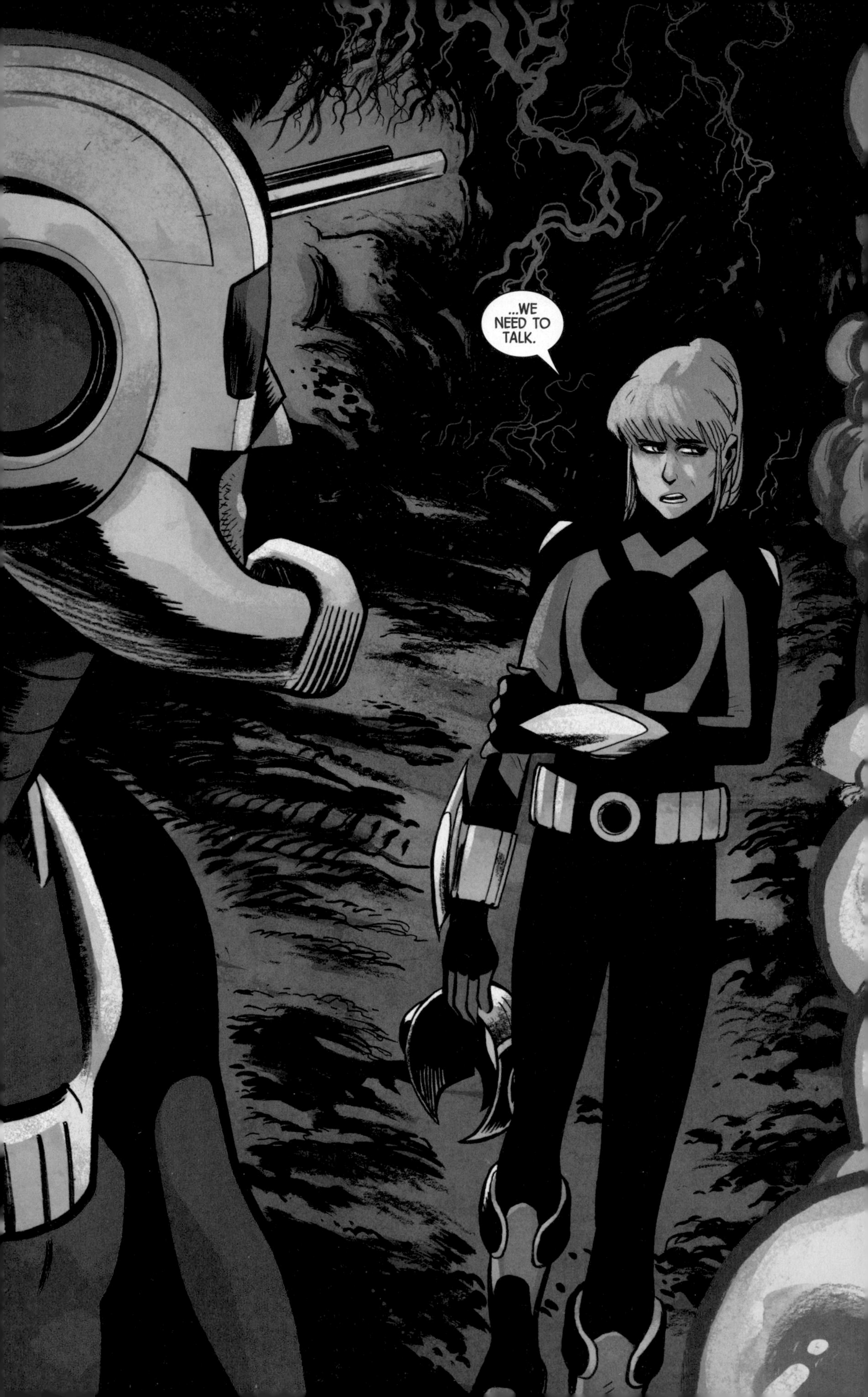
...WE NEED TO TALK.

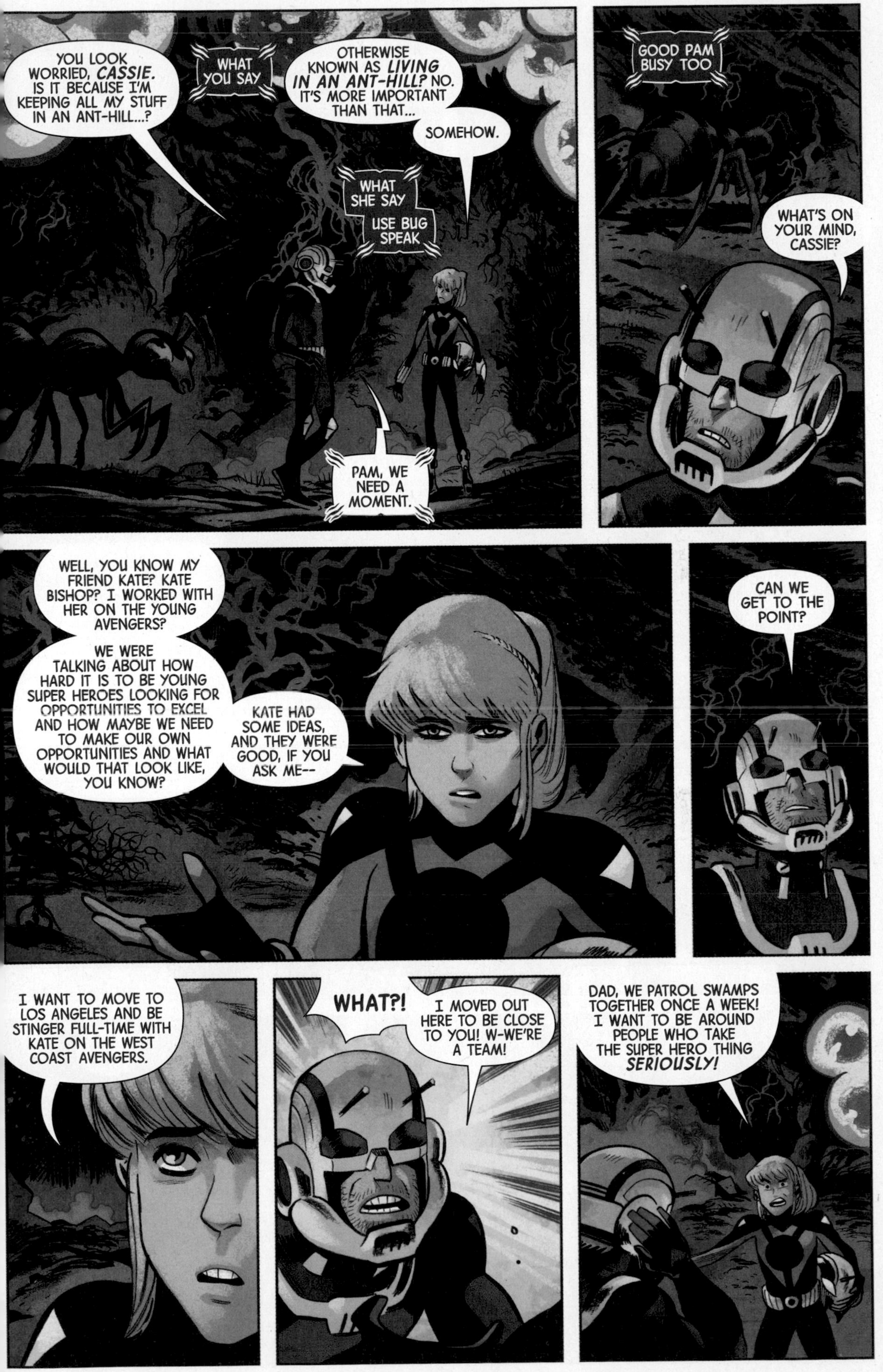
YOU LOOK WORRIED, CASSIE. IS IT BECAUSE I'M KEEPING ALL MY STUFF IN AN ANT-HILL...?
WHAT YOU SAY
OTHERWISE KNOWN AS LIVING IN AN ANT-HILL? NO. IT'S MORE IMPORTANT THAN THAT...
SOMEHOW.
WHAT SHE SAY
USE BUG SPEAK
PAM, WE NEED A MOMENT.
GOOD PAM BUSY TOO
WHAT'S ON YOUR MIND, CASSIE?
WELL, YOU KNOW MY FRIEND KATE? KATE BISHOP? I WORKED WITH HER ON THE YOUNG AVENGERS?
WE WERE TALKING ABOUT HOW HARD IT IS TO BE YOUNG SUPER HEROES LOOKING FOR OPPORTUNITIES TO EXCEL AND HOW MAYBE WE NEED TO MAKE OUR OWN OPPORTUNITIES AND WHAT WOULD THAT LOOK LIKE, YOU KNOW?
KATE HAD SOME IDEAS, AND THEY WERE GOOD, IF YOU ASK ME--
CAN WE GET TO THE POINT?
I WANT TO MOVE TO LOS ANGELES AND BE STINGER FULL-TIME WITH KATE ON THE WEST COAST AVENGERS.
WHAT?!
I MOVED OUT HERE TO BE CLOSE TO YOU! W-WE'RE A TEAM!
DAD, WE PATROL SWAMPS TOGETHER ONCE A WEEK! I WANT TO BE AROUND PEOPLE WHO TAKE THE SUPER HERO THING SERIOUSLY!

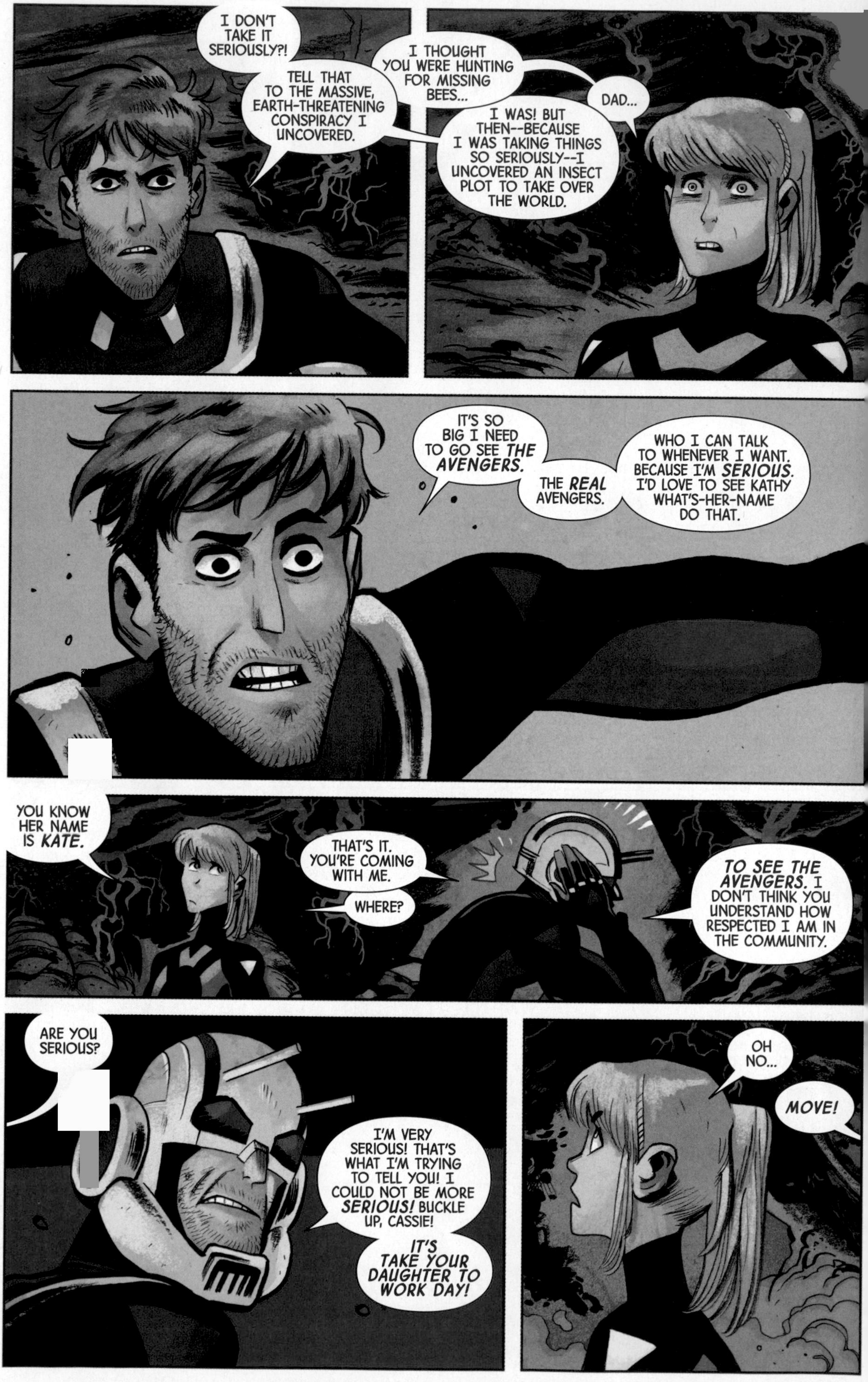
I DON'T TAKE IT SERIOUSLY?!
TELL THAT TO THE MASSIVE, EARTH-THREATENING CONSPIRACY I UNCOVERED.
I THOUGHT YOU WERE HUNTING FOR MISSING BEES...
DAD...
I WAS! BUT THEN--BECAUSE I WAS TAKING THINGS SO SERIOUSLY--I UNCOVERED AN INSECT PLOT TO TAKE OVER THE WORLD.
IT'S SO BIG I NEED TO GO SEE *THE AVENGERS.*
THE *REAL* AVENGERS.
WHO I CAN TALK TO WHENEVER I WANT. BECAUSE I'M *SERIOUS.* I'D LOVE TO SEE KATHY WHAT'S-HER-NAME DO THAT.
YOU KNOW HER NAME IS *KATE.*
THAT'S IT. YOU'RE COMING WITH ME.
WHERE?
TO SEE THE AVENGERS. I DON'T THINK YOU UNDERSTAND HOW RESPECTED I AM IN THE COMMUNITY.
ARE YOU SERIOUS?
I'M VERY SERIOUS! THAT'S WHAT I'M TRYING TO TELL YOU! I COULD NOT BE MORE *SERIOUS!* BUCKLE UP, CASSIE!
IT'S TAKE YOUR DAUGHTER TO WORK DAY!
OH NO...
MOVE!

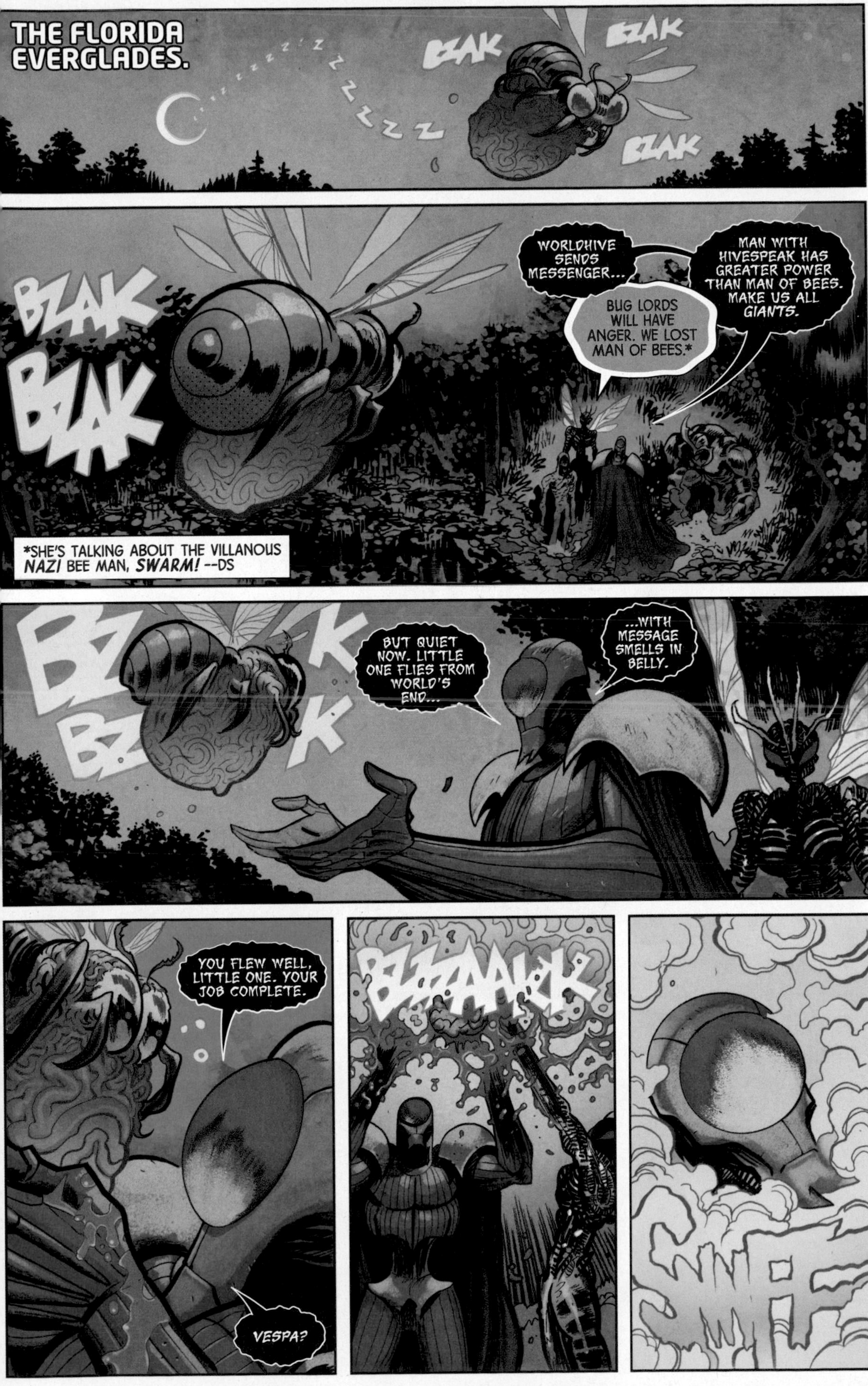
THE FLORIDA EVERGLADES.
ZZZZZZZZZ
BZAK
BZAK
BZAK
BZAK
BZAK
WORLDHIVE SENDS MESSENGER...
BUG LORDS WILL HAVE ANGER. WE LOST MAN OF BEES.*
MAN WITH HIVESPEAK HAS GREATER POWER THAN MAN OF BEES. MAKE US ALL GIANTS.
*SHE'S TALKING ABOUT THE VILLANOUS NAZI BEE MAN, SWARM! --DS
BUT QUIET NOW. LITTLE ONE FLIES FROM WORLD'S END...
...WITH MESSAGE SMELLS IN BELLY.
YOU FLEW WELL, LITTLE ONE. YOUR JOB COMPLETE.
VESPA?
BZZZAAKK

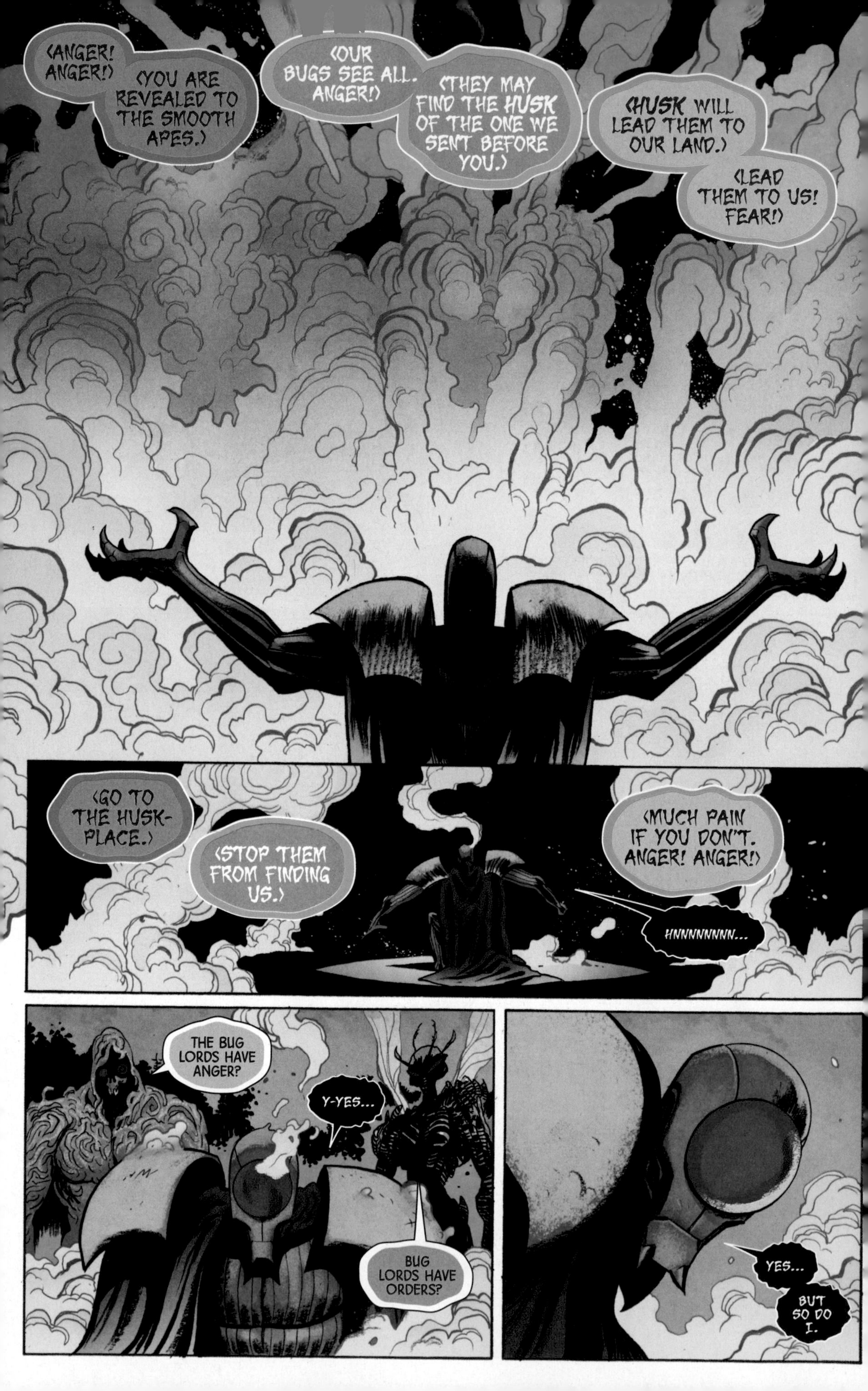
‹ANGER! ANGER!›
‹YOU ARE REVEALED TO THE SMOOTH APES.›
‹OUR BUGS SEE ALL. ANGER!›
‹THEY MAY FIND THE HUSK OF THE ONE WE SENT BEFORE YOU.›
‹HUSK WILL LEAD THEM TO OUR LAND.›
‹LEAD THEM TO US! FEAR!›
‹GO TO THE HUSK-PLACE.›
‹STOP THEM FROM FINDING US.›
‹MUCH PAIN IF YOU DON'T. ANGER! ANGER!›
HNNNNNNNN...
THE BUG LORDS HAVE ANGER?
Y-YES...
BUG LORDS HAVE ORDERS?
YES...
BUT SO DO I.

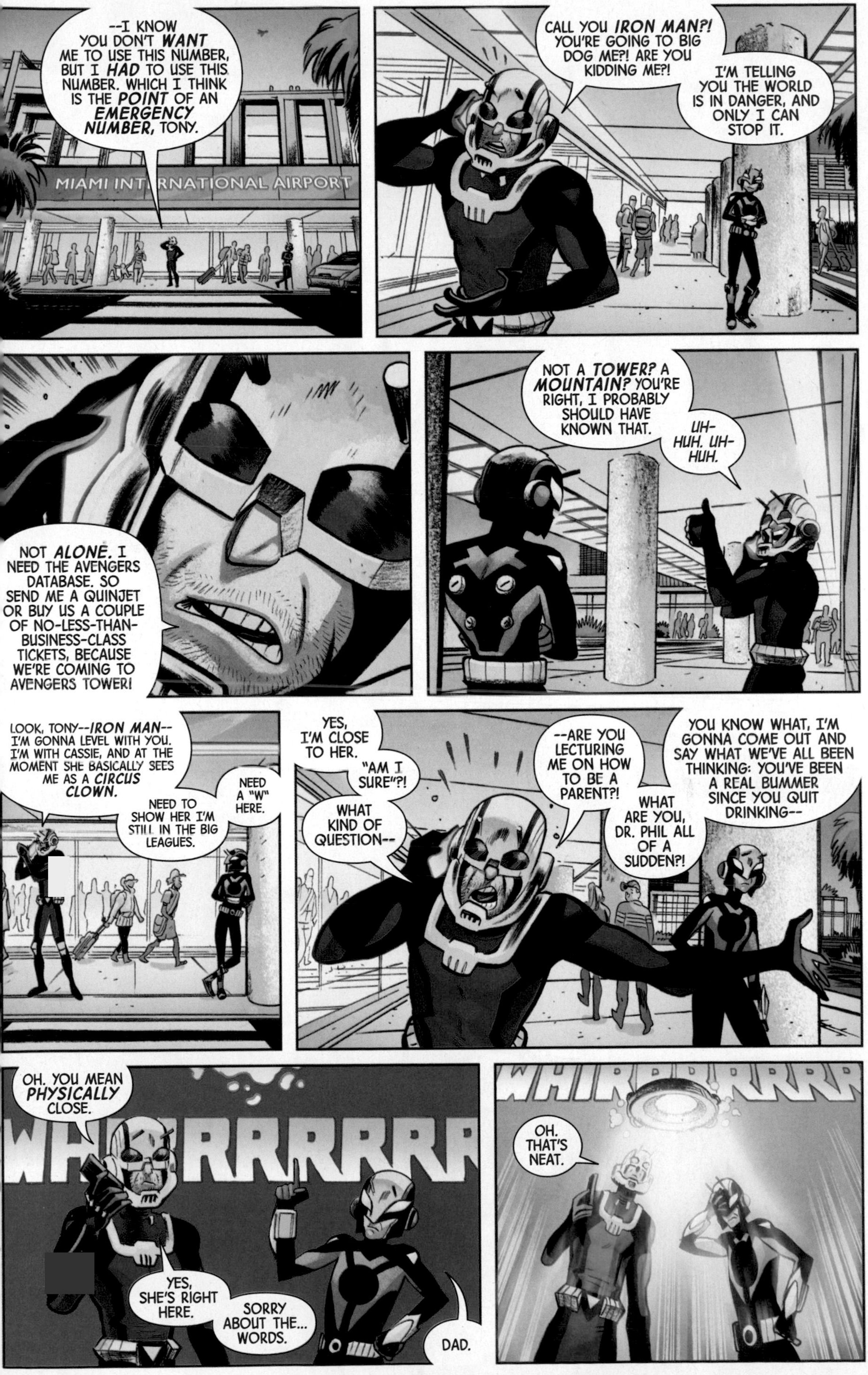

--I KNOW YOU DON'T WANT ME TO USE THIS NUMBER, BUT I HAD TO USE THIS NUMBER. WHICH I THINK IS THE POINT OF AN EMERGENCY NUMBER, TONY.
MIAMI INTERNATIONAL AIRPORT
CALL YOU IRON MAN?! YOU'RE GOING TO BIG DOG ME?! ARE YOU KIDDING ME?!
I'M TELLING YOU THE WORLD IS IN DANGER, AND ONLY I CAN STOP IT.
NOT ALONE. I NEED THE AVENGERS DATABASE. SO SEND ME A QUINJET OR BUY US A COUPLE OF NO-LESS-THAN-BUSINESS-CLASS TICKETS, BECAUSE WE'RE COMING TO AVENGERS TOWER!
NOT A TOWER? A MOUNTAIN? YOU'RE RIGHT, I PROBABLY SHOULD HAVE KNOWN THAT.
UH-HUH. UH-HUH.
LOOK, TONY--IRON MAN--I'M GONNA LEVEL WITH YOU. I'M WITH CASSIE, AND AT THE MOMENT SHE BASICALLY SEES ME AS A CIRCUS CLOWN.
NEED TO SHOW HER I'M STILL IN THE BIG LEAGUES.
NEED A "W" HERE.
YES, I'M CLOSE TO HER.
"AM I SURE"?!
WHAT KIND OF QUESTION--
--ARE YOU LECTURING ME ON HOW TO BE A PARENT?!
WHAT ARE YOU, DR. PHIL ALL OF A SUDDEN?!
YOU KNOW WHAT, I'M GONNA COME OUT AND SAY WHAT WE'VE ALL BEEN THINKING: YOU'VE BEEN A REAL BUMMER SINCE YOU QUIT DRINKING--
OH. YOU MEAN PHYSICALLY CLOSE.
YES, SHE'S RIGHT HERE.
SORRY ABOUT THE... WORDS.
DAD.
OH. THAT'S NEAT.

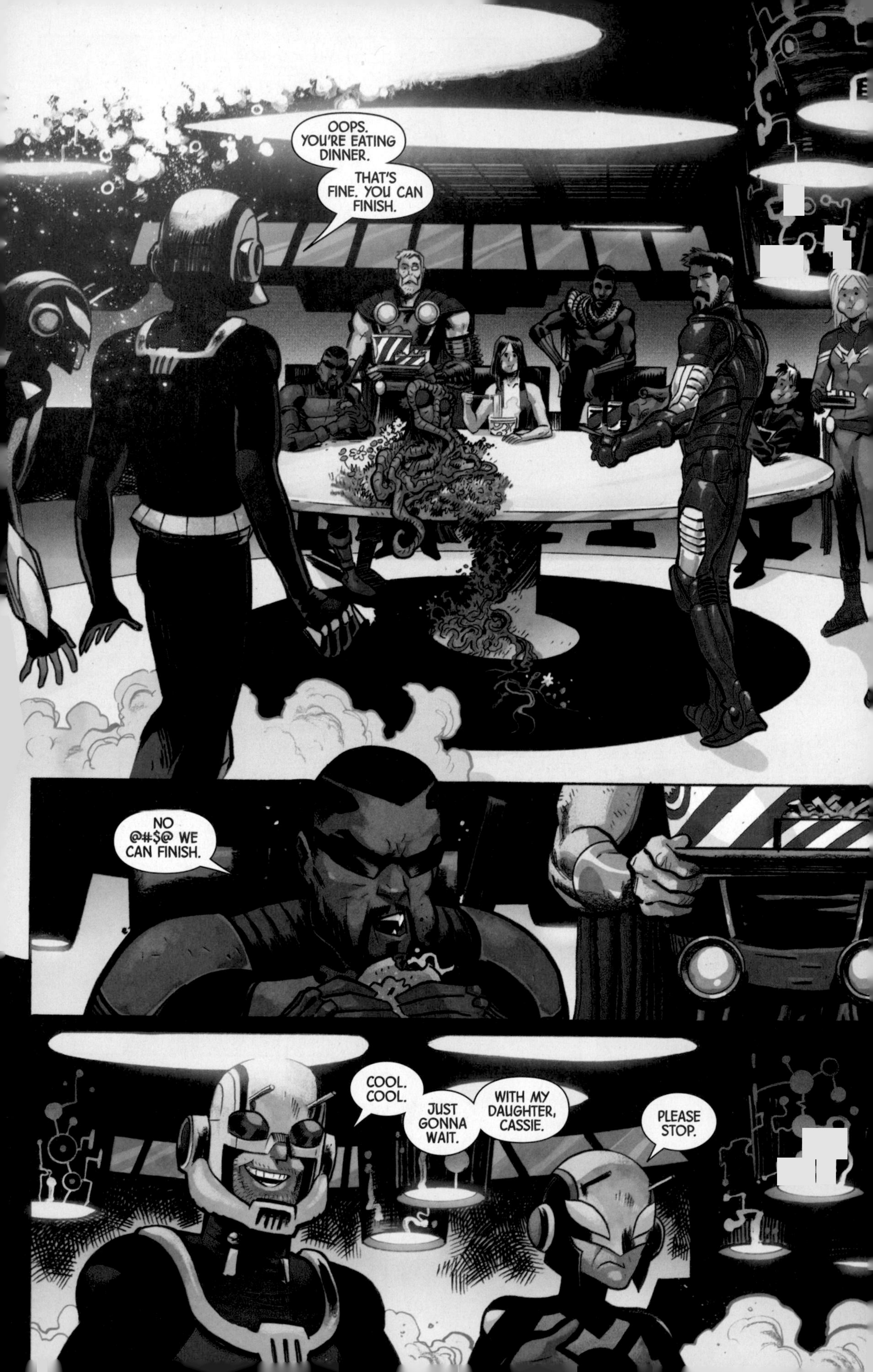
OOPS. YOU'RE EATING DINNER.
THAT'S FINE. YOU CAN FINISH.
NO @#$@ WE CAN FINISH.
COOL. COOL.
JUST GONNA WAIT.
WITH MY DAUGHTER, CASSIE.
PLEASE STOP.

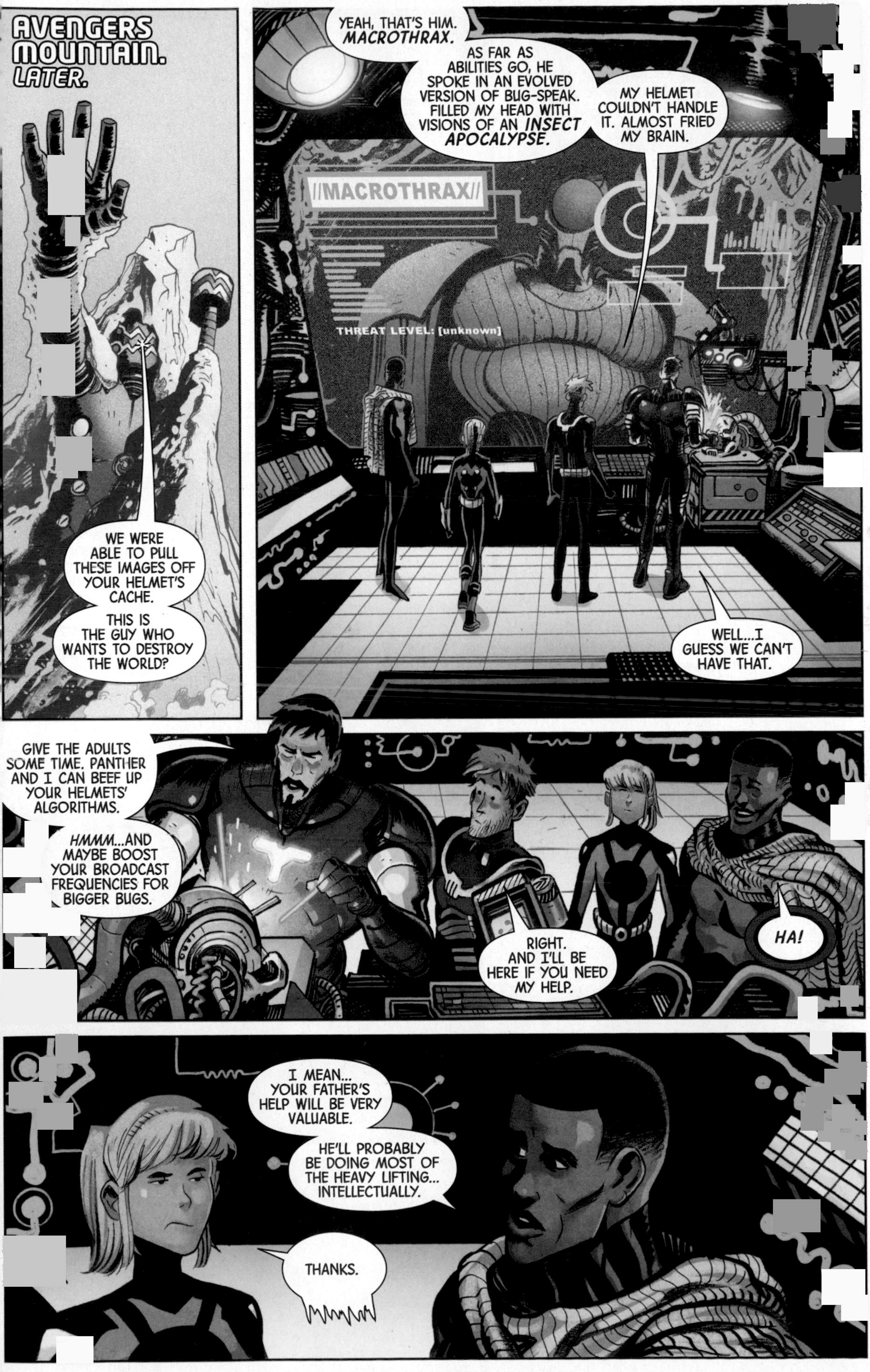
AVENGERS MOUNTAIN. LATER.
WE WERE ABLE TO PULL THESE IMAGES OFF YOUR HELMET'S CACHE.
THIS IS THE GUY WHO WANTS TO DESTROY THE WORLD?
YEAH, THAT'S HIM. MACROTHRAX.
AS FAR AS ABILITIES GO, HE SPOKE IN AN EVOLVED VERSION OF BUG-SPEAK. FILLED MY HEAD WITH VISIONS OF AN INSECT APOCALYPSE.
MY HELMET COULDN'T HANDLE IT. ALMOST FRIED MY BRAIN.
//MACROTHRAX//
THREAT LEVEL: [unknown]
WELL...I GUESS WE CAN'T HAVE THAT.
GIVE THE ADULTS SOME TIME. PANTHER AND I CAN BEEF UP YOUR HELMETS' ALGORITHMS.
HMMM...AND MAYBE BOOST YOUR BROADCAST FREQUENCIES FOR BIGGER BUGS.
RIGHT. AND I'LL BE HERE IF YOU NEED MY HELP.
HA!
I MEAN... YOUR FATHER'S HELP WILL BE VERY VALUABLE.
HE'LL PROBABLY BE DOING MOST OF THE HEAVY LIFTING... INTELLECTUALLY.
THANKS.

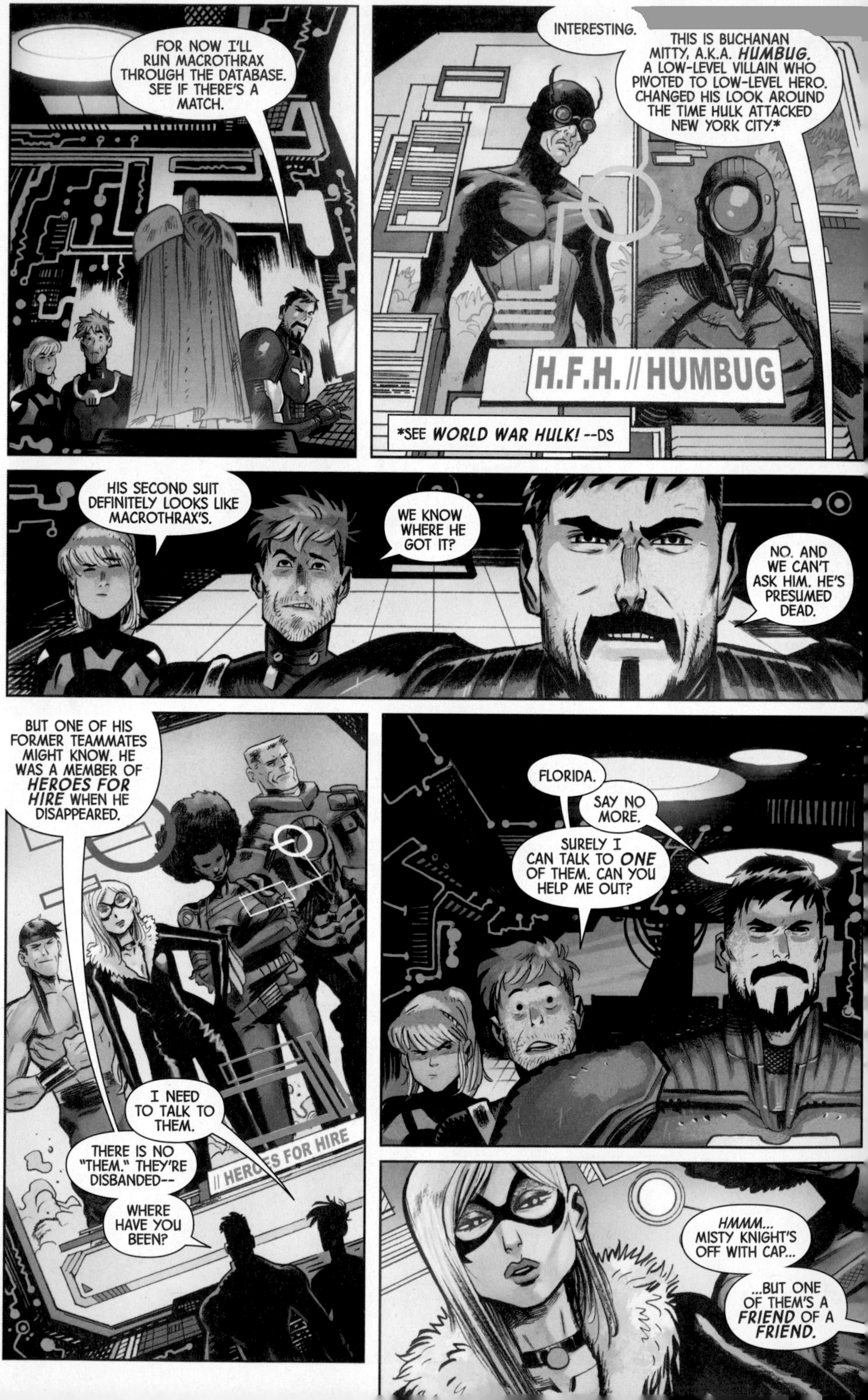
FOR NOW I'LL RUN MACROTHRAX THROUGH THE DATABASE. SEE IF THERE'S A MATCH.
INTERESTING.
THIS IS BUCHANAN MITTY, A.K.A. HUMBUG. A LOW-LEVEL VILLAIN WHO PIVOTED TO LOW-LEVEL HERO. CHANGED HIS LOOK AROUND THE TIME HULK ATTACKED NEW YORK CITY.*
H.F.H. // HUMBUG
*SEE WORLD WAR HULK! --DS
HIS SECOND SUIT DEFINITELY LOOKS LIKE MACROTHRAX'S.
WE KNOW WHERE HE GOT IT?
NO. AND WE CAN'T ASK HIM. HE'S PRESUMED DEAD.
BUT ONE OF HIS FORMER TEAMMATES MIGHT KNOW. HE WAS A MEMBER OF HEROES FOR HIRE WHEN HE DISAPPEARED.
I NEED TO TALK TO THEM.
THERE IS NO "THEM." THEY'RE DISBANDED--
WHERE HAVE YOU BEEN?
FLORIDA.
SAY NO MORE.
SURELY I CAN TALK TO ONE OF THEM. CAN YOU HELP ME OUT?
HMMM... MISTY KNIGHT'S OFF WITH CAP...
...BUT ONE OF THEM'S A FRIEND OF A FRIEND.

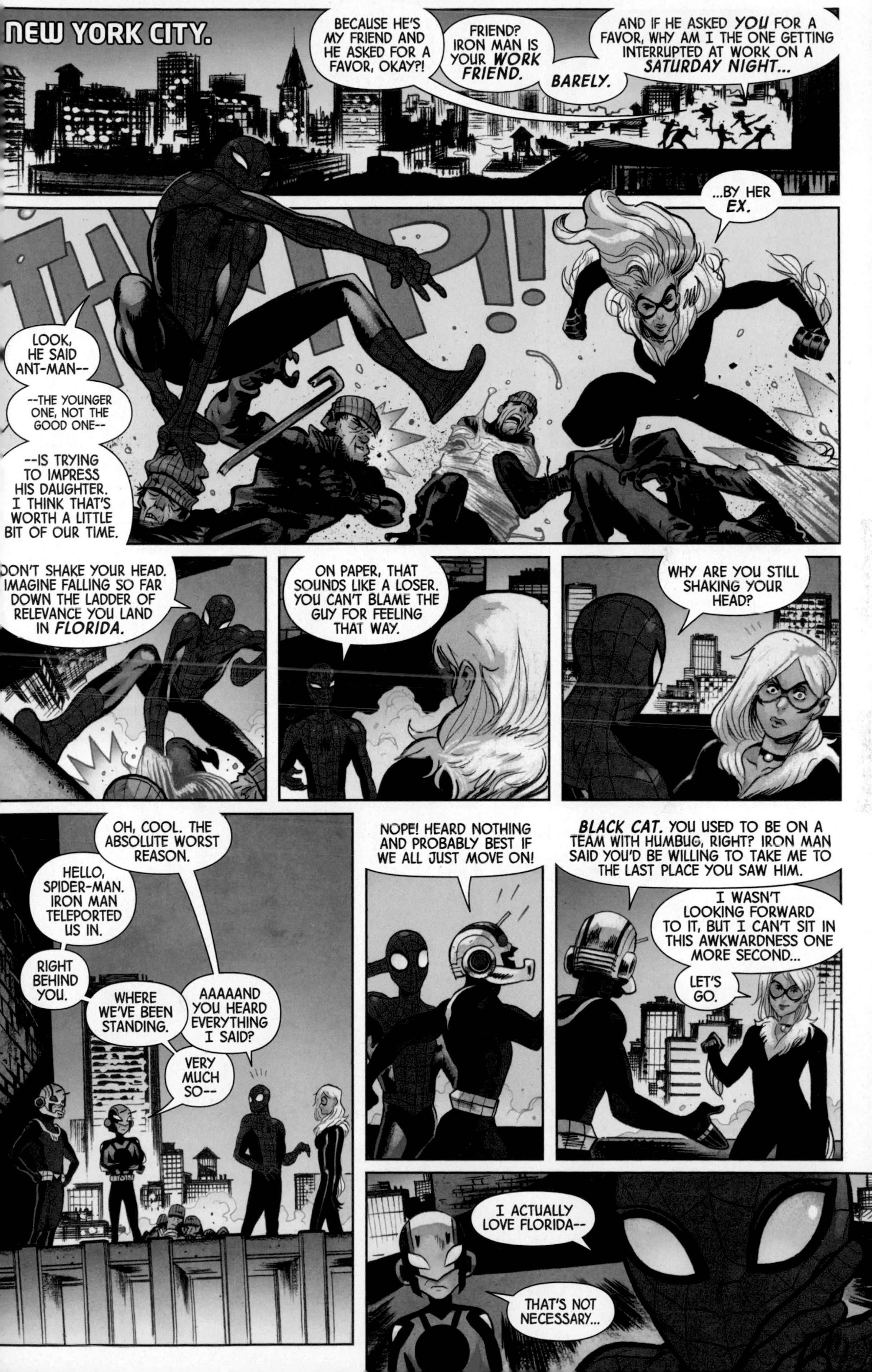
NEW YORK CITY.
BECAUSE HE'S MY FRIEND AND HE ASKED FOR A FAVOR, OKAY?!
FRIEND? IRON MAN IS YOUR WORK FRIEND.
BARELY.
AND IF HE ASKED YOU FOR A FAVOR, WHY AM I THE ONE GETTING INTERRUPTED AT WORK ON A SATURDAY NIGHT...
...BY HER EX.
LOOK, HE SAID ANT-MAN--
--THE YOUNGER ONE, NOT THE GOOD ONE--
--IS TRYING TO IMPRESS HIS DAUGHTER. I THINK THAT'S WORTH A LITTLE BIT OF OUR TIME.
DON'T SHAKE YOUR HEAD. IMAGINE FALLING SO FAR DOWN THE LADDER OF RELEVANCE YOU LAND IN FLORIDA.
ON PAPER, THAT SOUNDS LIKE A LOSER. YOU CAN'T BLAME THE GUY FOR FEELING THAT WAY.
WHY ARE YOU STILL SHAKING YOUR HEAD?
HELLO, SPIDER-MAN. IRON MAN TELEPORTED US IN.
OH, COOL. THE ABSOLUTE WORST REASON.
RIGHT BEHIND YOU.
WHERE WE'VE BEEN STANDING.
AAAAAND YOU HEARD EVERYTHING I SAID?
VERY MUCH SO--
NOPE! HEARD NOTHING AND PROBABLY BEST IF WE ALL JUST MOVE ON!
BLACK CAT. YOU USED TO BE ON A TEAM WITH HUMBUG, RIGHT? IRON MAN SAID YOU'D BE WILLING TO TAKE ME TO THE LAST PLACE YOU SAW HIM.
I WASN'T LOOKING FORWARD TO IT, BUT I CAN'T SIT IN THIS AWKWARDNESS ONE MORE SECOND...
LET'S GO.
I ACTUALLY LOVE FLORIDA--
THAT'S NOT NECESSARY...

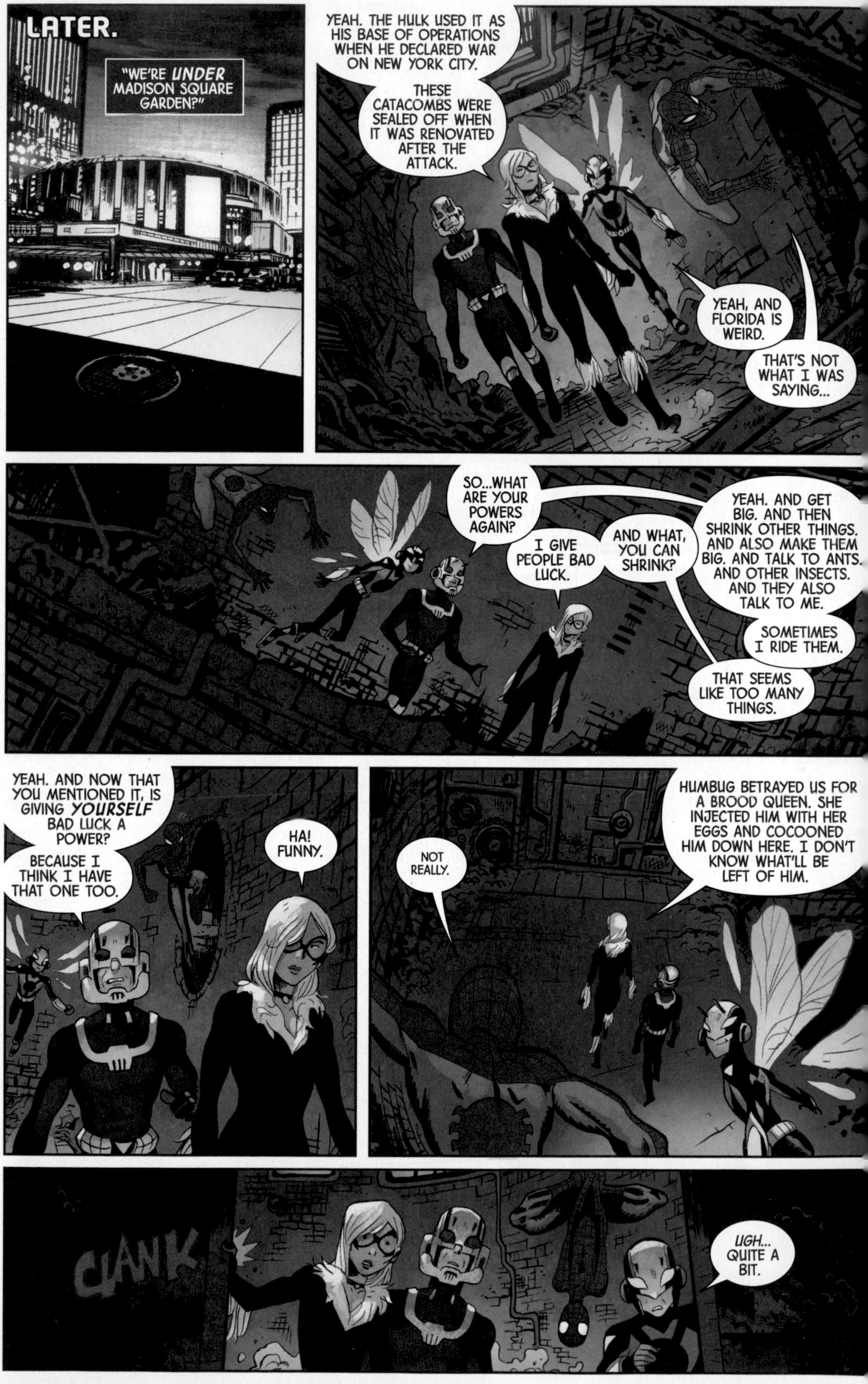
LATER.
"WE'RE UNDER MADISON SQUARE GARDEN?"
YEAH. THE HULK USED IT AS HIS BASE OF OPERATIONS WHEN HE DECLARED WAR ON NEW YORK CITY.
THESE CATACOMBS WERE SEALED OFF WHEN IT WAS RENOVATED AFTER THE ATTACK.
YEAH, AND FLORIDA IS WEIRD.
THAT'S NOT WHAT I WAS SAYING...
SO...WHAT ARE YOUR POWERS AGAIN?
I GIVE PEOPLE BAD LUCK.
AND WHAT, YOU CAN SHRINK?
YEAH. AND GET BIG. AND THEN SHRINK OTHER THINGS. AND ALSO MAKE THEM BIG. AND TALK TO ANTS. AND OTHER INSECTS. AND THEY ALSO TALK TO ME.
SOMETIMES I RIDE THEM.
THAT SEEMS LIKE TOO MANY THINGS.
YEAH. AND NOW THAT YOU MENTIONED IT, IS GIVING YOURSELF BAD LUCK A POWER?
BECAUSE I THINK I HAVE THAT ONE TOO.
HA! FUNNY.
NOT REALLY.
HUMBUG BETRAYED US FOR A BROOD QUEEN. SHE INJECTED HIM WITH HER EGGS AND COCOONED HIM DOWN HERE. I DON'T KNOW WHAT'LL BE LEFT OF HIM.
CLANK
UGH... QUITE A BIT.

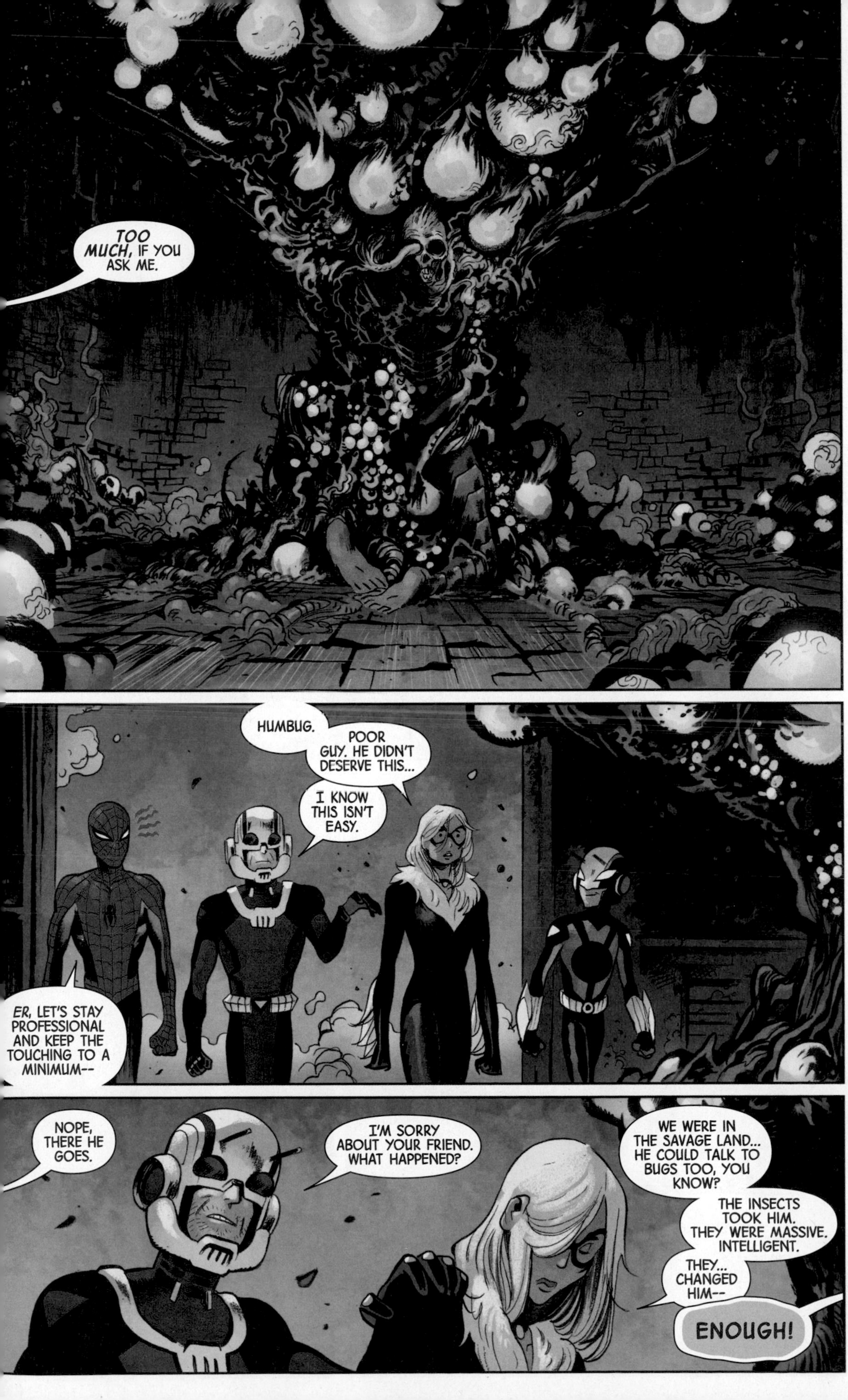
TOO MUCH, IF YOU ASK ME.
HUMBUG.
POOR GUY. HE DIDN'T DESERVE THIS...
I KNOW THIS ISN'T EASY.
ER, LET'S STAY PROFESSIONAL AND KEEP THE TOUCHING TO A MINIMUM--
NOPE, THERE HE GOES.
I'M SORRY ABOUT YOUR FRIEND. WHAT HAPPENED?
WE WERE IN THE SAVAGE LAND... HE COULD TALK TO BUGS TOO, YOU KNOW?
THE INSECTS TOOK HIM. THEY WERE MASSIVE. INTELLIGENT.
THEY... CHANGED HIM--
ENOUGH!

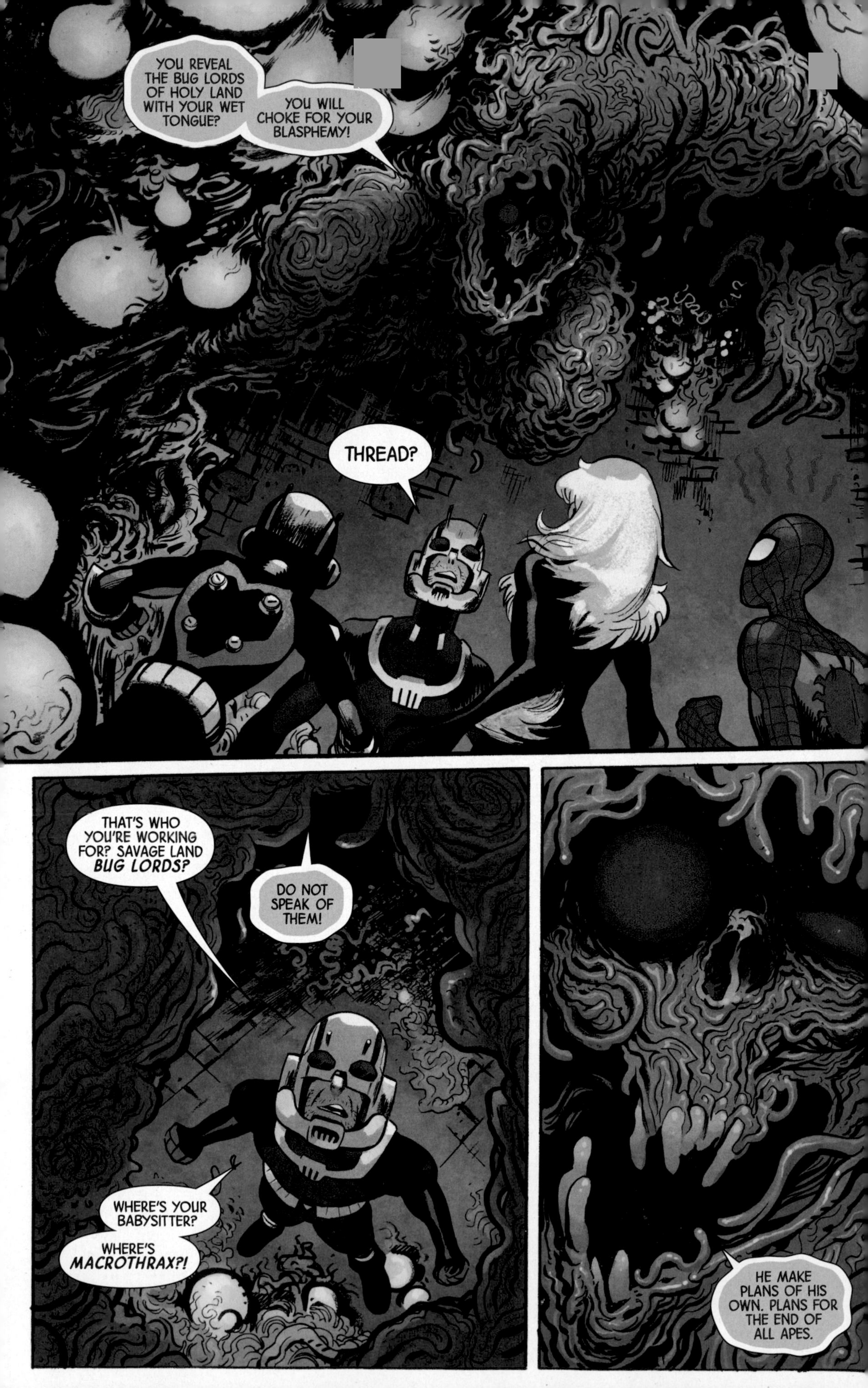
YOU REVEAL THE BUG LORDS OF HOLY LAND WITH YOUR WET TONGUE?
YOU WILL CHOKE FOR YOUR BLASPHEMY!
THREAD?
THAT'S WHO YOU'RE WORKING FOR? SAVAGE LAND *BUG LORDS?*
DO NOT SPEAK OF THEM!
WHERE'S YOUR BABYSITTER?
WHERE'S *MACROTHRAX?!*
HE MAKE PLANS OF HIS OWN. PLANS FOR THE END OF ALL APES.

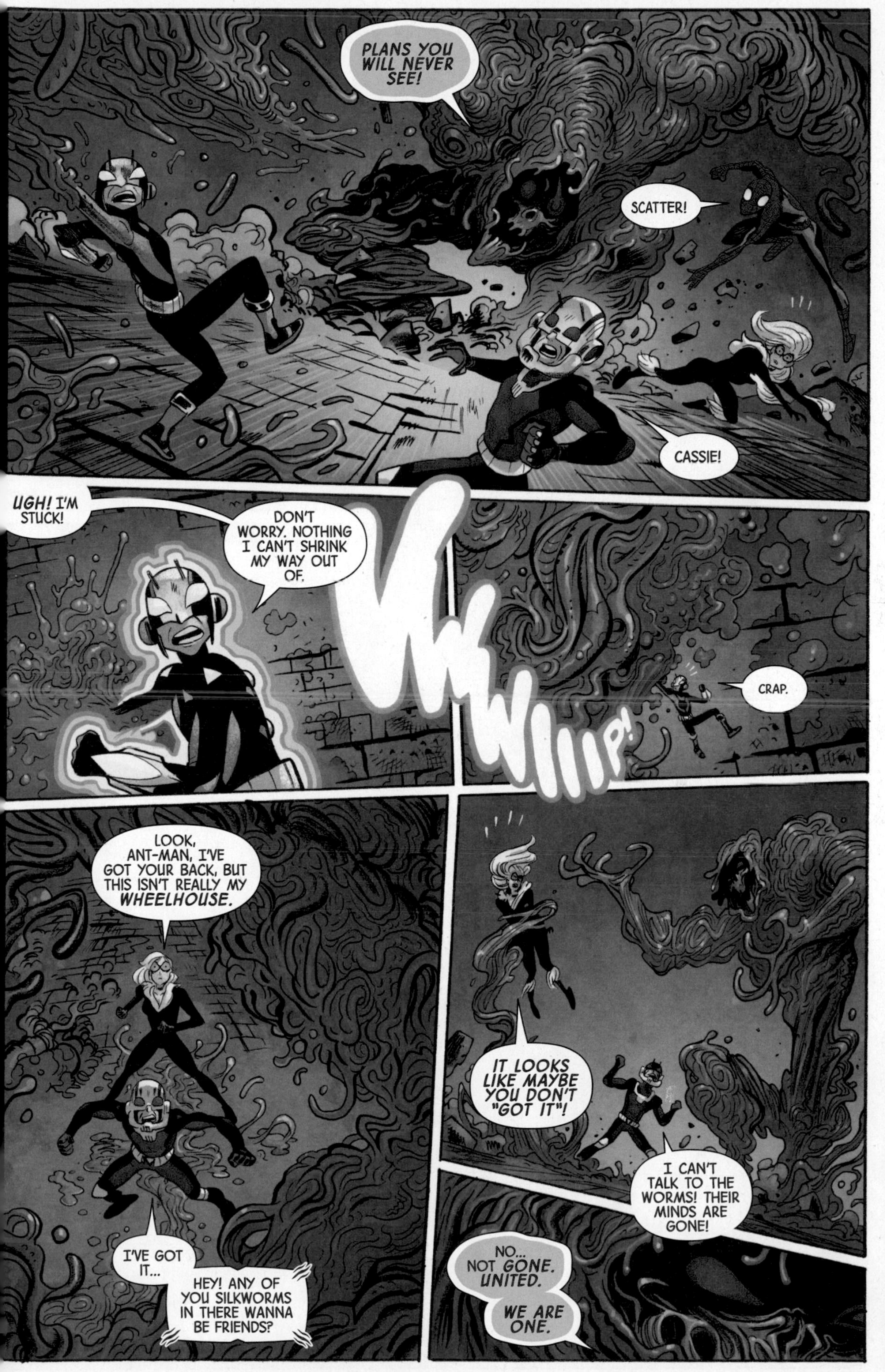
PLANS YOU WILL NEVER SEE!
SCATTER!
CASSIE!
UGH! I'M STUCK!
DON'T WORRY. NOTHING I CAN'T SHRINK MY WAY OUT OF.
VVWIIIP!
CRAP.
LOOK, ANT-MAN, I'VE GOT YOUR BACK, BUT THIS ISN'T REALLY MY WHEELHOUSE.
I'VE GOT IT...
HEY! ANY OF YOU SILKWORMS IN THERE WANNA BE FRIENDS?
IT LOOKS LIKE MAYBE YOU DON'T "GOT IT"!
I CAN'T TALK TO THE WORMS! THEIR MINDS ARE GONE!
NO... NOT GONE. UNITED.
WE ARE ONE.

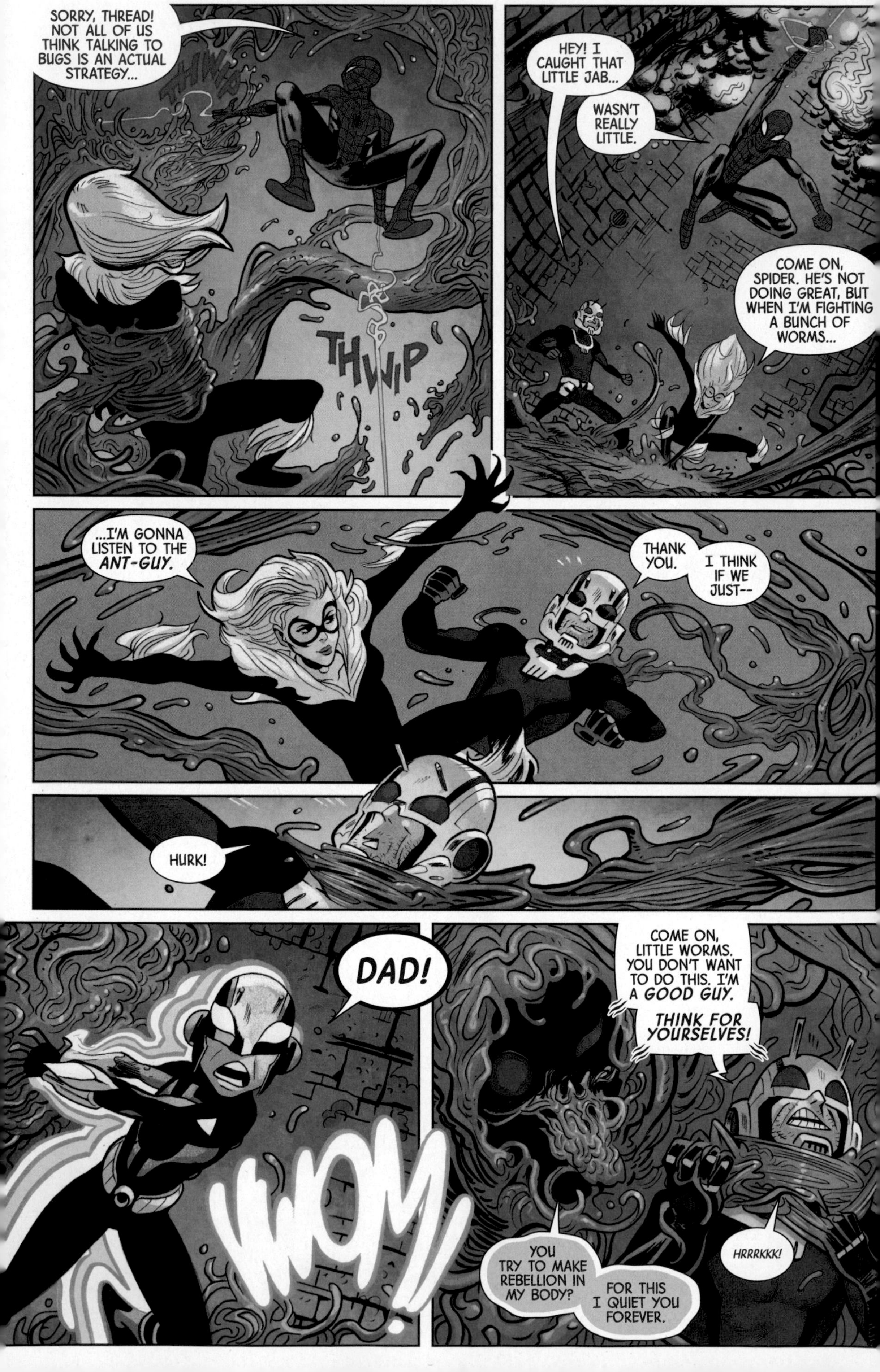
SORRY, THREAD! NOT ALL OF US THINK TALKING TO BUGS IS AN ACTUAL STRATEGY...
THWIP
HEY! I CAUGHT THAT LITTLE JAB...
WASN'T REALLY LITTLE.
COME ON, SPIDER. HE'S NOT DOING GREAT, BUT WHEN I'M FIGHTING A BUNCH OF WORMS...
...I'M GONNA LISTEN TO THE *ANT-GUY*.
THANK YOU.
I THINK IF WE JUST--
HURK!
DAD!
COME ON, LITTLE WORMS. YOU DON'T WANT TO DO THIS. I'M A *GOOD GUY*.
THINK FOR YOURSELVES!
YOU TRY TO MAKE REBELLION IN MY BODY?
FOR THIS I QUIET YOU FOREVER.
HRRRKKK!

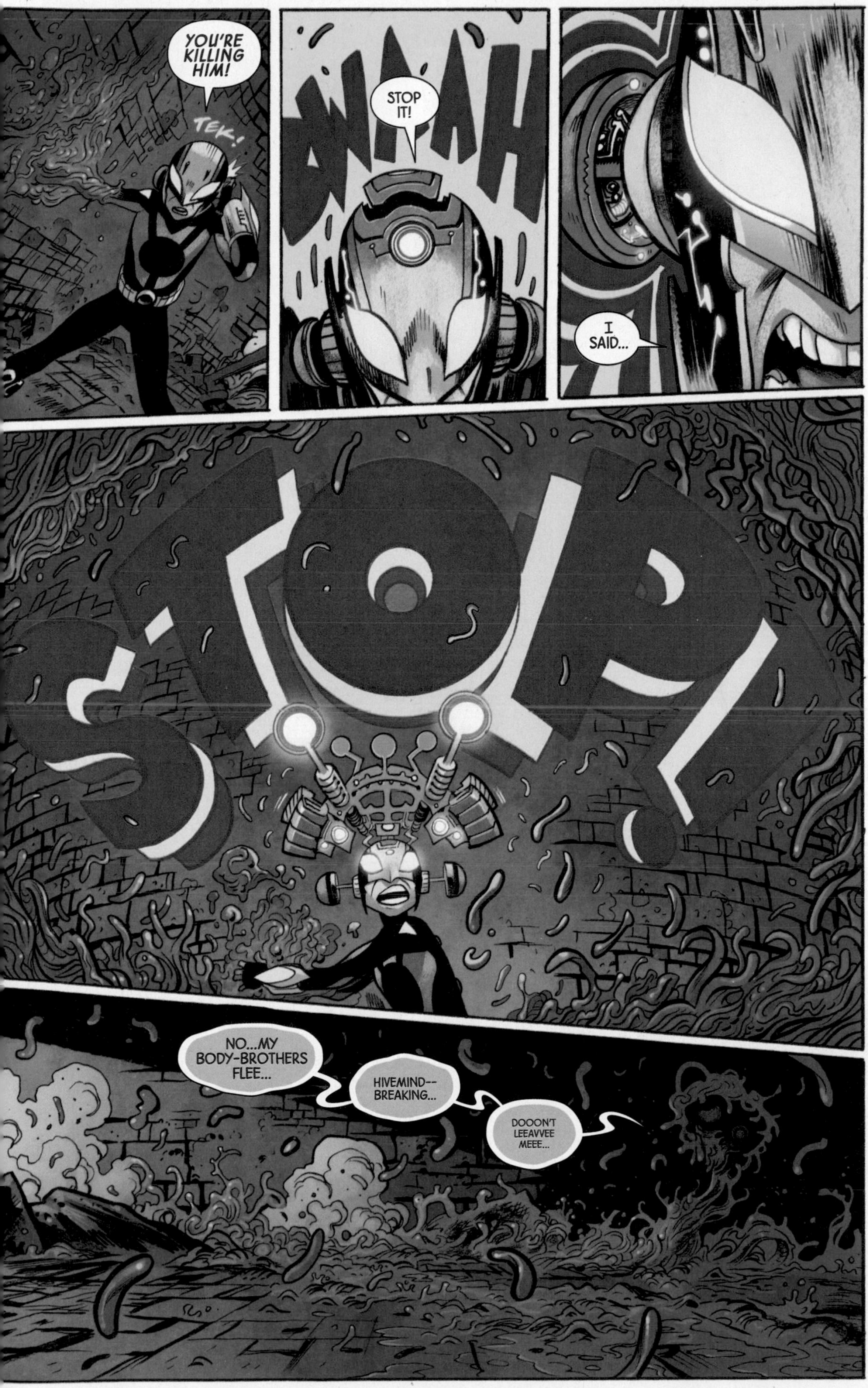
YOU'RE KILLING HIM!
TEK!
STOP IT!
I SAID...
STOP
NO...MY BODY-BROTHERS FLEE...
HIVEMIND-- BREAKING...
DOOON'T LEEAVVEE MEEE...

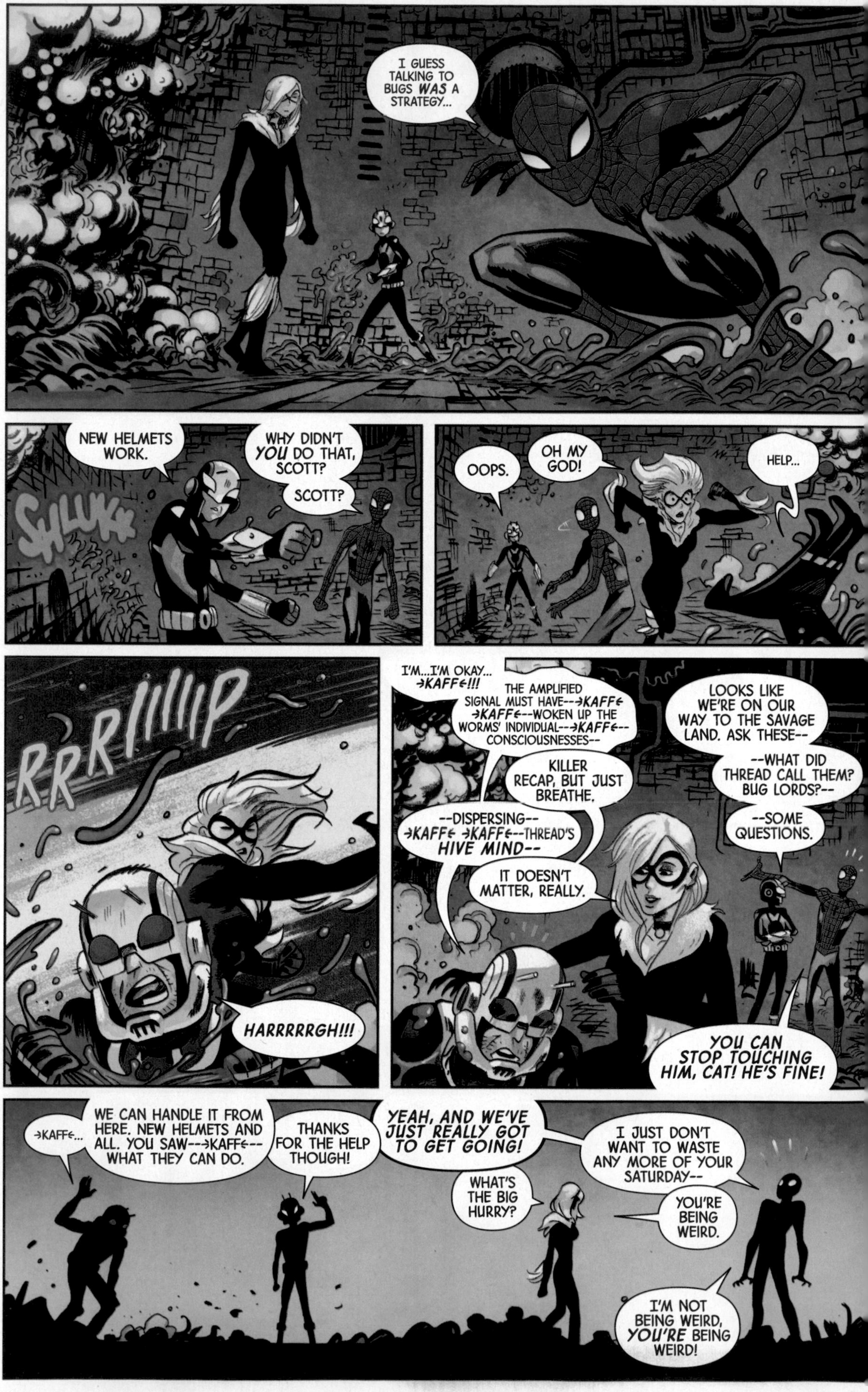
I GUESS TALKING TO BUGS *WAS* A STRATEGY...
NEW HELMETS WORK.
WHY DIDN'T *YOU* DO THAT, SCOTT?
SCOTT?
SHLUK
OOPS.
OH MY GOD!
HELP...
RRRIIIIIP
HARRRRRGH!!!
I'M...I'M OKAY... →KAFF←!!!
THE AMPLIFIED SIGNAL MUST HAVE--→KAFF← →KAFF←--WOKEN UP THE WORMS' INDIVIDUAL--→KAFF←--CONSCIOUSNESSES--
KILLER RECAP, BUT JUST BREATHE.
--DISPERSING-- →KAFF← →KAFF←--THREAD'S *HIVE MIND*--
IT DOESN'T MATTER, REALLY.
LOOKS LIKE WE'RE ON OUR WAY TO THE SAVAGE LAND. ASK THESE--
--WHAT DID THREAD CALL THEM? BUG LORDS?--
--SOME QUESTIONS.
YOU CAN STOP TOUCHING HIM, CAT! HE'S FINE!
→KAFF←...
WE CAN HANDLE IT FROM HERE. NEW HELMETS AND ALL. YOU SAW--→KAFF←--WHAT THEY CAN DO.
THANKS FOR THE HELP THOUGH!
YEAH, AND WE'VE JUST REALLY GOT TO GET GOING!
I JUST DON'T WANT TO WASTE ANY MORE OF YOUR SATURDAY--
WHAT'S THE BIG HURRY?
YOU'RE BEING WEIRD.
I'M NOT BEING WEIRD, *YOU'RE* BEING WEIRD!

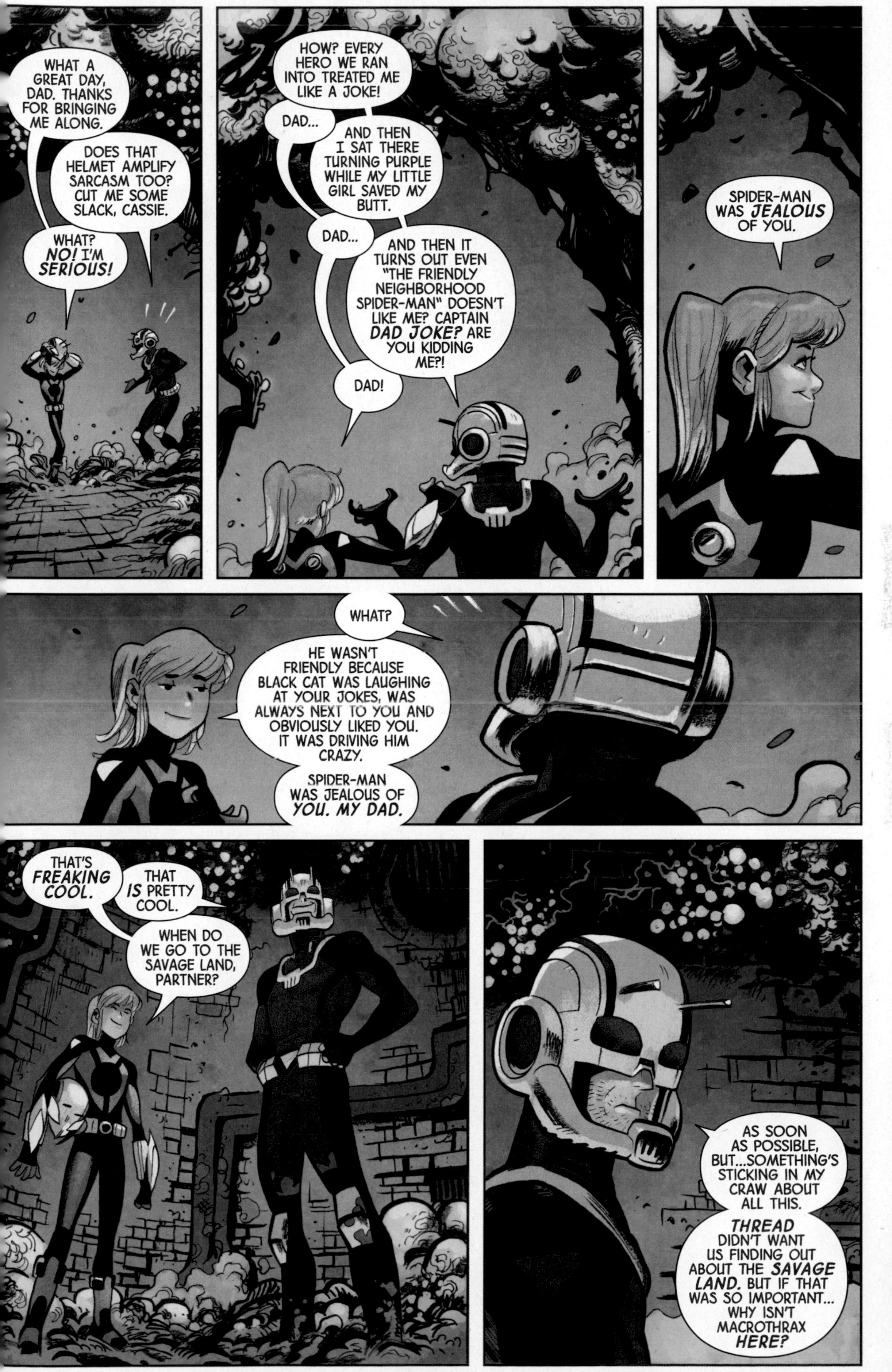
WHAT A GREAT DAY, DAD. THANKS FOR BRINGING ME ALONG.
DOES THAT HELMET AMPLIFY SARCASM TOO? CUT ME SOME SLACK, CASSIE.
WHAT? NO! I'M SERIOUS!
HOW? EVERY HERO WE RAN INTO TREATED ME LIKE A JOKE!
DAD...
AND THEN I SAT THERE TURNING PURPLE WHILE MY LITTLE GIRL SAVED MY BUTT.
DAD...
AND THEN IT TURNS OUT EVEN "THE FRIENDLY NEIGHBORHOOD SPIDER-MAN" DOESN'T LIKE ME? CAPTAIN DAD JOKE? ARE YOU KIDDING ME?!
DAD!
SPIDER-MAN WAS JEALOUS OF YOU.
WHAT?
HE WASN'T FRIENDLY BECAUSE BLACK CAT WAS LAUGHING AT YOUR JOKES, WAS ALWAYS NEXT TO YOU AND OBVIOUSLY LIKED YOU. IT WAS DRIVING HIM CRAZY.
SPIDER-MAN WAS JEALOUS OF YOU. MY DAD.
THAT'S FREAKING COOL.
THAT IS PRETTY COOL.
WHEN DO WE GO TO THE SAVAGE LAND, PARTNER?
AS SOON AS POSSIBLE, BUT...SOMETHING'S STICKING IN MY CRAW ABOUT ALL THIS.
THREAD DIDN'T WANT US FINDING OUT ABOUT THE SAVAGE LAND. BUT IF THAT WAS SO IMPORTANT... WHY ISN'T MACROTHRAX HERE?

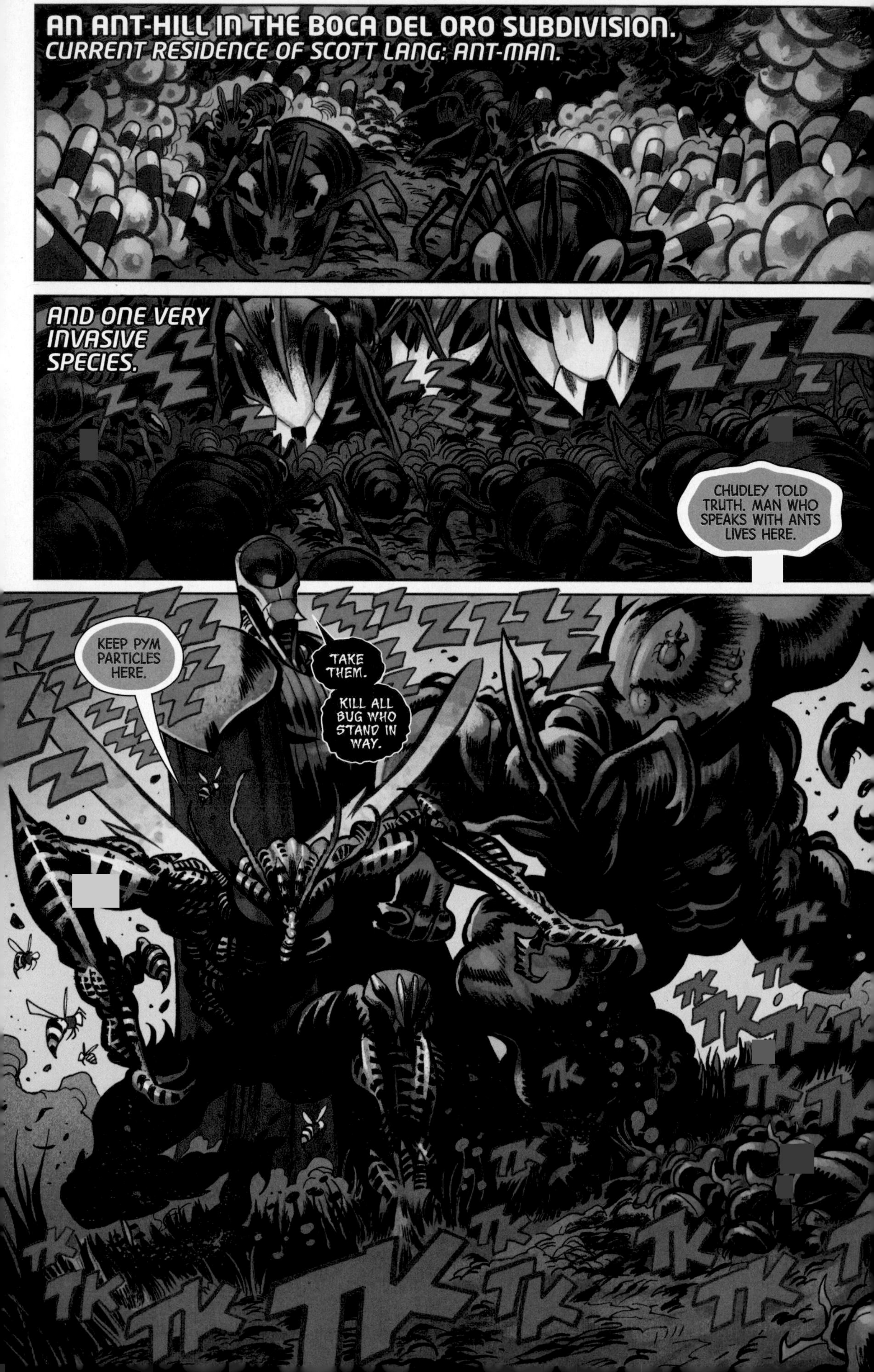
AN ANT-HILL IN THE BOCA DEL ORO SUBDIVISION.
CURRENT RESIDENCE OF SCOTT LANG: ANT-MAN.
AND ONE VERY INVASIVE SPECIES.
CHUDLEY TOLD TRUTH. MAN WHO SPEAKS WITH ANTS LIVES HERE.
KEEP PYM PARTICLES HERE.
TAKE THEM.
KILL ALL BUG WHO STAND IN WAY.

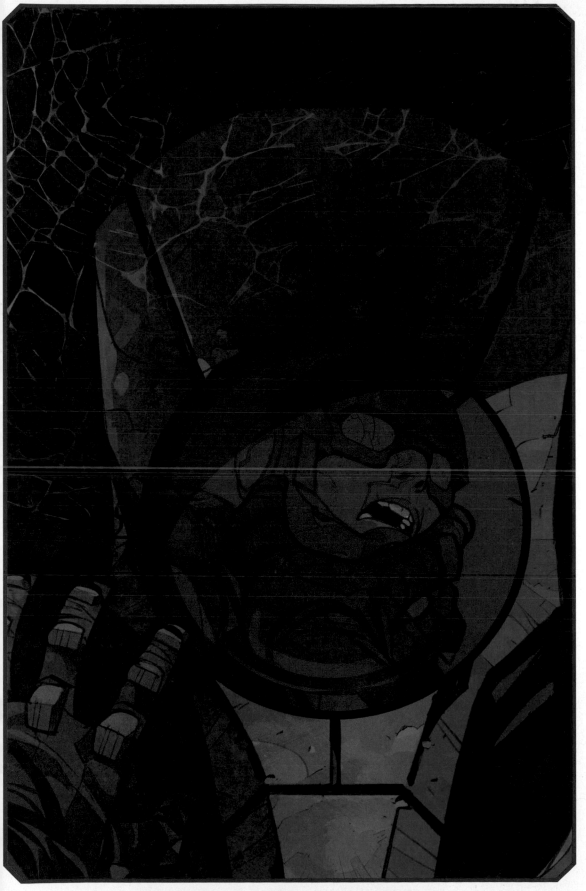

ANT-MAN #4 "WORLD HIVE PART 4"

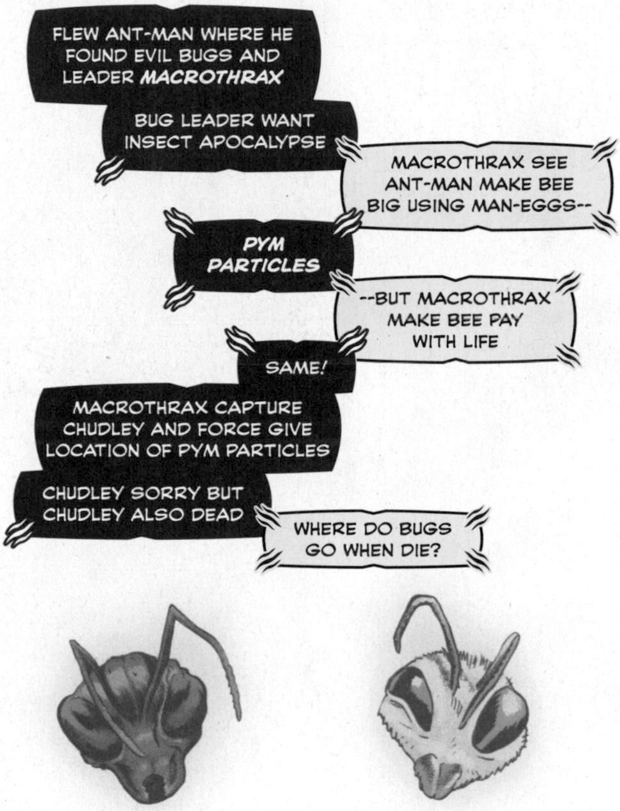
FLEW ANT-MAN WHERE HE FOUND EVIL BUGS AND LEADER *MACROTHRAX*
BUG LEADER WANT INSECT APOCALYPSE
MACROTHRAX SEE ANT-MAN MAKE BEE BIG USING MAN-EGGS--
PYM PARTICLES
--BUT MACROTHRAX MAKE BEE PAY WITH LIFE
SAME!
MACROTHRAX CAPTURE CHUDLEY AND FORCE GIVE LOCATION OF PYM PARTICLES
CHUDLEY SORRY BUT CHUDLEY ALSO DEAD
WHERE DO BUGS GO WHEN DIE?

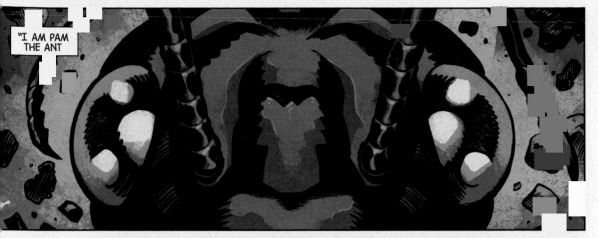

"I AM PAM THE ANT

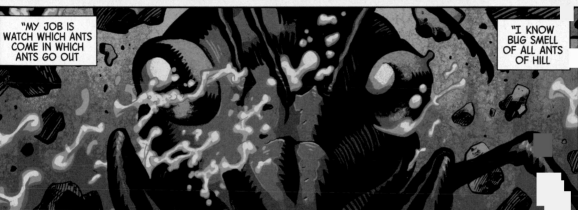

"MY JOB IS WATCH WHICH ANTS COME IN WHICH ANTS GO OUT

"I KNOW BUG SMELL OF ALL ANTS OF HILL

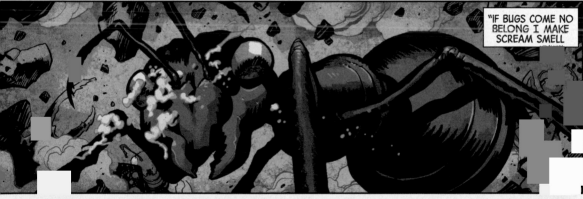

"IF BUGS COME NO BELONG I MAKE SCREAM SMELL

"I COULD NOT MAKE SCREAM SMELL ENOUGH

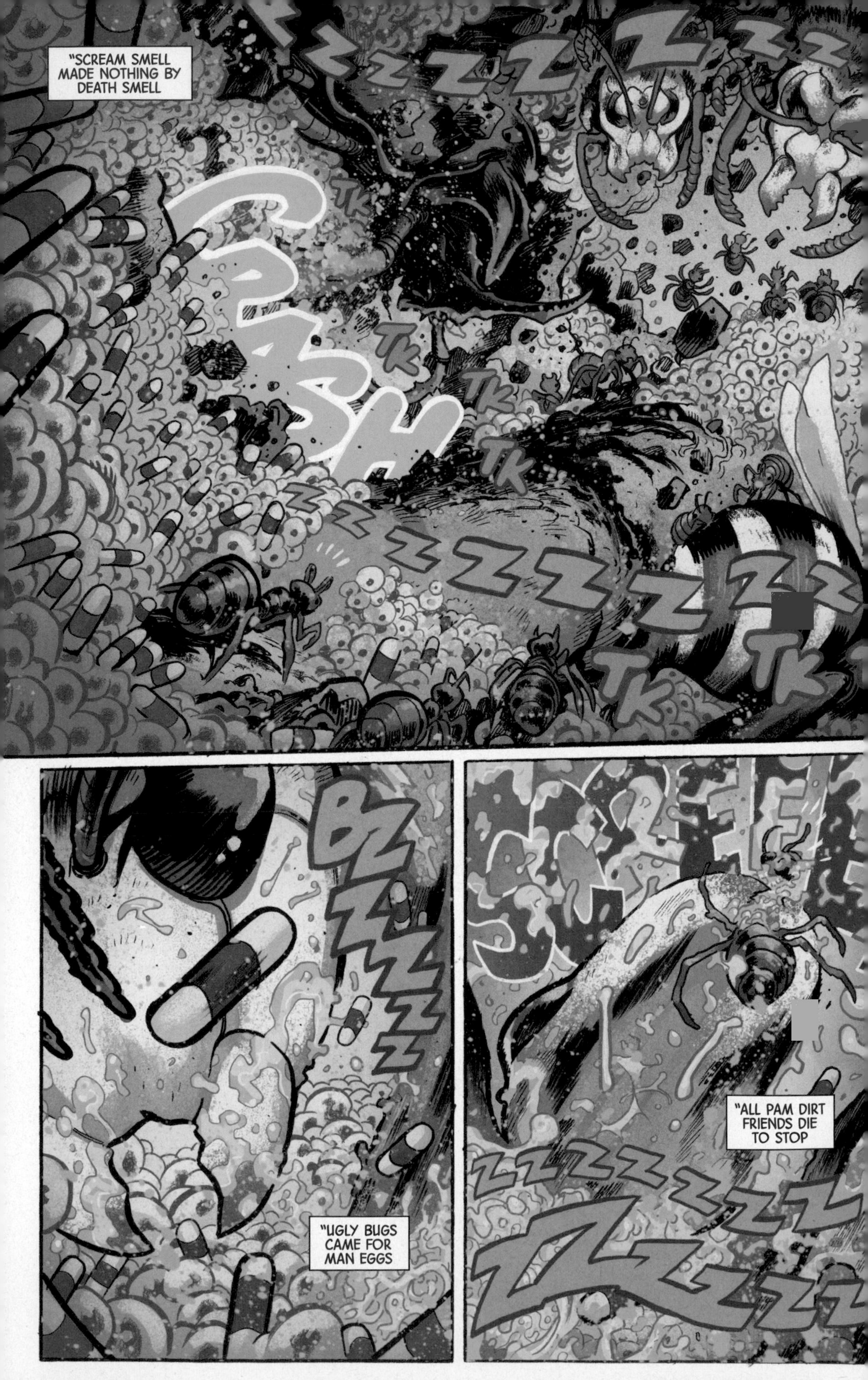
"SCREAM SMELL MADE NOTHING BY DEATH SMELL
CRASH
TK
TK
TK
TK
TK
TK
"UGLY BUGS CAME FOR MAN EGGS
"ALL PAM DIRT FRIENDS DIE TO STOP

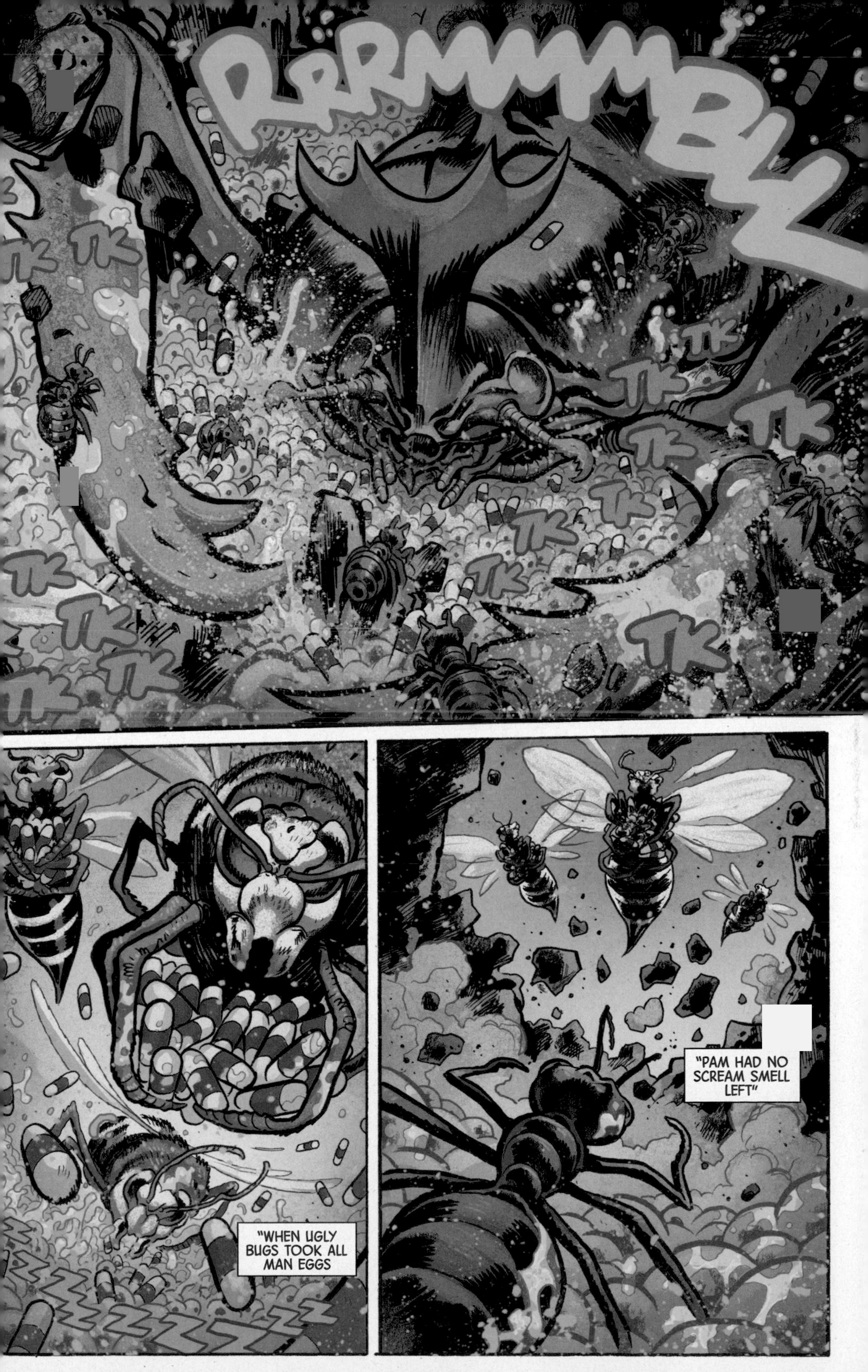
"WHEN UGLY BUGS TOOK ALL MAN EGGS
"PAM HAD NO SCREAM SMELL LEFT"

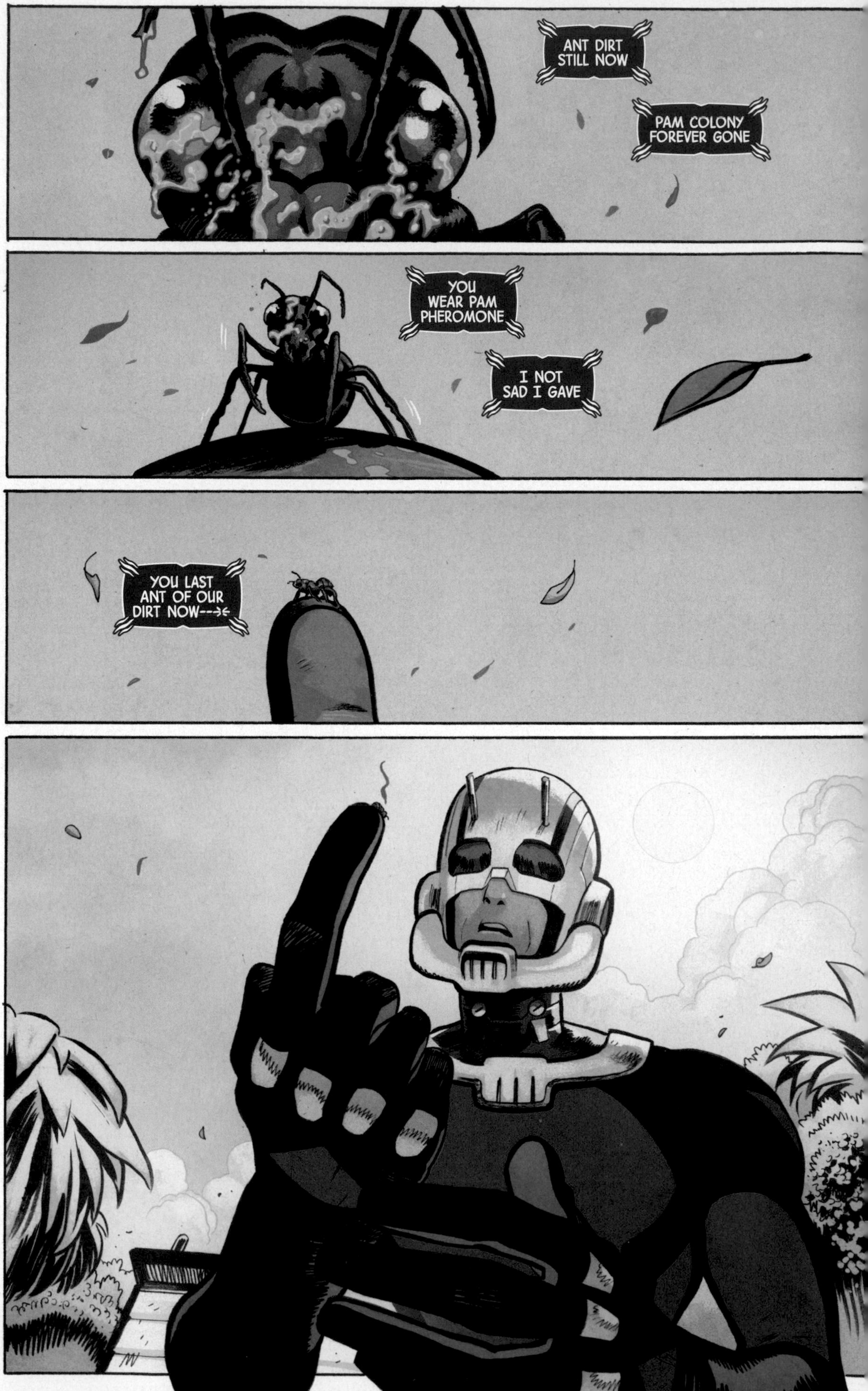
ANT DIRT STILL NOW
PAM COLONY FOREVER GONE
YOU WEAR PAM PHEROMONE
I NOT SAD I GAVE
YOU LAST ANT OF OUR DIRT NOW--

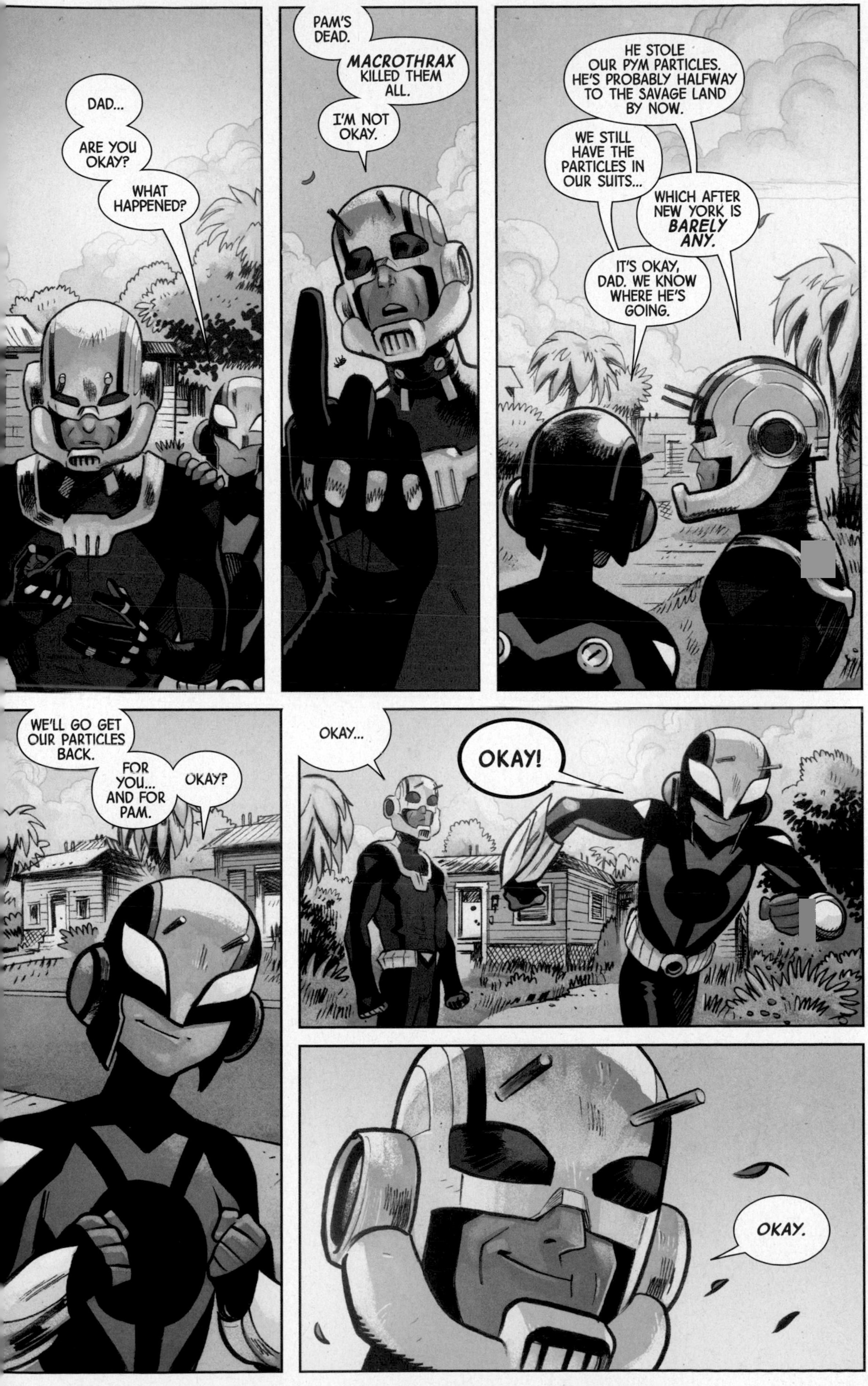
DAD...
ARE YOU OKAY?
WHAT HAPPENED?
PAM'S DEAD.
MACROTHRAX KILLED THEM ALL.
I'M NOT OKAY.
HE STOLE OUR PYM PARTICLES. HE'S PROBABLY HALFWAY TO THE SAVAGE LAND BY NOW.
WE STILL HAVE THE PARTICLES IN OUR SUITS...
WHICH AFTER NEW YORK IS BARELY ANY.
IT'S OKAY, DAD. WE KNOW WHERE HE'S GOING.
WE'LL GO GET OUR PARTICLES BACK.
FOR YOU... AND FOR PAM.
OKAY?
OKAY...
OKAY!
OKAY.

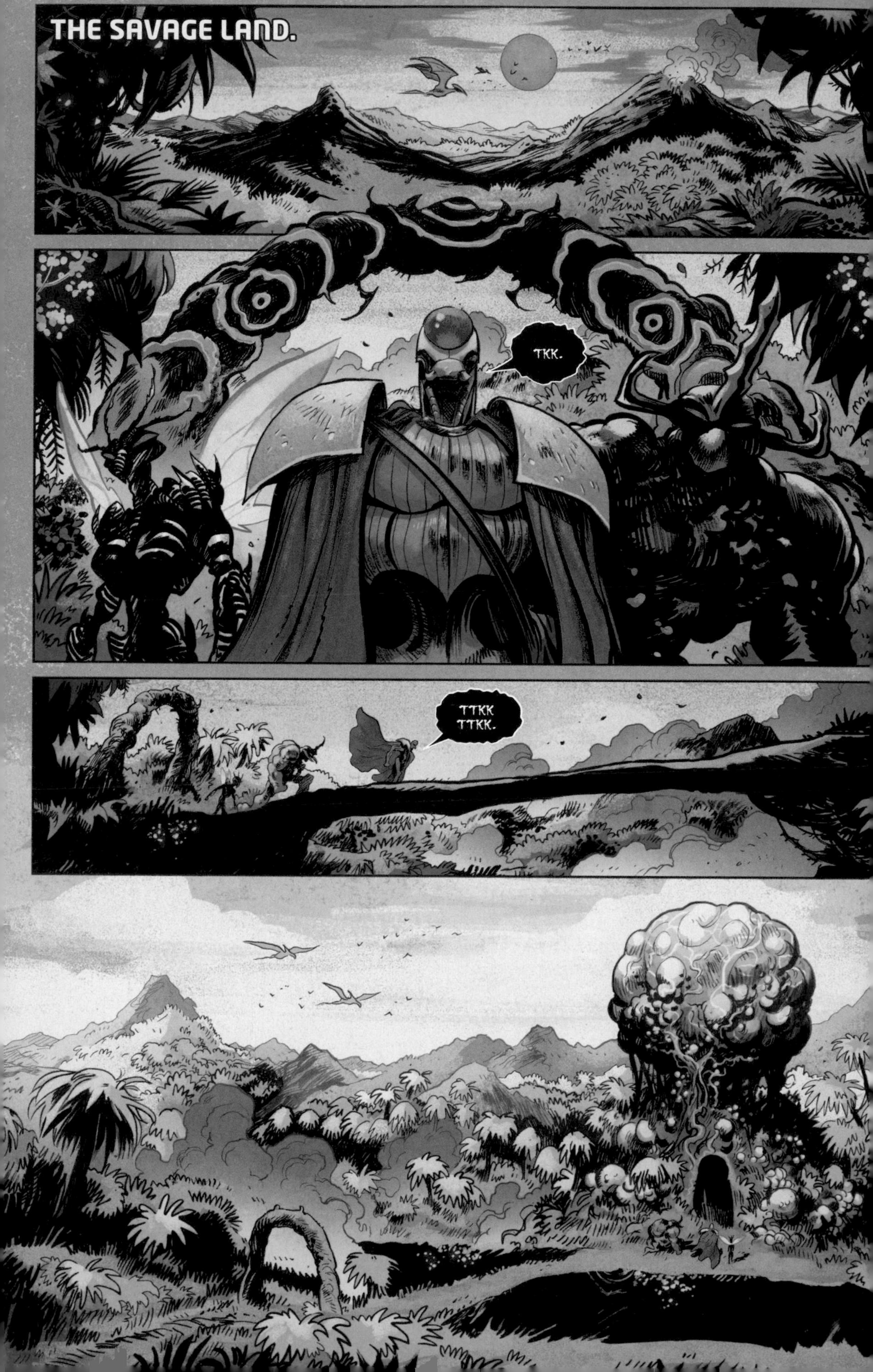
THE SAVAGE LAND.
TKK.
TTKK TTKK.

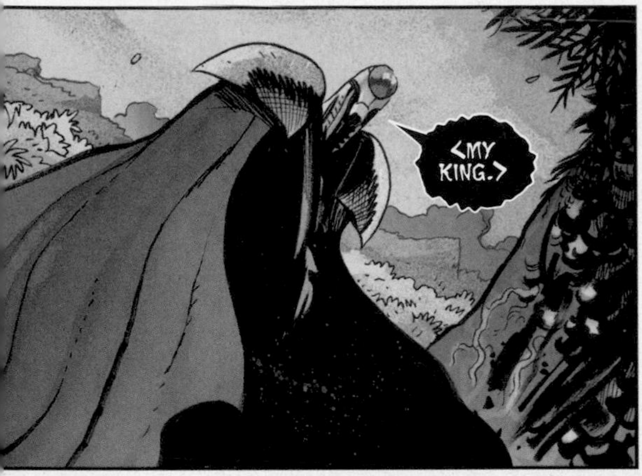
<MY KING.>

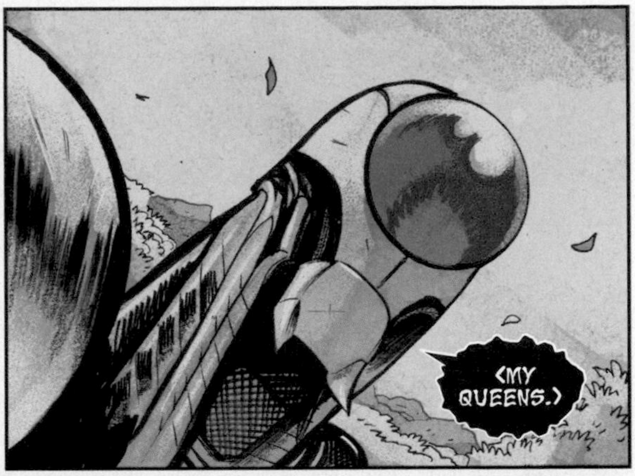
<MY QUEENS.>

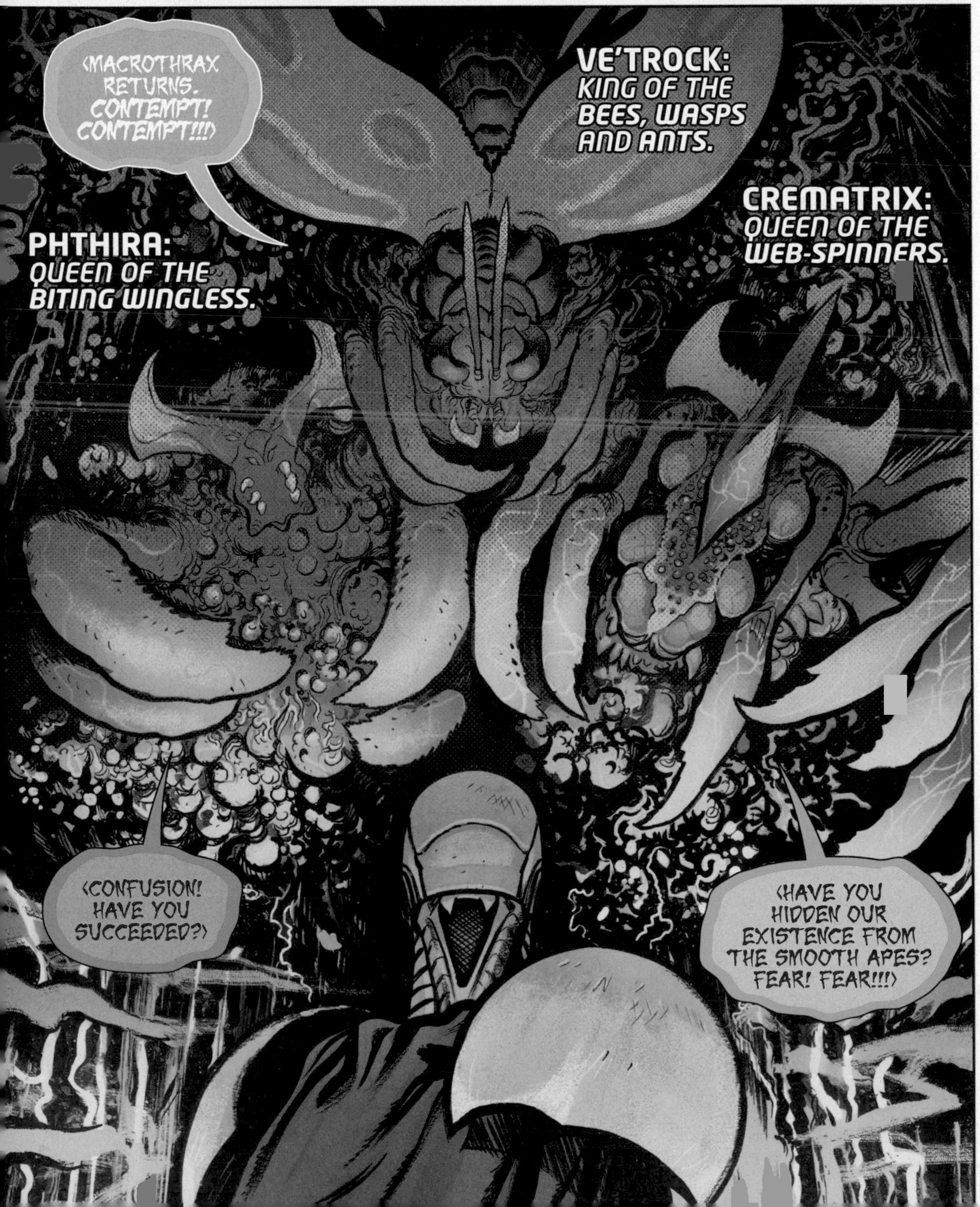
VE'TROCK: KING OF THE BEES, WASPS AND ANTS.
PHTHIRA: QUEEN OF THE BITING WINGLESS.
CREMATRIX: QUEEN OF THE WEB-SPINNERS.
<MACROTHRAX RETURNS. CONTEMPT! CONTEMPT!!!>
<CONFUSION! HAVE YOU SUCCEEDED?>
<HAVE YOU HIDDEN OUR EXISTENCE FROM THE SMOOTH APES? FEAR! FEAR!!!>

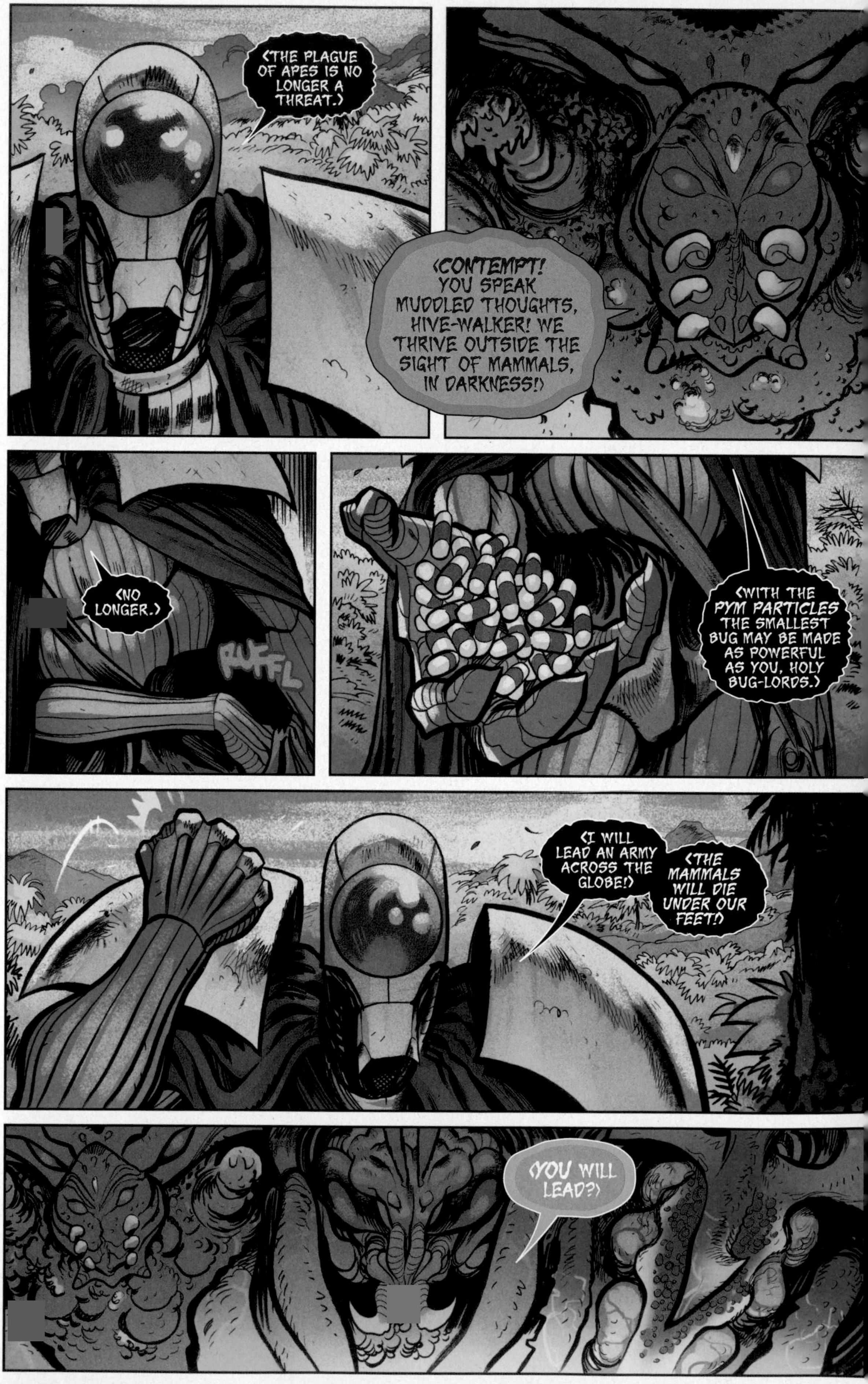

<THE PLAGUE OF APES IS NO LONGER A THREAT.>
<CONTEMPT! YOU SPEAK MUDDLED THOUGHTS, HIVE-WALKER! WE THRIVE OUTSIDE THE SIGHT OF MAMMALS, IN DARKNESS!>
<NO LONGER.>
RUFFL
<WITH THE PYM PARTICLES THE SMALLEST BUG MAY BE MADE AS POWERFUL AS YOU, HOLY BUG-LORDS.>
<I WILL LEAD AN ARMY ACROSS THE GLOBE!>
<THE MAMMALS WILL DIE UNDER OUR FEET!>
<YOU WILL LEAD?>

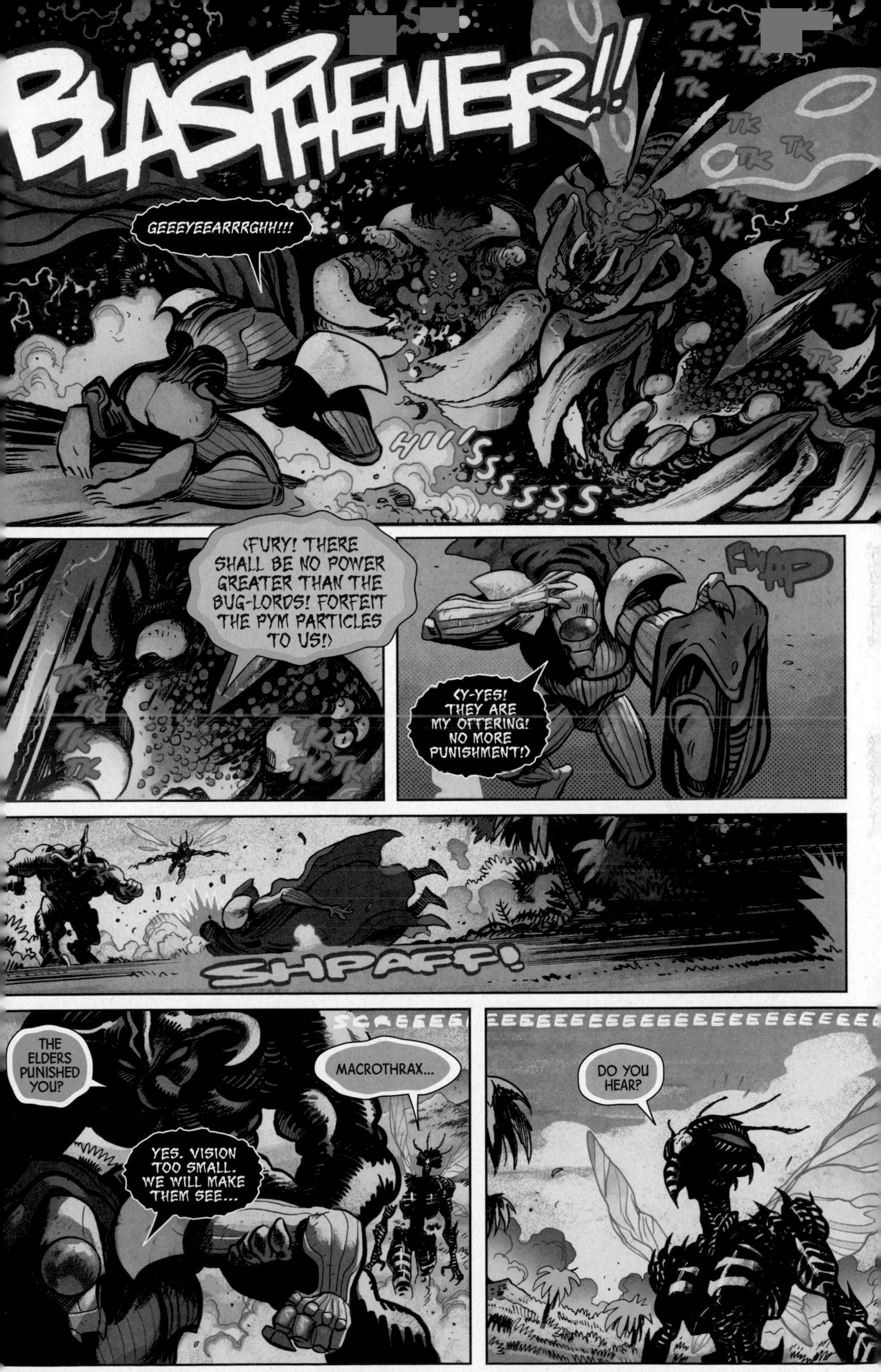

BLASPHEMER!!
TK TK TK TK
GEEEYEEARRRGHH!!!
TK TK TK TK TK TK TK TK TK
H'''SSSSSSS
‹FURY! THERE SHALL BE NO POWER GREATER THAN THE BUG-LORDS! FORFEIT THE PYM PARTICLES TO US!›
TK TK TK TK TK TK TK
FWAP
‹Y-YES! THEY ARE MY OFFERING! NO MORE PUNISHMENT!›
SHPAFF!
SCREEEEEEEEEEEEEEEEEEEEEEEEEEEE
THE ELDERS PUNISHED YOU?
MACROTHRAX...
YES. VISION TOO SMALL. WE WILL MAKE THEM SEE...
DO YOU HEAR?

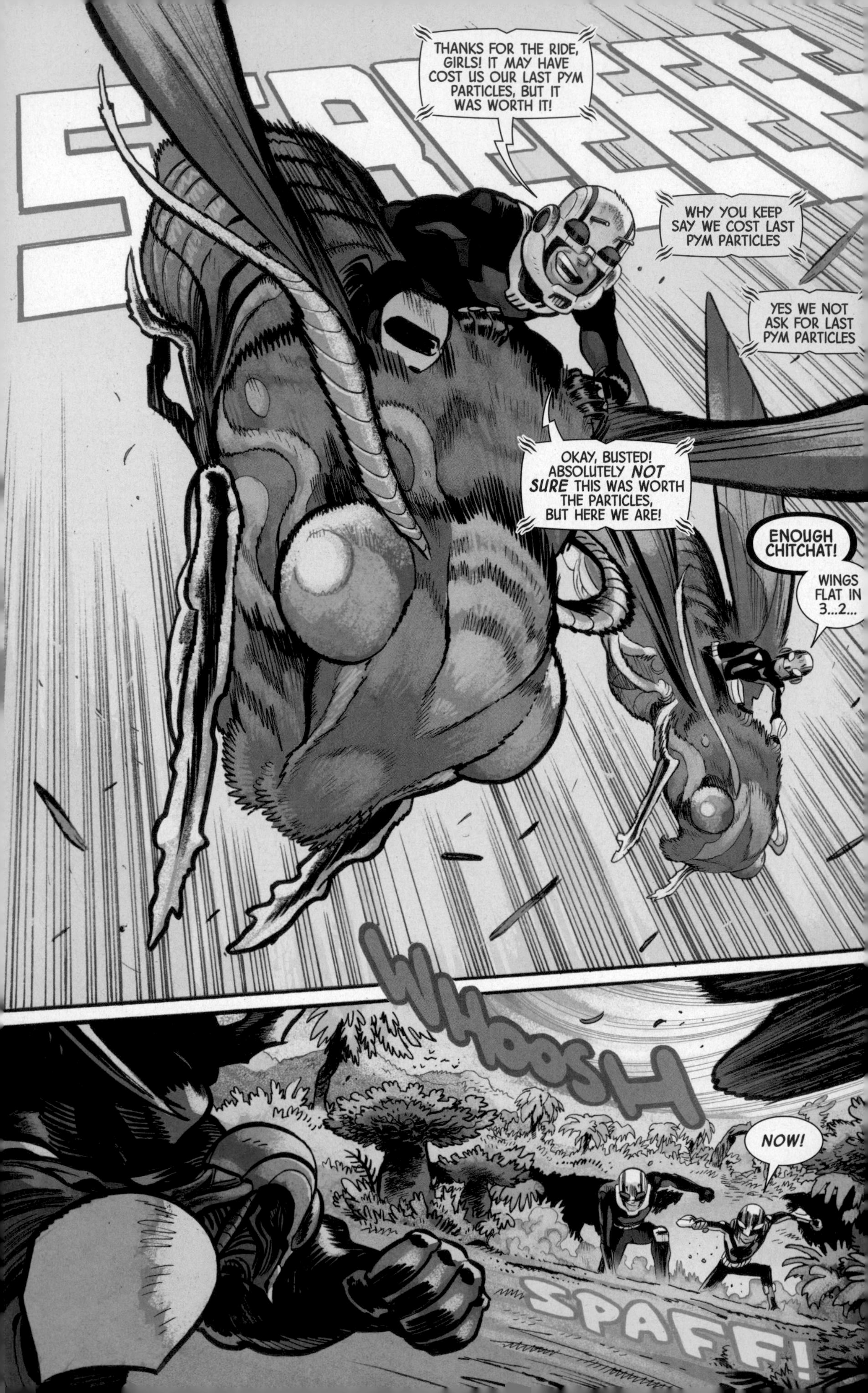
THANKS FOR THE RIDE, GIRLS! IT MAY HAVE COST US OUR LAST PYM PARTICLES, BUT IT WAS WORTH IT!
WHY YOU KEEP SAY WE COST LAST PYM PARTICLES
YES WE NOT ASK FOR LAST PYM PARTICLES
OKAY, BUSTED! ABSOLUTELY *NOT SURE* THIS WAS WORTH THE PARTICLES, BUT HERE WE ARE!
ENOUGH CHITCHAT!
WINGS FLAT IN 3...2...
WHOOSH
NOW!
SPAFF!

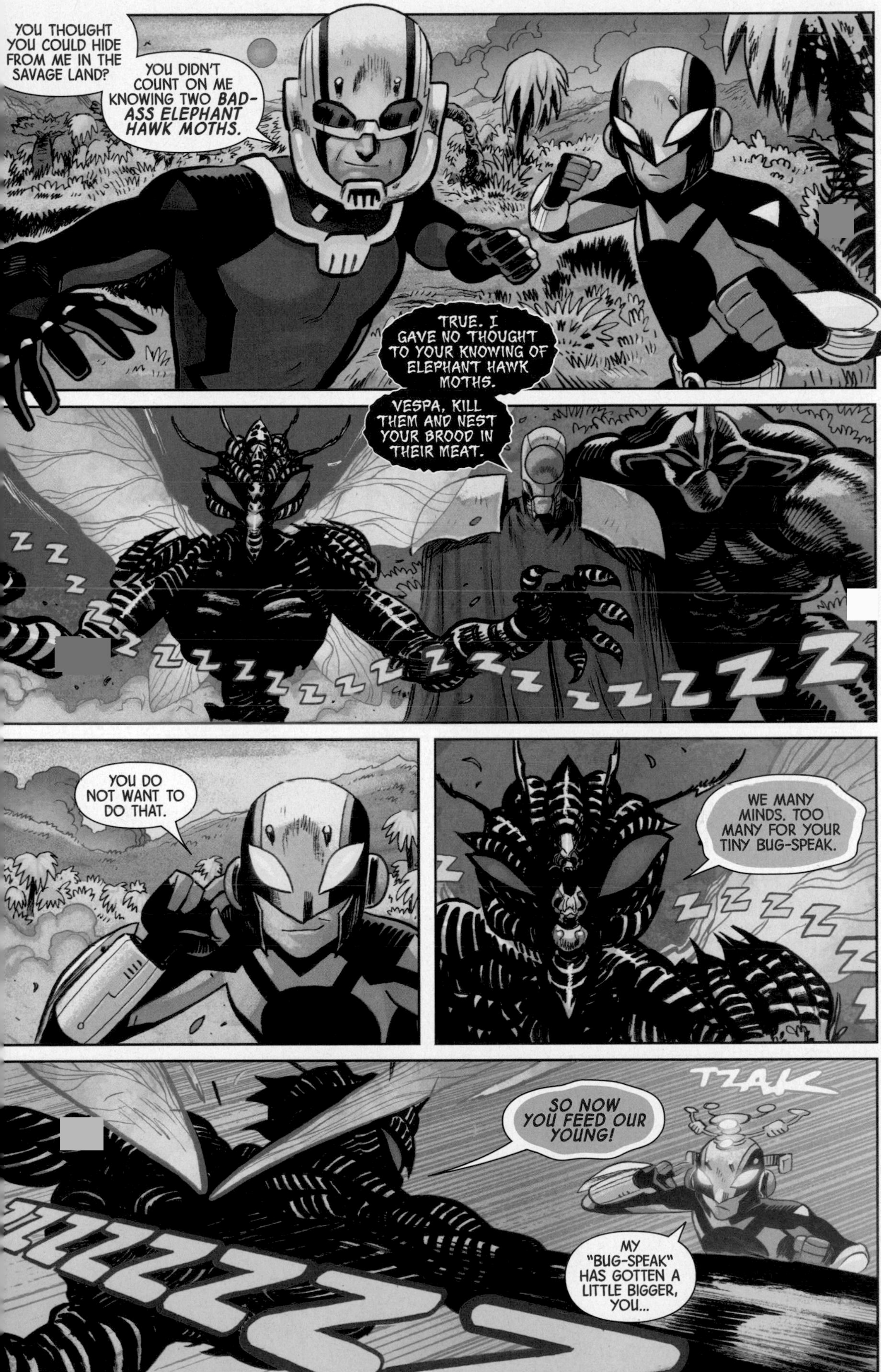

YOU THOUGHT YOU COULD HIDE FROM ME IN THE SAVAGE LAND?
YOU DIDN'T COUNT ON ME KNOWING TWO BAD-ASS ELEPHANT HAWK MOTHS.
TRUE. I GAVE NO THOUGHT TO YOUR KNOWING OF ELEPHANT HAWK MOTHS.
VESPA, KILL THEM AND NEST YOUR BROOD IN THEIR MEAT.
YOU DO NOT WANT TO DO THAT.
WE MANY MINDS. TOO MANY FOR YOUR TINY BUG-SPEAK.
TZAK
SO NOW YOU FEED OUR YOUNG!
MY "BUG-SPEAK" HAS GOTTEN A LITTLE BIGGER, YOU...

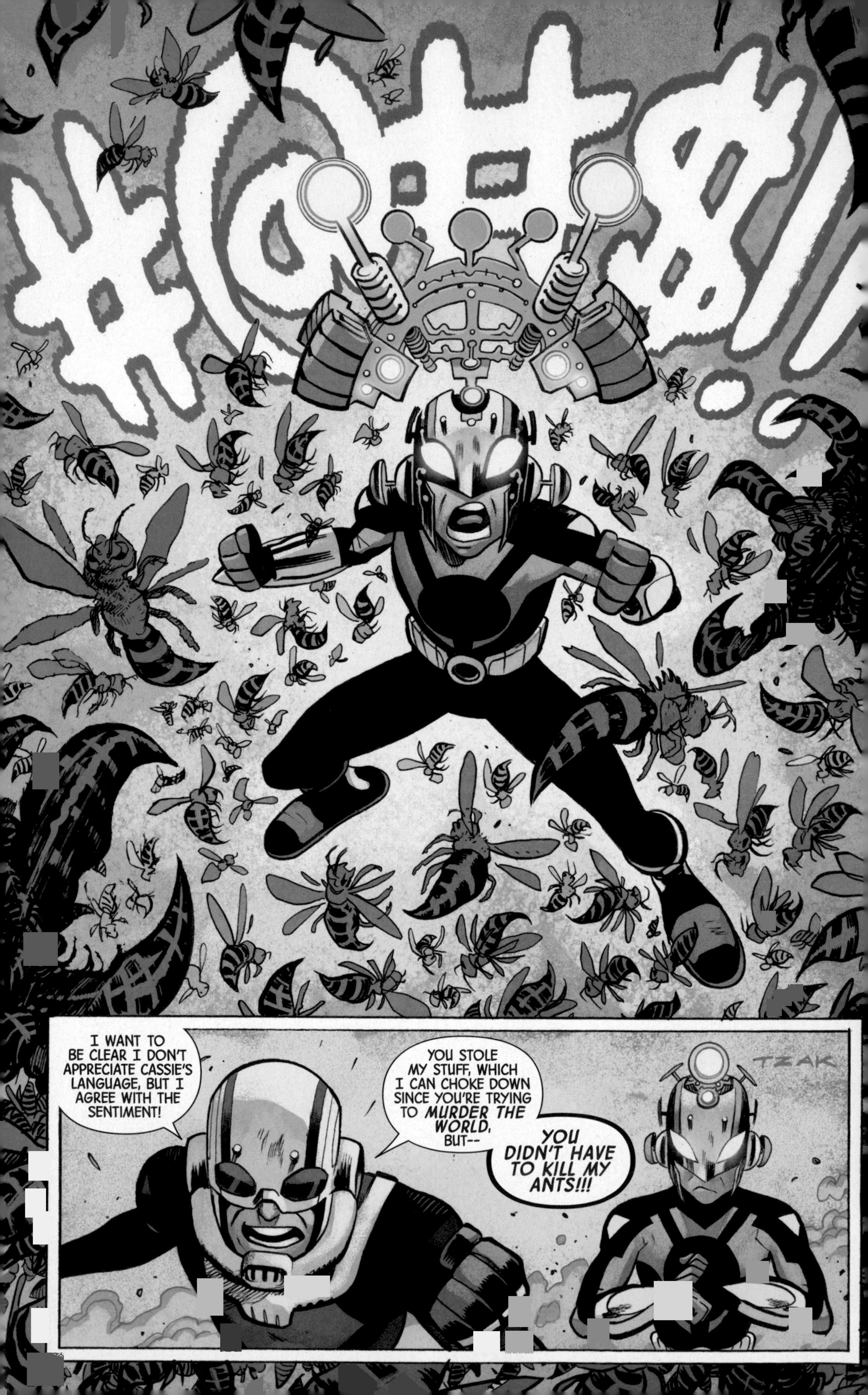
I WANT TO BE CLEAR I DON'T APPRECIATE CASSIE'S LANGUAGE, BUT I AGREE WITH THE SENTIMENT!
YOU STOLE MY STUFF, WHICH I CAN CHOKE DOWN SINCE YOU'RE TRYING TO *MURDER THE WORLD,* BUT--
YOU DIDN'T HAVE TO KILL MY ANTS!!!
TZAK

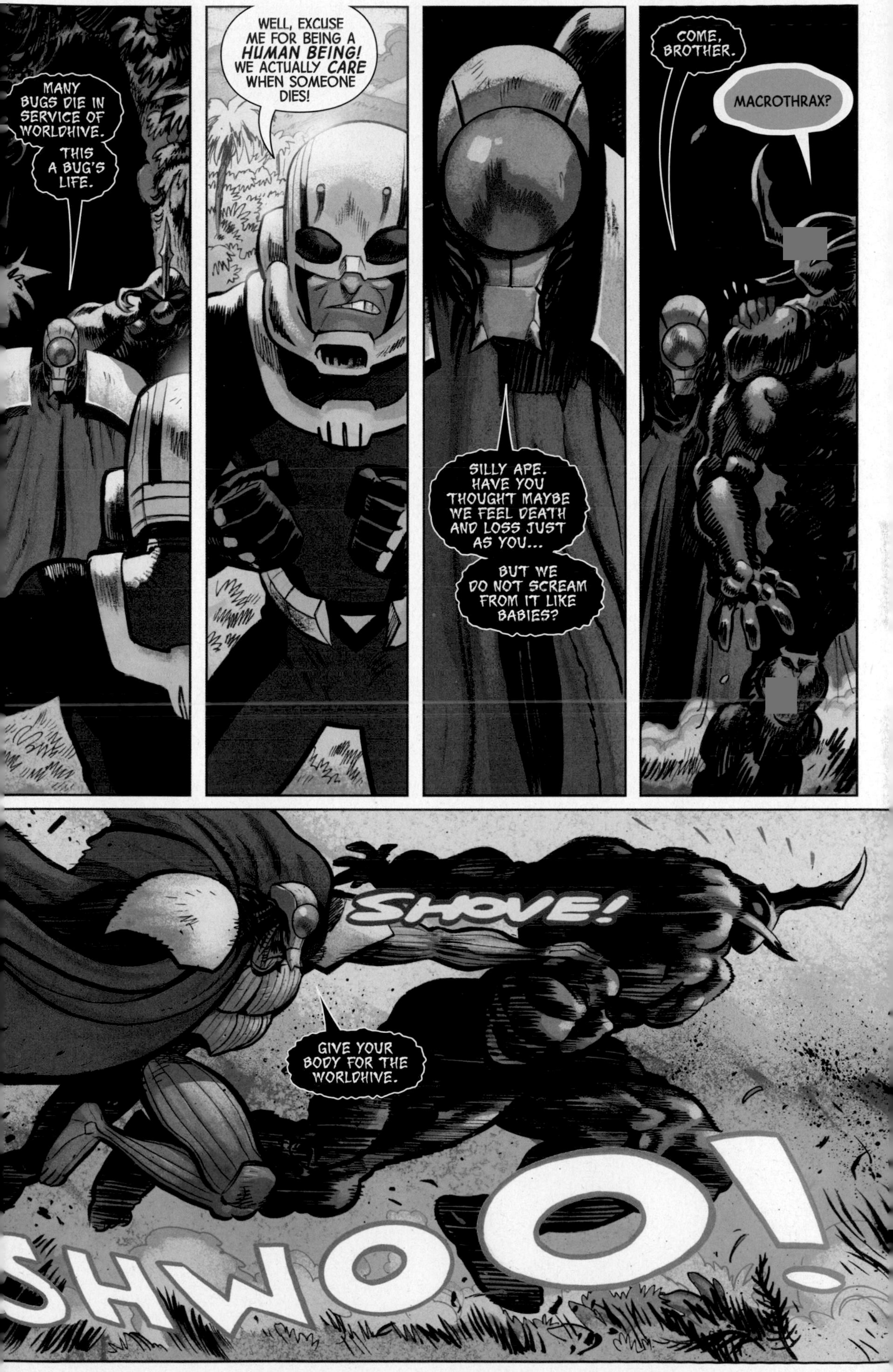
MANY BUGS DIE IN SERVICE OF WORLDHIVE.
THIS A BUG'S LIFE.
WELL, EXCUSE ME FOR BEING A HUMAN BEING! WE ACTUALLY CARE WHEN SOMEONE DIES!
SILLY APE. HAVE YOU THOUGHT MAYBE WE FEEL DEATH AND LOSS JUST AS YOU...
BUT WE DO NOT SCREAM FROM IT LIKE BABIES?
COME, BROTHER.
MACROTHRAX?
SHOVE!
GIVE YOUR BODY FOR THE WORLDHIVE.
SHWOOO!

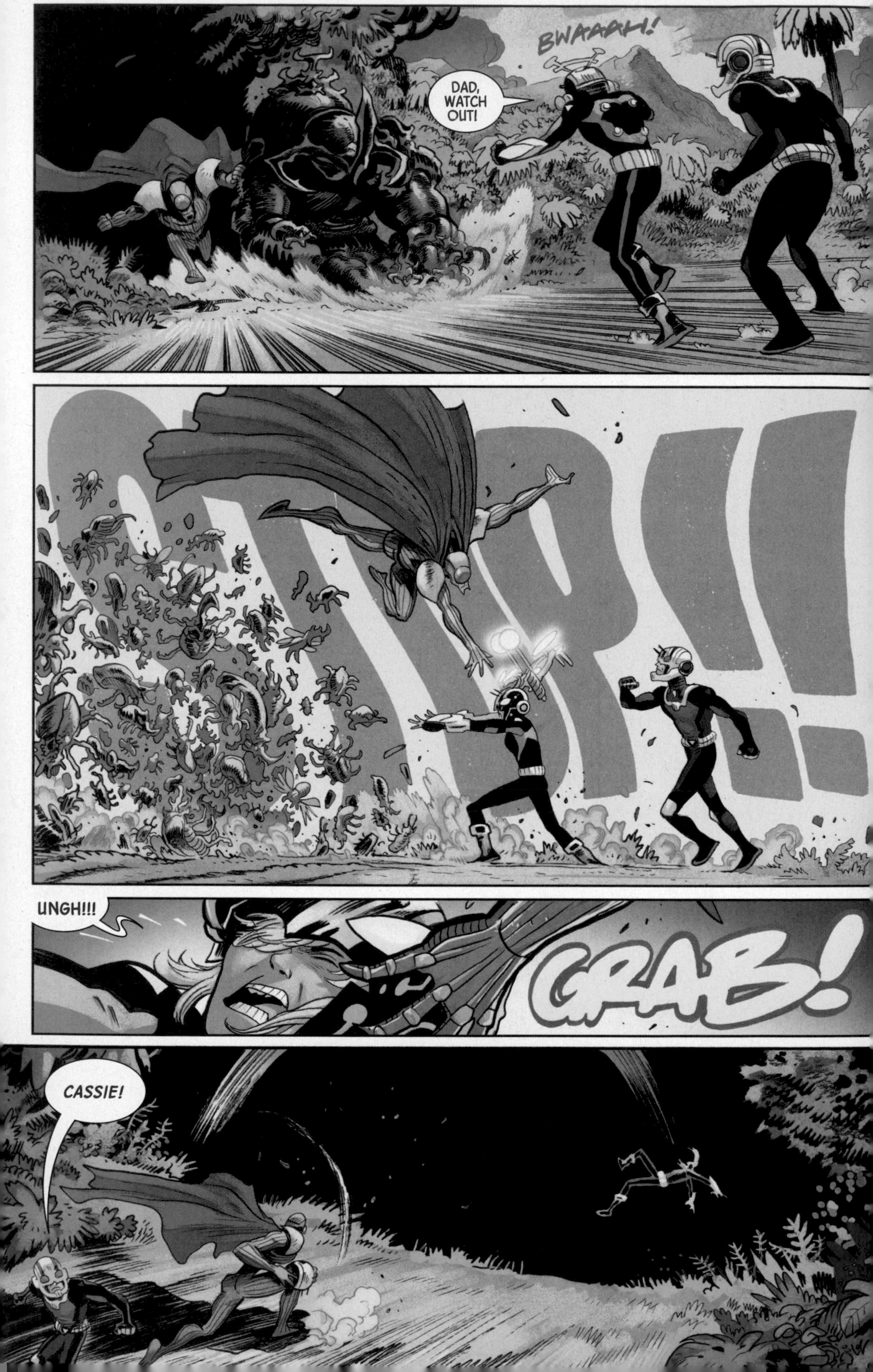
BWAAAH!
DAD, WATCH OUT!
UNGH!!!
GRAB!
CASSIE!

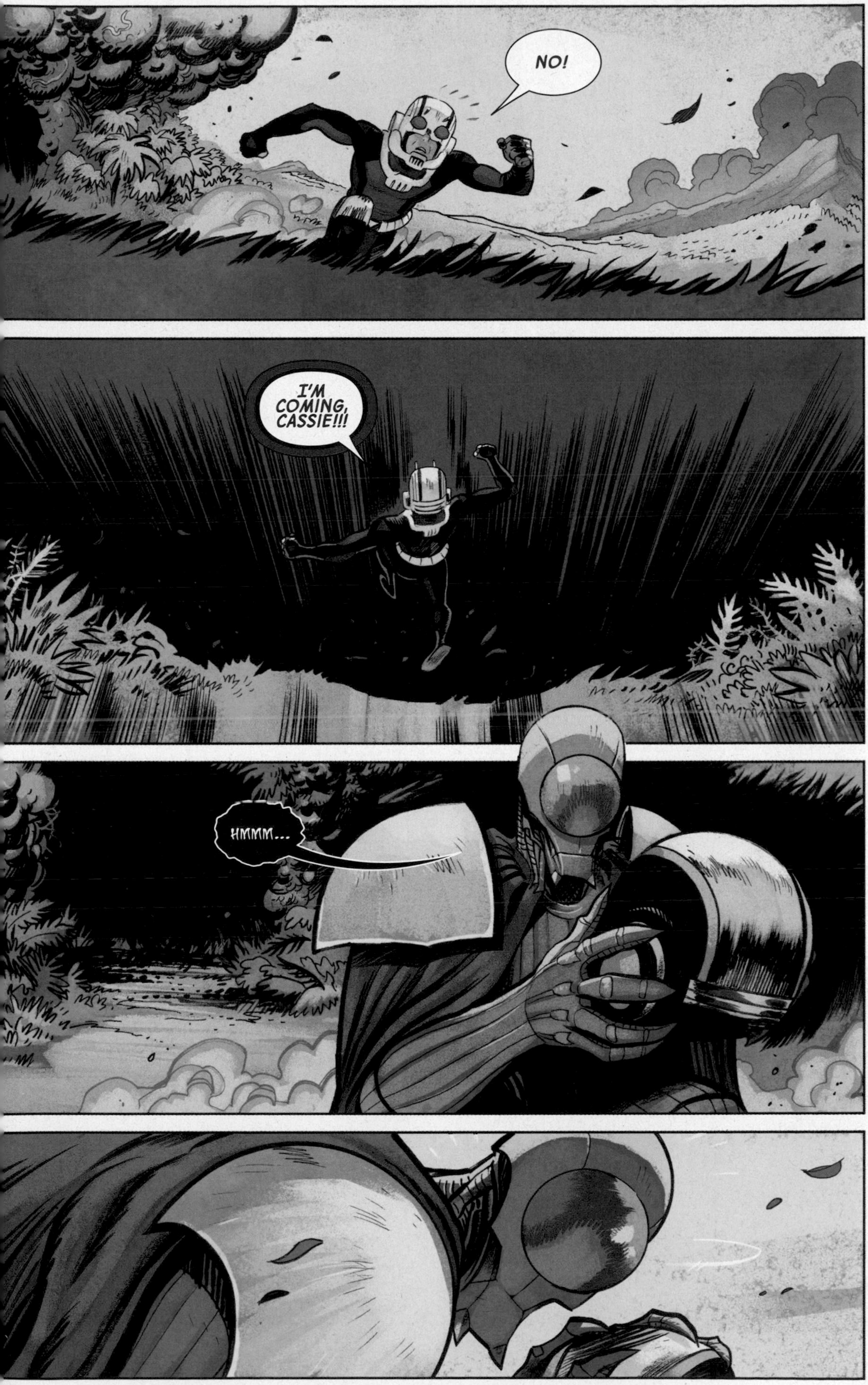
NO!
I'M COMING, CASSIE!!!
HMMM...

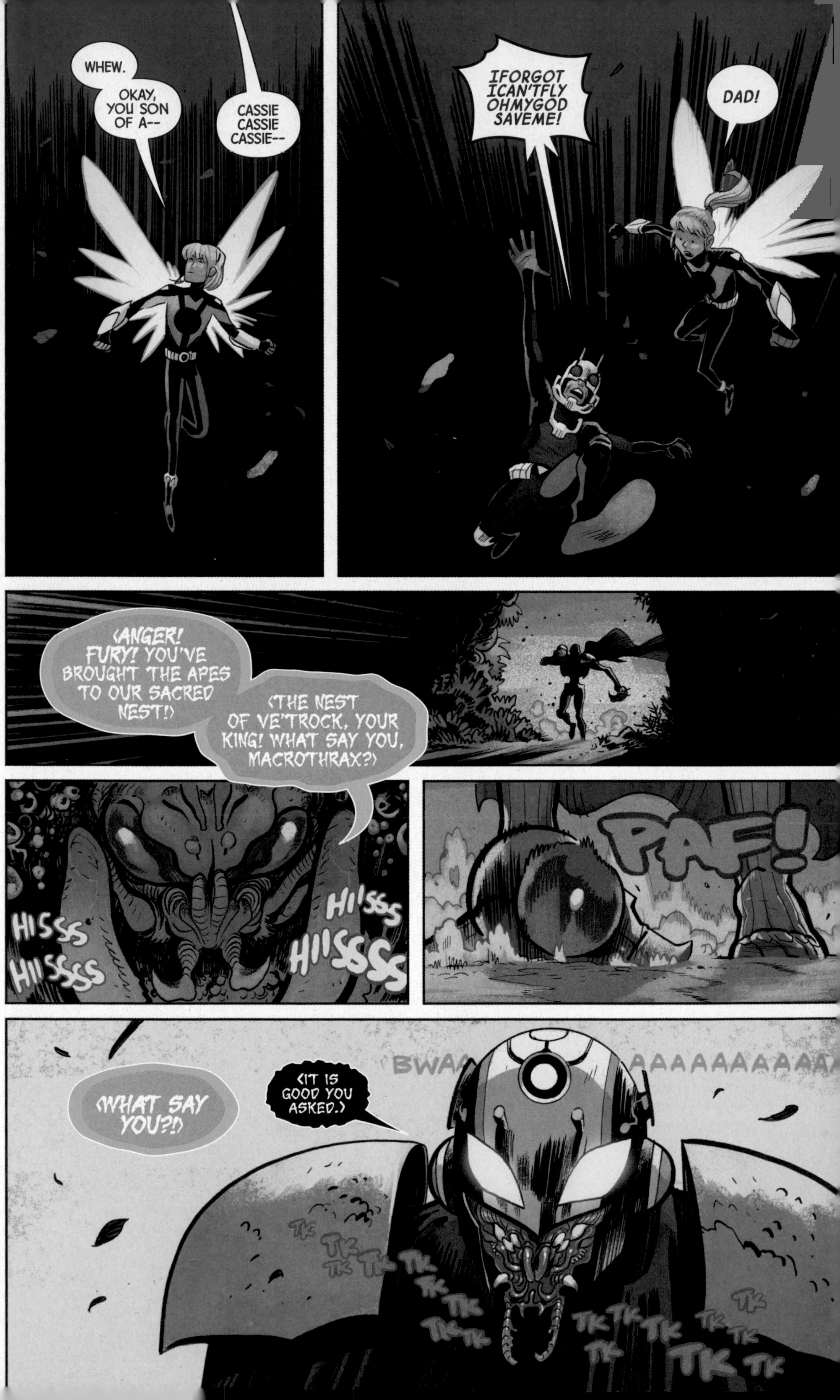
WHEW.
OKAY, YOU SON OF A--
CASSIE CASSIE CASSIE--
IFORGOT ICAN'TFLY OHMYGOD SAVEME!
DAD!
‹ANGER! FURY! YOU'VE BROUGHT THE APES TO OUR SACRED NEST!›
‹THE NEST OF VE'TROCK, YOUR KING! WHAT SAY YOU, MACROTHRAX?›
HISSSS HIISSSS
HI'SSS HIISSSS
PAF!
BWAAAAAAAAAAAAAA
‹WHAT SAY YOU?!›
‹IT IS GOOD YOU ASKED.›
TK TK TK TK TK TK TK TK TK TK TK TK TK TK TK TK TK

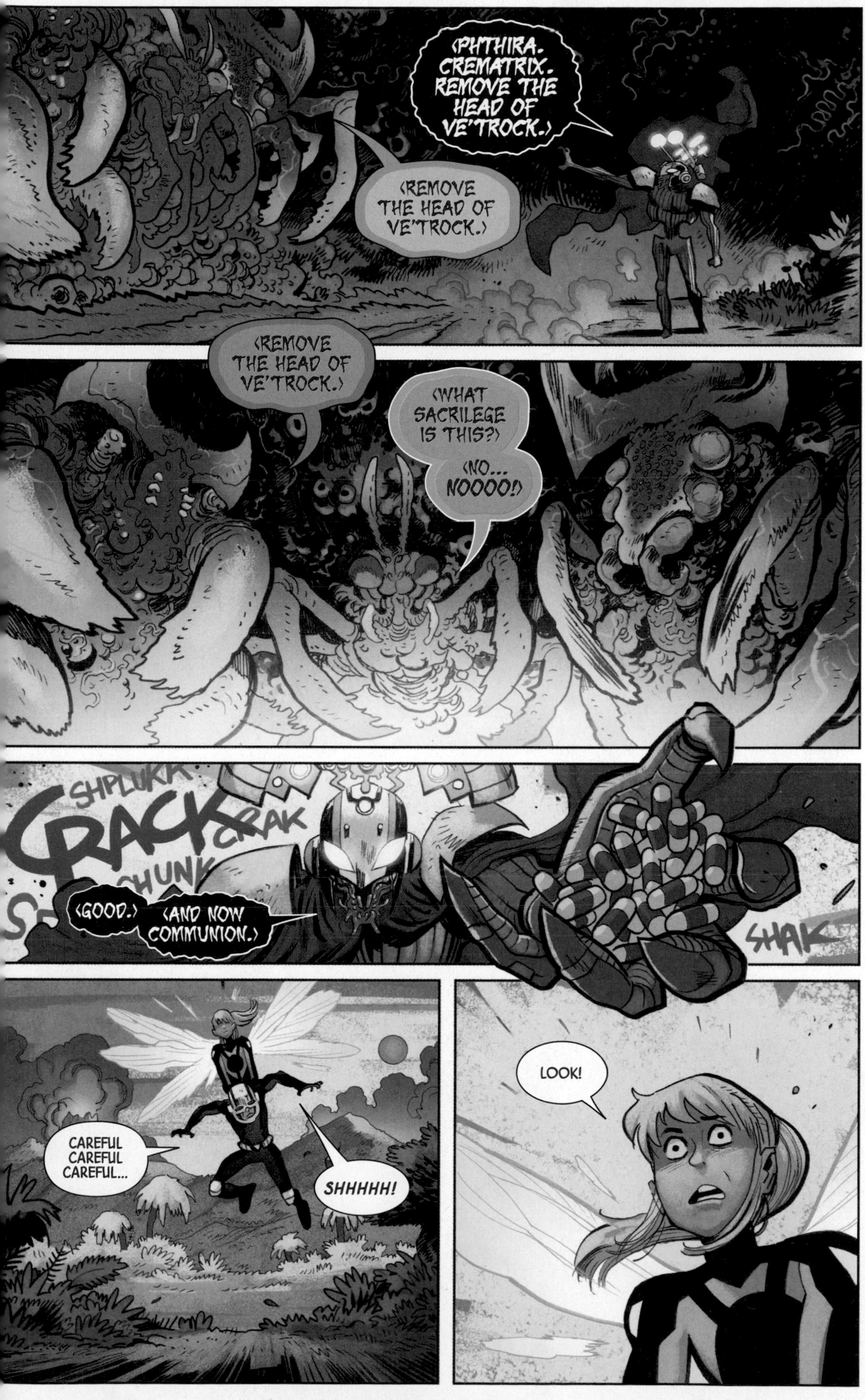
‹PH'THIRA. CREMATRIX. REMOVE THE HEAD OF VE'TROCK.›
‹REMOVE THE HEAD OF VE'TROCK.›
‹REMOVE THE HEAD OF VE'TROCK.›
‹WHAT SACRILEGE IS THIS?›
‹NO... NOOOO!›
SHPLUKK
CRACK
CRAK
CHUNK
‹GOOD.›
‹AND NOW COMMUNION.›
SHAK
CAREFUL CAREFUL CAREFUL...
SHHHHH!
LOOK!

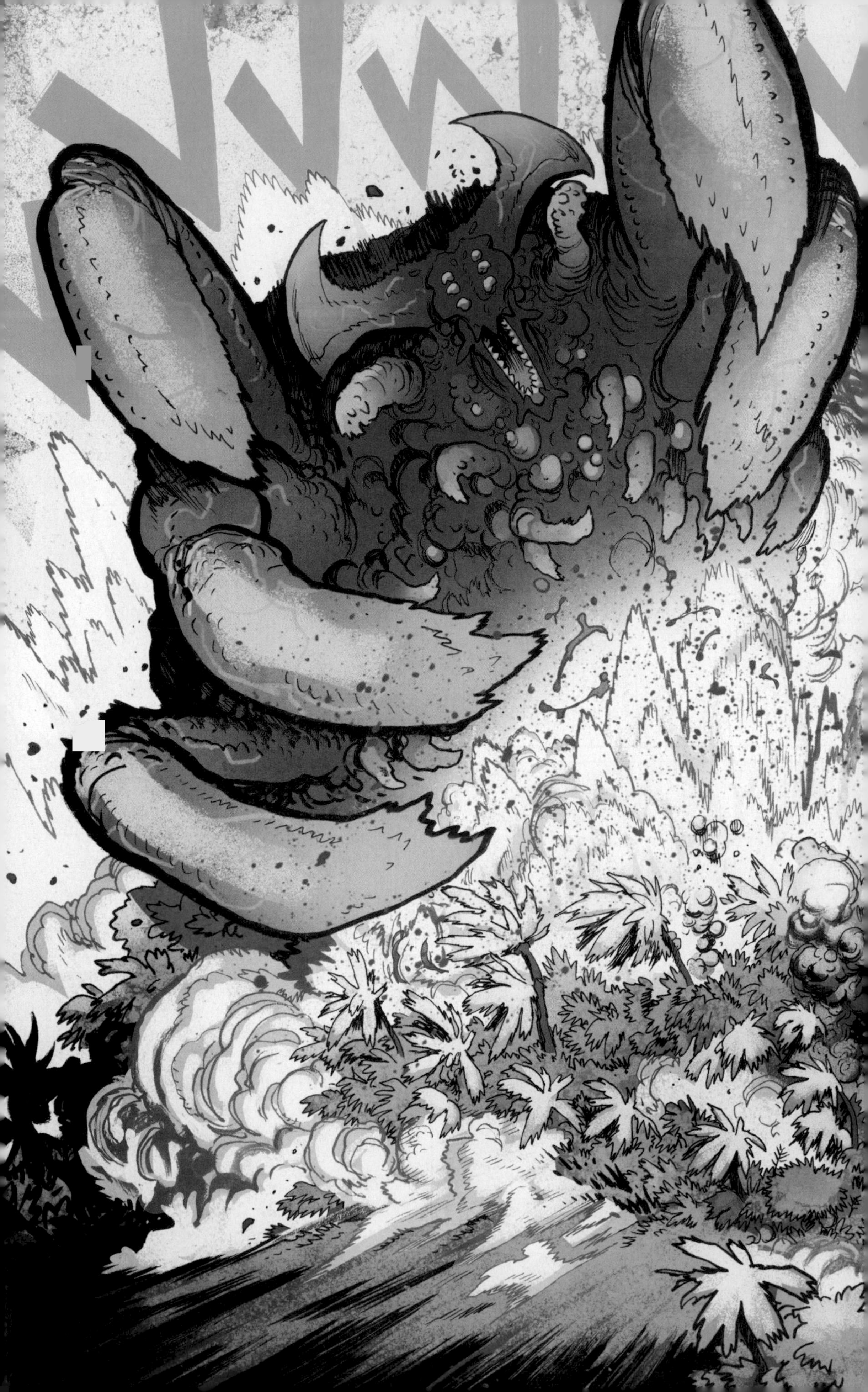

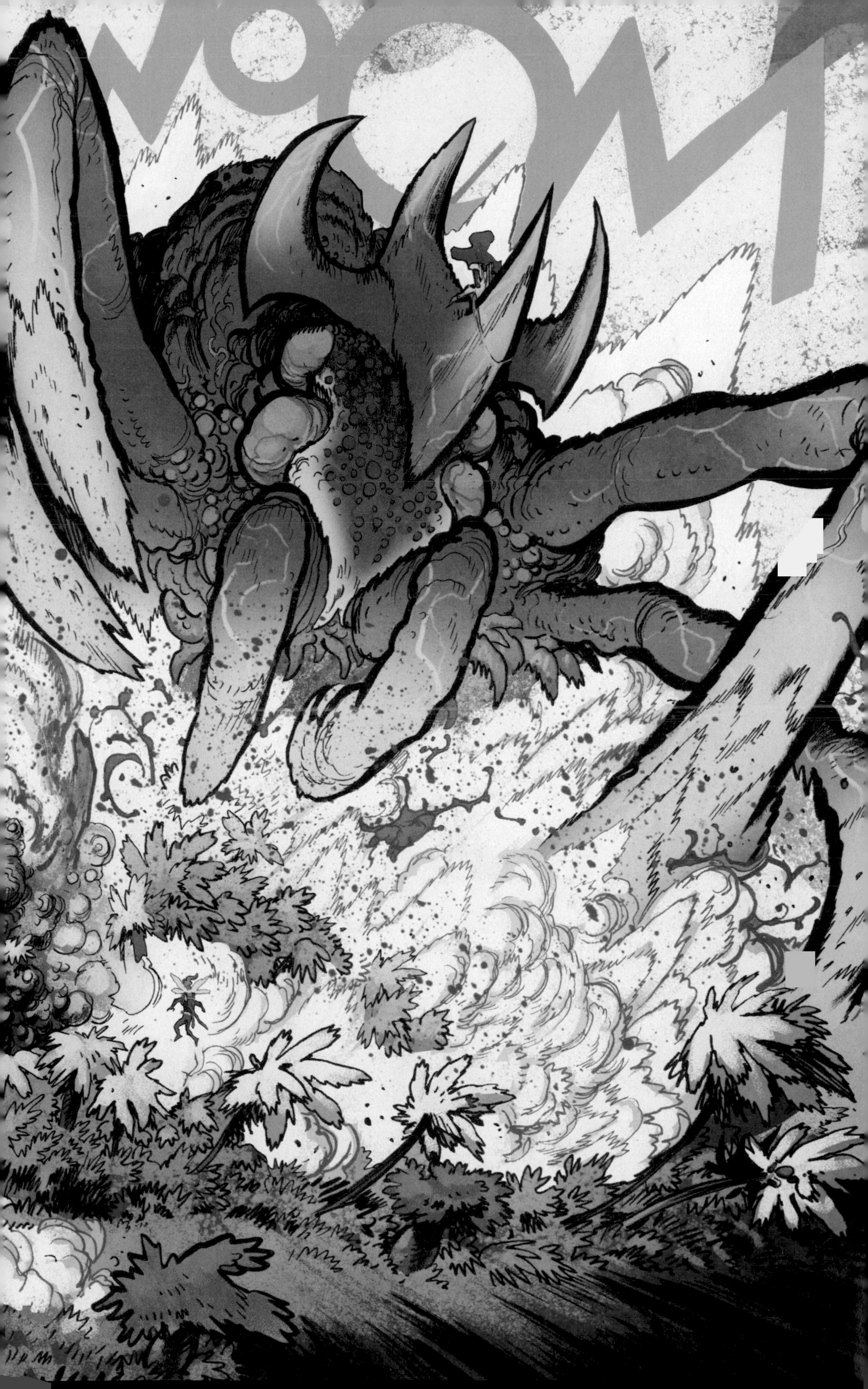
VOOM

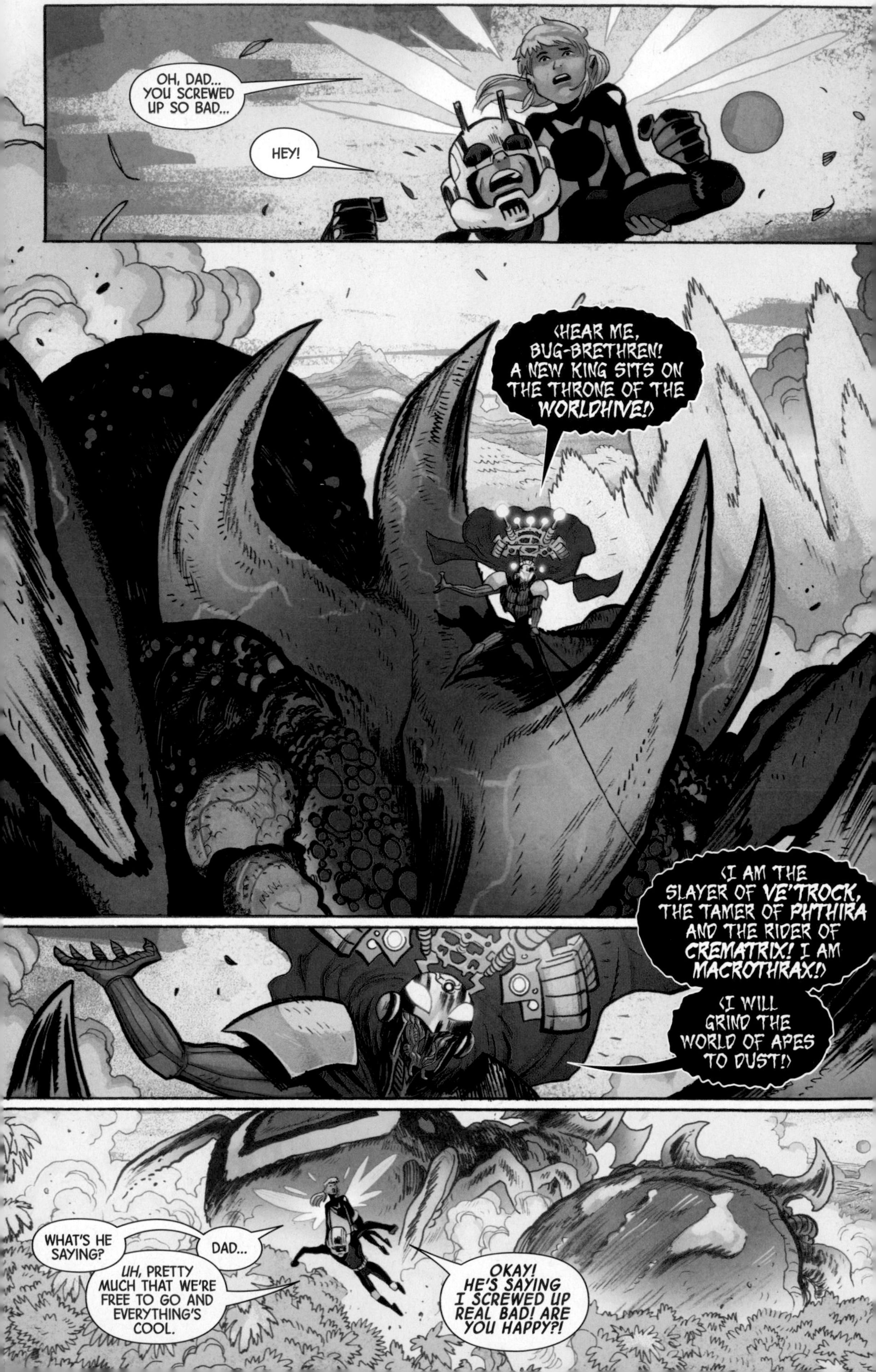
OH, DAD... YOU SCREWED UP SO BAD...
HEY!
‹HEAR ME, BUG-BRETHREN! A NEW KING SITS ON THE THRONE OF THE WORLDHIVE!›
‹I AM THE SLAYER OF VE'TROCK, THE TAMER OF PHTHIRA AND THE RIDER OF CREMATRIX! I AM MACROTHRAX!›
‹I WILL GRIND THE WORLD OF APES TO DUST!›
WHAT'S HE SAYING?
DAD...
UH, PRETTY MUCH THAT WE'RE FREE TO GO AND EVERYTHING'S COOL.
OKAY! HE'S SAYING I SCREWED UP REAL BAD! ARE YOU HAPPY?!

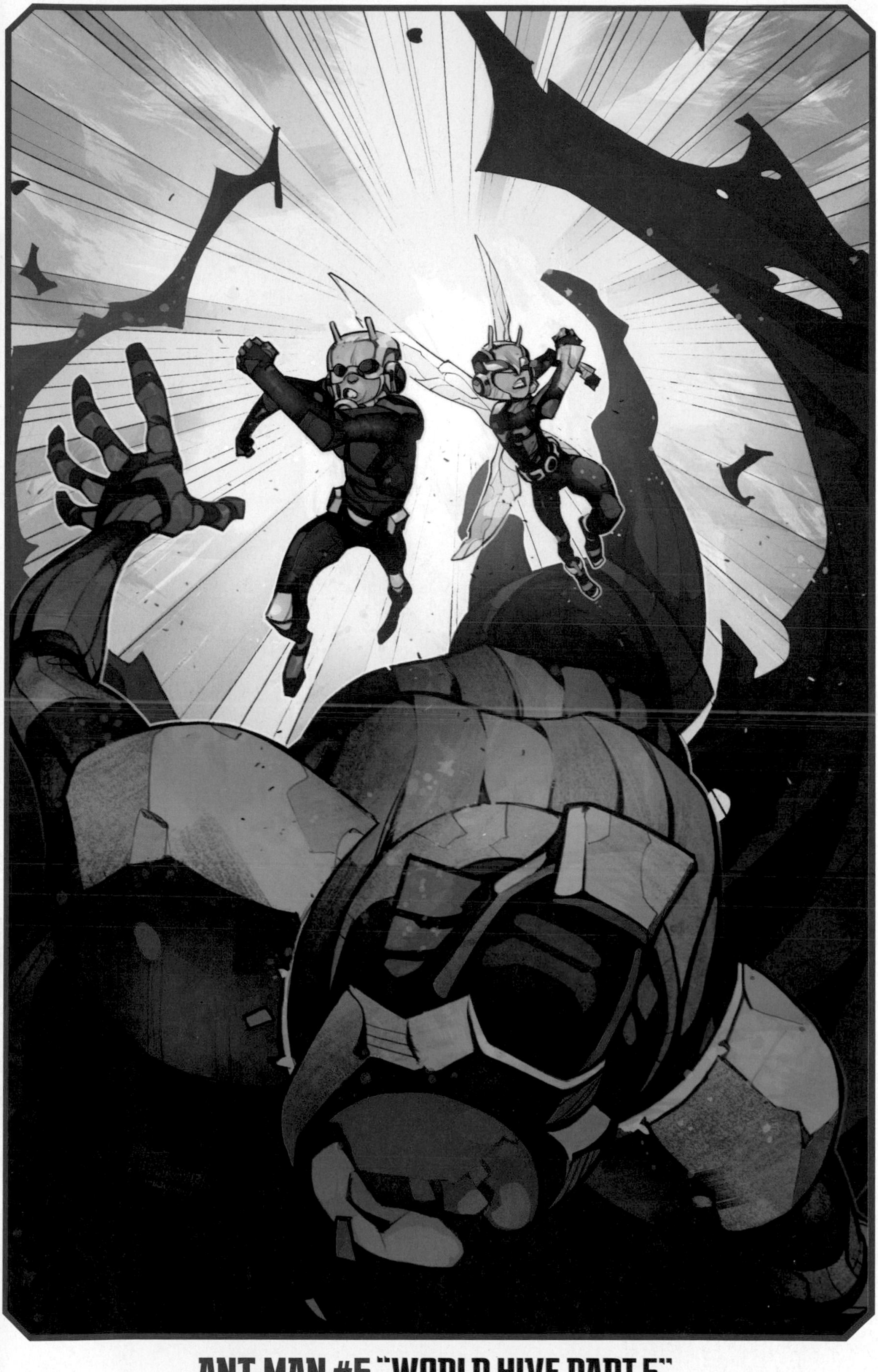

ANT-MAN #5 "WORLD HIVE PART 5"

'SUP
MACROTHRAX TOOK CONTROL OF BUG-LORDS TO TAKE OVER WORLD
ANT-MAN AND STINGER ONLY ONES STAND IN WAY
LOOK ELEPHANT HAWK MOTH KNOWS ANTS GOOD AT RECAPPING STORY BUT THAT NOT HOW THIS MOTH ROLLS
YOU READ FIRST FOUR ISSUES OR NO READ
MOTH HAS THINGS TO POLLINATE

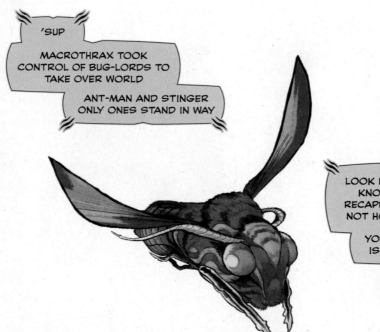

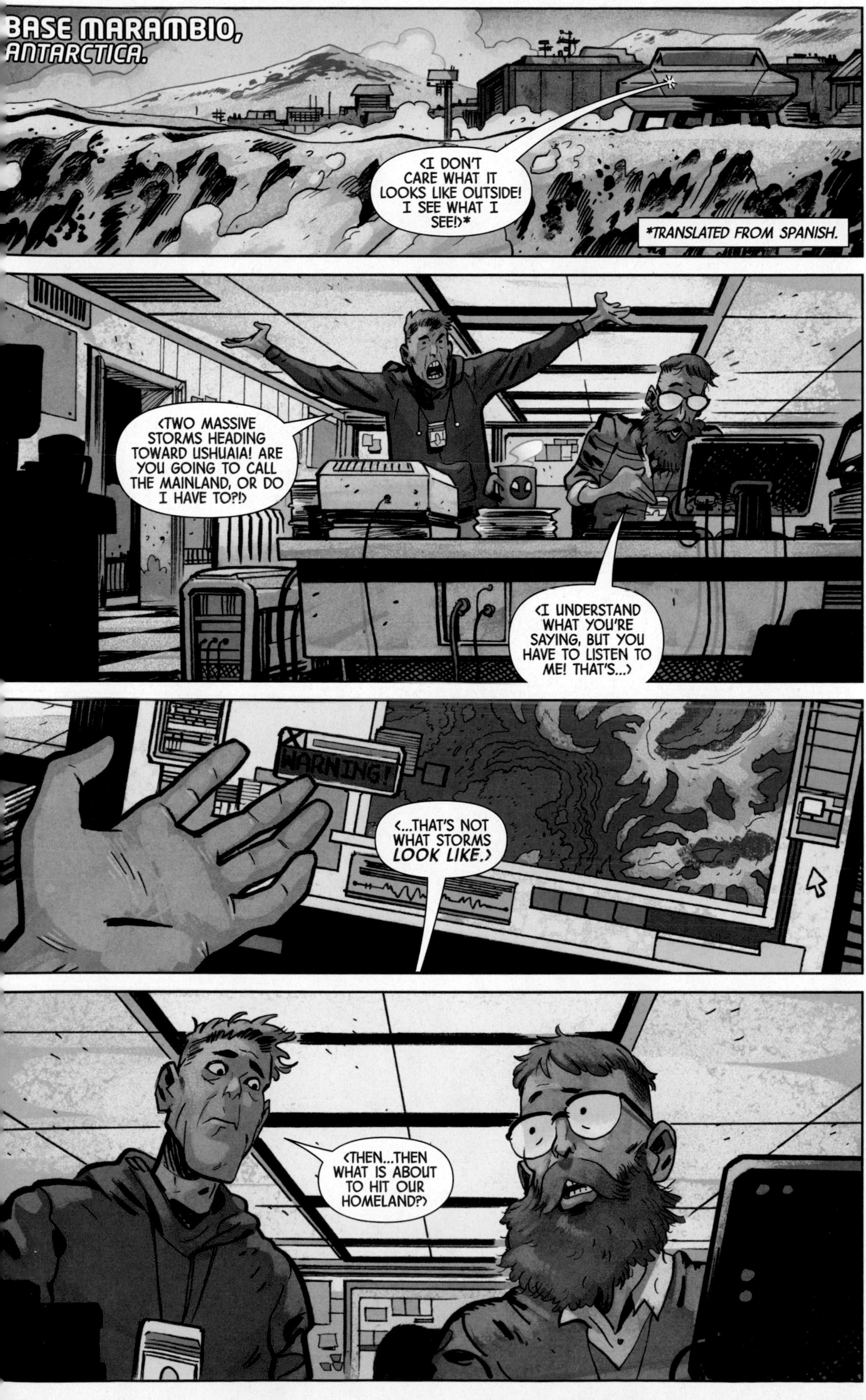
BASE MARAMBIO, ANTARCTICA.
<I DON'T CARE WHAT IT LOOKS LIKE OUTSIDE! I SEE WHAT I SEE!>*
*TRANSLATED FROM SPANISH.
<TWO MASSIVE STORMS HEADING TOWARD USHUAIA! ARE YOU GOING TO CALL THE MAINLAND, OR DO I HAVE TO?!>
<I UNDERSTAND WHAT YOU'RE SAYING, BUT YOU HAVE TO LISTEN TO ME! THAT'S...>
WARNING!
<...THAT'S NOT WHAT STORMS LOOK LIKE.>
<THEN...THEN WHAT IS ABOUT TO HIT OUR HOMELAND?>

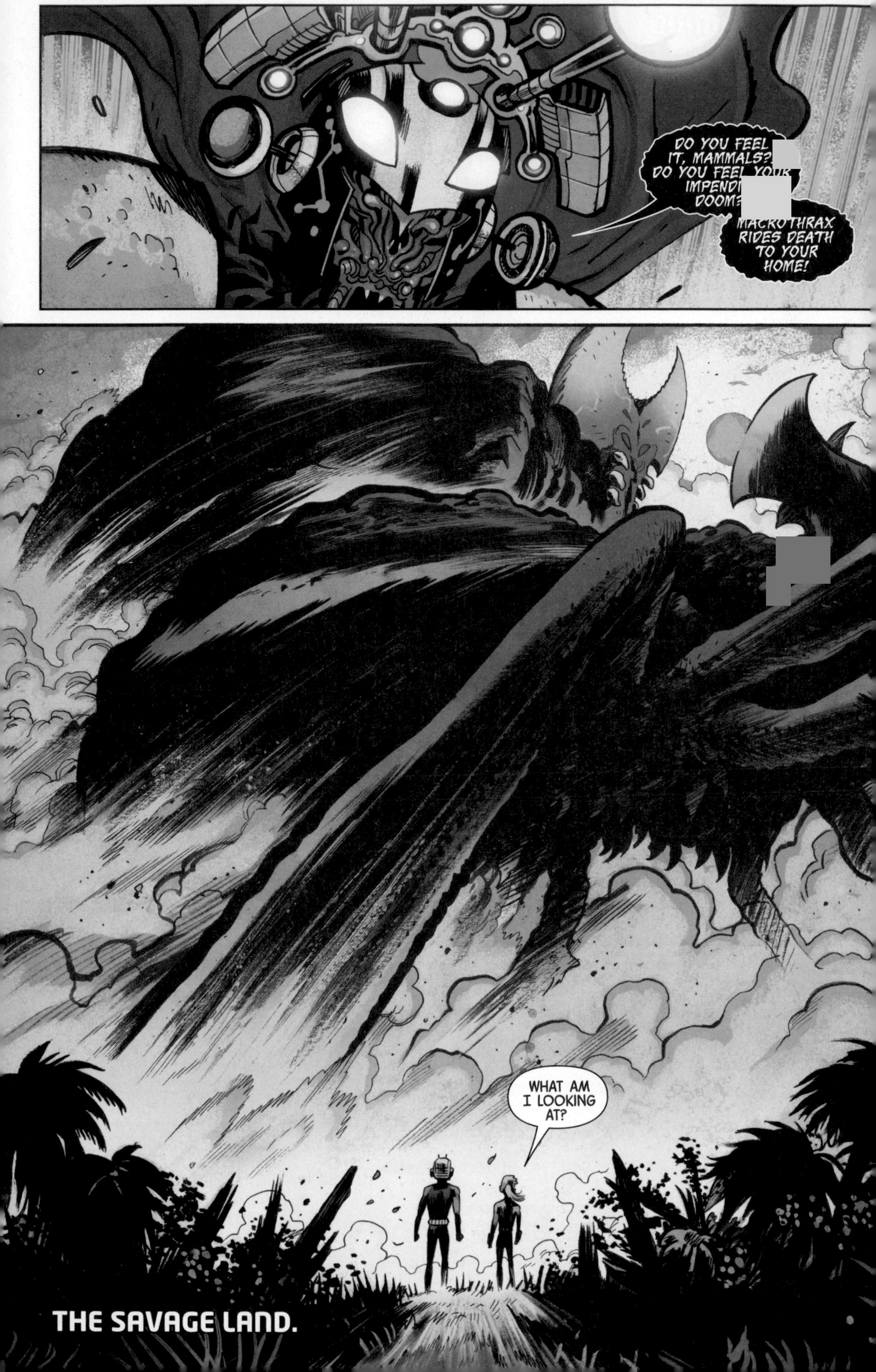
DO YOU FEEL IT, MAMMALS? DO YOU FEEL
DOOM?
MACROTHRAX RIDES DEATH TO YOUR HOME!
WHAT AM I LOOKING AT?
THE SAVAGE LAND.

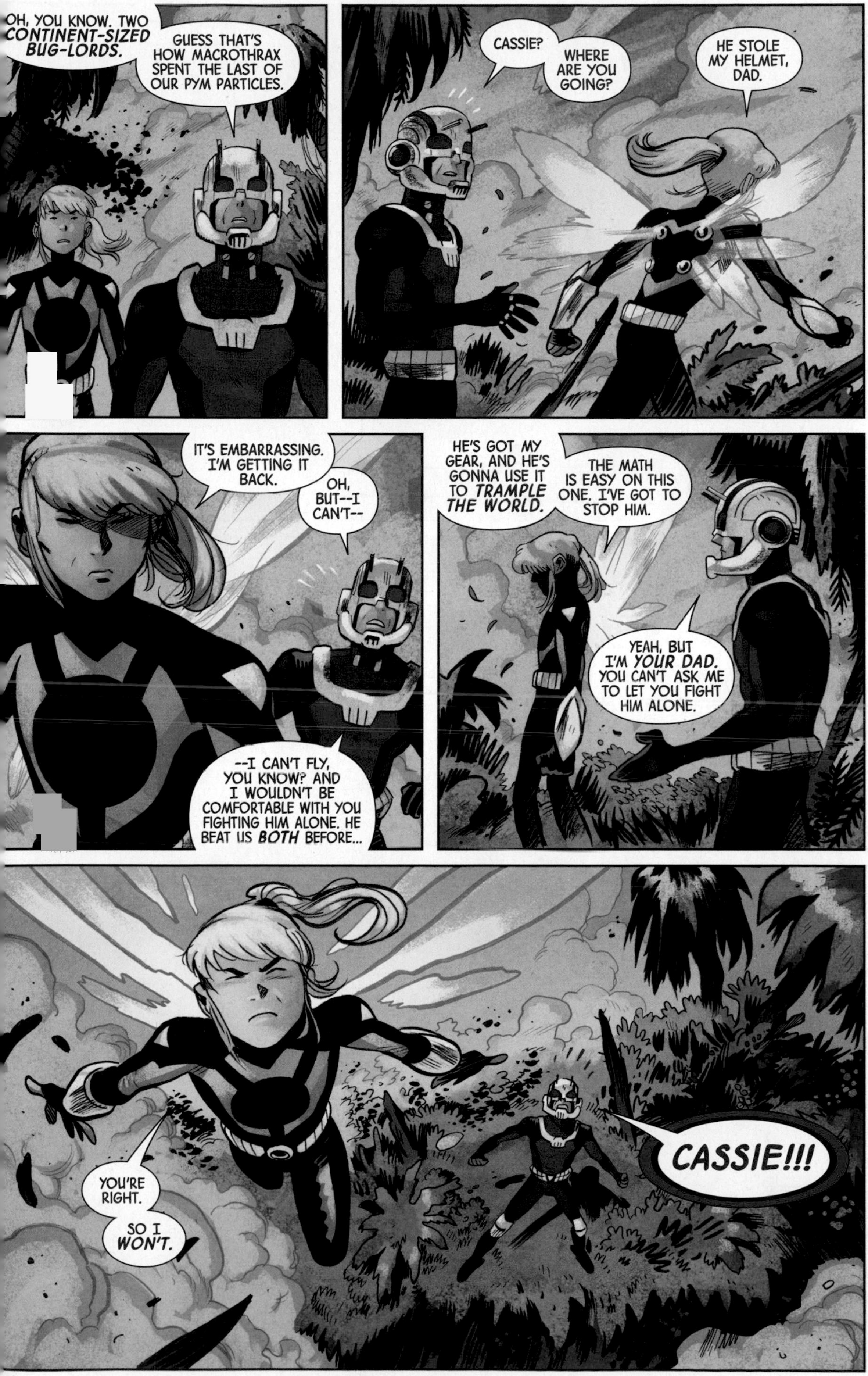

OH, YOU KNOW. TWO CONTINENT-SIZED BUG-LORDS.
GUESS THAT'S HOW MACROTHRAX SPENT THE LAST OF OUR PYM PARTICLES.
CASSIE?
WHERE ARE YOU GOING?
HE STOLE MY HELMET, DAD.
IT'S EMBARRASSING. I'M GETTING IT BACK.
OH, BUT--I CAN'T--
--I CAN'T FLY, YOU KNOW? AND I WOULDN'T BE COMFORTABLE WITH YOU FIGHTING HIM ALONE. HE BEAT US BOTH BEFORE...
HE'S GOT MY GEAR, AND HE'S GONNA USE IT TO TRAMPLE THE WORLD.
THE MATH IS EASY ON THIS ONE. I'VE GOT TO STOP HIM.
YEAH, BUT I'M YOUR DAD. YOU CAN'T ASK ME TO LET YOU FIGHT HIM ALONE.
YOU'RE RIGHT.
SO I WON'T.
CASSIE!!!

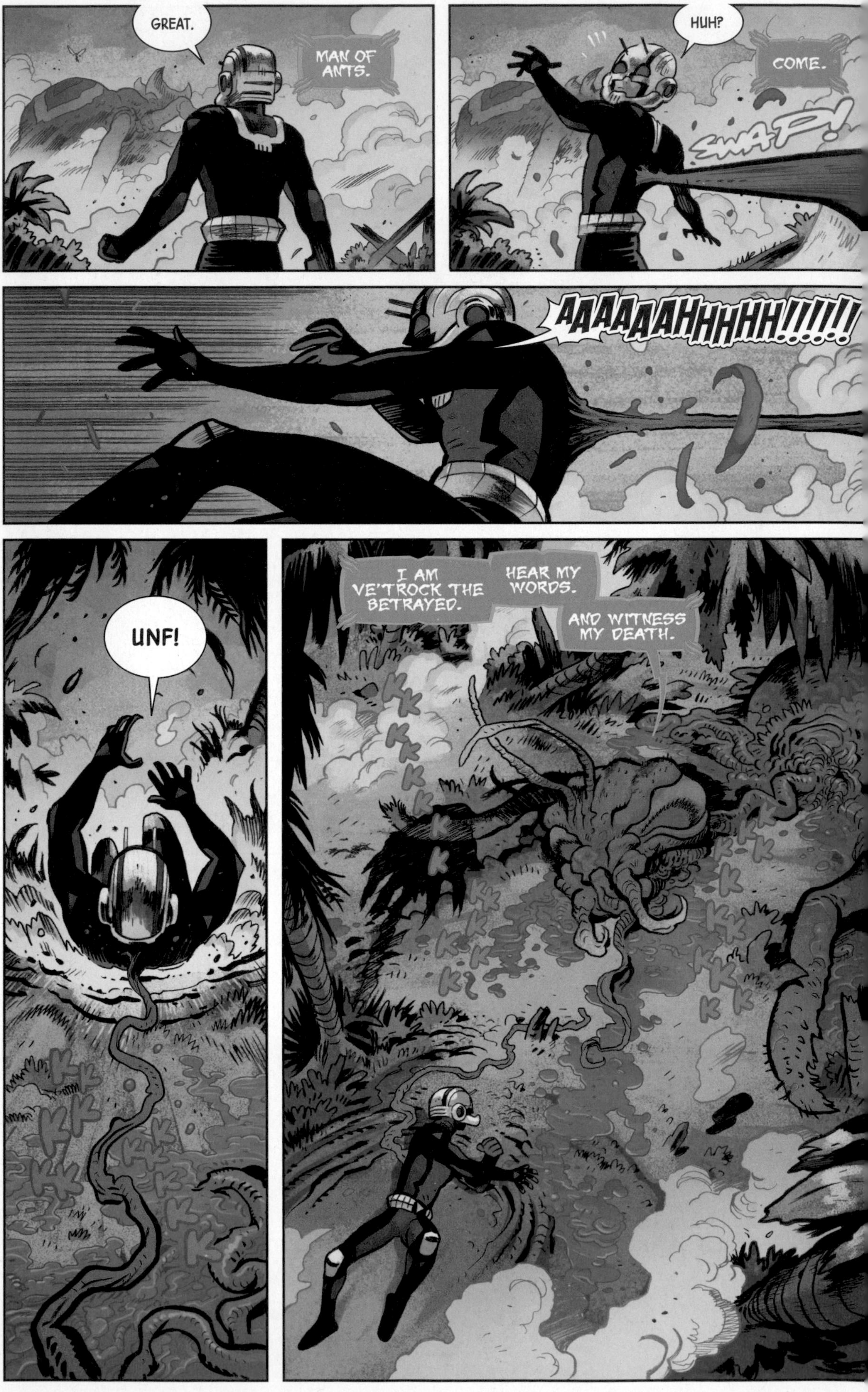
GREAT.
MAN OF ANTS.
HUH?
COME.
SWAP!
AAAAAAHHHHH!!!!!!
UNF!
I AM VE'TROCK THE BETRAYED.
HEAR MY WORDS.
AND WITNESS MY DEATH.

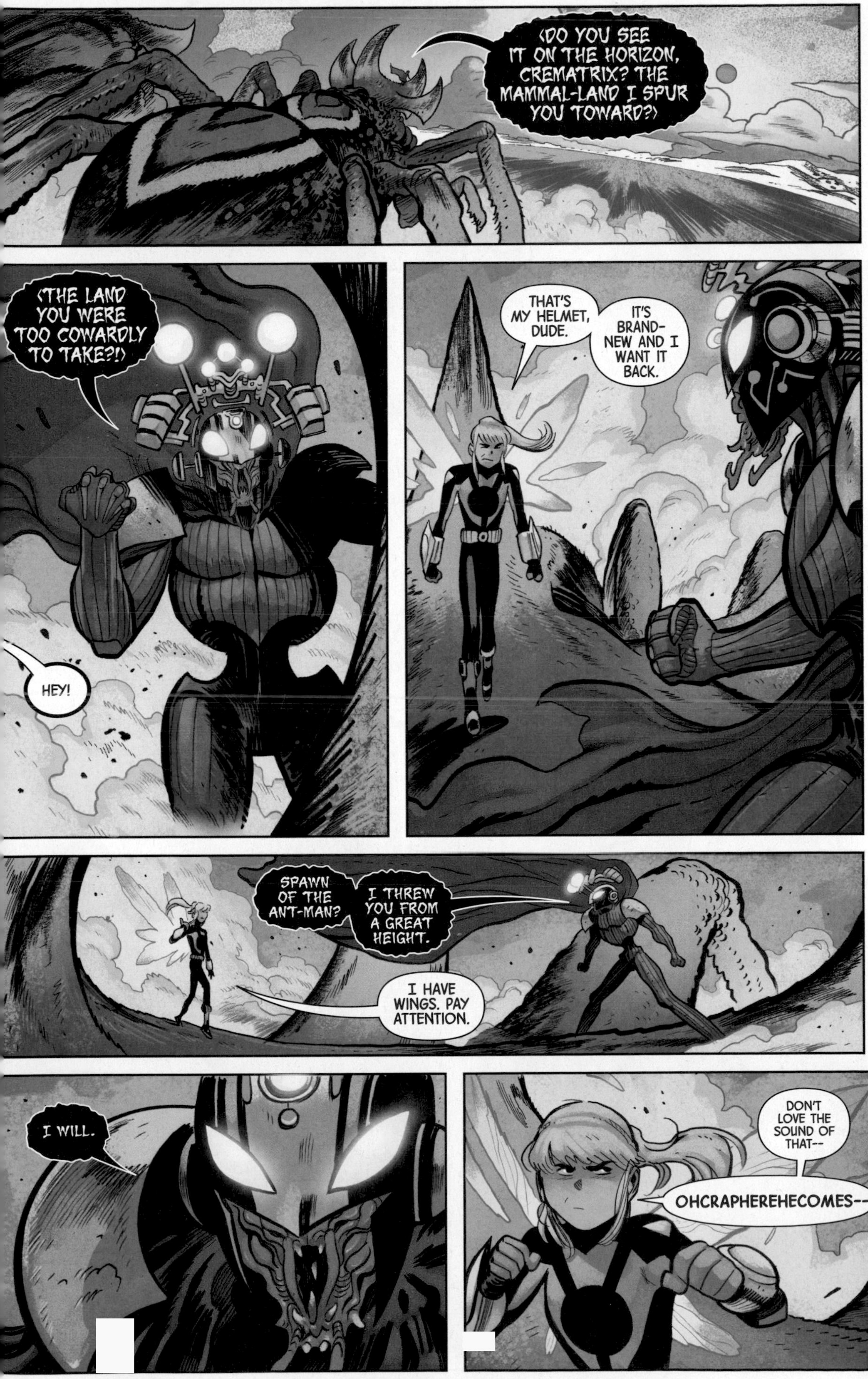
‹DO YOU SEE IT ON THE HORIZON, CREMATRIX? THE MAMMAL-LAND I SPUR YOU TOWARD?›
‹THE LAND YOU WERE TOO COWARDLY TO TAKE?!›
HEY!
THAT'S MY HELMET, DUDE.
IT'S BRAND-NEW AND I WANT IT BACK.
SPAWN OF THE ANT-MAN?
I THREW YOU FROM A GREAT HEIGHT.
I HAVE WINGS. PAY ATTENTION.
I WILL.
DON'T LOVE THE SOUND OF THAT--
OHCRAPHEREHECOMES--

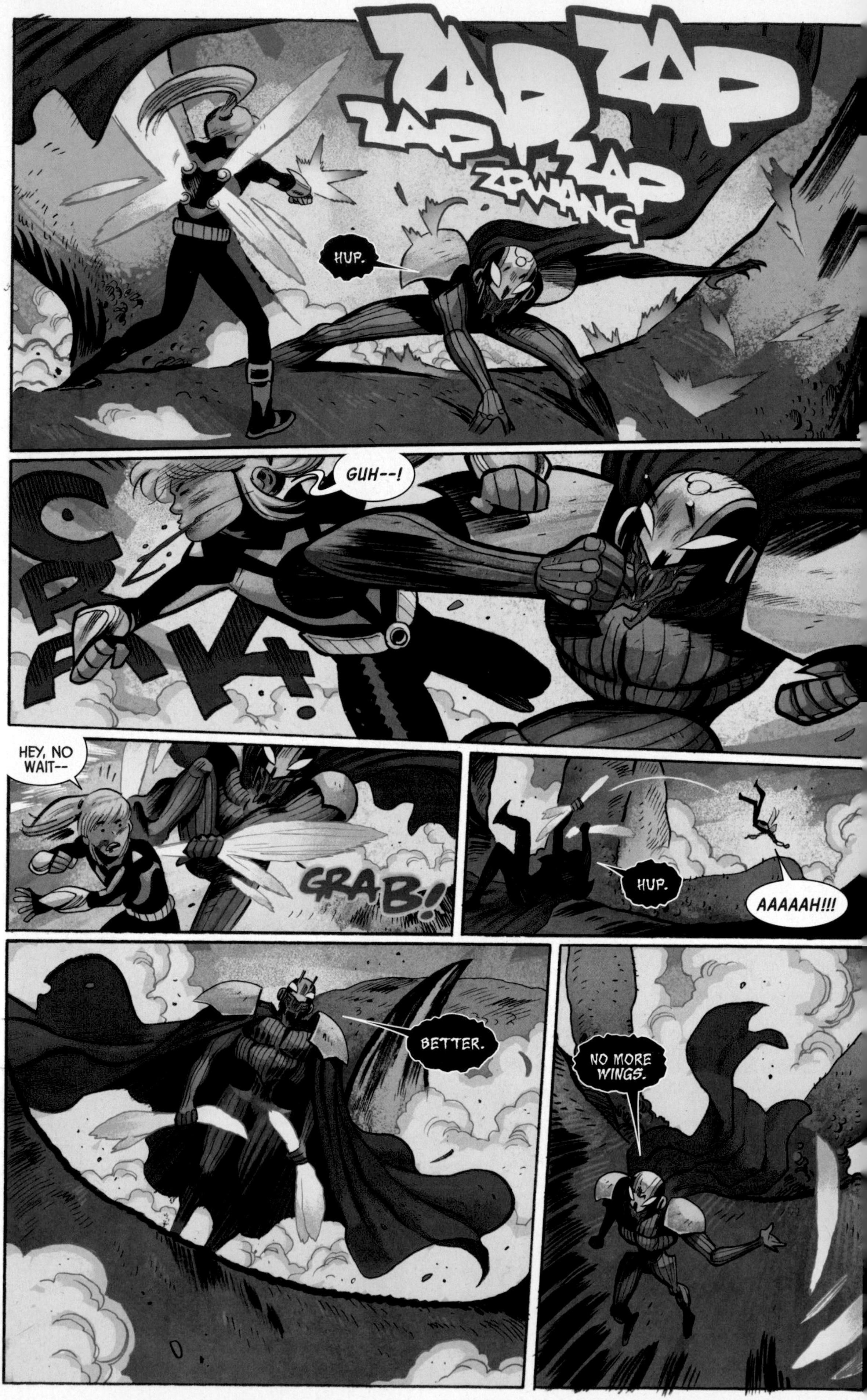
ZAP ZAP
ZAP ZAP ZAP
ZPWANG
HUP.
GUH--!
CRAK!
HEY, NO WAIT--
GRAB!
HUP.
AAAAAH!!!
BETTER.
NO MORE WINGS.

MAN, VE'TROCK, I'M SORRY, BUT YOU'RE *REALLY* MESSED UP. WISH I COULD BE MORE HELP, BUT I'VE GOTTA GO.

I DON'T MEAN TO BE INSENSITIVE, BUT MY DAUGHTER--

I KNOW WHY YOU ARE HERE, SCOTT LANG.

NOT BECAUSE MACROTHRAX STOLE YOUR PYM PARTICLES. NOT BECAUSE HE THREATENS THE SMOOTH APES.

BECAUSE HE SLAYED YOUR ANTS. HE SLAYED PAMELA.

YOU...YOU KNOW ABOUT PAMELA?

WORLDHIVE CONNECTS ALL. SEES ALL.

WORLDHIVE SEES YOU, SCOTT LANG.

YOU TRAVEL TO SAVAGE LAND BECAUSE YOU LOST AN ANT, AND YOU ARE SAD.

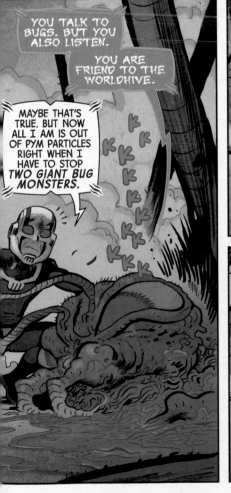

YOU TALK TO BUGS. BUT YOU ALSO LISTEN.

YOU ARE FRIEND TO THE WORLDHIVE.

MAYBE THAT'S TRUE. BUT NOW ALL I AM IS OUT OF PYM PARTICLES RIGHT WHEN I HAVE TO STOP *TWO GIANT BUG MONSTERS.*

NO. NOT ALL YOU ARE. YOU LISTEN. WORLDHIVE LISTENS TOO.

VE'TROCK JOIN THE UNDER-HIVE NOW. BUT I ASK WORLDHIVE FOR ONE LAST THING.

THAT WORLDHIVE HELP YOU.

BECAUSE YOU ARE WORTHY--"

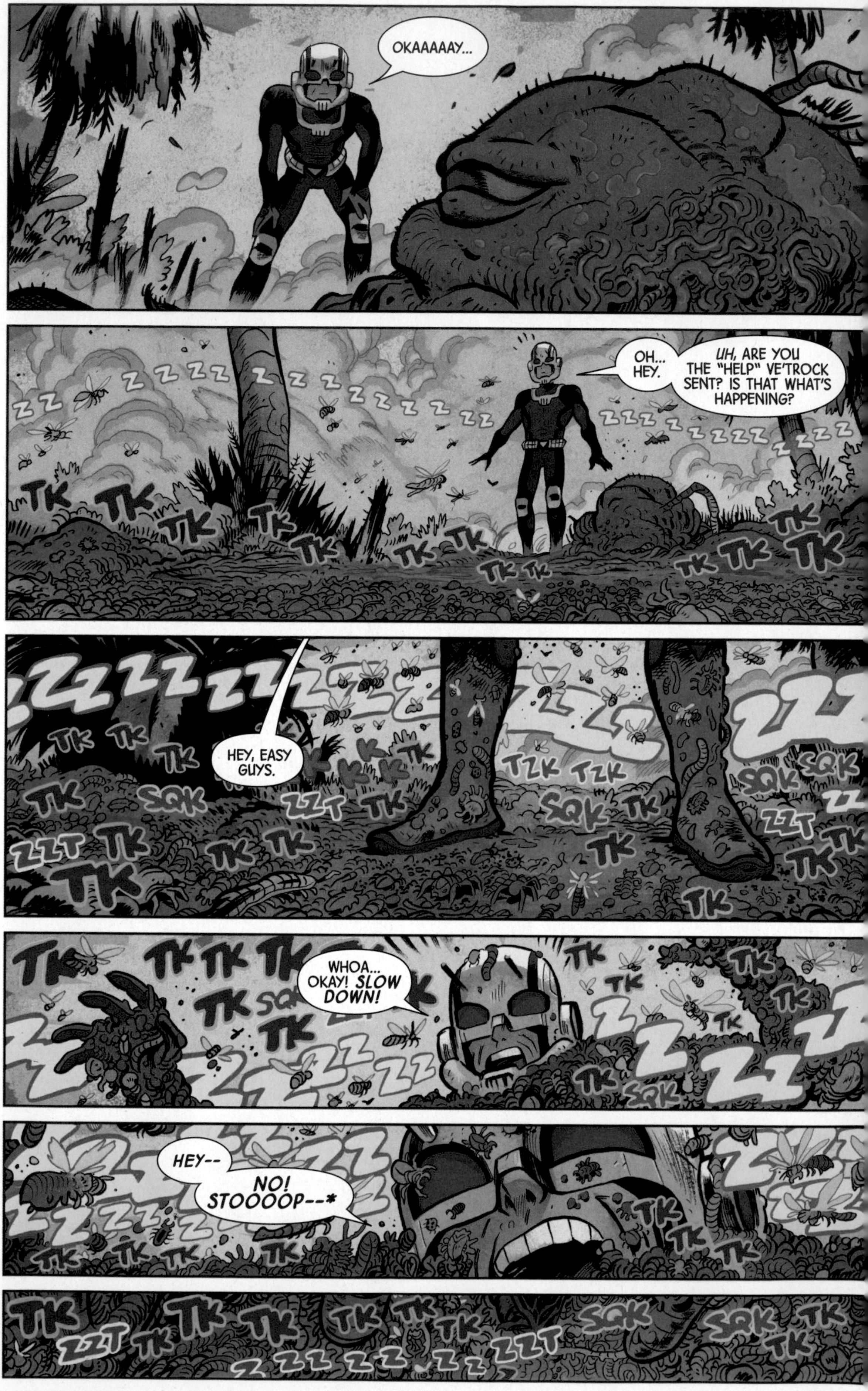
OKAAAAAY...
OH... HEY.
UH, ARE YOU THE "HELP" VE'TROCK SENT? IS THAT WHAT'S HAPPENING?
ZZZZZ
TK TK TK
HEY, EASY GUYS.
TK SQK ZZT TZK
WHOA... OKAY! SLOW DOWN!
HEY--
NO! STOOOOP--*
TK ZZT SQK

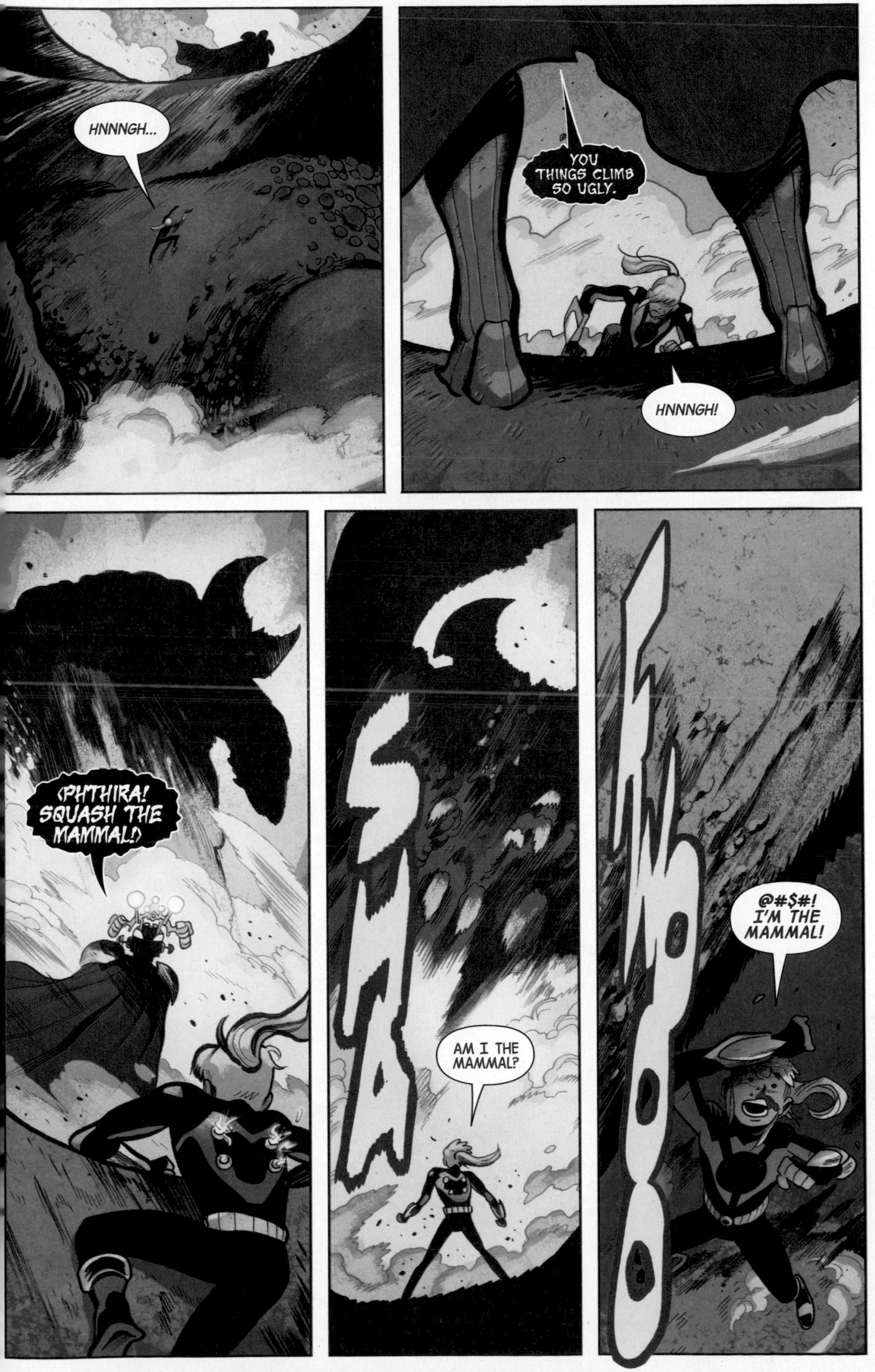
HNNNGH...
YOU THINGS CLIMB SO UGLY.
HNNNGH!
‹PHTHIRA! SQUASH THE MAMMAL!›
AM I THE MAMMAL?
@#$#! I'M THE MAMMAL!

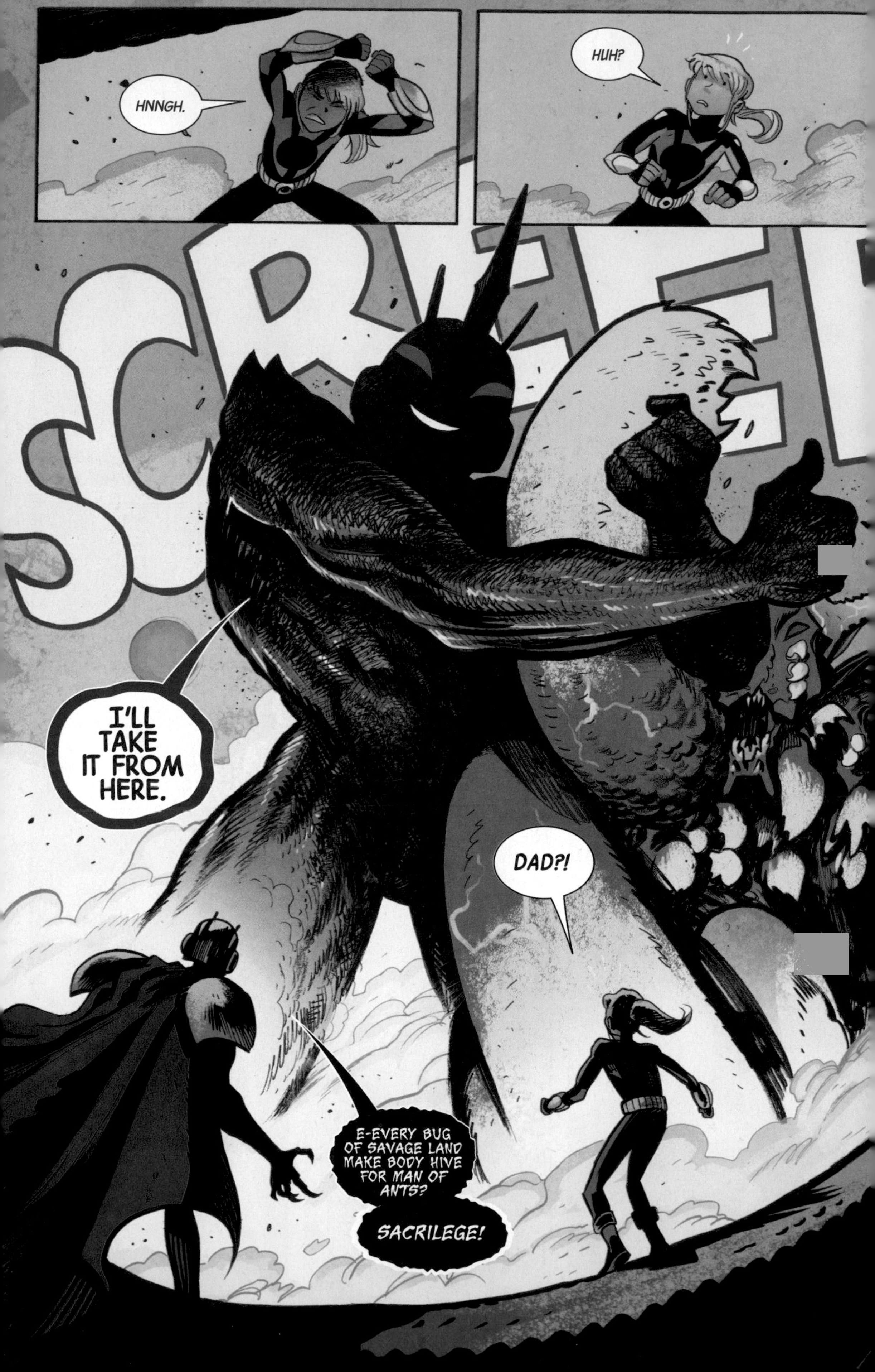
HNNGH.
HUH?
SCREEE
I'LL TAKE IT FROM HERE.
DAD?!
E-EVERY BUG OF SAVAGE LAND MAKE BODY HIVE FOR MAN OF ANTS?
SACRILEGE!

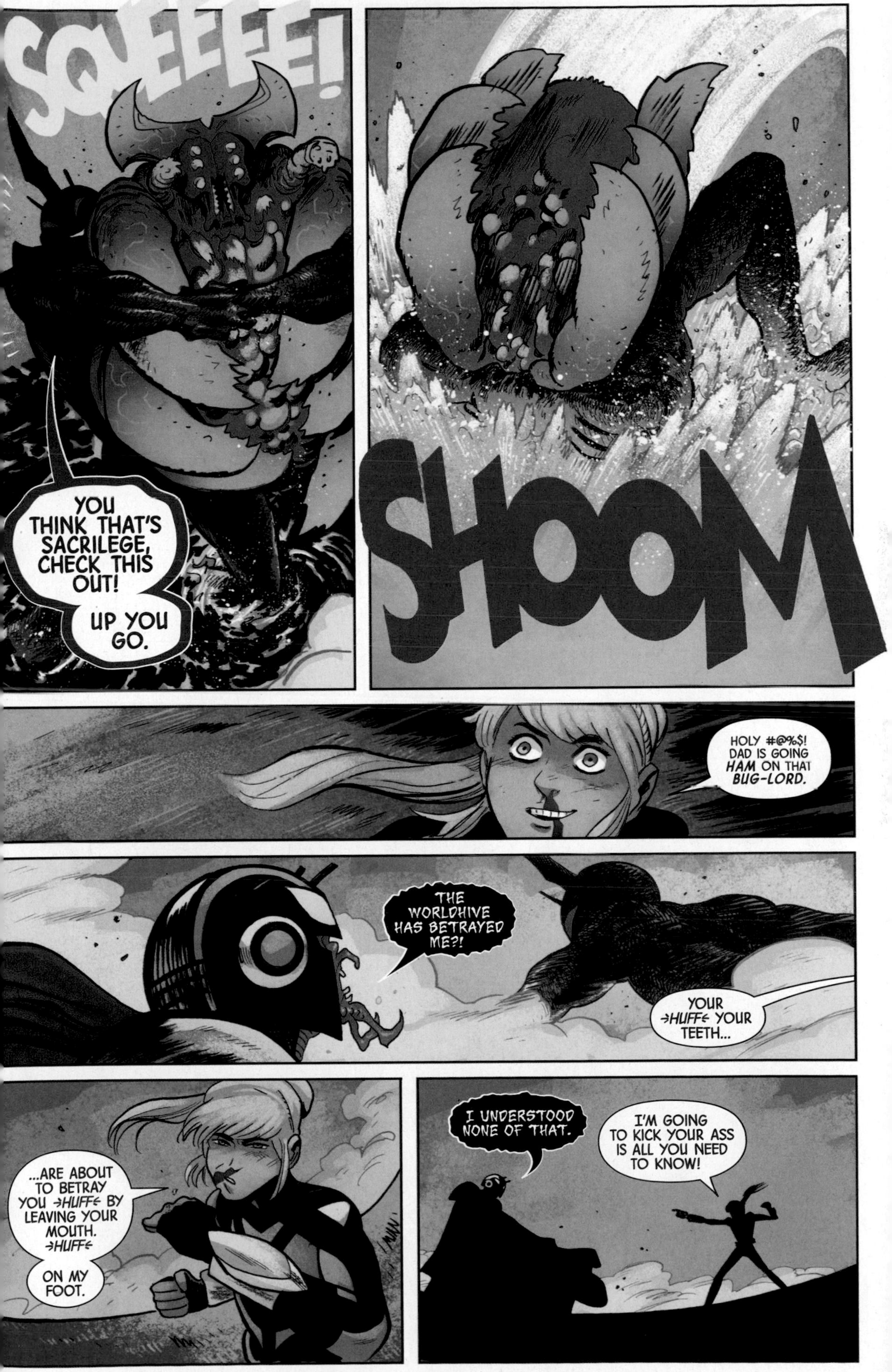
SQUEEEE!
YOU THINK THAT'S SACRILEGE, CHECK THIS OUT!
UP YOU GO.
SHOOM
HOLY #@%$! DAD IS GOING HAM ON THAT BUG-LORD.
THE WORLDHIVE HAS BETRAYED ME?!
YOUR →HUFF← YOUR TEETH...
...ARE ABOUT TO BETRAY YOU →HUFF← BY LEAVING YOUR MOUTH. →HUFF←
ON MY FOOT.
I UNDERSTOOD NONE OF THAT.
I'M GOING TO KICK YOUR ASS IS ALL YOU NEED TO KNOW!

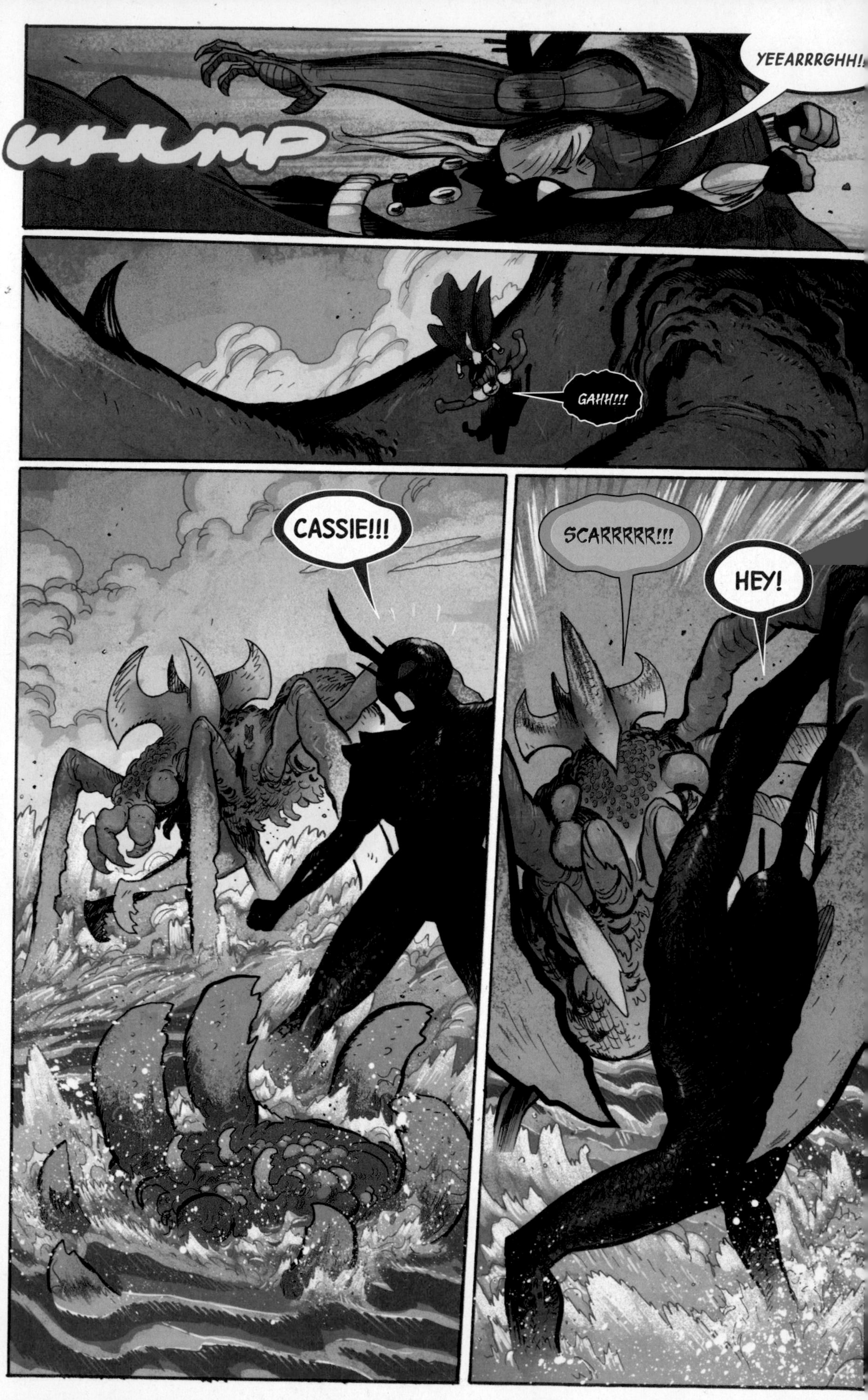
YEEARRRGHH!
WHUMP
GAHH!!!
CASSIE!!!
SCARRRRR!!!
HEY!

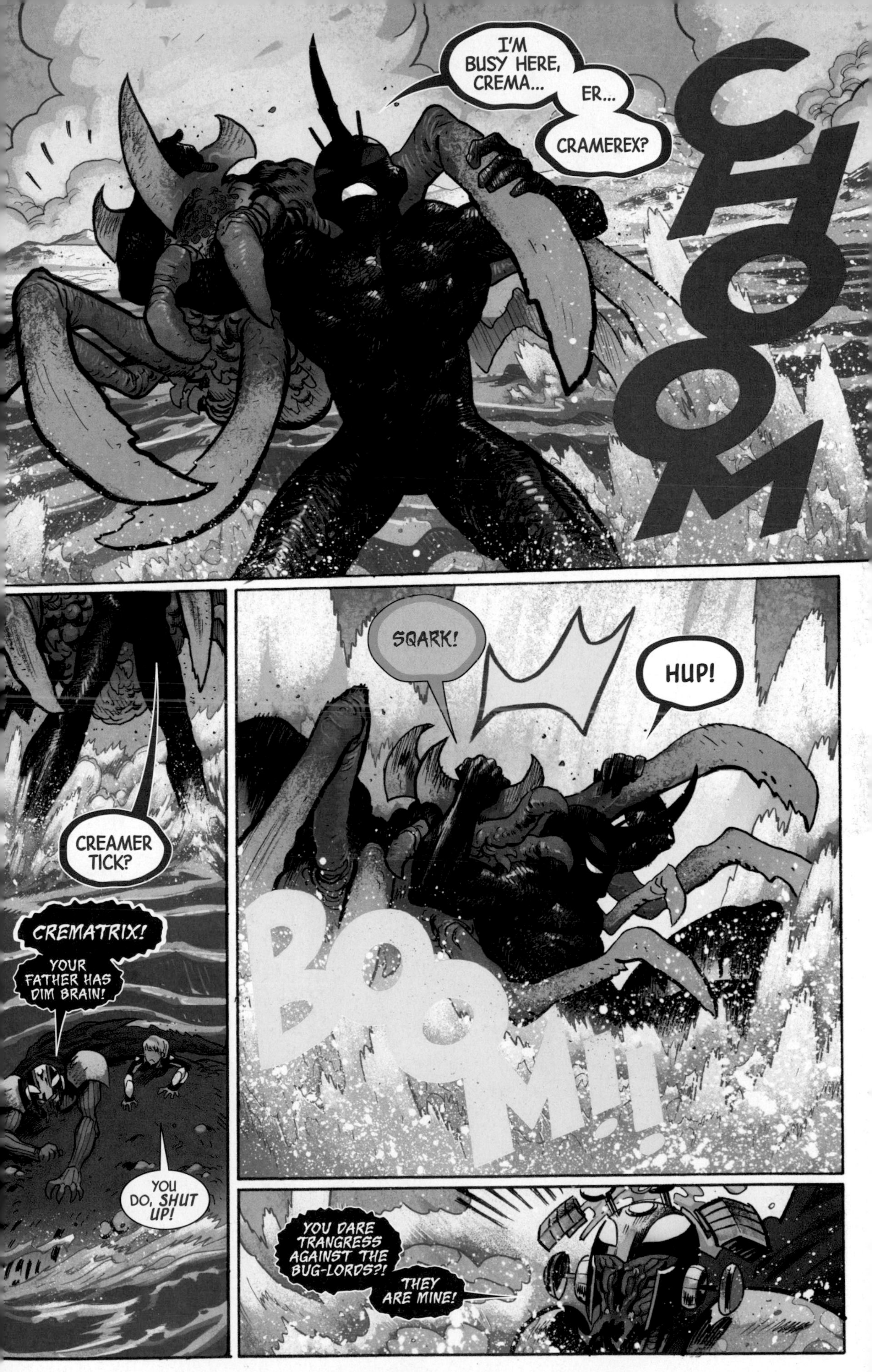

I'M BUSY HERE, CREMA...
ER...
CRAMEREX?
CHOOM
CREAMER TICK?
CREMATRIX!
YOUR FATHER HAS DIM BRAIN!
YOU DO, SHUT UP!
SQARK!
HUP!
BOOM!!
YOU DARE TRANGRESS AGAINST THE BUG-LORDS?!
THEY ARE MINE!

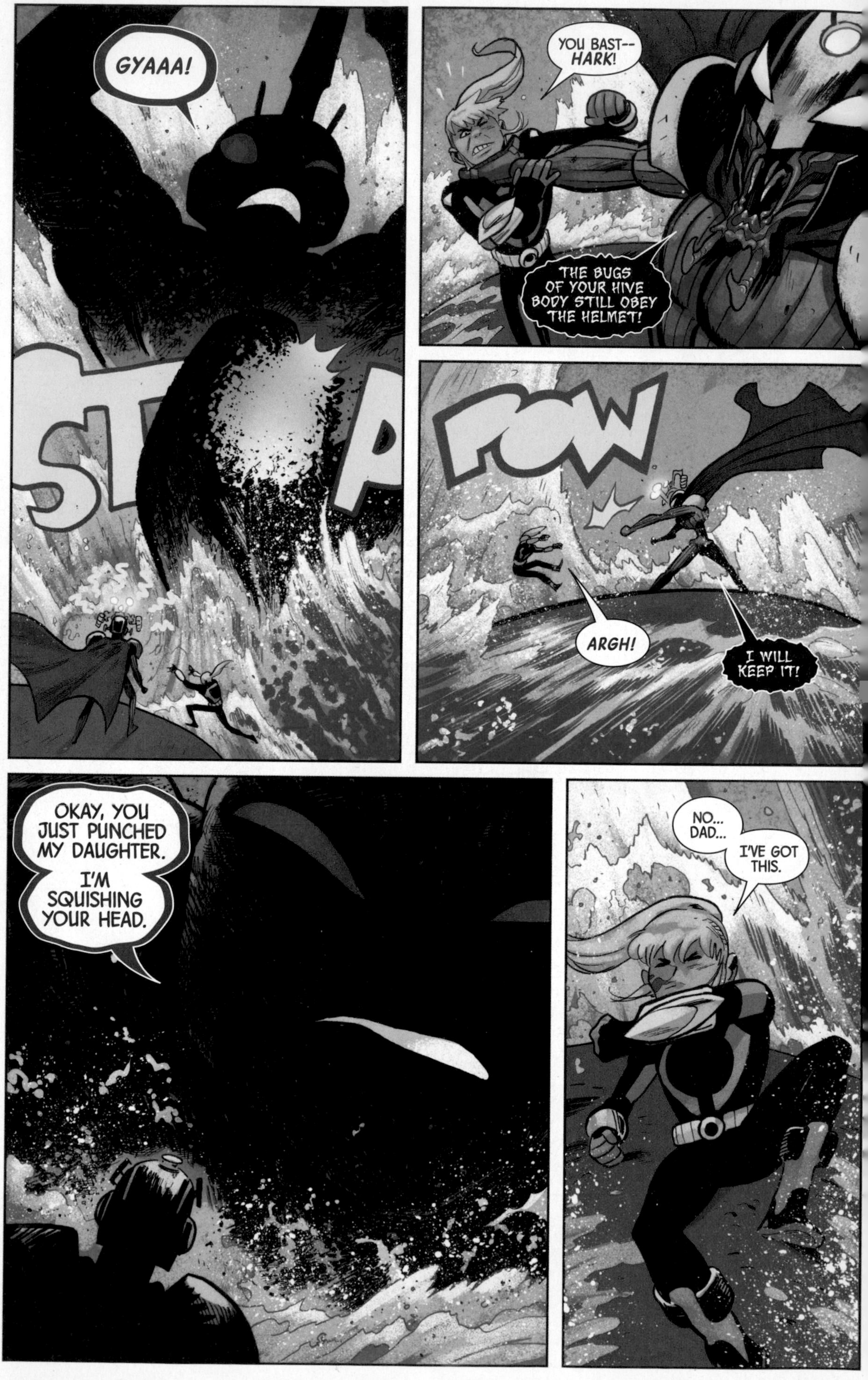

GYAAA!
STOMP
YOU BAST-- HARK!
THE BUGS OF YOUR HIVE BODY STILL OBEY THE HELMET!
POW
ARGH!
I WILL KEEP IT!
OKAY, YOU JUST PUNCHED MY DAUGHTER.
I'M SQUISHING YOUR HEAD.
NO... DAD...
I'VE GOT THIS.

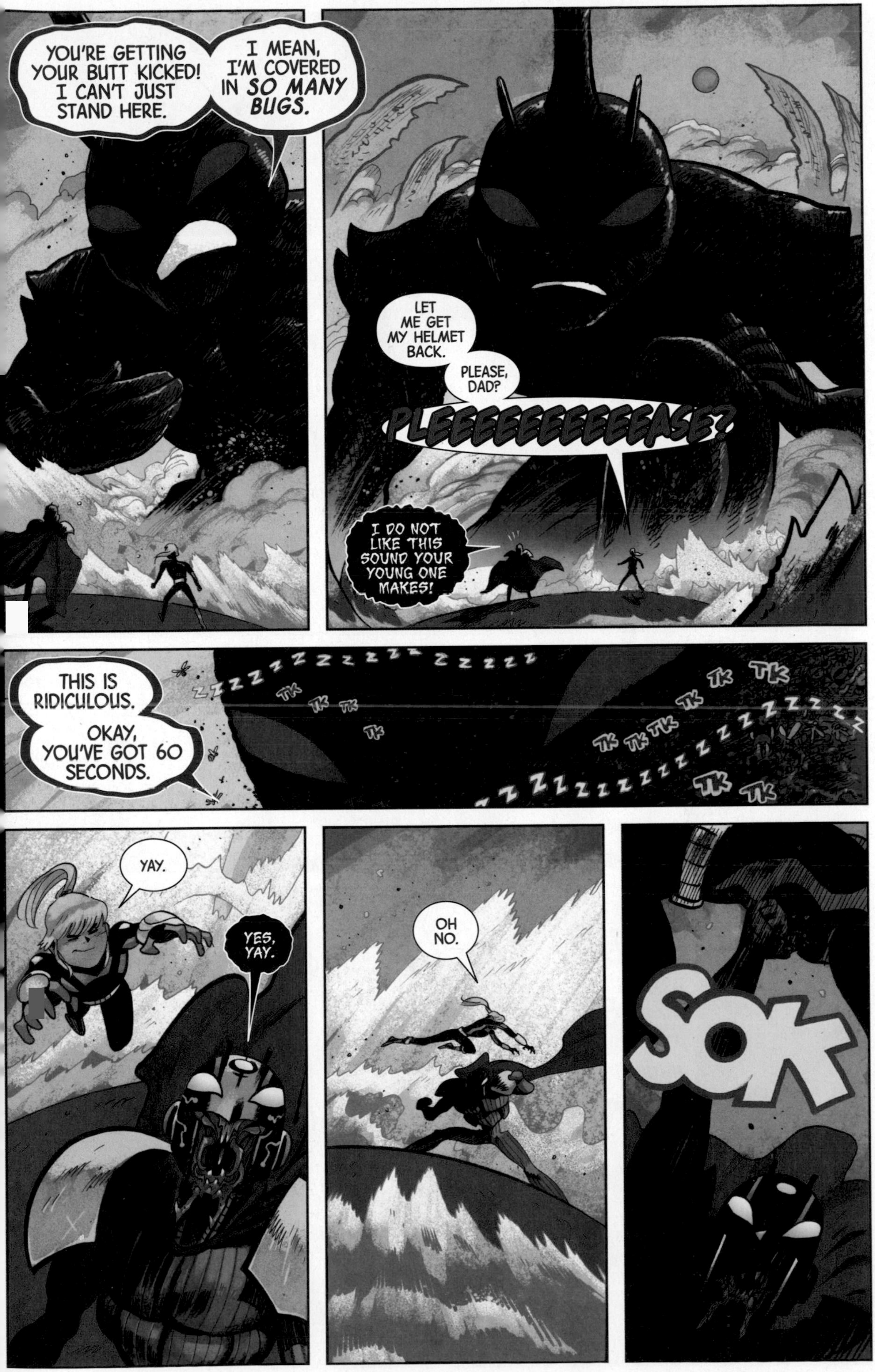
YOU'RE GETTING YOUR BUTT KICKED! I CAN'T JUST STAND HERE.
I MEAN, I'M COVERED IN SO MANY BUGS.
LET ME GET MY HELMET BACK.
PLEASE, DAD?
PLEEEEEEEEEEEEASE?
I DO NOT LIKE THIS SOUND YOUR YOUNG ONE MAKES!
THIS IS RIDICULOUS.
OKAY, YOU'VE GOT 60 SECONDS.
TK TK TK TK TK TK TK TK TK TK TK TK
YAY.
YES, YAY.
OH NO.
SOK

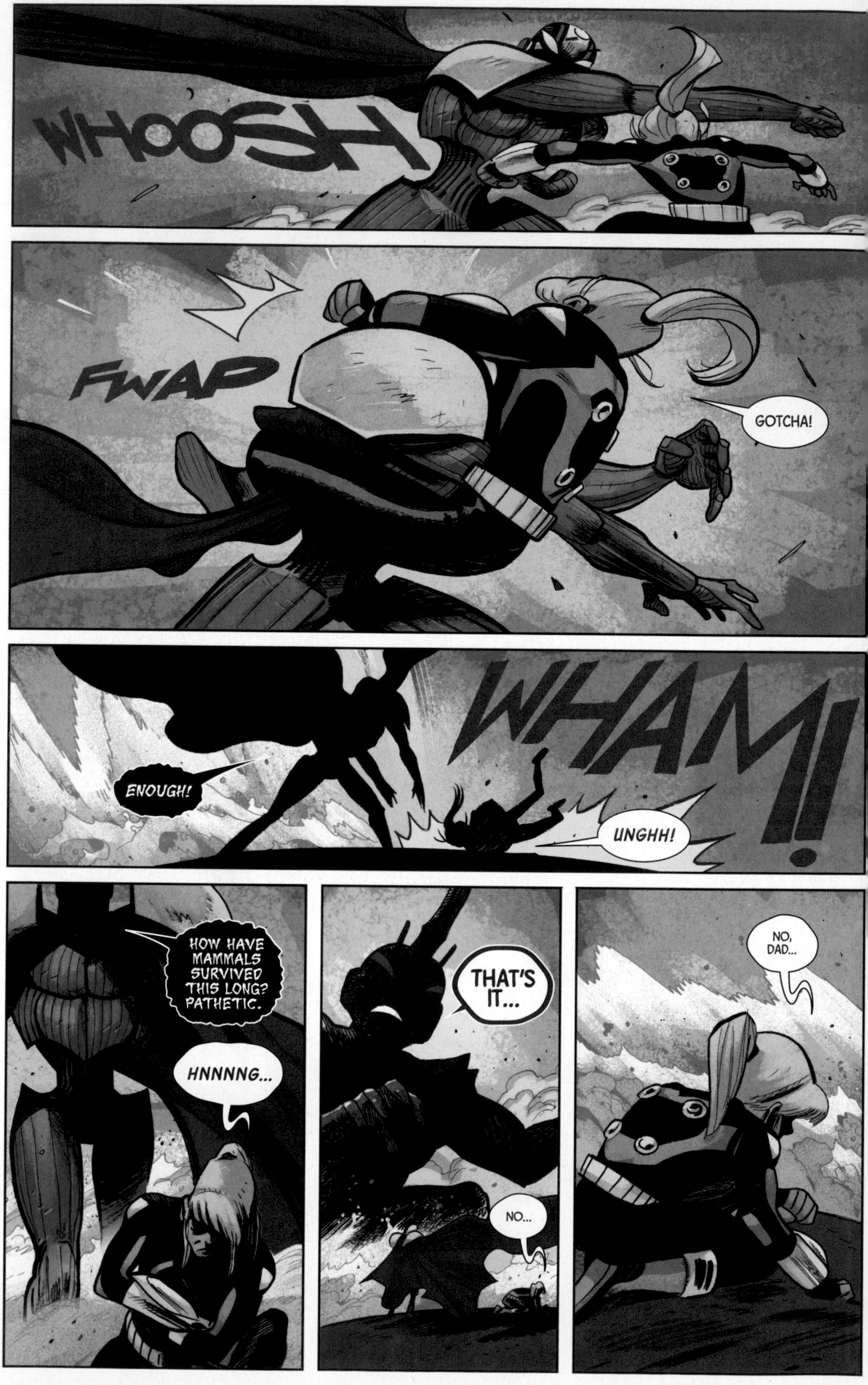
WHOOSH
FWAP
GOTCHA!
WHAM!
ENOUGH!
UNGHH!
HOW HAVE MAMMALS SURVIVED THIS LONG? PATHETIC.
HNNNNG...
THAT'S IT...
NO...
NO, DAD...

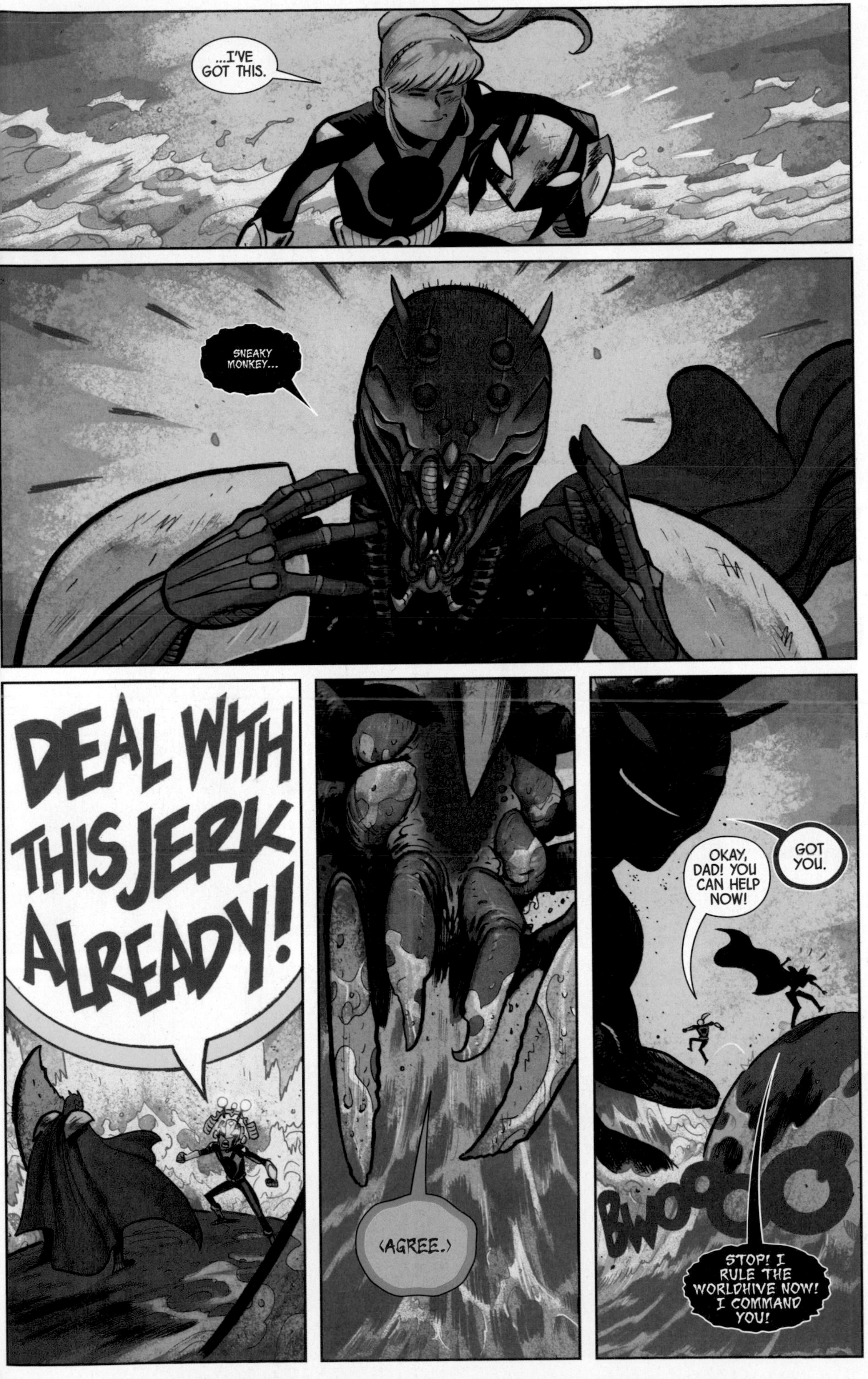
...I'VE GOT THIS.
SNEAKY MONKEY...
DEAL WITH THIS JERK ALREADY!
‹AGREE.›
OKAY, DAD! YOU CAN HELP NOW!
GOT YOU.
BWOOOO
STOP! I RULE THE WORLDHIVE NOW! I COMMAND YOU!

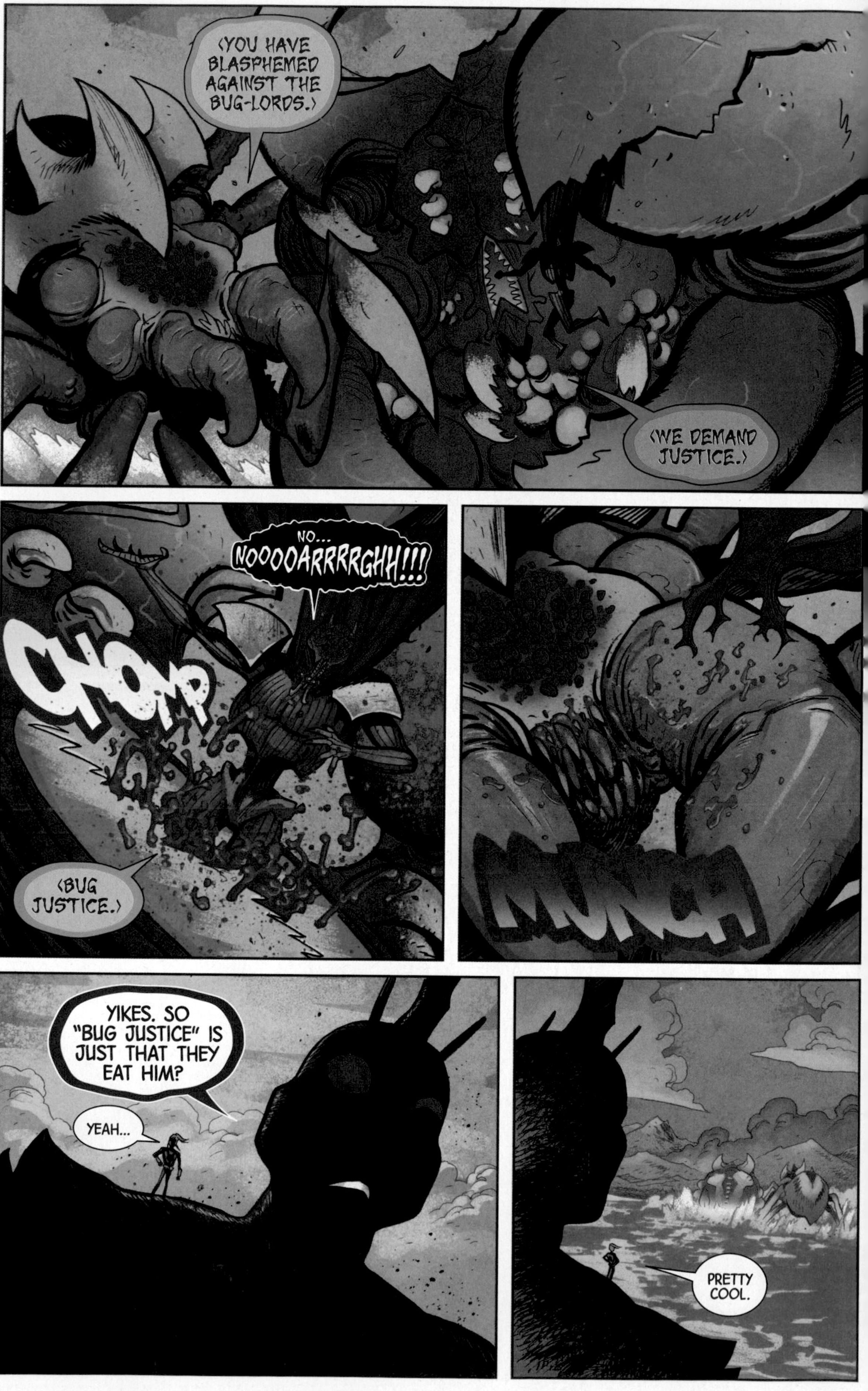
‹YOU HAVE BLASPHEMED AGAINST THE BUG-LORDS.›
‹WE DEMAND JUSTICE.›
NO... NOOOOARRRRGHH!!!!
CHOMP
‹BUG JUSTICE.›
MUNCH
YIKES. SO "BUG JUSTICE" IS JUST THAT THEY EAT HIM?
YEAH...
PRETTY COOL.

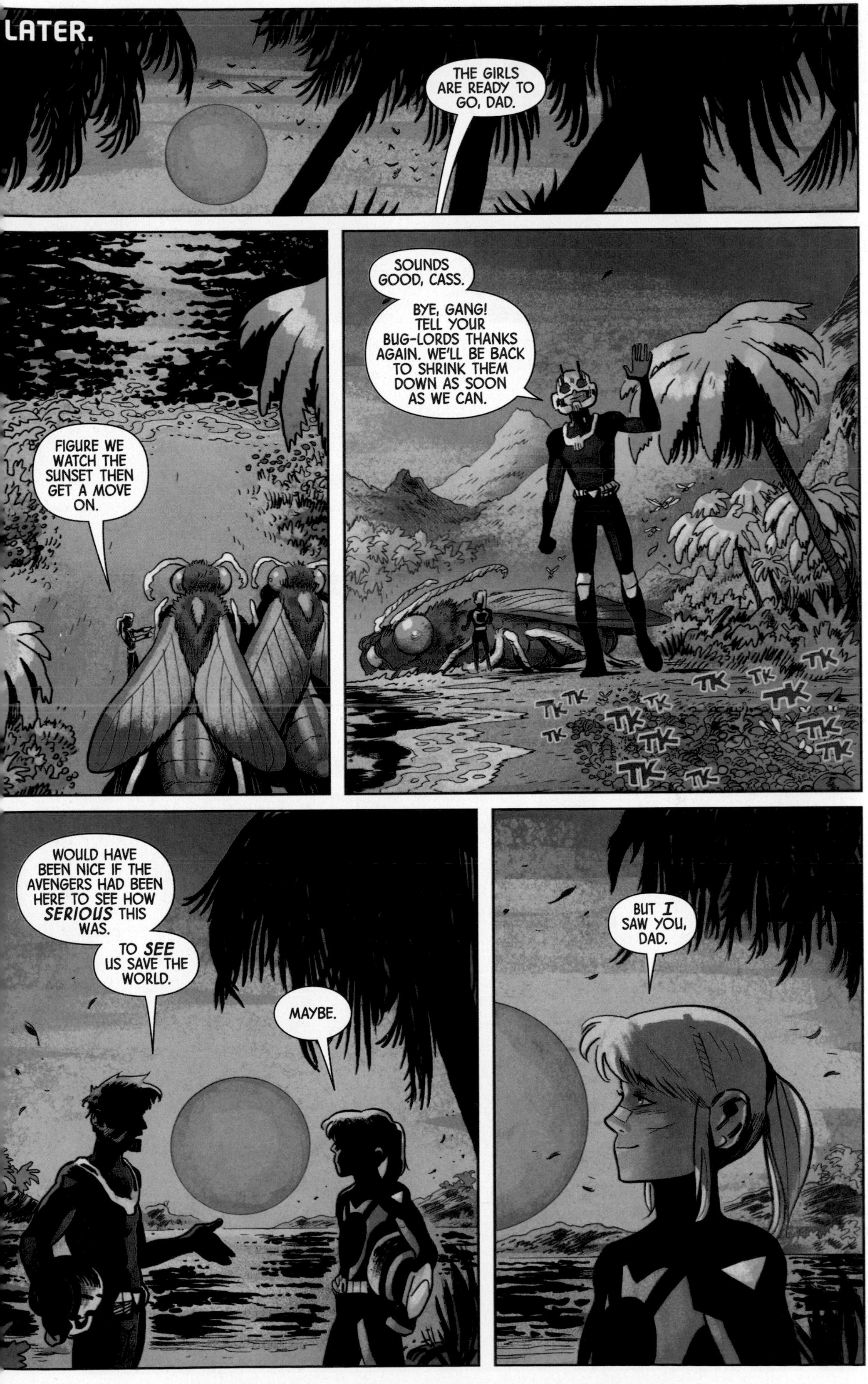
LATER.
THE GIRLS ARE READY TO GO, DAD.
FIGURE WE WATCH THE SUNSET THEN GET A MOVE ON.
SOUNDS GOOD, CASS.
BYE, GANG! TELL YOUR BUG-LORDS THANKS AGAIN. WE'LL BE BACK TO SHRINK THEM DOWN AS SOON AS WE CAN.
TK TK TK TK TK TK TK TK TK TK TK TK TK TK
WOULD HAVE BEEN NICE IF THE AVENGERS HAD BEEN HERE TO SEE HOW SERIOUS THIS WAS.
TO SEE US SAVE THE WORLD.
MAYBE.
BUT I SAW YOU, DAD.

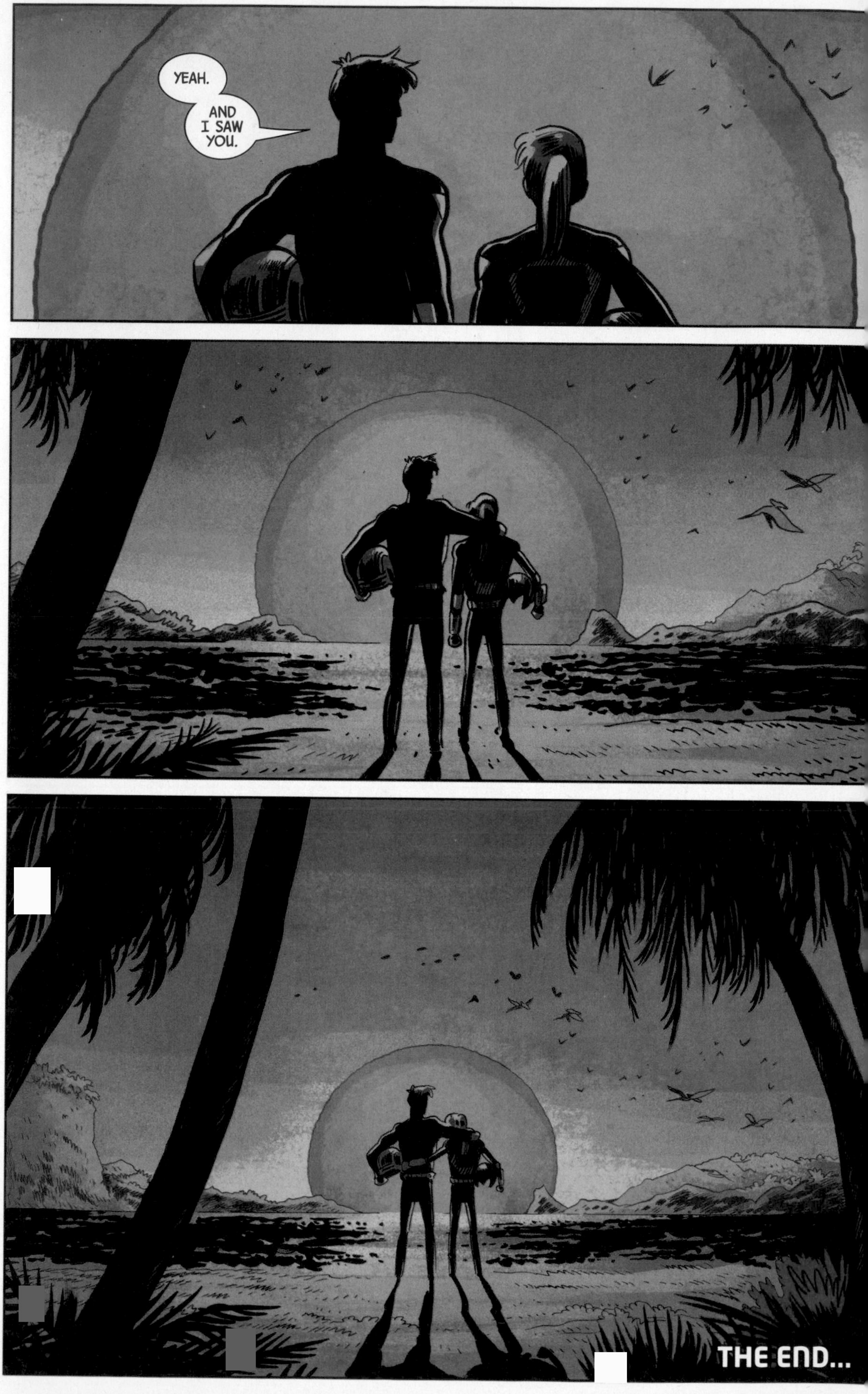
YEAH.
AND I SAW YOU.
THE END...

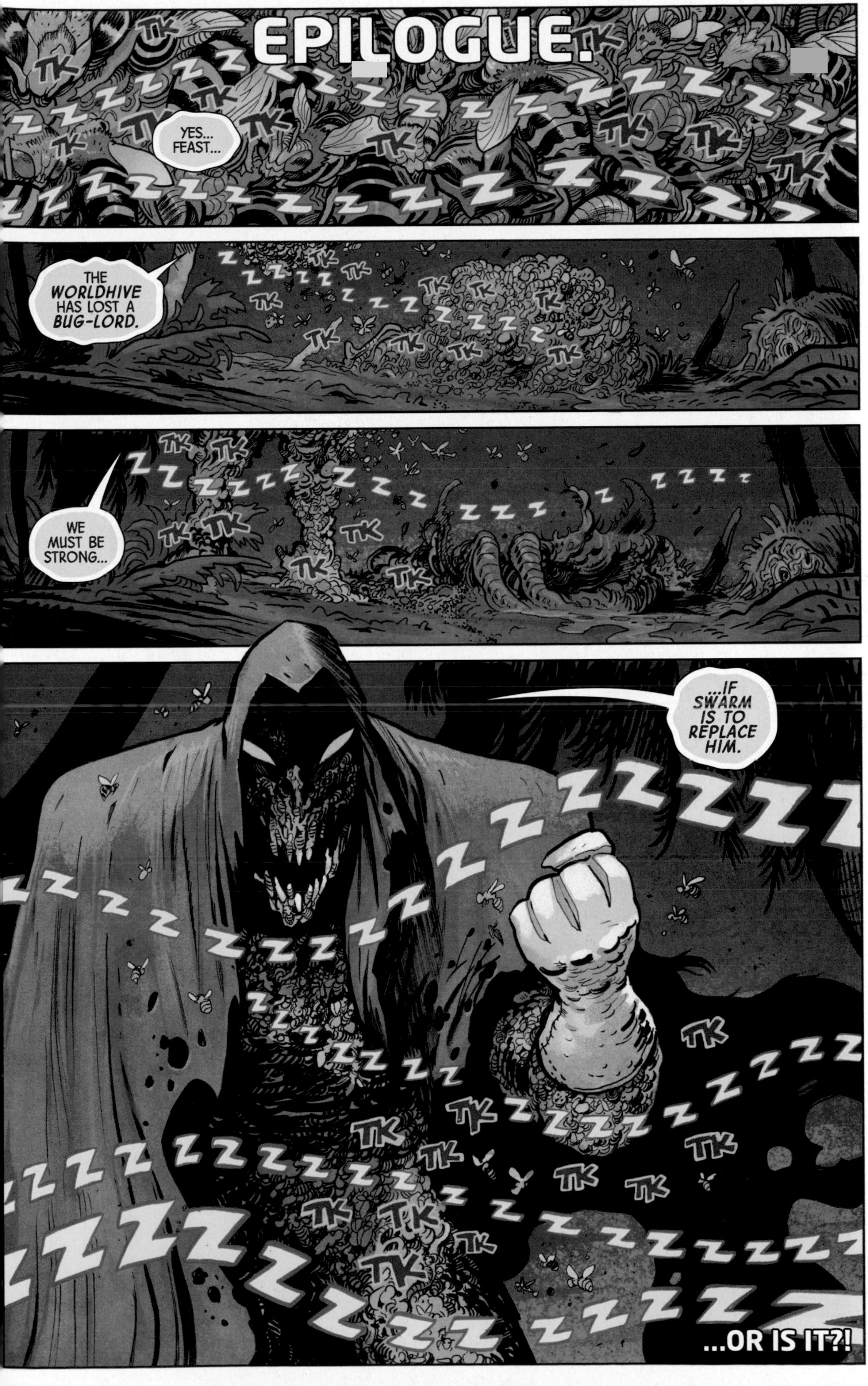
EPILOGUE!
YES... FEAST...
THE WORLDHIVE HAS LOST A BUG-LORD.
WE MUST BE STRONG...
...IF SWARM IS TO REPLACE HIM.
...OR IS IT?!

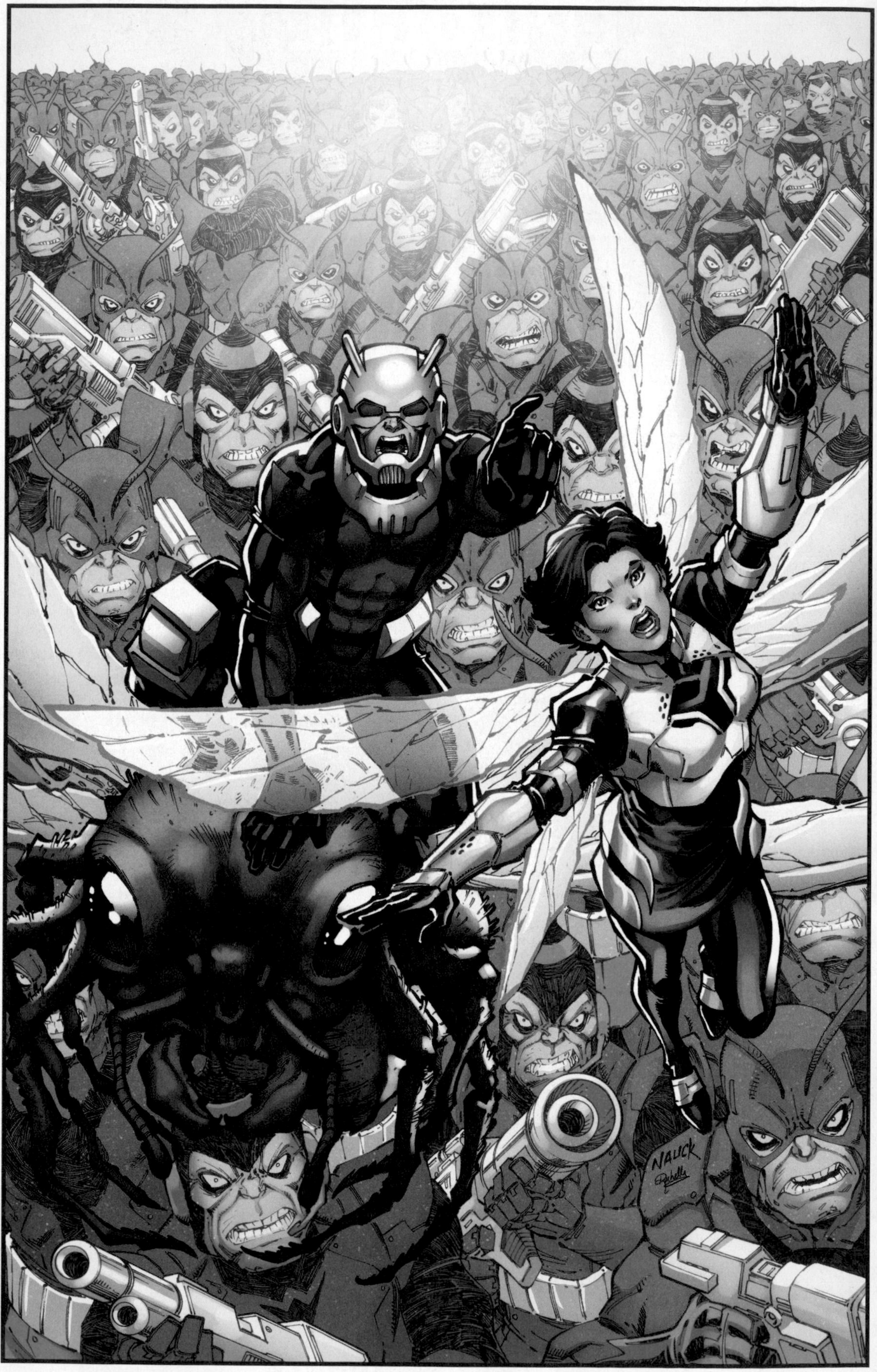
NAUCK

ANT-MAN & THE WASP: LIVING LEGENDS VARIANT BY **TODD NAUCK** & **RACHELLE ROSENBERG**

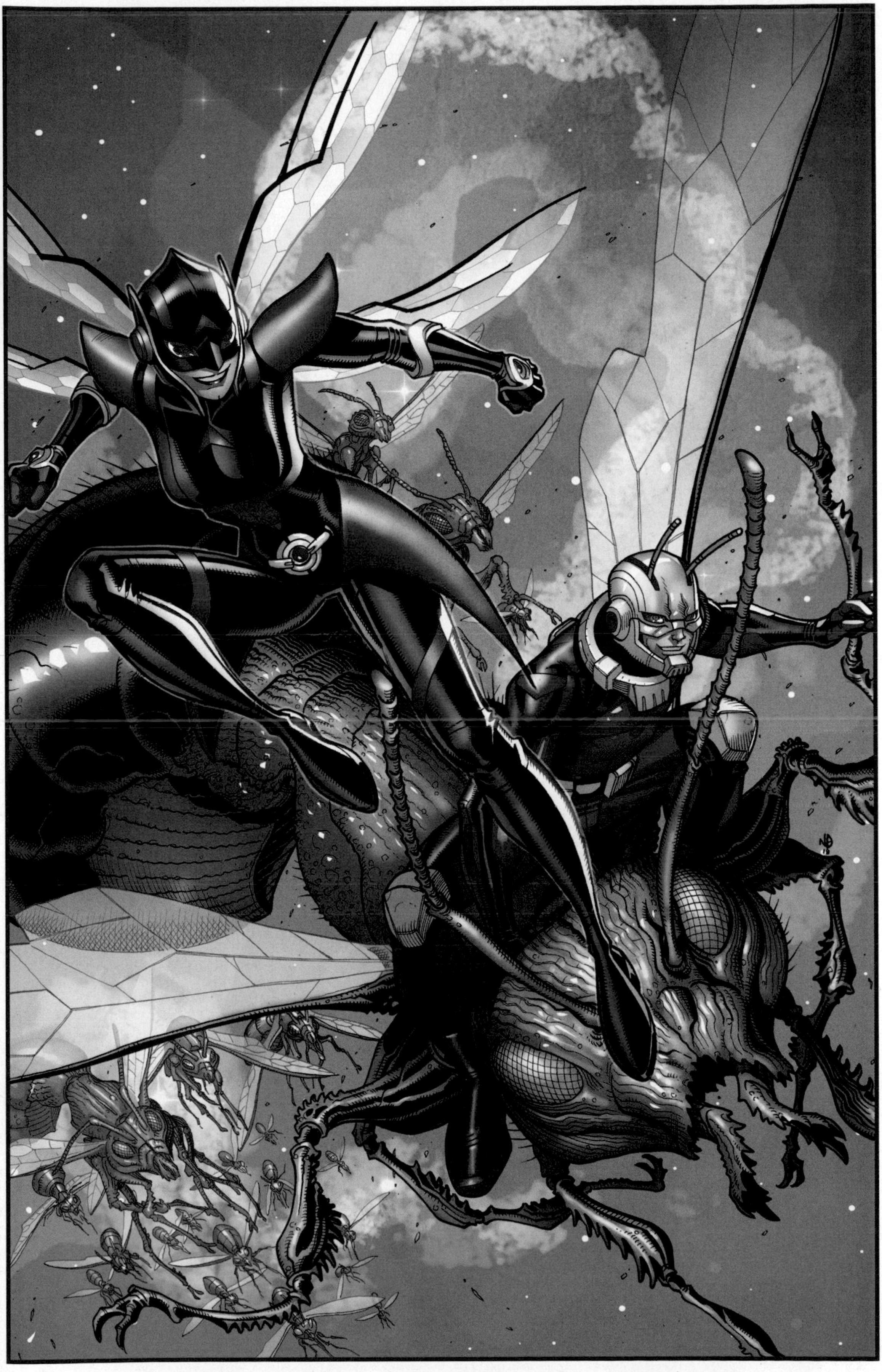

ANT-MAN AND THE WASP #1 VARIANT BY **NICK BRADSHAW** & **EDGAR DELGADO**

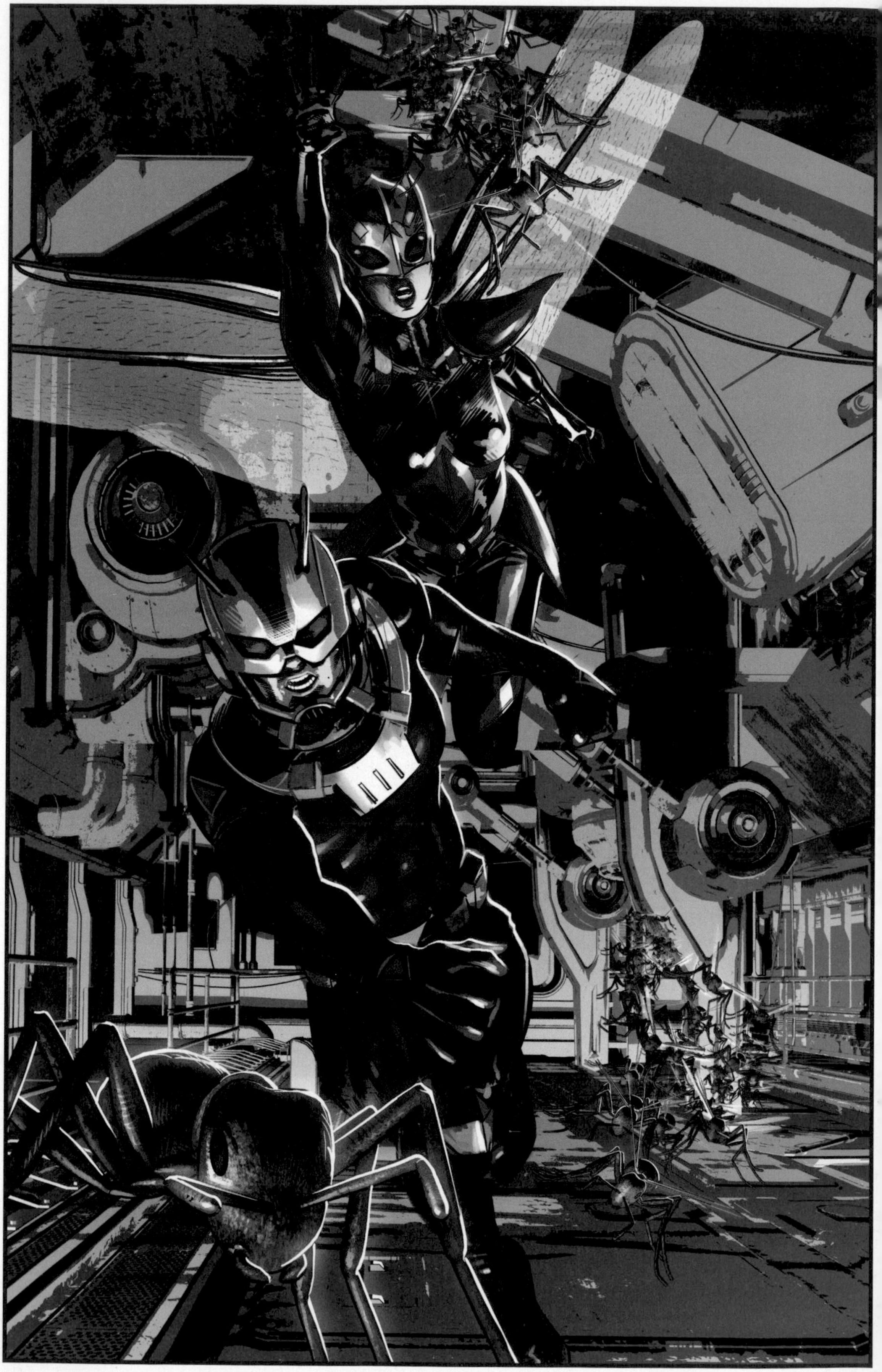

ANT-MAN AND THE WASP #1 VARIANT BY **MIKE DEODATO JR.** & **RAIN BEREDO**

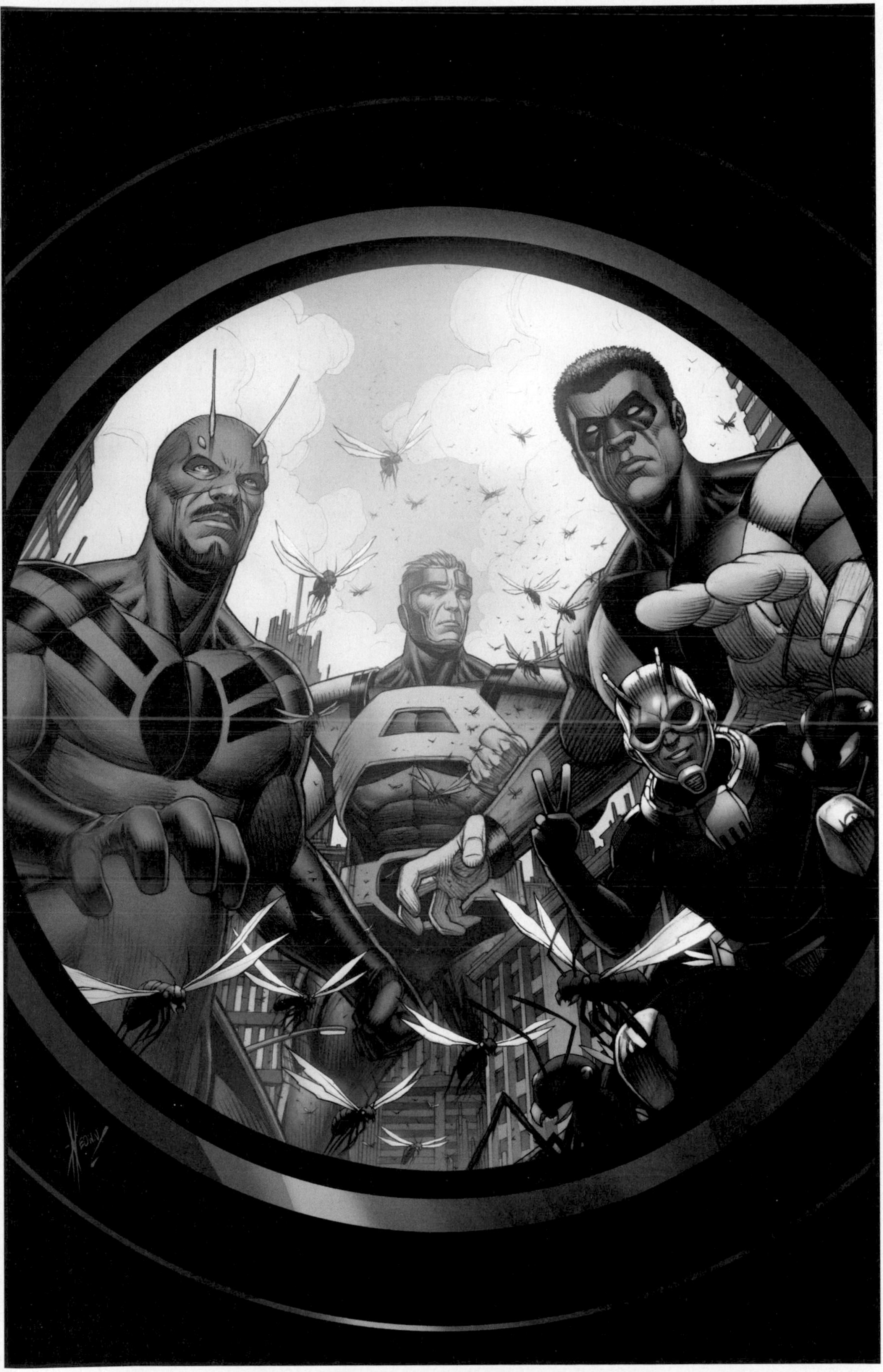

GIANT-MAN #1 VARIANT BY **DALE KEOWN** & **JASON KEITH**

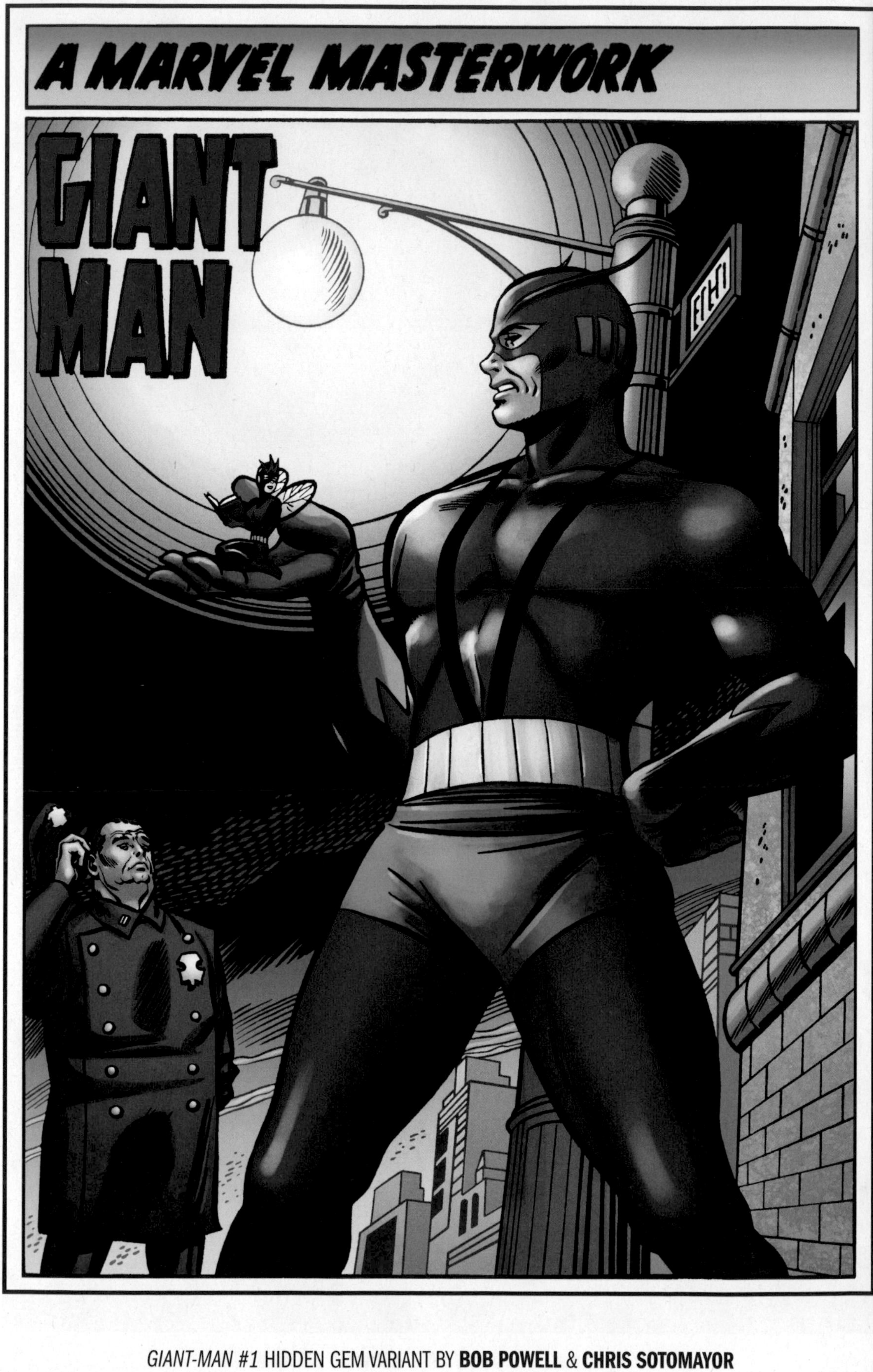
A MARVEL MASTERWORK
GIANT MAN

GIANT-MAN #1 HIDDEN GEM VARIANT BY **BOB POWELL** & **CHRIS SOTOMAYOR**

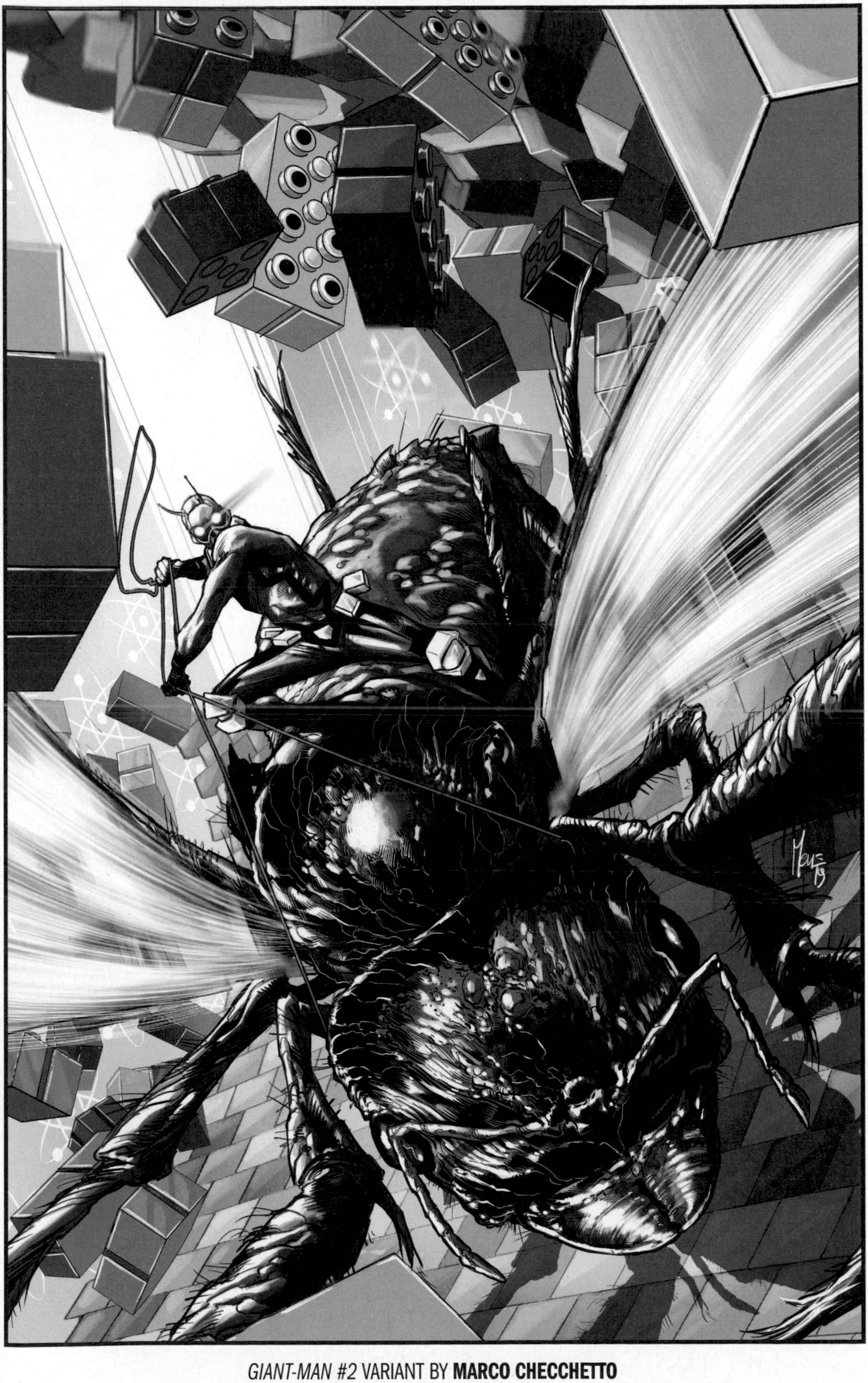

GIANT-MAN #2 VARIANT BY **MARCO CHECCHETTO**

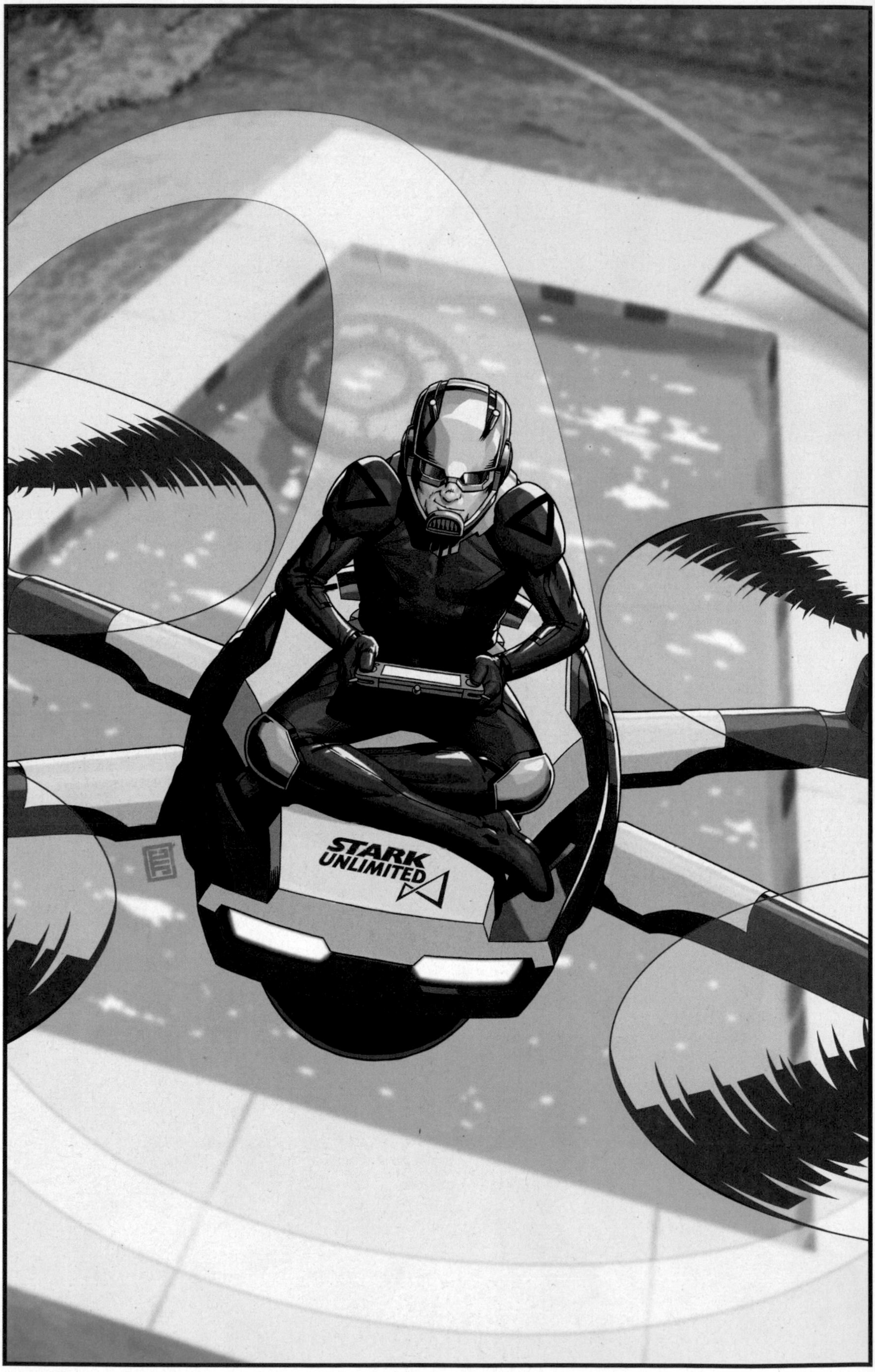
STARK
UNLIMITED

ANT-MAN #1 VARIANT BY **JOHN TYLER CHRISTOPHER**

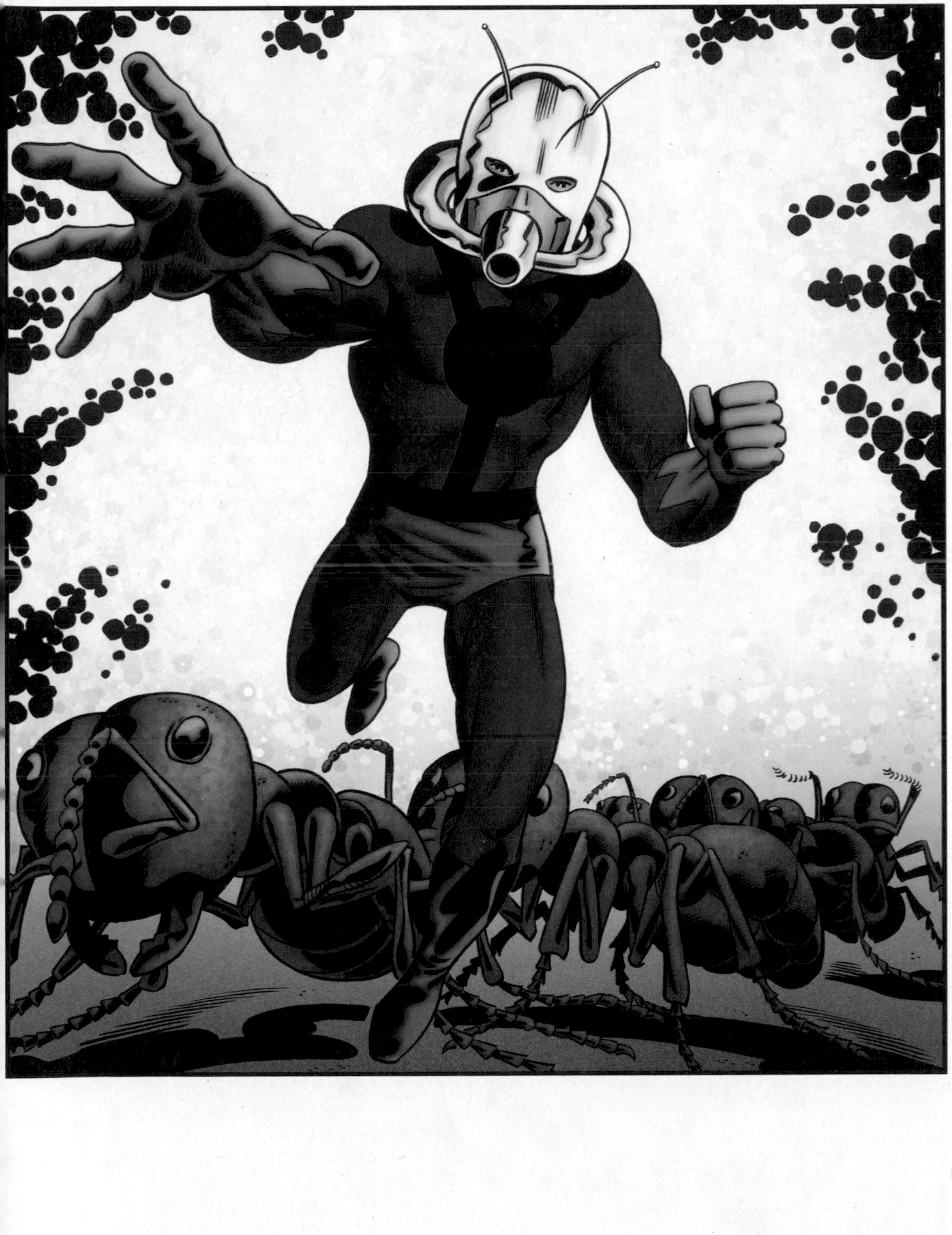

ANT-MAN #1 HIDDEN GEM VARIANT BY **HERB TRIMPE** & **MORRY HOLLOWELL**

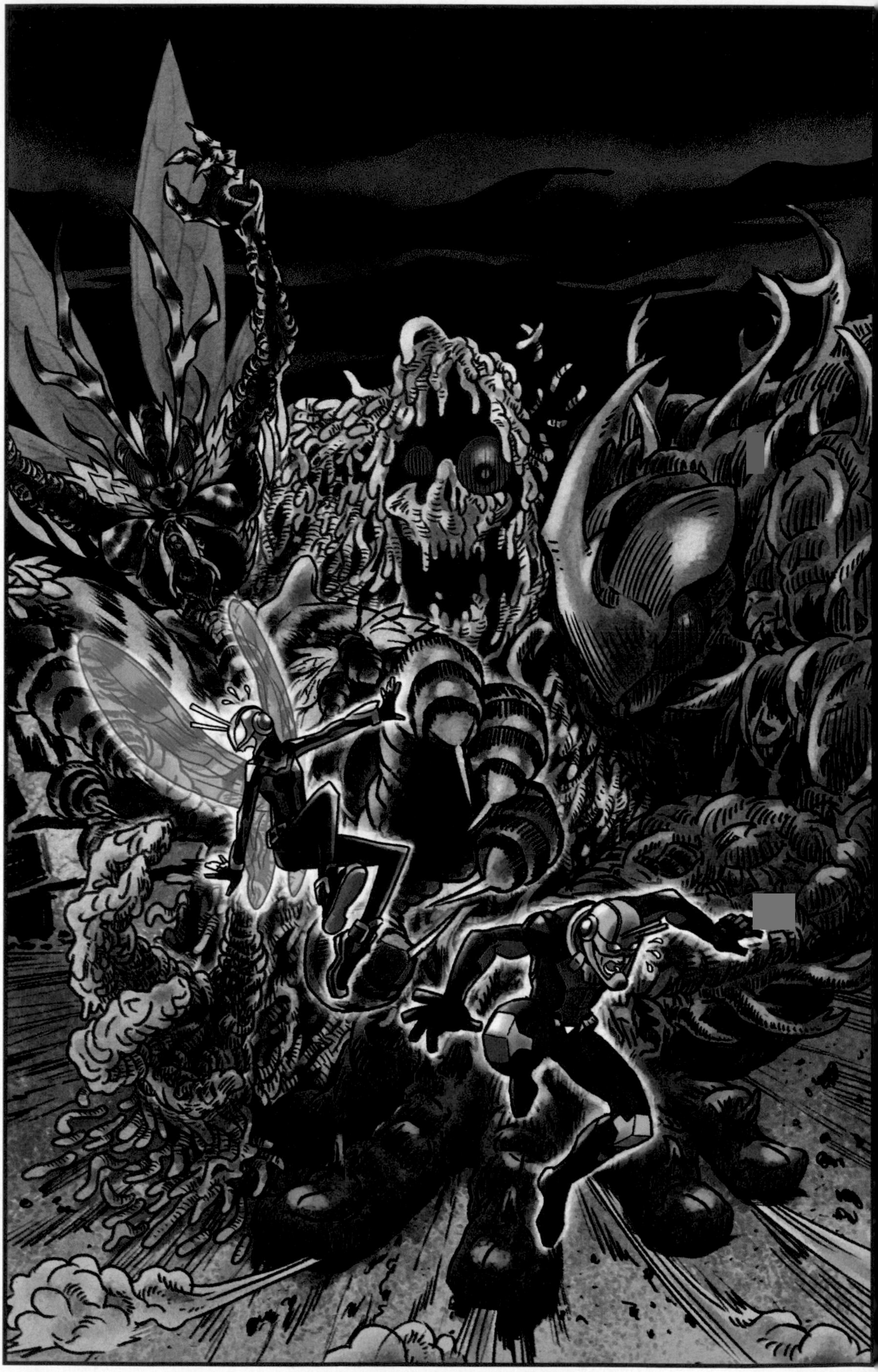

ANT-MAN #2 VARIANT BY **SUPERLOG**

Oh no!
Looks like some
errant Pym
Particles got into
the printer! Better
get your Mighty
Marvel Magnifying
Glasses*, True
Believers!
*Regular magnifying glasses

MICRO-FRIENDS!

Welcome to this new adventure! We assume you know Scott Lang, either from the many comics he's been in or...maybe...a big movie? With another one JUST MONTHS AWAY?!?! You may not know Nadia Pym, but you should! She's been on the Avengers over the last couple of years, but you have to check her out in Jeremy Whitley and Elsa Charretier's THE UNSTOPPABLE WASP! She's great and we're super excited for her to co-star here.

We here at Marvel would love to introduce you to a neophyte named Mark Waid. I'm sure he's written something, but I'm not familiar. Is he the guy who wrote that awesome AGE OF ULTRON A.I. Hank Pym one-shot? Couldn't be. Did he write those sweet AVENGERS issues that Nadia Pym was in? Can't be possible. He wasn't the guy who wrote DAREDEVIL and *Kingdom Come*, right? That's crazy talk. But I sure liked this issue.

Javier Garrón, on the other hand, is an accomplished and lovely man. Hailing from beautiful Barcelona, Javier has done some AMAZING SPIDER-MAN, SECRET WARRIORS, SECRET WARS and more! He was recently named one of our latest class of Marvel Young Guns and deservedly so. He has drawn some of the craziest things I've ever seen in upcoming issues.

And big thanks to Editor JORDAN D. WHITE, who did the hard editorial work and put this team together (including incredible cover artist David Nakayama, incredible colorist Israel Silva and our ever-faithful JOE CARAMAGNA, who lettered this while also lettering our 80-page AMAZING SPIDER-MAN #800)!

Mark, Javier and the rest of the team have so many astonishing plans for this book, and you're going to see a part of the Marvel Universe you've never seen before--THE MARVELOUS MICROVERSE!!! It helps that Mark, young and inexperienced in comics and the world in general as he is, is a huge physics nerd and has actually studied this sort of thing.

See you all in 30!
Nick

ANT-MAN AND THE WASP #1 INTRODUCTION LETTER

ANT-MAN AND THE WASP #4-5 COVER SKETCHES BY **DAVID NAKAYAMA**

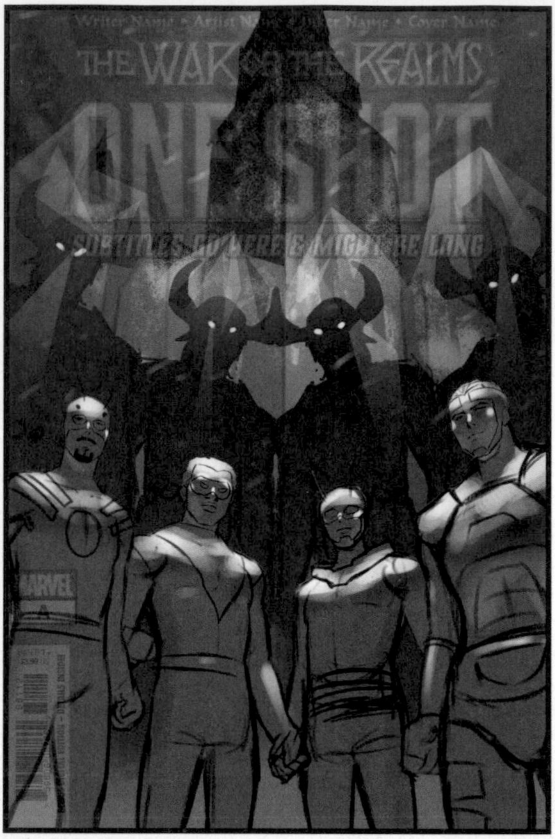
MARVEL

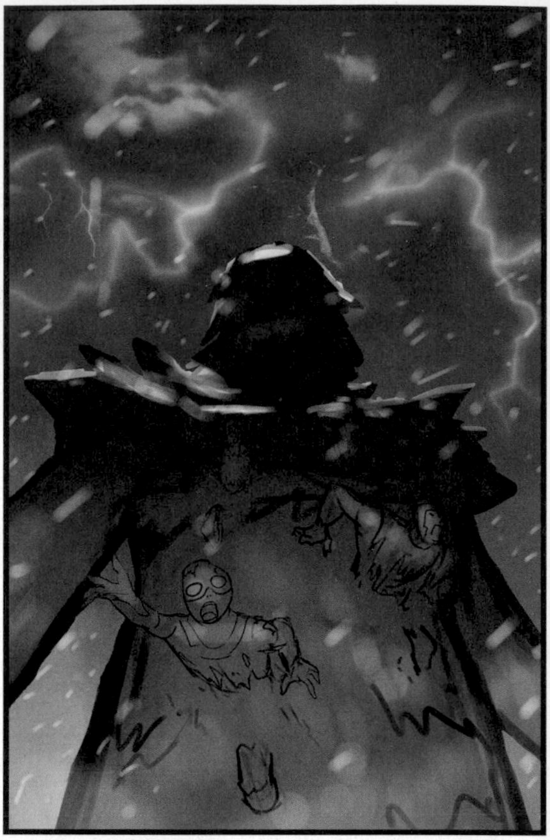

GIANT-MAN #1-2 COVER SKETCHES BY **WOO-CHUL LEE**

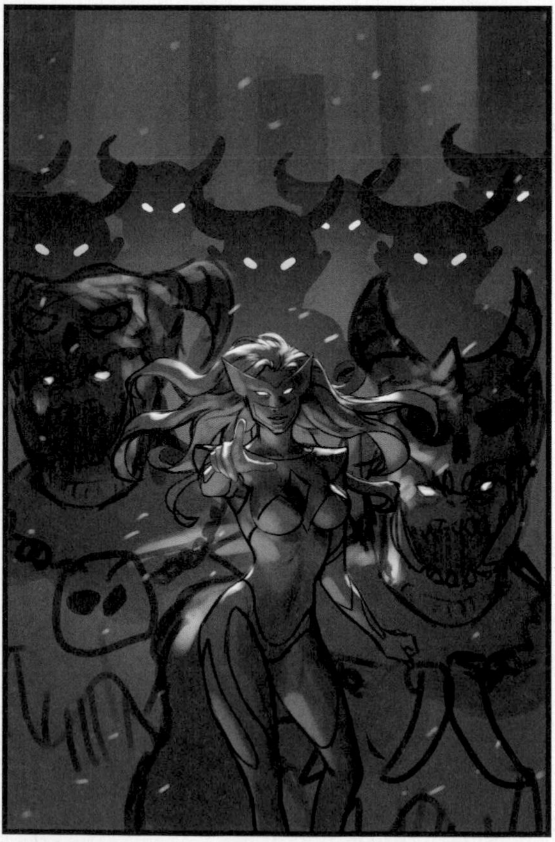

GIANT-MAN #3 COVER SKETCH BY **WOO-CHUL LEE**

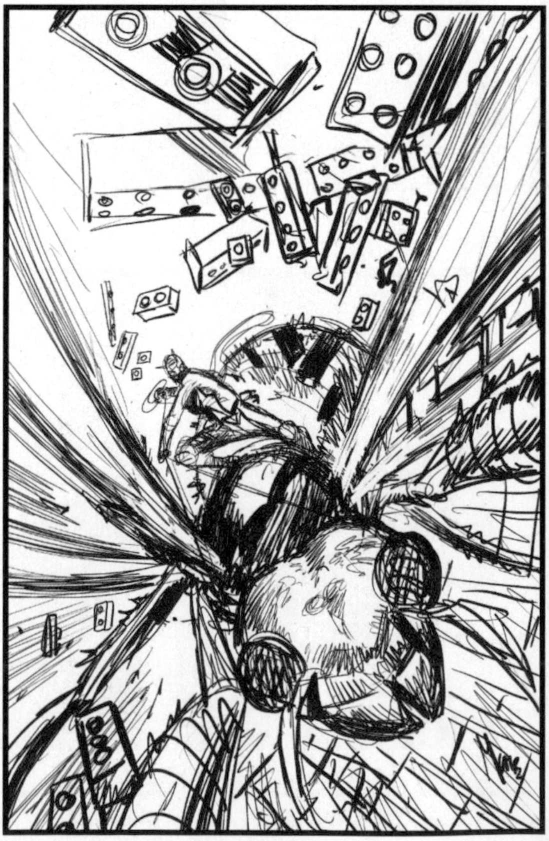

GIANT-MAN #3 VARIANT COVER SKETCH BY **MARCO CHECCHETTO**

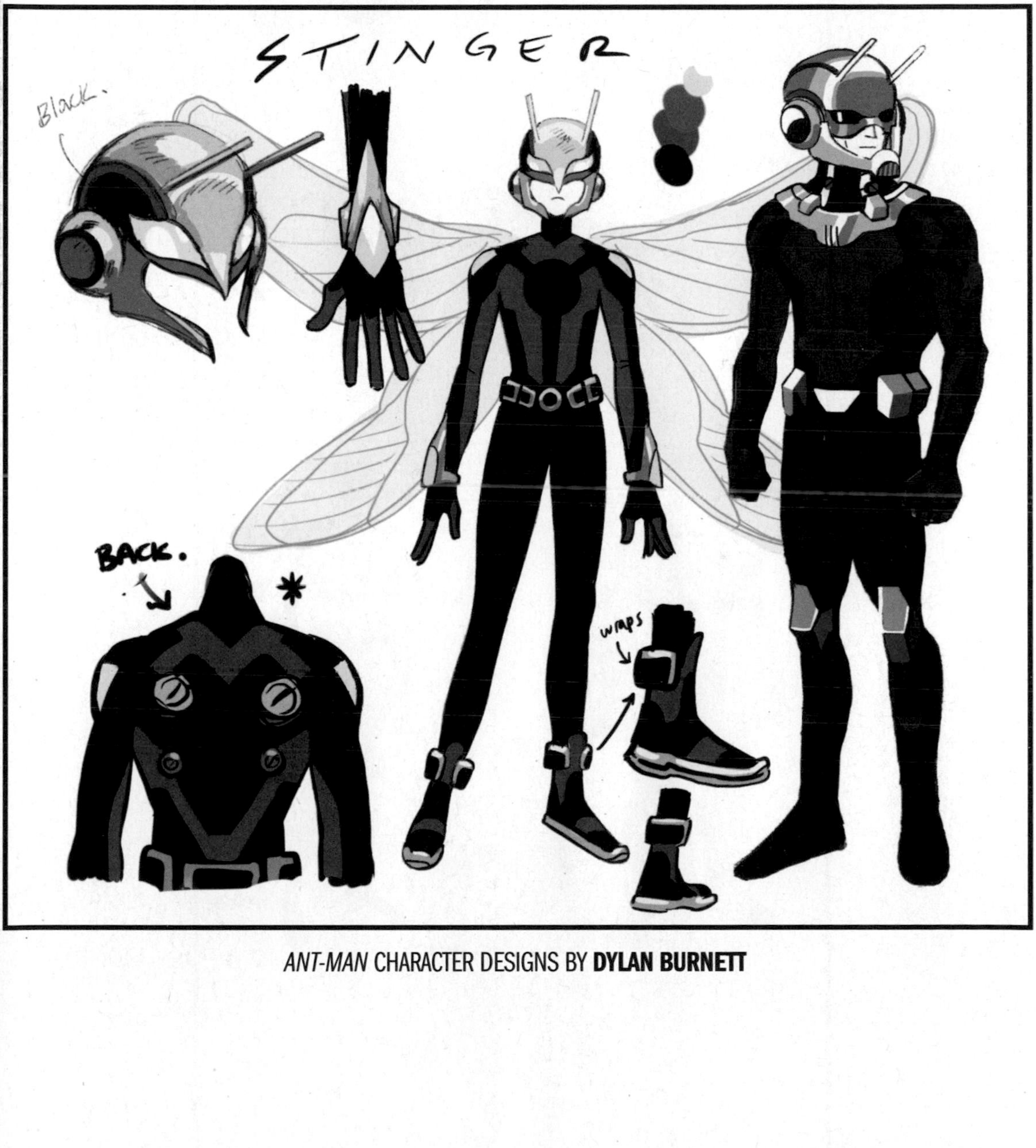
STINGER
Black.
BACK.
*
wraps

ANT-MAN CHARACTER DESIGNS BY **DYLAN BURNETT**

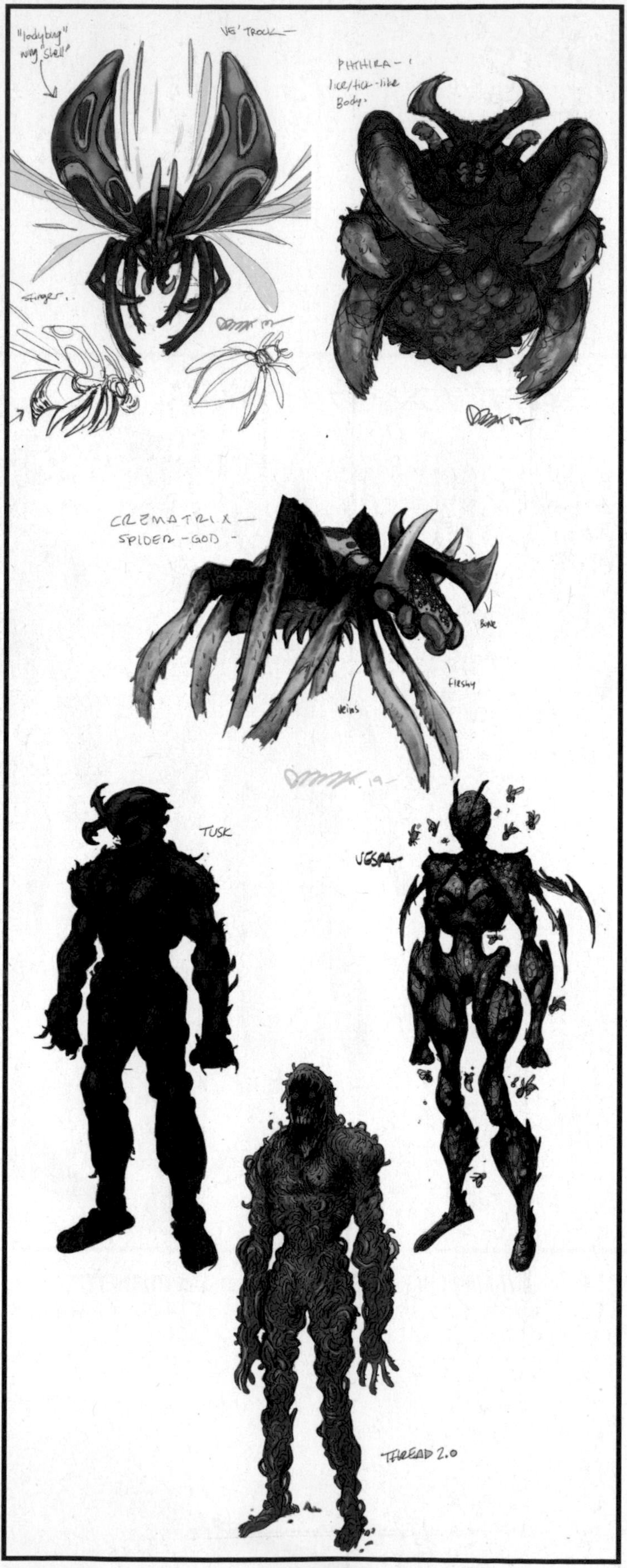
"ladybug" wing "shell"
VE'TROCK—
PHTHIRA—
lice/tick-like Body.
stinger.
CREMATRIX—
SPIDER-GOD—
Bone
Fleshy
Veins
TUSK
VESPA
THREAD 2.0

ANT-MAN CHARACTER DESIGNS BY **DYLAN BURNETT**